THE ORATIONS OF DEMOSTHENES

ON THE CROWN AND ON THE EMBASSY.

TRANSLATED, WITH NOTES, &c.,

BY

CHARLES RANN KENNEDY.

IN TWO VOLUMES.

VOL. II.

NEW YORK:
HARPER & BROTHERS, PUBLISHERS,
FRANKLIN SQUARE.
1857.

PREFACE.

The delay in bringing out this volume has been chiefly owing to the labor bestowed upon the Oration for the Crown, in which after all I feel I have but imperfectly succeeded. He is indeed a confident man who can satisfy himself upon such a task. The previous translations which I have consulted, I should rather say which I have constantly had before me, are those of Leland, Francis, Lord Brougham, Spillan, Auger, Jacobs, and Pabst. I believe there are some others, which I have not seen. These, however, I have carefully perused and compared; and to all the translators I am indebted for their assistance, but especially to Jacobs, of whose valuable notes and dissertations I have made ample use. It is a pity that his labors have been confined to the political speeches of Demosthenes.

Shilleto's edition of the Oration on the Embassy was unfortunately not put into my hands until I had completed the first half of the translation. The author has proved himself to be one of the profoundest of English scholars. His plan of writing critical notes in Latin, and explanatory in English, is novel, but not unattended with advantage.

CONTENTS.

THE

ORATIONS OF DEMOSTHENES.

THE ORATION ON THE CROWN.

THE ARGUMENT.

This has justly been considered the greatest speech of the greatest orator in the world. It derives an additional interest from the circumstance that it was the last great speech delivered in Athens. The subject matter of it is virtually a justification of the whole public policy and life of Demosthenes; while in point of form it is a defense of Ctesiphon for a decree which he proposed in favor of Demosthenes, B.C. 338, not long after the battle of Chæronea.

When the news of that disastrous battle reached Athens, the people were in the utmost consternation. Nothing less was expected than an immediate invasion of Attica by the conqueror; and strong measures were taken, under the advice of Hyperides, to put the city in a posture of defense. One of the most important was the repair of the walls and ramparts. Demosthenes at this time held the office of conservator of walls, having been appointed by his own tribe at the end of the year B.C. 339. The reparation, which had been commenced before, but suspended during the late campaign, was now vigorously prosecuted. He himself superintended the work, and expended on it three talents of his own money, beyond what was allowed out of the public treasury.

The fears of the people were not realized. Philip, while he chastised the Thebans, treated the Athenians with moderation and clemency; restoring their prisoners without ransom, burying their dead upon the field, and sending their bones to Athens. He deprived them indeed of most of their foreign possessions, but even enlarged their domestic territory by the addition of Oropus.

It seemed that the whole foundation upon which the credit and influence of Demosthenes had rested was overthrown. The hopes which he had held out of successful resistance to Philip, of re-establishing Athenian ascendency, or maintaining the independence of Greece, were now proved to be fallacious. The alliance of Thebes, his last great measure for the protection of Athens, appeared to have been the immediate cause of her defeat and disgrace. The very moderation with which Philip had used his victory looked like a reproach to the orator, who had so often denounced his cruelties before the Athenian assembly, and warned them of his deadly hostility to Athens.

The Macedonian party considered that the time was come for the humiliation of their adversary. They assailed him with prosecutions. The peace which Athens concluded with Macedonia was the signal for war against Demosthenes. But his enemies were mistaken in their reckoning, when they supposed that the people would feel resentment against him as the author of their misfortunes. The Athenians took a juster and nobler view of the matter: they judged not of his counsels by the result, but by their own intrinsic merit. Demosthenes came clear and triumphant out of every prosecution; and while Lysicles the general was condemned to capital punishment for his misconduct of the war, Demosthenes received from his countrymen a signal proof of their esteem and confidence, being appointed to pronounce the funeral oration in honor of the citizens who had fallen at Chæronea.

About the same time, and not many months after the battle, Ctesiphon introduced a bill to the Council of Five Hundred, proposing to reward Demosthenes for his gifts of money to the public, and for his general integrity and good conduct as a statesman. It is not unlikely that the very object of this measure was to stop the attacks upon Demosthenes, and to give him the opportunity, in case it should be opposed, of justifying the whole course of his political life. With that view was inserted the clause eulogizing his general character as a statesman. The Macedonian party naturally regarded this clause as a reflection upon themselves, and a virtual condemnation of the policy which they had for so many years espoused. They felt themselves therefore compelled to make a stand against it; and they resolved upon a course, which was open to them according to the Athenian laws, of indicting Ctesiphon as the author of an illegal measure. His bill, having been approved by the council, and then brought before the popular assembly, was passed in the shape of a decree, by which it was declared to be the will of the council and people of Athens, "that Demosthenes should be presented with a golden crown, and that a proclamation should be made in the theatre, at the great Dionysian festival, at the performance of the new tragedies, announcing that Demosthenes was rewarded by the people with a golden crown for his integrity, for the good-will which he had invariably displayed toward all the Greeks and toward the people of Athens, and also for his magnanimity, and because he had ever both by word and deed promoted the interests of the people, and been zealous to do all the good in his power." This decree, as the opposite party conceived, was open to three objections, two of which were chiefly of a legal nature; the other, while it equally assumed a legal form, called in question the real merits of Ctesiphon's motion. An indictment, embodying all the objections, was preferred before the archon, the chief magistrate of Athens, to whose cognizance a criminal proceeding of this kind appertained. The prosecutor was Æschines, the second of Athenian orators, the deadly enemy of Demosthenes, who would not only be considered by his party as the fittest person to conduct the cause, but was stimulated to it by every motive of rivalry and revenge. The indictment, after reciting the decree, alleged that it violated the Athenian laws in three points, as follows:—

First, because it was unlawful to make false allegations in any of the state documents:

Secondly, because it was unlawful to confer a crown upon any person who had an account to render of his official conduct; and Demosthenes was both a conservator of walls and the treasurer of the theoric fund:

Thirdly, because it was unlawful to proclaim the honor of a crown in the theatre at the Dionysian festival, at the performance of the new tragedies; the law being, that if the council gave a crown, it should be published in the council-hall; if the people, in the pnyx at the popular assembly.

The first of these points raised the substantial question at issue—viz., whether the decree of Ctesiphon had stated a falsehood, when it assigned the virtue and patriotism of Demosthenes as reasons for conferring public honor upon him. The other two, while they were mainly of a technical character, were strongly relied on by Æschines as affording him the means of securing a verdict.

Notice of intention to indict had probably been given at the time when the decree was passed. The bill was actually preferred on the sixth of Elaphebolion, B.C. 338, eight months after the battle of Chæronea, and a few days before the Dionysian festival, at which the honor conferred upon Demosthenes was to have been proclaimed. It had this immediate consequence, that the decree of Ctesiphon could not be carried into effect till after the trial; and thus one end, at least, was gained by Æschines and his party,—the satisfaction of having suspended their adversary's triumph. But whether they were deterred by the failure of other prosecutions against Demosthenes, or whether they judged from the temper of the people that they had but little chance of success, the indictment of Ctesiphon was suffered to lie dormant for more than seven years, and was not brought to trial till the year B.C. 330. It may seem strange that the law of Athens should have allowed a criminal prosecution to hang over a man for so long a period; but it must be borne in mind that the proceeding against Ctesiphon not only involved a charge personally affecting him, but had the further, and ostensibly the more important, object of maintaining the purity of the law itself, and preventing an unconstitutional decree from being recorded in the public archives. It is probable, however, that the case would never have been revived, but for the occurrence of political events which seemed to afford a favorable opportunity.

Within two years after his victory at Chæronea, Philip had perished by the hand of an assassin. The hopes that were excited in Greece by the news of his death were quickly dispelled by the vigorous measures of his successor. Notwithstanding the efforts of Demosthenes, it was found impossible to concert any feasible plan for a union of the Greek states against Macedonia. The rash revolt of the Thebans was punished by the extirpation of their city, which struck terror into the very heart of Greece. Athens, suspected of aiding the insurgents, hastened to appease the conqueror by humble submission; and when he insisted on the delivery up of their principal orators, including Demosthenes, it was with difficulty that he was prevailed upon to accept a less severe measure of satisfaction. The debate which took place in the Athenian assembly upon this demand of Alexander shows that Demosthenes must still have been in high esteem at Athens. The feelings of the people, notwithstanding their fears, were against the delivery of the orators: and Phocion's counsel, urging them to surrender themselves for the public good, was not well received. Alexander in the year following (B.C. 334) passed over into Asia, and commenced his career of conquest. Meanwhile Greece had a breathing time. The states that sighed for freedom looked with anxious expectation for every intelligence from the scene of war, as if all their hopes depended on the fate of one man. The farther he penetrated into Asia, the better chance there seemed to be of his being overwhelmed by the force of the Persian empire. While he was yet in the defiles of Cilicia, it was confidently asserted by Demosthenes at Athens, that his army would be trampled under foot by the cavalry of Darius. The battle of Issus belied this prophecy; yet it was still believed that the Persian monarchy had resources in itself sufficient to prevail in the war: and the length of time that Alexander was occupied in Phœnicia and Egypt, while Darius was collecting the strength of his empire in the East, seemed to favor these sanguine views.

About the time that Alexander was marching to fight his last and decisive battle against the Persian king in Mesopotamia, Agis, king of Sparta, put himself at the head of a confederacy, which comprised the greater part of the Peloponnesian states, and prepared to throw off the Macedonian yoke. Taking his opportunity, while Antipater was engaged in suppressing a Thracian insurrection, he raised his standard in Laconia, and declared war; but, after gaining some successes and laying siege to Megalopolis, which refused to join the league, he was defeated in a hard-fought battle by Antipater, and died fighting with the valor of an ancient Spartan. This was in the beginning of the year B.C. 330. The confederacy was dissolved, and the voice of freedom was again changed to that of submission.

Athens had taken no part in the last movement. The cause of her neutrality is not quite clear, though it is probably to be attributed to a want of proper concert and preparation. Had the Athenians sent their forces to assist Agis in Peloponnesus, they would have been exposed to the first attack of the enemy, and the dread of this may have restrained them from rising. A Macedonian garrison was maintained in the Cadmea, which would gain speedy intelligence of any movement on the part of the Athenians, and the people of the Bœotian towns were friendly to Macedonia. It is not quite clear either what part Demosthenes took upon this occasion. Æschines represents him as boasting that he had kindled the flames of war in Peloponnesus; and both Plutarch and Dinarchus intimate that he exerted himself for that purpose: yet Æschines accuses him also of neglecting so good an opportunity for engaging Athens in the contest. Demosthenes may in prudence have abstained from plunging the Athenians into a war, for which he saw they were ill prepared; and at the same time he might have encouraged the Peloponnesians to make an effort of which, in the event of success, his own country would equally have reaped the benefit. So timid a policy he would not certainly have adopted eight years before; but under existing circumstances it could hardly be a reproach to him, especially when he observed the timid and temporizing spirit which was gradually gaining ground among his countrymen. Presents of Persian spoil had been sent to Athens, to decorate the Acropolis. Phocion corresponded with Alexander as a friend; and it was generally represented by all who belonged to his party, that resistance to him was hopeless.

If such feelings prevailed to a great extent before the defeat of Agis, they must have been greatly strengthened after that event. Macedonian arms were every where triumphant. Alexander had seated himself on the throne of Darius; Antipater, his viceroy, was irresistible in Greece: Macedonian ascendency, which Demosthenes had exerted himself all his life to oppose, seemed now to be completely secured. Athens was not what she was even at the time of Chæronea, for sixteen years before that disastrous battle, the voice of Demosthenes had been continually resounding in the assembly, instructing, animating, improving, elevating the minds and hearts of his hearers; exerting such an influence over them, that he may be said to have raised up, by the force of his own eloquence, a new generation of patriots. But in the eight years that followed it was very different: his voice in the cause of freedom and glory had been little heard; and besides that the people were cowed by the events which had occurred, a lethargy had fallen on their spirit, for want of some one to rouse them.

This was the time chosen by Æschines for bringing to an issue the long-suspended cause. The aspect of affairs both at home and abroad seemed favorable to the undertaking; and he summoned up all his force and resolution for the contest. It was to be not only a trial of strength between the contending parties at Athens,—the favorers of Macedonian power, and those that regretted the loss of independence,—but a final and decisive struggle between two rival statesmen, exasperated against each other by a long series of hostilities. It was manifest that Ctesiphon was but the nominal defendant; the real object of attack was Demosthenes, his whole policy and administration. The interest excited was intense, not only at Athens, but throughout all Greece; and an immense concourse of foreigners flocked from all parts to hear the two most celebrated orators in the world. A jury (of not less than five hundred) was impanneled by the archon; and before a dense and breathless audience the pleadings began.

As the speeches of both the orators are preserved to us, we have the means of comparing one with the other, and forming our opinion of their respective merits. The world in general have decided as the people of Athens did, not only upon the oratorical merits of the two rivals, but upon the principal questions at issue between them. The accuser, who thought to brand his opponent with eternal infamy, has only added to the lustre of his renown. Independently of the internal evidence furnished by this and other orations of Demosthenes, which have carried to the hearts of most readers a conviction of his patriotism, we can not fail to be strongly influenced by the judgment of the Athenians themselves, whom neither their own past misfortunes, nor the terror inspired by the late victory of Antipater, could deter from giving a verdict, by which, while they acquitted Demosthenes from all blame, they in effect declared their approbation of his measures in opposition to Macedonia.

The reader who carefully examines the speech of Æschines will not fail to observe, that he betrays a consciousness of weakness in that part of his case where he attacks the political character of his rival. He seems to feel also that he is speaking in opposition to the general feeling of his hearers. His own character as a politician had been so dubious, his conduct so open to suspicion, that while he most bitterly assails his adversary, he is constantly under the necessity of defending himself. On the whole life, public and private, of Demosthenes, he pours a torrent of invective; to this the greater part of his speech is devoted: yet he seems to have been impelled to it rather by hate and revenge, than by any calculation of advantage. On the other hand, when he deals with the legal parts of his case, commenting on those specific violations of Athenian law which Ctesiphon's measure was charged with, it is evident that his strength lay there; he handles his subject temperately, skillfully, and carefully, laboring to make every point clear to the jury, and to impress them with the conviction that to uphold the laws was the sure way to maintain constitutional government. On these points he mainly relied, hoping by this means to secure a verdict, which would give him a triumph over his enemy, and carry the general opinion over Greece, that the credit and influence of Demosthenes were extinguished.

Demosthenes, feeling his weakness as to the legal questions, dexterously throws them into the middle of his speech, and passes lightly and rapidly over them, while he devotes his greatest efforts to the vindication of his own merits as a patriot and a statesman. Refusing to comply with the insidious demand of Æschines, that he should take the questions in the same order as his accuser, he insists upon his legal right to conduct his defense as he pleases. Opening with a modest exordium, to conciliate the favor of the jury, he launches gradually into the history of his own conduct and measures: presenting first a general view of the condition of Greece when he entered public life, and of the difficulties under which the Athenians labored in their contest with Philip; then setting forth his own views, plans, and objects, and showing that he had advised a course of action which both the circumstances of the time and the honor of the country required. He apologizes for the self-praise mixed up with his speech, on the ground that he was driven to it by his opponent. Entering on the Sacred War, and the peace of B.C. 346, he labors to exculpate himself from all share in the errors then committed, imputing them chiefly to the negligence of the other embassadors, and to the treachery of Philocrates and Æschines, who, by the false hopes which they excited at Athens, prevented the people from assisting the Phocians.

Coming to the events which brought on a renewal of the war, he shows how Philip's ambitious projects and encroachments in every part of Greece made it necessary to oppose him, especially for the Athenians, who were menaced at home as well as abroad by his aggressions in Thrace, Eubœa, and Megara. He pursues these topics until he has carried with him the feelings of his hearers, which must have been strongly on his side when he dilated on the glorious issue of the campaigns in Eubœa and the Propontis, and read to them the decrees of the Byzantines, Perinthians, and Chersonesites, in honor of Athens, all which were due to the vigorous measures of his own administration. Having thus secured the good-will and sympathy of his judges, he proceeds to discuss the legal charges against Ctesiphon. Dwelling on them but for a short time, he plunges into a personal attack upon Æschines, holding up to ridicule the meanness of his birth and parentage, and retorting on him the same coarse and opprobrious language which had been used toward himself. The bitterness of his invective is only to be excused on the ground of strong provocation, added to an assurance that his more grave charges of corruption and treason were well founded. Those charges, so often advanced before, he here repeats, denouncing more particularly the conduct of Æschines upon his mission to Delphi, B.C. 339, to which the disaster of Chæronea was attributable. The account which Æschines had given of this affair he shows to be false, and enters upon a minute examination of the proceedings which caused Philip to be appointed Amphictyonic general, and to march with an invading army, nominally against the Amphissian Locrians, really against Bœotia and Attica. A graphic description is given of the consternation at Athens on hearing that Philip had seized Elatea. The meeting of the people, the advice of Demosthenes to them, his embassy to Thebes, the success of his negotiations, and the conclusion of the alliance between Thebes and Athens are briefly recounted, Demosthenes forcibly pointing out the advantage of his measures, contending that they were not to be judged by the mere event of the battle, and that it was far more glorious for his country to be defeated in a struggle for the independence of Greece, than it would have been to keep aloof from the contest. Here he makes that noble adjuration, which has in all ages been admired, appealing to his countrymen by the deeds of their ancestors, of whom they would have acted most unworthily, had they without a struggle abandoned the post of honor bequeathed to them. He himself as a statesman would have deserved execration, had he advised such a course. The failure of their arms was not to be imputed to the minister, who had done all he could to insure their success, but rather to the commanders, or to evil fortune. As Æschines had said so much about the ill fortune which attended him, he draws a comparison between the different fortunes of himself and his rival, first, of their early life and education, next, of their career as public men. Æschines from the beginning had taken a part which put him in opposition to the true interests of Athens, which caused him to rejoice at her disasters, to quail and tremble at her successes. He never came forward to assist her by his counsels when she needed them, but only to censure others who had given their honest advice, because it had not turned out as well as was expected. It was a signal proof of his malignant disposition, that he had expatiated on the late disastrous events as if they were a subject of triumph to him, without shedding a single tear, without any faltering in his voice, without betraying the least emotion or symptom of grief. In reply to the challenge of Æschines, to say for what merit he claimed the reward of a crown, Demosthenes boldly declares, for his incorruptibility, by which he was distinguished not only from Æschines, but from the multitude of venal orators in the Grecian world. Had there been but a few more like himself in other states, Macedonia could never have risen to greatness upon their ruin. He had done all that was possible for a single man; and Athens, while she shared the misfortune of all the Greeks, had the consolation of reflecting, that she had striven gallantly and bravely to avert the common calamity. Æschines had lauded the great men of a by-gone age, drawing an invidious contrast between Demosthenes and them. This, says Demosthenes, was not a fair way of judging him: he should be tried by reference to his own acts, as compared with those of his contemporaries. Yet even from the former comparison he did not shrink; for he had acted on the same principles as the statesmen of olden time, striving always to maintain the honor and dignity of Athens. Attachment to his country, and earnest anxiety for her welfare, had been his constant and abiding motives of action: throughout his whole life, in the day of power, in the hour of trial and adversity, those feelings had never deserted him: that was the test of a good and honest citizen; by that he ought to be judged.

Such is, in substance, the argument of this celebrated Oration, as far as relates to the main question in the cause. Some remarks on the legal points will be found in an Appendix. The effect produced by the speech upon an Athenian audience can be but faintly imagined by us who read it at this distance of time. Although Athens was not then what she had once been; although she was humbled by defeat, shorn of her honors, stripped of her empire and dependencies, without allies, without resources, without means of resistance to that iron power under which all Greece had succumbed; there was still the remembrance of the past, not yet extinguished by habitual servitude; there were still vague hopes of future deliverance, and a fire of smothered indignation burning in the hearts of the people, ready to burst into a flame at the first favorable opportunity. That such were their feelings is proved by what occurred seven years afterward upon the death of Alexander; when Athens made one convulsive effort for freedom, ere she finally submitted to her fate. Demosthenes stood before his countrymen, representing all which remained of Athenian dignity and glory. If any man could help them, it was he. His advice had always been steady and constant; his warnings should have been earlier attended to; but even yet there might be need of him. He was their consolation for the past, their hope for the future. During the progress of his address, such thoughts rushed upon their minds with greater and greater force, till they were elevated above themselves, and all the spirit of their ancestors was for the moment regenerate within them.

They could forgive him all his egotism and self-praise. It was the praise of a life devoted to their service. Where he lauded his own acts most strongly, he identified them with the glories of his country. Whatever good results might have accrued from his measures, he ascribed the merit less to himself than to the fortune of Athens, or to the gods, of whom he was but the humble instrument in a righteous cause. His own eloquence would have been of no avail, had it not touched the true chord of Athenian feeling. Throughout his whole political career he had been supported by the judgment and convictions of the people. Thus he argued, and the people felt it was impossible for them to find him guilty, without passing sentence upon themselves, without condemning the policy which Athens had for a long series of years consistently pursued. The genius of Athens protected her from such disgrace; and by an overwhelming majority, which left the accuser no choice but to retire into exile, a verdict was given for the defendant.

I BEGIN, men of Athens, by praying to every God and Goddess, that the same good-will, which I have ever cherished toward the commonwealth and all of you, may be requited to me on the present trial.[1] I pray likewise—and this specially concerns yourselves, your religion, and your honor—that the Gods may put it in your minds, not to take counsel of my opponent touching the manner in which I am to be heard—that would indeed be cruel!—but of the laws and of your oath; wherein (besides the other obligations) it is prescribed that you shall hear both sides alike. This means, not only that you must pass no pre-condemnation, not only that you must extend your good-will equally to both, but also that you must allow the parties to adopt such order and course of defense as they severally choose and prefer.

Many advantages hath Æschines over me on this trial; and two especially, men of Athens. First, my risk in the contest is not the same. It is assuredly not the same for me to forfeit your regard, as for my adversary not to succeed in his in-

[1] Quintilian commends the modest opening of this oration, which he attributes to a cautious timidity. Cicero thus remarks upon it in the *Orator*:—

"Hic, quem præstitisse diximus cæteris, in illâ pro Ctesiphonte oratione longè optimâ, submissus à primo; deinde, dum de legibus disputat, pressus; post sensim incedens, judices ut vidit ardentes, in reliquis exultavit audacius."

It was not unusual with the ancient orators to commence with a prayer. Thus Lycurgus begins his speech against Leocrates; and Cicero his defense of Murena. Also, in the defense of Rabirius, (near the beginning,) there is an appeal, like this of Demosthenes, to all the Gods and Goddesses.

dictment. To me—but I will say nothing untoward[1] at the outset of my address. The prosecution however is play to him.[2] My second disadvantage is, the natural disposition of mankind to take pleasure in hearing invective and accusation, and to be annoyed by those who praise themselves. To Æschines is assigned the part which gives pleasure; that which is (I may fairly say) offensive to all, is left for me. And if, to escape from this, I make no mention of what I have done, I shall appear to be without defense against his charges, without proof of my claims to honor: whereas, if I proceed to give an account of my conduct and measures, I shall be forced to speak frequently of myself. I will endeavor then to do so with all becoming modesty: what I am driven to by the necessity of the case, will be fairly chargeable to my opponent who has instituted such a prosecution.[3]

I think, men of the jury, you will all agree that I, as well as Ctesiphon, am a party to this proceeding, and that it is a matter of no less concern to me. It is painful and grievous to be deprived of any thing, especially by the act of one's enemy; but your good-will and affection are the heaviest loss, precisely as they are the greatest prize to gain.

Such being the matters at stake in this cause, I conjure and implore you all alike, to hear my defense to the charge in that fair manner which the laws prescribe—laws, to which their author, Solon, a man friendly to you and to popular rights, thought that validity should be given, not only by the recording of them,[4] but by the oath of you the jurors: not that

[1] Auger: *sinistre.* Jacobs: *anstössiges.* Leland: *ominous.* There is a reference, of course, to the fear of an evil omen, which causes the orator to suppress what he would have said.

[2] Because he can afford to be beaten; he has not much to lose. He possesses not, like me, the esteem and affection of the people; and therefore has not the loss of these to fear. It is difficult to translate the phrase pointedly. Auger: "il m'accuse sans avoir rien à perdre." Spillan: "he accuses me without any risk." Brougham: "he brings his charge an unprovoked volunteer." Jacobs: *er klagt mich aus Muthwillen an.*

[3] Upon this Quintilian remarks: "Neque hoc dico, non aliquando de rebus a se gestis oratori esse dicendum, sicut eidem Demostheni pro Ctesiphonte: quod tamen ita emendavit, ut necessitatem id faciendi ostenderet, invidiamque omnem in eum regereret, qui hoc se coegisset."

[4] Leland and Spillan are wrong in translating *τῷ γράψαι* "by enacting;" and Lord Brougham, who has rendered it "by engraving on brazen tablets," has been unjustly and ignorantly censured. The only

he distrusted you, as it appears to me; but, seeing that the charges and calumnies, wherein the prosecutor is powerful by being the first speaker, can not be got over by the defendant, unless each of you jurors, observing his religious obligation, shall with like favor receive the arguments of the last speaker, and lend an equal and impartial ear to both, before he determines upon the whole case.

As I am, it appears, on this day to render an account both of my private life and my public measures, I would fain, as in the outset, call the Gods to my aid; and in your presence I implore them, first, that the good-will which I have ever cherished toward the commonwealth and all of you may be fully requited to me on the present trial; next, that they may direct you to such a decision upon this indictment, as will conduce to your common honor, and to the good conscience of each individual.

Had Æschines confined his charge to the subject of the prosecution, I too would have proceeded at once to my justification of the decree.[1] But since he has wasted no fewer words in the discussion of other matters, in most of them calumniating me, I deem it both necessary and just, men of Athens, to begin by shortly adverting to these points, that none of you may be induced by extraneous arguments to shut your ears against my defense to the indictment.

To all his scandalous abuse of my private life, observe my plain and honest answer. If you know me to be such as he alleged—for I have lived nowhere else but among you—let not my voice be heard, however transcendent my statesmanship! Rise up this instant and condemn me! But if, in your opinion and judgment, I am far better and of better descent than my adversary; if (to speak without offense) I am not inferior, I or mine, to any respectable[2] citizen; then

fault of such version is, that it has too many words. He probably followed Auger, who has "de les graver sur l'airain;" which, in fact, is the meaning. Jacobs and Pabst are right. The ordinary meaning of γράψαι νόμους, "to propose laws," is here manifestly inapplicable. I may here also observe that the censure of Lord Brougham for joining δικαίως with ἀκοῦσαι is equally absurd. The Germans both have it as he has; nor is it possible, with such a collocation of the words, to take it otherwise.

[1] The decree of the Senate procured by Ctesiphon in favor of Demosthenes.

[2] Jacobs: *der rechtlichen Bürger*. Auger: "aucune famille estimable."

give no credit to him for his other statements—it is plain they were all equally fictions—but to me let the same good-will, which you have uniformly exhibited upon many former trials, be manifested now. With all your malice, Æschines, it was very simple to suppose that I should turn from the discussion of measures and policy to notice your scandal. I will do no such thing: I am not so crazed. Your lies and calumnies about my political life I will examine forthwith; for that loose ribaldry I shall have a word hereafter, if the jury desire to hear it.

The crimes whereof I am accused are many and grievous: for some of them the laws enact heavy—most severe penalties. The scheme of this present proceeding includes a combination of spiteful insolence, insult, railing, aspersion, and every thing of the kind; while for the said charges and accusations, if they were true, the state has not the means of inflicting an adequate punishment, or any thing like it.[1] For

[1] Two ways of explaining this difficult passage have occurred to me. The first is as follows:—The whole scheme of the prosecution shows that it was instituted to gratify private enmity, not for the good of the public. If the charges of Æschines against me were true, you could not sufficiently punish him (Æschines) for preferring them in such a manner. Why? Because he prefers them by way of insult and slander, and would not let me be heard in answer to them, if he could have his way; a course which is most unjust and unconstitutional. He ought to have made such charges against me directly, and at the time when the offenses were committed; not to have assailed me through Ctesiphon so long after the time.

The second method has been partly indicated by a German critic, cited by Jacobs, and is thus:—The whole scheme of the prosecution bears the marks of private enmity and malice, while, if the charges were true, the prosecutor does not put you in a situation to punish me according to my deserts. Why? Because he does not prosecute me directly for the crimes which he lays to my charge. The penalties of the law for such crimes could not be enforced by means of the present prosecution, which is a collateral proceeding, not against me, but against a third party. The charges in question are made incidentally, and by way of slander and abuse. The very proposal of Æschines, that I should not be allowed to speak freely in defense of my political conduct, proves that his attack upon me is not for the public good; for he must know that you could never punish me for the crimes of which I am accused, without giving me a proper and full hearing. No such thing is allowed by the law, or could be tolerated on any principle of justice. His attack on me, therefore, can have no good object; it is manifestly dictated by personal hatred and malice, &c.

The latter method, I think, is preferable.

it is not right to debar another of access to the people and privilege of speech; moreover, to do so by way of malice and insult—by heaven! is neither honest, nor constitutional, nor just. If the crimes which he saw me committing against the state were as heinous as he so tragically gave out, he ought to have enforced the penalties of the law against them at the time; if he saw me guilty of an impeachable offense, by impeaching and so bringing me to trial before you; if moving illegal decrees, by indicting me for them. For surely, if he can prosecute Ctesiphon on my account, he would not have forborne to indict me myself, had he thought he could convict me. In short, whatever else he saw me doing to your prejudice, whether mentioned or not mentioned in his catalogue of slander, there are laws for such things, and punishments, and trials, and judgments, with sharp and severe penalties; all of which he might have enforced against me: and had he done so—had he thus pursued the proper method with me, his charges would have been consistent with his conduct. But now he has declined the straightforward and just course, avoided all proofs of guilt at the time,[1] and after this long interval gets up, to play his part withal, a heap of accusation, ribaldry, and scandal. Then he arraigns me, but prosecutes the defendant. His hatred of me he makes the prominent part of the whole contest; yet, without having ever met me upon that ground, he openly seeks to deprive a third party of his privileges. Now, men of Athens, besides all the other arguments that may be urged in Ctesiphon's behalf, this methinks, may very fairly be alleged—that we should try our own quarrel by ourselves; not leave our private dispute, and look what third party we can damage. That surely were the height of injustice.

It may appear from what has been said, that all his charges are alike unjust and unfounded in truth. Yet I wish

[1] In translating *τοὺς παρ' αὐτὰ τὰ πράγματα ἐλέγχους*, as just above in the expression *παρ' αὐτὰ τἀδικήματα*, I adhere to the interpretation of Wolf and Reiske, which is followed by Leland, Brougham, Spillan, and others. And so Pabst: *ist der Rüge gegen mich auf frischer That ausgewichen.* Taylor, however, understands *παρὰ* in the sense of "according to:" *τιμωρία παρὰ τὸ ἀδίκημα* he renders, *pœna juxta formam criminis.* Ἔλεγχος παρὰ τὸ πρᾶγμα would thus be "a proof applicable to the fact," "a proof by evidence." Jacobs has: *statt den Beweis aus wirklichen Thatsachen zu führen.*

to examine them separately, and especially his calumnies about the peace and the embassy, where he attributed to me the acts of himself and Philocrates. It is necessary also, and perhaps proper, men of Athens, to remind you how affairs stood at those times, that you may consider every single measure in reference to the occasion.

When the Phocian war[1] had broken out—not through me, for I had not then commenced public life—you were in this position: you wished the Phocians to be saved, though you saw they were not acting right; and would have been glad for the Thebans to suffer any thing, with whom for a just reason you were angry; for they had not borne with moderation their good fortune at Leuctra. The whole of Peloponnesus was divided: they that hated the Lacedæmonians were not powerful enough to destroy them; and they that ruled before by Spartan influence were not masters of the states: among them, as among the rest of the Greeks, there was a sort of unsettled strife and confusion.[2] Philip, seeing this—it was not difficult to see—lavished bribes upon the traitors in every state, embroiled and stirred them all up against each other; and so, by the errors and follies of the rest, he was strengthening himself, and growing up to the ruin of all. But when every one saw that the then overbearing, but now unfortunate, Thebans, harassed by so long a war, must of necessity have recourse to you; Philip, to prevent this, and obstruct the union of the states, offered to you peace, to them succor. What helped him then almost to surprise you in a voluntary snare? The cowardice, shall I call it? or ignorance—or both—of the other Greeks; who, while you were waging a long and incessant war—and that too for their common benefit, as the event has shown—assisted you neither with money nor men, nor any thing else whatsoever. You, being justly and naturally offended with them, lent a willing ear to Philip.

The peace then granted was through such means brought about, not through me, as Æschines calumniously charged. The criminal and corrupt practices of these men during the

[1] See Appendix I.

[2] The very words here seem to be borrowed from Xenophon, where he describes the result of the battle of Mantinea. *'Ακρισία καὶ ταραχὴ ἔτι πλειων μετὰ τὴν μάχην ἐγένετο ἢ πρόσθεν ἐν τῇ 'Ελλάδι.*

treaty will be found, on fair examination, to be the cause of our present condition. The whole matter am I for truth's sake discussing and going through; for, let there appear to be ever so much criminality in these transactions, it is surely nothing to me. The first who spoke and mentioned the subject of peace was Aristodemus the actor: the seconder and mover, fellow-hireling for that purpose with the prosecutor,[1] was Philocrates the Agnusian[2]—your associate, Æschines, not mine, though you should burst with lying. Their supporters—from whatever motives—I pass that by for the present—were Eubulus and Cephisophon. I had nothing to do with it.

Notwithstanding these facts, which I have stated exactly according to the truth, he ventured to assert—to such a pitch of impudence had he come—that I, besides being author of the peace, had prevented the country making it in a general council with the Greeks. Why, you—I know not what name you deserve!—when you saw me robbing the state of an advantage and connection so important as you described just now, did you ever express indignation? did you come forward to publish and proclaim what you now charge me with? If indeed I had been bribed by Philip to prevent the conjunction of the Greeks, it was your business not to be silent, but to cry out, to protest, and inform the people. But you never did so—your voice was never heard to such a purpose, and no wonder; for at that time no embassy had been sent to any of the Greeks—they had all been tested long before; and not a word of truth upon the subject has Æschines spoken.

Besides, it is the country that he most traduces by his falsehoods. For, if you were at the same time calling on the Greeks to take arms, and sending your own embassadors to treat with Philip for peace, you were performing the part of an Eurybatus,[3] not the act of a commonwealth, or of honest men. But it is false, it is false. For what purpose could

[1] Μετὰ τούτου is wrongly referred by most translators to Aristodemus.

[2] *I. e.* of the δῆμος, or township of Agnus. A brief account of the orators and statesmen of the period will be found in Appendix II.

[3] This name, having once belonged to a notorious thief and trickster, had passed into a by-word of reproach. See the comment of Eustathius on the Odyssey, T. 247. Suidas mentions a Ζεὺς Εὐρύβατος, who changed himself into all manner of shapes. Æschines had in his speech compared Demosthenes to Eurybatus.

ye have sent for them at that period? For peace? They all had it. For war? You were yourselves deliberating about peace. It appears therefore, I was not the adviser or the author of the original peace; and none of his other calumnies against me are shown to be true.

Observe again, after the state had concluded the peace, what line of conduct each of us adopted. Hence you will understand who it was that co-operated in every thing with Philip; who that acted in your behalf, and sought the advantage of the commonwealth.

I moved in the council that our embassadors should sail instantly for whatever place they heard Philip was in, and receive his oath: they would not however, notwithstanding my resolution.[1] What was the effect of this, men of Athens? I will explain. It was Philip's interest that the interval before the oaths should be as long as possible; yours, that it should be as short. Why? Because you discontinued all your warlike preparations, not only from the day of swearing peace, but from the day that you conceived hopes of it; a thing which Philip was from the beginning studious to contrive, believing—rightly enough—that whatever of our possessions he might take before the oath of ratification, he should hold securely; as none would break the peace on such account. I, men of Athens, foreseeing and weighing these consequences, moved the decree, to sail for whatever place Philip was in, and receive his oath without delay; so that your allies, the Thracians, might be in possession of the places which Æschines ridiculed just now, (Serrium, Myrtium, and Ergisce,) at the time of swearing the oaths; and that Philip might not become master of Thrace by securing the posts of vantage, nor provide himself with plenty of money and troops to facilitate his further designs. Yet this decree he neither mentions nor reads; but reproaches me, because, as Councilor, I thought proper to introduce the embassadors. Why, what should I have done? Moved not to introduce men who were come for the purpose of conferring with you? or ordered the Manager[2] not to assign

[1] It is implied that the motion was carried. It then became a resolution of the senate, on the motion of Demosthenes, and may be called *his* resolution.

[2] The ἀρχιτέκτων was the lessee of the theatre, who undertook to keep

them places at the theatre? They might have had places for their two obols, if the resolution had not been moved. Was it my duty to guard the petty interests of the state, and have sold our main interests like these men? Surely not. Take and read me this decree, which the prosecutor, knowing it well, passed over. Read.

THE DECREE.[1]

"In the Archonship of Mnesiphilus, on the thirteenth of Hecatombæon, in the presidency of the Pandionian tribe, Demosthenes son of Demosthenes of Pæania moved:—Whereas Philip hath sent embassadors for peace, and hath agreed upon

it in repair and proper order, he himself taking the profits. The entrance fee of two obols was paid to him.

Demosthenes, as member of the council, had introduced the Macedonian embassadors, Parmenio, Antipater, and Eurylochus, and moved that they should be invited to seats of honor at the Dionysian festival. This was no more than a necessary act of civility, due to the eminent ministers whom Philip had sent to treat with the Athenians; and there could not be a more fit person to make the motion than Demosthenes, who had been one of the ten embassadors to Philip, and (it seems) the only councilor among them. Nor did he confine himself to these formal acts, but during their stay at Athens hospitably entertained them at his own house, and on their departure accompanied them a part of the way on horseback. For these attentions he was reproached by Æschines, as if he had overacted his part, and either sought to curry favor with Philip, or to make an idle display of his wealth and importance.

[1] In this, as in most of the documents quoted in the first half of the present speech, there are found serious difficulties, which have led critics to the conviction that it is not genuine. In the first place, the name of the archon for the year B.C. 347 was not Mnesiphilus, but Themistocles. Secondly, not five, but ten embassadors, were sent to receive the oath of Philip; and indeed the same ten who had been on the previous embassy. Thirdly, it is called a resolution of the senate and people, whereas that which Demosthenes refers to was a resolution of the senate alone. Fourthly, the ten embassadors were sent to receive Philip's oath only, not to take the oath on behalf of their country, which had been done before. These and some other discrepancies have led to the conclusion, that the decree (which is not found in all the manuscripts) is an interpolation; and Böckh, in a treatise *De Archontibus Pseudeponymis*, suggests the following way of accounting for the error. He supposes that the decree in the text was found in some ancient collection by the interpolator; that he mistook the name of the Γραμματεὺς, or secretary of the council, which was usually appended to decrees, for the name of the archon; and that, for want of due attention to times and circumstances, he mistook one document for another. Thus, in the endeavor to supply the defect of his manuscript, he cor-

articles of treaty, it is resolved[1] by the Council and People of Athens, in order that the peace voted in the first assembly may be *ratified*, to choose forthwith from the whole body of Athenians five embassadors; and that the persons elected do repair, without any delay, wheresoever they shall ascertain that Philip is, and as speedily as may be exchange oaths with him, according to the articles agreed on between him and the Athenian people, comprehending the allies of either party. For embassadors were chosen, Eubulus of Anaphlestus, Æschines of Cothocidæ, Cephisophon of Rhamnus, Democrates of Phlya, Cleon of Cothocidæ."

Notwithstanding that I had passed this decree for the advantage of Athens, not that of Philip, our worthy embassadors so little regarded it, as to sit down in Macedonia three whole months, until Philip returned from Thrace after entirely subjugating the country, although they might in ten days, or rather in three or four, have reached the Hellespont and saved the fortresses, by receiving his oath before he reduced them: for he would never have touched them in our presence, or we should not have sworn him; and thus he would have lost the peace, and not have obtained both, the peace and the fortresses.

Such was the first trick of Philip, the first corrupt act of these accursed miscreants, in the embassy: for which I avow that I was and am and ever will be at war and variance[2] with

rupted the text of the author; but gave up the unprofitable work when he had got half through the speech: and so it happens that the latter half is free from such interpolation.

Jacobs, who concurs with this view of Böckh, appears to agree with him also in another conjecture, viz., that the peace referred to in this decree is the same which is stated by Diodorus (lib. xvi. 77) to have been concluded between the Athenians and Philip after his unsuccessful siege of Byzantium. Other writers have doubted the fact of such a peace having ever been made.

[1] The *δεδόχθαι* depends in construction upon *εἶπε*, "moved that it be resolved." Such was the style in which a decree was drawn up.

[2] Lord Brougham charges Leland with an anti-climax in translating *πολεμεῖν καὶ διαφέρεσθαι*, "war and opposition." But he has an incorrect notion of the meaning of *διαφέρομαι*, which he says "indicates a constant agitation—a restless enmity." The truth is, that *διαφέρομαι* is not a strong word, but means simply—"I differ with—I dispute with—I am at variance," or the like. People not familiar with a language may be misled by etymology; for example, the common meanings of *versari*,

them. But mark another and still greater piece of villainy immediately after. When Philip had sworn to the peace, having secured Thrace through these men disobeying my decree, he again bribes them not to leave Macedonia, until he had got all ready for his expedition against the Phocians. His fear was, if they reported to you his design and preparation for marching, you might sally forth, sail round with your galleys to Thermopylæ as before, and block up the strait: his desire, that, the moment you received the intelligence from them, he should have passed Thermopylæ, and you be unable to do any thing. And in such terror and anxiety was Philip, lest, notwithstanding he had gained these advantages, if you voted succor before the destruction of the Phocians, his enterprise should fail; he hires this despicable fellow, no longer in common with the other embassadors, but by himself individually, to make that statement and report to you, by which every thing was lost.

I conjure and beseech you, men of Athens, throughout the trial to remember this; that, if Æschines in his charge had not traveled out of the indictment,[1] neither would I have spoken a word irrelevant; but since he has resorted to every species both of accusation and calumny, it is necessary for me to reply briefly to each of his charges.

What then were the statements made by Æschines, through

conversant, prevaricate, discourse, would not be discovered from the mere derivation of the words. Familiarity only makes you acquainted with the conventional usages of language, with the ordinary meanings of words, and all their niceties and peculiarities. Lord Brougham was partly deceived by the lexicon, which gives *hinc inde jactor* as one of the meanings of *διαφέρομαι*, and partly by his assuming that Demosthenes himself would never have been guilty of an anti-climax. I have myself observed that the ancients were not so particular about climaxes as modern writers are. But it is further to be observed, that the force of the passage greatly depends upon the words *τότε καὶ νῦν καὶ ἀεί*, which are applicable to both the verbs; and also, that the war which Demosthenes denounces is only a political war, and, so understood, it does not in effect amount to more than political opposition or enmity.

Jacobs expresses *διαφέρεσθαι* by *Zwist,* Pabst by *Zwiespalt,* Auger by *opposition.*

[1] A lawyer-like phrase is suitable here; and I have adopted the one furnished by Lord Brougham's reviewer in the *Times.* Leland's version, "if Æschines had urged nothing against me foreign to his cause," is not so good. Jacobs *wenn nicht Æschines über die Grenzen der Klage ausgeschritten wäre.*

which every thing was lost? That you should not be alarmed by Philip's having passed Thermopylæ—that all would be as you desired, if you kept quiet; and in two or three days you would hear, he was their friend to whom he had come as an enemy, and their enemy to whom he had come as a friend—it was not words that cemented attachments, (such was his solemn phrase,) but identity of interest; and it was the interest of all alike, Philip, the Phocians, and you, to be relieved from the harshness and insolence of the Thebans. His assertions were heard by some with pleasure, on account of the hatred which then subsisted against the Thebans. But what happened directly, almost immediately, afterward? The wretched Phocians were destroyed, their cities demolished; you that kept quiet, and trusted to Æschines, were shortly bringing in your effects out of the country, while Æschines received gold; and yet more — while you got nothing but your enmity with the Thebans and Thessalians,[1] Philip won their gratitude for what he had done. To prove what I say, read me the decree of Callisthenes, and the letter of Philip, from both of which these particulars will be clear to you. Read.

THE DECREE.[2]

"In the Archonship of Mnesiphilus, an extraordinary assembly having been convened by the Generals, with the sanction of the Presidents[3] and the Council, on the twenty-

[1] The truth of the matter is a little warped by the verbal antithesis of the orator. It is not strictly true, that the enmity with the Thebans and Thessalians was caused by these proceedings; it existed before, the Athenians having all along favored the Phocians; though it was certainly increased by their display of ill-will upon the occasion referred to, as Demosthenes says in the Oration on the Embassy, *τὴν ἔχθραν τὴν πρός Θηβαίους μείζω πεποίηκεν* (368). The verb *γενέσθαι* applies well to the latter clause, but not to the former; as is frequently the case.

[2] This decree, like the last, appears to be spurious. Not only the name of the archon, but the date and other circumstances are incorrect. The assembly held after the news of the conquest of Phocis was not in the month here stated, but at the end of Scirrophorion (June). And the contents of the decree vary from those which Demosthenes himself mentions in the Oration on the Embassy (359, 379). Winiewski thinks that there may have been two decrees on the motion of Callisthenes, similar in character, but on different occasions.

[3] To explain the constant references to the *πρυτάνεις*, *πρόεδροι*, &c., &c., a brief account is given of the two Athenian Councils in Appendixes III. and IV., and of the Popular Assemblies in Appendix V.

first of Mæmacterion, Callisthenes, son of Eteonicus of Phalerum, moved:—No Athenian shall on any pretense sleep in the country, but all in the city and Piræus, except those who are stationed in the garrisons; and they shall every one keep the posts assigned to them, without absenting themselves by night or day. Whosoever disobeys this decree, shall be amenable to the penalties of treason, unless he can show that some necessity prevented him: the judges of such necessity shall be the General of Infantry, and he of the Finance department,[1] and the Secretary of the Council. All effects shall be conveyed out of the country as speedily as may be; those that are within a hundred and twenty furlongs into the city and Piræus, those that are beyond a hundred and twenty furlongs to Eleusis, and Phyle, and Aphidna, and Rhamnus, and Sunium. On the motion of Callisthenes of Phalerum."

Was it with such expectations you concluded the peace? Were such the promises this hireling made you? Come, read the letter which Philip sent after this to Athens.

[1] The duties of the generals were more numerous and varied in the time of Demosthenes than in the early period of the republic. Formerly (as mentioned in vol. I. p. 66, note 3) the ten generals were sent out all together on warlike service. But this practice was discontinued, as the wars of Athens began to be more frequent and on a larger scale. One, two, or three only were then put in command of a single armament. The generals had also various duties of a civil nature assigned to them, which required the presence of some of them at home. Such were the superintendence of all warlike preparations, and the collecting and dispensing of the military funds. The management of the property-tax was confided to them, on account of its being peculiarly a war-impost. (See Appendix IV. vol. I.) Like other Athenian magistrates, they had judicial functions to perform in matters under their administrative control; as in questions arising out of the property-tax assessments, and charges for breach of military duty. The power of convoking extraordinary assemblies of the people was given to them, as being the persons peculiarly intrusted with the defense of the city and commonwealth. In the time of Demosthenes it would seem that their functions were divided, probably for convenience; so that one commanded the infantry, ὁ ἐπὶ τῶν ὅπλων, or ὁπλιτῶν, another the cavalry, ὁ ἐπὶ τῶν ἱππέων, another took charge of the military chest and fund, ὁ ἐπὶ τῆς διοικήσεως. Perhaps others had other tasks assigned to them. See the page above referred to in vol. I. Reiske thinks ὁ ἐπὶ τῶν ὅπλων is simply "the general in military command." Jacobs renders it, *der befehlführende Strateg.*

THE LETTER OF PHILIP.

"Philip, king of Macedonia, to the Council and People of Athens, greeting. Ye know that we have passed Thermopylæ, and reduced Phocis to submission, and put garrisons in the towns that opened their gates; those that resisted we took by storm, and razed to the ground, enslaving their inhabitants. Hearing however, that ye are preparing to assist them, I have written unto you, that ye may trouble yourselves no farther in the business. For it seems to me, ye are acting altogether unreasonably; having concluded peace, and nevertheless taking the field, and that too when the Phocians are not comprehended in our treaty. Wherefore, if ye abide not by your engagements, ye will gain no advantage but that of being the aggressors."

You hear how plainly, in his letter to you, he declares and asserts to his own allies—"all this I have done against the will of the Athenians, and in their despite; therefore if ye are wise, ye Thebans and Thessalians, ye will regard them as enemies, and put confidence in me;" not writing in such words, but meaning so to be understood. And by these means he carried them away with him,[1] insomuch that they had neither foresight nor sense of the consequences, but suffered him to get every thing into his power: hence the misfortunes under which those wretched people at present are. The agent and auxiliary who helped to win for him such confidence—who brought false reports here and cajoled you—he it is who now bewails the sufferings of the Thebans, and dilates upon them so pathetically,[2] he himself being the cause both of these calamities, and those in Phocis, and all the rest which the Greeks have sustained. Truly must you, Æschines, grieve at these events, and compassionate the Thebans, when you hold property in Bœotia and farm their lands; and I rejoice at a work, whose author immediately required me to be delivered into his hands.[3]

[1] That is, "he won them completely over—he got them entirely under his influence, so that they had scarce a will of their own." The metaphorical use of our word *transported* is not dissimilar. Jacobs: *er Jene mit sich fortriss.* Pabst: *er diese ganz für sich einnahm.*

[2] "Describes at length how pitiable they are."

[3] After Thebes had been taken by Alexander, the Athenians, on the motion of Demades, sent embassadors to congratulate him. He sent them a letter, demanding that Demosthenes, and eight others (or nine

But I have fallen upon a subject which it may be more convenient to discuss by-and-by. I will return then to my proofs, showing how the iniquities of these men have brought about the present state of things.

When you had been deceived by Philip through the agency of these men, who sold themselves in the embassies, and reported not a word of truth to you—when the unhappy Phocians had been deceived and their cities destroyed—what followed? The despicable Thessalians and stupid Thebans looked on Philip as a friend, a benefactor, a saviour: he was every thing with them—not a syllable would they hear from any one to the contrary. You, though regarding his acts with suspicion and anger, still observed the peace; for you could have done nothing alone. The rest of the Greeks, cheated and disappointed like yourselves, gladly observed the peace, though they also had in a manner been attacked for a long time. For when Philip was marching about, subduing Illyrians and Triballians and some also of the Greeks, and gaining many considerable accessions of power, and certain citizens of the states (Æschines among them) took advantage of the peace to go there and be corrupted; all people then, against whom he was making such preparations, were attacked. If they perceived it not, that is another question, no concern of mine. I was for ever warning and protesting, both at Athens and wheresoever I was sent. But the states were diseased; one class in their politics and measures being venal and corrupt, while the multitude of private men either had

others, according to Diodorus) of the principal orators and statesmen of the anti-Macedonian party, among whom were Chares, Hyperides, and Lycurgus, should be delivered up to him. Phocion advised that they should be given up, and even urged them to surrender themselves for the good of their country. Demosthenes recited to the people the fable of Æsop, where the wolf required the sheep to give up their dogs. After some discussion Demades offered to intercede with the conqueror. He was sent on an embassy for that purpose, and by his entreaty Alexander was prevailed upon to withdraw the demand as to all but Charidemus.

That Demosthenes was obnoxious to Alexander can hardly be wondered at. Æschines relates that, on Alexander's first march to Thebes, Demosthenes was sent on an embassy to him from Athens, and went as far as Cithæron, where, apprehending danger to himself, he invented an excuse for turning back. There is no doubt that both then and afterward he had been concerting measures to shake off the yoke of Macedonia.

no foresight, or were caught with the bait of present ease and idleness; and all were under some such influence, only they imagined each that the mischief would not approach themselves, but that by the peril of others they might secure their own safety when they chose. The result, I fancy, has been, that the people, in return for their gross and unseasonable indolence, have lost their liberty: the statesmen, who imagined they were selling every thing but themselves, discovered they had sold themselves first; for, instead of friends, as they were named during the period of bribery, they are now called parasites, and miscreants, and the like befitting names. Justly. For no man, O Athenians, spends money for the traitor's benefit, or, when he has got possession of his purchase, employs the traitor to advise him in future proceedings: else nothing could have been more fortunate than a traitor. But it is not so—it never could be—it is far otherwise! When the aspirant for power has gained his object, he is master also of those that sold it; and then—then, I say, knowing their baseness, he loathes and mistrusts and spurns them.[1]

[1] In this, as in the passage a little below, I have in my version made no distinction between *φίλων* and *ξένων*, simply because the English language does not furnish me with the means. *Ξένοι* (in the sense here used) are absent friends, who would be *φίλοι*, if they dwelt in the same place, but being separated, can only correspond, or occasionally visit each other and exchange hospitality. The relation that exists between such persons is called *ξενία*, but we have not in our language any word which expresses that mutual relation; nor indeed any which expresses the relation between host and guest, as I have before observed. (Vol. I. p. 97, note 2.) Leland here renders *ξένος*, *guest*, (which is but half the sense,) and below, *intimate*, and *ξενία*, *intimacy*. Spillan makes *ξένος*, *friend*, and *φίλος*, *intimate*. Brougham has *guest* for *ξένος*, and *hospitality* for *ξενία*. Francis the same. But *hospitality* will not bear the enlarged sense necessary for *ξενία*. The *Gastfreund* of the German unfortunately can not be imitated in English. Auger (like Leland) is inconsistent. In the first passage he has "d'hôtes et d'amis;" in the next, "ami" for both. The true meaning of *ξένοι* is fully expressed by a paraphrase in the following passage of Shakspeare:

"Sicilia can not show himself over-kind to Bohemia. They were trained together in their childhood, and there rooted between them then such an affection, which can not choose but branch now. Since their more mature dignities and royal necessities made separation of their society, their encounters, though not personal, have been royally attornied, with interchange of gifts, letters, loving embassies; that they have seemed to be together, though absent, shook hands, as over a vast, and embraced, as it were, from the ends of opposed winds."—*Winter's Tale*, Act I. Scene 1.

Consider only—for, though the time of the events is past, the time for understanding them is ever present to the wise: Lasthenes was called the friend of Philip for a while, until he betrayed Olynthus—Timolaus for a while, until he destroyed Thebes—Rudicus and Simus of Larissa for a while, until they brought Thessaly under Philip's power. Since then the world has become full of traitors, expelled, and insulted, and suffering every possible calamity.[1] How fared Aristratus in Sicyon? how Perilaus in Megara? Are they not outcasts? Hence one may evidently see, it is the vigilant defender of his country, the strenuous opponent of such men, who secures to you traitors and hirelings, Æschines, the opportunity of getting bribes: through the number of those that oppose your wishes, you are in safety and in pay; for had it depended on yourselves, you would have perished long ago.

Much more could I say about those transactions, yet methinks too much has been said already. The fault is my adversary's, for having spirted over me the dregs,[2] I may say, of his own wickedness and iniquities, of which I was obliged to clear myself to those who are younger than the events. You too have probably been disgusted, who knew this man's venality before I spoke a word. He calls it friendship indeed; and said somewhere in his speech—"the man who reproaches me with the friendship of Alexander." I reproach you with friendship of Alexander! Whence gotten, or how merited? Neither Philip's friend nor Alexander's should I ever call you; I am not so mad; unless we are to call reapers and other hired laborers the friends of those that hire them. That however is not so—how could it be? It is nothing of the

[1] I agree with the German translators, who join the participles *ἐλαυνομένων*, &c. with *προδοτῶν*, not referring them to the persons above mentioned. Ἡ *οἰκουμένη*, as Schaefer truly remarks, is intended for Greece only; yet it is proper to translate it "the world." In like manner we use such expressions as "all the world says," "all the world knows," &c., when they apply to a very small portion of it.

With respect to the reproaches cast by Demosthenes on these men, there is an interesting passage in Polybius, which the reader will find in Appendix VI.

[2] Jacobs: *die schmutzigen Hefen über mich ausgeschüttet hat.* Pabst: *den ganzen Bodensatz ausgegossen.* Leland and Spillan: "disgorged the foulness." Brougham: "poured out the crapulous remains." Auger: "qui s'est déchargé sur moi de ses iniquités, qui m'a souillé de ses propres noirceurs."

kind. Philip's hireling I called you once, and Alexander's I call you now. So do all these men. If you disbelieve me, ask them; or rather I will do it for you. Athenians! is Æschines, think ye, the hireling, or the friend of Alexander? You hear what they say.[1]

I now proceed to my defense upon the indictment itself, and to the account of my own measures, that Æschines may hear, though he knows already, on what I found my title both to these which have been decreed and to far greater rewards. Take and read me the indictment itself.

THE INDICTMENT.

"In the archonship of Chærondas, on the sixth of Elaphebolion; Æschines son of Atrometus of Cothocidæ preferred before the archon an indictment against Ctesiphon son of Leosthenes of Anaphlystus, for an illegal measure:[2] for that he proposed a decree against law, to wit, that it was right to

[1] Auger remarks upon this as follows: "Après que les Athéniens ont répondu tout d'une voix qu'Eschine est un mercenaire, Demosthène reprend, en lui adressant la parole à lui-même: '*Vous entendez ce qu'ils disent?*' Il falloit être bien sûr de son éloquence et de son pouvoir sur les auditeurs, pour risquer une telle interrogation. Remarquons néanmoins que l'orateur ne se hasarde à la leur faire, que quand il a enflammé et embrasé leurs cœurs par la sortie la plus vive contre les traîtres, et que par-là il les a disposés à répondre suivant son désir."

Leland has the following note: "Commentators seem surprised at the boldness and the success of this appeal. Some tell us, that the speaker was hurried into the hazardous question by his impetuosity; some, that his friend Menander was the only person who returned the answer he desired; others again, that he pronounced falsely on purpose, and that the assembly intended but to correct his pronunciation, when they echoed back the word μισθωτὸς, hireling. But the truth is, he was too much interested in the present contest to suffer himself to be really transported beyond the strictest bounds of prudence and caution; he was too well supported to rely upon a single voice, if such could be at all heard in the assembly; and he had too much good sense to recur to a ridiculous and childish artifice. The assembly to which he addressed himself was of a quite different kind from one of our modern courts of law, where order and decorum are maintained. The audience were not at all concerned to suppress the emotions raised in them by the speaker: and Demosthenes had a large party present, who, he was well assured, would return the proper answer loudly."

The event seems to prove that Demosthenes could safely hazard the question.

[2] See Appendix VII.

crown Demosthenes son of Demosthenes of Pæania with a golden crown, and to proclaim in the theatre at the great Dionysian festival, at the exhibition of the new tragedies, that the people crown Demosthenes son of Demosthenes of Pæania with a golden crown, on account of his virtue, and of the good-will which he has constantly cherished toward all the Greeks as well as toward the people of Athens, and of his integrity, and because he has constantly by word and deed promoted the advantage of the people, and is zealous to do whatever good he can: all which clauses are false and illegal; the laws enacting, first, that no false allegations shall be entered in the public records; secondly, that an accountable officer[1] shall not be crowned (but Demosthenes is a conservator of the walls, and has charge of the theoric fund); thirdly, that the crown shall not be proclaimed in the theatre at the Dionysian festival, on the new exhibition of tragedies, but if the council confer a crown, it shall be published in the council-hall, if the people, in the Pnyx[2] at the assembly.

[1] All magistrates and public officers at Athens, whether civil or military, including the members of the two councils, were obliged, at the expiration of their term of office, to render an account to the people of the manner in which they had performed their duties. Thirty days was allowed for that purpose, and any citizen was at liberty to come forward within that period, and prefer an accusation against them. The scrutiny was not confined to pecuniary questions, but embraced an inquiry into their whole conduct and administration. It will easily however be understood, that with respect to general matters the accounting must in the first instance have been of a negative character, the magistrate having only to defend himself in case any charge was preferred; while, with respect to pecuniary transactions, he would have to give a positive account of all public moneys that had been received by him, or passed through his hands. There were officers specially appointed to superintend this business: *Λογισταὶ* and *Εὔθυνοι*, *Auditors* and *Scrutineers*, ten of each, and one for every tribe, elected by the council of five hundred. The auditors had a court under their jurisdiction, to which all charges for embezzlement, bribery, and malversation, as well as more general accusations for official misconduct, were referred by them to be tried by a jury. The scrutineers assisted the auditors, and were subordinate to them.

The importance attached by the framers of the Athenian laws to the institutions of the *Εὐθύνη*, which secured the responsibility of all functionaries to the people, is apparent from this law, which Æschines made the foundation of his indictment, as well as from divers other passages in the speeches of both the rival orators.

[2] The place where the assemblies of the people were commonly held. See Appendix V.

Penalty, fifty talents. Witnesses to the summons,[1] Cephisophon son of Cephisophon of Rhamnus, Cleon son of Cleon of Cothocidæ."

The clauses of the decree which he prosecutes are these, men of Athens. Now from these very clauses I think I shall immediately make it clear to you, that my whole defense will be just; for I shall take the charges in the same order as my adversary, and discuss them all one by one, without a single intentional omission.

With respect to the statement, "that I have constantly by word and deed promoted the advantage of the people, and am zealous to do whatever good I can," and the praising me[2] on such grounds, your judgment, I conceive, must depend on my public acts; from an examination of which it will be discovered whether what Ctesiphon has alleged concerning me is true and proper, or false. As to his proposing to give the crown without adding "when he has passed his accounts," and to proclaim the crown in the theatre, I imagine that this also relates to my political conduct, whether I am worthy of the crown and the public proclamation, or not. However, I deem it necessary to produce the laws which justified the defendant in proposing such clauses.

Thus honestly and simply, men of Athens, have I resolved to conduct my defense. I now proceed to my own actual measures. And let no one suppose that I wander from[3] the

[1] These were persons who accompanied the prosecutor when he summoned the defendant to appear before the magistrate. Anciently they were sureties also for the proper carrying on of the cause, like our ancient pledges to prosecute. In later times they were mere servers of the citation or summons; but the plaint, or bill of indictment, always had their names subscribed.

[2] *'Επαινεῖν* is connected with *τοῦ*, and not governed by *γράψαι*, as Schaefer thinks. *Τοῦ γράψαι* depends in construction upon *κρίσιν*. In the clause below, I make *στεφανοῦν* dependent on *κελεῦσαι*. Spillan connects it with *τό*. Jacobs joins it with *προσγράψαντα*.

[3] Literally: "Disconnect my speech from the indictment." Leland had a wrong idea when he translated it, "that I am suspending the discussion of this cause." So had Francis, who renders it: "that I propose to evade the force of the indictment."

With respect to the anxiety shown by the orator to justify this line of defense, Lord Brougham remarks as follows: "The extreme importance to Demosthenes' case of the skillful movement, so to speak, by which he availed himself of Æschines' error, and at once entered on the general subject of his whole administration—thus escaping the immediate

indictment, if I touch upon Grecian questions and affairs: he who attacks that clause of the decree, "that by word and deed I have promoted your good"—he who has indicted this for being false—he, I say, has rendered the discussion of my whole policy pertinent and necessary to the charge. Moreover, there being many departments of political action, I chose that which belonged to Grecian affairs: therefore I am justified in drawing my proofs from them.

The conquests which Philip had got and held before I commenced life as a statesman and orator, I shall pass over, as I think they concern not me. Those that he was baffled in from the day of my entering on such duties, I will call to your recollection, and render an account of them; premising one thing only—Philip started, men of Athens, with a great advantage. It happened that among the Greeks—not some, but all alike—there sprang up a crop[1] of traitors and venal wretches, such as in the memory of man had never been before. These he got for his agents and supporters: the Greeks, already ill-disposed and unfriendly to each other, he brought into a still worse state, deceiving this people, making presents to that, corrupting others in every way; and he split them into many parties, when they had all one interest, to prevent his aggrandizement. While the Greeks were all in such a condition—in such ignorance of the gathering and growing mischief—you have to consider, men of Athens, what policy and measures it became the commonwealth to adopt, and of this to receive a reckoning from me; for the man who assumed that post in the administration was I.

Ought she, Æschines, to have cast off her spirit and dignity, and, in the style of Thessalians and Dolopians, helped to acquire for Philip the dominion of Greece, and extinguished the honors and rights of our ancestors? Or, if she did not

charge, to which he had no answer, and overwhelming his adversary by a triumphant defense on ground of his own choosing—requires that he should again and again defend this movement, which he here does very carefully."

[1] I have adopted Lord Brougham's word. Leland and Spillan: *supply*. Francis: *harvest*. Jacobs: *Fülle*. Pabst: *ein reichlicher Nachwuchs*. Reiske: *proventus*.

The same expression is used by Diodorus, in reference to the corruption of Greek statesmen at this time. (XVI. 54.) He evidently had the words of Demosthenes before his eye.

this—which would indeed have been shameful—was it right, that what she saw would happen if unprevented, and was for a long time, it seems, aware of, she should suffer to come to pass?[1]

I would gladly ask the severest censurer of our acts, with what party he would have wished the commonwealth to side —with those who contributed to the disgraces and disasters of the Greeks, the party, we may say, of the Thessalians and their followers—or those who permitted it all for the hope of selfish advantage, among whom we may reckon the Arcadians, Messenians, and Argives? But many of them, or rather all, have fared worse than ourselves. If Philip after his victory had immediately marched off and kept quiet, without molesting any either of his own allies or of the Greeks in general, still[2] they that opposed not his enterprises would have merited some blame and reproach. But when he has stripped all alike of their dignity, their authority, their liberty—nay, even of their constitutions, where he was able—can it be doubted that you took the most glorious course in pursuance of my counsels?

But I return to the question—What should the commonwealth, Æschines, have done, when she saw Philip establishing an empire and dominion over Greece? Or what was your statesman to advise or move?—I, a statesman at Athens?—for this is most material—I who knew that from the earliest time, until the day of my own mounting the platform, our country had ever striven for precedency and honor and renown, and expended more blood and treasure for the sake of glory and the general weal than the rest of the Greeks had expended on their several interests?—who saw that Philip himself, with whom we were contending, had, in the strife for power and empire, had his eye cut out,[3] his collar-bone frac-

[1] Pabst is the only translator who has rendered *περιιδεῖν γιγνόμενα* accurately: *aber das, was er bevorstehen sah, wenn Niemand Widerstand leistete, und was er lange voraus erkannte, ungehindert geschehen lassen?*

[2] Ὅμως and *οὐκ* are omitted in some manuscripts. Without them, the sense is: "If Philip had quietly withdrawn after his victory, some blame might have fallen on you for opposing him; because it would then have appeared that he had no evil designs."

[3] Philip lost his eye at the siege of Methone. (See vol. I. Appendix I.) The other wounds were inflicted on his return from Scythia, in a battle with the Triballi, B.C. 340.

tured, his hand and leg mutilated, and was ready and willing to sacrifice any part of his body that fortune chose to take, provided he could live with the remainder in honor and glory? Hardly will any one venture to say this—that it became a man bred at Pella, then an obscure and inconsiderable place, to possess such inborn magnanimity, as to aspire to the mastery of Greece and form the project in his mind, while you, who were Athenians, day after day in speeches and in dramas reminded of the virtue of your ancestors, should have been so naturally base, as of your own free-will and accord to surrender to Philip the liberty of Greece. No man will say this![1]

The only course then that remained was a just resistance to all his attacks upon you. Such course you took from the beginning, properly and becomingly; and I assisted by

[1] Lord Brougham's reviewer censures him for translating *θεωρήμασι* "spectacles," taking it in the more general sense of "every thing which you see," which is in accordance with Schaefer's opinion. Undoubtedly it would make very good sense, if Demosthenes referred to every thing which might be seen in Athens reminding the people of their ancient glory, such as their public buildings, their walls, the Parthenon, Propylæa, and the like. But *θεώρημα* is more commonly used to signify a theatrical spectacle or exhibition; and perhaps in connection with *ὁρῶσι* one rather expects a word of a confined signification. I am therefore inclined to prefer Lord Brougham's version, which agrees with those of Jacobs, Pabst, Spilland, Leland and Auger. *Λόγοι* and *θεωρήματα* are aptly joined together; the "public harangues," and the "dramatic exhibitions." In such dramas as the Persæ, the Supplices, the Heraclidæ, Athenians were constantly hearing the praises of their ancestors.

Lord Brougham has been censured likewise for translating *ὁρῶσι* "contemplate." No doubt he did so purposely, in order to avoid the use of a verb which would not suit *λόγοις*. And he was right. The application of a word to two clauses, which strictly is applicable to one only, is a Greek idiom, but not an English. It might be rendered, "having before you." I have given it a turn, for brevity's sake.

The same critic, correcting Lord Brougham's version of *Φιλίππῳ παραχωρῆσαι*, "surrender to Philip," (which I have adopted,) proposes, "let slip out of your own keeping into that of Philip;" which shows that he does not even understand the true sense of *παραχωρεῖν*, which is, "to yield to another by retiring, or stepping out of the way," *loco cedere*. A yet more amusing essay at translation is the following:—*οὐδ' ἂν εἱς ταῦτα φήσειεν*, "that no man would have dared to assert." In this, which the critic designates as a literal and verbatim translation, there is one pleonasm and one gross error, which any good school-boy will point out. Lord Brougham certainly has committed the same error, but then he does not set it up as a verbatim and literal version.

motions and counsels during the period of my political life:—I acknowledge it. But what should I have done? I put this question to you, dismissing all else: Amphipolis, Pydna, Potidæa, Halonnesus—I mention none of them: Serrium, Doriscus, the ravaging of Peparethus, and any similar wrongs which the country has suffered—I know not even of their occurrence. You indeed said, that by talking of these I had brought the people into a quarrel, although the resolutions respecting them were moved by Eubulus and Aristophon and Diopithes—not by me, you ready utterer of what suits your purpose! Neither will I speak of these now. But I ask—the man who was appropriating to himself Eubœa, and making it a fortress against Attica, and attempting Megara, and seizing Oreus, and razing Porthmus, and setting up Philistides as tyrant in Oreus, Clitarchus in Eretria, and subjugating the Hellespont, and besieging Byzantium, and destroying some of the Greek cities, restoring exiles to others—was he by all these proceedings committing injustice, breaking the truce, violating the peace, or not? Was it meet that any of the Greeks should rise up to prevent these proceedings, or not? If not—if Greece was to present the spectacle (as it is called) of a Mysian prey,[1] while Athenians had life and being, then I have exceeded my duty in speaking on the subject—the commonwealth has exceeded her duty, which followed my counsels—I admit that every measure has been a misdeed, a blunder of mine. But if some one ought to have arisen to prevent these things, who but the Athenian people should it have been? Such then was the policy which I espoused. I saw him reducing all men to subjection, and I opposed him: I continued warning and exhorting you not to make these sacrifices to Philip.

It was he that infringed the peace by taking our ships: it was not the state, Æschines. Produce the decrees themselves, and Philip's letter, and read them one after another. From an examination of them, it will be evident who is chargeable with each proceeding. Read.

[1] A proverbial expression applied to a people in an utterly helpless and defenseless state. It was derived, we are told, from the times of the Trojan war, when the Mysians were exposed to the enemy by the absence of their king Telephus.

THE DECREE.[1]

"In the archonship of Neocles, in the month Boedromion, an extraordinary assembly having been convened by the generals, Eubulus son of Mnesitheus of Cytherus[2] moved; Whereas the generals have reported in the assembly, that Leodamas the admiral, and the twenty vessels dispatched with him to the Hellespont for the safe-conduct of the corn, have been carried to Macedonia by Philip's general Amyntas, and are detained in custody, let the presidents and the generals take care that the council be convened, and embassadors to Philip be chosen, who shall go and treat with him for the release of the admiral, vessels, and troops: and if Amyntas has acted in ignorance, they shall say that the people make no complaint against him; if the admiral was found wrongfully exceeding his instructions, that the Athenians will make inquiry, and punish him as his negligence deserves: if it be neither of these things, but a willful[3] trespass on the part of him who gave or him who received the commission, let them state this also,[4] that the people, being apprised, may deliberate what course to take."

This decree Eubulus carried, not I. The next, Aristophon: then Hegesippus, then Aristophon again, then Philocrates, then Cephisophon, then the rest. I had no concern in the matter. Read the decree.

[1] The archon mentioned in this and the two following decrees is incorrect. Nicomachus was archon of that year. For an account of the events, see Vol. I. Appendix III. p. 293.

[2] Cytherus was one of the δῆμοι of Attica. The common reading is Κύπριος. Reiske seems to think that Eubulus might be called a Cyprian, though a citizen of Athens, if he had been educated or long resided at Cyprus. However that may be, such would not be his description in a state paper.

[3] The term *willful* applies to Philip as well as Amyntas. "In his own person," or "on his own account," would hardly be suitable to Philip. The student should notice the use of the plural ἀγνωμονοῦσιν, followed by the disjunctive clauses. It is perhaps an expression of the following thought:—"If it be a trespass on the part of the captors, whether committed by Amyntas on his own account, or under the special orders of Philip."

[4] The clause καὶ τοῦτο γράψαι λέγειν depends on εἶπεν, and is to be construed thus: γράψαι, "to insert an order in the decree," λέγειν, "for the embassadors to state," &c.

THE DECREE.[1]

"In the archonship of Neocles, on the last day of Boedromion, at the desire of the council, the presidents and generals introduced their report of the proceedings of the assembly, to wit, that the people had resolved to appoint embassadors to Philip for the recovery of the ships, and to furnish them with instructions and with the decrees of the assembly; and they appointed the following: Cephisophon son of Cleon of Anaphlystus; Democritus son of Demophon of Anagyrus; Polycritus son of Apemantus of Cothocidæ. In the presidency of the Hippothoontian tribe, on the motion of Aristophon of Colyttus, committee-man."

Now then, as I produce these decrees, so do you, Æschines, point out what decree of my passing makes me chargeable with the war. You can not find one: had you any, there is nothing you would sooner have produced. Why, even Philip makes no charge against me on account of the war, though he complains of others. Read Philip's own letter.

THE LETTER OF PHILIP.

"Philip, king of Macedon, to the Council and People of Athens, greeting. Your embassadors, Cephisophon, Democritus, and Polycritus, came to me and conferred about the release of the galleys which Laomedon commanded. Upon the whole, I think you must be very simple, if you imagine I do not see that those galleys were commissioned, under the pretense of conveying corn from the Hellespont to Lemnos, to relieve the Selymbrians, whom I am besieging, and who are not included in the friendly treaty subsisting between us.

[1] We have seen that by the last decree the people had ordered a meeting of the council to be convened, to elect embassadors to Philip. The presidents and generals, to whom that task was intrusted, convene the council accordingly, and lay before them the business for which they were called—(χρηματίζειν is the usual word, signifying "to introduce the topic of discussion, the business of the day"). The council proceed to execute the order of the people, and elect the embassadors. That is their ψήφισμα, the senatorial decree containing their appointment of embassadors, pursuant to the decree of the popular assembly. The document has perplexed commentators, but really has no difficulty. Schömann explains it in his treatise "De Comitiis" (94). As to πρόεδρος, which I translate "committee-man," see Appendix IV.

And these instructions were given, without leave of the Athenian people, by certain magistrates and others who are not now in office, but who are anyways desirous for the people to exchange our present amity for a renewal of war, and are far more anxious for such a consummation than to relieve the Selymbrians. They suppose it will be a source of income to themselves: however, I scarcely think it is for your advantage or mine. Wherefore I release you the vessels carried into my port; and for the future, if, instead of allowing your statesmen to adopt malignant measures, you will punish them, I too will endeavor to maintain the peace. Farewell."

Here is no mention by him of Demosthenes, or any charge against me. Why then, while he complains of the others, makes he no mention of my acts? Because he must have noticed his own aggressions, had he written aught concerning me; for on these I fixed myself—these I kept resisting. And first I proposed the embassy to Peloponnesus,[1] when into Peloponnesus he began to steal; next that to Eubœa,[2] when on Eubœa he was laying his hands; then the expedition (no longer an embassy) to Oreus, and that to Eretria, when he established rulers in those cities. Afterward I dispatched all the armaments, by which Chersonesus was preserved, and Byzantium, and all our allies; whence to you there accrued the noblest results—praises, eulogies, honors, crowns, thanks from those you succored; while the people attacked—those that trusted you then obtained deliverance, those that disregarded you have had often to remember your warnings, and to be convinced that you were not only their friends, but wise men also and prophets: for all that you predicted has come to pass.

That Philistides would have given a great deal to keep Oreus—Clitarchus a great deal to keep Eretria—Philip himself a great deal to have these vantage-posts[3] against you, and

[1] This was the embassy referred to in the third Philippic, which prevented the advance of Philip into the Peloponnese, B.C. 343. For a brief account of Philip's proceedings in Peloponnesus, see Appendix VIII.

[2] As to Eubœa, see vol. I. pp. 107, 128, 150.

[3] Or perhaps simply "these advantages." Jacobs: *um diese Vortheile gegen Euch zu erhalten.* Pabst: *um dieses alles gegen Euch auszuführen.*

in other matters to avoid exposure, and any inquiry into his wrongful acts in general—no man is ignorant, and least of all you. For the embassadors who came here then from Clitarchus and Philistides lodged with you, Æschines, and you were their host. The commonwealth regarded them as enemies, whose offers were neither just nor advantageous, and expelled them; but they were your friends. None of their designs then were accomplished;[1] you slanderer—who say of me, that I am silent when I have got something, and bawl when I have spent it![2] That is not your custom. You bawl when you have something, and will never stop, unless the jury stop you by disfranchisement to-day.[3]

When you crowned me then for those services, and Aristonicus drew up the same words that Ctesiphon here has now drawn up, and the crown was proclaimed in the theatre—for this now is the second proclamation in my favor[4]—Æschines, being present, neither opposed it, nor indicted the mover. Take this decree now and read it.

THE DECREE.

"In the archonship of Chærondas, son of Hegemon, on the twenty-fifth of Gamelion, in the presidency of the Leontian

[1] The argument is—Philistides and Clitarchus were unable to accomplish their purpose, and that chiefly through my opposition. Yet it is notorious, they would have given a large bribe to have obtained powerful support at Athens. Then what becomes of your charge of corruption against me?

[2] Æschines, defending himself against the reproach of having retired from public affairs, said that his own habits were so simple, and his desires so moderate, that he was not compelled to speak in public for lucre's sake—Demosthenes, on the contrary, never opened his mouth but when he was hired. The words here referred to are: *σὺ δ' οἶμαι λαβὼν μὲν σεσίγηκας, ἀναλώσας δὲ κέκραγας.*

Many idle stories to the same effect were circulated against Demosthenes, besides the celebrated charge in the affair of Harpalus. There is one told by Aulus Gellius, that he had been bribed by the Milesian embassadors to withdraw his opposition to them in the assembly, and afterward, hearing from Aristodemus the actor that he had received a talent for his performance—"I," said he, "have received more than that for being silent."

[3] If the prosecutor failed to obtain a fifth part of the votes, besides a fine of a thousand drachms, he incurred a partial disfranchisement, which incapacitated him to prefer a similar charge in future.

[4] Τούτου means "this of Ctesiphon." So Schaefer rightly explains it. Pabst's version is: *so dass dies schon die zweite Verkündigung dieser Ehre für mich ist.* I have adopted the turn of Leland.

tribe, Aristonicus of Phrearrii moved: Whereas Demosthenes son of Demosthenes of Pæania hath rendered many important services to the people of Athens, and to divers of her allies heretofore, and hath also on the present occasion aided them by his decrees, and liberated certain of the cities in Eubœa, and perseveres in his attachment to the people of Athens, and doth by word and deed whatever good he can for the Athenians themselves and the rest of the Greeks: It is resolved by the Council and People of Athens, to honor Demosthenes son of Demosthenes of Pæania with public praise[1] and a golden crown, and to proclaim the crown in the theatre at the Dyonysian festival at the new tragedies, and the proclamation of the crown shall be given in charge to the presiding tribe and the prize-master.[2] On the motion of Aristonicus of Phrearrii."

Is there one of you that knows of any disgrace falling on the state by reason of this decree, or any scorn or ridicule—consequences which this man now predicts, if I am crowned? It is when acts are recent and notorious that, if good, they obtain reward, if the contrary, punishment; and it appears that I then obtained reward, not blame or punishment. So, up to the period of those transactions, I am acknowledged on all occasions to have promoted the interests of the state—because my speeches and motions prevailed in your councils—because my measures were executed, and procured crowns for the commonwealth and for me and all of you—because you have offered sacrifices and thanksgivings to the gods for their success.

When Philip therefore was driven out of Eubœa, with arms by you, with counsels and decrees—though some persons there should burst![3]—by me, he sought some new

[1] The epithet "public" seems necessary in our language to express the distinction conferred upon Demosthenes; though indeed we say "to praise God," in the sense of "to glorify:" and Shakspeare has,

I come to bury Cæsar, not to praise him.

Leland has: "pay public honors." Brougham: "signalize." Spillan: "bestow honors." Auger: "accorder publiquement des louanges." Jacobs: *Lob zu ertheilen*. Pabst: *beloben*.

[2] The person who adjudged the prizes in the various contests during the festival.

[3] Demosthenes is fond of this expression. Compare Virgil, Eclog. vii. 26.

Invidiâ rumpantur ut ilia Codro.

position of attack upon Athens.[1] Seeing that we use more foreign corn than any people, and wishing to command the passage of the corn-trade, he advanced to Thrace; the Byzantines being his allies, he first required them to join in the war against you, and when they refused, saying (truly enough) that they had not made alliance on such terms, he threw up intrenchments before the city, planted batteries, and laid siege to it. What course hereupon it became you to take, I will not ask again; it is manifest to all. But who was it that succored the Byzantines, and rescued them? who prevented the alienation of the Hellespont at that crisis? You, men of Athens. When I say you, I mean the commonwealth. But who advised, framed, executed the measures of state, devoted himself wholly and unreservedly to the public business?—I!—What benefits thence accrued to all, you need no further to be told; you have learned by experience. For the war which then sprang up, besides that it brought honor and renown, kept you in a cheaper and more plentiful supply of all the necessaries of life than does the present peace, which these worthies maintain to their country's prejudice in the hope of something to come. Perish such hope! Never may they share the blessings for which you men of honest wishes pray to the gods, nor communicate their own principles to you!

Read them now the crowns of the Byzantines, and those of the Perinthians, which they conferred upon the country as a reward.

THE BYZANTINE DECREE.

"In the Presbytership[2] of Bosporichus, Damagetus moved

[1] Leland: "he raised another engine against this state." Spillan follows him. Francis has "battery." So has Auger. Jacobs: *versuchte er einen Angriff andrer Art gegen die Stadt.* Pabst: *andere Schutzwehr zum Kampf.* Brougham: "some new mode of beleaguering our state." A critic in the *Times* suggests: "another mode of annoyance." That, no doubt, is the general meaning; but in the translation we should not lose sight of the strict signification of *ἐπιτειχισμόν*. The occupation of Byzantium would be, in reference to the corn-trade, what the occupation of Eubœa might have been for the purpose of a more direct attack upon Athens. See my observations in the Preface to the First Volume, p. 5.

[2] Hieromnemon (the word in the original) appears to have been the name of the chief magistrate at Byzantium, whose term of office furnished the date of the year, as the archon did at Athens. The name

in the assembly, having obtained permission of the Council: Whereas the people of Athens have ever in former times been friendly to the Byzantines and their allies, and to their kinsmen the Perinthians, and have rendered them many signal services, and also, on the present occasion, when Philip of Macedon attempted by invasion and siege to exterminate the Byzantines and Perinthians, and burned and ravaged their country, they succored us with a hundred and twenty ships and provisions and weapons and soldiers, and rescued us from grievous perils, and preserved our hereditary constitution, our laws, and our sepulchres: it is resolved by the people of Byzantium and Perinthus to grant unto the Athenians the right of intermarriage, citizenship, purchase of land and houses, the first seat at the games, first admission to the Council and People after the sacrifices, and exemption from all public services to such as wish to reside in the city: and that three statues of sixteen cubits be erected in the harbor,[1] representing the People of Athens crowned by the People of Byzantium and Perinthus:[2] and deputations sent to the general assemblies of Greece, the Isthmian, Nemean, Olympian, and Pythian, to proclaim the crowns wherewith the people of Athens hath been honored by us, that all the Greeks may know the virtue of the Athenians, and the gratitude of the Byzantines and Perinthians."

Now read the crowns given by the people of Chersonesus.

THE DECREE OF THE CHERSONESITES.

"The Chersonesites, inhabitants of Sestus, Eleus, Madytus, and Alopeconnesus, crown the Council and People of Athens with a golden crown of the value of sixty talents,[3] and build

(which was held by the magistrates of some other Dorian states) imports the performance of some priestly or religious duties. As it sounds harsh in English, I have ventured to translate it at the risk of cavil. With respect to the Amphictyonic deputies so called see Appendix I.

[1] Such, perhaps, is the meaning of ἐν τῷ Βοσπορίχῳ. Others would read Βοσπόρῳ.

[2] Statues of countries and people are often mentioned. Thus, Pausanias saw in the Piræus a statue of the Athenian Demus by Leochares, and another by Lyson. (Lib. i. c. 1 and 3.) Polybius mentions a statue of the Rhodian People crowned by the Syracusan, which Hiero and Gelo erected in the great square of Rhodes. (Lib. v. 88.) And there was a celebrated one of the Athenian by Parrhasius.

[3] According to Gronovius, Böckh, and Jacobs, we are not to suppose

an altar to Gratitude and the Athenian People, because that People hath helped the Chersonesites to obtain the greatest of blessings, by rescuing them from the power of Philip, and restoring their country, their laws, their liberty, their sanctuaries: and in all future time they will not fail to be grateful, and do what service they can. Decreed in general Council."

Thus the saving of Chersonesus and Byzantium, the preventing Philip's conquest of the Hellespont, and the honors therefore bestowed on this country, were the effects of my policy and administration; and more than this—they proved to all mankind the generosity of Athens and the baseness of Philip. He, the ally and friend of the Byzantines, was before all eyes besieging them—what could be more shameful or outrageous?—You, who might justly on many grounds have reproached them for wrongs done you in former times, instead of bearing malice and abandoning the oppressed, appeared as their deliverers; conduct which procured you glory, good-will, honor from all men. That you have crowned many of your statesmen, every one knows; but through what other person (I mean what minister or orator), besides myself, the commonwealth has been crowned, no one can say.

To prove now the malignity of those calumnies, which he urged against the Eubœans and Byzantines, reminding you of any unkindness which they had done you—prove it I shall, not only by their falsehood, which I apprehend you know already, but (were they ever so true) by showing the advantages of my policy—I wish to recount one or two of the noble acts of your own state, and to do it briefly; for individuals, as well as communities, should ever strive to model their future conduct by the noblest of their past.

Well then, men of Athens—when the Lacedæmonians had the empire of land and sea, and held the country round Attica by governors and garrisons, Eubœa, Tanagra, all Bœotia, Megara, Ægina, Cleonæ, the other islands; when our state possessed neither ships nor walls; you marched out

that a crown was given of the actual weight or value of sixty talents, but that six drachms of gold are (by a form of speech usual in some cases) called a talent. A similar crown of a hundred talents, given by the Carthaginians to Demareta, the wife of Gelo, is mentioned by Diodorus. (Lib. xi. 26.)

to Haliartus,[1] and again not many days after to Corinth; albeit the Athenians of that time had many causes of resentment against both Corinthians and Thebans for their acts in the Decelean war:[2] but they showed no resentment, none. And yet neither of these steps took they, Æschines, for benefactors, nor were they blind to the danger; but they would not for such reasons abandon people who sought their protection; for the sake of renown and glory they willingly exposed themselves to peril; just and noble was their resolve! For to all mankind the end of life is death, though one keep one's self shut up in a closet;[3] but it becomes brave men to strive always for honor, with good hope before them,[4] and to endure courageously whatever the Deity ordains.

Thus did your ancestors, thus the elder among yourselves. For, though the Lacedæmonians were neither friends nor benefactors, but had done many grievous injuries to our state, yet when the Thebans, victorious at Leuctra, sought their destruction, you prevented it, not fearing the power and reputation then possessed by the Thebans, nor reckoning up the merits of those whom you were about to fight for. And so you demonstrated to all the Greeks, that, however any people may offend you, you reserve your anger against them for other occasions; but should their existence or liberty be imperiled, you will not resent your wrongs or bring them into account.

[1] This was B.C. 395, at the breaking out of the war, in which Athens, Thebes, Corinth, and Argos, combined against Lacedæmon. (See vol. I. p. 64.) The battle of Corinth, in which the Lacedæmonians defeated the allies, took place in the year following the siege of Haliartus.

[2] The latter part of the Peloponnesian war, so called from the occupation of Decelea, a fortress in Attica, fifteen miles from Athens, B.C. 413. By means of this post the enemy got the command of the territory round Athens, and reduced the Athenians to great distress by cutting off supplies of corn and provisions.

[3] Spillan, Jacobs, and Pabst render *οἰκίσκῳ* "a cage," *Käfich;* an interpretation found in Harpocration. Compare the lines of Propertius:

Ille licet ferro cautus se condat et ære,
Mors tamen inclusum protrahit inde caput.

[4] I have here taken *προβαλλομένους* in the simple sense of "proposing to themselves," or "having before their eyes." So Spillan has it. And Jacobs: *mit froher Hoffnung vor Augen.* But Reiske understood it in the more ordinary sense of "putting before them as a defense." And so Leland renders it: "armed in fair hopes of success." And Pabst: *sich dazu mit dem Schilde der guten Hoffnung waffnen.*

And not in these instances only hath such been your temper. Again, when the Thebans were taking possession of Eubœa,[1] you looked not quietly on—you remembered not the wrongs done you by Themison and Theodorus in the affair of Oropus,[2] but assisted even them. It was the time when the volunteer captains[3] first offered themselves to the state, of whom I was one;—but of this presently. However, it was glorious that you saved the island, but far more glorious that, when you had got their persons and their cities in your power, you fairly restored them to the people who had ill-used you, and made no reckoning of your wrongs in an affair where you were trusted.

Hundreds of cases which I could mention I pass over—sea-fights, land-marches, campaigns, both in ancient times and in your own, all of which the commonwealth has undertaken for the freedom and safety of the Greeks in general. Then, having observed the commonwealth engaging in contests of such number and importance for the interests of others, what was I to urge, what course to recommend her, when the question in a manner concerned herself?—To revive grudges, I suppose, against people who wanted help, and to seek pretenses for abandoning every thing. And who might not justly have killed me, had I attempted even by words to tarnish any of the honors of Athens? For the thing itself, I am certain, you would never have done—had you wished, what was to hinder you?—any lack of opportunity?—had you not these men to advise it?

I must return to the next in date of my political acts; and here again consider what was most beneficial for the state. I saw, men of Athens, that your navy was decaying, and that, while the rich were getting off[4] with small payments, citizens

[1] As to the war in Eubœa, see vol. I. pp. 114, 275.

[2] Themison and Theodorus were the rulers of Eretria, who seized upon Oropus, B.C. 366. See vol. I. p. 210.

[3] The exertions of these voluntary trierarchs enabled the Athenians to ship off their troops in three days. The orators frequently boasted of this expedition: for example, Demosthenes in the speech against Androtion; Æschines in the speech against Ctesiphon.

[4] Schaefer rightly explains ἀτελεῖς, "qui tam pauca contribuerent, nihil ut dare viderentur." My translation expresses this by a vernacular phrase. We might say, "escaping with." Brougham has "escaping all taxes by paying an insignificant contribution." Leland: "purchase

of moderate or small fortunes were losing their substance, and the state, by reason thereof, missing her opportunities of action. I therefore proposed a law, by which I compelled the one class (the rich) to perform their duty, and stopped the oppression of the poor; and—what was most useful to the country—I caused her preparations to be made in time. And being indicted for it, I appeared on the charge before you, and was acquitted; and the prosecutor did not get his portion[1] of the votes. But what sums, think ye, the chief men[2] of the Boards, or those in the second and third degrees, offered me, first, not to propose that law, secondly, when I had recorded it, to drop it on the abatement-oath?[3] Such sums, men of Athens, as I should be afraid to tell you. And no wonder they did so; for under the former laws they might divide the charge between sixteen, spending little or nothing

a total exemption from public taxes at the expense of a trifling contribution." But they should have avoided a reference to any other payments than what relate to the trierarchy.

[1] The fifth part, to save him from the penalty.

[2] According to Ulpian, the first three hundred among the Symmoriæ were called ἡγεμόνες. See as to this subject, vol. I. Appendix V.

[3] Ὑπωμοσία commonly meant an oath or affidavit sworn by a party to a cause, in order to obtain some adjournment or delay. But, according to the explanation of Julius Pollux, it was applied also to the oath sworn by a person who threatened another with a γραφὴ παρανόμων or indictment for an illegal measure. Any citizen was at liberty to indict the author of a decree, though passed by the popular assembly, within a twelvemonth after the passing; and it became void, if the indictment succeeded. He gave notice of his intention to prosecute by a public declaration, supported by oath, that he believed the decree in question to be illegal or unconstitutional; and this had the effect of suspending the validity of the decree until after the trial. Therefore, as Schömann observes (De Comitiis, 159), this oath, which had the effect of adjourning a law, was so called by analogy to the legal oath. See the Appendix to this volume on the γραφὴ παρανόμων.

In none of the translations do I find any explanation of καταβαλόντα. I take it to mean, "having entered it in the public register," *i. e.* in the temple of the Mother of the Gods, ἐν τῷ Μητρῴῳ, where the records of all decrees were kept. (See Schömann, De Comitiis, 129.)

Demosthenes, after carrying his measure in the assembly, and depositing it according to custom in the public archives, might have abandoned the defense of it, had he chosen to compromise the matter with his opponents; as Wolf rightly explains it—"Quo pacto impune tulisset Demosthenes prævaricationem istam? Si collusisset cum adversario, is actionem non persecutus esset, ac Demosthenes, anno elapso, indemnis fuisset."

themselves, and grinding down the needy citizens; whereas under my law every one had to pay a sum proportioned to his means, and there was a captain for two ships, where before there was a partner with fifteen others for one ship; for they were calling themselves not captains any longer, but partners. They would have given any thing then to get these regulations annulled, and not be obliged to perform their duties. Read me, first, the decree for which I appeared to the indictment, then the service-rolls, that of the former law, and that under mine. Read.

THE DECREE.[1]

"In the archonship of Polycles, on the sixteenth of Boedromion, in the presidency of the Hippothoontian tribe, Demosthenes son of Demosthenes of Pæania introduced a law for the naval service,[2] instead of the former one under which there were the associations of joint-captains; and it was passed by the council and people. And Patrocles of Phlyus preferred an indictment against Demosthenes for an illegal

[1] Schömann, in his chapter on Decrees (De Comitiis, 130), after mentioning the ordinary signification of the word *ψήφισμα*, viz., "a law passed by the people in assembly," and "a bill or decree of the council," proceeds to say, that it has a third and more extended meaning. "By that name," he says, "the Athenians designated those public records which did not contain the actual bill or decree, but merely an account of the circumstances connected with the proposal or adoption thereof, or a statement of the measures passed in consequence by the people. The object of this was, to have at hand always, in case they should be wanted again, authentic documents of the whole transaction." In support of his assertion, he refers to this and some other of the records cited in the Oration on the Crown. Their genuineness, however, has been questioned. In this one, as well as in others, the name of the archon is false. I doubt whether the word ever bore the extended meaning assigned to it by Schömann. Suppose the record in the text could be called *ψήφισμα*, it could hardly be the *ψήφισμα καθ' ὃ εἰσῆλθον τὴν γραφὴν*, which Demosthenes requires to be read, but of which it contains only a short recital. It is possible, indeed, that Demosthenes, though he calls on the clerk to read the decree, produced in fact only the document which is preserved to us, and which might answer his purpose quite as well, and even better, because it contained a memorial of his own acquittal, and the consequent establishment of his decree.

[2] Reiske understands *ἀρχεῖον*. Taylor translates it "for the admiralty." Schaefer adopts Stephens' explanation, that *τὸ τριηραρχικὸν* is nothing more than *τοὺς τριηράρχους*. Then it means "a law for the regulation of the trierarchs."

measure, and, not having obtained his share of the votes, paid the penalty of five hundred drachms."

Now produce that fine roll.

THE ROLL.

"Let sixteen captains be called out for every galley, as they are associated in the companies,[1] from the age of twenty-five to forty, defraying the charge equally."

Now for the roll under my law.

THE ROLL.

"Let captains be chosen according to their property by valuation, taking ten talents to a galley: if the property be valued at a higher sum, let the charge be proportionate, as far as three ships and a tender; and let it be in the same proportion for those whose property is less than ten talents, joining them in a partnership to make up ten talents."[2]

Think ye I but slightly helped the poor of Athens, or that the rich would have spent but a trifling sum to escape the doing what was right? I glory, however, not only in having refused this compromise, and having been acquitted on the indictment, but because my law was beneficial, and I have proved it so by trial. For during the whole war, while the armaments were shipped off according to my regulations, no captain ever appealed to you[3] against oppression, or took sanctuary at Munychia,[4] or was imprisoned by the clearing-officers;[5] no galley was lost to the state by capture abroad,

[1] Literally, "according to the associations in the companies." Λόχοι here are the same as συμμορίαι, according to Wolf.

[2] The ten talents, which are made the basis of this regulation, are the ratable value of the property, as Böckh explains it, which would be one-fifth of the whole for the highest class, if the valuation of B.C. 379 was in force; so that a man possessing fifty talents would have the charge of one ship, a hundred talents, of two ships, a hundred and fifty talents, of three ships; and a tender would have to be found in addition for a certain sum beyond, which is not specified. Higher the charge was not carried. Those who had less than ten talents of ratable capital clubbed together for one ship, but the rating was in a lower proportion. See Vol. I. Appendixes IV. and V.

[3] Ἱκετηρίαν θεῖναι is literally, "to deposit (at the altar or elsewhere) an olive bough wrapped with wool," which was the symbol of supplication.

[4] In a temple of Diana in the port of Munychia.

[5] The ἀποστολεῖς were ten officers, whose business it was to expedite the equipment of the fleet, and its clearance out from port—a Board of Dispatch.

or left behind from unfitness to go to sea. Under the former laws all these things happened—because the burden was put upon the poor, and therefore difficulties frequently arose. I transferred the charge from the poor to the wealthy, and then every duty was done. For this itself too I deserve praise, that I adopted all such measures as brought glory and honor and power to the state: there is no envy, spite, or malice in any measure of mine, nothing sordid or unworthy of Athens. The same character is apparent in my home and in my foreign policy. At home, I never preferred the favor of the wealthy to the rights of the many: abroad, I valued not the presents or the friendship of Philip above the general interests of Greece.

I conceive it remains for me to speak of the proclamation and the accounts: for, that I acted for the best—that I have throughout been your friend and zealous in your service—is proved abundantly, methinks, by what I have said already. The most important part of my policy and administration I pass by, considering that I have in regular course to reply to the charge of illegality; and besides—though I am silent as to the rest of my political acts—the knowledge you all have will serve me equally well.

As to the arguments which he jumbled together about the counter-written laws,[1] I hardly suppose you comprehend them—I myself could not understand the greater part. However I shall argue a just case in a straightforward way. So far from saying that I am not accountable, as the prosecutor just now falsely asserted, I acknowledge that I am all

[1] The laws alleged to have been violated were copied out and hung on a board side by side with the impugned decree, as Æschines clearly describes it in his speech against Ctesiphon (82). *Ὥσπερ γὰρ ἐν τῇ τεκτονικῇ, ὅταν εἰδέναι βουλώμεθα τὸ ὀρθὸν καὶ τὸ μή, τὸν κανόνα προσφέρομεν ᾧ διαγινώσκεται, οὕτω καὶ ἐν ταῖς γραφαῖς ταῖς τῶν παρανόμων παράκειται κανὼν τοῦ δικαίου τουτὶ τὸ σανίδιον καὶ τὸ ψήφισμα καὶ οἱ παραγεγραμμένοι νόμοι.* Compare Demosth. cont. Aristoc. 640. There is no doubt of this being the true meaning; the only difficulty is to translate *παραγεγραμμένοι* neatly. Spillan has: "the transcribed laws." Francis the same. Leland: "authentic transcript." Brougham: "his comparative exhibition of the laws;" which expresses the meaning more fully. The German translators would seem to have followed Wolf's interpretation. Jacobs has *über den Widerspruch mit den Gesetzen.* Pabst: *über die Gesetzwidrigkeiten.* Perhaps we might render it, "contrasted;" or, "put in counterview."

my life accountable for what as your statesman I have undertaken or advised; but for what I have voluntarily given to the people out of my own private fortune, I deny that I am any day accountable—do you hear, Æschines?—nor is any other man, let him even be one of the nine archons.[1] For what law is so full of injustice and inhumanity as to enact, that one who has given of his private means, and done an act of generosity and munificence, instead of having thanks, shall be brought before malignants, appointed to be the auditors of his liberality? None. If he says there is, let him produce it, and I will be content and hold my tongue. But there is none, men of Athens. The prosecutor in his malice, because I gave some of my own money when I superintended the theatre fund, says—"the Council praised him before he had rendered his account." Not for any matters of which I had an account to render, but for what I spent of my own, you malignant!

"Oh, but you were a Conservator of Walls!" says he. Yes; and for that reason was I justly praised, because I gave the sums expended and did not charge them. A charge requires auditing and examiners; a donation merits thanks and praise: therefore the defendant made this motion in my favor.

That this is a settled principle in your hearts as well as in the laws, I can show by many proofs easily. First, Nausicles has often been crowned by you for what he expended out of his own funds while he was general. Secondly, Diotimus was crowned for his present of shields; and Charidemus too. Again, Neoptolemus here, superintendent of divers works, has been honored for his donations. It would indeed be cruel, if a man holding an office should either, by reason of his office, be precluded from giving his own money to the state, or have, instead of receiving thanks, to render an account of what he gave. To prove the truth of my statements, take and read me the original decrees made in favor of these men.

A DECREE.[2]

"Archon, Demonicus of Phlyus. On the twenty-sixth of Boedromion, with the sanction of the council and people, Cal-

[1] The archons were not only liable to the εὐθύνη, but to an examination by the council previous to admission to their office.

[2] The event referred to in this decree seems to have taken place

lias of Phrearrii moved: That the council and people resolve to crown Nausicles, general of foot, for that, there being two thousand Athenian troops of the line in Imbrus, for the defense of the Athenian residents in that island, and Philo of the finance department being by reason of storms unable to sail and pay the troops, he advanced money of his own, and did not ask the people for it again; and that the crown be proclaimed at the Dionysian festival, at the new tragedies."

ANOTHER DECREE.[1]

"Callias of Phrearrii moved, the presidents declaring it to be with the sanction of the council: Whereas Charidemus, general of foot, having been sent to Salamis, he and Diotimus, general of horse, after certain of the troops had in the skirmish by the river been disarmed by the enemy, did at their own expense arm the young men with eight hundred shields: It hath been resolved by the council and people to crown Charidemus and Diotimus with a golden crown, and to proclaim it at the great Panathenaic festival, during the gymnastic contest, and at the Dionysian festival, at the exhibition of the new tragedies: the proclamation to be given in charge to the judges,[2] the presidents, and the prize-masters."

during the Social War, B.C. 355, when the Chians, Rhodians, and Byzantines made a descent upon Lemnos and Imbrus. In that year Callistratus was archon. The heading Ἀρχων, instead of ἐπὶ Ἀρχοντος, is noticed by Jacobs as unusual. Nausicles is frequently mentioned by Æschines and Demosthenes in terms of praise. He commanded an Athenian force in the Sacred War, B.C. 352.

[1] As this decree was moved by the same person as the preceding one, it is perhaps referable to the same period. Winiewski has conjectured that, while Nausicles was sent to Imbrus, some hostile neighbors, perhaps the Megarians, took the opportunity of invading Salamis. Reiske understands it of the Cyprian Salamis; but this is not so probable. The Charidemus here mentioned is not to be confounded with Charidemus of Oreus, but is the person who, with Demosthenes and others, was demanded by Alexander after the taking of Thebes, and thereupon fled to the court of Darius, by whom he was afterward put to death. (Diodorus, xvii. 30.) Diotimus also was one of the men demanded by Alexander.

[2] Such is the name which I give to the six junior archons, to avoid the uncouth title of Thesmothetes. It does not indeed (any more than Thesmothetes itself) convey a perfect idea of the official duties which they had to discharge; yet it is by no means inappropriate, seeing that the most important part of them were of a judicial character.

Each of these men, Æschines, was accountable for the office which he held, but not accountable for the matters in respect of which he was crowned. No more then am I; for surely I have the same rights, under the same circumstances, as other men. Have I given money? I am praised for that, not being accountable for what I gave. Did I hold office? Yes; and I have rendered an account of my official acts, not of my bounties. Oh, but I was guilty of malpractices in office! And you, present when the auditors brought me up,[1] accused me not?

To show you that he himself bears testimony to my having been crowned for what I had no account to render of, take and read the whole decree drawn up in my favor. By the portions of the bill which he never indicted it will appear that his prosecution is vexatious. Read.

THE DECREE.[2]

"In the archonship of Euthycles, on the twenty-second of Pyanepsion, in the presidency of the Œneian tribe, Ctesiphon son of Leosthenes of Anaphlystus moved: Whereas Demosthenes son of Demosthenes of Pæania, having been superintendant of the repair of the walls, and having expended on the works three additional talents out of his own money, hath given that sum to the people; and whereas, having been

[1] Either before the popular assembly, or before their own court, the *Λογιστήριον*. But I rather think the former. The accounts having been sent in to the *Λογισταὶ*, and there not appearing to be any pecuniary deficit, they were passed as a matter of course, unless some accuser appeared; but the law afforded an opportunity for an accusation at the popular assembly, before which the *Λογισταὶ* were obliged to bring the parties as a matter of form, and by public proclamation to ask whether any citizen desired to accuse them. (Æsch. contra Ctesiph. 57.)

Schömann indeed (De Comitiis, 293) appears to take a different view. Demosthenes had passed the scrutiny of the Logistæ, and had no charge preferred against him at the close of his official year. This however, in point of law, was no answer to his opponent's argument; for the legality of Ctesiphon's measure was to be tried by reference to the time when he introduced it, at which time Demosthenes had not cleared himself of his official responsibility.

[2] The name of the archon is wrong here, and the decree is not in all manuscripts. The terms of it do not agree with the recital in the indictment, though it is the same in substance. It may possibly be that in one we have the *προβούλευμα*, in the other the *ψήφισμα* as sanctioned by the assembly.

appointed treasurer of the theoric fund, he hath given to the theoric officers[1] of the tribes a hundred minas toward the sacrifices, the council and people of Athens have resolved to honor Demosthenes son of Demosthenes of Pæania with public praise, for the goodness and generosity which he has shown throughout on every occasion toward the people of Athens, and to crown him with a golden crown, and to proclaim the crown in the theatre, at the Dionysian festival, at the performance of the new tragedies: the proclamation to be given in charge to the prize-master."

These were my donations; none of which have you indicted: the rewards which the council says I deserve for them are what you arraign. To receive the gifts then you confess to be legal; the requital of them you indict for illegality. In the name of heaven! what sort of person can a monster of wickedness and malignity be, if not such a person as this?

Concerning the proclamation in the theatre, I pass over the fact, that thousands of thousands have been proclaimed, and I myself have been crowned often before. But by the Gods! are you so perverse and stupid, Æschines, as not to be able to reflect, that the party crowned has the same glory from the crown wherever it be published, and that the proclamation is made in the theatre for the benefit of those who confer the crown? For the hearers are all encouraged to render service to the state, and praise the parties who show their gratitude more than the party crowned. Therefore has our commonwealth enacted this law. Take and read me the law itself.

THE LAW.

"Whensoever any of the townships bestow crowns, proclamations thereof shall be made by them in their several townships, unless where any are crowned by the people of Athens or the council; and it shall be lawful for them to be proclaimed in the theatre at the Dionysian festival."

Do you hear, Æschines, the law distinctly saying—"unless where any are voted by the people or the council; such may

[1] Reiske prefers taking θεωρικοῖς as the neuter gender, "the theoric contributions from all the tribes." Schaefer, Jacobs, and Pabst read θεωροῖς.

be proclaimed?" Why then, wretched man, do you play the pettifogger? Why manufacture arguments? Why don't you take hellebore[1] for your malady? Are you not ashamed to bring on a cause for spite, and not for any offense?—to alter some laws, and to garble others, the whole of which should in justice be read to persons sworn to decide according to the laws? And you that act thus describe the qualities which belong to a friend of the people, as if you had ordered a statue according to contract, and received it without having what the contract required; or as if friends of the people were known by words, and not by acts and measures! And you bawl out, regardless of decency,[2] a sort of cart-language,[3] applicable to yourself and your race, not to me.

Again, men of Athens — I conceive abuse to differ from

[1] Hellebore was used by the ancients to purge the brain, and cure people of insanity; and because it grew abundantly in the island of Anticyra, "to send a person to Anticyra," was as good as saying he was mad. Horace, Sat. II. iii. 82:—

> Dum doceo insanire omnes, vos ordine adite.
> Danda est Hellebori multo pars maxima avaris:
> Nescio an Anticyram ratio illis destinet omnem.

And ibid. 166:—

> Naviget Anticyram: quid enim differt, barathrone
> Dones quicquid habes, an nunquam utare paratis?

[2] With the expression in the original compare Virgil, Æn. IX. 595:—

> Digna atque indigna relatu
> Vociferans.

[3] Billingsgate, as the Londoners would say.

It was the custom of the Athenian women, in divers solemn processions, especially at the Eleusinian mysteries, when they were conveyed in open wagons or carts, to amuse themselves by jeering and joking one another, without the slightest regard to modesty or propriety of language. Hence *τὰ ἐκ τῶν ἁμαξῶν σκώμματα* came to signify licentious and indecent abuse. *Πομπεύειν* is used in the like sense, and also *γεφυρίζειν*, because at a certain bridge over the Cephisus, where the procession stopped, the bantering of the ladies waxed peculiarly warm. Leland observes—"The French translator is extremely shocked at this interpretation, and can not persuade himself that the Athenian ladies could so far forget the modesty and reserve peculiar to their sex. But it is well if this were the worst part of their conduct, or if they were guilty of no greater transgression of modesty in the course of their attendance on these famous rites." Dionysius of Halicarnassus, in his Roman Antiquities (VII. 72), compares this custom of the Athenians with the license allowed at a Roman triumph, where those who followed the procession were permitted to make fun of the generals and other men of distinction by squibs and jests.

accusation in this, that accusation has to do with offenses for which the laws provide penalties, abuse with the scandal which enemies speak against each other according to their humor.[1] And I believe our ancestors built these courts, not that we should assemble you here and bring forth the secrets of private life for mutual reproach,[2] but to give us the means of convicting persons guilty of crimes against the state. Æschines knew this as well as I, and yet he chose to rail rather than to accuse.

Even in this way he must take as much as he gives;[3] but before I enter upon such matters, let me ask him one question — Should one call you the state's enemy, or mine, Æschines? Mine, of course. Yet, where you might, for any offense which I committed, have obtained satisfaction for the people according to the laws, you neglected it—at the audit, on the indictments and other trials; but where I in my own person am safe on every account, by the laws, by time, by prescription,[4] by many previous judgments on every point, by my never having been convicted of a public offense—and where the country must share, more or less, in the repute of measures which were her own—here it is you have encountered me. See if you are not the people's enemy, while you pretend to be mine!

Since therefore the righteous and true verdict is made

[1] Compare Cicero pro Cœlio: "Aliud est maledicere, aliud accusare. Accusatio crimen desiderat, rem ut definiat, hominem ut notet, argumento probet, teste confirmet; maledictio autem nihil habet propositi, præter contumeliam; quæ si petulantius jactatur, convicium, si facetius, urbanitas nominatur."

[2] Literally: "speak to the reproach of one another secrets from private life;" adhering to Bekker's reading of *κακῶς*. Jacobs: *und schmähend die Geheimnisse des Privatlebens gegenseitig aufzudecken.* Pabst, to the same effect.

[3] Lord Brougham justly censures the English translators, who have not preserved the familiar expression in the Greek, that so well corresponds with our own. They are all upon stilts. He himself has: "But even in this kind of conflict it is right that he should get as good as he brings."

[4] "By the Statute of Limitations," as we should say. The *γραφὴ παρανόμων* could only be brought within a year after the decree. The *εὐθόνη* was to take place within thirty days after the expiration of the term of office, and the accuser was bound to appear when the accounts were rendered, or before they were passed. See my article *Προθεσμία* in the Arch. Dict., also article *Εὐθύνη*.

clear to all;[1] but I must, it seems—though not naturally fond of railing, yet on account of the calumnies uttered by my opponent—in reply to so many falsehoods, just mention some leading particulars concerning him, and show who he is, and from whom descended, that so readily begins using hard words—and what language he carps at, after uttering such as any decent man would have shuddered to pronounce.[2]—Why, if my accuser had been Æacus, or Rhadamanthus, or Minos, instead of a prater,[3] a hack of the market, a pestilent scribbler, I don't think he would have spoken such things, or found such offensive terms, shouting, as in a tragedy, "O Earth! O Sun! O Virtue!"[4] and the like; and again appealing to Intelligence and Education, by which the honorable is distinguished from the base:—all this you undoubtedly heard from his lips. Accursed one![5] What have you or

[1] Leland, following Wolf, infers from this passage that there had been some acclamation in the court, which Demosthenes affects to consider as the general voice of the jury. I agree with Lord Brougham, that this is not a necessary inference from the text, where the connection with what goes before is plain and easy.

[2] I have preserved the anacoluthon of the original. In *τίς οὐκ ἂν ὤκνησε* I have converted the interrogative, which is unsuitable to our language, into an affirmative. This weakens the sentence, but as a compensation I strengthen *ὤκνησε*.

[3] The word *σπερμολόγος* in the same sense occurs in the Acts of the Apostles, xvii. 18, where our version is "babbler." The origin of this meaning is uncertain. *Περίτριμμα ἀγορᾶς* describes a low fellow who frequented the market, where loose and dissolute characters of all sorts used to congregate. Jacobs and Pabst render it, *Marktschreier*, "mountebank," or "blackguard," as we should say. Aristophanes says in the Knights:

ὁτιὴ πονηρὸς κἀξ ἀγορᾶς εἶ καὶ θρασύς.

[4] This occurs at the end of the speech against Ctesiphon.

[5] Lord Brougham's translation of *κάθαρμα* is—"You abomination;" upon which his reviewer has the following note:—

"It is quite clear that Lord Brougham himself has no notion of the real meaning of the word. We refer for explanation of it to Mitchell's edition of the Knights of Aristophanes, v. 708 and v. 1099. He will there see that *κάθαρμα* was an expiatory victim, offered up to atone for the guilt, and avert the punishment, of the parties sacrificing. Two such victims—both men, according to some writers, but a male and female, according to others—were provided annually by the Athenian state for this purpose. A feeling of the utmost contempt and horror was attached to these *καθάρματα*. But of all this Lord Brougham seems perfectly unconscious. We can not translate, we can only approximate to the meaning of *κάθαρμα*. It is a sort of frozen word, which, as Mr.

yours to do with virtue? How should you discern what is honorable or otherwise? How were you ever qualified? What right have you to talk about education? Those who really possess it would never say as much of themselves, but rather blush if another did: those who are destitute like you, but make pretensions to it from stupidity, annoy the hearers by their talk, without getting the reputation which they desire.

I am at no loss for materials concerning you and your family, but am in doubt what to mention first—whether how your father Tromes, being servant to Elpias, who kept a reading-school in the temple of Theseus, wore a weight of fetters and a collar;[1] or how your mother, by her morning spousals in the cottage by Hero Calamites,[2] reared up you, the beautiful statue, the eminent third-rate actor![3]—But all

Mitchell remarks on another occasion, requires the warm breath of commentatorship to come over it before it can be thawed into life and animation."

This is a most unfair attack upon his Lordship. There is not the least objection to his translation, nor does it at all appear that the meaning of *κάθαρμα* was unknown to him. The observation about frozen words is good enough, but it is misapplied. Comment is different from translation. Jacobs renders it: *Du Schandfleck.* Pabst: *Scheusal.* Auger: "Scélérat."

[1] *Ξύλον*, according to Reiske, is a round board with a hole in the middle, put on the necks of thievish slaves, to prevent them from reaching their hands to their mouths. Or it may be, as Jacobs says, the stocks; as in the Knights of Aristophanes, v. 702.

ἐν τῷ ξύλῳ δήσω σε, νὴ τὸν οὐρανόν.

where the Scholiast interprets *ἐν τῇ ποδοκάκῃ.* Or simply a collar worn as a badge of servitude. Compare Plautus, Captivi, Act II. Sc. 3, v. 107:—

Dî tibi omnes omnia optata afferant,
Cum me tanto honore honestas, cumque ex vinclis eximis.
Hoc quidem haud molestum est jam, quod collus collariâ caret.

[2] A Hero of that name is the common interpretation. Schaefer, however, referring to the oration of Demosthenes on the Embassy (419), where Atrometus is said to have taught his boys *πρὸς τῷ τοῦ Ἥρω τοῦ ἰατροῦ*, thinks that Heros was the name of a physician, who received the title of Calamites, because he set fractured bones with splinters of reeds. Dissen's explanation, to which Pabst inclines, is, that there was a statue surrounded with reeds, of some unknown hero, a sort of Æsculapius, to whom the people ascribed a healing power.

[3] A *τριταγωνιστής* was an actor of the lowest description. The reader will remember that the characters in an Athenian tragedy were few in number: the dialogue was never carried on by more than three persons besides the chorus, generally by two only.

know these things without my telling—Or how the galley-piper Phormio, the slave of Dion of Phrearrii, removed her from that honorable employment. But, by Jupiter and the gods! I fear, in saying what is proper about you, I may be thought to have chosen topics unbecoming to myself. All this therefore I shall pass by, and commence with the acts of his own life; for indeed he came not of common parents, but of such as are execrated by the people.[1] Very lately—lately do I say?—it is but yesterday that he has become both an Athenian and an orator—adding two syllables, he converted his father from Tromes to Atrometus,[2] and dignified his mother by the name of Glaucothea, who (as every one knows) was called Empusa;[3] having got that title (it is plain) from her doing and submitting to any thing—how else could she have got it? However, you are so ungrateful and wicked by nature, that after being raised through the people from servitude to freedom, from beggary to affluence, instead of returning their kindness, you work against them as a hireling politician.

Of the speeches, which it may possibly be contended he has made for the good of the country, I will say nothing: of the acts which he was clearly proved to have done for the enemy, I will remind you.

What man present but knows of the outcast Antiphon,[4] who came into the city under promise to Philip that he

[1] Reiske's interpretation is, "*οὐκ ἦν εἷς τις τῶν τυχόντων*, non enim est Æschines de genere hominum triviali, vulgari, sed unus illorum inventu rarorum hominum, quos populus per præconem publicè devovet." Dissen refers these words to *ἃ βεβίωκεν*. Schaefer and Jacobs understand *ὧν ἔτυχεν* of the parents of Æschines, but, on the authority of one manuscript, transpose the clause *οὐδὲ—καταρᾶται* immediately after *λόγους*. According to my view, there is no necessity for the transposition, the argument running thus—I will pass by this topic: his parentage was so disgraceful that he himself was ashamed of it; and so he changed the names of his parents, to escape the shame.

[2] Tromes, from *τρέμω*, would be a fit name for a slave; *'Ατρόμητος*, "Intrepid," for a freeman. The lengthening of names was often resorted to by the ancients, as it is now, as a device to exalt the dignity of the party.

[3] This denoted a frightful spectre or hobgoblin. According to Aristophanes (Frogs, 293), it could change itself into various shapes.

[4] *'Αποψηφισθέντα* is, "ousted from the register by the votes of his fellow-townsmen," *δημόται*. The members of each *δῆμος*, or township, of Attica occasionally assembled to revise their register, and if any member was adjudged by a majority of votes not to be a true citizen, his name was expunged. He might still appeal to a court of justice at

would burn your arsenal? I found him concealed in Piræus, and brought him before the Assembly; when this mischief-maker, shouting and clamoring that it was monstrous in a free state that I should ill-treat unfortunate citizens, and enter houses without warrant,[1] procured his release. And had not the Council of Areopagus, discovering the fact, and perceiving your ill-timed error, made search after the man, seized and brought him before you, a fellow like that would have been rescued, would have slipped through the hands of justice, and been sent out of the way by this declaimer. As it was, you put him to torture and to death, as you ought this man also. The Council of Areopagus were informed what Æschines had done, and therefore, though you had elected him for your advocate on the question of the Delian temple,[2] in the same ignorance by which you have sacrificed many of the public interests, as you referred the matter to the council, and gave them full powers, they immediately removed him for his treason, and appointed Hyperides to plead; for which purpose they took their ballots from the altar,[3] and not a single

Athens; but if the court affirmed the decision of the townsmen, he was sold for a slave.

Antiphon (as it would appear) had been thus degraded from his rank as a citizen, and, in resentment of such usage, had entered into a treasonable engagement with the king of Macedon. Plutarch calls this proceeding of Demosthenes a very arbitrary measure, *σφόδρα ἀριστοκρατικὸν πολίτευμα*. Dinarchus brings it up against him in the speech upon his trial, but does not deny the guilt of Antiphon.

[1] Without the authority of the Council.

[2] The Athenians claimed the superintendence of the temple of Delos, which the Delians disputed with them. The question was referred to the decision of the Amphictyonic Council at Thermopylæ, and each of the two states sent a deputy to plead their cause. Some fragments remain of a speech made by Hyperides on this occasion, entitled Deliacus.

[3] This was the most solemn method of voting. An example is mentioned by Herodotus (VIII. 123), on a memorable occasion, when the Greek generals met at the Isthmus after the battle of Salamis, to declare what two men had done the greatest service in the war. They voted standing at the altar of Neptune; and while each awarded the first place to himself, the great majority concurred in allowing the second place to Themistocles.

Another example may be seen in the speech of Demosthenes against Macartatus, 1054.

Compare Cicero pro Balbo, 5: "Athenis aiunt, cùm quidam apud eos, qui sanctè graviterque vixisset, et testimonium publicè dixisset, et, ut mos Græcorum est, jurandi causâ ad aras accederet," &c.

ballot was given for this wretch. To prove the truth of my statements, call me the witnesses.

WITNESSES.

"We, Callias of Sunium, Zenon of Phlyus, Cleon of Phalerum, Demonicus of Marathon, testify for Demosthenes in the name of all, that, the people having formerly elected Æschines for their advocate before the Amphictyons on the question of the Delian temple, we in council determined that Hyperides was more worthy to plead on behalf of the state, and Hyperides was commissioned."

Thus, by removing this man when he was about to plead, and appointing another, the council pronounced him a traitor and an enemy.

Such is one of this boy's[1] political acts, similar—is it not?—to what he charges me with. Now let me remind you of another. When Philip sent Python[2] of Byzantium, together with an embassy from all his own allies, with the intention of putting our commonwealth to shame, and proving her in the wrong, then—when Python swaggered and poured a flood of abuse[3] upon you—I neither yielded nor gave way; I rose and answered him, and betrayed not the rights of the commonwealth. So plainly did I convict Philip of injustice, that his very allies rose up and acknowledged it; while Æschines fought his battle, and bore witness, ay, false witness, against his own country.

Nor was this enough. Again, some time afterward, he was found meeting Anaxinus the spy at Thraso's house.[4] A

[1] It means "a fine fellow," as we say ironically. Jacobs preserves the original term: *des Jünglings.* Pabst: *Buben.* Leland and Spillan: "this noble personage." Francis: "You have here one gallant instance of his politics."

[2] Probably on the same occasion when the second Philippic was spoken.

[3] With the original πολλῷ ῥέοντι compare Horace, Sat. I. vii. 28:—

Tum Prænestinus salso multoque fluenti
Expressa arbusto regerit convicia.

[4] Anaxinus was an Orite. The transaction is supposed to have occurred B.C. 342. Æschines, in his speech (85), asserts that the whole affair was a contrivance of Demosthenes, to prevent an impeachment with which he had threatened him; and he reproaches Demosthenes with having put a man to the rack, at whose house in Oreus he had lodged and received hospitality.

man, I say, who had a private meeting and conference with an emissary of the foe, must himself have been a spy by nature and an enemy to his country. To prove these statements, call me the witnesses.

WITNESSES.

"Teledemus, son of Cleon, Hyperides son of Callæschrus, Nicomechus son of Diophantus, testify for Demosthenes, as they swore before the generals, that Æschines son of Atrometus of Cothocidæ did, to their knowledge, meet by night in Thraso's house, and confer with Anaxinus, who was adjudged to be a spy of Philip. These depositions were returned before Nicias,[1] on the third of Hecatombæon."

A vast deal besides that I could say about him I omit. For thus (methinks) it is. I could produce many more such cases, where Æschines was discovered at that period assisting the enemy and harassing me. But these things are not treasured up by you for careful remembrance or proper resentment. You have, through evil custom, given large license to any one that chooses to supplant and calumniate your honest counselors, exchanging the interest of the state for the pleasure and gratification of hearing abuse; and so it is easier and safer always to be a hireling serving your enemies, than a statesman attached to you.

That he should co-operate openly with Philip before the war, was shocking—O heaven and earth! could it be otherwise?—against his country! Yet allow him if you please, allow him this. But when the ships had openly been made prize, Chersonesus was ravaged, the man was marching against Attica, matters were no longer doubtful, war had begun—nothing that he ever did for you can this malicious iambic-mouther[2] show—not a resolution has Æschines, great or small,

[1] It is uncertain whether this Nicias is the name of a spurious archon, or the secretary of the council, or an error for Nicomachus, who was archon B.C. 341. Jacobs translates it: *unter dem Nikias.* Pabst, Auger, Leland, and Francis, the same. Spillan is with me.

[2] Some of the translators, following an interpretation given by the grammarians (*ὑβριστής, φιλολοίδορος*), take this word as having reference to the acrimonious language of Æschines, the Iambic metre having anciently been the vehicle of satire, as we learn from Horace, Ars Poet. 79,

Archilochum proprio rabies armavit Iambo.

But it is better to understand the epithet as having reference to the

concerning the interests of the state. If he asserts it, let him prove it now while my waterglass is running.[1] But there is none. He is reduced to an alternative;—either he had no fault to find with my measures, and therefore moved none against them; or he sought the good of the enemy, and therefore would not propose any better.

Did he abstain from speaking as well as moving, when any mischief was to be done to you? Why, no one else could speak a word. Other things, it appears, the country could endure, and he could accomplish without detection: but one last act he achieved, O Athenians, which crowned all he had done before; on which he lavished that multitude of words, recounting the decrees against the Amphissian Locrians, in hopes of distorting the truth. But the thing admits it not. No! never will you wash yourself clean[2] from your performances there—talk as long as you will!

In your presence, men of Athens, I invoke all the gods and goddesses to whom the Attic territory belongs, and Pythian

theatrical profession of Æschines. Schaefer takes it to signify a person who spoils the verses by bad pronunciation ("an iambic-gulper"—*Iamben-verschlucker*). Passow, in his dictionary, explains it of one who learns by heart and repeats a great number of Iambics. Jacobs follows Schaefer. Pabst: *Iamben-schnapper*. Leland: "theatrical ranter."

[1] The Athenians, to prevent the parties from saying more than was necessary, timed them by a glass, in which water trickled through a narrow tube, like sand in one of our minute-glasses. The measure of water was not always the same, and varied according to the importance of the cause. Mention is made of a certain quantity of water being allowed in certain causes; but this gives us no idea of the length of time, as we do not know the construction of the glass. Our best evidence of this is the length of the speeches which have come down to us. Each party was commonly allowed to have two speeches, the defendant having the last reply; and the second speech might be half as long as the first. If either got a friend to plead for him, he gave up so much of his own time as the friend's speech would occupy. The admeasurement of the water was seen to by the superintending magistrate. An officer of the court stood by the glass, and stopped it whenever a witness was called, or a law or other document was read to the jury.

[2] The reviewer of Lord Brougham very appositely quotes the lines in *Macbeth*, Act II. Scene 2—

> "Will all great Neptune's ocean wash this blood
> Clean from my hand?"

Compare also what Lady Macbeth says, Act V. Scene I—

> "Out! damned spot," &c.

Apollo the Father-god[1] of our state; and I implore them all! As I shall declare the truth to you, as I declared it in your assembly at the time, the very moment I saw this wretch putting his hand to the work—for I perceived, instantly perceived it—so may they grant me favor and protection! If from malice or personal rivalry I bring a false charge against my opponent, may they cut me off from every blessing!

But wherefore this imprecation, this solemn assurance? Because, though I have documents lying in the public archives, from which I shall clearly prove my assertions, though I know you remember the facts, I fear this man may be considered unequal to the mischiefs which he has wrought; as before happened, when he caused the destruction of the unhappy Phocians by his false reports to you.

The Amphissian war,[2] I say—which brought Philip to Elatea, which caused him to be chosen general of the Amphictyons, which ruined every thing in Greece—was this man's contrivance. He is the single author of all our heaviest calamities. I protested at the time, and cried out in the assembly—"You are bringing a war, Æschines, into Attica, an Amphictyonic war"—but his packed party[3] would not let me be heard; the rest wondered, and supposed that I was bringing an idle charge against him out of personal enmity. However, the real character of those transactions, the purpose for which they were got up, the manner in which they were accomplished, hear ye now, men of Athens, as ye were prevented then. You will see that the thing was well concerted, and it will help you much to get a knowledge of public affairs, and what craftiness there was in Philip you will observe.

Philip could neither finish nor get rid of the war with Athens, unless he made the Thebans and Thessalians her enemies. Though your generals fought against him without

[1] So called as being the father of Ion, the ancient king of Athens. See the Ion of Euripides.

[2] See Appendix IX.

[3] Literally, "those who had come on request and were sitting together," *i. e.* at the special request or invitation of Æschines and his friends—by appointment or concert. Pabst has: *welche der Verabredung gemäss zusammenhielten.* Jacobs: *die zufolge der Aufforderung zusammenhielten.* Francis, the only English translator who expresses the meaning, has: "some of his party, convened by him for that purpose." But the *some* is wrong, for *οἱ* goes with *συγκαθήμενοι*.

fortune or skill, yet from the war itself and the cruisers he suffered infinite damage. He could neither export any of the produce of his country, nor import what he needed. He was not then superior to you at sea, nor able to reach Attica, unless the Thessalians followed him and the Thebans gave him a passage; so that, while he overcame in war the generals whom you sent out—such as they were—I say nothing about that—he found himself distressed by the difference of your local position and means.[1] Should he urge either Thessalians or Thebans to march in his own quarrel against you, none, he thought, would attend to him: but should he, under the pretense of taking up their common cause, be elected general, he trusted partly by deceit and partly by persuasion to gain his ends more easily.[2] He sets to work therefore—observe how cleverly—to get the Amphictyons into a war, and create a disturbance in the congress. For this he thought they would immediately want him. Now, if any of the presbyters commissioned by himself or any of his allies brought it forward, he imagined that both Thebans and Thessalians would suspect the thing, and would all be on their guard; whereas, if the agent were an Athenian and commissioned by you his opponents, it would easily pass unnoticed. And thus it turned out.

How did he effect his purpose? He hires the prosecutor. No one (I believe) was aware of the thing or attending to it, and so—just as these things are usually done at Athens—Æschines was proposed for Pylæan deputy, three or four held up their hands for him, and his election was declared. When clothed with the dignity of the state he arrived among the Amphictyons, dismissing and disregarding all besides, he hastened to execute what he was hired for. He makes up a pretty speech and story, showing how the Cirrhæan plain came to be consecrated; reciting this to the presbyters, men unused to speeches and unsuspicious of any consequences, he procures a vote from them to walk round the district, which

[1] That is, the position of the countries that were the seat of war, and the different character of the resources which each of the belligerent parties possessed. For example, Philip's standing army could not prevent the Athenians annoying him with their fleets and cruisers. Jacobs: *durch die Natur der Oertlichkeit und durch das, was Beiden zu Gebot stand.*

[2] Jacobs: *so hoffe er leichter, hier durch Berückung, dort durch Ueberredung, zum Ziele zu kommen.*

the Amphissians maintained they had a right to cultivate, but which he charged to be parcel of the sacred plain. The Locrians were not then instituting any suit against us, or any such proceeding as Æschines now falsely alleges.[1] This will show you—It was impossible (I fancy) for the Locrians to carry on process against our commonwealth without a citation. Who summoned us then? In whose archonship? Say who knows—point him out. You can not. Your pretense was flimsy and false.

When the Amphictyons at the instance of this man walked over the plain, the Locrians fell upon them and well-nigh speared them all; some of the presbyters they carried off captive. Complaints having followed, and war being stirred up against the Amphyssians, at first Cottyphus led an army composed entirely of Amphictyons; but as some never came, and those that came did nothing, measures were taken against the ensuing congress by an instructed gang, the old traitors of Thessaly and other states, to get the command for Philip.[2] And they had found a fair pretext: for it was necessary, they said, either to subsidize themselves and maintain a mercenary force and fine all recusants, or to elect him. What need of many words? He was thereupon chosen general; and immediately afterward collecting an army, and marching professedly against Cirrha, he bids a long farewell to the Cirrhæans and Locrians, and seizes Elatea. Had not the Thebans, upon seeing this, immediately changed their minds and sided with us, the whole thing would have fallen like a torrent upon our country. As it was, they for the instant[3] stopped him; chiefly, O Athenians, by the kindness of some divinity to Athens, but secondly,[4] as far as it could depend on

[1] Æschines had stated in his speech (70), that the Amphissian Locrians proposed to fine the Athenians fifty talents, for an inscription which they had put on a golden shield in the temple, commemorating the alliance of the Thebans with Persia. This he alleged to have been the cause of his own proceeding against them. See, as to all these details, Appendix IX.

[2] Pabst: *wirkten die von den Thessaliern und aus andern Städten, welche dazu schon angeleitet und längst schlecht gesinnt waren, dass Philipp zum Feldherrn erwählt ward.*

[3] Jacobs: *hielten Jene ihn wenigstens vom plötzlichen Vordringen ab.* Pabst: *hielten Jene wenigstens den plötzlichen Andrang auf.*

[4] Brougham expresses εἶτα by "under Providence." Leland had given the same turn before him. And it is a good one.

a single man, through me. Give me those decrees, and the dates of the several transactions, that you may know what mischief this pestilent creature has stirred up with impunity. Read me the decrees.

THE DECREE OF THE AMPHICTYONS.

"In the priesthood of Clinagoras, at the spring congress, it hath been resolved by the deputies and councilors[1] of the Amphictyons, and by the assembly of the Amphictyons, seeing that the Amphissians trespass upon the sacred plain and sow and depasture it with cattle, that the deputies and councilors do enter thereupon and define the boundaries with pillars, and enjoin the Amphissians not to trespass for the future."

ANOTHER DECREE.

"In the prieshood of Clynagoras,[2] at the spring congress, it hath been resolved by the deputies and councilors of the Amphictyons and by the assembly of the Amphictyons, seeing that the people of Amphissa have partitioned among themselves the sacred plain and cultivate and feed cattle upon the same, and on being interrupted have come in arms, and with force resisted the general council of the Greeks, and have wounded some of them: that Cottyphus the Arcadian,[3] who hath been elected general of the Amphictyons, be sent embassador to Philip of Macedon, and do request him to come to the aid of Apollo and the Amphictyons, that he may not suffer the god to be insulted by the impious Amphissians; and do announce that the Greeks who are members of the Amphictyonic Council appoint him general with absolute powers."

Now read the dates of these transactions. They correspond with the time when Æschines was deputy. Read.

[1] As to the constitution of the Amphictyonic Council, see Appendix I.

[2] The name of the priest seems to mark the year, as that of the archon at Athens. As this decree must have been passed at a different congress from the one first cited, it has been conjectured that either the name of the priest is wrong, or that ὀπωρινῆς should be read here instead of ἐαρινῆς. See Appendix IX.

[3] Æschines calls Cottyphus a Pharsalian. Winiewski supposes he may have migrated from Arcadia to Pharsalus. Or Φαρσάλιος may be an error for Παῤῥάσιος.

DATES.

"Mnesithides[1] archon, on the sixteenth of the month Anthesterion."

Now give me the letter which, when the Thebans would not hearken to Philip, he sends to his allies in Peloponnesus, that you may plainly see even from this, how the true motives of his enterprise, his designs against Greece and the Thebans and yourselves, were concealed by him, while he affected to be taking measures for the common good under a decree of the Amphictyons. The man who furnished him with these handles and pretexts was Æschines. Read.

THE LETTER OF PHILIP.

"Philip, king of Macedon, to the magistrates[2] and councilors of the confederate Peloponnesians and to all the other allies greeting: Whereas the Locrians surnamed Ozolian, dwelling in Amphissa, commit sacrilege against the temple of Apollo at Delphi, and coming with arms despoil the sacred plain, I propose with your assistance to avenge the god, and to chastise people who violate any part of our recognized religion. Wherefore meet me with arms in Phocis, bringing provisions for forty days, in the ensuing month of Lous, as we style it, Boedromion, as the Athenians, Panemus, as the Corinthians. Those who do not meet us with all their forces, we shall visit with punishment.[3] Farewell."

You see, he avoids all private pleas, and has recourse to an Amphictyonic. Who was it, I say, that helped him to this contrivance—that lent him these excuses? Who is most to blame for the misfortunes which have happened? Surely Æschines. Then[4] go not about saying, O Athenians, that

[1] The archon is wrong. It was Theophrastus, as we learn from the speech of Æschines.

[2] *Δημιοῦργοι* was the title given to magistrates in many of the Peloponnesian states, especially in Elis and Achaia.

[3] I have followed the reading of Schaefer and Jacobs, who omit the words *τοῖς δὲ συμβούλοις ἡμῖν κειμένοις*. Pabst follows Wolf and Taylor, who read *τοῖς δὲ ἡμῖν συναντήσασι πανδημεὶ χρησόμεθα συμβούλοις, τοῖς δὲ μὴ προσθεμένοις ἐπιζημίοις*. Spillan renders it: "Such as attend us with all their forces we shall use as our advisers, those who obey us not we shall fine."

[4] Leland renders this: "Yet mistake me not, Athenians: when our public calamities are the subject of your conversation, say not that we

one man has inflicted these calamities on Greece. Heaven and earth! It was not a single man, but a number of miscreants in every state. Æschines was one of them; and, were I obliged to speak the truth without reserve, I should not hesitate to call him the common pest[1] of all that have since been ruined, men, places, cities: for whoever supplies the seed, to him the crop is owing. I marvel indeed you turned not your faces away the moment you beheld him. But there is a thick darkness, it seems, between you and the truth.

The mention of this man's treasonable acts brings me to the part which I have myself taken in opposition to him. It is fair you should hear my account of it for many reasons, but chiefly, men of Athens, because it would be a shame, when I have undergone the toil of exertions on your behalf, that you should not endure the bare recital of them.

When I saw that the Thebans, and I may add the Athenians, were so led away by Philip's partisans and the corrupt men of either state, as to disregard and take no precaution against a danger which menaced both, and required the utmost precaution, (I mean the suffering Philip's power to increase,) and were readily disposed to enmity and strife with each other; I was constantly watchful to prevent it, not only because in my own judgment I deemed such vigilance expedient, but knowing that Aristophon, and again Eubulus, had all along desired to bring about that union, and, while they were frequently opposed upon other matters, were always agreed upon this. Men whom in their lifetime—you reptile!—you pestered with flattery, yet see not that you are accusing them in their graves:[2] for the Theban policy that

owe them entirely to a single person." From this it appears that he understood ὑφ' ἑνὸς to mean Æschines. I agree with those interpreters who understand it of Philip.

[1] Compare Virgil, Æneid II. 573:

Trojæ et patriæ communis Erinnys.

And Cicero, Philippic II. "Ut Helena Trojanis, sic iste huic reipublicæ causa belli, causa pestis atque exitii fuit." That Cicero had this passage of Demosthenes in his eye, appears also from another sentence, occurring shortly before—"Ut igitur in seminibus est causa arborum et stirpium, sic hujus luctuosissimi belli semen tu fuisti."

[2] Κίναδος has been variously rendered by the translators. The idea intended to be conveyed is that of a sly, sneaking fellow. Spillan has:

you reproach me with is a charge less affecting me than them, who approved that alliance before I did. But I must return.—I say, when Æschines had excited the war in Amphissa, and his coadjutors had helped to establish enmity with Thebes, Philip marched against us—that was the object for which these persons embroiled the states—and had we not roused up a little in time, we could never have recovered ourselves: so far had these men carried matters. In what position you then stood to each other, you will learn from the recital of these decrees and answers. Here, take and read them.

DECREE.[1]

"In the archonship of Heropythus, on the twenty-fifth of the month Elaphebolion, in the presidency of the Erechtheian tribe, by the advice of the Council and the Generals: Whereas Philip hath taken possession of certain neighboring cities, and is besieging others, and finally is preparing to advance against Attica, setting our treaty at nought, and designs to break his oaths and the peace, in violation of our common engagements: The Council and People have resolved to send unto him embassadors, who shall confer with him, and exhort him above all to maintain his relations of amity with us and his convention, or if not, to give time to the Commonwealth for deliberation, and conclude an armistice until the month Thargelion. These have been chosen from the Council; Simus of Anagyrus, Euthydemus of Phlyus, Bulagoras of Alopece."

ANOTHER DECREE.

"In the archonship of Heropythus, on the last day of the month Munychion, by the advice of the Polemarch: Whereas Philip designs to put the Thebans at variance with us, and hath prepared to advance with his whole army to the places nearest to Attica, violating the engagements that subsist between us, the Council and People have resolved to send

"base wretch." Francis: "vile animal." Leland: "scandal to humanity." Brougham: "crafty creature." Jacobs: *Schlange.* Pabst: *schlauer Fuchs.* Auger: "cœur faux et perfide."

I have followed Bekker's reading of *αἰσθάνει*. But the other translators read *αἰσχύνει*, which is found in most manuscripts.

[1] The archon in this and the following decree is wrong, Lysimachides having been archon in the year when these events happened.

unto him a herald and embassadors, who shall request and call upon him to conclude an armistice, so that the people may take measures according to circumstances; for now they do not purpose to march out in the event of any thing reasonable.[1] Nearchus, son of Sosinomus and Polycrates son of Epiphron have been chosen from the Council; and for herald, Eunomus of Anaphlystus from the People."

Now read the answers:—

THE ANSWER TO THE ATHENIANS.

"Philip king of Macedon to the Council and People of Athens greeting: Of the part which you have taken in reference to me from the beginning I am not ignorant, nor what exertions you are making to gain over the Thessalians and Thebans, and also the Bœotians. Since they are more prudent, and will not submit their choice to your dictation, but stand by their own interest, you shift your ground, and sending embassadors and a herald to me, you talk of engagements and ask for an armistice, although I have given you no offense. However I have given audience to your embassadors, and I agree to your request and am ready to conclude an armistice, if you will dismiss your evil counselors and degrade them as they deserve. Farewell."

THE ANSWER TO THE THEBANS.

"Philip king of Macedon to the Council and People of Thebes greeting: I have received your letter, wherein you renew peace and amity with me. I am informed however that the Athenians are most earnestly soliciting you to accept their overtures. I blamed you at first, for being inclined to put faith in their promises and to espouse their policy. But since I have discovered that you would rather maintain peace with me than follow the counsels of others, I

[1] That is, "if Philip conducts himself with moderation—with tolerable forbearance—grants reasonable conditions—or the like." The commentators have been puzzled by this sentence. Lord Brougham thinks it was purposely made obscure by the Athenians, to avoid committing themselves. Schaefer sees in it the symptoms of irresolution and despondency. Jacobs: *denn jetzt hat es noch nicht beschlossen auszurücken bei irgend mässigen Bedingungen.* Pabst: *denn jetzt ist das Volk bei Bewilligung erträglicher Bedingungen keineswegs entschlossen gegen Philipp auszurücken.*

praise you the more on divers accounts, but chiefly because you have consulted in this business for your safety, and preserve your attachment to me, which I trust will be of no small moment to you, if you persevere in that determination. Farewell."

Philip having thus disposed the states toward each other by his contrivances, and being elated by these decrees and answers, came with his army and seized Elatea, confident that, happen what might, you and the Thebans could never again unite. What commotion there was in the city you all know; but let me just mention the most striking circumstances.

It was evening. A person came with a message to the presidents, that Elatea was taken. They rose from supper immediately, drove off the people from their market-stalls, and set fire to the wicker-frames;[1] others sent for the generals and called the trumpeter; and the city was full of commotion. The next morning at daybreak the presidents summoned the council to their hall, and you went to the assembly, and before they could introduce or prepare the question,[2] the whole people were up in their seats.[3] When the council had entered, and the presidents had reported their intelligence and presented the courier, and he had made his statement, the crier asked—"Who wishes to speak?"—and no one came forward. The crier put the

[1] Reiske thinks the object of this proceeding was to clear the ground of the market, that the people might be stationed there in arms during the night. Leland says it was "to clear the place for an assembly, and in their confusion and impatience they took the speediest and most violent method." But the assembly was held in the Pnyx, and not in the market. Another writer has conjectured that the presidents meant to force the citizens to attend to public business. Schaefer's is the more probable explanation, that the stalls were burned for a fire-signal, to bring the people from the rural districts into the city.

[2] According to the usual course of law, the council prepared and drew up some formal question or bill to be submitted to the people. This was the προβούλευμα. In the present case, being a special meeting on a sudden emergency, they would probably draw up nothing more than the heads of a question, to be afterward put in the shape of a decree if necessary. Jacobs translates these words: *ehe der Senat noch sein Geschäft vollbracht und einen voläufingen Beschluss gefasst hatte.* Pabst: *ehe noch der Senat seine Verhandlungen beendigt und ein Gutachten abgefasst hatte.* See Schömann, de Comitiis, chap. ix.

[3] On the hill of the Pnyx.

question repeatedly—still no man rose, though all the generals were present and all the orators, and our country with her common voice called for some one to speak and save her—for when the crier raises his voice according to law, it may justly be deemed the common voice of our country. If those who desired the salvation of Athens were the proper parties to come forward, all of you and the other Athenians would have risen and mounted the platform; for I am sure you all desired her salvation—if those of greatest wealth, the three-hundred[1]—if those who were both, friendly to the state and wealthy, the men who afterward gave such ample donations; for patriotism and wealth produced the gift. But that occasion, that day, as it seems, called not only for a patriot and a wealthy man, but for one who had closely followed the proceedings from their commencement, and rightly calculated for what object and purpose Philip carried them on. A man who was ignorant of these matters, or had not long and carefully studied them, let him be ever so patriotic or wealthy, would neither see what measures were needful, nor be competent to advise you.

Well then—I was the man called for upon that day. I came forward and addressed you. What I said, I beg you for two reasons attentively to hear—first, to be convinced, that of all your orators and statesmen I alone deserted not the patriot's post[2] in the hour of danger, but was found in the very moment of panic speaking and moving what your necessities required—secondly, because at the expense of a little time you will gain large experience for the future in all your political concerns.[3]

I said—those who were in such alarm under the idea that Philip had got the Thebans with him did not, in my opinion,

[1] See Vol. I. pp. 52, 301.

[2] Auger has the following note, whether fanciful or not, I leave to the judgment of the reader:—"On doit remarquer que Démosthene affecte de se servir de ce mot *poste* dans plusieurs endroits de son discours, comme pour faire entendre que s'il avoit, comme guerrier, abandonné son poste à la bataille de Chéronée, il ne l'avoit jamais abandonné, comme ministre, à la tête des affaires."

[3] *Τῆς πάσης πολιτείας*, "the whole range of politics—that political knowledge which concerned the Athenian public." As Lord Brougham expresses it: "you may acquire a fuller insight into our whole polity for the future." Leland and Spillan refer it wrongly to the political actions of Demosthenes.

understand the position of affairs; for I was sure, had that really been so, we should have heard not of his being at Elatea, but upon our frontiers: he was come however, I knew for certain, to make all right for himself in Thebes. "Let me inform you," said I, "how the matter stands.—All the Thebans whom it was possible either to bribe or deceive he has at his command;[1] those who have resisted him from the first and still oppose him he can in no way prevail upon: what then is his meaning, and why has he seized upon Elatea? He means, by displaying a force in the neighborhood, and bringing up his troops, to encourage and embolden his friends, to intimidate his adversaries, that they may either concede from fear what they now refuse, or be compelled. Now"—said I—"if we determine on the present occasion to remember any unkindness which the Thebans have done us, and to regard them in the character of enemies with distrust, in the first place, we shall be doing just what Philip would desire; in the next place, I fear, his present adversaries embracing his friendship and all Philippizing with one consent, they will both march against Attica. But if you will hearken to me, and be pleased to examine (not cavil at) what I say, I believe it will meet your approval, and I shall dispel the danger impending over Athens. What then do I advise?—First, away with your present fear; and rather fear all of ye for the Thebans—they are nearer harm than we are—to them the peril is more immediate:—next I say, march to Eleusis, all the fighting-men and the cavalry, and show yourselves to the world in arms, that your partisans in Thebes may have equal liberty to speak up for the good cause, knowing that, as the faction who sell their country to Philip have an army to support them at Elatea, so the party that will contend for freedom have your assistance at hand if they are assailed. Further I recommend you to elect ten embassadors, and empower them in conjunction with the generals to fix the time for going there and for the out-march. When the embassadors have arrived at Thebes, how do I advise that you should treat the matter? Pray attend particularly to this—Ask nothing of the Thebans; (it would be dishonorable at this time;) but offer to assist them if they require it, on the plea

[1] So Lord Brougham, whom I have followed; and so Jacobs expresses it: *hat er alle in seiner Gewalt.*

that they are in extreme danger, and we see the future better than they do. If they accept this offer and hearken to our counsels, so shall we have accomplished what we desire, and our conduct will look[1] worthy of the state: should we miscarry, they will have themselves to blame for any error committed now, and we shall have done nothing dishonorable or mean."

This and more to the like effect I spoke, and left the platform. It was approved by all; not a word was said against me. Nor did I make the speech without moving, nor make the motion without undertaking the embassy, nor undertake the embassy without prevailing on the Thebans.[2] From the beginning to the end I went through it all; I gave myself entirely to your service, to meet the dangers which encompassed Athens.

Produce me the decree which then passed. Now, Æschines, how would you have me describe you, and how myself, upon that day? Shall I call myself Batalus,[3] your nickname of reproach, and you not even a hero of the common sort, but one of those upon the stage, Cresphontes or Creon, or the

[1] I have taken *προσχήματος* as Jacobs, Pabst, Auger, Leland, and Spillan have taken it. Compare Sophocles, Electra, 680, and Brunck's note.

ἐπεὶ γὰρ ἦλθον εἰς τὸ κλεινὸν Ἑλλάδος
πρόσχημ' ἀγῶνος.

But the sense of "pretext," in which Schaefer understands the word, is by no means unsuitable to the passage.

[2] Lord Brougham has a good note on the different modes of turning this famous climax, which is cited as an example by Quinctilian, and thus imitated by Cicero, pro Milone,—"Neque vero se populo solum sed etiam Senatui commisit; neque Senatui modo, sed etiam publicis præsidiis et armis; neque iis tantum, verum etiam ejus potestati cui Senatus totam rempublicam, omnem Italiæ pacem, cuncta populi Romani arma commiserat."

[3] The origin of this nickname is doubtful. The early critics were not agreed upon it, as we learn from Plutarch. Libanius, in the Life of Demosthenes, says that Batalus was an effeminate flute-player in Asia Minor; which seems to agree with the words of Æschines, in his speech on the Embassy, (p. 41,) where he says that Demosthenes was called Batalus when a boy, *δι' αἰσχρουργίαν καὶ κιναιδίαν*; afterward he received the name of *Ἀργᾶς* (a sort of serpent), on account of the unnatural action against his guardians; and, in his later years, *Συκοφάντης*, "the common name of all scoundrels." Compare page 45 of the same speech; and pages 17 and 18 of the speech against Timarchus, where it is alleged, that Demosthenes himself joked about the name of Batalus, and said it was a term of endearment used by his aunt.

Œnomaus whom you execrably murdered once at Colyttus?[1] Well; upon that occasion I the Batalus of Pæania was more serviceable to the state than you the Œnomaus of Cothocidæ. You were of no earthly use; I did every thing which became a good citizen. Read the decree.

THE DECREE OF DEMOSTHENES.

"In the archonship of Nausicles,[2] in the presidency of the Æantian tribe, on the sixteenth of Scirophorion, Demosthenes son of Demosthenes of Pæania moved: Whereas Philip king of Macedon hath in time past been violating the treaty of peace made between him and the Athenian people, in contempt of his oaths and those laws of justice which are recognized among all the Greeks, and hath been annexing unto himself cities that no way belong to him, and hath besieged and taken some which belong to the Athenians without any provocation by the people of Athens, and at the present time he is making great advances in cruelty and violence, forasmuch as in certain Greek cities he puts garrisons and overturns their constitution, some he razes to the ground and sells the inhabitants for slaves, in some he replaces a Greek population with barbarians, giving them possession of the temples and sepulchres, acting in no way foreign to his own country or character, making an insolent use of his present fortune, and forgetting that from a petty and insignificant person he has come to be unexpectedly great: and the people of Athens, so long as they saw him annexing barbarian or private cities of their own,[3] less seriously regarded the

[1] Cresphontes, king of Messenia, and one of the Heraclidæ, was the hero of a lost play of Euripides; Creon is the well known character in the Œdipus and Antigone of Sophocles: Œnomaus, the king of Elis, and father of Hippodamia, was the hero of a tragedy of Ischander, in the performance of which Æschines was hissed off the stage at Colyttus, one of the Attic townships.

[2] The archon was Lysimachides.

[3] Jacobs: *dass er nur barbarische, wenn gleich ihm angehörige Städte wegnahm.* Pabst: *die zwar diesem Volke gehörten, aber von Barbaren bewohnt waren.* They have both adopted Schaefer's interpretation of ἰδίας, as I have done. Schaefer thus comments on the passage: "Scilicet totius psephismatis hæc vis, hic tenor est, ut Athenienses arma sumere videantur, non suorum causâ commodorum, quæ amissa recuperent, sed ob communem Græciæ salutem. Ceterum hoc decretum numerem in illustrissimis monumentis summæ Atheniensium vanitatis, cui oratores ita velificarenter, ut vel e mythicis temporibus mellitos verborum globulos repeterent."

offense given to themselves, but now that they see Greek cities outraged and some destroyed, they think it would be monstrous and unworthy of their ancestral glory to look on while the Greeks are enslaved: Therefore it is resolved by the Council and People of Athens, that having prayed and sacrificed to the gods and heroes who protect the Athenian city and territory, bearing in mind the virtue of their ancestors, who deemed it of greater moment to preserve the liberty of Greece than their own country, they will put two hundred ships to sea, and their admiral shall sail up into the straits of Thermopylæ, and their general and commander of horse shall march with the infantry and cavalry to Eleusis, and embassadors shall be sent to the other Greeks, and first of all to the Thebans, because Philip is nearest their territory, and shall exhort them without dread of Philip to maintain their own independence and that of Greece at large, and assure them that the Athenian people, not remembering any variance which has formerly arisen between the countries, will assist them with troops and money and weapons and arms, feeling that for them (being Greeks) to contend among themselves for the leadership is honorable, but to be commanded and deprived of the leadership by a man of foreign extraction is derogatory to the renown of the Greeks and the virtue of their ancestors: further, the people of Athens do not regard the people of Thebes as aliens either in blood or race; they remember also the benefits conferred by their ancestors upon the ancestors of the Thebans; for they restored the children of Hercules who were kept by the Peloponnesians out of their hereditary dominion, defeating in battle those who attempted to resist the descendants of Hercules; and we gave shelter to Œdipus and his comrades in exile; and many other kind and generous acts have been done by us to the Thebans: wherefore now also the people of Athens will not desert the interests of the Thebans and the other Greeks: And let a treaty be entered into with them for alliance and intermarriage, and oaths be mutually exchanged. Embassadors: Demosthenes son of Demosthenes of Pæania, Hyperides son of Cleander of Spettus, Mnesithides son of Antiphanes of Phrearrii, Democrates son of Sophilus of Phlyus, Callæschrus son of Diotimus of Cothocidæ."

That was the commencement and first step in the negotiation with Thebes:[1] before then the countries had been led by these men into discord and hatred and jealousy. That decree caused the peril which then surrounded us to pass away like a cloud. It was the duty of a good citizen, if he had any better plan, to disclose it at the time, not to find fault now. A statesman and a pettifogger,[2] while in no other respect are they alike, in this most widely differ. The one declares his opinion before the proceedings, and makes himself responsible to his followers, to fortune, to the times, to all men: the other is silent when he ought to speak; at any untoward event he grumbles. Now, as I said before, the time for a man who regarded the commonwealth, and for honest counsel, was then: however I will go to this extent[3]—if any one now can point out a better course, or indeed if any other was practicable but the one which I adopted, I confess that I was wrong. For if there be any measure now discovered, which (executed then) would have been to our advantage, I say it

[1] Jacobs: *Dies war der Anfang und das erste Verfahren in der thebäischen Sache.* Pabst: *Dies war der Anfang und der erste Schritt, der in den Angelegenheiten der Thebener gethan wurde.*

[2] Lord Brougham, objecting to Leland's translation of "sycophant," says, "he might as well call a player a 'hypocrite,' or a peasant a 'villain.'" This criticism I assent to; yet it is not easy to find an apt word for *συκοφάντης*, and hence the German translators, as well as some of the English, have retained the Greek term. It has various modifications of meaning in the Orators, all having reference, more or less remote, to the original meaning of an "informer." (See my article *Συκοφάντης* in the Archæological Dictionary, where this is fully explained.) It may often be rendered "a slanderer," and so Auger renders it here, "calomniateur." Sometimes it denotes a "vexatious meddler," a "malignant and sneaking enemy." Thus Demosthenes says, *πονηρὸν ὁ συκοφάντης καὶ βάσκανον*. And again, *συκοφάντης τοῦτ' ἔστιν, αἰτιᾶσθαι μὲν πάντα, ἐξελέγχειν δὲ μηδέν*. And (as we have seen) Æschines says it was a common name for all scoundrels.

As contrasted with *σύμβουλος*, an honest adviser or statesman, it signifies a factious politician, one who seeks his own interest or that of his party, or the gratification of private malice, rather than the good of his country; one capable of doing the things which Demosthenes charges his adversary with. Such a person may be called a pettifogger in politics, just as a dirty practitioner is called a pettifogger in the law. The version, I must admit, is not perfectly satisfactory, yet it seems preferable to any other single word. Lord Brougham's "partisan" is too weak. If I chose to use two words, I would say "an honest politician and a factious one," &c.

[3] "I will go to this extreme length in making concession." Or as Lord Brougham has it: "I will go to such an excess of candor."

ought not to have escaped me. But if there is none, if there was none, if none can be suggested even at this day, what was a statesman to do? Was he not to choose the best measures within his reach and view? That did I, Æschines, when the crier asked, "Who wishes to speak?"—not, "Who wishes to complain about the past, or to guarantee the future?" While you on those occasions sat mute in the assembly, I came forward and spake. However, as you omitted then, tell us now. Say, what scheme that I ought to have devised, what favorable opportunity was lost to the state by my neglect?—what alliance was there, what better plan, to which I should have directed the people? But no! The past is with all the world given up; no one even proposes to deliberate about it: the future it is, or the present, which demands the action of a counselor. At the time, as it appeared, there were dangers impending, and dangers at hand. Mark the line of my policy at that crisis; don't rail at the event. The end of all things is what the Deity pleases: his line of policy it is that shows the judgment of the statesman. Do not then impute it as a crime to me that Philip chanced to conquer in battle: that issue depended not on me, but on God. Prove that I adopted not all measures that according to human calculation were feasible—that I did not honestly and diligently and with exertions beyond my strength carry them out—or that my enterprises were not honorable and worthy of the state and necessary. Show me this, and accuse me as soon as you like. But if the hurricane that visited us hath been too powerful, not for us only, but for all Greece besides, what is the fair course?[1] As if a merchant, after taking every precaution, and furnishing his vessel with every thing that he thought would insure her safety, because afterward he met with a storm and his tackle was strained or broken to pieces, should be charged with the

[1] The Orator, as Schaefer rightly observes, suppresses the answer to his own question, which, if fully expressed, would be as follows:—"The fair thing is, not to blame me for events which were inevitable. You might as well blame a shipowner," &c. Leland saw the true meaning, and expresses it in his translation: "What then? Am I to be accused? With equal justice might the trader," &c. And thus Auger: "Que faire, je vous prie? Faut il m'imputer ce contre-temps?" &c. Other translators have read χρῆν apparently, and misconceived the sense of the passage. I have thought it better to preserve the looseness of the original, which is not at all unnatural, and will not mislead the intelligent reader.

shipwreck! "Well, but I was not the pilot"—he might say—just as I was not the general.—"Fortune was not under my control: all was under hers."

Consider and reflect upon this—If, with the Thebans on our side, we were destined so to fare in the contest, what was to be expected, if we had never had them for allies, but they had joined Philip, as he used every effort of persuasion to make them do?[1] And if, when the battle was fought three days' march from Attica, such peril and alarm surrounded the city, what must we have expected, if the same disaster had happened in some part of our territory? As it was (do you see?) we could stand, meet, breathe; mightily did one, two, three days, help to our preservation:[2] in the other case—but it is wrong to mention things, of which we have been spared the trial by the favor of some deity, and by our protecting ourselves with the very alliance which you assail.

All this, at such length, have I addressed to you, men of the jury, and to the outer circle of hearers; for, as to this contemptible fellow, a short and plain argument would suffice.

If the future was revealed to you, Æschines, alone, when the state was deliberating on these proceedings, you ought to have forewarned us at the time. If you did not foresee it,

[1] That is, Philip, by his letters and by his embassies. Compare p. 301, 'Αλλὰ μὴν οἵας τότ' ἠφίει φωνὰς ὁ Φίλιππος κ. τ. λ. Most of the translators take *ἐκεῖνος* to mean Æschines. The writer of an article in the *Edinburgh Review*, vol. xxxvi. p. 483, said to have been the late Justice Williams, has the following note:—"If *ἐκεῖνος* be the true reading, we are aware that Philip must be meant. But the spirit of the passage itself, and the analogy of the whole oration, lean to *οὗτος*, as we translate it." I can not assent to this criticism. The orator wishes to impress upon his hearers the great importance which Philip attached to the alliance of Thebes. He does not mean to charge Æschines with openly advocating Philip's cause: on the contrary, he represents Æschines as having then held his tongue. Leland saw the true meaning. His version is: "but united with our enemy in compliance with all his urgent solicitations." So did Auger, whom the Edinburgh reviewer calls "a babbling, cackling Frenchman." His version is: "ce prince alors épuisoit sa politique pour s'attacher ce peuple." The Germans are wrong.

[2] The infinitives, *στῆναι, συνελθεῖν, ἀναπνεῦσαι*, depend upon *ἔδοσαν*. I have given a turn in the translation to preserve the force of the original. The translators, all but Jacobs, have made a shocking mess of this passage. Jacobs: *Weisst Du nicht, dass jetz ein und zwei und drei Tage uns aufrecht zu stehn, zusammen zu kommen, aufzuathmen, und vieles Andre der Stadt zur Rettung verschafft haben?*

you are responsible for the same ignorance as the rest. Why then do you accuse me in this behalf, rather than I you? A better citizen have I been than you in respect of the matters of which I am speaking, (others I discuss not at present,) inasmuch as I gave myself up to what seemed for the general good, not shrinking from any personal danger, nor taking thought of any; while you neither suggested better measures, (or mine would not have been adopted,) nor lent any aid in the prosecuting of mine: exactly what the basest person and worst enemy of the state would do, are you found to have done after the event; and at the same time Aristratus in Naxos and Aristolaus in Thasos, the deadly foes of our state, are bringing to trial the friends of Athens, and Æschines at Athens is accusing Demosthenes. Surely the man, who waited to found his reputation upon the misfortunes of the Greeks,[1] deserves rather to perish than to accuse another; nor is it possible that one, who has profited by the same conjunctures as the enemies of the commonwealth, can be a well-wisher of his country. You show yourself by your life and conduct, by your political action, and even your political inaction.[2] Is any thing going on that appears good for the people? Æschines is mute. Has any thing untoward happened or amiss? Forth comes Æschines; just as fractures and sprains are put in motion, when the body is attacked with disease.

But since he insists so strongly on the event, I will even assert something of a paradox: and I beg and pray of you not to marvel at its boldness, but kindly to consider what I say. If then the results had been foreknown to all, if all had foreseen them, and you, Æschines, had foretold them and protested with clamor and outcry—you that never opened your mouth—not even then should the Commonwealth have abandoned her design, if she had any regard for glory, or ancestry, or futurity. As it is, she appears to have failed in

[1] Literally: "for whom the misfortunes of the Greeks were kept in store to get repute by." Pabst: *Wer auf die Unglücksfälle der Hellenen gewartet, um durch dieselben berühmt zu werden.*

[2] The Edinburgh reviewer: "by what you do in public affairs, and by what you decline doing." Auger: "Par vos discours, et même par votre silence." Jacobs: *was im Staate treibst und wiederum nicht treibst.* Pabst: *durch Deine Theilnahme und Nichttheilnahme an der Verwaltung des Staats.*

her enterprise, a thing to which all mankind are liable, if the Deity so wills it: but then—claiming precedency over others, and afterward abandoning her pretensions—she would have incurred the charge of betraying all to Philip. Why, had we resigned without a struggle that which our ancestors encountered every danger to win, who would not have spit upon you? Let me not say, the commonwealth or myself![1] With what eyes, I pray, could we have beheld strangers visiting the city, if the result had been what it is, and Philip had been chosen leader and lord of all, but other people without us had made the struggle to prevent it; especially when in former times our country had never preferred an ignominious security to the battle for honor? For what Grecian or what barbarian is ignorant, that by the Thebans, or by the Lacedæmonians who were in might before them, or by the Persian king, permission would thankfully and gladly have been given to our commonwealth, to take what she pleased and hold her own, provided she would accept foreign law and let another power command in Greece? But, as it seems, to the Athenians of that day such conduct would not have been national, or natural, or endurable: none could at any period of time persuade the commonwealth to attach herself in secure subjection to the powerful and unjust: through every age has she persevered in a perilous struggle for precedency and honor and glory. And this you esteem so noble and congenial to your principles, that among your

[1] *I. e.* "Let me not say any thing so shocking, so revolting to my feelings, as to suppose that the commonwealth or myself could deserve such an indignity!" According to the natural course of the argument we should rather have expected the orator to conclude by saying—"the commonwealth would have acted a despicable part," or the like. But adopting a strong expression, he takes care to preserve a respectful euphemism toward the Athenian people, and surprises his adversary by suddenly denouncing him as the supposed adviser of the degenerate policy. Immediately afterward he reverts (but in milder language) to the disgrace which would have fallen upon the country.

This I take to be a better interpretation than Schaefer's, who understands *καταπτύσειε*. Another, to which, if it were borne out by the words, I should be much inclined, is offered by the Edinburgh reviewer, who translates it: "to say nothing of the state or myself," and observes, "The meaning is, not that the state and I are blameless, but if such a line of policy had been adopted, who would not have regarded even you, Æschines, the most worthless animal in the city, with new and additional contempt, *à fortiori*, me, and *à fortissimo*, the city itself?"

ancestors you honor most those who acted in such a spirit; and with reason. For who would not admire the virtue of those men, who resolutely embarked in their galleys and quitted country and home, rather than receive foreign law, choosing Themistocles who gave such counsel for their general, and stoning Cyrsilus to death who advised submission to the terms imposed—not him only, but your wives also stoning his wife?[1] Yes; the Athenians of that day looked not for an orator or a general, who might help them to a pleasant servitude: they scorned to live, if it could not be with freedom. For each of them considered, that he was not born to his father or mother only, but also to his country.[2] What is the difference? He that thinks himself born for his parents only, waits for his appointed or natural end: he that thinks himself born for his country also, will sooner perish than behold her in slavery, and will regard the insults and indignities, which must be borne in a commonwealth enslaved, as more terrible than death.

Had I attempted to say, that I instructed you in sentiments worthy of your ancestors, there is not a man who would not justly rebuke me. What I declare is, that such principles are your own; I show that before my time such was the spirit of the commonwealth; though certainly in the execution of the particular measures I claim a share also for myself. The prosecutor, arraigning the whole proceedings, and imbittering you against me as the cause of our alarms and dangers, in his eagerness to deprive me of honor for the moment, robs you of the eulogies that should endure forever.

[1] Cicero (de Officiis, III. 11) has borrowed this anecdote from Demosthenes. The same story is related by Herodotus (IX. 4, 5), who calls the person not Cyrsilus, but Lycidas. The terms were offered by Mardonius to the Athenians, while they were in Salamis. The advice of Lycidas was given to the council, and the people outside hearing of it, proceeded immediately to inflict summary punishment upon him.

[2] Compare Cicero pro Milone—"Hiccine vir patriæ natus usquam nisi in patriâ morietur?" The "necessaria mors" of Cicero is the same as the τὸν τῆς εἱμαρμένης θάνατος of Demosthenes. These expressions are illustrated by Aulus Gellius, XIII. 1, who quotes the following passage from the first Philippic of the Roman:—

"Hunc igitur ut sequerer properavi, quem præsentes non sunt secuti; non ut proficerem aliquid; neque enim sperabam id, nec præstare poteram; sed ut, si quid mihi humanitus accidisset, (multa autem impendere videntur præter naturam præterque fatum,) hujus diei vocem testem reipublicæ relinquerem meæ perpetuæ erga se voluntatis."

For should you, under a disbelief in the wisdom of my policy, convict the defendant, you will appear to have done wrong, not to have suffered what befell you by the cruelty of fortune. But never, never can you have done wrong, O Athenians, in undertaking the battle for the freedom and safety of all! I swear it by your forefathers—those that met the peril at Marathon, those that took the field at Platæa, those in the sea-fight at Salamis, and those at Artemisium, and many other brave men who repose in the public monuments, all of whom alike, as being worthy of the same honor, the country buried, Æschines, not only the successful or victorious! Justly! For the duty of brave men has been done by all: their fortune has been such as the Deity assigned to each.[1]

Accursed scribbler![2] you, to deprive me of the approbation and affection of my countrymen, speak of trophies and battles and ancient deeds, with none of which had this present trial the least concern; but I!—O you third-rate actor!—I, that rose to counsel the state how to maintain her pre-eminence! in what spirit was I to mount the hustings? In the spirit of one having unworthy counsel to offer?[3]—I should

[1] So much criticism has been lavished, both in ancient and modern times, on the beauty of this celebrated passage, that even to refer to all that has been said would be impossible. I shall content myself with transcribing the remarks of the writer, whom I have before adverted to, of the *Edinburgh Review*:—"The whole passage," he says, "is teeming and bursting with proofs of superhuman high-mindedness and devotion." But he observes further—"The argument is not lost sight of for an instant in the midst of this inflammation. The sentence containing the apostrophe is not closed, before we find it recurring, and in such a shape as induces us to suppose, that for its sake the oratory is introduced. Longinus says that Demosthenes here gives a proof of the necessity of keeping sober even in excesses, *διδάσκων ὅτι κἂν βακχεύμασι νήφειν ἀναγκαῖον.* He notices also the dexterity and address with which the difference of success in the two cases is managed. They are not called *conquerors* of Marathon, &c., but the *combatants;* and then the orator is beforehand with any objection, (*τὸν ἀκροατὴν φθάνων,*) by turning short round upon Æschines, and reminding him that all, whether successful or not, had equal honors."

[2] *Γραμματοκύφων* is "one that stoops or pores over papers and writing." He alludes to the office of clerk, formerly held by Æschines, not to his father's school, as some have supposed. Jacobs renders the word *Buchstabenhocker.* Pabst: *Aktenhocker.*

[3] Literally: "intending to offer counsel unworthy of these (*τούτων*) my countrymen?" Let the student be careful not to connect *τούτων* with *πρωτείων.* The orator looking, or pointing with his hand, to the

have deserved to perish! You yourselves, men of Athens, may not try private and public causes on the same principles: the compacts of every-day life you are to judge of by particular laws and circumstances; the measures of statesmen, by reference to the dignity of your ancestors. And if you think it your duty to act worthily of them, you should every one of you consider, when you come into court to decide public questions, that together with your staff and ticket[1] the spirit of the commonwealth is delivered to you.

But in touching upon the deeds of your ancestors, there were some decrees and transactions which I omitted. I will return from my digression.

On our arrival at Thebes, we found embassadors there from Philip, from the Thessalians and from his other allies; our friends in trepidation, his friends confident. To prove that I am not asserting this now to serve my own purposes, read me the letter which we embassadors dispatched on the instant. So outrageous is my opponent's malignity, that, if any advantage was procured, he attributes it to the occasion, not to me;

plaintiff, or defendant, (who were always in court,) or to their respective friends and supporters who stood near them, or to the jury or surrounding spectators, designates them simply as *οὗτος* or *οὗτοι*, and is easily understood by his hearers. But in a translation for English readers, these terms require to be varied according to circumstances. Jacobs here has: *Sollt' ich sagen was der Stadt unwürdig war?*

[1] There were 6000 jurors chosen by lot for the service of the year, 600 from each of the Attic tribes. The whole number was then divided into ten sections of 500 each, a thousand being left as supernumeraries, to supply deficiencies occasioned by death or any other cause. There were ten courts at Athens, among which the services of these jurors were to be distributed; and it was managed in the following way. Each court was designated by a color, and also by a letter over the doorway. Each of the jury sections was likewise designated by a letter. When the juries had to be impanneled, the letters indicating the different sections were drawn out of one box, and the letters indicating the different courts were drawn out of another: each pair of lots so drawn out determined what section should be assigned to what court. When the whole section was not required, the individual jurors who were to form the pannel were chosen by lot, each juror having a counter with his section and name marked upon it. The courts being thus allotted, every juryman received a staff and a ticket. The staff, on which was marked the letter and color of his court, served to distinguish him from the crowd, and procure him instant admission. The ticket, which he returned to the magistrate when the business was concluded, entitled him to his fee.

while all miscarriages he attributes to me and my fortune. And according to him, as it seems, I, the orator and adviser, have no merit in results of argument and counsel, but am the sole author of misfortunes in arms and strategy. Could there be a more brutal calumniator or a more execrable? Read the letter.

[*The letter is read.*][1]

On the convening of the assembly, our opponents were introduced first, because they held the character of allies. And they came forward and spoke, in high praise of Philip and disparagement of you, bringing up all the hostilities that you ever committed against the Thebans. In fine, they urged them to show their gratitude for the services done by Philip, and to avenge themselves for the injuries which you had done them, either—it mattered not which—by giving them a passage against you, or by joining in the invasion of Attica; and they proved, as they fancied, that by adopting their advice the cattle and slaves and other effects of Attica would come into Bœotia, whereas by acting as they said we should advise Bœotia would suffer pillage through the war. And much they said besides, tending all to the same point. The reply that we made I would give my life to recapitulate, but I fear, as the occasion is past, you will look upon it as if a sort of deluge had overwhelmed the whole proceedings, and regard any talk about them as a useless troubling of you.[2] Hear then what we persuaded them and what answer they returned. Take and read this:

[*The answer of the Thebans.*]

After this they invited and sent for you. You marched to their succor, and—to omit what happened between—their reception of you was so friendly, that, while their infantry and cavalry were outside the walls, they admitted your army into their houses and citadel, among their wives and children and all that was most precious. Why, upon that day three of the noblest testimonies were before all mankind borne in your favor by the Thebans, one to your courage, one to

[1] This, and all the documents subsequently referred to by the Orator, are lost.

[2] Spillan: "useless trouble." Leland: "useless and odious." Francis: "idle impertinence." Jacobs: *eitle Belästigung.*

your justice, one to your good behavior.[1] For when they preferred fighting on your side to fighting against you, they held you to be braver and juster in your demands than Philip; and when they put under your charge what they and all men are most watchful to protect, their wives and children, they showed that they had confidence in your good behavior. In all which, men of Athens, it appeared they had rightly estimated your character. For after your forces entered the city, not so much as a groundless complaint was preferred against you by any one; so discreetly did you behave yourselves: and twice arrayed on their side in the earlier battles, that by the river and the winter-battle,[2] you proved yourselves not irreproachable only, but admirable in your discipline, your equipments, and your zeal: which called forth eulogies from other men to you, sacrifice and thanksgiving from you to the Gods. And I would gladly ask Æschines—while these things were going on, and the city was full of enthusiasm and joy and praise, whether he joined with the multitude in sacrifice and festivity, or sat at home sorrowing and moaning and repining at the public success. For if he was present and appeared with the rest, is not his conduct monstrous, or rather impious, when measures, which he himself called the Gods to witness were excellent, he now requires you to condemn—you that have sworn by the Gods? If he was not present, does he not deserve a thousand deaths for grieving to behold what others rejoiced at?[3] Read me now the decrees.

[*The decrees for sacrifice.*]

[1] Σωφροσύνης is variously rendered by the translators: "continence;" "self-command;" "virtue;" "honor." Auger; "sagesse;" and afterward, "vertu." Jacobs: *Enthaltsamkeit.* Pabst: *Mässigung.* And in truth the word includes more or less of all these meanings.

[2] See Appendix IX.

[3] Lord Brougham observes as follows:—

"The beauty of this passage is very striking. Not merely the exquisite diction—the majesty of the rhythm—the skillful collocation—the picturesque description of Æschines' dismay and skulking from the public rejoicings; but the argument is to be observed and admired. It is a dilemma, and one which would be quite sufficient for the momentary victory at which alone an orator often aims. It is not closely reasoned; it is not a complete dilemma; a retort is obvious, (to use the language of the logicians,) and this is always fatal, being the test before which no bad dilemma can stand. Æschines had only to em-

We thus were engaged in sacrifice; the Thebans were in the assurance that they had been saved through us; and it had come about, that a people, who seemed likely to want assistance through the practices of these men, were themselves assisting others in consequence of my advice which you followed. What language Philip then uttered, and in what trouble he was on this account, you shall learn from his letters which he sent to Peloponnesus. Take and read them, that the jury may know what my perseverance and journeys and toils, and the many decrees which this man just now pulled to pieces, accomplished.

Athenians, you have had many great and renowned orators before me; the famous Callistratus, Aristophon, Cephalus, Thrasybulus, hundreds of others; yet none of them ever thoroughly devoted himself to any measure of state: for instance, the mover of a resolution would not be embassador; the embassador would not move a resolution; each one left for himself some relief, and also, should any thing happen, an excuse.[1] How then—it may be said—did you so far surpass others in might and boldness as to do every thing yourself? I don't say that: but such was my conviction of the danger impending over us, that I considered it left no room or thought for individual security; a man should have been only too happy to perform his duty without neglect.[2] As to

brace the second alternative—the second horn—and it never could have transfixed him.

" 'I did remain at home, not mourning over the success of your measures, but their wickedness; not grudging the people their short-lived joy, but grieved to see them deluded by your arts to their ruin.' This answer was complete. Nevertheless, there are but very few complete dilemmas in the whole course of any argument upon any subject: and the one under consideration is quite good enough to pass with an audience in a speech. Many much less complete are every day used with us both in the senate, in popular assemblies, and even at the bar, and with sufficient success. This whole passage would be of certain success in our parliament."

I may add, that Demosthenes was safe from the retort, Æschines having no reply.

[1] Ἀναφορὰ means "power of casting or shifting the blame upon some other person or thing." This is not sufficiently expressed by the word "resource," which Leland and other translators have: nor indeed have we any word exactly corresponding. Auger: "une sûreté." Jacobs: *Rückenhalt.*

[2] Schaefer explains this differently: "sed boni consulendum esse, si

myself I was persuaded, perhaps foolishly, yet I was persuaded, that none would move better resolutions than myself, none would execute them better, none as embassador would show more zeal and honesty. Therefore I undertook every duty myself. Read the letters of Philip.

[*The letters.*]

To this did my policy, Æschines, reduce Philip. This language he uttered through me, he that before had lifted his voice so boldly against Athens! For which I was justly crowned by the people; and you were present and opposed it not, and Diondas who preferred an indictment obtained not his share of the votes. Here, read me the decrees which were then absolved, and which this man never indicted.

[*The decrees.*]

These decrees, men of Athens, contain the very words and syllables, which Aristonicus drew up formerly, and Ctesiphon the defendant has now. And Æschines neither arraigned these himself, nor aided the party who preferred an indictment. Yet, if his present charge against me be true, he might then have arraigned Demomeles the mover and Hyperides with more show of reason than he can the defendant. Why? Because Ctesiphon may refer to them, and to the decisions of the courts, and to the fact of Æschines not having accused them, although they moved the same decrees which he has now, and to the laws which bar any further proceedings in such a case,[1] and to many points besides:—whereas then the question would have been tried on its own merits, before any such advantages had been obtained.[2] But then, I imagine, it would have been impossible to do what Æschines now does

quis, nullâ non curâ adhibitâ, sorte fatali uteretur." And so Jacobs: *sondern dass man sich gefallen lassen müsse, bei dem Bewusstseyn nichts unterlassen zu haben, das, was syen muss, zu leiden.* I do not assent to this interpretation, which would give too emphatic a sense to the words *μηδὲν παραλείπων*. As I take it, they refer to *ἃ δεῖ*, so that we understand *τῶν δεόντων* after *μηδέν*.

[1] Spillan has it literally: "concerning matters thus transacted." Brougham: "for things so settled." Pabst: *gegen das, was schon also verhandelt worden ist.* It refers undoubtedly to the previous decision of the courts, though *πραχθέντων* does not signify "decided," as Leland, Auger, and Jacobs express it in their translations.

[2] *Πρίν τι τούτων προλαβεῖν*, "before it [*i. e.* before the party accused] had secured any of these advantages," *i. e.* any of those preliminary ob-

—to pick out of a multitude of old dates and decrees what no man knew before, and what no man would have expected to hear to-day, for the purpose of slander—to transpose dates, and assign measures to the wrong causes instead of the right, in order to make a plausible case. That was impossible then. Every statement must have been according to the truth, soon after the facts, while you still remembered the particulars and had them almost at your fingers' ends. Therefore it was that he shunned all investigation at the time, and has come at this late period; thinking, as it appears to me, that you would make it a contest of orators, instead of an inquiry into political conduct; that words would be criticised, and not interests of state.

Then he plays the sophist,[1] and says, you ought to disregard the opinion of us which you came from home with—that, as when you audit a man's account under the impression that he has a surplus, if it casts up right and nothing remains, you allow it,[2] so should you now accept the fair conclusion of the argument. Only see, how rotten in its nature (and justly so) is every wicked contrivance! For by this very cunning simile he has now acknowledged it to be your conviction, that I am my country's advocate and he is Philip's. Had not this been your opinion of each, he would not have tried to persuade you differently. That he has however no reasonable ground for requiring you to change your belief, I can easily show, not by casting accounts—for that mode of reckoning applies not to measures—but by calling the circumstances briefly to mind, taking you that hear me both for auditors and witnesses.

Through my policy, which he arraigns, instead of the Thebans invading this country with Philip, as all expected,

jections which enable the accused to defend himself irrespectively of the merits of the question. Schaefer reads προσλαβεῖν, and renders it: "priusquam horum quidquam subsidio assumpsisset." Pabst follows him. If I adopted that reading, I would translate thus: "before it got any of these points mixed up with it."

[1] So Spillan: and Jacobs: *spielt er den Sophisten.*

[2] The illustration is taken, not from common tradesmen's accounts, as Reiske supposes, nor from the census for classification of citizens, as Schaefer thinks, but rather from the audit of official accounts by the Λογισταὶ at Athens. To them he clearly refers in the expression below, λογισταῖς ἅμα καὶ μάρτυσι χρώμενος. The passage in Æschines cont. Ctesiph. (62) confirms this view.

they joined our ranks and prevented him;—instead of the war being in Attica, it took place seven hundred furlongs from the city on the confines of Bœotia;—instead of corsairs issuing from Eubœa to plunder us, Attica was in peace on the coast-side during the whole war;—instead of Philip being master of the Hellespont by taking Byzantium, the Byzantines were our auxiliaries against him. Does this computation of services, think you, resemble the casting of accounts? Or should we strike these out on a balance,[1] and not look that they be kept in everlasting remembrance? I will not set down, that of the cruelty, remarkable in cases where Philip got people all at once into his power, others have had the

The expressions τιθεὶς ψήφους, ἀνταναιρεῖν, refer to the use of counters by the ancients in their arithmetical processes. Hence comes our word "calculation," from *calculus*, a stone or counter used for such purpose. A literal translation of these expressions would hardly be intelligible in our language, and therefore I have avoided it.

[1] *I. e.* strike them out of the credit side of the account, by means of a set-off on the debit side. Lord Brougham: "must these events be taken out of the opposite side of my account?" The meaning is properly explained by Reiske: "Existimasne, res has præclare a me gestas ex hominum memoriâ tolli debere propter ingentes clades quas passi sumus?" Schaefer, who is followed by Jacobs and Pabst, has given a different interpretation. Ταῦτα, according to him, means both the services of Demosthenes, and the malpractices of Æschines; and ἀνταναιρεῖν ταῦτα is to set them off against one another, to mutually cancel them. Pabst introduces this amplification of ταῦτα into his text, feeling perhaps that the reader would not gather it from the context: *glaubst Du, dass man Das, was ich für, Du gegen das Vaterland gethan hast, gegen einander aufheben müsse.* This interpretation is not only not borne out by the words, but contrary to the scope of the whole passage. Demosthenes is not saying any thing here about the misdeeds of Æschines; and the notion of setting them off against his own services was too palpably absurd to suggest for a moment. He has been enumerating certain good results of his administration. His argument is: "These are positive services which I have rendered you, deserving gratitude and permanent record. You can not treat them as credits, to be canceled by a debit side of the question. Such a mode of reckoning is well enough for an arithmetical computation, but is inapplicable to a case of this kind." Here he stops short, and why? He felt that at this very moment Chæronea and its results, constantly present to his own thoughts, might cross the minds of his hearers; and that he might be met with the objection,—"If you take credit for the victories, you must have the discredit of the defeats: your policy must be judged of as a whole." To this indeed he had an answer, but not exactly in the present line of argument; therefore he turns it off, spurning the bare idea of Æschines' illustration.

trial; while of the generosity, which, casting about for his future purposes, he assumed toward Athens, you have happily enjoyed the fruits. I pass that by.

Yet this I do not hesitate to say; that any one desirous of truly testing an orator, not of calumniating him, would never have made the charges that you advanced just now, inventing similes, mimicking words and gestures: (doubtless it hath determined the fortune of Greece, whether I spoke this word or that, whether I moved my hand one way or the other!) no! he would have examined the facts of the case, what means and resources our country possessed, when I entered on the administration, what, when I applied myself to it, I collected for her, and what was the condition of our adversaries. Then, if I had lessened her resources, he would have shown me to be guilty; if I had greatly increased them, he would not have calumniated me. However, as you have declined this course, I will adopt it. See if I state the case fairly.

For resources—our country possessed the islanders; not all, but the weakest; for neither Chios, nor Rhodes, nor Corcyra was with us: subsidies[1] she had amounting to five-and-forty talents; and they were anticipated: infantry or cavalry, none besides the native. But what was most alarming and wrought most in favor of the enemy—these men had got all our neighbors to be hostile rather than friendly to us; Megarians, Thebans, Eubœans. Such were the circumstances of our state; no man can say any thing to the contrary: look now at those of Philip, whom we had to contend with. In the first place, he ruled his followers with unlimited sway, the most important thing for military operations: in the next place, they had arms always in their hands: besides, he had plenty of money, and did what he pleased, not giving notice by decrees, not deliberating openly, not brought to trial by calumniators, not defending indictments for illegal measures, not responsible to any one, but himself absolute master, leader, and lord of all. I, who was matched against him—for it is right to examine this—what had I under my control? Nothing. Public speech, for instance, the only thing open to me—even to this you invited his hirelings as well as myself; and whenever they prevailed over me, (as often happened

[1] The tribute from the islanders. See vol. I: p. 77, note 1.

for some cause or other,) your resolutions were passed[1] for the enemy's good. Still under these disadvantages I got you for allies Eubœans, Achæans, Corinthians, Thebans, Megarians, Leucadians, Corcyræans; from whom were collected fifteen thousand mercenaries and two thousand horse, besides the national troops.[2] Of money too I procured as large a contribution as possible.

If you talk about just conditions with the Thebans,[3] Æschines, or with the Byzantines or Eubœans, or discuss now the question of equal terms, first I say—you are ignorant that of those galleys formerly which defended Greece, being three hundred in number, our commonwealth furnished two hundred, and never (as it seemed) thought herself injured by having done so, never prosecuted those who advised it or expressed any dissatisfaction;—shame on her if she had!—but was grateful to the gods, that, when a common danger beset the Greeks, she alone furnished double what the rest did for the preservation of all. Besides, it is but a poor favor you do your countrymen by calumniating me. For what is the use of telling us now what we should have done?—Why, being in the city and present, did you not make your proposals then; if indeed they were practicable at a crisis when we had to accept not what we liked but what the circumstances allowed? Remember, there was one ready to bid against us, to welcome eagerly those that we rejected, and give money into the bargain.

But if I am accused for what I have actually done, how would it have been, if, through my hard bargaining, the states had gone off and attached themselves to Philip, and he had become master at the same time of Eubœa, Thebes, and Byzantium? What, think ye, these impious men would have said or done? Said doubtless, that the states were abandoned—that they wished to join us and were driven away—that he had got command of the Hellespont by the Byzantines, and be-

[1] Literally: "You left the assembly, having passed resolutions." See my observations in the Preface, p. 14.

[2] I believe this means the national troops of the allies. See Appendix IX. Schaefer, however, takes πολιτικῶν to be the same as οἰκείων just above.

[3] Æschines, in his speech (73), complains that the terms of the treaty, concluded by Demosthenes with the Thebans, were most disadvantageous to Athens.

come master of the corn-trade of Greece—that a heavy neighbor-war had by means of the Thebans been brought into Attica—that the sea had become unnavigable by the excursion of pirates from Eubœa! All this would they have said sure enough, and a great deal besides. A wicked, wicked thing, O Athenians, is a calumniator always, every way spiteful and fault-finding. But this creature is a reptile by nature, that from the beginning never did any thing honest or liberal; a very ape of a tragedian, village Œnomaus, counterfeit orator![1] What advantage has your eloquence[2] been to your country? Now do you speak to us about the past? As if a physician should visit his patients, and not order or prescribe any thing to cure the disease, but on the death of any one, when the last ceremonies were performing, should follow him to the grave and expound, how, if the poor fellow had done this and that, he never would have died! Idiot! do you speak now?

Even the defeat—if you exult in that which should make you groan, you accursed one!—by nothing that I have done will it appear to have befallen us. Consider it thus, O Athenians. From no embassy, on which I was commissioned by you, did I ever come away defeated by the embassadors of Philip—neither from Thessaly, nor from Ambracia, nor from the kings of Thrace, nor from Byzantium,

[1] Leland renders this passage as follows: "A false accuser, my countrymen, is a monster, a dangerous monster, querulous and industrious in seeking pretenses of complaint. And such is the very nature of this fox in human shape,—a stranger to every thing good or liberal,—this theatrical ape, this strolling player, this blundering haranguer!" Jacobs: *Ein boshaftes Wesen, Ihr Männer Athens, ist der Sycophant, boshaft immer und überall, misgünstig und schmähsüchtig; aber dieser Wicht hier ist eine Bestie von Natur; von Anbeginn hat er nichts Gesundes, nichts Freisinniges gethan, dieser leibhafte Affe der Tragödie, dieser dörfische Oenomaus, dieser Redner von schlechtestem Schrot und Korn.*

As to κίναδος, see page 65, note 2; and as to Œnomaus, see page 72, note 1.

[2] Δεινότης is used not only to signify craft and cleverness in general, but specially to describe the quality of a powerful and effective speaker. So it occurs several times in Dionysius. It is applied, however, both in a good and in a bad sense, according to circumstances, as many other words are. Thus we may call a man an orator, either simply, meaning a public speaker, or by way of praise, meaning a good speaker, or invidiously, meaning to say that he is an artful speaker, able to make the worse appear the better cause. Compare Æschines cont. Ctes. 73, 83; Demosth. De Cor. 318.

nor from any other place, nor on the last recent occasion from Thebes; but where his embassadors were vanquished in argument, he came with arms and carried the day. And for this you call me to account; and are not ashamed to jeer the same person for cowardice, whom you require single-handed to overcome the might of Philip—and that too by words! For what else had I at my command? Certainly not the spirit[1] of each individual, nor the fortune of the army, nor the conduct of the war, for which you would make me accountable; such a blunderer are you!

Yet understand me. Of what a statesman may be responsible for I allow the utmost scrutiny; I deprecate it not. What are his functions? To observe things in the beginning, to foresee and foretell them to others—this I have done: again; wherever he finds delays, backwardness, ignorance, jealousies, vices inherent and unavoidable in all communities, to contract them into the narrowest compass, and on the other hand, to promote unanimity and friendship and zeal in the discharge of duty. All this too I have performed; and no one can discover the least neglect on my part. Ask any man, by what means Philip achieved most of his successes, and you will be told, by his army, and by his bribing and corrupting men in power. Well; your forces were not under my command or control; so that I can not be questioned for any thing done in that department. But by refusing the price of corruption I have overcome Philip: for as the offerer of a bribe, if it be accepted, has vanquished the taker, so the person who refuses it and is not corrupted has vanquished the person offering. Therefore is the commonwealth undefeated as far as I am concerned.

These, and such as these, (besides many others,) are the grounds furnished by myself to justify the defendent's motion in my behalf. Those which you my fellow-citizens furnished, I will proceed to mention. Immediately after the battle the people, knowing and having witnessed every thing which I did, in the very midst of their alarm and terror, when it would not have been surprising if the great body of them had even treated me harshly, passed my resolutions for the safety of the country; all their measures of defense, the disposition of the

[1] Jacobs: *Muth.* Pabst: *Gesinnung.* Augur: "valeur." Other translators take ψυχῆς to signify "life."

garrisons, the trenches, the levies for our fortifications, were carried on under my decrees: and further, upon the election of a commissioner of grain, they chose me in preference to all. Afterward, when those who were bent to do me a mischief conspired, and brought indictments, audits, impeachments and the rest of it against me, not at first in their own persons, but in such names as they imagined would most effectually screen themselves, (for you surely know and remember, that every day of that first period I was arraigned, and neither the desperation of Sosicles, nor the malignity of Philocrates, nor the madness of Diondas and Melantus, nor any thing else was left untried by them against me;) on all those occasions, chiefly through the Gods, secondly through you and the other Athenians, I was preserved. And with justice! Yes, that is the truth, and to the honor of the juries who so conscientiously decided. Well then: on the impeachments, when you acquitted me and gave not the prosecutors their share of the votes, you pronounced that my policy was the best: by my acquittal on the indictments my counsels and motion were shown to be legal; by your passing of my accounts you acknowledged my whole conduct to have been honest and incorruptible. Under these circumstances, what name could Ctesiphon with decency or justice give to my acts? Not that which he saw the people give—which he saw the jurors give—which he saw truth establish to the world?

Ay, says he; that was a fine thing of Cephalus, never to have been indicted. Yes, and a lucky one too. But why should a man, who has often been charged, but never convicted of crime, be a whit the more liable to reproach? However, men of Athens, against my opponent I have a right to use the boast of Cephalus; for he never preferred or prosecuted any indictment against me; therefore I am a citizen as good as Cephalus by his admission.

From many things one may see his unfeelingness and malignity, but especially from his discourse about fortune. For my part, I regard any one, who reproaches his fellow-man with fortune, as devoid of sense. He that is best satisfied with his condition, he that deems his fortune excellent, can not be sure that it will remain so until the evening: how then can it be right to bring it forward, or upbraid another man with it? As Æschines, however, has on this subject (besides many others) expressed himself with insolence, look, men of Athens, and observe how much more truth and humanity there shall be in my discourse upon fortune[1] than in his.

I hold the fortune of our commonwealth to be good, and so I find the oracles of Dodonæan Jupiter and Pythian Apollo declaring to us. The fortune of all mankind, which now prevails, I consider cruel and dreadful: for what Greek, what barbarian, has not in these times experienced a multitude of evils? That Athens chose the noblest policy, that she fares better than those very Greeks who thought, if they abandoned us, they should abide in prosperity, I reckon as part of her good fortune: if she suffered reverses, if all happened not to us as we desired, I conceive she has had that share of the general fortune which fell to our lot. As to my fortune (personally speaking) or that of any individual among us, it should, as I conceive, be judged of in connection with personal matters. Such is my opinion upon the subject of fortune, a right and just one, as it appears to me, and I think you will agree with it. Æschines says that my individual fortune is

[1] "Les anciens donnoient beaucoup à la fatalité: c'étoit une force aveugle qui entraînoit les hommes dans le malheur, et même dans le crime, sans qu'il fût possible de résister à sa violence. Cette fatalité est le mobile presque unique de leurs tragédies, et c'est peut-être, pour le dire en passant, ce qui les a rendus un peu trop uniformes. Non seulement ils croyoient que le destin s'attachoit à poursuivre un homme, mais encore que la mauvaise fortune, que le sort malheureux qui le suivoit, se communiquoit à ceux qui l'approchoient. Oreste, dans Racine, dit à Pylade:—

Je ne sais de tous temps quelle injuste puissance
Laisse le crime en paix et poursuit l'innocence.
De quelque part sur moi que je tourne les yeux,
Je ne vois que malheurs qui condamnent les Dieux.
Mais toi, par quelle erreur veux-tu toujours sur toi
Détourner un courroux qui ne cherche que moi?

"En conséquence de ces principes Eschine, méchamment, a représenté Démosthene, dans un endroit de son discours, comme un misérable poursuivi par la fortune, et qui communiquoit son malheur à tous ceux qui lui confioient leurs affaires.

"Démosthene lui répond ici en faisant voir, 1°. que quand même il auroit été poursuivi par la fortune, il seroit cruel de lui reprocher son malheur: 2°. qu'il est ridicule de prétendre que la destinée d'un particulier influe sur la destinée de la république: 3°. qu'il n'a pas été si malheureux pendant sa vie, que sa fortune n'a pas été si misérable; et de là il prend occasion de comparer sa fortune à celle d'Eschine."—*Auger.*

paramount to that of the commonwealth, the small and mean to the good and great. How can this possibly be?

However, if you are determined, Æschines, to scrutinize my fortune, compare it with your own, and, if you find my fortune better than yours, cease to revile it. Look then from the very beginning. And I pray and entreat that I may not be condemned for bad taste.[1] I don't think any person wise who insults poverty, or who prides himself on having been bred in affluence: but by the slander and malice of this cruel man I am forced into such a discussion; which I will conduct with all the moderation which circumstances allow.

I had the advantage, Æschines, in my boyhood of going to proper schools, and having such allowance as a boy should have who is to do nothing mean from indigence. Arrived at man's estate, I lived suitably to my breeding; was choir-master, ship-commander, rate-payer; backward in no acts of liberality public or private, but making myself useful to the commonwealth and to my friends. When I entered upon state affairs, I chose such a line of politics, that both by my country and many people of Greece I have been crowned many times, and not even you my enemies venture to say that the line I chose was not honorable. Such then has been the fortune of my life: I could enlarge upon it, but I forbear, lest what I pride myself in should give offense.

But you, the man of dignity, who spit upon others, look what sort of fortune is yours compared with mine. As a boy you were reared in abject poverty, waiting with your father on the school, grinding the ink, sponging the benches, sweeping the room, doing the duty of a menial rather than a freeman's son. After you were grown up, you attended your mother's initiations,[2] reading her books and helping in all the

[1] Most of the commentators take ψυχρότητα in the sense of "insipidity or absurdity." Jacobs has: *abgeschmackten Frostes.* Pabst: *Abgeschmacktheit.* Schaefer compares the ψυχρὰ λέγειν of Xenophon, Conviv. vi. 7. Francis translates it, "any thing offensive," which is not the meaning of the word, though undoubtedly it was the object of Demosthenes to deprecate giving offense. He knew that a large number, perhaps the majority, of the jurors were taken from the humbler class of citizens, and they might be offended if he boasted too much of his wealth and origin. Therefore he is anxious to show that he was forced into this comparison by Æschines himself.

[2] The rites, which Demosthenes represents to have been performed by the mother of Æschines, were brought into Greece from Phrygia and

ceremonies: at night wrapping the noviciates in fawn-skin, swilling, purifying, and scouring them with clay and bran, raising them after the lustration, and bidding them say, "Bad

the east, and from Thrace. They appear not to have been of the most reputable kind, at all events the officiating parties were a low class of people. Plato, in the second book of his Republic, tells us, that at this period there were a multitude of jugglers and adventurers going about Greece, who acquired influence over ignorant men by pretending to the exercise of supernatural power. They carried books with them, the authorship of which they ascribed to Musæus and Orpheus, and which contained directions as to various rites of sacrifice and purification, and other mystic ceremonies. These, they said, had the effect of expiating crime and averting evil. Bacchus and Ceres were the divinities to whose worship these mysteries were devoted, especially the former, as appears abundantly from the passage before us.

Νεβρίζων is putting on the fawn-skin worn by the Bacchanalians. Compare the Bacchæ of Euripides, 137, 176, and Statius Theb. II. 664:

> Nebridas et fragiles thyrsos portare putâstis
> Imbellem ad sonitum.

Κρατηρίζων was a species of Bacchic baptism, either by immersion, or pouring the bowl over the head.

Ἀπομάττων πηλῷ καὶ πιτύροις refers, according to Harpocration, to the Orphic myth of *Διόνυσος Ζαγρεὺς*, the infernal Bacchus, son of Proserpine, whom the Titans tore to pieces, having plastered their own faces with clay to escape detection. Jupiter destroyed the Titans with his thunder, and from the smoke of their burning bodies man was generated. See Orph. Hymn. 29, Procli Hymn. ad Athen. and Olympiodorus on the Phædo. Taylor, whom Leland and Francis follow, interprets *ἀπομάττων* in the sense of modeling images or idols for the mysteries. Reiske thinks the clay and bran was nothing more than a kind of soap, used for lustration. Jacobs says the bran reminds him of the flour (*παιπάλη*) with which Strepsiades is powdered in the Clouds of Aristophanes (v. 265), where it is evident that the poet is ridiculing some initiatory or mystic ceremony.

Ἔφυγον κακὸν εὗρον ἄμεινον, is a form of words pronounced by the initiated, a sort of thanksgiving for the blessings of civilized life introduced by Ceres and Bacchus, mystically referring to religious blessings. To this there is a manifest allusion in the chorus of the Bacchæ, v. 900.

> *εὐδαίμων μὲν ὃς ἐκ θαλάσσας*
> *ἔφυγε κῦμα, λιμένα δ' ἔκιχεν.*

Taylor compares Cicero de Legibus, II. 24,—"Nam mihi cum multa eximia divinaque videntur Athenæ tuæ peperisse atque in vitam hominum attulisse, tum nihil melius iis mysteriis, quibus ex agresti immanique vitâ exculti ad humanitatem et mitigati sumus, initiaque ut appellantur, ita re verâ principia vitæ cognovimus, neque solum cum lætitiâ vivendi rationem accepimus, sed etiam cum spe meliori moriendi."

Ὀλολύξαι is the religious or orgiastic howl. See Bacchæ, 24, 688.

I have scaped, and better I have found;" priding yourself that no one ever howled so lustily—and I believe him! for don't suppose that he who speaks so loud is not a splendid howler! In the daytime you led your noble orgiasts, crowned with fennel and poplar, through the highways, squeezing the big-cheeked serpents, and lifting them over your head, and shouting Evœ Sabœ, and capering to the words Hyes Attes, Attes Hyes, saluted by the beldames as Leader, Conductor, Chest-bearer, Fan-bearer, and the like, getting as your reward tarts and biscuits and rolls; for which any man might well bless himself and his fortune![1]

When you were enrolled among your fellow-townsmen—by

Claudian, Raptus Pros. lib. i. *Ululatibus Ide Bacchatur*, and lib. ii. *ululantia Dindyma Gallis.*

Poplar, supposed to be the growth of the infernal region, was sacred (as Harpocration says) to the son of Proserpine. Fennel was supposed to have a peculiar virtue. A species of fennel is mentioned by Virgil (Eclog. X. 25) as carried by Sylvanus:

Florentes ferulas et grandia lilia quassans.

As to the serpents, see Bacchæ, v. 697. Ceres is drawn by serpents in Claudian Rapt. Pros. lib. i. Compare Plutarch, Vit. Alex. 2.

The exclamations *εὐοῖ σαβοῖ* are Thracian, perhaps of eastern origin. Bacchus is called Evius and Sabazius. See Orph. Hymn 47, Plut. Symp. iv. 5. *Ὕης ἄττης* are Phrygian. *Θίασος* is the common term for a troop of Bacchanals (Bacchæ, 56). The god himself is called *ἔξαρχος* (Bacchæ, 141). *Λίκνος* is the "mystica vannus Iacchi" (Virgil Georg. I. 166). He is called *Λικνίτης Διόνυσος* in Orph. Hymn 45. See Callimach. Hymn. ad Jovem, 48. The *κίστα* contained the arcane symbols of the mysteries. Such was the *κάλαθος* of Ceres (Callimach. Hymn. ad Cererem, 1, Taylor's Eleusinian and Bacchic Mysteries, 119).

[1] I consider it better to give this turn than to write, "for which who would not," &c., which suits not the English idiom so well. But you may keep the interrogative, if you turn "for which" into "for such things," as Pabst and Jacobs do.

Here I can not forbear noticing the fulsome eulogy pronounced by the *Times* reviewer upon Mitchell's version of this passage. I concede that it is clever, but it certainly deserves not the epithets of "terse and pointed," which have been applied to it. He himself would disdain such an encomium, for he insists that it is necessary to expand and dilute the expressions of the original, and he translates upon that system. Thus, *ὁ διαπτύων* is, "who considers worthy only of the spittle of his mouth;" *ἐτράφης* must be enlarged into "born and bred;" *γραδίων*, "all the crones and beldames of the quarter," and so on. I suppose these are questions of taste. For my own part, I think there was much wisdom in the saying of the clergyman, who excused himself to his congregation for preaching longer than usual, on the plea that he had not had time to make his sermon shorter.

what means I stop not to inquire—when you were enrolled however, you immediately selected the most honorable of employments, that of clerk and assistant to our petty magistrates. From this you were removed after a while, having done yourself all that you charge others with; and then, sure enough, you disgraced not your antecedents by your subsequent life, but hiring yourself to those ranting players, as they were called, Simylus and Socrates, you acted third parts, collecting figs and grapes and olives like a fruiterer from other men's farms, and getting more from them than from the playing, in which the lives of your whole company were at stake; for there was an implacable and incessant war between them and the audience, from whom you received so many wounds, that no wonder you taunt as cowards people inexperienced in such encounters.[1]

But passing over what may be imputed to poverty, I will come to the direct charges against your character. You espoused such a line of politics, (when at last you thought of taking to them,) that, if your country prospered, you lived the life of a hare, fearing and trembling and ever expecting to be scourged for the crimes of which your conscience accused you; though all have seen how bold you were during the misfortunes of the rest. A man who took courage at the death of a thousand citizens—what does he deserve at the hands of the living? A great deal more that I could say about him I shall omit: for it is not all I can tell of his turpitude and infamy which I ought to let slip from my tongue, but only what is not disgraceful to myself to mention.

[1] The commentators and translators have all misunderstood this passage, imagining that Æschines and his troop are charged with strolling about the country and robbing orchards. Nothing could be more foreign to the meaning. Taking Bekker's text, and omitting the first *τραύματα*, the explanation is simply as follows:—

Æschines and his fellow-players acted so badly, that they were pelted by the audience with figs, grapes, and olives,—as we should say, with oranges. The players picked up these missiles, and were glad to pocket the affront. Such quantities were showered upon the stage, that they got enough to stock a fruiterer's shop; so they were supplied, *ὥσπερ ὀπωρώνης ἐκ τῶν ἀλλοτρίων χωρίων*, like a dealer in fruit, who purchases his stock from various farmers and gardeners. From this source Æschines derived more profit, *πλείω λαμβάνων ἀπὸ τούτων*, than from the dramatic contests, *τῶν ἀγώνων*, for which the company were ill paid, and in which they ran the risk of their lives every day from the indignation of the audience.

Contrast now the circumstances of your life and mine, gently and with temper, Æschines; and then ask these people whose fortune they would each of them prefer. You taught reading, I went to school: you performed initiations, I received them: you danced in the chorus, I furnished it: you were assembly-clerk, I was a speaker: you acted third parts, I heard you: you broke down, and I hissed: you have worked as a statesman for the enemy, I for my country.[1] I pass by the rest; but this very day I am on my probation for a crown, and am acknowledged to be innocent of all offense; while you are already judged to be a pettifogger, and the question is, whether you shall continue that trade, or at once be silenced by not getting a fifth part of the votes. A happy fortune, do you see, you have enjoyed, that you should denounce mine as miserable!

Come now, let me read the evidence to the jury of public services which I have performed. And by way of comparison do you recite me the verses which you murdered:

From Hades and the dusky realms I come.

And

Ill news, believe me, I am loth to bear.

Ill betide thee, say I, and may the Gods, or at least the Athenians, confound thee for a vile citizen and a vile third-rate actor![2]

[1] The best version of this series of antitheses is, I think, that of Jacobs:

Du hieltest Schule; ich besuchte die Schulen; Du besorgtest die Weihungen; ich empfing sie; Du tanztest im Chor; ich stattete Chöre aus; Du dientest als Schreiber; ich sprach vor dem Volke; Du spieltest die dritten Rollen; ich sah zu; Du fielst durch, und ich zischte; Du wirktest für die Feinde; ich für das Vaterland.

Milton has imitated this passage in the Apology for Smectymnuus (vol. i. p. 221, Symmons' Edition). Speaking of the young divines and students at college, whom he had seen so often upon the stage prostituting the shame of that ministry, which they either had or were nigh having, to the eyes of courtiers and court ladies, he proceeds thus:—

"There while they acted and overacted, among other young scholars, I was a spectator: they thought themselves gallant men, and I thought them fools; they made sport, and I laughed; they mispronounced, and I misliked; and, to make up the Atticism, they were out, and I hissed."

[2] The first quotation is from the beginning of the Hecuba. The words κακὸν κακῶς are supposed by Wolf to be the beginning of another quotation which the orator converts abruptly into an imprecation upon Æschines. The position of the words however is against this inter-

Read the evidence.

[*Evidence.*]

Such has been my character in political matters. In private, if you do not all know that I have been liberal and humane and charitable to the distressed, I am silent, I will say not a word, I will offer no evidence on the subject, either of persons whom I ransomed from the enemy, or of persons whose daughters I helped to portion, or any thing of the kind. For this is my maxim. I hold that the party receiving an obligation should ever remember it, the party conferring should forget it immediately, if the one is to act with honesty, the other without meanness. To remind and speak of your own bounties is next door to reproaching.[1] I will not act so; nothing shall induce me. Whatever my reputation is in these respects, I am content with it.

I will have done then with private topics, but say another word or two upon public. If you can mention, Æschines, a single man under the sun, whether Greek or barbarian, who has not suffered by Philip's power formerly and Alexander's now, well and good; I concede to you, that my fortune, or misfortune (if you please), has been the cause of every thing. But if many that never saw me or heard my voice have been grievously afflicted, not individuals only but whole cities and nations; how much juster and fairer is it to consider, that to the common fortune apparently of all men, to a tide of events overwhelming and lamentable,[2] these disasters are to

pretation: for *μάλιστα μὲν* must be connected with what follows, and *σὲ* standing alone could not have the required emphasis. Schaefer with greater probability supposes *κακὸν κακῶς σε* to be the commencement of a verse. I have followed Bekker, who throws them into the next clause. Demosthenes, after repeating two Iambic lines, and ridiculing his opponent's declamatory style, suddenly, as if he was weary of such stuff, breaks into the curse, the introductory words being suggested by the *κακαγγελεῖν*.

[1] Compare Terence, Andria, Act I. Sc. i. 16:—

Sed mî hoc molestum est; nam isthæc commemoratio
Quasi exprobratio est immemoris beneficî.

[2] Brougham: "some force of circumstances untoward and difficult to resist." Leland: "torrent of unhappy events that bore down upon us with irresistible violence." Francis: "the rapid impetuosity of particular conjunctures, cruel and unaccountable,"—a lame version indeed! Auger: "concours fatal de circonstances malheureuses." Jacobs: *einer harten und widrigen Gewalt der Ereignisse.* Pabst: *einen gewaltsamen Umschwung der Ereignisse, wie er nicht hätte stattfinden sollen.*

be attributed. You, disregarding all this, accuse me whose ministry has been among my countrymen,[1] knowing all the while, that a part (if not the whole) of your calumny falls upon the people, and yourself in particular. For if I assumed the sole and absolute direction of our counsels, it was open to you the other speakers to accuse me: but if you were constantly present in all the assemblies, if the state invited public discussion of what was expedient, and if these measures were then believed by all to be the best, and especially by you; (for certainly from no good-will did you leave me in possession of hopes and admiration and honors, all of which attended on my policy, but doubtless because you were compelled by the truth and had nothing better to advise;) is it not iniquitous and monstrous to complain now of measures, than which you could suggest none better at the time?

Among all other people I find these principles in a manner defined and settled—Does a man willfully offend? He is the object of wrath and punishment. Hath a man erred unintentionally? There is pardon instead of punishment for him. Has a man devoted himself to what seemed for the general good, and without any fault or misconduct been in common with all disappointed of success? Such a one deserves not obloquy or reproach, but sympathy. These principles will not be found in our statutes only: Nature herself has defined them by her unwritten laws and the feelings of humanity. Æschines however has so far surpassed all men in brutality and malignity, that even things which he cited himself as misfortunes he imputes to me as crimes.

And besides—as if he himself had spoken every thing with candor and good-will—he told you to watch me, and mind

[1] The meaning is—"you charge me with this universal ruin, though I was merely an Athenian citizen who took my share, together with my fellow-citizens, in the politics of my own country, but could have nothing to do with the affairs of other people, on whom similar calamities fell." So Reiske interprets παρὰ τουτοισί—"designat pro more judices civesque Athenienses." Pabst however takes these words to refer to the φορὰν πραγμάτων, and thus translates: *der ich unter dem Einflusse dieses Umschwunges der Ereignisse die Staatsverwaltung führte.* Lord Brougham, following Francis, translates to the same effect: "called upon, as I was, to carry on the government in such a crisis." The words do not favor such an interpretation. Ἅπασι refers to τουτοισὶ, and, if it stood alone, could be hardly understood to signify "all the Athenians."

that I did not cajole and deceive you, calling me a great orator,[1] a juggler, a sophist, and the like: as though, if a man says of another what applies to himself, it must be true, and the hearers are not to inquire who the person is that makes the charge. Certain am I, that you are all acquainted with my opponent's character, and believe these charges to be more applicable to him than to me. And of this I am sure, that my oratory—let it be so: though indeed I find, that the speaker's power depends for the most part on the hearers; for according to your reception and favor it is, that the wisdom of a speaker is esteemed—if I however possess any ability of this sort, you will find it has been exhibited always in public business on your behalf, never against you or on personal matters; whereas that of Æschines has been displayed not only in speaking for the enemy, but against all persons who ever offended or quarreled with him. It is not for justice or the good of the commonwealth that he employs it. A citizen of worth and honor should not call upon judges impanneled in the public service to gratify his anger or hatred or any thing of that kind; nor should he come before you upon such grounds. The best thing is not to have these feelings; but, if it can not be helped, they should be mitigated and restrained.

On what occasions ought an orator and statesman to be vehement? Where any of the commonwealth's main interests are in jeopardy, and he is opposed to the adversaries of the people.[2] Those are the occasions for a generous and brave citizen. But for a person, who never sought to punish me for any offense either public or private, on the state's behalf or on his own, to have got up an accusation because I am crowned and honored, and to have expended such a multitude of words—this is a proof of personal enmity and spite and meanness, not of any thing good. And then his leaving the controversy with me, and attacking the defendant, comprises every thing that is base.[3]

I should conclude, Æschines, that you undertook this

[1] See p. 90, note 2.

[2] Or, "he has to do with the adversaries of the people," omitting τι with Bekker. But with τι the sense is as Jacobs, Reiske, and others give it: *wo es der Sache des Volkes gegen die Feinde gilt.*

[3] "This once more pressed, because, after the brilliant declamation that precedes, it was sure to be doubly effective."—*Lord Brougham.*

cause to exhibit your eloquence and strength of lungs, not to obtain satisfaction for any wrong. But it is not the language of an orator, Æschines, that has any value, nor yet the tone of his voice, but his adopting the same views with the people, and his hating and loving the same persons that his country does. He that is thus minded will say every thing with loyal intention: he that courts persons from whom the commonwealth apprehends danger to herself, rides not on the same anchorage with the people, and therefore has not the same expectation of safety. But—do you see?—I have: for my objects are the same with those of my countrymen; I have no interest separate or distinct. Is that so with you? How can it be—when immediately after the battle you went as embassador to Philip, who was at that period the author of your country's calamities, notwithstanding that you had before persisted in refusing that office,[1] as all men know?

And who is it that deceives the state? Surely the man who speaks not what he thinks. On whom does the crier pronounce a curse?[2] Surely on such a man. What greater crime can an orator be charged with, than that his opinions and his language are not the same? Such is found to be your character. And yet you open your mouth, and dare to look these men in the faces! Do you think they don't know you?—or are sunk all in such slumber and oblivion, as not to remember the speeches which you delivered in the assembly, cursing and swearing that you had nothing to do with Philip, and that I brought that charge against you out of personal enmity without foundation? No sooner came the news of the battle, than you forgot all that; you acknowledged and avowed that between Philip and yourself there subsisted a relation of hospitality and friendship—new names these for

[1] This is to be understood only of the last six years before Chæronea.

[2] This curse was pronounced at every assembly of the people and every meeting of the council, before the business began. It was included in a form of prayer prescribed by law, in which the gods were implored to bless and prosper the consultations of the citizens, and to destroy and extirpate all persons who were ill-affected to the commonwealth, or plotted or conspired against the people, or were bribed to mislead or deceive them. There are many allusions to this curse in the Attic orators. In the speech on the Embassy (p. 363), Demosthenes causes it to be read to the jury. At the meeting of ladies in the Thesmophoriazusæ of Aristophanes, there is an amusing mock prayer read by the crier, vv. 295—351. See Schömann De Comitiis, 92.

your contract of hire. For upon what plea of equality or justice could Æschines, son of Glaucothea the timbrel-player,[1] be the friend or acquaintance of Philip? I can not see. No! You were hired to ruin the interests of your countrymen: and yet, though you have been caught yourself in open treason, and informed against yourself after the fact, you revile and reproach me for things which you will find any man is chargeable with sooner than I.[2]

Many great and glorious enterprises has the commonwealth, Æschines, undertaken and succeeded in through me; and she did not forget them. Here is the proof—On the election of a person to speak the funeral oration immediately after the event, you were proposed, but the people would not have you, notwithstanding your fine voice, nor Demades, though he had just made the peace, nor Hegemon, nor any other of your party—but me. And when you and Pythocles came forward in a brutal and shameful manner, (O merciful heaven!) and urged the same accusations against me which you now do, and abused me, they elected me all the more. The reason—you are not ignorant of it—yet I will tell you. The Atheni-

[1] The drum or timbrel was an instrument peculiarly used in the orgies of Bacchus and Cybele, derived from Phrygia. Compare Bacchæ, 58:—

> *αἴρεσθε τἀπιχώρι' ἐν πόλει Φρυγῶν.*
> *τύμπανα; 'Ρέας τε μητρὸς ἐμά θ' εὑρήματα·*

and Virgil, Æn. IX. 619:—

> Tympana vos buxusque vocat Berecynthia matris
> Idææ.

Compare also Virgil, Georg. IV. 64; Apulei. de Gen. 49, "Ægyptia numina gaudent plangoribus, Græca choreis, barbara strepitu cymbalistarum et tympanistarum et ceraularum."

[2] "Here is the same leading topic once more introduced; but introduced after new topics and fresh illustrations. The repetitions, the enforcement again and again of the same points, are a distinguishing feature of Demosthenes, and formed also one of the characteristics of Mr. Fox's great eloquence. The ancient however was incomparably more felicitous in this than the modern; for in the latter it often arose from carelessness, from ill-arranged discourse, from want of giving due attention, and from having once or twice attempted the topic and forgotten it, or perhaps from having failed to produce the desired effect. Now in Demosthenes this is never the case: the early allusions to the subject of the repetition are always perfect in themselves, and would sufficiently have enforced the topic, had they stood alone. But new matter afterward handled gave the topic new force and fresh illustration, by presenting the point in a new light."—*Lord Brougham.*

ans knew as well the loyalty and zeal with which I conducted their affairs, as the dishonesty of you and your party; for what you denied upon oath in our prosperity, you confessed in the misfortunes of the republic. They considered therefore, that men who got security for their politics by the public disasters had been their enemies long before, and were then avowedly such. They thought it right also, that the person who was to speak in honor of the fallen and celebrate their valor, should not have sat under the same roof or at the same table[1] with their antagonists; that he should not revel there and sing a pæan over the calamities of Greece in company with their murderers, and then come here and receive distinction; that he should not with his voice act the mourner of their fate, but that he should lament over them with his heart. This they perceived in themselves and in me, but not in any of you: therefore they elected me, and not you. Nor, while the people felt thus, did the fathers and brothers of the deceased, who were chosen by the people to perform their obsequies, feel differently. For having to order the funeral banquet (according to custom)[2] at the house of the nearest relative to the deceased, they ordered it at mine. And with reason: because, though each to his own was nearer of kin than I was, none was so near to them all collectively. He that had the deepest interest in their safety and success, had upon their mournful disaster the largest share of sorrow for them all.[3]

[1] Literally: "joined in the same libations." Brougham: "drunk out of the same cup." Pabst has happily expressed the two words: *Haus- und Tisch-Genosse*, "house and board-fellows." We might say, "shared house and board with." I have adopted the turn of Jacobs.

[2] Literally: "as other funeral banquets [*i. e.* as funeral banquets in general] are wont to be held."

[3] This passage, which has not been particularly noticed by any of the critics, appears to me one of the most touching in the whole oration. The sentiment is like that which Œdipus expresses in the beautiful lines of Sophocles (Œd. Rex, 58), which very possibly were in the mind of the orator:—

ὦ παῖδες οἰκτροὶ, γνωτὰ κοὐκ ἄγνωτά μοι
προσήλθεθ' ἱμείροντες· εὖ γὰρ οἶδ' ὅτι
νοσεῖτε πάντες, καὶ νοσοῦντες, ὡς ἐγὼ
οὐκ ἔστιν ὑμῶν ὅστις ἐξ ἴσου νοσεῖ.
τὸ μὲν γὰρ ὑμῶν ἄλγος εἰς ἕν' ἔρχεται
μόνον καθ' αὑτὸν, κοὐδέν' ἄλλον· ἡ δ' ἐμὴ
ψυχὴ πόλιν τε κἀμὲ καὶ σ' ὁμοῦ στένει.

Read him this epitaph, which the state chose to inscribe on their monument, that you may see even by this, Æschines, what a heartless and malignant wretch you are. Read.

THE EPITAPH.[1]

These are the patriot brave, who side by side
Stood to their arms, and dash'd the foeman's pride:
Firm in their valor, prodigal of life,
Hades they chose the arbiter of strife;
That Greeks might ne'er to haughty victors bow,
Nor thraldom's yoke, nor dire oppression know;
They fought, they bled, and on their country's breast
(Such was the doom of heaven) these warriors rest.
Gods never lack success, nor strive in vain,
But man must suffer what the fates ordain.

Do you hear, Æschines, in this very inscription, that "Gods never lack success, nor strive in vain?" Not to the statesman does it ascribe the power of giving victory in battle, but to the Gods. Wherefore then, execrable man, do you reproach me with these things? Wherefore utter such language? I pray that it may fall upon the heads of you and yours.

Many other accusations and falsehoods he urged against

[1] The reader will doubtless be pleased to see the lines of Campbell, which appeared in Lord Brougham's translation, and therefore I take the liberty of subjoining them:—

These are the brave, unknowing how to yield,
Who, terrible in valor, kept the field
Against the foe, and higher than life's breath
Prizing their honor, met the doom of death,
Our common doom, that Greece unyoked might stand,
Nor shuddering crouch beneath a tyrant's hand.
Such was the will of Jove; and now they rest
Peaceful enfolded in their country's breast.
Th' immortal gods alone are ever great,
But erring mortals must submit to fate.

The following also is submitted for the judgment of the reader:—

These for their country stood in war-array,
And check'd the fierce invader on his way;
Into the battle rush'd at glory's call,
With firm resolve to conquer or to fall;
That Greeks should ne'er to tyrants bend the knee,
But live, as they were born, from thraldom free.
Now in the bosom of their fatherland
These warriors rest; for such was Jove's command.
The Gods in all succeed and have their will,
But mortals must their destiny fulfill.

me, O Athenians, but one thing surprised me more than all, that, when he mentioned the late misfortunes of the country, he felt not as became a well-disposed and upright citizen, he shed no tear, experienced no such emotion: with a loud voice exulting, and straining his throat, he imagined apparently that he was accusing me, while he was giving proof against himself, that our distresses touched him not in the same manner as the rest. A person who pretends, as he did, to care for the laws and constitution, ought at least to have this about him, that he grieves and rejoices for the same cause as the people, and not by his politics to be enlisted in the ranks of the enemy, as Æschines has plainly done, saying[1] that I am the cause of all, and that the commonwealth has fallen into troubles through me, when it was not owing to my views or principles that you began to assist the Greeks; for, if you conceded[2] this to me, that my influence caused you to resist the subjugation of Greece, it would be a higher honor than any that you have bestowed upon others. I myself would not make such an assertion—it would be doing you injustice—nor would you allow it, I am sure; and Æschines, if he acted honestly, would never, out of enmity to me, have disparaged and defamed the greatest of your glories.

But why do I censure him for this, when with calumny far more shocking has he assailed me? He that charges me with Philippizing—O heaven and earth!—what would he not say? By Hercules and the Gods! if one had honestly to inquire, discarding all expression of spite and falsehood, who the persons really are, on whom the blame of what has happened may by common consent fairly and justly be thrown, it would be found, they are persons in the various states like Æschines, not like me—persons who, while Philip's power was feeble and exceedingly small, and we were constantly warning and exhorting and giving salutary counsel, sacrificed the general interests for the sake of selfish lucre, deceiving and corrupting their respective countrymen,[3] until they made them slaves—Daochus, Cineas, Thrasylaus, the Thessalians; Cercidas, Hieronymus, Eucampidas, the Arcadians; Myrtis, Teledamus, Mnaseas, the Argives; Euxitheus, Cleotimus,

[1] Confer Æschines contr. Ctes. 61.
[2] Perhaps "attributed;" as Jacobs and Pabst render it.
[3] Schaefer explains τοὺς ὑπάρχοντας πολίτας, "cives suæ factionis."

Aristæchmus, the Eleans; Neon and Thrasylochus, sons of the accursed Philiades, the Messenians; Aristratus, Epichares, the Sicyonians; Dinarchus, Demaratus, the Corinthians; Ptœodorus, Helixus, Perilaus, the Megarians; Timolaus, Theogiton, Anemœtas, the Thebans; Hipparchus, Clitarchus, Sosistratus, the Eubœans. The day will not last me to recount the names of the traitors.[1] All these, O Athenians, are men of the same politics in their own countries as this party among you,—profligates, and parasites, and miscreants, who have each of them crippled[2] their fatherlands; toasted away[3] their liberty, first to Philip and last to Alexander; who measure happiness by their belly and all that is base, while freedom and independence, which the Greeks of olden time regarded as the test and standard of well-being, they have annihilated.

Of this base and infamous conspiracy and profligacy—or rather, O Athenians, if I am to speak in earnest, of this betrayal of Grecian liberty—Athens is by all mankind acquitted, owing to my counsels; and I am acquitted by you. Then do you ask me, Æschines, for what merit I claim to be honored? I will tell you. Because, while all the statesmen in Greece, beginning with yourself, have been corrupted formerly by Philip and now by Alexander, me neither opportunity, nor fair speeches, nor large promises, nor hope, nor fear, nor any thing else could tempt or induce to betray aught that I considered just and beneficial to my country. Whatever I have advised my fellow-citizens, I have never advised like you men, leaning as in a balance to the side of profit: all my proceedings have been those of a soul upright, honest,

[1] See the opinion of Polybius in Appendix VI.

Cicero appears to have imitated this passage in the oration against Verres, Act. II. lib. 4,—"Nulla domus in Siciliâ locuples fuit, ubi iste non textrinum instituerit. Mulier est Segestana, perdives et nobilis, Lamia nomine; per triennium isti, plena domo telarum, stragulam vestem confecit: nihil nisi conchylio tinctum. Attalus, homo pecuniosus, Neti; Lyso Lilybæi; Critolaus Ennæ; Syracusis Æschrio, Cleomenes, Theomnastus; Elori Archonides, Megistus. Vox me citius defecerit quam nomina."

[2] Literally: "mutilated."

[3] I have given for *προπεπωκότες* the version of Lord Brougham, who justly censures the paraphrases of the other translators. Jacobs renders it *darbot*, but says in a note: *wörtlich: zutrank.* Pabst: *wie ein Geschenk beim Zutrinken hingegeben haben.*

and incorrupt: intrusted with affairs of greater magnitude than any of my contemporaries, I have administered them all honestly and faithfully. Therefore do I claim to be honored.

As to this fortification, for which you ridiculed me,[1] of the wall and fosse, I regard them as deserving of thanks and praise, and so they are; but I place them nowhere near my acts of administration. Not with stones nor with bricks did I fortify Athens: nor is this the ministry on which I most pride myself. Would you view my fortifications aright, you will find arms, and states, and posts, and harbors, and galleys, and horses, and men for their defense.[2] These are the bulwarks with which I protected Attica, as far as was possible by human wisdom; with these I fortified our territory, not the circle of Piræus or the city.[3] Nay more; I was not beaten by Philip in estimates or preparations; far from it; but the generals and forces of the allies were over-

[1] Æschines had urged in his speech—"that the merit of repairing the fortifications was far outweighed by the guilt of having rendered such repairs necessary; that a good statesman should not seek to be honored for strengthening the ramparts, but for doing some real service to the commonwealth."—P. 87.

[2] I have here taken τούτων as Wolf, Reiske, Jacobs, and Pabst do. But Taylor, Markland, and Schaefer understand it to mean "these men," *i. e.* the Athenians.

[3] I subjoin Lord Brougham's note:—

"The fame of this noble passage is great and universal. It is of a beauty and force made for all times and all places; its effect with us may be imagined by supposing Mr. Pitt to have been attacked for his Martello towers, the use of which was far more doubtful than Demosthenes' τειχισμὸς and ταφρεία, and to have indignantly and proudly appealed to the other services he had rendered and the other outworks he had erected for our internal protection against foreign and domestic enemies. One seems to hear him nobly pour forth his magnificent periods, alike majestic in structure and in tone, upon the 'lines of circumvallation far mightier than any fortress, lines which the energy of a united people and the wisdom of a British parliament had drawn around our glorious constitution, placing it in proud security above all the assaults either of an insulting enemy from without, or a more desperate foe at home,'—and 'desiring that his title to the gratitude of his country should be rested on foundations like these, far more imperishable than any works which the hands of men could raise.' Or would he haply have spoken figuratively of 'the loftier towers which he had raised in the people's hearts, and the exhaustless magazines of their loyalty and valor?'"

come by his fortune. Where are the proofs of this? They are plain and evident. Consider.

What was the course becoming a loyal citizen—a statesman serving his country with all possible forethought and zeal and fidelity? Should he not have covered Attica on the seaboard with Eubœa, on the midland frontier with Bœotia, on the Peloponnesian with the people of that confine? Should he not have provided for the conveyance of corn along a friendly coast all the way to Piræus? preserved certain places that belonged to us by sending off succors, and by advising and moving accordingly,—Proconnesus, Chersonesus, Tenedos? brought others into alliance and confederacy with us,—Byzantium, Abydus, Eubœa?—cut off the principal resources of the enemy, and supplied what the commonwealth was deficient in? All this has been accomplished by my decrees and measures; and whoever will examine them without prejudice, men of Athens, will find they were rightly planned and faithfully executed; that none of the proper seasons were lost or missed or thrown away by me, nothing which depended on one man's ability and prudence was neglected. But if the power of some deity or of fortune, or the worthlessness of commanders, or the wickedness of you that betrayed your countries, or all these things together, injured and eventually ruined our cause, of what is Demosthenes guilty? Had there in each of the Greek cities been one such man as I was in my station among you; or rather, had Thessaly possessed one single man, and Arcadia one, of the same sentiments as myself, none of the Greeks either beyond or within Thermopylæ would have suffered their present calamities; all would have been free and independent, living prosperously in their own countries with perfect safety and security, thankful to you and the rest of the Athenians for such manifold blessings through me.

To show you that I greatly understate my services for fear of giving offense, here—read me this—the list of auxiliaries procured by my decrees.

[*The list of auxiliaries.*]

These and the like measures, Æschines, are what become an honorable citizen; (by their success—O earth and heaven!—we should have been the greatest of people incontestably, and deserved to be so: even under their failure the result is glory, and no one blames Athens or her policy: all condemn fortune that so ordered things:) but never will he desert the interests of the commonwealth, nor hire himself to her adversaries, and study the enemy's advantage instead of his country's; nor on a man who has courage to advise and propose measures worthy of the state, and resolution to persevere in them, will he cast an evil eye, and, if any one privately offends him, remember and treasure it up; no, nor keep himself in a criminal and treacherous[1] retirement, as you so often do. There is indeed a retirement just and beneficial to the state, such as you, the bulk of my countrymen, innocently enjoy: that however is not the retirement of Æschines; far from it. Withdrawing himself from public life when he pleases, (and that is often,) he watches for the moment when you are tired of a constant speaker, or when some reverse of fortune has befallen you, or any thing untoward has happened (and many are the casualties of human life): at such a crisis he springs up an orator, rising from his retreat like a wind; in full voice,[2] with words and phrases collected, he rolls them out audibly and breathlessly, to no advantage or good purpose whatsoever, but to the detriment of some or other of his fellow-citizens and to the general disgrace.

[1] As to the meaning of *ὕπουλος*, the Edinburgh reviewer, whom I have before quoted, remarks as follows (vol. xxxvi. p. 493):—

"He accuses Æschines of maintaining *an unfair and hollow silence*, or *quiet*, *ἡσυχίαν ἄδικον καὶ ὕπουλον*. This translation we consider a very tolerable one, but how far it falls short of the original will be seen when, in order to express the literal meaning of that single word, we are of necessity driven to this periphrasis—*a hollow silence, like that particular state of a wound which has just skinned over, as if about to heal, but which is nevertheless rankling underneath, and just upon the point of breaking out into fresh mischief.*"

Leland renders it "insidious." Brougham: "traitorous." Auger: "perfide." Jacobs: *heimtückische*. Pabst: *arglistige*.

[2] Leland renders this aptly enough: "his voice is already exercised." Spillan follows him; and Pabst is to the same effect. It is not correct to say, "raising his voice," or the like, as others have it.

It appears from the testimony of ancient writers, as well as from the sneers of Demosthenes, that Æschines had a remarkably fine voice, and was not a little proud of it. A good voice must indeed have been a great advantage to an Athenian speaker, who had to address thousands of people in the open air. But Æschines not only possessed a voice that was loud and clear, but had a wonderful ease and fluency of speech, in these natural gifts surpassing Demosthenes himself.

Yet from this labor and diligence, Æschines, if it proceeded from an honest heart, solicitous for your country's welfare, the fruits should have been rich and noble and profitable to all—alliances of states, supplies of money, conveniences of commerce, enactment of useful laws, opposition to our declared enemies. All such things were looked for[1] in former times; and many opportunities did the past afford for a good man and true to show himself; during which time you are nowhere to be found, neither first, second, third, fourth, fifth, nor sixth[2]—not in any rank at all—certainly on no service by which your country was exalted. For what alliance has come to the state by your procurement? What succors, what acquisition of good-will or credit? What embassy or agency is there of yours, by which the reputation of the country has been increased? What concern domestic, Hellenic, or foreign, of which you have had the management, has improved under it? What galleys? what ammunition? what arsenals? what repair of walls? what cavalry? What in the world are you good for? What assistance in money have you ever given, either to the rich or the poor, out of public spirit or liberality? None. But, good sir, if there is nothing of this, there is at all events zeal and loyalty. Where?

[1] Ἐξέτασις ἦν, "there was an inquiry after—they were wanted,"—the word being strictly applicable to a search or muster, where the names of persons are called over—the things needed or missing are inquired for. Hence ἐξετάζεσθαι gets the meaning of "to be found;" being strictly, "to be called over at muster," and more loosely, "to appear in your place at call." Leland's translation is: "such were the services which the late times required." Spillan: "for all these services there was a demand." Francis: "these were objects of great attention." The Germans, however, understand it differently. Jacobs: *Alle diese Gegenstände dienten in früherer Zeit zur Prüfung.* Pabst: *Durch alles dies konnte man in den frühern Zeiten sich erproben*, which is pretty nearly the same thing as is expressed by the next clause. Compare the passage below (p. 331, Orig.), *ἐπειδὴ οὐκέτι συμβούλων ἀλλὰ τῶν τοῖς ἐπιταττομένοις ὑπηρετούντων καὶ τῶν κατὰ τῆς πατρίδος μισθαρνεῖν ἑτοίμων καὶ τῶν κολακεύειν ἑτέρους βουλομένων ἐξέτασις ἦν, τηνικαῦτα σὺ καὶ τούτων ἕκαστος ἐν τάξει.*

[2] Auger contents himself with rendering this: "ni le premier, ni le second, ni le dernier, dans aucun rang enfin," and observes, "il me semble que cette énumération arithmétique n'auroit eu aucune grace en françois." It refers, however, to an ancient answer of the Delphic oracle, which to an inquiry, what rank the Ægæans held, responded, that "they were neither third, nor fourth, nor twelfth; of no number or account at all."

when? You infamous fellow! Even at a time when all who ever spoke upon the platform gave something for the public safety, and last Aristonicus gave the sum which he had amassed to retrieve his franchise,[1] you neither came forward nor contributed a mite—not from inability—no! for you have inherited above five talents from Philo, your wife's father, and you had a subscription of two talents from the chairmen of the Boards for what you did to cut up the navy-law. But, that I may not go from one thing to another and lose sight of the question, I pass this by. That it was not poverty prevented your contributing, already appears: it was, in fact, your anxiety to do nothing against those to whom your political life is subservient. On what occasions then do you show your spirit? When do you shine out?[2] When aught is to be spoken against your countrymen!—then it is you are splendid in voice, perfect in memory, an admirable actor, a tragic Theocrines.[3]

You mention the good men of olden times; and you are right so to do. Yet it is hardly fair, O Athenians, that he should get the advantage of that respect which you have for the dead, to compare and contrast me with them,—me who am living among you; for what mortal is ignorant, that toward the living there exists always more or less of ill-will, whereas the dead are no longer hated even by an enemy?[4] Such being human nature, am I to be tried and judged by

[1] His civic privileges were suspended, until he had discharged the debt due from him to the state.

[2] *Νεανίας—λαμπρός.* Leland: "spirited and shining." Brougham: "bold and munificent." Francis: "on what occasions has your spirit been excited and your abilities displayed?" Jacobs: *wacker—kräftig.* Pabst: *Bei welchen Gelegenheiten zeigtest Du Dich also mit jugendlicher Kraft, bei welchen glänzend und ausgezeichnet.* See note 1, p. 57.

[3] Theocrines was a notorious informer and slanderer. There is an oration attributed to Demosthenes against such a person. Reiske in his Index says, apparently from conjecture—"Videtur Athenis Roscius ævi sui fuisse, *i. e.* perfectus histrio comicus; cum quo Demosthenes Æschinem comparans Theocrinem tragicum appellat, ut agentem histrionicam in rebus seriis et funestis."

[4] Compare Thucydides ii. 45.—*φθόνος γὰρ τοῖς ζῶσι πρὸς τὸ ἀντίπαλον τὸ δὲ μὴ ἐμποδὼν ἀνανταγωνίστῳ εὐνοίᾳ τετίμηται*; and the declamation attributed to Cicero against Sallust: "Quare noli mihi antiquos viros objectare. Neque me cum iis conferre decet, Patres Conscripti, qui jam decesserunt, omnique odio carent et invidiâ, sed cum iis qui mecum una in republicâ versati sunt."

the standard of my predecessors? Heaven forbid! It is not just or equitable, Æschines. Let me be compared with you, or any persons you like of your party who are still alive. And consider this—whether it is more honorable and better for the state, that because of the services of a former age, prodigious though they are beyond all power of expression, those of the present generation should be unrequited and spurned, or that all who give proof of their good intentions should have their share of honor and regard from the people? Yet indeed—if I must say so much—my politics and principles, if considered fairly, will be found to resemble those of the illustrious ancients, and to have had the same objects in view, while yours resemble those of their calumniators; for it is certain there were persons in those times, who ran down the living, and praised people dead and gone, with a malignant purpose like yourself.

You say that I am nothing like the ancients. Are you like them, Æschines? Is your brother, or any of our speakers? I assert that none is. But pray, my good fellow, (that I may give you no other name,) try the living with the living and with his competitors, as you would in all cases—poets, dancers, athletes. Philammon did not, because he was inferior to Glaucus of Carystus and some other champions of a by-gone age, depart uncrowned from Olympia, but, because he beat all who entered the ring against him, was crowned and proclaimed conqueror.[1] So I ask you to compare me with the orators of the day, with yourself, with any one you like: I yield to none. When the commonwealth was at liberty to choose for her advantage, and patriotism was a matter of emulation, I showed myself a better counselor than any, and every act of state was pursuant to my decrees and laws

[1] An anecdote of this Glaucus is told by Pausanias (vi. 10). He used to drive his father's plow, and one day, when the coulter was loose, he knocked it in with his fist. His father, having seen this feat, took him to Olympia, and entered him in the ring as a pugilist. He was nearly beaten for want of skill, when his father called out, "Strike as you did the coulter," on which he redoubled his efforts, and won the battle.

The argument here advanced is anticipated by Æschines, (cont. Ctes. 81,) who asserts that on questions of political merit the true test is, not a mere comparison with men of the day, but a positive standard of excellence.

and negotiations: none of your party was to be seen, unless you had to do the Athenians a mischief. After that lamentable occurrence, when there was a call no longer for advisers, but for persons obedient to command, persons ready to be hired against their country and willing to flatter strangers, then all of you were in occupation, grand people with splendid equipages; I was powerless, I confess, though more attached to my countrymen than you.[1]

Two things, men of Athens, are characteristic of a well-disposed citizen:—so may I speak of myself and give the least offense:—In authority, his constant aim should be the dignity and pre-eminence of the commonwealth; in all times and circumstances his spirit should be loyal. This depends upon nature; power and might upon other things. Such a spirit, you will find, I have ever sincerely cherished. Only see. When my person was demanded—when they brought Amphictyonic suits against me—when they menaced—when they promised—when they set these miscreants like wild beasts upon me—never in any way have I abandoned my affection for you. From the very beginning I chose an honest and straightforward course in politics, to support the honor, the power, the glory of my fatherland, these to exalt, in these to have my being. I do not walk about the market-place gay and cheerful because the stranger has prospered, holding out my right hand and congratulating those who I think will report it yonder, and on any news of our own success shudder and groan and stoop to the earth, like these impious men, who rail at Athens, as if in so doing they did not rail at themselves; who look abroad, and if the foreigner thrives by the distresses of Greece, are thankful for it, and say we should keep him so thriving to all time.

Never, O ye Gods, may those wishes be confirmed by you! If possible, inspire even in these men a better sense and feeling! But if they are indeed incurable, destroy them by themselves; exterminate them on land and sea; and for the

[1] Æschines declares (cont. Ctes. 76) that soon after the battle of Chæronea Demosthenes rose in the assembly, trembling and half-dead, and asked that he might be appointed to draw up the terms of peace; but the Athenians would not allow his name to be subscribed to their decrees.

rest of us, grant that we may speedily be released from our present fears, and enjoy a lasting deliverance![1]

[1] Lord Brougham's version of this concluding passage is spirited, though not free from faults:

"Let not, O gracious God, let not such conduct receive any measure of sanction from thee! Rather plant even in these men a better spirit and better feelings! But if they are wholly incurable, then pursue them, yea, themselves by themselves, to utter and untimely perdition, by land and by sea; and to us who are spared vouchsafe to grant the speediest rescue from our impending alarms, and an unshaken security."

'Επινεύσειε ταῦτα is not translated quite correctly, and *μάλιστα* is omitted. "Themselves by themselves" is a Greek idiom, not an English. For example, *αὐτὸς αὑτὸν ἀπέκτεινεν* is, in plain and good English, "he killed himself," not, "he himself killed himself." We might say, "by themselves alone;" and Leland's turn is not bad: "on them, on them only discharge your vengeance."

It may be thought that my own version of the *ἐξώλεις καὶ προώλεις ποιήσατε* is too wide. I look upon it as a phrase, like *ἄγειν καὶ φέρειν* and many others, to be represented by some general equivalent, and not by taking the words piecemeal. There is no advantage that I see in giving a particular verbal expression to the *πρὸ* in *προώλεις*, since in any form of imprecation, such as "perdition seize," or the like, it is necessarily implied that the destruction is to be premature, or before the ordinary course of nature.

Lord Brougham justly says that "the music of this passage is almost as fine as the sense is impressive and grand, and the manner dignified and calm;" and he remarks upon the difficulty of preserving this in a translation. The last two lines are perhaps the most difficult of all. I have resorted to a little expansion, in the attempt to preserve their harmony; yet I am unable to satisfy myself. *'Ασφαλῆ σωτηρίαν* is variously rendered—by Spillan: "safe security"—Leland: "blessings of protection and tranquillity." Lord Brougham's "unshaken security" is a good expression, and sounds well at the close. "Inviolable security" had occurred to me; but I rather think that *σωτηρίαν* indicates the idea of divine protection, or safety derived from the Gods. The prayer of Demosthenes is, that his countrymen may not only be extricated from their present state of suspense and anxiety, but may have the insurance of divine protection for the future. In effect, he prays for the deliverance of Athens from a foreign yoke, and the restoration of her ancient dignity. His language is purposely vague, but was not the less felt and understood by his hearers. The very prayer which invokes a blessing upon the Athenians is designed to impress the conviction upon them, that Æschines was their deadly enemy, who would regard their welfare as his own ruin.

The version of Jacobs is subjoined. He has been bold enough, like Leland, to omit "by land and sea;" which, perhaps, to modern ears, does not much add to the force. It means, that the whole gang of traitors should be destroyed, in whatever part of the world they might be, without chance or possibility of escape.

Möchte doch, o all' ihr Götter! keiner von Euch dieses billigen, son-

THE ORATION ON THE EMBASSY.

THE ARGUMENT.

Demosthenes appears in this cause as the conductor of a prosecution against Æschines for treasonable practices in the embassy which preceded the peace of B.C. 346. The circumstances connected with that embassy are so fully explained in the third Appendix to Volume I., and in the first Appendix to this Volume, that it will be sufficient to advert briefly to them, while we inquire more particularly into certain matters that took place after the conclusion of the peace and before this prosecution. An interval of three years elapsed between those two events. Æschines was then accused and brought to trial, not only for neglect and misconduct in the performance of his duty as embassador, but for positive corruption and betrayal of his country's interests to Philip. It will naturally be asked why the proceeding against him on such grave charges was so long delayed. For this various causes may be assigned.

Notwithstanding the dissatisfaction of the Athenians at the conditions and consequences of the peace, and at the triumph and advantage which Philip had obtained, there was a general reluctance to bring on any public discussion of the matter, which might possibly provoke a new quarrel, for which the Athenians were ill prepared. It was felt that an exposure of the artifices by which the people were deluded would reflect some disgrace upon them for their credulity. All parties concerned in the negotiation for peace were in some measure respons-

---

dern Ihr vor allen Dingen auch diesen hier einen bessern Sinn und besseres Gemüth verleihen; wenn sie aber unheilbar sind, sie allein für sich dem Verderben überliefern, uns, den Uebrigen, aber die schnellste Befreiung von den obschwebenden Besorgnissen und unerschütterte Wohlfahrt gewähren.

Now let the reader compare with this the peroration of the first Catilinarian speech:

"Hisce ominibus, Catilina, cum summâ reipublicæ salute et cum tuâ peste ac pernicie, cumque eorum exitio, qui se tecum omni scelere parricidioque junxerunt, proficiscere ad impium bellum ac nefarium. Tum tu, Jupiter, qui iisdem, quibus hæc urbs, auspiciis a Romulo es constitutus; quem Statorem hujus urbis atque imperii vere nominamus; hunc et hujus socios a tuis aris ceterisque templis, a tectis urbis ac mœnibus, a vitâ fortunisque civium omnium arcebis: et omnes inimicos bonorum, hostes patriæ, latrones Italiæ, scelerum fœdere inter se ac nefariâ societate conjunctos, æternis suppliciis vivos mortuosque mactabis."

ible for it, and among these Demosthenes himself: and therefore, while he was the first to call the attention of his countrymen to the misdeeds of his colleagues, he forbore for some time to take any active steps against them. Again, whatever ground there might be for suspecting Æschines and Philocrates of corrupt practices, there appeared no substantial proof against them, at least none such as would be sufficient to convict them in a court of justice. Moreover, they were supported by a powerful party, at the head of which were Eubulus and Phocion, and which comprised most of those citizens who were anxious to preserve peace with Macedonia. Demosthenes, although he had acquired a great reputation both as a statesman and an orator, had not yet attained that high position as minister of the commonwealth, to which a few more years served to raise him. These were the causes which for a long time prevented any formal proceeding against the suspected parties.

The discontent at Athens however continued to increase. The complaints against the embassadors were kept alive, not only by private discussion, but by frequent indirect attacks upon them in the public debates. Thus, in the Oration on the Peace, Demosthenes reminded the people how they had been deluded by false reports and promises. In the second Philippic, without expressly naming either Æschines or Philocrates, but in language that could not fail to be understood, he publicly denounced them, and declared that they ought to be called to account. The part which Æschines took when Python came to Athens, his addressing the people in support of the Macedonian envoys, and defending Philip's conduct, by no means tended to increase his popularity. News was continually arriving at Athens of some warlike or ambitious movement of Philip, plainly showing that he would not rest contented even with his present position, but was making advances in every direction to extend his influence and power. All this, while it excited the alarm of the Athenians, exalted Demosthenes in their estimation as a man who possessed more foresight than his adversaries, and brought them in a corresponding degree into disrepute. Before the close of the year B.C. 343, many important events had occurred, showing what advantage Philip had gained by terminating the Sacred War, and how the safety of Athens was endangered by his influence in Southern Greece. Such were, the division of Thessaly into tetrarchies, and the establishment of Philip's adherents in the government—the conspiracy of Ptœdorus at Megara, which nearly threw that city into Philip's hands—his intrigues in Eubœa—and those in Elis, where a Macedonian faction had become predominant. Negotiations had been entered into between Philip and the Athenians, with a view to amend the articles of the peace, and put them on a basis which should preclude future disputes; but they had proved wholly ineffectual. Philip was so incensed at the demands made by the Athenian embassadors, that he treated them with rudeness, and even banished from his dominions the poet Xenoclides, because he had received them into his house. These events are alluded to in the speech of Demosthenes. Before the trial came on, it is clear that the Athenian people had begun to regard Philip with increased suspicion and anger.

It would appear also, from a particular passage in the Oration on the Embassy, that the affair of Antiphon (related more fully in the Oration on the Crown, ante p. 55) occurred shortly before the present trial. The part which Æschines took in it caused him to be deprived of an honorable appointment, that of pleader before the Amphictyonic council; so that, if the date which has been assigned is correct, he must about this time have been in no little disgrace with the public. The allusions of Demosthenes, however, are not so distinct as to enable us to speak with much certainty upon the point.

Notwithstanding all the suspicion under which Æschines might lie, it is very doubtful whether any legal proceeding would ever have been taken against him, but for the imprudence of his colleague Philocrates, who by his conduct at Athens, by open talk and conversation, afforded the strongest evidence against himself, and almost provoked his enemies to bring him to justice. Of the treason of Philocrates there remains no historical doubt. He had received from Philip large sums of money and grants of land in Phocis, which brought him in a considerable income; all this wealth he displayed ostentatiously, and made no secret of the quarter from which it was derived. About two years after the peace, and probably not long after the delivery of the second Philippic, Hyperides undertook to prosecute him. The law of Athens, in case of high crimes and misdemeanors against the state, afforded a method of proceeding not unlike an impeachment in our own law. This method Hyperides adopted. He brought Philocrates before the popular assembly, and there charging him with treasonable conspiracy, procured a decree of the people ordering him to be brought to trial. Philocrates, having (as we may presume) given bail for his appearance to answer the charge, was so conscious of guilt, and so hopeless of escape, that he sought safety in voluntary exile.

This confession of crime on the part of one with whom on the most important occasions he had acted in concert was a severe blow to Æschines. He had already been menaced with a similar accusation: for at the time when Hyperides preferred his impeachment, Demosthenes rose in the assembly, and declared, that there was one thing in it which dissatisfied him, and this was, that Philocrates was the only person accused; for it was certain, there must have been accomplices among the embassadors. "Let those," said he, "who disapprove the conduct of Philocrates, and disclaim connection with him, come forward and declare themselves, and I will acquit them from all blame." No one responded to this challenge; and Demosthenes stood pledged to follow up his own words, and bring another delinquent to justice. The flight of Philocrates left no room for hesitation; and the only question was, what sort of criminal process it was most advisable to adopt.

It was open to him to take the same course against Æschines which Hyperides had taken against Philocrates, viz. to proceed by impeachment. But the more regular way of proceeding against a public functionary for any crime or misdemeanor relating to his office, was to prefer an accusation against him when he presented himself before the logistæ, or auditors, to render an account of his official duties.

We have seen that every person holding an office of importance at Athens was compelled, after the expiration of his term, to render an account of the manner in which he had acquitted himself. Embassadors were subject to the same liability as other servants of the public, except that no particular time was fixed for their submission to the audit, as in other cases. The reason for such difference may be found in the nature of their employment; embassadors not being appointed like ordinary magistrates for any stated term, or at regular periods, but occasionally, as circumstances might require. Therefore, while it was competent for any citizen to summon an embassador before the auditors, and call him to account for the manner in which he had executed his mission, the law prescribed no positive time for the embassador himself to tender his accounts.

Many embassies must have been simple affairs, involving little or no responsibility; and we may presume, the ministers employed upon them would hardly be called upon to go through the ceremony of an audit. On the other hand, we may reasonably suppose, that persons commissioned to represent their country on questions of moment, and to conduct arduous and critical negotiations, would for their own sakes come before the auditors at the earliest opportunity, and offer themselves to that public inquiry which the Athenian law in all such cases invited or allowed. Æschines had not done so; on the contrary, he had suffered three years to elapse without submitting to this ordeal. But he had raised a point of law, on which his excuse partly rested. He contended that there was no necessity to render an account of the second embassy, as all the substantial part of the business had been transacted upon the first; the second journey to Macedonia was for a matter of form only, to receive the oath of Philip: having therefore obtained his legal discharge as to the first embassy, he was to all intents and purposes discharged as to both. Demosthenes took a different view of the question, and presented himself before the auditors as having a distinct account to render of his conduct upon the second embassy. Æschines, seeing that this might be turned into a precedent against him, came with a large number of friends to the audit-room, and objected that the account of Demosthenes could not be received, he being no longer accountable. The objection was overruled; Demosthenes went through the necessary forms, and his account was passed. It does not appear however that this decision had any immediate influence upon the conduct of Æschines. The time when Demosthenes presented himself to the auditors is not stated; yet I should be disposed to think, it was a considerable time before the commencement of this prosecution. It was not the legal precedent, but the force of circumstance, which afterward determined Æschines to follow his adversary's example. Finding after the flight of Philocrates, that a prosecution against himself was inevitable, he deemed it the most prudent policy to take a bold step; and accordingly he demanded his audit, thereby challenging any accuser who dared to come forward and arraign him.

Several accusers appeared, the principal among them being Timarchus and Demosthenes. Timarchus had long been known as an active politician, and for the last few years had zealously exerted himself in opposition to Philip. He was however a man of profligate habits, and notoriously guilty of certain infamous practices, which by an old statute of Solon incapacitated him to appear as a speaker in the public assembly. Æschines seized the opportunity, which this law afforded him, of striking a blow, which might at the same time crush a formidable adversary, and create a prejudice that should help him materially in his own defense. He demanded, according to the form of the Attic law, a judicial scrutiny into the character of Timarchus, and a jury being summoned to try the case, he accused and convicted him of the crimes above mentioned. The legal consequence of such conviction was disfranchisement; and Æschines thus in a summary way got rid of one of his accusers. Demosthenes remained: and his own trial soon afterward came on.

The nature of the case is best learned from the speeches of the rival orators. Demosthenes, feeling what difficulties he had to contend with, and how much his own credit was at stake, uses every exertion to bring home to Æschines those charges which he had been for three years proclaiming incessantly to the Athenian public, and labors to supply the want of direct proof by close reasoning, and inferences from a variety of facts and circumstances. He calls attention at the outset to the efforts which the defendant's party were making to screen him from justice. Timarchus had been destroyed, he says, not for the good of society, but to deter any other accuser from taking up the case. Notwithstanding the lapse of time, he undertakes to prove the following points—that Æschines had deceived the Athenians by false reports; that he had given treacherous counsel; that he had neglected his instructions; that he had lost precious opportunities by delay; and that he had done all this from corrupt motives. The charge is in terms confined to the transactions upon the second embassy; but the discussion is by no means confined to them. Æschines, according to his opponent's view, was bribed by Philip on the first embassy, but no one suspected him till some time after. Dionysius, in his treatise on Rhetoric, commends the skill shown by Demosthenes in dealing with this part of the subject. It would not have lain in his mouth to complain of any thing done upon the first journey to Pella, as on his return he had expressed himself satisfied with all the proceedings, and praised the embassadors for their conduct. The prosecution therefore is nominally directed to the affairs of the second embassy, and the orator, contending that Æschines had previously hired himself to Philip, excuses his own apparent inconsistency by alleging that up to a certain time he, in common with the rest of his fellow-citizens, had been deceived as to the defendant's motives. He comments upon the remarkable change which Æschines had undergone in his political views:—he had been sent embassador to Peloponnesus, to rouse the Arcadians against Philip; he had made a brilliant speech at Megalopolis, in which he assailed the king of Macedon with the fiercest invective; he talked in the same strain when he returned to Athens, and boasted of what he had done; he was appointed on that very account to be one of the embassadors to Pella, that he might be a check upon his colleagues, who were suspected of being too favorable to Philip; yet, after all this, he was found suddenly acting in concert with Philocrates, and doing every thing to secure Philip's advantage in the negotiations. Among other circumstances, prominently advanced as evidence of guilt, are—the time which the embassadors wasted on their journey to Pella, in disobedience to the decree of the council; their lingering afterward at Pella, until Philip returned from Thrace; their consenting to accompany him to Pheræ, and postponing the signature of the treaty until their arrival at that city. By all this delay Philip was enabled to reduce Thrace into subjection, and complete the preparations for his march southward. It was the duty of the embassadors to apprise their countrymen of Philip's preparations and objects; yet not only had they neglected to do so themselves, but they refused to permit a letter, which Demosthenes had written for that purpose, to be sent to Athens. Philip had sent a letter to the Athenians, apologizing for their delay: this, says Demosthenes, was an argument that they were colluding with him, and it was plain that Æschines had dictated the letter.

Æschines had had many private interviews with Philip, and on one particular occasion, at Pheræ—of this Demosthenes gives evidence—he had been watched coming out of the king's tent at midnight. It is further asserted by Demosthenes, that on the first embassy Philip offered a sum of money to the whole body of the embassadors; that he also sounded them each separately, himself among the rest, with a view to seduce them from their allegiance. Æschines was known to have received land in Phocis, yielding an income of thirty minas; (this apparently is not denied by Æschines;) it could not be doubted that this was the price of corruption. The conduct of Æschines after his return home could only be explained on the supposition of treachery. He professed to be perfectly acquainted with Philip's intentions; he assured the people that Philip meant to deprive the Thebans of their sovereignty in Bœotia, and to punish them for their designs upon Delphi; to restore Thespiæ and Platæa, and to give Eubœa and Oropus to Athens. Afterward, when it turned out that these promises were nugatory—when Philip had destroyed the Phocian cities, and confirmed Thebes in her sovereignty over Bœotia—how had Æschines acted? Instead of denouncing Philip for breach of faith,—which would have been the natural course if he had been himself deceived by Philip—he remained quite silent: and not only that; he had gone to Phocis, and shared the festivities of Philip's camp, and continued ever after to sound his praises at Athens. Not very long ago he had supported the Macedonian envoys before the popular assembly, and, to gratify them, had spoken disparagingly of his own countrymen. He had throughout assisted and upheld Philocrates, clearly because he was the partner of his treason, and had been afraid to disclaim connection with him, lest his royal master should be displeased.

Such are the principal matters of fact adduced by Demosthenes in support of the charge. Many stories are told, not bearing directly upon the case, but tending to throw discredit on the character of the defendant and his supposed accomplices, Philocrates and Phrynon. Great pains also are taken by the orator to explain the part which he himself took in the same transactions, with a view to clear himself from all imputation of connection with the guilty parties, or any other share of the blame. His anxiety on this head rendered it more difficult for him to confine himself to the question properly at issue; and the speech has not that clear order and arrangement which is commonly observable in Demosthenes. The arguments indeed are often pointed and forcible, but they are not well put together. He dwells with much emphasis on the destruction of the Phocians, on the evil consequences resulting from Philip's possession of Thermopylæ, and the great extension of his power; all which are attributed to Æschines and his colleagues. If, after they had discovered the designs of Philip, they had given immediate information to the Athenians, there was plenty of time to send a fleet and army to Thermopylæ, and prevent his passing the straits: even after he had passed, they might have saved Phocis, if they had not been prevented by false intelligence and insidious counsels. The men who had thus deceived their countrymen had been hired to betray a sacred trust, and they ought not to be spared. It was urged, that their punishment would excite the resentment of Philip: but, says Demosthenes, they deserved punishment on this very account, that they had made Philip's resentment a thing to be dreaded; and Philip should be made to see that it would not answer his purpose to bribe the citizens of Athens. He reminds the jury how severely Timarchus had been dealt with, and how Æschines had in his case insisted upon general notoriety as a sufficient ground of conviction: if they tried Æschines upon his own principles, they must convict him, for his guilt was known to all. He comments at great length upon the general increase of corruption in the Greek states, showing what baneful effects it had produced in Chalcidice, Peloponnesus, and elsewhere, and how perilous it would be to themselves, if they suffered it to spread yet further. Strong measures should be taken to check the progress of the mischief; and now that Æschines was brought before them on a clear charge of treason, they should, without regard to his abilities, his position, or his party, make a signal example of him, and strike terror into the host of traitors in the Hellenic world.

Æschines replied, in a speech little, if at all, inferior to that of his adversary; and, as we are informed by Idomeneus the Epicurean, he was acquitted by a majority of thirty votes. Nor can this surprise us, when we look at the circumstances of the case—the length of time which had elapsed—the lack of any direct proof of criminality—the able defense made by Æschines—the advantage which he had gained by the conviction of Timarchus—and the powerful aid of Eubulus and other friends, who appeared in his behalf, or supported him by their influence.

Notwithstanding the express testimony of Idomeneus, who wrote not very long after the event, and who is confirmed by Ulpian, there are writers, both ancient and modern, who have inclined to the opinion that Æschines was never brought to trial, but the orations on both sides were only published. The doubt was first suggested by Plutarch, who thought it strange that no mention of this trial should be made in either of the speeches on the Crown. The same view is espoused by Albert Gerhard Becker, in his treatise on the character of Demosthenes, (*Demosthenes als Staatsman und Redner*, p. 320,) who argues the matter more fully. It appears to me, that the negative evidence on which they rely has but little force under the circumstances, for the reason assigned by Auger, (which Becker does not satisfactorily answer,) viz., that both the orators had motives for their silence: Demosthenes had lost the verdict, and therefore had nothing to boast of; Æschines had so small a majority—the whole number of jurors being not less probably than five hundred—that he was considered not to have obtained an honorable acquittal.

As to the title to this oration, and further information as to the law, see my article *Parapresbeia* in the Archæological Dictionary.

Of the intrigue and canvassing which there has been about this trial, men of Athens, I imagine you are all aware, having seen what a throng assailed you at the ballot just now.[1] I shall only ask at your hands—what those who don't ask it are entitled to—that you will value no person and no one's favor more highly than justice and the oath which each juror has sworn, remembering that this is for the good of yourselves and the community; whereas all this intrigue and importunity of partisans is to get advantages for some persons over the rest, which the laws assemble you here to prevent, not to secure for the benefit of the unjust.

Other men, who enter honestly upon the service of the public, even after their audit, I see, profess a continued responsibility: Æschines does the very reverse; for before he appeared in court to give a reckoning of his actions, one of the persons who came to demand it he has removed out of the way;[2] others he goes about threatening, and thus introduces into the commonwealth a practice most flagitious and injurious to you; for if a man who has discharged or administered any public office can by intimidation, and not by honesty, keep people from accusing him, you will be deprived of all authority.

That I shall prove the defendant to be guilty of many grave misdemeanors, and to merit the severest punishment, I am confident and persuaded: what, notwithstanding such conviction, I am afraid of, I will tell you without disguise. It appears to me, O Athenians, that all the causes which come before you depend on the time of bringing them as much as

[1] For the election of jurors. See page 81, note 1.

[2] Timarchus. See Appendix II.

upon the merits, and I fear, the length of time since the embassy may have caused you to forget or become reconciled to your wrongs. Yet, even under these circumstances, you may, I think, arrive at a correct judgment and decision: I will tell you how. You must consider among yourselves, men of the jury, and reflect for what things the commonwealth should receive an account from an embassador. First, it should be, on the subject of his reports; secondly, of his counsels; thirdly, of your instructions to him; next, as to the circumstances of time; and after all, whether in each of these points he has acted incorruptly or not. Why these inquiries? Because, from his reports you have to deliberate on your course of action; if they are true, you determine rightly, if not so, otherwise. The advice of embassadors you give more credit to, because you listen to them as to men who understand what they were sent about: never then ought an embassador to be convicted of giving bad or mischievous advice. And of course, whatever you instructed him either to do or say, whatever commission you expressly gave him, it is his duty to have executed. But why the account of time? Because it often happens, men of Athens, that the season for many important measures falls in a short space, and if it be sacrificed and betrayed to the enemy, do what you will, it can not be recalled. As to the absence of corrupt motive—I am sure you will all agree, that to take reward for acts which injure the commonwealth is shocking and abominable. The legislator indeed does not define it so, but absolutely forbids the taking of bribes in any way, considering, as it appears to me, that a person who is once bribed and corrupted ceases to be even a safe judge of what is useful for the state. If then I shall prove and demonstrate clearly, that Æschines the defendant has reported what is untrue, and prevented the people hearing the truth from me—that he has given advice totally opposed to your interests, and fulfilled none of your instructions on the embassy—that he has wasted time in which many important opportunities have been lost to the commonwealth—and that for all this he has received presents and wages in conjunction with Philocrates,—convict him, punish him as his crimes deserve: if I prove not these statements, or not all of them, look with contempt on me, and acquit the defendant.

Many grievous things can I lay to his charge besides those which I have mentioned, O Athenians—enough to make every one detest him—but before I enter upon other topics, I will remind you (though nearly all indeed must remember) what character Æschines first assumed in politics, and what language he thought proper to address to the people against Philip, that you may see, his own early acts and speeches will most surely convict him of taking bribes.

He is the first Athenian (as he declared in his speech) who discovered that Philip was plotting against the Greeks, and corrupting certain of the leading men in Arcadia. He it is who, having Ischander, son of Neoptolemus, to play second part to him,[1] applied to the council on this matter, and also to the people, and persuaded you to send embassadors every where to assemble a congress at Athens for consulting about war with Philip; who afterward, on his return from Arcadia, reported those fine long speeches, which he said he had delivered on your behalf before the ten thousand at Megalopolis,[2] in answer to Philip's advocate Hieronymus, and dwelt on the enormous injury done, not only to their own countries, but to the whole of Greece, by the men who took presents and money from Philip. Such being his politics then, such the specimen which he had given of himself, when Aristodemus, Neoptolemus, Ctesiphon, and the rest, who brought reports from Macedonia, without a word of truth, prevailed on you to send embassadors to Philip for peace, this man is put into the embassy, not as one of a party who would sell your interests, not as one of those who trusted Philip, but as one who would help to watch the others; for, on account of his former speeches and hostility to Philip, you all naturally held that opinion of him. He came then to me, and arranged that we should act in the embassy together; and strongly

[1] Pabst: *indem er dem Ischander dem Sohne des Neoptolemus die zweite Rolle bei seinen Umtrieben zu spielen übertrug.* Others connect *δευτεραγωνιστὴν* with *τὸν* Νεοπτολέμου, and understand it literally, as if Ischander had been an actor, as Photius says he was. See Thirlwall's Gr. Hist. v. 326. Taylor takes *τὸν Νεοπτολέμου* to mean "the servant or assistant of Neoptolemus."

[2] The general Pan-Arcadian assembly, which met at Megalopolis, and had power to determine questions of peace and war. See Diodorus, xv. 59. And as to the embassy of Æschines to Peloponnesus, see Appendix VIII.

urged, that we should both watch that impudent profligate Philocrates. And until his return home from the first embassy, men of Athens, I certainly never discovered that he was corrupted and had sold himself; for, besides the speeches which, as I said, he had made before, he rose in the first of the assemblies in which you debated on the peace, and began —I think I can repeat his opening to you in the very same words which he used—"Had Philocrates been meditating ever so long, men of Athens, upon the best means of opposing the peace, he could not, methinks, have found a better way than a motion like the present. Never will I, while a single Athenian is left, advise the commonwealth to make a peace like this: peace, however, I do advise"—and to such purport briefly and fairly he expressed himself. Yet the same man who had thus spoken on the first day in the hearing of you all, on the next, when the peace was to be ratified, when I supported the resolution of our allies, and exerted myself to make the peace equitable and just, and you were of my opinion, and would not even hear the voice of the despicable Philocrates, —he then got up and addressed the people in support of Philocrates, and said what (O heavens!) deserved a thousand deaths—that you ought not to remember your ancestors, nor put up with persons who talked about trophies and sea-fights, and that he would propose and pass a law to prevent your succoring any Greeks who had not previously succored you. All which this impudent wretch dared to utter in the presence and hearing of the embassadors, whom you sent for out of Greece at his persuasion before he had sold himself.

How he wasted the time, O Athenians, after you had appointed him again to receive the oaths; how he ruined all the affairs of the commonwealth, and quarreled with me about it when I sought to prevent him, you shall hear presently. But when[1] we had returned from that embassy for the oaths, which is the subject of your present inquiry—we not having obtained a particle, great or small, of what was promised and expected when you made the peace, but having been cheated in every thing, and these men having a second

[1] Auger's turn of the passage is a good one: "écoutez auparavant ce qui a suivi le retour de cette seconde ambassade, dont je lui demande compte aujourd'hui. Nous étions revenu," &c.

time outstepped their duty as embassadors, and neglected your orders—we went before the council. What I am about to say is known to many people; for the council-hall was full of strangers.[1] I came forward and reported the whole truth to the council, and accused these men, and reckoned every thing up, beginning with those first hopes which Ctesiphon and Aristodemus brought you, showing what speeches Æschines had made at the time of your concluding peace, and into what position they had brought the commonwealth; and as to what remained, that is, the Phocians and Thermopylæ, I advised that we should not sacrifice them and repeat our errors, not keep hanging on hopes and promises, till we let things come to an extremity. And so I persuaded the council. But when the assembly came, and we had to address you, Æschines advanced before any of us: and do, I entreat you, try and recollect, as I go on, whether I am telling the truth; for what marred and utterly ruined all our affairs is just this. From any report of our proceedings on the embassy, from any mention of what was said in the council, whether or no he disputed the truth of my statements, he altogether abstained; but told a tale promising such mighty advantages, that he carried you all away with him. He said that he had brought Philip entirely over to the interests of Athens, both on Amphictyonic questions and all others; and he went through a long speech, which he said he had addressed to Philip against the Thebans, and repeated to you the heads, and computed that in two or three days (thanks to his own diplomacy) you would hear without leaving home or having any field-service or trouble, that Thebes, alone and separately from the rest of Bœotia, was besieged, that Thespiæ and Platæa were having their people restored, and the treasures of the God were demanded not from the Phocians, but from the Thebans, who had formed the design of seizing his temple; for he had taught Philip, he said, that those who designed were guilty of as much impiety as those who executed; and on that account the Thebans had set a price upon his head. He declared further, he had heard some of the Eubœans, who were frightened and alarmed at the connection of our state

[1] *I. e.* people not councilors. As Thirlwall expresses it, (Gr. Hist. v. 363,) "thronged with spectators." Auger: "plein de peuple." Pabst: *mit Bürgern ohne Staatsamt angefüllt.*

with Philip, say to the embassadors, "We are not unaware of the terms on which you have concluded peace with Philip; we are not ignorant, that you have given Amphipolis to him, and Philip has agreed to surrender Eubœa to you:" there was indeed another thing which he had arranged, but he would not mention it yet a while; for some of his colleagues were jealous of him—hinting in obscure words at Oropus. Exalted in your opinion by this plausible tale, judged to be a consummate orator and a wonderful man, he quitted the platform with much solemnity. I rose, and declared that I knew none of those things, and was proceeding to tell what I had reported to the council; but the defendant standing up on one side, and Philocrates on the other, shouted and clamored me down, and at last mocked me. You laughed, and would neither hear nor believe any thing but what Æschines had reported. And, by the Gods! I think your behavior was not unnatural; for who could have endured, with such splendid prospects of advantage, to hear any one say they were delusive, or arraign what these men had done? Every thing else, I fancy, at that time was secondary to the hopes and prospects before you; opposition looked like spite and annoyance merely;[1] the results achieved for the country were so marvelously advantageous, as it seemed.

Why have I begun by reminding you of these things, and going over these speeches? Chiefly and principally, men of Athens, for this reason, that when you hear me speak of any proceeding, and it appears outrageously bad, you may not cry in astonishment, "Why didn't you speak at the moment, and inform us?" but remembering the promises of these men, by means of which on every occasion they prevented others from being heard, and also that specious announcement of Æschines, you may see that he has injured you in this way among others, because you were not suffered to learn the truth at

[1] I do not agree with Schaefer, in thinking that *οἱ δ' ἀντιλέγοντες ὄχλος ἄλλως* are to be separated from the following words. *Οἱ ἀντιλέγοντες* is, in effect, the same as *τὸ ἀντιλέγειν*, and the sentence, though loose, is not inelegant. Pabst expresses it at too great length: *und von denen die dem widersprachen nahm man an, dass sie ohne hinlänglichen Grund als widerwärtige und hämische Menschen sich benähmen.* Auger is much neater: "les contredire, c'étoit vous troubler inutilement, c'étoit jalousie." Francis: "whoever contradicted them appeared actuated merely by a spirit of opposition and envy."

the instant when it was needful, but cheated by hopes and impostures and promises. Such was the chief and principal cause of my entering into these details. What was the second? One of no less importance; that, while you remember his political principles before he was corrupted—how wary, how mistrustful he was of Philip—you may observe his sudden conversion to confidence and friendship; and if his reports to you have been verified, and the results are all right, you may hold his conversion to have been honest and for the country's good; but if the events have all been contrary to what he said, and are fraught with deep disgrace and grievous peril to the country, you may see that he has changed from sordid avarice and bartering of the truth for money.

As I have been led into these topics, I would take the earliest opportunity of mentioning how they took the Phocian business out of your hands. And you must not suppose, men of the jury, when you look at the magnitude of that affair, that the crimes and charges imputed to Æschines are too great for his character, but consider, that any person whom you had placed in that position and made the arbiter of events, had he sold himself, like Æschines, for the purpose of cheating and deceiving you, would have wrought the same mischief as Æschines. It is not because you often put mean persons in public employments, that the affairs which other people deem our state worthy to administer are mean; quite otherwise. And again—Philip, I grant, has destroyed the Phocians; but these men helped him: and we must look and see, whether such chance of saving the Phocians as depended on the embassy was sacrificed and lost by the treachery of these men; not that Æschines[1] destroyed the Phocians by himself—how could he?

Give me the resolution which the council passed on my report, and the deposition of the person who drew it up—to show you, I am not repudiating acts which I was silent about before, for I denounced them immediately, and

[1] Ὅδε means Æschines, as Reiske, Auger, and Pabst take it; not Philip, as Schaefer and Francis. The argument is—It is not necessary to make out, for the purpose of conviction, that Æschines was the sole destroyer of the Phocians; of course he was not, and could not be. Philip was the principal author of that result. The question is, whether Æschines and his accomplices did not help to bring it about by their treacherous conduct in the embassy.

foresaw the consequences; and the council, who were not prevented hearing the truth from me, would neither vote thanks to these men, nor invite them to the city-hall.[1] Such an indignity is not known to have befallen any embassadors since the foundation of the city, not even Timagoras,[2] whom the people condemned to death: yet it has been suffered by these men.

Read them first the evidence, and then the resolution.

[*The evidence.*]

[*The resolution of the council.*]

Here is no vote of thanks, no invitation of the embassadors by the council to the city-hall. If Æschines says there is, let him show and produce it, and I will sit down. But there is none. I allow, if we all acted alike, in the embassy, the

[1] The Prytaneum, or town-hall of Athens. This was a public building near the market-place, where the Prytanes, or presidents of the council, met to dine every day during their term of office, in company with a few select citizens, to whom the state gave the honor of a public dinner. This honor was sometimes given for life, to men who had done some signal service, or to the children of such persons; but it was a reward reserved for rare occasions. Hence the Athenians were so incensed with Socrates, when, being asked after his conviction what penalty he deserved, he replied, "Dinner in the Prytaneum." Cicero de Oratore, i. 54:—"Respondit sese meruisse ut amplissimis honoribus et præmiis decoraretur, et ei victus quotidianus in Prytaneo publice præberetur; qui honos apud Græcos maximus habetur. Cujus responso sic judices exarserunt, ut capitis hominem innocentissimum condemnarent." Here also the presidents, representing the hospitality of the state, entertained embassadors and other foreigners of distinction. And it appears from this passage of Demosthenes, that it was usual to invite the Athenian embassadors after their return home, unless they had misconducted themselves, and the omission to give such invitation would be regarded as a stigma.

[2] Timagoras and Leon were the Athenian embassadors to the court of Persia, at the same time when the Thebans and their allies sent a joint embassy with Pelopidas at their head, B. C. 367. According to Xenophon, (Hell. vii. 38,) Leon, upon his return to Athens, accused Timagoras of having refused to lodge with him, and having acted in concert with Pelopidas; and the Athenians for this put him to death. Plutarch, in the life of Pelopidas, relates that the Athenians condemned Timagoras for receiving a large number of presents from Artaxerxes, and traveling to the coast in a carriage provided by the king; though the real cause of their displeasure was, that Pelopidas, by means of his superior credit and abilities, had gained greater success than the Athenian envoys.

council did right in thanking none of us; for the conduct of all was truly shameful: but if some of us acted uprightly and some not, through the rogues, it would seem, honest men have come in for a share of the disgrace. How then may you easily distinguish who is the knave? Recollect among yourselves, who it is that denounced the proceedings from the beginning: for it is clear that the guilty party was content to be silent, to elude the present time, and never afterward submit his conduct to inquiry; while to a man conscious of nothing wrong it occurred, that possibly by holding his tongue he might seem to be an accomplice in misdemeanor and crime. Well then, I am the person who accused these men from the beginning; none of them accused me.

The council had passed their resolution. The assembly was convened, and Philip already at Thermopylæ. This indeed was their prime offense, that they gave the conduct of such an affair to Philip, and when the proper course was, that you should have information, and then deliberate, and afterward execute what you determined, you received intelligence only at the moment of his arrival, and it was difficult even to advise what should be done. And besides, no one ever read to the people that resolution of the council; the people never heard it; but Æschines got up and harangued as I have just told you, stating what immense advantages he had persuaded Philip to grant, and that the Thebans on that account had set a price upon his head; at which you, though terrified at first by Philip's arrival, and angry with these men for having given no warning, became as gentle as possible,[1] in the expectation of getting all that you desired, and would not suffer me or any one else to speak. And then was read Philip's letter, which Æschines wrote without our privity,[2] and which is in terms a plain and direct apology for

[1] "As gentle as any thing." The familiar expression in English is like that of the Greek. And it is the same in German: see Reiske's note. But Schaefer prefers the reading of τινὰς, "some of you;" the orator confining his observation to a part of the assembly, to avoid giving offense. Pabst adopts the same reading, and translates: *aber gar bald gewissermassen milder gestimmt wurdet.*

[2] I follow Reiske, Auger, and Schaefer. Pabst renders it: *während seines Zurückbleibens nach unserer Abreise.* And Francis the same. It does indeed appear that Æschines staid behind with Philip after the departure of Demosthenes. See p. 396, orig.

these men's faults. For it states, that he hindered them from going to the cities as they wished and receiving the oaths, and that he kept them to assist him as mediators between the Halians and Pharsalians; and he adopts and takes upon himself all their delinquencies: but as to the Phocians or Thespians, or the defendant's reports to you, there is not a syllable. And it was not done in this way by accident: but where you ought to have punished these men for non-performance and neglect of your positive instructions, Philip takes the blame off their shoulders, and says that he himself was in fault, because (as I imagine) you were not likely to punish him: when he desired to cheat and surprise us out of some advantage, Æschines made the report, that you might have no charge or complaint against Philip afterward, the statements not being in a letter or any other communication of his. Read them the letter itself, which this man wrote and Philip sent. You will see, it is just as I explained. Read.

[*The letter.*]

You hear the letter, O Athenians—how fair and friendly it is. About the Phocians however, or the Thebans, or the other matters which this man reported, there is not a word: and therefore there is nothing honest in it, as you shall see directly. He kept them, as he says, to help him in making up the quarrel of the Halians: but a pretty making-up the Halians have got—they have been outcast, and their city has been razed to the ground. As to the prisoners, this man who was considering what he could do to oblige you says, he never thought of ransoming them: but it has often, as you know, been testified before the assembly, that I went with a talent to redeem them, and it shall be testified now: therefore, to deprive me of the credit of a generous act, Æschines persuaded him to insert this.[1] But here is the most important

[1] "*Λύσασθαι* idem valere quod activum *λῦσαι*, ut Kusteri doctrinam convellat, ait Clericus, antestans Æschinem, qui diserte affirmet, *Φίλιππον ἐν τῷ πολέμῳ οὐδένα πώποτε Ἀθηναίων λύτρα πράξασθαι.* Sed vera illum ratio fugit. Scilicet Philippus gratis potuit dimittere eos qui ipsius mancipia essent; qui essent aliorum, si vellet liberare, a dominis redimere debuit pretio soluto. Illos igitur *ἔλυσεν*, hos *ἐλύσατο.* Omnem tollit dubitationem quod legitur p. 393."—Schaefer, App. Crit. And compare what Thirwall says, Gr. Hist. v. 356,—"Demosthenes wished

thing:—He that wrote in the first letter which we brought—"I should have expressly mentioned what benefits I had in store for you, had I been sure of the alliance also"—after the alliance had been concluded says, he knows not what he can do to oblige you; he knows not even his own promise! Of course he knew that, if he was not playing false.[1] To prove that he wrote so at first—here, read the passage out of the letter—begin here—read.

[*The passage from the letter.*]

You see, before he obtained peace, he promised, if alliance also was granted him, he would write and say what benefits he had in store for you. Now that both have been granted him, he says he knows not what he can do to oblige you, but, if you will tell him, he will do any thing that is not disgraceful or dishonorable; having recourse to these pre-

it to be believed that the debates on the peace had raised such suspicions in his mind as to the integrity of his former colleagues, especially Philocrates and Æschines, that he would have declined the office, if he had not undertaken to procure the release of some of the Athenian prisoners who were detained in Macedonia. Æschines treats this as an empty pretext, because Philip had never been used to exact ransom for his Athenian prisoners during the war; and a promise had been given in his name that all should be released as soon as peace should be concluded. But it is clear that this related only to those whom he kept in his own hands; and Æschines himself admits that, among the instructions of the second embassy, one was to negotiate for the release of the prisoners."

The distinction between λῦσαι and λύσασθαι is properly explained by Schaefer; and the first part of the charge here made against Philip is perfectly clear. Philip had said he was considering what service he could render to the Athenians: and yet in his letter he states that he never thought of redeeming the prisoners. How could this obvious method of obliging them have escaped him, if he had really desired to do so? But what does Demosthenes mean when he says that Philip put that clause in his letter, in order to deprive him of credit for his liberality? We should have the whole letter before us, to understand this fully; but perhaps the meaning of Philip was as follows: It did not occur to me to redeem the prisoners who were in the hands of my subjects; the moment it was suggested, however, I acceded to the request: there could be no occasion for Demosthenes, or any one else, to come to Pella for the purpose of effecting their ransom. Compare what Demosthenes says at pp. 393, 394, which looks like an answer to this very argument.

[1] The γὰρ might be expressed more fully, thus—"a likely thing, indeed! Surely he must have known that!" &c.

tenses, and (should you mention any thing and be induced to make a proposal) leaving himself an escape.

These and many other tricks one might then instantly have exposed, and enlightened you on the subject, and not permitted you to abandon every thing, had not Thespiæ and Platæa and the expectation of immediate punishment being inflicted on Thebes blinded you to the truth. If these things were merely to be heard, and the commonwealth to be deluded, it was proper enough to tell you of them: but if they were really to be performed, they should not have been talked about. For if matters had gone so far, that the Thebans even discovering the design could not have helped themselves, why has it not been executed? If they discovered it in time to prevent the execution, who let out the secret? Was it not Æschines? But no—he never had any such meaning or intention,[1] and Æschines never expected it: so I acquit him entirel yof letting the secret out. The fact is—it was necessary that you should be amused by these statements, and refuse to hear the truth from me, and that you should yourselves remain at home, and a decree pass by which the Phocians would be destroyed. Therefore were these statements fabricated, and therefore publicly announced.

I, when I heard the defendant making such magnificent promises, being quite certain of their falsehood—and I will tell you why: first because, when Philip was about to swear the oath of peace, the Phocians were by these men expressly excluded from the treaty, a thing they should have been quite silent about, if the Phocians were to be saved—secondly, because Philip's embassadors used no such language, nor Philip's letter, but only the defendant.[2] Making my conjectures accordingly, I got up to speak, and attempted to answer him: but, as you refused to hear me, I held my tongue, protesting only—I pray and entreat you to recollect—that I had no knowledge of these things, that I had no

[1] I follow Markland, Auger, and Pabst, in understanding Philip as the nominative to *ἤμελλεν* and *ἠβουλήθη*. It is true that Philip has not been mentioned in the sentences preceding; but then he was throughout in the orator's thoughts as the party promising and designing the things alluded to. Schaefer explains *οὔτ' ἤμελλεν*, "nec futura erant quæ fore Æschines jactaverat;" and connects *ἠβουλήθη* with *οὗτος*. But there is not much sense in saying that "Æschines never desired."

[2] I preserve the anacoluthon of the original.

concern in them, and what was more, I did not expect them. At this (the not expecting) you fired up. "Athenians," I said, "if any of this comes true, be sure you praise and honor and crown these men, and not me; but if it turns out differently, let them feel your resentment. I am out of it altogether."[1] "Don't be out of it now," said Æschines, interrupting—"Mind you don't want to be in it another time." "Certainly," said I, "or I should be acting unfairly;" at which Philocrates rose in a flippant manner and said, "No wonder, men of Athens, that I and Demosthenes agree not in opinion; for he drinks water, and I drink wine"[2]—and you laughed.

Read the decree, which Philocrates presented afterward, of his own drawing.[3] It is very well just to hear: but when one takes into account the occasion on which it was prepared, and the promises which the defendant then made, it will appear, they plainly delivered up the Phocians to Philip and the Thebans, all but tying their hands behind them. Read the decree.

[*The decree.*]

You see, men of Athens, how full the decree is of fair and flattering words; that it extends the peace with Philip to his descendants, and the alliance, and awards praise to Philip for offering to do what was just. But Philip offered nothing at all—so far from offering, he says he knows not what he can do to oblige you: it was the defendant that spoke and

[1] "I wash my hands of it," as we familiarly say. "I disclaim all connection with the business; (that is) with what Æschines has been telling you." The reply of Æschines might be rendered with equal force, but with a turn of expression, thus—"Don't disclaim connection now and claim it hereafter." Pabst: *Ich für meinen Theil sage mich los von der ganzen Sache! Hierauf sprach dieser Æschines: sage Dich jetzt nicht los davon, und siehe zu, dass Du nicht hernach daran Antheil wirst haben wollen.* Francis, without either force or accuracy: "For my part I retire. Not yet, replied Æschines: do not yet retire: only remember not to claim any of these rewards, when they are distributed."

[2] Demosthenes was often joked about his water-drinking. Thus, in allusion to the Clepsydra (as to which, see page 59, note 1), it was said, that other men spoke by water, but Demosthenes composed by it.

[3] Philocrates had drawn it up, and then put it in the hands of the assembly-clerk, to be read as his own motion before the people. See Appendix V.

promised in his name. Philocrates, seeing you jump at the defendant's promise,[1] inserts in the decree, that, unless the Phocians did what was right and gave up the temple to the Amphictyons, the Athenian people would send forces against those who resisted. So, men of Athens, as you were staying at home and had never been out, as the Lacedæmonians seeing the artifice had withdrawn, and no other Amphictyons were present besides Thessalians and Thebans, he has proposed[2] in the blandest possible language to deliver up the temple to them, proposing (as he does) to deliver it up to the Amphictyons—what Amphictyons? for none were there but Thebans and Thessalians—not that you should convoke the Amphictyonic body, or wait till they assembled; not that Proxenus should carry succor to the Phocians, or that the Athenians should take the field, or any thing of the kind. Philip however twice summoned you by letter—not to induce you to march, most assuredly: or he would never have destroyed your opportunities of marching and summoned you then; he would not have prevented my sailing home when I desired it, or ordered Æschines to make statements calculated to stop your march: no—it was that you, under the belief that he would do all you desired, might vote nothing against him; that the Phocians might not be encouraged by hopes from you to hold out and resist, but might in utter despair surrender themselves into his hands. Read Philip's letters, and let them speak for themselves.

[*The letters.*]

You see, the letters summon you, and verily for the first time: but these men—had there been any thing honest about it—ought surely to have pressed for your going out,[3] and moved that Proxenus, whom they knew to be in the neighborhood, should immediately carry succor. Yet it appears, they have done just the contrary: and no wonder. They heeded not his epistles, for they understood his intentions in writing them: those intentions they seconded and strove to forward.

[1] Pabst: *der Euch durch die Reden des Æschines angelockt sah.*

[2] This tense is used because the decree, which Demosthenes had caused to be read, was before the court. Francis translates inaccurately: "then did Æschines write in the gentlest language in the world." The mover of the decree was not Æschines, but Philocrates.

[3] More literally: "what else should they have done but second his request for your march?" &c.

The Phocians, when they learned your views from the assembly,[1] and received this decree of Philocrates, and heard the defendant's report and his promises, were in every way undone. Consider only. There were some intelligent persons there who distrusted Philip: they were induced to put faith in him—why?—because they supposed that, if Philip deceived them ten times over, he would at all events not dare to deceive the Athenian envoys, but that the defendant's reports to you were correct, and destruction menaced the Thebans, not themselves. There were others inclined to resist at any price: but even their zeal was slackened by the persuasion that Philip was on their side, and that, if they refused compliance, you would attack them, you from whom they had expected succor. Some however believed, that you repented having made peace with Philip: to these they showed, that you had voted the same peace with his posterity, so that all hope from you must have been despaired of. Therefore they got all this into one decree. And here, in my opinion, have they done you the most grievous wrong. In drawing a treaty of peace with a mortal man raised to power by certain accidents, to have covenanted for an immortality of disgrace to the commonwealth!—to have deprived her not merely of other things, but also of the chances of fortune!—to have been so wantonly wicked as to injure not only the existing Athenians, but all hereafter to come in being![2]—is not this most dreadful? Never afterward would you have consented to add to the treaty this clause, "and to his pos-

[1] "They got intelligence about you from the proceedings in the assembly, which were reported to them." Others construe it differently, joining τὰ παρ' ὑμῶν with ἐκ τῆς ἐκκλησίας. Francis: "what you had determined in your assembly." Pabst, to the same effect.

[2] "Selon la formule assez ordinaire, les Athéniens avoient inséré dans leur traité de paix les mots de *paix perpétuel*, de *paix conclue avec eux et leur descendants.* Ce n'étoit à-peu-près qu'une formule; car cette perpétuité se bornoit souvent à un petit nombre d'années. La déclamation de Démosthène, quoiqu'éloquente, n'est donc dans la réalité qu'une déclamation."—*Auger.*

These observations are not quite correct. It was common enough among the Greeks to conclude a peace for a limited number of years; and when for a small term, it was little better than an armistice. (See Thucydides, v. 18, 23, 41; Aristophanes, Acharn. 186—202, 251.) The argument of Demosthenes is good, assuming the peace with Philip to have been a dishonorable and injurious one. Had the peace been satisfactory, it could not be too firmly cemented.

terity," had you not relied on the promises announced by Æschines. On these the Phocians relied, and were ruined: for, after they had surrendered to Philip and put their cities into his hands, they met with treatment the very opposite of what he assured them.

To convince you that all has been lost in this manner and through these men, I will compute to you the dates of the several transactions. Whoever disputes any of these particulars, may get up and speak while my water is running. The peace was concluded on the nineteenth of Elaphebolion, and we were away to receive the oaths three whole months; and during all that time the Phocians were safe. We returned from the embassy for the oaths on the thirteenth of the month Scirophorion, and Philip was by that time at Thermopylæ, and making promises to the Phocians, of which they believed not a single word. The proof is this;—they would not otherwise have come here to you. The assembly, in which these men ruined all by their false and delusive statements to you, was held afterward, on the sixteenth of Scirophorion. On the fifth day after that, as I reckon, intelligence of your proceedings reached the Phocians; for the Phocian envoys were here, and it much concerned them to know what these men would report, and what resolution you would pass. I reckon then, it was on the twentieth that the Phocians heard of your proceedings, for that is the fifth day from the sixteenth.[1] Then comes the twenty-first, twenty-second, twenty-third: on this the convention[2] took place, and it was all over with Phocis. How does this appear? On the twenty-seventh you were assembled in Piræus on the business of the arsenal, and Dercylus came from Chalcis, and reported to you that Philip had put every thing into the hands of the Thebans; and he computed it to be the fifth day from the convention. Twenty-three, twenty-four, twenty-five, twenty-six, twenty-seven—that makes it exactly the fifth. So, you see, by the date of their report, by the date of their motion, by all the dates,[3] are they convicted of having acted in concert with Philip, and assisted in the destruction of the Phocians.

[1] Reckoning inclusive, according to custom.

[2] Between Philip and the Phocians. See Appendix I.

[3] I follow Pabst in connecting *οἷς* with *χρόνοις*, not Reiske, who takes it neutrally. But I differ with Pabst as to *πᾶσιν*. He explains it, "by

Again, the circumstance that not a city of the Phocians was taken by storm or blockade, but that they were utterly destroyed by the convention, is a decisive proof that they suffered because these men had persuaded them that they would be saved by Philip. For of his character they were certainly not ignorant. Give me the treaty of alliance with the Phocians, and the decrees[1] under which they dismantled the fortifications—to show you in what relation you stood to them, and how they were treated notwithstanding through these accursed men. Read.

[*The treaty of alliance between the Athenians and the Phocians.*]

That is what they had to expect from you—friendship, alliance, succor. Now hear what treatment they got through this man who prevented your succoring them. Read.

[*The convention between Philip and the Phocians.*]

You hear, O Athenians. A convention between Philip and the Phocians, it says, not between the Thebans and Phocians, nor Thessalians and Phocians, nor Locrians, nor any other of the people present. And again it says, that the Phocians shall deliver up these cities to Philip; not to the Thebans, nor the Thessalians, nor any other people. Why? Because this man reported to you that Philip had come to save the Phocians. To him they trusted for all; to him they looked for all; with him they concluded peace. Now for the rest. Look what they trusted to, and what they got. Any thing like was it or similar to this man's assurance? Read.

[*The decree of the Amphictyons.*]

Results more awful and momentous, O Athenians, have not been wrought in Greece within our time, nor I should think in any time heretofore. Yet such mighty results has Philip singly been able to accomplish during the existence of the Athenian commonwealth, whose hereditary privilege it is

all the circumstances." But Demosthenes is here summing up his argument as to the dates only. See the clause just above, near the beginning of p. 359 (orig.), Τοὺς χρόνους ὑμῖν λογιοῦμαι καθ' οὓς ἐγίγνεθ' ἕκαστα.

[1] The Amphictyonic.

to take the lead in Greece, and not permit any proceeding of this kind.

The ruin which has fallen on the poor Phocians may be seen not only by these decrees, but by what has actually been done—a shocking and pitiable spectacle, O Athenians! On our late journey to Delphi[1] we were forced to see it all—houses razed to the ground, walls demolished, a country stripped of its adult population, a few women and little children and miserable old men. No language can come up to the wretchedness now existing there. I hear you all say, that once this people gave the opposite vote to the Thebans on the question of enslaving us.[2] How think ye then, O Athenians?—could your ancestors return to life, what vote or judgment would they pass upon the authors of this destruction? In my opinion, though they stoned them with their own hands, they would consider themselves pure. For is it not disgraceful—is it not, if possible, worse than disgraceful—that people who had then saved us, who gave the vote for our preservation, should have met with an opposite return through these men, and been suffered to incur greater misfortunes than any Greeks ever knew? Who then is the author of them? Who was the deceiver? Æschines—who but he?

For many things, men of Athens, might one felicitate Philip on his fortune, but for one thing with the greatest justice—one piece of luck which (by the gods and goddesses!) I don't think has fallen to any other man in our time. To have taken great cities and subdued a large territory, these and the like feats are wonderful, I allow, and splendid—how can they help being? Yet they have been achieved, it may be said, by many others. This however is a peculiar good fortune which has occurred to no other mortal—what?—That, when he wanted base men for his purposes, he found baser than he desired. Can we avoid holding such an opinion of these men, when falsehoods which Philip dared not utter in his own behalf, notwithstanding their importance to him—

[1] To the Amphictyonic meeting.

[2] In the council of war, after the capture of Athens by Lysander, when the Thebans proposed that Athens should be razed to the ground, and Attica thrown into pasture. See Xenophon, Hell. ii. 2. As to the phrase ψῆφον προτεθεῖσαν, see Schömann, De Comitiis, 104.

which he neither wrote in any letter nor commissioned any embassador to state—they lent themselves to for hire, and deceived you by them? Antipater and Parmenio, who were serving a master, and not likely to encounter you afterward, contrived not to be the instruments of your deception: yet embassadors appointed by the Athenian state, the freest in the world, had the hardiness to deceive you—you whom they were certain to look upon face to face, and to pass the remainder of their lives with, and before whom they would have to render an account of their conduct. Could any men be more wicked or abandoned?

To show that he is devoted by you to execration, that after such falsehoods you could not with any regard to sanctity or religion acquit him—recite the curse—read it from the law here.

[*The curse.*][1]

This imprecation, men of Athens, the crier pronounces on your behalf according to law in every assembly, and also before the council when it sits. Æschines can't say that he was not well acquainted with it: for as your clerk and servant to the council, he himself dictated this law to the crier. Would it not be a strange and monstrous proceeding, if what you enjoin, or rather request the gods to do in your behalf, you should fail to do yourselves when it is in your power today, and acquit a man whom you implore the gods to extirpate with his house and family? Don't think of such a thing. When a man escapes you, leave the gods to punish him: when you catch him yourselves, trouble them about him no more.

So far will he carry his impudence and audacity, I am told, that, leaving the facts of the case, his reports, his promises, his impostures upon the state, as if he were tried before some other people, and not before you who know it all, he will accuse first the Lacedæmonians, then the Phocians, then Hegesippus. But this is mockery, or rather abominable effrontery. For, whatever he may say now about the Phocians, or the Lacedæmonians or Hegesippus—that they would not receive Proxenus, that they are guilty of impiety, or any thing else against them surely it had all taken place before these embassadors returned, and was no obstacle to the Phocians being saved, as

[1] See page 102, note 2.

is said—by whom?—by Æschines the defendant himself. For he did not then report, that but for the Lacedæmonians, or but for their not receiving Proxenus, or but for Hegesippus, or but for this thing and the other, the Phocians would have been saved—No: he passed over all that, and said expressly that he had prevailed on Philip to save the Phocians, to re-people Bœotia, to arrange things to your advantage;[1] that it would all be accomplished in two or three days, and on that account the Thebans had set a price upon his head. Therefore, if he talks about what the Lacedæmonians or what the Phocians had done before he made these reports, don't listen to him nor hear a word; and don't suffer him to make charges of immorality against the Phocians. It was not for their merit that you rescued the Lacedæmonians formerly, or these accursed Eubœans, or many others, but because their safety was for the interest of the commonwealth, as that of the Phocians was lately. And what fault did the Phocians or the Lacedæmonians or yourselves or any other people commit after this man's statements, to cause the miscarriage of what he then told you? Ask him this: he won't be able to explain. There have been but five days in which he made his false report, you believed him, the Phocians got the news, yielded themselves up, and perished. From this, I imagine, it appears clearly, that the whole fraud and artifice was contrived for the purpose of destroying the Phocians. For in the interval after the peace, while Philip was unable to march, but was making preparations, he sent for the Lacedæmonians, and promised to do every thing for them, that the Phocians might not get them for auxiliaries through you. But when he arrived at Thermopylæ, and the Lacedæmonians perceiving the snare withdrew, he then put this man forward[2] to deceive you; for he

[1] Pabst: *Euch Einfluss auf die dortigen Angelegenheiten zu verschaffen.* Auger: "à vous rendre maîtres des affaires."

[2] Reiske in his Index gives the following explanation of the verb *προκαθιέναι*: "aliquem præmittere, summittere, subornare, qui ante tuum adventum omnia quæ tu parata velis præparet atque instruat; ut si tu exempli causâ fratrem in puteum demittas explorandi aut elimandi ergo, antequam tute temet eo demittas. Τοῦτον *προκαθῆκεν ἐξαπατᾶν ὑμᾶς*, ericulum facturum, possitne Philippus vobis imponere." Pabst renders it: *sandte er diesen Menschen wieder voran, um Euch listig zu betrügen.* Francis: "he secretly employed Æschines to deceive you."

feared, if you discovered that he was acting for the Thebans, he might get into war and delay and embarrassment, by the Phocians defending themselves and your assisting them, and he wished rather to complete his conquest without a struggle; which indeed has been the case. Don't then, because Philip deceived the Lacedæmonians and the Phocians also, let this man escape punishment for his deception of you. That would hardly be just.

If, to compensate for the Phocians and Thermopylæ and the rest of our losses, he alleges that the Chersonese is preserved to us, by heavens! men of the jury, don't admit the excuse; don't endure that, in addition to the injuries which you have sustained by the embassy, he should by his defense cast reproach upon the state, as if you made a reservation for certain of your own possessions, while you sacrificed the welfare of your allies. You did no such thing: for, after the peace was made and the Chersonese was in security, the Phocians were safe during the four ensuing months, and the falsehoods of this man afterward, by imposing on you, caused their ruin.[1] Besides, you will find the Chersonese is in greater danger now than it was then. For let me ask, would it have been easier to punish Philip for attacking it before he had snatched any of

[1] "Si quid cerno, argumentum hoc, cui tantum tribuit Demosthenes, parum aut nil valet. Ecquis enim non videt in arcanis Philippo cum Atheniensibus condictis, quæ non fuerunt publicata, hoc fuisse, ut Athenienses pro Cherrhoneso Phocidem Philippo permitterent? Et renuntiatio legationis falsa ab Æschine ad populum Atheniensem potuerunt esse meræ præstigiæ ad oculos Græciæ occæcandos et invidiam ab Atheniensibus avertendam commissæ erga socios proditionis. Tales mimi aguntur inter optimates. Quæ intra siparium fiunt, multum ab iis diversa sunt, quæ foris."—*Reiske.*

"Non cogitavit Reiskius Atheniensium illis temporibus publice, hoc est, in concionibus, talia transigentium esse non potuisse arcana πολιτεύματα. Quidquid igitur hoc in negotio fraudis fuit, commissum est a Philippo, non consciis Atheniensibus, sed parariis τοῖς παραπρεσβεύσασιν."—*Schaefer.*

Reiske was undoubtedly quite mistaken in his view of this transaction. There is not the slightest evidence of any instructions having been given by the Athenians to their ministers, to effect a peace with Philip by which their allies were intentionally sacrificed. They acted foolishly indeed and weakly, in suffering themselves to be deceived, and not seeing their real interests; and it is true also that they were prejudiced in some degree by the forms of their political government, by reason of which their embassadors were not sufficiently checked by a vigorous executive power.

these advantages from us, or is it easier now? I imagine it was much easier before. What sort of preservation then is it for the Chersonese, when he that would violate it is released from fear and danger?

I understand however, that he intends to say something of this kind—that he wonders how it is Demosthenes accuses him, and not any of the Phocians. It is better you should hear the explanation from me beforehand. Among the expatriated Phocians, the best and most respectable being in exile and consequent distress keep themselves quiet, and none of them would like to incur private hostility on account of the public misfortunes; while those who would do any thing for money can find no one to give it them. I certainly would not have feed any of them, to stand up for me here and cry out what they had suffered: for the truth and the facts cry out of themselves. As to the Phocian commonalty, they are in such a wretched and deplorable condition, that they have no thought of being prosecutors at Athenian audits, but are every one of them slaves, frightened to death at the Thebans and the mercenaries of Philip, whom they are forced to maintain, scattered themselves over villages, and deprived of their arms. Don't allow him then to use that argument, but make him show that the Phocians have not been ruined, or that he never promised that Philip would save them. These are the questions at the account of an embassy—What has been negotiated? what was your report? If true, take your acquittal; if false, pay the penalty. What matters it whether the Phocians are present or not? They are in such a plight, I fancy—and you did your best to bring them into it—they can neither help their friends nor punish their enemies.

But besides the general discredit and disgrace which these proceedings are attended with, it is easy to show that serious perils consequently menace the state. For which of you is ignorant that by the Phocian war, and the Phocians being masters of Thermopylæ, we were out of all apprehension from the Thebans; never could they or Philip make their way to Peloponnesus, nor to Eubœa, nor Attica? This security, which place and circumstances guaranteed to the commonwealth, you, trusting to the falsehoods and artifices of these men, abandoned; fortified though it was by arms, by continued war, by great cities of an allied people, and by an extensive territory, you suffered it to be overthrown.[1] And your former expedition to Thermopylæ has become fruitless, which cost you more than two hundred talents, reckoning the private expenses of those who served. Your hopes about the Thebans are fruitless also. But what, among many shameful services which this man has performed for Philip, involves really the most contemptuous treatment of the commonwealth, and all of you, I beg you to hear—it is this: that Philip having determined from the beginning to do all that he has done for the Thebans, Æschines, by reporting the contrary, and making it manifest that you were against what he did, has increased your enmity with the Thebans and their friendliness to Philip. How could a man have treated you more contumeliously?

Take and read the decree of Diophantus, and that of Callisthenes, to show you that when you performed your duties, you were recompensed with thanksgivings and praise both at Athens and elsewhere, but after you had been deluded by these men, you brought in your women and children from the country, and decreed to perform the Heraclean sacrifice within the city in time of peace: which makes me wonder whether you will let off with impunity a man who caused even the gods to be deprived of their customary worship. Read the decree.

[*The decree.*]

Thus worthily of your conduct, O Athenians, you voted then. Now read the next.

[*The decree.*]

Such was the vote you then passed through the conduct of these men; though it was not with such prospects that you

[1] The emendation of Reiske, who for καὶ χώρᾳ πολλῇ substitutes χώραν πολλήν, has met the approval of some critics, and among others, of Pabst, who thus renders the passage: *und ein durch Waffen und fortdauernden Krieg geschütztes Land, was mit bedeutenden Stadten und verbündeten Bewohnern bevölkert, und von ansenhlichem Umfange war, habt Irh ruhig, ohne es zu hindern, verheeren lassen.* I agree with Schaefer, that it is much better to preserve the old reading and understand ἀσφάλειαν as the subject of the whole sentence. The metaphor, he observes, is by no means harsh, but suitable to the dignity of the argument. And he refers to the famous passage τὸν δὲ τειχισμὸν τοῦτον, κ. τ. λ. (p. 325 Orig. and p. 108 in this volume.)

either originally concluded peace and alliance, or were afterward persuaded to insert the clause, "and to his posterity," but under the belief that through these men you would get marvelous benefits. You all know how often afterward you were alarmed by hearing of Philip's army and mercenaries in the neighborhood of Porthmus or Megara.[1] Therefore, though he may not yet have invaded Attic ground, it is not that you must look at, nor relax in your vigilance: you must see whether he has through these men got the opportunity of doing it when he pleases; this peril you must keep in view, and abhor and punish the guilty person who has furnished him with such opportunity.

I know indeed that Æschines will avoid all discussion of the charges against him; that, seeking to withdraw you as far as possible from the facts, he will rehearse what mighty blessings accrue to mankind from peace, and, on the other hand, what evils from war; in short, he will pronounce a panegyric on peace, and take up that line of defense. Yet even these are so many arguments to convict him. For if the cause of blessings to others has been the cause of so many troubles and such confusion to us, what else can one suppose, but that by taking bribes these men have spoiled a thing in its own nature excellent?

Oh, but—he may say perhaps—have you not preserved, and won't you preserve through the peace three hundred galleys, with stores for them and money?—In regard to this you must understand, that Philip's resources likewise have been largely augmented through the peace, in supplies of arms, in territory, in revenues, of which he has gained an abundance. True, some have come in to us also. But that establishment of power and alliances, through which people hold their good things either for themselves or their superiors[2]—ours has been sold by these men, and gone to ruin

[1] See vol. i. pp. 119, 128.

[2] Schaefer explains it: "*Potentioribus*, ubi aut unus regnat, aut oligarchis civitas subjecta est." Pabst renders it thus: *durch welchen einst Alle, theils für sich, theils für einen mächtigern Staat, Güter und Vortheile gewonnen haben.* And with this latter interpretation I agree. Thus the whole Athenian empire is that establishment of power and alliances, *κατασκευὴ πραγμάτων καὶ συμμάχων*, through which the Lemnians, Imbrians, and other subject people, hold what they have, (their country, their harbors, their revenues, &c.,) partly for themselves,

and decay;[1] his hath become formidable and mightier by far. It is not just, that Philip should through these men have augmented both his alliances and his revenues, while what Athens must naturally have gained by the peace they set off against what was sold by themselves. The one has not come to us in exchange for the other—very far from it: one we should equally have had, and the other in addition, but for these men.

Speaking generally, men of Athens, I presume you will agree, that on the one hand, however many and grievous have been the misfortunes of the commonwealth, if Æschines be not to blame for any, your resentment ought not to fall upon him; and, on the other hand, if any advantages have been achieved through others, they ought not to save him. Consider what the defendant has been the cause of; look favorably on him, if favor he deserves, but with anger, if he has done aught to excite it. How will you ascertain the truth of the matter? In this way—you must not let him confound all things together—the misdeeds of the generals, the war with Philip, the blessings of peace—but you must consider each point by itself. For example—Was Philip at war with us? He was. Does any man complain of Æschines on that account? Would any man wish to arraign him for the transactions of the war? No man. Well then; upon those points he is acquitted, and has no need to say any thing: for it is a defendant's business to produce witnesses and proofs upon the matters in issue, not to mystify the court by pleading

partly for the Athenians, who are at the head of the empire. The power of the general confederacy supports every constituent part of it.

[1] On the expression, *ἀπόλωλε καὶ γέγονεν ἀσθενὴς*, Schaefer observes: "Gravius præcedit, sequitur levius. Sic passim Orator. *'Απώλλυε καὶ ἐλυμαίνετο*, p. 119. *'Απόλωλε καὶ νενόσηκεν*, p. 121. *'Απόλωλε καὶ διέφθαρται*, p. 372. Qualia non mirer si nostris Technicis parum probentur. Sed Critici caveant, ne hæc similiaque transponendo corrumpant: nam sunt longè sanissima."

See my observations about Anti-climaxes, p. 18, n. 2. In the ancient writings, both Greek and Roman, the weaker word or clause often follows to explain or qualify the preceding. Compare Virgil, Æneid II. 353,—

> Moriamur et in media arma ruamus;

and Æneid VII. 50,—

> Filius huic fato Divûm prolesque virilis
> Nulla fuit, primâque oriens erepta juventâ est.

what no one disputes. Mind then, that you say nothing about the war; for no one charges you with any thing concerning it. Afterward certain persons advised us to make peace; we followed their advice; we sent embassadors; they brought people to Athens to conclude peace. Here again, does any one blame Æschines for this? No one. Does any man say that he introduced the question of peace, or is guilty of crime for having brought people here to conclude it? No man. No more should he say any thing about the fact of our concluding peace: for he is not chargeable with it.

What then do you say, man?—suppose I were asked—from what point do you commence your accusation? From this, men of Athens—when, at the time you were deliberating, not whether you should make peace or no, (for that had already been resolved upon,) but what sort of a peace you should have, he opposed the men who offered honest advice, and supported the mover of a corrupt resolution, himself being bribed; and afterward, on being chosen to receive the oaths, he entirely neglected your instructions, destroyed those allies who had come safe through the whole war, and told such huge falsehoods as no mortal ever did either before or after. At first indeed, until Philip got leave to negotiate for peace, Ctesiphon and Aristodemus commenced the beginning of the plot; but when things were ripe for execution, they handed it over to Philocrates and the defendant, who took up the matter and ruined every thing. Now that he must render an account of what has been done, and stand his trial for it, the defendant, I imagine, like a rascally and abominable clerk[1] as he is, will plead his defense as if he were tried for the peace—not that he may render an account of more than he is accused of; that were madness—but he sees, that in his own conduct there is nothing good and every thing criminal, while a defense of peace, if it have nothing else about it, has in name at least a show of humanity. I fear indeed, O

[1] In Bekker's edition *καὶ* stands before *γραμματεὺς*, which appears to be thrown in as an additional term of reproach. And so Reiske understands it: "erat convicium usurpatum pro nomine vilissimâ stirpe, quæstûs sordidi, versuto, impuro, scelerato, audaci." Schaefer dissents from this view, and expunges *καί*. Demosthenes does often refer to the early occupation of Æschines, but rather contemptuously than by way of strong reproach. Where he means the latter, he adds an epithet, as *ὄλεθρος γραμματεύς*. See page 80, note 2.

Athenians, I fear, that without knowing it, like persons who borrow money, we are enjoying the peace at a high rate: for these men betrayed what constituted its strength and security, the Phocians and Thermopylæ. However, it was not through the defendant we originally made it: for what I am about to say is strange, yet perfectly true—if any one is really glad of the peace, let him thank the generals for it, whom all accuse. Had they carried on the war as you desired, the very name of peace would have been intolerable to you. Peace therefore is owing to them: perilous and unstable and insecure has it become through these men having taken bribes. Bar him then, bar him from any argument in favor of peace, and put him to his defense for what he has done. For Æschines is not tried for the peace; no: the peace is discredited through Æschines. Here is the proof—if the peace had been concluded without any deception being afterward practiced on you, or any of your allies being ruined, what mortal would the peace have aggrieved, independently of its being dishonorable? Of this indeed the defendant was in part the cause, by supporting Philocrates: nothing fatal however would have taken place. Now, I conceive, he is answerable for a great deal.

That these men have shamefully and basely wrought all this ruin and mischief, I suppose you are all satisfied. I however, men of the jury, am so far from entering upon these questions in a vexatious spirit, or wishing you to do so, that if it has all been brought about through thoughtlessness or good nature or any kind of ignorance, I acquit Æschines myself and I advise you also. Though indeed none of these excuses is constitutional or just, for no one is required or compelled by you to perform public business; but when a man has persuaded himself of his ability and applies for it, you, acting the part of worthy and benevolent people, receive him with favor and without envy; you elect him, and put your affairs into his hands. Then if a man be successful, he will be honored and have an advantage over the bulk of the people in this respect; if he fails, shall he set up excuses and apologies? That would not be fair. It would be no satisfaction to our ruined allies or to their wives or children or any other parties, that my incapacity (not to say the defendant's) had brought such misfortune upon them—far from it indeed. However, you may forgive Æschines these dreadful and monstrous things, if it appears that he has damaged the cause through stupidity or any kind of ignorance: but if he has done it from a base motive, having received money and presents, and if he is clearly convicted by the facts themselves, put him to death if it be possible, or if that can not be, make him a living example to others. Now consider in your minds, how convincing the proof of his guilt will be.

I presume that Æschines the defendant must have addressed those speeches to you, those about the Phocians and Thespiæ and Eubœa, (supposing he was not from a corrupt motive intentionally playing false,) from one of two causes; either because he had heard Philip expressly promise to effect and do the things in question, or else because he was charmed and beguiled by Philip's general liberality, and therefore expected those things from him also. There is no other alternative. Now in either of these cases he ought beyond all other men to detest Philip. Why? Because, so far as it depended on Philip, he has suffered the utmost indignity and disgrace. He has deceived you; he has become infamous; he is judged to be a lost man, if he had his deserts.[1] Had due proceedings been taken, he would have been impeached long ago; but now through your simplicity and good nature he attends his audit, and chooses his time for it. Is there one of you who has heard the voice of Æschines accusing Philip?—who has seen him pressing any charge or speaking to the point? No one. Every Athenian is more ready to accuse Philip—any indeed that you like—though none of them assuredly has sustained any personal injury. I should have expected language like this from him, if he had not sold himself—"Men of Athens, deal with me as you please: I believed, I was deluded, I was in error, I confess it: but beware of the man, O Athenians: he is not to be trusted, he is a juggler, a villain. See you not how he has treated me? how he has cajoled me?" I hear no language of this kind, nor do you. Why? Because he was not cajoled or deceived, but had hired himself and taken money when he made those statements, and betrayed you to Philip, and has been a good, true

[1] According to Bekker's reading, *δικαίως*. But I rather incline to *δίκαιος*, with Wolf and Schaefer.

and faithful hireling to him, but a traitorous embassador and citizen to you, deserving to perish not once but three times over.

Nor is this the only proof that he was bribed to make all those statements. There came to you lately some envoys from Thessaly, and some of Philip's with them, requiring you to acknowledge Philip as an Amphictyon. Now of all men who was most especially bound to oppose them? Æschines here. Why? Because his reports to you were contradicted by Philip's acts. This man said that he would fortify Thespiæ and Platæa, and not destroy the Phocians, but humble the insolence of the Thebans: whereas Philip has made the Thebans greater than they should be, the Phocians he has utterly destroyed; and instead of fortifying Thespiæ and Platæa, he has reduced Orchomenus and Coronea also to slavery. How could any things be more contrary to one another? Yet he opposed them not; he never opened his mouth or uttered a word against them. And this, bad as it is, is not the worst:—he spoke on their side, he and no other person in the state. Even the profligate Philocrates ventured not to do this; Æschines, the man before you, did: and when you clamored and refused to hear him, he came down from the platform, and said, showing himself off to Philip's embassadors who were present—"There were many to clamor, but few to fight when it was needful:" this you surely remember—he himself doubtless being a wonderful soldier, O Jupiter!

Yet more—if we were unable to show that any of the embassadors had got any thing, and it was not plain enough for all men to see, we must have resorted to question by torture[1] and the like. But if Philocrates not only confessed his gains frequently in your assembly, but even displayed them before you, selling wheat, building houses, declaring that he would

[1] This refers to the practice, common not only in criminal but also in civil proceedings at Athens, of examining slaves by torture. The parties to a cause were at liberty either to give up their own slaves to be examined in this way, or to demand those of the adversary; and though it was not compulsory to give up a slave, the refusal might be attributed to fear of the truth coming out. No slave was admissible as a witness, except on this condition; such was the degraded state to which men were reduced by servitude in Greece. On the other hand, it was not lawful to apply the torture to freemen, except under extraordinary circumstances, when the necessities of the commonwealth required it.

make his journey,[1] whether you elected him or not, importing timber, changing gold openly at the banks; he surely can not deny that he has had money, he that himself makes a confession and display of it. Then is there any man so senseless or infatuate, that, to procure money for Philocrates, and bring discredit and danger upon himself, when he might appear in the ranks of the innocent, he would rather be at enmity with them, and side with Philocrates to be prosecuted? There is no such man, I believe. All these, if you examine them rightly, O Athenians, you will find to be clear and ample proofs that Æschines has taken bribes.

A thing which has last occurred, but is as good a proof as any that he has sold himself to Philip, I beg you to consider. You know of course, that when Hyperides lately impeached Philocrates, I came forward and said, I was dissatisfied with one point in the impeachment, if it alleged that Philocrates had alone been guilty of so many grave misdemeanors, and the other nine embassadors were entirely innocent. And I declared it was not so; for he by himself would have been of no account, if he had not had some of these men to co-operate with him. "However," said I, "that I may neither acquit nor accuse any man, but that facts themselves may discover the guilty, and clear those who are not implicated, let any man that pleases get up and declare before you, that he has no concern in the acts of Philocrates, and approves them not. And whoever does so, I will acquit him," I said. This you remember, I suppose. Well: no one came forward or showed himself. And the rest have each an excuse: one was not accountable; one perhaps was not present; another had a son-in-law yonder.[2] The defendant however has no such

[1] *I. e.* to Macedonia. When Philocrates said this does not appear. In the construction I follow Auger and Pabst. But Francis connects *ξυληγῶν* with *βαδιεῖσθαι*.

Philip had abundance of timber in the Macedonian forests, of which he made presents to his friends at Athens and elsewhere. Compare the passages which follow in this oration, pp. 386, 426.

[2] This, according to Ulpian, is a piece of bitter irony against Phrynon, who is accused by Demosthenes of prostituting his own son to the king of Macedon. Taylor, Reiske, Francis, and Pabst adopt Ulpian's interpretation. Others read *ἐκεῖνος*, meaning Philocrates. Schaefer thinks that the supposed reflection upon Phrynon would be beneath the dignity of an orator. The charge itself is distinctly made at page 412 (Orig.).

reason. So completely hath he sold himself, and not only received wages for past services, but makes it plain that hereafter, should he now get off, he will help Philip against you, that, to avoid letting fall even a word in opposition to Philip, he accepts not even acquittal when we offer it, but chooses to incur infamy, prosecution, any kind of indignity at Athens, rather than do any thing to give Philip displeasure.

But what is this connection, this over-anxiety for Philocrates? Had he done ever such great things, and got every advantage by his diplomacy, yet, if he confessed having made money by it, as he does confess, this is the very thing[1] from which an incorrupt embassador should have kept himself aloof and clear, and protested against it for his own part. Æschines however has not done so. Are not these facts plain, men of Athens? Don't they cry aloud, that Æschines has taken bribes and is a scoundrel systematically for lucre's sake, not in thoughtlessness, nor in ignorance, nor by reason of failures?

And what witness proves that I have taken bribes?—says he. This is his grand point.—The facts, Æschines, which are the surest of all things; and it is impossible to charge or allege, that they are what they are in obedience or out of favor to any person. No: just what your treason and mischief has made them, they on examination appear to be. But in addition to the facts, you shall bear testimony against yourself immediately. Come, stand up and answer me.[2] You can't urge that from inexperience you have nothing to say. You that conduct new prosecutions, like new dramas, and win them without witnesses even, in the division of a day, you must surely be a prodigy of an orator.[3]

[1] That is, the money-making, as I understand it. But Schaefer refers it to the connection with Philocrates, *τὴν κοινωνίαν καὶ τὴν πολλὴν πρόνοιαν ὑπὲρ Φιλοκράτους.*

[2] The question does not follow, probably because Æschines did not step forward to intimate that he was ready to answer questions.

[3] "He alludes to the extraordinary prosecution of Timarchus, unsupported by evidence, and founded only upon general reports of the impurity of his life. He alludes also to the theatrical profession of Æschines, who treated such prosecutions as if they were only dramatic performances, but in which however he is allowed to have performed a principal character, and to have appeared a very powerful orator."—*Francis.*

Taylor supposes *καινοὺς* to refer to the first appearance of Æschines

Many dreadful things hath Æschines the defendant perpetrated, involving a high degree of baseness, as I think you will agree; yet there is nothing in my judgment so dreadful as what I am about to mention; nothing that will so palpably convict him of having taken bribes and sold every thing.

When you were for the third time again dispatching envoys to Philip, under those great and splendid expectations which the defendant had held out, you elected him and me and most of the others the same as before. I came forward directly and excused myself,[1] and when certain persons clamored and called on me to go, I declared I would not leave Athens: the defendant had then been elected. After the assembly had broken up, these men met and consulted whom they should

as prosecutor in a court of justice; but it refers rather to the novelty of the proceeding itself, as Francis understands it. The credit due to Æschines was enhanced by the circumstance that he had a very limited time allowed him to plead in. This may have been for the reason assigned by Reiske, that the causes for that day were so numerous, they were obliged to circumscribe the time for each. Or perhaps the time allowed for that species of trial (viz. a δοκιμασία) was shorter than for ordinary causes. Harpocration explains διαμεμετρημένη ἡμέρα by stating, that the whole time for a cause was divided by the Clepsydra into three portions,—one for each of the parties, and one for the jury. Whether such explanation suits this passage may be doubtful. Demosthenes seems rather to speak of something out of the common course, or there would be no point in the words πρὸς δ. τ. ἡ. I understand πρὸς in the sense of "against," the limitation of time being an adverse circumstance against which the orator had to contend: so we say, "to speak against time." Francis takes these words in quite a different sense. His version is: "which were of such importance as to demand a particular day for their determination." Pabst: *in abgemessenen Tagestunden.*

Auger translates the whole passage as follows: "Puisque dans un temps limité vous plaidez des causes toutes neuves avec l'art d'un poëte qui compose un drame, et que vous les gagnez sans le secours des temoins; peut-on douter un moment de la subtilité de votre éloquence?"

As to the Clepsydra, see p. 59, note 1. And as to πάνδεινος, see p. 90, note 2.

[1] Literally: "excused myself on oath—swore off." As Francis has it: "declared upon oath I could not accept the employment." A man desirous of excusing himself from such an appointment as the one in question was obliged to assign some reason for it, as illness or the like, and to put in an affidavit stating such reason. The affidavit was called ἐξωμοσία, and was recorded. It would appear from this passage, that almost any formal excuse was admitted.

leave behind: for, while things were yet in suspense and the future was uncertain, conferences and discussions of all kinds took place in the market; they feared therefore that an extraordinary assembly[1] might be convened on a sudden, that you might hear the truth from me, and pass some proper resolutions in favor of the Phocians, and so things would slip out of Philip's hands. Indeed, had you but voted and shown them a glimpse of hope, they would have been saved. For impossible, impossible was it for Philip to remain, if you had not been tricked; as there was neither any grain in the country, it not having been sown on account of the war, nor could any grain be brought while your galleys were there and commanded the sea; and the Phocian cities were numerous and hard to take, except by a long siege; for if he took a city in a day, they are twenty-two in number. For all these reasons, that you might not change the course into which you had been entrapped, they left Æschines at home. Well, but to excuse himself without some ground was dangerous, and fraught with suspicion.—"What say you? aren't you going, after these mighty advantages of your own announcing, and won't you be on the embassy?"—Still it was necessary to stay. How to act then?—He pretends to be ill, and his brother, taking Execestus the physician and going to the council, made affidavit of the defendant's illness, and was himself appointed. Five or six days after, when the Phocians had been destroyed, and this man's hire had come to an end like any thing else, and Dercylus had returned from Chalcis, and reported to you, in assembly at Piræus, that the Phocians were destroyed, and you, men of Athens, naturally on receiving that intelligence were smitten with compassion for them and terror on your own account, and passed a vote to bring in your women and children from the country, and to repair the garrisons and fortify Piræus, and offer the Heraclean sacrifice within the city,—in this state of things, when the commonwealth was in the midst of such confusion and alarm, this clever and powerful and loud-voiced orator, without any appointment by the council or the people, went off as embassador to the author of all the mischief, taking into account neither the illness on which he grounded his excuse, nor the fact that another embassador had been chosen in his stead,

[1] See Appendix V.

nor that the law provides the penalty of death for such conduct, nor how monstrous it was, after reporting that a price had been set upon his head in Thebes, when the Thebans had in addition to the lordship of all Bœotia become masters also of the Phocian territory, to take a journey then to the heart of Thebes and the Theban camp: so insane was he, so intent upon his pelf and reward, that in defiance and despite of all these considerations he took himself off.

Such is the character of this proceeding: but what he did on his arrival there is far more shocking. For when all of you here, and the Athenians in general, considered the poor Phocians so shamefully and cruelly treated, that you would not send either members[1] of the council or the judges to represent you at the Pythian games, but abstained from your customary deputation to the festival, Æschines went to the sacrifice which Philip and the Thebans offered in honor of their success and conquest, and was feasted, and joined in the libations and prayers which Philip offered up in thanksgiving for the lost fortresses and territory and troops of your allies, and donned the garland and sang the pæan in company with Philip, and pledged to him the cup of friendship.

Nor is it possible that I should state the matter thus, and the defendant otherwise. With respect to the affidavit, there is an entry in your public register in the temple of Cybele, which is given in charge to the superintendent, and a decree has been specially drawn concerning that name.[2] With respect

[1] The Athenians, as well as all the other people who belonged to the Hellenic community, sent deputies regularly to the great periodical festivals—the Olympian, Pythian, Isthmian, and Nemean. These deputies represented the state, and it would appear that certain members of the council, and of the six junior archons, (whom I call in my translation the judges,) or at least persons chosen from one or the other of these bodies, formed part of the deputation. They were called Θεωροί, which name signifies simply "spectators," derived from *θέα, a spectacle,* unless we adopt the explanation of Pollux, who derives it from *θεὸς* and *ὤρα*, as if it properly designated parties concerned in some divine service or ceremony. The common uses of the word *θεωρεῖν* and its derivatives perhaps favor the former derivation, though it is true that the spectacles which these deputies were sent to attend partook always of a religious character; and persons dispatched on more purely religious missions—as to consult an oracle, or the like—received the same appellation. For further information, see the Archæological Dictionary, title *Theori*. Pabst translates the word, *Festgesandte*.

[2] A decree (probably of the council) was drawn up, ordering the name

to his doings yonder, there will be evidence against him by his colleagues and persons present, who told the particulars to me; for I did not go with them on the embassy, but excused myself. Now read me the decree and the register, and call the witnesses.

[*The Decree. The Public Register. The Witnesses.*]

What prayer do you suppose Philip offered to the gods when he poured his libation? What do you suppose the Thebans? Did they not pray for might and victory in battle for them and their allies; the contrary for the allies of the Phocians? Well then; Æschines joined in that prayer, and invoked a curse upon his country, which you ought now to make recoil upon his head.

He departed therefore in violation of the law which makes such an act punishable with death: on his arrival, it has been shown, he did what he deserves to die for a second time: and his former acts and measures in this behalf[1] as embassador will justify his execution. Consider then what penalty there can be of severity enough to be deemed adequate to all his crimes. For would it not be shameful, O Athenians, that you and the whole people should publicly condemn all the proceedings consequent upon the peace, and refuse to take any part in Amphictyonic business, and regard Philip with displeasure and distrust, because the proceedings are impious and shocking, opposed at the same time to your interests and to justice; yet, when you have come into court to adjudicate at the audit of these matters, a sworn jury on behalf of the commonwealth, you should acquit the author of all the mischief, whom you have caught in the very act when his guilt was complete? And which of your fellow-citizens, or

of Æschines to be expunged from the list of embassadors, and that of his brother to be substituted.

[1] *Ὑπὲρ τοὺτων.* "Dubium est, ad quos referatur, Philippumne et Thebanos, *pro his*, an ad Athenienses, *horum nomine*."—*Reiske.* "Posterius malim."—*Schaefer.*

There is a difficulty about either of these interpretations. If it meant the Athenians, we should rather expect *ὑμῶν*; if Philip and the Thebans, *ἐκείνων*. I am therefore more inclined to the explanation suggested by Wolf: *τῶν νῦν γεγενημένων ἐν Φωκεῦσι.* If Schaefer is right, we must suppose Demosthenes to be making a sort of computation to himself, instead of directly addressing the jury.

rather of the Greeks at large, will not have reason to complain of you, seeing that you are wroth with Philip, who, in the transition from war to a treaty of peace, purchased his advantages from those that would sell them, a thing very venial in him; yet you will acquit this man, who so disgracefully sold your interests, although the laws prescribe the heaviest penalties for such conduct.

Perhaps however an argument of the following kind may be advanced by these men—that it will cause enmity with Philip, if you convict the embassadors who negotiated peace. If this be true, I can't imagine any thing stronger to be urged against the defendant. For if the man who expended money to obtain the peace has now become so formidable and mighty that you must disregard your oaths and obligations, and consider only what you can do to gratify Philip, in what way can the authors of such a result be sufficiently punished? Though I think indeed I can show, that it will more probably lead to a friendship advantageous for you. For it should be understood, men of Athens, that Philip does not despise your commonwealth, and did not prefer the Thebans to you, because he thought you less capable of serving him; but he was instructed by these men and informed—as I told you once before in the assembly, and none of them contradicted me—"that the people[1] is of all things the most unstable and

[1] The word "people," notwithstanding a little ambiguity, is preferable to "populace," or "mob," because it increases the odium sought to be thrown upon Æschines, that he spoke thus disrespectfully of the sovereign people of Athens by the very name that constitutionally belonged to them. The comparison in the text reminds one of the famous simile in Virgil, Æneid I. 148. The fickleness of the *vulgus infidum* has been a theme for innumerable orators and poets. Even Jack Cade exclaims, after he has been deserted by his followers, "Was ever feather so lightly blown to and fro as this multitude?"—*Henry VI.* Part II. Act IV. Sc. 8.

Shilleto cites Cicero pro Muren. 17 (35), pro Planc. 6 (15), Liv. xxviii. 27, and the following passage from Clarendon's History of the Rebellion:—"The Duke of Buckingham was utterly ignorant of the ebbs and floods of popular councils, and of the winds that move those waters."

Of the words *οἱον αὐτὸς δή* he gives the following explanation in the same note:—"It is for his advantage to have ready at hand certain friends who will transact and manage every thing for him with you, for instance, myself (the speaker)."—So Dobree nearly: "Your Majesty," say these persons, "wants able managers" (each of them of course meaning such a one as himself).

The same was my own impression originally, and it was with some

inconstant, like a restless wind in the sea, put in motion by any accident—one comes and another goes; no one cares for the public interests, or keeps them in mind—he should have friends to transact every thing for him with you, and manage just as he would himself: if that were contrived for him, he would accomplish all that he desired with you easily."—If he had heard, I fancy, that the persons who used such language to him then had immediately after their return home been cudgelled to death, he would have done the same as the Persian king. What did the Persian king? He had been deceived by Timagoras, and given him forty talents, as report says; but when he heard that Timagoras[1] had been put to death at Athens, and had not the means even to insure his own safety, much less to perform his late promise to him, he saw that he had not given his fee to the party with whom the power rested. So, in the first place, he made Amphipolis again your subject, which before he had registered as his own ally and friend;[2] and, in the next place, he never afterward gave money to any man. And Philip would have done the

hesitation that I took a different view. There is an awkwardness in the change from the plural τούτων to the singular αὐτός. Again, it would be clumsy to make αὐτὸς refer to the speaker, when there is an αὐτῷ so close both before and after it referring to Philip. And there would be a little difficulty in the construction. It is true, there is some harshness in the other method. I should prefer reading οἵ' ἄν.

[1] As to this story, see p. 130, note 2.

[2] I adhere to Bekker's reading, and understand it thus: "Artaxerxes, seeing the fate of Timagoras, sought to conciliate the people of Athens by acknowledging their right to the possession of Amphipolis, which before he had treated as independent, and registered in the archives of the kingdom as his own ally. When he made such acknowledgment does not appear. After the embassy of Pelopidas to Susa, the Persian king sent a letter to Greece, containing the terms on which he desired a general peace to be established. This was publicly read at Thebes, at which city the Greek states had been invited to hold a congress, the Thebans hoping to be placed in the same situation as the Lacedæmonians had been at the peace of Antalcidas. The king's wishes were entirely in favor of Thebes, and there was a clause in the letter which virtually required the disarming of the Athenian naval power. The Athenians however and the Greeks in general refused to abide by the terms which Artaxerxes sought to impose; and it may be that he, on receiving intelligence of this, as well as of the execution of Timagoras, and the probability of some new combination among the Greek states, which might increase the influence of Athens, adopted a different tone, and expressed his willingness to consent to a different settlement of affairs, acknowledging (among other things) her title to Amphipolis.

same, if he had seen any of these men punished; and now, if he sees it, he will do so. But when he hears that they enjoy reputation among you as speakers, as prosecutors of other men, what should he do? Seek to incur large expenses, when he may incur less, and volunteer to court all, instead of two or three? Why, he would be mad.

Even the Thebans Philip had no desire to serve as a people —far from it; but he was persuaded by the embassadors, and I will tell you in what manner. Embassadors came to him from Thebes, at the same time that we were there from you. He offered them money, and (according to their statement) a great deal. The Theban envoys would not accept or receive it. Afterward at a certain sacrifice or banquet, when Philip was drinking and making himself agreeable to them, he offered them over the cup divers things, such as captives and the like, and lastly some gold and silver goblets. All these things they rejected, and would in no way compromise themselves. At length Philon, one of the embassadors, made a speech worthy, O Athenians, to have been spoken not on behalf of the Thebans, but on yours. He said he was delighted and rejoiced to see Philip liberally and generously disposed to them: they, for their part, were his friends already without those gifts; but they desired him to apply his generosity to the affairs of the commonwealth, in which he was then engaged,[1] and to do something worthy both of himself and the Thebans; and they promised then that the whole commonwealth as well as themselves would be attached to him. Now only see what has come of this, what events have happened, to the Thebans; and consider in good sooth, what an important thing it is not to sell the interests of the state. First, they have obtained peace when they were distressed and harassed by the war and getting the worst of it; secondly, their enemies the Phocians have been utterly destroyed, and all their fortifications and cities demolished. Is that all? No indeed! Besides that they have Orchomenus, Coronea, Corsiæ, Tilphossæum, as much of the Phocian territory as they please. Such advantages have the Thebans gained by the peace: greater they could not wish for, I

[1] ἐν οἷς ἦν τότε. So Francis: "which were then before him." It is possible however, that ἡ πόλις may be the nominative to ἦν, and thus Auger has taken it.

imagine: but what have the Theban embassadors gained? The advantage of having done so much for their country—that is all; but that is honorable and glorious, O Athenians, in regard to praise and renown, which these men bartered away for gold.

Now let me contrast what the Athenian commonwealth has gained by the peace, and what the Athenian embassadors; and see if the commonwealth and these men themselves have fared alike. To the commonwealth the result has been, that she has relinquished all her possessions and all her allies, and has sworn to Philip, that, should any one else interfere ever to preserve them, you will prevent it, and will regard the person who wishes to restore them to you as an adversary and a foe, the person who has deprived you of them as an ally and a friend. These are the terms which Æschines the defendant supported, and his coadjutor Philocrates proposed; and when I prevailed on the first day and had persuaded you to confirm the resolution[1] of your allies, and to summon Philip's embassadors, the defendant drove it off to the following day, and persuaded you to adopt the decree of Philocrates, in which these clauses, and many others yet more shameful, are contained. To the state then such consequences have resulted from the peace:—consequences more disgraceful could not easily be found: but what to the embassadors who caused them? I pass by all the other matters which you have seen—houses—timber—grain; but in the territory of our ruined allies they have estates and farms of large extent, bringing in to Philocrates an income of a talent, to Æschines here thirty minas. Is it not shocking and dreadful, O Athenians, that the misfortunes of your allies have become a source of revenue to your embassadors; that the same peace has to the country which sent them proved to be destruction of allies, cession of dominions, disgrace instead of honor, while to the embassadors, who wrought these mischiefs to the country, it

[1] Schaefer interprets this, "decretum de sociis," taking it, I suppose, to mean the decree of the Athenians that all the allies should be included in the peace; as to which see page 391 (orig.). But there had been a resolution passed by the deputies of the allies themselves, then assembled at Athens, which Demosthenes says he supported. See page 345 (orig.). To this he refers again.

For further particulars on the subject, the reader is referred to Appendix I.

has produced revenues, resources, estates, riches, in exchange for extreme indigence? To prove the truth of my statements, call me the Olynthian witnesses.

[*Witnesses.*]

I shall not be surprised however, if he ventures to say something of this kind—that it was not possible to conclude the peace honorably or in the manner I desired, as the generals had conducted the war badly. Should he say this, pray remember to ask him, whether he went embassador from any other state, or from this only. If he went from another, which he can say had been victorious in war and possessed generals of ability, he has taken money with good reason:[1] but if he went from this, why on a treaty, where the state which sent him renounced her own rights, did he receive presents into the bargain? The state which sent the embassy should have got the same advantages as her embassadors, if any justice were done.

And again, consider this, men of Athens,—Which, think ye, more prevailed in the war, the Phocians over the Thebans, or Philip over you? I am quite clear, the Phocians over the Thebans. They held Orchomenus and Coronea and Tilphossæum, and had cut off the Theban force at Neones,[2] and had slain two hundred and seventy at Hedyleum, and a trophy was erected, and their cavalry were masters of the field, and an Iliad[3] of misfortunes beset the Thebans. You had suffered nothing of the kind, and I trust you never may: the worst

[1] The argument is somewhat lame. The point of it is, that there is more excuse when a minister of the victorious party is bribed to make concessions to the enemy, than when a minister of the vanquished party does the same thing. The former only diminishes his country's gain, the other augments his country's loss. The moral delinquency is the same in both cases; the positive mischief done may be less in the latter case.

[2] A city of Phocis, also called Neon. Reiske prefers the reading of *αὐτῶν*, with which the meaning is,—"they had recovered their own troops captured at Neon." Auger, Francis, and Pabst adopt that reading; but it does not so well suit this passage, where the orator is recounting the positive disasters inflicted on the Thebans.

[3] The expression "Iliad of misfortunes" was proverbial, and is plain enough.

Shilleto cites Cicero ad Attic. VIII. 11,—"Tanta malorum impendet Ἰλιάς." And Ovid, II. Epist. ex Pont. 7:—

Ilias est fatis longa futura meis.

thing in the war with Philip was, that you could not do him harm when you desired; but you were perfectly secure against being damaged yourselves. How comes it then, that by the same peace the Thebans, who were so much beaten in the war, have recovered their own possessions and won those of their enemies, while you, the Athenians, have lost in time of peace even what was preserved in war? It is because their interests were not sold by their embassadors, while these men have bartered yours away. That such has been the character of these transactions, you will learn yet more clearly from what follows.[1]

When this treaty of Philocrates, which the defendant spoke in favor of, was concluded, and Philip's embassadors had received the oaths and departed, (and up to this point no incurable mischief had been done, but, though the peace was dishonorable and unworthy of the state, yet we were to have those wonderful advantages by way of compensation,) I asked your leave,[2] and urged these men to sail with the utmost speed for the Hellespont, and not to sacrifice or let Philip get possession of any of the places there in the interval. For I knew well, that whatever is sacrificed in the transition from war to peace is lost to the neglectful parties: for when once people have made up their minds on the whole for peace, they won't renew the war for what has been abandoned, but that remains the property of the captors. Besides, I believed the state would be sure to get one of two advantages, if we sailed;—for either, we being on the spot and having sworn him according to the decree, he would restore the places which he had taken from the republic, and forbear to attack

[1] The preceding clause, which Bekker has included in brackets, and which does not appear to fit the passage, I have omitted, as Francis has. Auger's translation shows how little it suits the context, though he tries to make it more intelligible by expansion: "Contre la vérité des faits qui précedent, Eschine aura le front de dire que vos alliés étoient fatigués et harassés par le guerre. Au reste, vous verrez encore mieux, par ce qui suit, que vos députés, gagnés par l'or de Philippe, ont prévariqué dans leur embassade."

[2] So Schaefer rightly explains ἠξίουν ὑμᾶς: and Auger: "Je demandois au peuple." But it must not be understood of a request to the assembly, but rather of an application to the proper authorities, as the generals, or the council, to expedite the preparations for sail, provide the traveling expenses, &c.

the rest, or, if he did not, we should immediately report it to Athens; and so you, seeing his rapacity and perfidy in those distant and less important matters, would not be careless about these more important and nearer home—I mean the Phocians and Thermopylæ: on the other hand, if he had not captured those places and you had not been tricked, all your interests would be secure, and your just demands cheerfully accorded by him. And I had reason for supposing it would be so. For if the Phocians were safe, as they were then, and masters of Thermopylæ, Philip could have held out no threat to prevent your insisting upon any of your rights: neither a land march nor a victory by sea would have opened him the road to Attica, while you, if he refused to give you satisfaction, would instantly close his ports, and again reduce him to distress for money and to a state of general blockade; so that he would be the party dependent on the benefits of peace, not you. That I am not now inventing and assuming the merit of these things after the event, but that they were perceived by me at the time, and foreseen on your behalf and communicated to these men, I will now give you the proof:—As all the assemblies had been exhausted,[1] and therefore no new one could be had, and these men were not gone, but lingering here, I as councilor frame a decree, (the people having given full power to the council,) ordering the embassadors to depart without delay, and the general Proxenus to convey them to whatever place they should hear Philip was in; and I drew it up just as I am telling you, in those express words. Here—read me the decree.

[*The Decree.*]

[1] *διὰ τὸ προκατακεχρῆσθαι*—*i. e.* *ταῖς ἐκκλησίαις*: "by reason that the people had already held all the assemblies appointed by law,"—*i. e.* all the ordinary assemblies; and therefore none but an extraordinary one could be called. As to the Athenian law, see Appendix V. Reiske in his Index explains these words as follows: "propterea quod, concionibus antea nimis multis incassum habitis, salutare nihil neque decretum neque effectum esset." In his notes he suggests another interpretation: "propterea quod omnia huc facientia peracta et absoluta essent." Schaefer renders it: "propterea quod omne tempus concionibus habendis destinatum abierat." So Francis: "When there no longer remained any assembly to be called, the days of convening them being already past." And Pabst: *da keine Versammlung des Volks mehr bevorstund, weil die ganze Zeit, wo dergleichen stattfinden, schon abgelaufen war.*

I carried them from Athens downright against their will, as you will see clearly by what they did afterward. When we arrived at Oreus and joined Proxenus, these men, instead of sailing and performing your instructions, took a circuitous journey, and before we came to Macedonia we wasted three-and-twenty days; all the rest of the time before Philip came we sat down in Pella, making fifty days altogether with those of the journey. In that interval Doriscus, Thrace, the Fortresses,[1] the Sacred Mountain—every thing, in short, during a time of peace and truce was taken and disposed of by Philip; though I was constantly speaking and remonstrating, at first giving my opinion as in consultation, afterward by way of instruction to ignorant men, lastly as if I were addressing venal and impious wretches without any reserve. The man who openly opposed what I said, who thwarted all my counsels and your decrees, was the defendant. Whether that pleased the other embassadors, you will know presently; for as yet I say nothing about any one—I make no accusation—there is no need for any of them to appear honest to-day by compulsion, but of their own choice, and by having had no connection with the crimes. For that the acts done are disgraceful and flagitious and not unpaid for, you have all seen: the thing itself will disclose who have been concerned in them.[2]

But, forsooth, in that interval they received the oaths from the allies, or performed other duties. Very far from it. Although they were absent for three whole months, and had received from you a thousand drachms for their traveling expenses, from not a single state, either on the journey there or on the journey back, did they receive the oaths; but in the inn before the temple of Castor and Pollux—if any of

[1] "Fuisse tractum Thraciæ τὰ Τείχη dictum, ut in Belgio sunt *les Barrières*, e. p. 397, constat."—*Reiske.*

[2] The reader will notice the artifice of the orator. He was apprehensive that the colleagues of Æschines might support him by their testimony or influence. He seeks to deter them from such a course, by insinuating that it would prove them to be accomplices. He affects to suspend his own judgment, as if he waited to see the result. But this affectation is not consistent with the general tenor of the speech, in which Demosthenes is continually talking of *these men* (meaning the embassadors in general, or at least the greater number of them, who were doubtless in court and supporting Æschines) as being all more or less associated with him, and participators in his misconduct.

you has been at Pheræ, he knows the place I mean—here the oaths were administered, when Philip was marching hither with his army, in a manner disgraceful, O Athenians, and unworthy of you. Philip indeed would have given a great deal to have it managed in this way. For when they were unable to draw up the treaty as these men attempted at first, excluding the Halians and Phocians, but Philocrates was compelled by you to expunge that clause and insert expressly the Athenians and allies of the Athenians, he did not wish any of his own allies to have sworn that oath, (for then they would not have marched with him to attack those possessions of yours which he now holds, but would have made the oaths an excuse,) nor did he wish them to witness the promises on which he was obtaining the peace, nor to have it shown to all, that in fact the Athenian commonwealth had not been beaten in war, but it was Philip who desired peace, and was making large promises to the Athenians if he could obtain peace. So, for fear what I say might be publicly known, he objected to these men going any where; and they did every thing to gratify him with an ostentation of zeal and extravagant servility.

I say then—when they are convicted of all these things—having wasted the time, sacrificed the posts in Thrace, done nothing that you directed or that your interests required, brought false intelligence to Athens—how is it possible for them to escape with intelligent and conscientious judges? To prove the truth of these statements, read first the decree prescribing how the oath was to be administered, then the letter of Philip, then the decree of Philocrates and that of the people.

[*The Decree prescribing the Oath.*]

[*The Letter of Philip.*]

[*The Decree of Philocrates.*]

[*The Decree of the People amending that of Philocrates.*]

To show that we should have caught Philip in the Hellespont, if they had followed my advice and executed your commands as expressed in the decrees, call the witnesses there present.

[*Witnesses.*]

Now read the other deposition, what answer Philip made to Euclides here, who came afterward.[1]

[*The Deposition.*]

They can't deny they did all this to serve Philip—attend, and you will see. When we started on the former embassy for the peace, you sent a herald before us to stipulate for our safe conduct. On that occasion, as soon as they arrived at Oreus, they did not wait for the herald or create any delay, but, though Halus[2] was under siege, they crossed over to it, and again coming out of that city to Parmenio, who was besieging it, they set off through the hostile army for Pagasæ, and going on met the herald at Larissa: with such expedition and diligence they proceeded then. Yet when there was peace and every security for traveling, and your command to make haste, it never occurred to them either to expedite their journey or to go by sea. How came this about? Because on the former occasion it was Philip's interest that the peace should be concluded as quickly as possible, but on this it was for his advantage that the interval before demanding the oaths should be as much as possible protracted. To show that these statements are also true, here—take this deposition.

[*The Deposition.*]

Is there any evidence to convict men of entire subservience to Philip stronger than this—that on the same journey they loitered when they ought to have made haste in your service, and hurried when they ought not even to have traveled[3] before the arrival of the herald?

During the time that we were there and loitering in Pella,

[1] Euclides was sent by the Athenians to remonstrate with Philip for having invaded the dominions of Cersobleptes. He replied, that his embassadors had not informed him that peace had been concluded, and therefore he had a right to pursue his conquests. The deposition of Euclides to this effect is now read, he being present to confirm it.

[2] Halus was near the coast, about the centre of the Pagasæan bay, and a few miles from Pagasæ.

[3] The opposition here is between σπεύδειν and οὐδὲ βαδίζειν, "to hasten," and "not to travel at all—not to begin the journey." Therefore there is no necessity to express (as Schaefer would have us) the opposition between πλεῖν and βαδίζειν, which elsewhere occurs. (See pp. 392, 398 orig.)

see what different employments we each chose for ourselves. Mine was to deliver the captives and seek them out, to expend money of my own, and request Philip to ransom them with what he would have given in presents to us. What the defendant made it his business to accomplish, you shall hear immediately. What was it? That Philip should make us a common present of money. For you must know, among other things, Philip sounded us all—in what way?—by sending to each privately, and offering, O Athenians, a heap of gold. Failing with one, no matter whom—(for it is not for me to mention myself; the facts and circumstances will show;)—he thought that a common present would be accepted without suspicion[1] by all, and thus there would be security for those who had privately sold themselves, if in ever so small a degree we all joined in the acceptance. Therefore the offer was made, under pretense of being a gift of hospitality. I having stopped it, these men divided the money among themselves—this besides what they had had before. Philip, when I requested him to expend it upon the captives, could neither inform against these men with honor, or say—"Oh! but this and that person have it"—nor yet escape the outlay; so he consented, giving an evasive promise to send them home by the Panathenæan festival. Read the deposition of Apollophanes, then that of the other persons who were present. Read.

[*The Deposition.*]

Now let me tell you how many of the prisoners I ransomed myself. During the time that we staid in Pella, before the arrival of Philip, some of the captives who were out on bail, doubting (I suppose) whether they should afterward be able to prevail on Philip, said they should like to ransom themselves, and not be under an obligation to Philip; and they applied for loans, one of three minas, another of five, and so on, according to what each man's ransom came to. When Philip therefore consented to redeem the rest, I called the

[1] *εὐήθως*,—"without scruple or misgiving—in simple and thoughtless honesty of heart." Pabst: *in gutmüthiger Einfalt.* But Schaefer connects it with *ἡγεῖτο*, and renders it, "pro eâ ouâ erat stultitiâ existimabat."

men together, to whom I had advanced[1] the money, and reminding them of what had been done, that they might not seem to be in a worse position for their haste, or to have been ransomed (poor as they were) out of their own private means, while the others expected to be released by Philip, I made them a present of the redemption-money. To prove my statements, read these depositions.

[*The Depositions.*]

The sums that I forgave and made a present of to our unfortunate fellow-citizens are what you hear. Should the defendant say to you presently—"How comes it, Demosthenes, having discovered (as you say) from my supporting Philocrates, that we were after no good, you went with us on the subsequent embassy for the oaths, and did not excuse yourself?"—remember, I had promised the men whom I ransomed, that I would come and bring the redemption-money, and do my best to deliver them. It would have been shameful then to break my word, and abandon fellow-citizens in misfortune. But, had I got off the appointment, I could not have made a private excursion there with propriety or safety: for, but that I desired to release the captives, perdition seize me, if I would have taken a very large sum of money to be the colleague of these men. And I can prove it—for you twice elected me for the third embassy, and I twice excused myself; and during the whole of my absence on this I opposed them in every thing.

Thus went your affairs, so far as I had the control on the embassy: what these men carried by being the majority has ruined all. Indeed all our measures would have been consistent with what I have just stated, had my advice been followed. For I was not such a wretched idiot, as to give money, when I saw others receiving it, for the sake of standing well with you, while things that might be accomplished without expense, and that drew with them far greater advantages to the commonwealth, I was in my wishes opposed to. I wished for them earnestly, O Athenians; but these men, I trow, were too many for me.

[1] Demosthenes had lent the money as a friend (ἔχρησε, not ἐδάνεισε). We have not the same distinction in our language. *To lend* is indifferently used, whether the loan be with interest or without.

Come now—see what have been the defendant's acts in comparison with mine, and what those of Philocrates; for in contrast they will appear more glaring. First, they excluded the Phocians and the Halians and Cersobleptes from the treaty, contrary to your decree and the declaration[1] made to you: secondly, they attempted to disturb and alter the decree, which we had been commissioned to execute: further, they set down the Cardians as allies of Philip. And the letter written by me to you they determined not to send, while they sent one written by themselves without a word of truth. Then this brave fellow here said I had promised Philip to overturn your democracy, because I denounced those acts, not only regarding them as disgraceful, but fearing I might be involved in the ruin of these men through their fault; while he himself never ceased during the whole time holding private interviews with Philip. And the rest I say nothing about—but Dercylus, (not I,) with the assistance of this boy of mine, watched him during the night at Pheræ, and having caught him coming out of Philip's tent, told the boy to report it to me and keep it in his own remembrance; and finally this abominable and shameless fellow for a night and day after our departure stayed behind with Philip.[2] To prove

[1] *I. e.* by Philip's embassadors, as Pabst understands it. Francis renders it: "in contradiction to the assurances they themselves had given you."

[2] Reiske in his Index gives a different explanation of these words: "quoties nos a Philippo discederemus, sive interdiu sive noctu cum eo congressi essemus, Æschines cum eo solus remanebat totum illum reliquum diem noctemve." This would require ἀπελείπετο.

Æschines, in his answer (p. 44), states the charge of Demosthenes to have been, that he went in a boat by night down the river Lydias, on purpose to assist Philip in writing the letter. If this was the charge, it must have appeared in the deposition read to the jury. Æschines ridicules the idea of it being necessary for Philip to have his assistance in composing the letter, when there was Python of Byzantium and the exile Leosthenes, either of them fully capable of writing it; and indeed Philip could easily have done it himself. And it would have been absurd (he argues) to go by night for such a purpose, when the day would have suited quite as well. Yet neither of these arguments touches the point of the matter; for it might be necessary to Philip's objects to concert things with the person who was to be his agent at Athens, and the night might, for more than one reason, be more suitable than the day. He proceeds next to confute the charge, by direct counter evidence, calling Aglacreon and Iatrocles to prove what we call an *alibi;* that it was impossible he could have passed the night in

the truth of my statements, in the first place, I will draw up my own deposition and make myself responsible as a witness; in the next place, I call each of the other embassadors, and will force them to do one or the other, to give testimony or swear they are unable.[1] If they swear they are unable, I shall convict them of perjury before you clearly.

[*The Deposition.*]

With what annoyances and troubles I was beset during the whole of the expedition, you have seen. You may guess indeed what they did in the neighborhood of their paymaster,

Philip's company, because he lodged in the same apartment with them, and was never absent for a single night. The value of such evidence depends in some measure upon the terms in which it was expressed; but the proof of an *alibi*, without cross-examination, could never be satisfactory.

The use of *ἀπελείφθη* in this passage tends certainly to confirm the translation of Pabst and Francis in the former passage (*ante*, p. 131).

[1] To make this passage intelligible, it is necessary to explain the method of giving evidence in Athenian courts of law. Any party intending to call a witness in court drew up his evidence in the shape of a deposition, and summoned him before the magistrate who had cognizance of the cause. The deposition having been sworn to was put into a box, together with other documents in the cause, to be produced when the trial came on before the jury. On the day of trial the witness again attended, his deposition was read out, and he confirmed it by signifying his assent. No *vivâ voce* testimony (in our sense of the term) was permitted. It was required to be in writing, in order that there might be no mistake about what the witness deposed to, and to afford the opposite party the means of obtaining redress in case he lost his cause by false evidence. A party might be a witness for himself; and then he prepared his own deposition in the same way, and, having sworn to it, produced and had it read in court, making himself answerable, like any other witness, to a charge of perjury.

Where a man called a doubtful or unfriendly witness, he drew up a statement of the facts which he supposed him capable of proving, and, having caused it to be read by the clerk of the court, he asked the witness whether he would swear to it. The witness was then required either to give his testimony to that effect, or swear that the statement was untrue, or not true to his knowledge.

While some advantages attended this method of proceeding, and, among others, a saving of time, (for the evidence was all produced and read during the course of the party's address to the jury, though excluded from the measurement of time allotted to him,) there were other obvious disadvantages, one of which was the absence of cross-examination, and another (in the case of a hostile witness) was the extreme difficulty of preparing such a deposition as he could not escape from.

when such are their doings before your eyes, in whose power it is either to reward or to punish.

I will now reckon up the charges from the beginning, to show you I have performed all that I promised in the outset of my speech. I have shown by the evidence not of words, but of the facts themselves, that his reports have been utterly false and that he imposed on you. I have shown, that owing to him you refused to hear the truth from me, being influenced by his promises and assurances; that all his advice was contrary to what it should have been: that he opposed the peace of the allies and supported that of Philocrates; he wasted the time, to prevent your marching to Phocis, even if you desired it; he has committed many grievous things besides during his absence; he has betrayed and sold every thing, taken bribes, stopped short of nothing that is villainous. All these things I promised in the beginning; all I have made out. Mark then what follows—this that I have next to say to you is simple:—You have sworn to give your verdict according to the laws and the decrees of the people and the council of five hundred: the defendant is proved by his whole conduct as embassador to have violated the laws, the decrees, the obligations of justice: it is fit therefore he should be convicted before an intelligent jury.

Were he guilty of nothing else, two of his acts are sufficient to kill him: for he has betrayed not only the Phocians, but Thrace also to Philip. Two places in the world more important to our commonwealth could not be pointed out than Thermopylæ by land, and the Hellespont by sea: both which together have these men disgracefully sold and delivered into Philip's hands against you. What an offense even this is, without any thing further—the sacrificing of Thrace and the Fortresses—would be an infinite topic of discussion: and it were easy to show, how many persons have on that account been sentenced to death before you, or incurred heavy fines—Ergophilus, Cephisodotus, Timomachus, in ancient times Ergocles, Dionysius,[1] and others, all of whom together (I may

[1] As to the first three persons named in the text, see vol. i. pp. 271—274.

Ergocles is a person against whom there is an extant oration of Lysias, and who, it appears, was condemned by the Athenians for peculation. Of Dionysius nothing is known.

nearly say) have injured the commonwealth less than this man. But then, O Athenians, you were still, on calculation, wary and provident of danger: while now, what for the day gives you no trouble, no present annoyance, you disregard; and here you pass idle votes:—that Philip shall take the oaths to Cersobleptes—that he shall not interfere in Amphictyonic business—that you will amend the peace. But there would have been no necessity for any of these decrees, if the defendant had chosen to sail and perform his duty: what might have been preserved by sailing, he has lost by advising a land-journey; what might have been saved by telling truth, he has lost by lying.

He will make it a grievance presently, as I am informed, that he should be the only orator in the assembly who is called to account for words. I will not press the argument, that all men should be made responsible for their words, if they speak for lucre; but I say this—If Æschines in his private capacity played the fool or made any slip, don't be over-nice; let it pass, forgive him: but if in the character of embassador he has for lucre's sake purposely deceived you, don't let him off, don't tolerate that he is not to be brought to trial for what he said. For what else ought we to call embassadors to account but for words? Embassadors have not galleys or post or soldiers or citadels under their control, (for no one intrusts embassadors with these things,) but only words and times. With respect to time—if he never destroyed the opportunities of the state, he is innocent; if he has destroyed them, he is guilty. And as to words—if his reports have been true or serviceable, let him be acquitted; if false and corrupt and injurious, let him be convicted. A man can do you no greater wrong than by telling falsehoods: for where the government depends on words, how is it possible, if these be untrue, to carry it on safely? And if speakers will even take bribes for the interest of the enemy, how can you avoid being in peril? Nor indeed is it the same thing to rob oligarchs or despots of their opportunities, as it is to rob you: nor any thing like. For in those governments, I take it, every thing is done sharply according to order: but with you, first the council must hear of all matters and frame their previous order, and that only after publication of notice for heralds and embassies,[1] not always; then they must convene an assembly, and that only when it is allowable by the laws: then your honest counselors must get the day, and prevail over those who ignorantly or wickedly oppose them. And after all this, when a resolution has passed, and its advantage is apparent, time has to be allowed for the indigence of the multitude to provide themselves with what is needful, that they may be able to execute your resolve. A man, I say, who destroys these times of action in a government such as ours, has done more than destroy times of action; he has absolutely robbed you of your main chance.

There is a ready argument however for all who wish to deceive you—"the disturbers of the commonwealth!—the persons who prevent Philip from doing the state a service!" To them I shall offer not a word in reply, but read you Philip's letters, and remind you of the occasions on which in every instance you have been cheated, that you may see, by cajoling you, he has forfeited that boastful title that one got sick of hearing.[2]

[*Letters of Philip.*]

His acts in the embassy having been thus disgraceful, so many, nay all of them, having been treason against you, he goes about saying—"What name does Demosthenes deserve, who accuses his colleagues?" Verily I accuse, whether I will or no, having been so plotted against by you during the

[1] A *program* or notice was always posted up in the city, to announce the holding of an assembly. But where heralds or embassadors from foreign states were to have reception, a notice was required to be published before the council could meet on the business, and frame their preliminary decree. *Προβουλεῦσαι* is, "to pass the decree or order of council, which was necessary before it could be laid before the people." It was called then *Προβούλευμα*. (See Schömann, De Comitiis, 58, 97.) I take *κήρυξι καὶ πρεσβείαις* to refer only to foreign heralds and embassies. Pabst otherwise; whose version is: *bei Euch muss über Alles erst der Senat gehört, und Alles durch ihn zuvor berathen werden, und zwar nur dann, wenn dies für Absendung von Herolden und für Gesandtschaften zuvor angekündigt ist, und nicht immer.*

[2] *I. e.* the title of "friend" or "benefactor of Athens," which Philip was continually assuming in his letters, and which the Macedonian party at Athens studiously repeated. Such is Reiske's interpretation of this obscure passage, which I have followed as being, though not wholly satisfactory, yet the best.

whole of my absence, and having the choice of two things left me, either in acts of such a description to be thought your accomplice, or to accuse. I say that I have not been your colleague at all in the embassy, but that you did many heinous things as embassador, and I did what was best for these people. Philocrates has been your colleague, and you his, and Phrynon: for you all did these things, and approved of them.

But where is the salt? where the social board and libations?[1] Such is the rant he goes about with: as if doers of justice, and not doers of iniquity, were the betrayers of these things! I know that all the presidents on every occasion sacrifice in common, and sup with each other, and pour libations together; and the good do not on this account imitate the bad, but if they find any of their body committing an offense, they inform the council and the people. In like manner the council offer their opening sacrifice,[2] banquet together, join in libations and ceremonials. So do the generals, and I may say nearly all the magistrates. But do they on such account allow impunity to their members who commit crime? Far from it. Leon accused Timagoras,[3] after having been four years his co-embassador: Eubulus accused Tharrex and Smicythas, after having been their messmate:

[1] To have eaten salt together, sat at the same table, and poured the same drink-offering, have in most countries been regarded as sacred obligations of mutual friendship or good faith. Compare Odyssey, xiv. 158:—

> Ἴστω νῦν Ζεὺς πρῶτα Θεῶν ξενίη τε τράπεζα,
> Ἱστίη τ' Ὀδυσῆος ἀμύμονος ἣν ἀφικάνω,
> Ἦ μέν τοι τάδε πάντα τελείεται ὡς ἀγορεύω.

Eurip. Hecub. 787:—

> Κοινῆς τραπέζης πολλάκις τυχὼν ἐμοί.

Cicero quotes an old saying having reference to this (De Amicitiâ, 19): "Verum illud est, quod dicitur, multos modios salis simul edendos esse, ut amicitiæ munus expletum sit."

Æschines frequently reproaches Demosthenes with his disregard of these obligations. De Fals. Leg. 31, 52; Cont. Ctes. 85.

[2] Εἰσιτήρια are the sacrifices offered by the council at the opening of their session in honor of Jupiter and Pallas. Suidas however, whose account is adopted by Schömann, says it was the first day of every year, when the magistrates entered upon their offices.

[3] As to Leon and Timagoras, see ante, p. 130. Of Tharrex and Smicythas nothing is known.

the famous Conon of old accused Adimantus,[1] after having shared the command with him. Which then violated the salt and the cup, Æschines—the traitors, the false embassadors and acceptors of bribes, or their accusers? Assuredly the men of iniquity violated, as you have done, the sanctities of their whole country, not merely those of private fellowship.[2]

To show you however, that these men have been the vilest and basest not only of all public deputies to Philip, but of all (without exception) who ever privately visited him, let me tell you a little circumstance unconnected with the embassy.

When Philip took Olynthus, he celebrated Olympic games, and invited all kinds of artists[3] to the sacrifice and the festival. While he was feasting them and crowning the conquerors, he asked Satyrus,[4] our comic actor, why he was the

[1] Adimantus was one of the commanders at the fatal battle of Ægospotamos. In the general massacre of the Athenian prisoners ordered by Lysander, he alone was spared, because he had opposed the order for cutting off the thumbs of the Peloponnesian captives. He was suspected however of having betrayed the fleet to the enemy, and afterward brought to trial on such charge by Conon.

[2] Others take σπονδὰς to be governed by ἀδικοῦντες, as Pabst, who thus renders the passage: *Gewiss Diejenigen, welche, wie Du, alle heiligen Verbindlichkeiten gegen ihr Vaterland verletzten und nicht etwa nur die gegen einzelne Bürger.*

[3] Theatrical people were often specially called *artists* among the Greeks, just as painters are in these days.

[4] The person of whom this pleasing anecdote is told was an early friend of Demosthenes, who first directed his attention to his faults in elocution, and showed him how to overcome them. Plutarch, in the Life of Demosthenes, relates that the young orator, after making one of his earliest essays at speaking in the assembly, and having been ill received by his audience, was returning home in a melancholy humor, when he met Satyrus, and complained to him of his misfortune, saying how hard it was that, after having spent so much time in the study of oratory, he was unable to please the people of Athens: the most ignorant and illiterate persons were heard with pleasure, while he was not listened to. "Ay," said Satyrus; "but I can remedy this. Just repeat me some verses of Sophocles or Euripides." Demosthenes did so, but without that accompaniment of graceful action and pronunciation, by which Satyrus was accustomed to charm his hearers on the stage. Satyrus then repeated the same verses himself, showing how it ought to be done, and making the orator see his own deficiencies. Demosthenes had the wisdom to profit by this lesson, and from that hour set himself resolutely to work to overcome all his natural impediments, to perfect his organs of speech, and to acquire the external graces of address and

only person who preferred no request, whether it was that he had observed in him any meanness or discourtesy toward himself. Satyrus (they say) replied, that he wanted none of the things which the others asked, that what he should like to propose it would be very easy for Philip to oblige him with, but he was fearful of being refused. Philip bade him speak out, assuring him in handsome terms, that there was nothing he would not do; upon which (they say) he declared, that Apollophanes of Pydna was his friend; that, after he had been assassinated, his relations in alarm secretly removed his daughters, then little children, to Olynthus. "They," said he, "now that the city is taken, have become prisoners, and are in your hands: they are of marriageable age. Give me them, I pray and beseech you. Yet I wish you to hear and understand, what sort of a present you will give me, if you do give it. I myself shall derive no profit from the grant; for I shall give them in marriage with portions, and not suffer them to be treated in any manner unworthy of myself or their father." When the company at the banquet heard this, there was a clapping of hands and tumult of applause from all sides, insomuch that Philip was touched, and gave him the girls. Yet this Apollophanes was one of the persons who killed Philip's brother Alexander.[1]

Now let us contrast with this banquet of Satyrus another banquet, which these men held in Macedonia; and see if it has any likeness or resemblance.

These men were invited to the house of Xenophron, the son of Phædimus,[2] one of the Thirty, and off they went. I did not go. When they came to the drinking, he introduces a certain Olynthian woman, good-looking, and well-born also and modest, as the case proved. At first (I believe) they only

manner. He even shut himself up, refusing to see any of his friends, and keeping his head shaved for several months together, that he might have perfect leisure to pursue his training without interruption. In the result he acquired a style of delivery which fully recompensed him for all this exertion, and proved the justice of the player's advice.

The story which Demosthenes tells appears to have been introduced more for the purpose of doing honor to Satyrus, than for any purpose connected with the trial; and we may regard it as being really a tribute of gratitude to the man to whom he was so much indebted.

[1] See Vol. I. Appendix I. pp. 232, 250.

[2] In the list of the thirty tyrants given by Xenophon, occurs the name of Phædrias.

made her drink quietly and eat dessert; so Iatrocles told me the next day: but as it went on, and they became heated, they ordered her to sit down and sing a song. The woman was in a sad way; she neither would do it nor could; whereupon the defendant and Phrynon said it was an insult, and not to be tolerated that a captive woman, one of the accursed and pestilent Olynthians, should give herself airs; and—"Call the boy;" and—"A lash here." A servant came with a whip: and as they were in liquor, I imagine, and it took but little to exasperate them, upon her saying something or other and bursting into tears, the servant rips off her tunic and gives her several cuts on the back. The woman, maddened by the pain and the whole treatment, jumps up, throws herself at the knees of Iatrocles, and overturns the table: and had he not snatched her away, she would have perished by drunken violence; for the drunkenness of this scoundrel is terrible. There was a talk about this female in Arcadia before the Ten Thousand; and Diophantus made a report to you, which I will compel him now to give evidence of; and there was much talk in Thessaly and every where.[1]

[1] In support of this charge, as it appears, Demosthenes gives no evidence, though he asserts that he heard the story from Iatrocles, whom he calls as his witness for another purpose. Æschines declares the whole story to be a fabrication, and produces the evidence of an Olynthian, named Aristophanes, to prove that Demosthenes had offered him a bribe to come forward as a witness, and that he had refused. It is remarkable however, that Æschines produces none of the embassadors who were present at the party to disprove the statement. (See his reply, pp. 48, 49.) In the opening of his speech Æschines adverts to the indignant reception which the charge had met with from the jury, stating that they had hissed the accuser, and expressed their confidence in his innocence. This is apparently confirmed by Ulpian, who states that when the charge was preferred, Eubulus instantly got up and appealed to the jury, whether they would permit his friend to be slandered in such a way; the jury then rose and stopped it.

Many topics of remark suggest themselves as we peruse these contradictory statements. In the first place, Demosthenes was wrong and unfair in lugging in this story at all; and the Athenians, if they stopped him, did perfectly right, though they were not always so scrupulous about what the speakers chose to say. The tale itself, apart from some exaggerations, is not so very improbable. Demosthenes may have made some inquiries of Aristophanes respecting the parentage and condition of the female; but he could not have been a witness to the facts themselves which took place at Xenophron's house. It is an odd thing that Æschines should have been prepared with the evidence of Aristophanes;

Notwithstanding his guilty conscience, this polluted wretch will dare to look you in the face, will raise his voice presently and talk about the life that he has lived; which chokes me to listen to. Don't these people know, that in early life you used to read the books for your mother at her initiations, and as a boy were rolled about among orgiasts and drunkards?—that afterward you were an office under-clerk, and did dirty work for two or three drachms?—that it is but lately you got a wretched livelihood for your services as third-rate player on the boards of other men?[1] What sort of a life can you mention which you have not lived, when that which you have lived appears to be of such a character? But his assurance forsooth! He brought another man to trial before you for infamous practices! But of that by-and-by. Read me first these depositions.

[*Depositions.*]

Such being the number, men of the jury, such the character of the offenses which he has committed against you, including every species of criminality—a receiver of bribes, a

and it seems like a confirmation of what Demosthenes says that the story had been talked about. The cruel treatment of the woman would have been equally reprehensible, whether she was an Olynthian or not, though the prejudice which Demosthenes helped to raise against his opponent might have been enhanced by that circumstance; and it is strange that Æschines brings no witness to disprove the occurrence.

These and many other points may naturally occur to the reader, but it is perhaps waste of time to dwell upon them too long. The difficulty of ascertaining the truth is increased by the absence of the depositions, and the uncertainty how far the speeches which have come down to us are correct reports of the speeches which were actually delivered; for even the orators themselves, when they published their own speeches, may have added or omitted what suited their purpose. The discrepancies which we find in these very passages, between what Demosthenes says, and what Æschines represents him to have said, may be accounted for possibly in this way.

[1] Literally, "in the training-rooms of other choirmasters—*choregi.*" Χορηγεῖον, or *χορήγιον*, was the place which the *choregus* provided to train the youths who formed his chorus. He also maintained them during that time, and found the dresses and accoutrements. The words mean nothing more in effect than "in the theatres found by other men," who hired Æschines to take third parts. In the Oration on the Crown, (ante, p. 97,) he says that Æschines hired himself out to Simylus and Socrates. Reiske renders it: "alliis choregos agentibus." Shilleto: "in the green-rooms of other choregi." *Παρατρέφεσθαι* is, "to be maintained as a dependent."

flatterer, under the curse, a liar, a betrayer of his friends—all the most heinous crimes are included;—from none of these charges will he defend himself, no plain and honest defense will he be able to plead: what I have heard he intends to say amounts almost to madness, though perhaps a person who has no other plea to urge is obliged to employ what artifices he can. I am told he will say, that I have been a partner in all that I denounced, that I approved of all and co-operated with him, but I have suddenly changed and become accuser. This is no fair or proper justification of his conduct, but only an accusation of me: for if I had so acted, I am a good-for-nothing man, and yet the proceedings are none the better for that; quite otherwise. However, I consider it my duty to show to you, both that the assertion, if he makes it, will be false, and what the fair line of defense is. The fair and honest defense is, to show either that the things alleged against him have not been done, or that, being done, they benefit the state. Neither of these points can he establish. For neither surely can he say, that it is to our advantage for the Phocians to be destroyed and Philip to hold Thermopylæ and the Thebans to be strong and troops to be in Eubœa and forming designs on Megara and the peace to be unsworn ;[1] the contrary to all which his reports to you announced as being to your advantage and about to take place: nor can he persuade you, who have yourselves seen and known all the circumstances, that these results have not been accomplished. It remains then for me to prove that I have had no connection with these men in any thing. Would you like me to pass over all the rest—how I spoke against them before you, how I quarreled on the journey, how I have opposed them all along—and produce these men themselves as witnesses, that my acts and theirs have been entirely different, and that they have received money to be your enemies while I refused to take it? Mark then.

What man in the commonwealth should you say was the most odious blackguard, with the largest stock of impudence and insolence? Not one of you, I am certain, could even by mistake name any other than Philocrates. What man speaks the loudest, and can utter what he likes with the clearest

[1] *I. e.* to have remained so long unsworn, owing to the dilatoriness of the embassadors.

voice? Æschines the defendant, I am sure. Whom do these men call spiritless and cowardly with the mob, while I call him reserved? Myself: for never was I intrusive in any way; never have I done violence to your inclinations. Well: in all the assemblies, whenever there has been a discussion upon these matters, you hear me always both accusing and convicting these men, and positively declaring that they have taken money and sold all the interests of the state. And none of them hearing my statements ever contradicted them, or opened his mouth or showed himself. What can be the reason that the most odious blackguards in the commonwealth and the loudest speakers are overpowered by me, who am the timidest of men, and speak no louder than any one else? It is that truth is strong, and, on the other hand, the consciousness of having sold your interests is weak. This takes off from the audacity of these men, this warps their tongue, stops their mouths, chokes and keeps them silent. You know of course, on the late occasion in Piræus,[1] when you would not allow him to be your envoy, how he shouted out that he would impeach and indict me, with cries of "Shame! shame!" Yet all that[2] is the prelude to numerous contests and arguments, whereas these are simple, and perhaps but two or three words, which a slave bought yesterday might have spoken:—"Athenians, it is atrocious: here is a man accusing me of what he has himself been concerned in; and saying that I have taken money, when he has taken it himself."—Nothing of this kind did he say or utter; none of you heard him; but he threatened something different. Why? Because he was conscious of guilt, and not independent enough to speak those words:[3] his resolution

[1] This, it is supposed, refers to the story of Antiphon, which Demosthenes speaks of more fully in the Oration on the Crown (ante, pp. 55, 56). Æschines threatened to impeach Demosthenes for his own unconstitutional proceedings against Antiphon in that affair.

[2] "Sensus—Atqui hæc quæ mihi tunc minatus est, scilicet ἡ εἰσαγγελία καὶ ἡ γραφή, sunt longi temporis multæque operæ; poteratque me, nisi culpæ sibi conscius esset, continuo vel tribus verbis prosternere."—*Schaefer.*

Pabst: *Doch eine solche Anklage würde der Anfang vieler und grosser Kämpfe und langer Reden seyn.*

I rather understand *ταῦτα* to mean "that declaration—that kind of talk."

[3] Literally: "he was the slave of those words." "In hæc ei verba non magis quidquam quam mancipio in dominum licebat, h.e. hæc in

never reached that point, but shrank back, for his conscience checked it. No one however prevented him from indulging in general abuse and calumny.

The strongest point of all, a matter not of argument but of fact, I am about to mention:—Upon my offering to do what was just, namely, as I had been twice embassador, to render my account twice, Æschines the defendant came up to the auditors with divers witnesses, and warned them not to summon me into court, on the ground that I had passed my audit and had no further liability. And the thing was beyond measure ridiculous. What was the meaning of it? He having rendered his account of the former embassy, which no one arraigned, did not wish to attend a fresh audit for that which he is now tried upon, which included all his misdeeds: but if I attended twice, the consequence would be that he too must come into court again; therefore he would not let them summon me. Now, men of Athens, this circumstance proves both points clearly to you, both that Æschines has condemned himself, so that none of you can conscientiously acquit him now, and that he will not utter a word of truth about me; for had he any thing to say, he would have come forward with it then and accused me, never have given notice not to summon me into court. In support of my statements, call the witnesses to them.

[*Witnesses.*]

Should he speak any slander about me foreign to the embassy, on many accounts you should refuse to hear him. I am not on my trial to-day; and after this no water is poured in for me.[1] What is it then but lack of honest arguments? For who upon his trial would elect to accuse, if he had a good defense? Again, consider this, men of the jury.

me jactare reformidabat ut *δοῦλος ἀπαρρησίαστος* cui *ἡ γλῶττα δέδεται*: nam si in me jactaret, suo se gladio jugulaturus erat."—*Schaefer.*

Auger gives the sense of the passage well enough: "C'est qu'intimement convaincu de ses délits, il appréhendoit, il trembloit de rien dire qui y eût rapport. Si la pensée par hasard le portoit de ce côté là, un remords importun le repoussoit aussi-tôt."

Pabst: *weil er sich bewusst war, dies begangen zu haben, und diese Worte aus sklavischer Furcht vor ihnen nicht auszusprechen wagte, so wendete sich sein Sinn nicht dazu, sondern bebte zurück und wurde von seinem Gewissen übermannt.*

[1] Into the water-glass. See p. 59, note 1.

If I were tried, and Æschines accusing, and Philip the judge, and I, having no means of showing my innocence, began maligning Æschines and trying to blacken his character, don't you think Philip would on this very account be indignant, that any one before him should malign his benefactors?[1] Do not you then be worse than Philip, but compel him to make his defense upon the points in issue.

[*The Deposition.*][2]

You see, I, because I was conscious of no wrong, thought proper to render my account, and submit to all that the laws required: Æschines did the reverse. How then can his actions and mine have been the same? or how can he possibly maintain before you what he has never even alleged against me before? Surely he can not. He will, however; and verily I don't wonder. For you surely know this—that since the creation of man, and since trials have been instituted, no one ever was found guilty confessing his crime: no; they put on a bold face, deny the charge, tell lies, invent excuses, do any thing to escape punishment.[3]

You must not be duped by any thing of this sort to-day, but decide the case by your own knowledge, and pay no heed to my statements or the defendant's, no, nor to the witnesses whom he will have ready to prove what he likes, with Philip for his paymaster; (you'll see how promptly they will give evidence for him:) neither care whether Æschines has a loud and fine voice, or I a poor one. For it is not your business, if you are wise, to have a trial of orators or speeches to-day, but to regard the dire and shameful ruin of your affairs, and to cast back the infamy upon its authors, having inquired into these doings that are within your own knowledge. What doings? These which you know, and need not be informed by me. If all which they promised you has resulted from the peace, and you confess yourselves to be so full of cowardice

[1] The *petitio principii* is remarkable in this argument.

[2] This is the deposition of the witnesses called just above. While they are coming up, or standing for a minute or two, the orator interposes a few more words to the jury. This is common.

[3] Compare *Winter's Tale*, Act III. Scene 2:—

I ne'er heard yet,
That any of these bolder vices wanted
Less impudence to gainsay what they did,
Than to perform it first.

and baseness, that without enemies in the country, without being blockaded by sea, without the city being in any danger, while you were purchasing cheap corn, and in other respects no worse off than at present, when you knew and had been told by these men, that your allies would be ruined and the Thebans would become powerful and that Philip would take the fortresses in Thrace and that sallying-places would be established against you in Eubœa and that all which has been done would happen, you were content to make the peace notwithstanding—acquit Æschines, and do not in addition to so many disgraces incur the sin of perjury: for he does you no wrong; I am a fool and a madman to accuse him. But if just the reverse—if they spoke in the kindest manner of Philip, saying that he loved the commonwealth, he would save the Phocians, he would humble the pride of Thebes, yet more, he would confer benefits on you beyond the value of Amphipolis, if he obtained the peace, and would restore Eubœa and Oropus—if after saying and promising all this they have cheated and cajoled you, and all but stripped you of Attica, pronounce your verdict against him, and let it not be that, in addition to the other outrages put upon you, (for I know not what else to call them,) you, for the bribes taken by these men, carry home the curse and the perjury.[1]

Consider again, men of the jury: for what object could I have chosen to accuse these men, if they were innocent? You can find none. Is it pleasant to have many enemies? It is not even safe. Was there any quarrel subsisting between Æschines and me? None. What then? You feared for yourself, and through cowardice thought this was your security:—that I have heard he says.—Well, but without there being any danger or crime, Æschines, as you allege![2]

[1] This is a fine sentence, pregnant with meaning. Don't let it happen, says the orator, that, instead of taking vengeance on these men for their venality, you take their sins upon your own heads; for if you acquit Æschines, the curse to which he is liable (ταῖς ἀραῖς ἔνοχος, p. 404, orig.) will justly be transferred to you, and by violating your oaths as jurors and giving a verdict contrary to the evidence you will have incurred the crime of perjury.

[2] The supposed assertion of Æschines involved the assumption of crime having been committed, which was adverse to his case. If the embassadors had done nothing wrong, as Æschines would make out, then Demosthenes could have had nothing to fear, and the last assigned motive for accusation was absurd.

Should he repeat that, consider, men of the jury, whether for crimes, which I who am innocent feared would be my ruin through those persons—what ought they to suffer who are the guilty parties?[1] But it is for no such reason. Wherefore then do I accuse you? Vexatiously, forsooth, that I may get money from you! And pray, was it better for me to receive a large sum, as large as any of these men, from Philip who offered it, and have both him and these for my friends, (for they would, they would have been my friends, if I had been their accomplices: even now the feud between us is not hereditary, but because I have not been a partner in their acts:) or to beg from them a portion of their receipts, and be at enmity both with Philip and them?—and while I ransomed the prisoners at such an expense out of my own means, to ask these men for a disgraceful pittance which made them my enemies? Impossible. I reported what was true, and abstained from taking presents out of regard to justice and truth and my future life, believing that, if I was virtuous, I should be honored among you no less than certain other people,[2] and that I must not barter away my public spirit for any lucre: and these men I abhor, because I saw them in the embassy to be villainous and execrable, and I have been deprived too of my personal distinctions,[3] since through the corruption of these men your displeasure has fallen upon the whole embassy: and I accuse now and am come to the audit foreseeing the future, and wishing to have it determined by the verdict of this tribunal, that my actions have been the opposite of theirs. And I fear, I fear, (all my thoughts shall be declared to you,) hereafter you may drag me who am innocent along with them, but you will remain passive now.[4]

[1] I have kept the *anacoluthon* of the original; but it is not very elegant in this passage.

[2] This is a modest way of saying that he hoped to receive the same honors as other distinguished citizens.

[3] Φιλοτιμία, like ἀρετή, signifies not only the meritorious quality or action of the person himself, but also the honorable distinction attending it.

Demosthenes had lost not only the vote of thanks and invitation to dine in the City Hall (as Schaefer observes, see ante, p. 130), but suffered in his general credit and reputation, through the misconduct of the embassadors.

[4] Ἀναπεπτωκότες, "fallen back." Reiske: "remissi, supini." Pabst: *nachlässig und nachsichtig.*

For it seems to me, O Athenians, you are wholly paralyzed, waiting till calamity falls upon you; and while you see other people suffer, you take no precaution, nor give a thought to the commonwealth, now so long in many fearful ways declining.

Don't you think it dreadful and monstrous?—for though I had resolved to be silent, I am led on to speak:—You must know Pythocles[1] the son of Pythodorus. With him I was on very friendly terms, and up to this day nothing unpleasant has passed between us. He turns out of my way now when he meets me, ever since he has been with Philip; and if he is compelled to cross my path, he starts away in a moment, for fear some one should see him speaking to me: yet with Æschines he walks all round the market, and holds consultation. It is really dreadful and shocking, O Athenians—while people who have chosen Philip's service have this advantage, that his perception is in either case so keen, they believe each of them, as surely as if he were standing at their side, that nothing they do even here can escape him, and they regard as friends whom he thinks proper, and as enemies likewise—those who are devoted to you, who are ambitious of your esteem and have never sacrificed it, find in you such a deafness and blindness, that these miscreants are here contending on equal terms with me, and that too before a jury who know all the circumstances. Would you like to know and hear the reason? I will tell you; and pray be not offended at my speaking the truth. It is because Philip, I take it, having one body and one soul, loves with his whole heart the people that do him good, and hates those that do the contrary; whereas any one of you never thinks that a person serving the state serves him, or that a person damaging the state damages him; each individual has things of greater importance to himself by which you are frequently led astray—compassion, envy, resentment, granting favors, a thousand things besides—indeed, should one escape every thing else, there is no escaping persons who don't like one to be such.[2]

[1] Mentioned in the Speech on the Crown (p. 320, orig.) as an adversary of Demosthenes. His stately manner of walking is noticed further on in this speech (p. 442, orig.). He was many years after condemned to death.

[2] This sentence, which perplexed Taylor, and which Francis omits from his translation, is explained by Reiske, and not badly rendered by Auger, "Quand on échapperoit à tout le reste, pourroit on échapper

The fault in each of these instances gradually undermines and ends in being the total ruin of the commonwealth.[1]

Do not, O Athenians, commit any such error to-day; do not acquit the man who has so greatly wronged you. For really what will be said of you, if you do acquit him?—Certain embassadors went from Athens to Philip; Philocrates, Æschines, Phrynon, Demosthenes. What then? One of them, besides that he made no profit by the embassy, redeemed the captives out of his own private means: another with the money for which he sold the country's interests went about purchasing harlots and fish. Another sent his son to Philip, before he had entered him in the roll of citizens;[2] the brutal Phrynon: while the first did nothing unworthy of the commonwealth or himself. One, though choir-master and captain, thought it right in addition to incur these voluntary expenses, to redeem the captives, and not permit any of his fellow-countrymen to be in distress for want: another, so far from delivering any already in captivity, helped to bring a whole district, and more than ten thousand infantry and nearly a thousand cavalry of an allied nation, into the power of Philip. What followed? The Athenians got hold of them—having known all about it long before—well?—the men who

à l'envie, qui ne peut souffrir un citoyen integre et zélé!"—The orator partly alludes to himself, as being the patriotic citizen whose vocation did not please a certain class of the people. And it is not impossible he might have been led to this remark by some signs of displeasure which he observed in some of the jurors. Pabst makes him speak expressly of himself (*wie ich bin*); but it is better not to introduce this into the text.

[1] I have followed the interpretation of ὑποῤῥέουσα indicated by F. A. Wolf in his note on the Leptines, p. 471. Shilleto, who quotes F. A. Wolf, and adopts his view, misapplies his learning, when he desires us to translate—"The error in each of these cases gradually giving way from under you, results in a universal and momentary destruction to the state." The transitive force of ὑποῤῥεῖν is derived from the notion of "slipping from under;" but to translate it so here is not advisable.

Reiske, in his Index, agreeing with F. A. Wolf as to the meaning in the Leptines, here renders ὑποῤῥέουσα simply *subrepens*, in which he has been generally followed. Francis: "These particular and separate errors advancing by degrees, fall at last in one collected ruin on the republic." Pabst: *Aber solche bei allen einzelnen Sachen dieser Art begangenen Fehltritte bringen, wenn sie allmählig und unmerklich weiter schreiten, dem Staat endlich in seiner Gesammtheit Verderben.*

[2] At the age of eighteen an Athenian citizen was enrolled in the register of his township (δῆμος).

had taken money and presents, who had disgraced themselves and the country and their own children, they acquitted, considering them to be men of sense and the country to be in a flourishing state;—but what of the man who accused them?—him they judged to be an idiot, ignorant of the country, not knowing how to throw his own away.[1]

And who, O Athenians, after seeing this example, will wish to prove himself an honest man? Who will be an embassador for nothing, if he is neither to take reward, nor with you to be held more trustworthy than persons who have taken it? Therefore you are not only trying these men to-day; no: you are legislating for all time to come, whether embassadors should take money to work disgracefully for the enemy, or do their best in your behalf without bribe or fee.

Upon the other matters you require no witness: but as to Phrynon sending his son, call me the witnesses to that.[2]

[*Witnesses.*]

Æschines never prosecuted this man on the charge of sending his son to Philip for dishonor. But if one being in his youth better looking than another, not foreseeing what suspicion might arise from such comeliness, hath been a little wild in after-life, Æschines must prosecute him for infamous crime.

Now let me speak of the entertainment and the decree: I had nearly forgotten what was most material to say to you.

[1] *Τὴν πόλιν ἀγνοεῖν* is explained thus by Reiske: "non nôsse mores civium degeneres, inimicos suos ornantium, bene de se meritos abjicientium." By Schaefer otherwise: "ignorare quam prosperæ sint res civitatis."

Οὐκ ἔχειν ὅποι τὰ ἑαυτοῦ ῥίπτῃ refers to the boasted liberality of Demosthenes, in ransoming the prisoners, &c. His enemies represented him as a fool, who threw away his money, and even didn't know how to throw it away. Auger: "qui ne savoit où jeter son argent."

[2] It may seem strange to an English reader that Demosthenes should call witnesses to a fact so remote from the point at issue. But the Athenians appear to have admitted all kinds of evidence which tended to show the general character of the parties. Demosthenes seeks to create a prejudice against Æschines, as being connected with such an infamous person as Phrynon, and he turns this to still better account, when he comments upon his prosecution of Timarchus. This (says he) could only have been for the purpose of screening himself. Had his motive been the pure love of virtue, he would have proceeded against Phrynon also.

In drawing up the order of council concerning the first embassy, and again before the people at the assemblies in which you were to debate the question of peace, when nothing either spoken or done wrong by these persons was known, I according to customary usage commended and invited them to the city-hall. And what is more, I entertained Philip's embassadors, and very splendidly too, O Athenians: for when I saw them in Macedonia glorying even in such things as proofs of wealth and splendor, it occurred to me that I should begin directly to surpass them in these things, and display greater magnificence myself: however, the defendant now will bring the matter forward, and say, "Demosthenes himself commended us, himself feasted the embassadors"—not distinguishing the when. It was before the country had sustained an injury, before it was discovered that these men had sold themselves; when the embassadors had just arrived for the first time, and the people had to hear what they proposed, and it was not yet known that the defendant would support Philocrates, or that he would make such a motion. If therefore he should bring this forward, remember the dates; they are earlier than the offenses: since that time there has not been the slightest connection or communion between these men and me. Read the deposition.

[*The Deposition.*]

Perhaps his brothers Philochares and Aphobetus[1] will plead for him. To both of them there is much that you may with justice reply: (I must speak freely, O Athenians, without any reserve:)—Aphobetus and Philochares! you being a painter of perfume-boxes and drums, your brothers under-clerks and common persons; (there is no reproach in these things, yet they hardly deserve a general's rank); we dignified you with embassies, generalships, and the highest honors. Now supposing that none of you committed any crime, we should have nothing to be grateful for to you, but you for these things ought to be grateful to us; for we, passing by many persons more worthy of honor, exalted you. But if in the very exercise of your dignities one of you has committed crime, and crime too of such a nature, don't

[1] See Appendix II.

you much more deserve execration than pardon? Much more, in my opinion.

They will be violent perhaps, with their loud voices and impudence, and with the plea that "it is pardonable to assist a brother." But don't you give way: remember, while it is their duty to regard Æschines, it is yours to regard the laws and the whole commonwealth, and (above all) the oaths that you have yourselves sworn as jurors. If indeed they have requested any of you to save the defendant, see whether they mean, in case he is not shown to have injured the commonwealth, or even in case he is. If they mean in case of innocence, I am also for saving him; if unconditionally and however guilty he has been, they have asked you to commit perjury. For though the ballot is secret, it will not be hidden from the gods. Most wisely was it seen by him that enacted the law of secret voting, that none of these men[1] will know which of you has obliged him, but the gods and the divine spirit will know who has voted iniquitously: from whom it is better for each of you to secure good hopes for himself and his children by giving a righteous and proper judgment, than to confer a secret and uncertain obligation upon these men, and to acquit a person who has given evidence against himself. For what stronger witness, Æschines, can I produce, to prove your misconduct as embassador, than you against yourself? You that thought it necessary to involve in such a dreadful calamity the man who would have brought some of your deeds to light, certainly expected some heavy punishment yourself, should the people hear what you had done.

This proceeding, if you are wise, will turn out to his own prejudice, not only on this account, that it is a flagrant indication of what his acts as embassador have been, but because in conducting the accusation he used those arguments which stand good against him now: for surely the same principles, which you laid down when you prosecuted Timarchus, are available also for others against yourself. You then said to the jury—"Demosthenes will defend him, and will arraign my conduct as embassador: and then, if he misleads you by his speech, he will brag and go about saying—how? what do

[1] Τούτων means here not only Æschines and his colleagues, but all criminals brought to the bar of justice.

you think?[1] I led the jurors right away from the question, and stole the case out of their hands." Don't yourself act thus. Confine your defense to the subject of your trial. When you were prosecuting him, then was the time for accusing and saying what you pleased.

Again you recited before the jury, having no witness to bring in support of your charge against the accused—

Rumor which many people noise abroad
Not wholly dies: a goddess eke is she.[2]

Well, Æschines; and all these people say that you have received money from the embassy; so that against you too, I should think, Rumor which many people noise abroad not wholly dies. For inasmuch as more accuse you than him, see how the matter stands. Timarchus even his neighbors did not all know; but of you embassadors there is no Greek or barbarian who does not say, that you have received money from the embassy. If rumor therefore is true, that of the

[1] These words πῶς; τί; which have puzzled the critics, are understood by most to be put in the mouth of Demosthenes. Perhaps the better way is to understand them as referring to what precedes, thus: "how will he brag! what will he say? why, as follows."

[2] These lines are from Hesiod, Opera et Dies, 761. Æschines, in the passage referred to (cont. Timarch. 18), quotes also Homer and Euripides on the subject of Fame or Rumor. Compare the celebrated lines of Virgil, Æneid IV. 173.

Whether this goddess, the personification of common rumor or report, should in English be rendered *Fame*, as it more generally is, or *Rumor*, I have entertained some doubt: *Fame* is nearer in point of form to the Greek and Latin original; and it may be said that *Rumor*, derived from the Latin *Rumor*, can not so well be made feminine. But on the other hand, the meaning of our *Fame* is not so like the *Fama* of Virgil and Hesiod as *Rumor* is. And with respect to the gender, we have as much right to follow the French *Rumeur* as the Latin *Rumor*, or perhaps to exercise an arbitrary discretion upon such a matter. Shakspeare, no doubt, makes his *Rumor* a male personage, in the Introduction to Henry IV. Part 2, and one of a character more like Virgil's than Hesiod's deity. The lines are quite equal to Virgil's. I make no apology for quoting some of them:—

Open your ears; for which of you will stop
The vent of hearing, when loud Rumor speaks?
I from the orient to the drooping west,
Making the wind my post-horse, still unfold
The acts commenced on this ball of earth.
Upon my tongues continual slanders ride,
The which in every language I pronounce,
Stuffing the ears of men with false reports, &c. &c.

multitude is against you all; and that such rumor is credible, and that a goddess eke is she, and that the poet who wrote this was a wise man, you have yourself laid down.

And besides, he got up a number of Iambics, and repeated them; for instance—

IAMBICS FROM THE PHŒNIX OF EURIPIDES.

Who loves the fellowship of evil men,
Of him I never ask, assured that whom
He seeks for comrades he resembles most.

"The man[1] who frequented the cockpits and walked about with Pittalacus"—these were his words and others like them —"don't you know," said he, "what sort of a person to consider him?" Well, Æschines: these iambics will suit me now against you; and I shall speak fitly and properly, if I recite to the jury—Who loves the fellowship of Philocrates, and that too on an embassy, of him I never ask, assured that he has received money like Philocrates who confesses it.

When he calls other men speech-writers[2] and sophists, and attempts to vilify them, he will prove to be himself liable to these reproaches. For those iambics are from the Phœnix of Euripides: and that drama was never acted by either Theodorus or Aristodemus, to whom the defendant used to take third parts, but Molon played in it, and other old performers whoever they were. The Antigone of Sophocles however Theodorus has often acted, and so has Aristodemus; in which there are iambics beautifully written and in a strain

[1] Æschines (cont. Timarch. 8, 9) charges Timarchus with cock-fighting and gambling, and with a disgraceful intimacy with Pittalacus, a town-slave.

Others, following Reiske, made τοὺς ὄρνις "the bird-market," which does equally well. A cock-fighter would naturally frequent the market where cocks were sold. Francis: "aviaries."

[2] "Λογογράφους. Properly, persons who wrote speeches either forensic or epideictic, *i. e.* which turn on praise or censure, such as those of Isocrates. Such persons would probably introduce into their written speeches many far-fetched allusions and passages from the old poets, who were generally neglected in those stirring and active and therefore unreading times. Hence the word would nearly get the meaning of our *pedant.* That it was used in an opprobrious sense (compare our *pamphleteer*) is stated by Thom. Mag. p. 580, and is attested by Plato, (Phædr. p. 257,) which shows that λογογράφος and σοφιστής were used to convey the same idea."—*Shilleto.*

The passage here referred to by Demosthenes is from the speech against Timarchus, p. 13.

useful to you, which, though he has himself often spoken and knows them quite by heart, he omitted. You are of course aware, that in all tragic pieces it is a sort of special privilege for third-rate actors to come on as tyrants and sceptre-bearers. See then what the verses are in this drama, which the poet has put into the mouth of Creon Æschines, which he neither conned over to himself to serve him in the embassy, nor repeated to the jury. Read:

IAMBICS FROM THE ANTIGONE OF SOPHOCLES.

Ye can not tell the spirit of a man,
His wisdom, nor his worth, till they be tried
In public life and acts of policy.
The statesman, who to serve the common we l
Adopts not what in counsel is the best,
But closes up his mouth for fear of danger,
Base have I ever deem'd, and deem him still.
And whoso dearer than his country loves
A private friend, as nothing I esteem.
For I (bear witness, thou all-seeing Jove!)
Should not keep silence, if I saw destruction
Advancing toward my people 'stead of safety;
Nor e'er would I accept as friend of mine
My country's enemy: for well I know,
'Tis she preserves us all; in her embark'd,
While steadily she sails, we lack not friendship.

None of these verses did Æschines repeat to himself on the embassy: instead of the commonwealth, he deemed Philip's friendship of the greatest importance and advantage to himself, bidding a long farewell to the wise Sophocles: when he saw destruction advancing nigh, the expedition against Phocis, he gave no warning or notice, but on the contrary helped to conceal and forward it, and those who wished to give information he prevented; not remembering that she it is who preserves us all, and in her his mother initiating[1] and purifying, and making a profit from the houses of her employers, reared up all these children,[2] and

[1] This turn is Aristophanic. As to the father and mother's occupations, and as to Heros the physician, see ante, pp. 54, 94—96, and the notes. Shilleto observes: "Schaefer is, in my judgment, right in erasing from the Greek Hero-Calendar one unknown Calamites, and restoring to the contemporary chirurgeons the name of Heros. Καλαμίτης appears to have been a by-word for ἰατρὸς from the κάλαμοι used for surgical purposes."

[2] I refer τοσούτους, as Reiske does, to number. Francis: "these her

that his father teaching the alphabet, as I am informed by older men, lived how he could next door to Heros the physician, but lived at all events in this city; and they themselves got money by being under-clerks and servants to all the public functionaries, and at last having been appointed clerks by you were maintained for two years in the Round-room,[1] and from this city was the defendant sent but just now as embassador. None of these things did he consider; no care he took that the commonwealth should sail steadily, but overturned and sank her, and did his utmost to throw her into the power of her enemies. Are not you then a sophist, and a vile one too? Are not you a speech-writer, ay, and one hated by the gods? you that passed over what you had often played and knew perfectly by heart, while what you never acted in your life you searched out and quoted to injure one of your fellow-citizens?

Come, consider now his remarks about Solon. He said there was a statue of Solon exemplifying the decorous style of the orators of that day, with his hand folded inside the mantle;[2] this by way of reproach and rebuke to the forwardness of Timarchus. But the Salaminians say the statue has not been erected fifty years, and it is nearly two hundred and forty years from Solon to the present time, so that the artist who shaped that figure was not only himself no contemporary of Solon, but his grandfather was not either. However, he said this to the jury, and gave an imitation: but what was of far greater advantage to the state than Solon's attitude, to see (namely) his heart and mind — of them he gave no imitation, quite the contrary. Solon[3] (after Salamis had re-

illustrious sons." Auger: "de merveilleux personnages." Pabst: *diese stattlichen Söhne.*

[1] The room in the centre of the Prytaneum, where the Prytanes dined. See ante, p. 130, note 1.

[2] Literally: "having his mantle wrapped round him, with his hand inside."

[3] Here we have the celebrated legislator of Athens introduced to our notice in the character of a poet and a warrior. Of his poetry a few fragments only remain, and are remarkable for elegance and simplicity rather than for any merit of a higher description. The story respecting the recovery of Salamis is told in Plutarch's Life of Solon, as follows:— The Megarians had wrested the island of Salamis from the Athenians, who, after many unsuccessful attempts to retrieve their loss, became heartily sick of the war, and passed a decree making it punishable with

volted from the Athenians, and they had decreed to punish with death whoever advised its recovery,) at the risk of his own life composed and sang an elegy, and preserved that country to Athens, and removed the disgrace which had fallen upon her. Æschines, although the Persian king and all the Greeks had acknowledged Amphipolis to be yours, gave up and sold it, and supported Philocrates who moved the resolution. Worth his while (was it not?) to mention Solon! And not

death for any one to advise its renewal. Solon, who was a native of Salamis, was greatly discontented; and by-and-by, having observed that the youth of Athens were beginning to change their minds but afraid to violate the law, counterfeited insanity, and, keeping himself at home, composed an elegy on the loss of the island. It contained a hundred verses, and is said to have been a poem of considerable merit. Having these verses by heart, he suddenly ran into the market-place with a cap on his head,—(the cap was a sign of sickness,)—and mounting the herald's platform, sang them out in a loud voice to the people. His supposed madness and the exciting character of the verses gave it the appearance of inspiration. Pisistratus, then a young man, was among the hearers, and urged them to obey the voice of Solon. In the moment of their enthusiasm the people repealed the decree, and prepared for war. Solon recovered Salamis by a stratagem, which is variously related. According to one account, he by a false message enticed a large body of Megarians to the Attic coast, and having put them to the sword, sailed instantly to Salamis and took it. After some further struggles, the belligerent parties referred their claims to the arbitration of Sparta. Solon pleaded his country's cause before the arbitrators, and urged (among other arguments in favor of the Athenian title to Salamis) that the Salaminians buried their dead in the Athenian fashion, turning their faces to the west, and not to the east, as the Megarians did; and also that they had separate tombs for each body, whereas the Megarians put several bodies into one tomb. He urged also that Salamis was called Ionian in some of the Delphic oracles. A further story is told, that he inserted a line in the catalogue of ships in the second book of the Iliad, which is now read thus:—

Αἴας δ' ἐκ Σαλαμῖνος ἄγεν δυοκαίδεκα νῆας,
Στῆσε δ' ἄγων ἵν' 'Αθηναίων ἵσταντο φάλαγγες.

The second of these lines is said to have been Solon's interpolation, to prove that Salamis was, even so early as the Trojan war, subject to, or at least connected with Athens; and some critics have thought that the spuriousness of the line appears from other passages of Homer, where the Salaminians are made to occupy a station separate from the Athenians. (See Heyne's learned note to Iliad, II. 553.) The Megarians are said to have contended for a different reading in Homer, which established their own connection with Salamis. Judgment was given by the arbitrators in favor of Athens.

The cap which Æschines went out with was, as Demosthenes hints (below, p. 196), an affected imitation of Solon.

only here acted he so, but on his arrival there he never uttered the name of the place which he came to negotiate about. And so he himself reported to you; for you must remember his saying—"I too had something to say about Amphipolis, but I omitted it, to give Demosthenes an opportunity of taking up the subject."—I came forward and said, that he had left nothing for me that he wished to say to Philip; for he would sooner give a part of his blood than a part of his speech to any one. The fact, I apprehend, was —having received money, he could say nothing on the other side of the question to Philip, who had paid him on purpose that he might not restore Amphipolis. Here—take and read these elegiacs of Solon, and let the jury see, that Solon abhorred men like the defendant.

Not to speak with the hand folded, Æschines—not that—but to perform your embassage with the hand folded, is needful. You, after extending and holding it open yonder and disgracing your countrymen, talk pompously here, and, having got up and spouted some wretched phrases, imagine you can escape punishment for all these grievous crimes, if you put a cap on your head and walk about and abuse me.

Read, if you please:

THE ELEGIACS OF SOLON:

Our city everlastingly shall stand;
So Jupiter and all the Gods command:
Athenian Pallas lends her guardian aid,
She of the mighty Father, heavenly Maid.
Yet the fair city breedeth for her bane
A generation covetous and vain,
Ill-minded statesmen, who shall yet be tried
In many sorrows to rebuke their pride;
Insatiable, in riot they devour
The fleeting pleasures of the festal hour,
Indulge their lustful appetence of gain,
And sparing neither sacred nor profane,
By spoil and rapine thrive, nor hold in awe
Omniscient Themis and her holy law,
Who sits in watchful silence, and the day
Of vengeance bides, more dreadful for delay.
Thus on a people creeps the dire disease,
Till perish all their ancient liberties:
Or civil strife or warfare is at hand,
To waste the youthful promise of the land.
A factious race the sword shall overthrow;
Who wrong their friends are pillaged by the foe.

Over the country these misfortunes brood:
The poor meanwhile, a hapless multitude,
Are dragg'd to foreign shores and long exile,
To slavery sold, and bound in fetters vile.
The common Pest of all comes home to each;
No door can guard him from the Fury's reach;
She leaps the lofty wall; hide where he will,
In cell or chamber, she shall find him still.
Fain am I thus, Athenians, to advise,
What evils under Anarchy arise,
How Discipline the public weal maintains,
Curbs wicked men with penance and with chains;
How she can tame the wild, the proud put low,
And wither mischief ere to strength it grow;
How straighten crooked justice, and assuage
The might of passion and unruly rage:
Under her sway confusion, discord cease,
And men abide in fellowship and peace.[1]

---

[1] These are not from the Salamis, but verses of a purely political character, addressed to the Athenians during some period of discord and trouble. The future legislator, preparing the way for that great work which has transmitted his name to all ages, endeavors to kindle the flame of patriotism in his countrymen, rebukes the leading statesmen for their selfishness and vicious conduct, and exhorts all classes to maintain civil harmony and obedience to the laws. Whether this was the whole poem, or is but an extract, we can not determine. There are errors in the text, and some verses manifestly lost. Pabst in his version, which is in hexameter and pentameter, leaves the hiatuses as he finds them. I have taken a different course, and have not kept so close to the original as he. Francis has given a spirited version, which I subjoin:—

Nor Jove supreme, whose secret will is Fate,
Nor the blest Gods have doom'd th' Athenian State;
For Pallas, with her Father's glories crown'd,
Spreads the protection of her Ægis round.
But dire Corruption wide extends its sway;
Athenians hear its dictates, and obey.
Oppressive demagogues our counsels guide,
Though various mischiefs wait to quell their pride.
Untaught with cheerful appetite to taste
The calm delights that crown the temperate feast,
A lust of gold their restless bosoms fires;
A lust of gold their guilty schemes inspires.
Vain are all laws, or human or divine,
To guard the public wealth, or sacred shrine,
While private life is fill'd with mutual fraud,
By Justice and her sacred laws unawed.
Silent she sits, the past, the present views,
And in her own good time the guilty scene pursues.

You hear, O Athenians, what Solon declares of such men, and of the gods who (he says) protect the commonwealth. For myself, I believe as I hope, that his statement is eternally true; that the gods do indeed protect our commonwealth: and in some sort I believe, that all which has taken place upon this audit has been a manifestation to the commonwealth of divine benevolence. Only see:—A man who has grossly violated his duty as embassador, who has given up places in which the gods had ought to be worshiped by you and your allies, disfranchised an accuser who obeyed his challenge.[1] To what end? That he may obtain neither pity nor pardon for his own offenses. Further, in accusing that person he chose to speak ill of me, and again before the

Thus other states their mortal wound receive,
And servile chains their free-born sons enslave;
Sedition rages; wars, long-slumbering, rise,
And the loved youth in prime of beauty dies;
For soon the foe lays waste that hapless state,
Where joyless Discord dwells, and foul Debate.
For the poor wretch a harder lot remains,
Sold like a slave to pine in foreign chains.
His proper woes the man of wealth await,
Bound o'er his walls, and thunder at his gate;
Close on th' unhappy fugitive they press,
And find him in his chamber's dark recess.
Thus my good genius speaks, and bids advise
The sons of Athens to be just and wise;
To mark attentive what a stream of woes
From civil discord and contention flows;
What beauteous order shines, where Justice reigns,
And binds the sons of Violence in chains:
Folly, of thousand forms, before her flies,
And in the bud the flowering mischief dies.
She guides the judge's sentence, quells the proud,
And midst sedition's rage appalls the crowd;
While clamorous Faction and Contention cease,
And man is blest with Happiness and Peace.

[1] When the embassador presented himself to the Logistæ to pass his audit, it was in effect a challenge to any of his fellow-citizens who thought proper to come forward and accuse him. Schaefer explains it differently: "Sensum pulchre intellexit Marklandus, citans p. 434. Orator dicit, Timarchum non sponte suâ, non ut petulantem sycophantam, sed rogatum ab amicis invitatumque a bonis civibus ad accusandum Æschinem prodiisse." Shilleto follows him, interpreting ὑπακούειν "to get up to speak when called upon." I scarcely think it can bear such a meaning, unless connected with other words. In the passage cited from p. 434, it is ὑπακοῦσαι καλούμενος.

people he threatened to prefer indictments and the like. For what purpose? That when I accuse him, who thoroughly know his villainies and have closely watched them all, I may be received by you with the utmost indulgence. Furthermore, by pushing off his trial during all the former period he has been led on to a crisis, at which, out of regard to future consequences, if to nothing else, it is neither safe nor possible for you to let him escape punishment for his bribery.[1] You ought indeed, O Athenians, at all times to execrate and to punish men guilty of corruption and treason; but now it will be most especially seasonable and for the common benefit of all mankind. For a plague, O Athenians, has fallen upon Greece, a grievous and severe one, that requires some extraordinary good fortune and carefulness on your part. The notables intrusted with the administration of state affairs are betraying their own liberty, unhappy men, and bringing upon themselves a voluntary servitude, which they call friendship and intimacy and connection with Philip, and other flattering names: the rest of the people and the authorities (whatever they are) in the several states, who ought to punish those men and put them instantly to death, so far from doing any thing of the kind, admire and envy them, and would like every one to be in their places.

This sort of thing, this kind of ambition, men of Athens, until but the other day had destroyed the sovereignty and national dignity of the Thessalians, and is at this moment stealing away their liberty; for the citadels of some of them are garrisoned by Macedonians. It has entered Peloponnesus, and caused the massacres in Elis; and with such frenzy and

[1] The skill of the orator in this passage is worthy of observation. There were three points greatly to the advantage of his opponent, as he could not fail to see: first, the successful proceeding against Timarchus; secondly, the invidious character of the present prosecution, being against a colleague with whom he had acted harmoniously in the beginning; thirdly, the length of time which had elapsed since the commission of the supposed offense. Demosthenes, briefly adverting to these points, turns them skillfully to his own account, without any laborious argument, and without any appearance of doubt as to the effect which they might produce on the minds of his hearers. He then launches out into that splendid description of the state of Greece, and the baneful effects of subservience to Philip, (beginning *νόσημα γὰρ ὦ ἄνδρες, Ἀθηναῖοι,*) which has been praised by most critics, and especially by Pliny, IX. Epist. 26.

madness did it inspire those wretched people, that, to get dominion over each other and gratify Philip, they would spill the blood of their kindred and fellow-countrymen. And it stops not even here. It entered into Arcadia, and has turned every thing there upside down; and now many of the Arcadians, (who ought like yourselves to be eminently proud of freedom, for the only indigenous people are you and they,) hold Philip in admiration, and set him up in brass, and crown him; and to complete all, should he visit Peloponnesus, they have passed resolutions to receive him in their cities. The Argives have done the same. By Ceres, if one must speak in earnest, these matters require no little precaution; as the plague, advancing in a circle, has entered, men of Athens, even here. While then you are yet in safety, be on your guard, and punish with infamy the persons who first introduced it; or else, see that my words be not deemed to have been wisely spoken, when you have no longer any resource.

See you not, O men of Athens, how notable and striking an example the poor Olynthians are; who owe their destruction, unhappy men, to nothing so much as to conduct of this kind? You may discover it plainly by what has befallen them. When they had only four hundred horse, and were not more than five thousand altogether in number, the Chalcidians not yet being all united, although the Lacedæmonians attacked them with a considerable army and fleet,—for of course you know that the Lacedæmonians had the command (so to speak) both of sea and land at that period,—notwithstanding the attack of so mighty a force, they lost neither their city nor a single fortress, but even won many battles, and killed three of the enemy's generals, and at last put an end to the war upon their own terms.[1] But when certain men had begun to receive bribes, and the multitude, through stupidity or through ill fortune rather, regarded them as more trustworthy than their honest counselors, when Lasthenes roofed his house with timber given from Macedonia, and Euthycrates fed herds of kine without paying a price to any one, and one man came with sheep, another with horses, and the mass of the people, against whom these treasons were

[1] This, as well as several other statements of Demosthenes on the subject of Olynthus, is not in exact accordance with the truth of history. See vol i. Appendix I.

committed, instead of being incensed or calling for punishment of the traitors, looked on them with respect and admiration, honored and esteemed them for manliness,—when things proceeded thus far and corruption got the ascendency, although they possessed a thousand horse and were more than ten thousand in number, and you sent to their assistance ten thousand mercenaries and fifty galleys and four thousand citizens besides, all of it could not save them; before a year of the war had expired, the betrayers had lost all the cities in Chalcidice; Philip could no longer be at the call of the betrayers, and was puzzled what he should first take possession of. Five hundred horse, betrayed by their own leaders, did Philip capture with all their arms, such a number as no mortal ever did before. And the perpetrators of all this were not ashamed to look at the sun, or at the earth (their country) on which they stood, or at her temples or sepulchres, or at the infamy that upon such doings was sure to follow. So mad and senseless, O Athenians, are people rendered by the taking of bribes! You therefore, you the people, must be wise, and not permit such practices, but punish them by public sentence. It would indeed be monstrous, if, having passed so many severe resolutions against the betrayers of Olynthus, you should fail to punish criminals in your own country. Read me the decree concerning the Olynthians.

[*The Decree.*]

These resolutions, men of the jury, you have in the opinion of all people, whether Greek or barbarian, righteously and nobly passed against traitors and miscreants. Since therefore the acceptance of bribes precedes such practices, and it is on that account that people are found to commit such acts, whomsoever you see accepting bribes, men of Athens, look upon him as a traitor. If one person betrays opportunities, another measures, another troops, each of you, I take it, ruins that of which he has the management: but all persons of this kind ought equally to be detested. You, O Athenians, are the only people in the world who upon such matters may take examples from home, and imitate in action the forefathers whom you justly praise. Though the battles, the campaigns, the adventures, by which they were renowned, there is no occasion for imitating, since for the present you are at peace, imitate at least their wisdom. This there is always need for, and a wise judgment is not a whit more troublesome or irksome than a foolish one: each of you will sit here for as long a time, whether by a right decision and verdict upon the case he improves the condition of the commonwealth and acts worthily of your forefathers, or by an improper decision he damages the public interests and acts unworthily of your forefathers. What then was their judgment upon such a case? Take and read this inscription, clerk. You ought to know, that the acts which you regard with apathy are such as your ancestors have passed capital sentence upon. Read.

[*The Inscription.*][1]

You hear, men of Athens, the inscription declaring Arthmius the son of Pythonax of Zelea to be an enemy and a foe to the people of Athens and their allies, himself and all his race. On what account? Because he brought the gold of the barbarians among the Greeks. You may see then, as it appears from this, that your forefathers were anxious to prevent even strangers being hired to injure Greece; while you make no provision even to prevent your fellow-citizens doing wrong to the state.

Oh, but this inscription stands in some ordinary place! No. While the whole of yonder citadel is sacred and of considerable extent, it stands on the right by the great bronze statue of Pallas, which the republic offered up as the chief memorial of their war with the barbarians, the Greeks having given the money. At that time then justice was so revered, so honorable was it to punish people who did such things, that the same station was appropriated to the prize-offering of the goddess and the sentence against offenders of that kind: now all is mockery, impunity, disgrace, unless you repress these extravagant liberties to-day.

I think therefore, ye men of Athens, you will do right to imitate your ancestors, not in one point only, but in the whole series of their conduct. They—I am sure you have all heard the story — after Callias the son of Hipponicus had negotiated that peace[2] which is in the mouths of all men,

[1] The inscription on the pillar recording the decree against Arthmius; as to which see vol. i. p. 125, note 1.

[2] See vol. i. p. 200, note 3.

providing that the king should not approach within a day's ride of the sea-coast, nor sail with a vessel of war within the Chelidonian islands and Cyanean rocks, because it appeared that he had taken gifts on his embassy, they fined him fifty talents at his audit, and were near putting him to death. Yet no man can say, that the commonwealth has ever made a better peace either before or after: but it was not that they looked at. For that they considered was owing to their own valor and the reputation of the commonwealth; while the taking or not taking of money depended on the disposition of the embassador; they expected therefore of any man who entered on public duties, that he should show a disposition for honesty and integrity. Your ancestors thus considered bribe-taking so inimical and injurious to the state, that they would not suffer it upon any occasion or in any person; but you, O Athenians, though you have seen that the same peace has demolished the walls of your allies and is building the houses of your embassadors, that it has taken away the possessions of the commonwealth and has earned for these men what they never imagined even in a dream, have not spontaneously put these men to death, but require an accuser, and hear on their trial persons whose crimes are actually beheld by all.

But one needs not confine one's self to ancient events, nor by such examples incite you to vengeance, for in the time of you that are here present and still living many have been brought to justice; the rest of whom I will pass by, and mention only one or two, sentenced to death upon an embassy which has wrought far less mischief to the state than this. Take and read me this decree.

[*The Decree.*]

According to this decree, men of Athens, you condemned to death those embassadors, of whom one was Epicrates,[1] a

[1] This (though Pabst thinks otherwise) must be the same Epicrates referred to in Athenæus (vi. 229, 251), where it is said, that he received divers presents from the Persian king, and paid him the coarsest flattery; and even ventured to say (partly in joke, no doubt) that there ought to be an annual election, not of nine archons, but of nine embassadors to the king. The writer expresses his wonder that the Athenians should not have brought him to trial; which seems not to agree with this passage of Demosthenes; but he may have been ignorant of the fact.

man (as I hear from my elders) of good character, who was on many occasions serviceable to the state, one of those that marched from Piræus[1] and restored the democracy, and generally a friend to the people. However, none of these things helped him; and justly: for one who undertakes to manage such important concerns should not be honest by halves, nor take advantage of your confidence to do greater mischief, but should never do you any wrong at all willfully.

Well: if these men have left undone any part of what those have been sentenced to death for, kill me this very moment. Just see. "Since those men," it says,[2] "acted contrary to their instructions on the embassy:" and this is the first of the charges. And did not these act contrary to their instructions? Did not the decree say, "for the Athenians and allies of the Athenians," and did not these men exclude the Phocians expressly from the treaty? Did not the decree order them to swear the magistrates in the states, and did not they swear the persons whom Philip sent to them? Did not the decree say, that they should nowhere meet Philip alone, and did not they incessantly hold private conferences with him? "And some of them were convicted of making false reports in the council"—ay, and these men before the people too, and by what evidence?—for this is the grand point—By the facts themselves: for surely the very reverse of what they reported has taken place. "And sending false intelligence by letter," it says. So have these men. "And calumniating the allies and taking bribes."—Well; instead of calumniating, say, having completely ruined: and this surely is far more dreadful than calumniating. With respect to the having taken bribes, I can only say, if they denied it, proof would have been necessary; since they confess it, they should have been led off to punishment surely.[3]

[1] When Thrasybulus and his band of exiles marched from Phyle, and occupied the Piræus, until by consent of the Lacedæmonians the Thirty Tyrants were expelled, and popular government restored at Athens.

[2] The decree of condemnation against Epicrates and his accomplices. Passages from this are contrasted with the charges against Æschines.

[3] See Reiske's Index ἀπάγειν and ἀπαγωγή. And the Archæological Dictionary, under title Ἔνδειξις. By the Athenian law, if a man confessed his crime, or was caught in the fact (*flagrante delicto*), he might in some cases have immediate punishment inflicted by the magistrate; not as in our law, which requires proof of such facts to be given on the trial.

How say ye then, O Athenians? Under these circumstances, you being the descendants of these men, yourselves being some of them still living, will you endure that Epicrates, the benefactor of the people and the liberator from Piræus, should be degraded and punished?—that again lately Thrasybulus, the son of Thrasybulus the people's friend, who marched from Phyle and restored the democracy, should have incurred a penalty of ten talents?—and that the descendant of Harmodius and Aristogiton[1] and men who have conferred on you the greatest benefits, whom, on account of their meritorious services, you have by law adopted to be partakers of the cup and libations in all your temples at the sacrifices, whom you celebrate and honor equally with your heroes and gods, should all have suffered punishment according to law; and that neither mercy nor pity, neither weeping children named after your benefactors, nor any thing else should have helped them?—and shall the son of Atrometus the pedagogue and Glaucothea (the assembler of Bacchanals for performances which another priestess has died for,[2]) shall he, when you have caught him, be let off, he, the issue of such parents, he that in no single instance has been useful to the state, neither himself, nor his father, nor any other of his family? For what horse, what galley, what expedition, what chorus, what state service, what contribution, what present, what feat of valor, what thing of the kind has at any time come from these men to the republic? Even though he possessed all these merits, without the addition that he has been an honest and incorrupt embassador, he ought assuredly to suffer death. But if he has neither the one nor the other, will you not avenge yourselves on him? Will you not remember what he

[1] What person is here alluded to is not known. The reader will notice the peculiarity of calling a descendant of one of these men a descendant of both. Pabst cites other instances. Shilleto comments upon it as follows:—

"The names of these miscalled patriots and worthless men were so intimately associated in the minds of an Athenian audience, that they could hardly be disunited even in such a passage as the present. The reader will probably recollect that the heiress of a partner in a noted firm rejoiced in the name *Miss A and B.*"

[2] Ulpian says this refers to a woman of the name of Nino, who was brought to trial for mixing a love-potion. As to Glaucothea, see ante, p. 94, note 2.

said on his accusation of Timarchus,[1] that there was no good in a commonwealth which had not sinews to stretch against malefactors, or in a government where mercy and canvassing had greater power than the laws; and that you ought to have no pity either for the mother of Timarchus, an old woman, or for his children or any one else, but consider this, that, should you abandon the laws and the constitution, you would find none to have pity on yourselves. And shall that unhappy man remain in infamy, because he saw the defendant to be a criminal, and will you allow the defendant to go unscathed? For what reason? If Æschines thought fit to demand such heavy satisfaction from trespassers against him and his party, what should you, sworn judges, demand from such heinous trespassers against the state, of whom the defendant is proved to be one? Oh, but our young men will be all the better for that trial! Well; and this will improve our statesmen, on whom the most important chances of the commonwealth depend. They also need your attention.

To convince you however, that he destroyed this man Timarchus, not (good heavens!) out of any desire to make your children virtuous, (for they are virtuous already, O Athenians: never may such misfortune befall the commonwealth, that her younger members should need Aphobetus and Æschines to reform them!) but because he moved in the council, that whoever should be convicted of carrying arms or naval implements to Philip should be punishable with death. To prove this, let me ask—how long was Timarchus a public speaker? A considerable time. Well: during all that time Æschines was in the city, and never took umbrage, or thought it a shocking matter that such a person should open his mouth, until he went to Macedonia and became a hireling. Here, take and read me the decree of Timarchus itself:

[*The Decree.*]

You see, the person who proposed on your behalf, that no one, on pain of death, should carry arms to Philip in time of war, has been ruined and disgraced; and this man, who delivered up to Philip the arms of your allies, was his accuser,

[1] These statements are not in the extant speech of Æschines.

and declaimed upon prostitution, (O heaven and earth!) while by him were standing his two brothers-in-law,[1] at the sight of whom you would cry out with astonishment, the odious Nicias, who hired himself to Chabrias to go to Egypt, and the accursed Cyrebion, who plays his part in the procession revels without his mask. But this is nothing — he did it with his brother Aphobetus before him! Verily, upon that day all the haranguing about prostitution was a flowing up the stream.[2]

To show you what dishonor our commonwealth has been brought to by this man's wickedness and falsehood, I will pass by every thing else, and mention a thing which you all know. Formerly, men of Athens, what you had decreed was looked for by the people of Greece; now we go about inquiring what the others have resolved, listening what news there is of the Arcadians, what of the Amphictyons, where Philip is about to march, whether he is alive or dead. Is it not thus we employ ourselves? I for my part am afraid, not if Philip is alive, but if the abhorring and punishing of criminals is dead in the commonwealth. Philip alarms me not, if all is sound with you; but if you allow impunity to men who are willing to be his hirelings, if certain of the people in your confidence will plead for these men, and, after denying all along that they are Philip's agents, will get up for them now—this alarms me. How comes it, Eubulus,

[1] Æschines, in allusion to this passage, (De fals. Leg. 48,) speaks of Philon, and not Nicias. As to Philon, see Demosthenes, De Coron. p. 329; this volume, p. 112. Cyrebion is a nickname, derived from κυρήβια, *bran*, denoting a worthless, good-for-nothing person, applied to Epicrates, brother-in-law of Æschines, not the same Epicrates as the one mentioned above, p. 203. Æschines describes him as an easy, good-natured sort of man.

[2] That is, was unnatural and absurd, coming from the mouth of such a person; perhaps further intimating that the whole trial was a perversion of justice. The expression was proverbial: the words are found in Euripides, Medea, 411:—

Ἄνω ποταμῶν ἱερῶν
χωροῦσι παγαί,
καὶ δίκα καὶ πάντα πάλιν στρέφεται.

Francis translates · "But all remarks that day upon impudicity ran upward like rivers against their fountain-heads." Pabst: *Freilich flossen auch an jenem Tage die Reden über Unzucht wie Strom-aufwärts aus seinem Munde.*

that on the trial of Hegesilaus,[1] who is your cousin, and on that of Thrasybulus lately, the uncle of Niceratus, on the first voting[2] you would not even hearken to their call, and on the question of punishment you got up, yet never spoke a word on their behalf, but begged the jury to excuse you? And do you refuse then to get up for relatives and connections, but will stand up for Æschines, who, when Aristophon was prosecuting Philonicus and through him assailing your conduct, joined him in accusing you, and appeared as one of your enemies? And when you having terrified the Athenians, and told them they must immediately go down to Piræus and pay a property tax and make the theatric fund a military one, or vote for the measures which this man supported and the odious Philocrates moved, it came about that the peace was made on disgraceful instead of honorable terms, and these men by their subsequent misdeeds have ruined every thing[3] — then is it that you are reconciled? And before the people you cursed Philip, and swore with imprecations on your children, that you would like him to be destroyed, and now will you help the defendant? How can he be destroyed, when you come to the rescue of those who take his bribes? Yes! How on earth could you prosecute Mœrocles, because he got the mine-tenants[4] to give him twenty drachms each—and indict Cephisophon for embezzlement of sacred moneys,[5] because three days after the time he

[1] Hegesilaus, according to Ulpian, supported Plutarch of Eretria at Athens, and led troops to his assistance in Eubœa.

[2] On the question of "guilty or not guilty." In many cases, where the Athenian law did not fix the penalty, the jury had to give a second verdict, to decide what sentence should be passed on the convict.

[3] In the original there is a *nominativus pendens*, σὺ—δεδιξάμενος—φήσας, after which one would, in the usual course of grammar, have expected ἐποίησας, instead of συνέβη γενέσθαι. But Shilleto well observes that, "probably Demosthenes, at the outset of the sentence, intended to signify that Eubulus had caused the people, by the alternative which he suggested, to pass the disgraceful measure; yet he prudently thought proper to disguise this as he proceeded under the vague language, *it so resulted*, especially as he could then with more weight contrast the anti-Macedonic feeling which Eubulus had or pretended to have evinced, with his becoming reconciled to and advocating the Philippizing party."

[4] Mœrocles seems to have been guilty of some extortion in getting money from the lessees of the Laurian mines: as to which see vol. i., Appendix II.

[5] Cephisophon may have been a treasurer of some temple, ταμίας

paid seven minas into the bank; while persons who have received money, who confess it, who are caught in the fact, and proved to have done it on purpose to ruin your allies, these, instead of bringing to trial, you desire us to acquit? That the charges in this case are fearful, and require a deal of prudence and precaution, whereas what you prosecuted those men for were laughing matters, will appear from the following considerations:—There were persons in Elis who plundered the public? Very probably. Well: were any of those persons concerned in overthrowing the democracy there lately? Not one. Again: while Olynthus existed, there were persons of the same kind? I should think so. Did Olynthus fall through them? No. At Megara, again, think ye not there was a thief or two who pilfered the public moneys? Undoubtedly; and it has come to light. Which of them caused the events which have occurred there? Not one. What sort of people then are they who commit these heavy crimes? The men who deem themselves of importance enough to be called friends and acquaintances of Philip,—men who covet command and are invested with civic dignity, and who consider they ought to be greater than the common people. Was not Perilaus tried lately at Megara[1] before the Three

ἱερῶν χρημάτων, and had the management of its revenues, or he may have been a mere collector. He would be required by law to pay certain moneys in his custody into the bank within a given time; and being a defaulter, though for a few days only, was liable to a fine or other penalty.

[1] Philip's attempt on Megara, which appears to have been made in, or just before, the year B.C. 343, is thus described by Thirlwall, History of Greece, vi. 15:—

"It seems to have been while he was still occupied with the affairs of Thessaly, or at least before he withdrew from the country, that he made an attempt in another quarter, which, if it had succeeded, would have brought him nearer by a great step to one of his principal objects. Megara was at this time, as it had probably never ceased to be, divided between rival factions, which however seem not to have been so turbulent as to prevent it from enjoying a high degree of prosperity, and there are indications that its form of government was not unhappily tempered. The old animosity against Athens had perhaps now in a great measure subsided: Philip indeed had his adherents; but there was a strong party which opposed them, and which looked to Athens for protection. The contending interests, however, seem not to have been exactly those of democracy and aristocracy or oligarchy. Philip's leading partisans appear to have been some of the most powerful citizens, who hoped with his aid to rise to sovereign power, which they would have been content

Hundred, because he had gone to Philip; and did not Ptœodorus, a man for wealth, birth, and reputation the first of the Megarians, come forward and beg him off, and again send him out to Philip; and afterward the one came with his mercenary troops, while the other was cooking up[1] matters in the city? That is one example. There is nothing, nothing in the world, more to be guarded against than allowing any one to be exalted above the people. Don't let me have men saved or destroyed at the pleasure of this or that individual; but whoever is saved by his actions, or the contrary, let him be entitled to the proper verdict at your hands. That is constitutional. Besides, many men have on occasions become powerful with you: Callistratus, again, Aristophon, Diophantus, others before them: but where did they each exercise their sway? In the popular assembly. In courts of justice no man up to the present day has ever had an authority greater than yourselves or the laws or your oaths. Then don't suffer this man to have it now. To show you that it will be more reasonable to take such precaution than

to hold under him. Ptœodorus, the foremost man in Megara, in birth, wealth, and reputation, was, according to Demosthenes, at the head of a conspiracy for the purpose of placing the city in Philip's hands, and had opened a correspondence with him, in which he employed another Megarian, Perilaus, as his agent. Perilaus was brought to trial for his unauthorized dealings with a foreign court, but was acquitted through the influence of Ptœodorus, who sent him again to obtain a body of Macedonian troops, while he himself staid to prepare for their reception at Megara. The plot appears to have been baffled by some unusually vigorous measures of the Athenians. It is difficult to determine, whether an expedition which they made about this time to their frontier on the side of Drymus and Panactus was connected with these movements at Megara; and equally uncertain, though perhaps more probable, that it was on this occasion Phocion was sent, at the request of their Megarian partisans, to guard the city. Though he could not secure it from treachery within, he took the most effectual precautions against a surprise from without: he fortified Nicæa, and again annexed it to the city by two long walls. However this may be, the attempt of Ptœodorus failed, and Philip's hopes in this quarter were for the time frustrated."

[1] In the original the literal expression is, "cheese-making." The same metaphor is used by Aristophanes, and very likely it was common. So we are in the habit of saying familiarly, "to hatch a plot," "to concoct," "to dress up," and the like. Pabst: *so grosse Verwirrung anrichtete.* Auger: "intriguitp our lui." Francis: "had totally changed the civil constitution of his country;" which is wide of the meaning.

to put confidence in these men, I will read you an oracle of the gods, who always protect the commonwealth far better than her statesmen. Read the verses:

[*The Oracle.*]

You hear, O Athenians, what the gods admonish you. If now they have given you this response during a time of war, they mean that you should beware of your generals; for the generals are conductors of war: but if after the conclusion of peace, they mean your chief statesmen; for they have the lead, their counsels you follow, by them are you in danger of being deceived.

And you are told by the oracle to hold the commonwealth together, so that all may have one mind, and not cause gratification to the enemy. Think ye now, O Athenians, that the preserving, or the punishing, of a man who has done all this mischief would cause gratification to Philip? I think the preserving. The oracle however says, you should do your best to prevent the enemy rejoicing. So it exhorts all with one mind to punish those who have in any way been subservient to the enemy: Jupiter, Dione, all the gods. They that intend you evil are outside, their supporters are inside; the business of the former is to give bribes, of the latter to receive, and get off those who have received them.

Besides, even by human reasoning one may see, that the most mischievous and dangerous of all things is, to suffer a leading statesman to become attached to those who have not the same objects with the people. Consider by what means Philip has become master of every thing, and by what means he has achieved the greatest of his works. By purchasing success from those who would sell it; by corrupting and exciting the ambition of leading statesmen: by such means. Both these however it is in your power, if you please, to render ineffective to-day: if to one class of men you will not listen, when they plead for people of this kind, but show that they have no authority with you (for now they say they have authority): and if you will punish him that has sold himself, and this shall be seen by all.

With any man you might well be wroth, O Athenians, who had done such deeds, and sacrificed allies and friends and opportunities, which make or mar the fortunes of every people, but with none more strongly or more justly than the defendant. A man who took his place with the mistrusters of Philip — who first and singly discovered him to be the common enemy of all the Greeks, and then deserted and turned traitor, and has suddenly become a supporter of Philip—can it be doubted that such a man deserves a thousand deaths? The truth of these statements he himself will not be able to gainsay. Who is it that brought Ischander to you in the beginning, whom he represented to have come here from the country's friends in Arcadia? Who cried out, that Philip was packing[1] Greece and Peloponnesus, while you were sleeping? Who was it that made those fine long orations before the assembly, and read the decree of Miltiades and Themistocles, and the young men's oath in the temple of Aglauros?[2] Was it not this man? Who persuaded you to send embassies almost to the Red Sea, urging that Greece was plotted against by Philip, and that it became you to foresee it and not abandon the interests of the Greeks? Was not the mover of the decree Eubulus, and the envoy to Peloponnesus the defendant Æschines? What he may have talked and harangued about when he got there, is best known to himself; but what he reported to you I am sure you all remember. Several times in his speech he called Philip a barbarian and a pest,[3] and told you the Arcadians were delighted that the Athenian commonwealth was now attending to her affairs and rousing herself. But what most of all had made him indignant, he said, — coming home he met Atrestidas on his way from Philip's court, and there were about thirty women and children walking with him; and he was astonished, and asked one of the travelers who the man was, and who the crowd

[1] συσκευάζεσθαι. Reiske: "convasare, compilare, in manticam infercire, tanquam fures solent furta raptim auferre festinantes. Sententia est: alia Peloponnesi oppida ex aliis sibi devincire et in servitutem pertrahere." Auger: "envahissoit." Francis: "pillaging." Perhaps it rather means "packing against you," as in the oration on the Chersonese, p. 91,—συσκευάζεται πάντας ἀνθρώπους ἐφ' ὑμᾶς.

[2] Athenian youths, before they were enrolled in the register of citizens, underwent a scrutiny with regard to their birth and other matters. If approved, they received a shield and lance, and took a solemn oath in the temple of Aglauros, daughter of Cecrops, by which they bound themselves to defend their country, to obey her laws, and respect all her civil and religious institutions.

[3] So Pabst and Francis render ἀλάστορα. Auger: "fléau."

that followed him; but when he heard that these were Olynthian captives, whom Atrestidas was bringing away as a present from Philip, he thought it shocking, and wept, and bewailed the miserable condition of Greece, that she should regard such calamitous events with indifference. And he advised you to send persons to Arcadia to denounce the agents of Philip; for he heard, he said, from his friends, that if the commonwealth would turn their attention to it and send an embassy, they would be punished. Such was then his language, honorable indeed, O Athenians, and worthy of the state. But after he had gone to Macedonia, and beheld this Philip, the enemy of himself and the Greeks, was it like or similar? Very far from it. He said you were not to remember your ancestors, not to talk of trophies or succor any one; and he was surprised at the men who advised you to consult with the Greeks about peace with Philip, as if any one else had to be persuaded on a question that concerned you alone; and that Philip himself was (O Hercules!) a thorough Greek,[1] an eloquent speaker, a warm friend of Athens, and that there were some men in the city so unreasonable and perverse, as not to be ashamed of abusing him and calling him a barbarian.

Is it possible that the same man, after having made the former speeches, could have ventured to make these, without having been corrupted? But further; is there a man who, after having then execrated Atrestidas on account of the women and children of the Olynthians, could have endured now to co-operate with Philocrates, who brought free-born Olynthian women hither for dishonor, and is so notorious for his abominable life, that I have no need to say any thing scandalous or offensive about him, but let me only say that Philocrates brought women, you and the by-standers know all the rest, and feel pity, I am sure, for those poor unhappy creatures, whom Æschines pitied not, nor wept for Greece on their account, that among an allied people they should be outraged by the embassadors.

But he will shed tears for himself, such an embassador as

[1] Auger: "le meilleur ami des Grecs." And so Francis: "best affected to Greece." But it rather has reference, I think, to the character and manners of Philip, and perhaps also to his parentage. Shilleto: "a most genuine Greek."

he has been: perhaps he will bring forward his children and mount them up on the bar. But remember, ye men of the jury—against his children—that you had many friends and allies, whose children are wanderers, roaming about in beggary, having suffered cruel injuries through this man; who are far more deserving of your compassion than the sons of such a malefactor and traitor; and that these men, by adding to the treaty the words "and to his posterity," have deprived your children even of their hopes. Against his own tears harden yourselves by reflecting, that you have in your power a man who bade you send accusers into Arcadia against the agents of Philip. Now then you need not send an embassy to Peloponnesus, or go a long journey, or incur traveling expenses, but only advance each of you up to the bar here, and give your righteous and just verdict for your country against a man, who, (O heaven and earth!) after having declaimed, as I told you in the outset, about Marathon, Salamis, battles, and trophies, all of a sudden, when he had set foot in Macedonia, used the very opposite language—that you should not remember your ancestors, not talk of trophies, not succor any one, not deliberate in conjunction with the Greeks, but should almost dismantle your city walls. Surely more disgraceful language has never at any period of time been spoken among you. For what Greek or barbarian is there so stupid, so uninformed, so bitter an enemy of our state, who, if the question were asked—"Tell me, of this present land and country of Greece is there a part which would have had the name, or been occupied by the Greeks who now possess it, if the heroes of Marathon and Salamis, our ancestors, had not enacted those feats of valor on their behalf?"—there is not one, I am certain, who would not answer, "No; it must all have been taken by the barbarians!" Persons that even an enemy would not rob of their praise and honor, are you their descendants, I say, forbidden to remember by Æschines, for the sake of his own pelf? And observe, other advantages are not shared in by the dead, but praise for glorious actions is the peculiar property of those who have died in achieving it; for then even envy opposes them no longer; and the defendant, for depriving them of this, deserves now to be deprived of his rank, and you will do well to inflict this punishment upon him on behalf of your ancestors. But by such language, you miscreant, while of the deeds of our ancestors you made spoil and havoc with your tongue, you ruined all our affairs. And out of all this you are a land-owner and become a considerable personage. For here again: Before he had wronged the state so grievously, he acknowledged that he had been a clerk and was under obligation to you for electing him, and he behaved himself with decency; but since he has wrought such infinite mischief, he has drawn up his eyebrows, and if any one says, "the ex-clerk Æschines," he is at once his enemy, and says he has been slandered; and he traverses the market with his robe down to his ankles, walking as stately as Pythocles, puffing out his cheeks, one of the friends and acquaintances of Philip for you,—that's what he is now,—one of those that would be rid of the people, and regard the present establishment as a raging sea:[1] he that formerly worshiped the dining-hall![2]

Let me now recapitulate to you, in what manner Philip outmanœuvred you by getting these abominable men to assist him. It is well worth your while to examine and look into the whole artifice. At first when he wanted peace, his dominions being pillaged by corsairs, and his ports having been closed so that he could enjoy none of their advantages, he sent those men who made such friendly declarations in his name, Neoptolemus, Aristodemus, Ctesiphon; but after we embassadors had been with him, he engaged the defendant's services directly, to second and support the beastly Philocrates, and to overpower us whose intentions were honest; and he composed a letter to you, through which he mainly expected to obtain peace. Yet even this did not enable him to do any thing important against you without destroying the Phocians; and that was not easy; for his affairs had been brought as it were by accident to such a critical point, that either it was impos-

[1] Literally: "storm and madness." Francis: "confusion and madness." Pabst: *ein wildes Getümmel und sinnlose Raserei.* See ante, p. 158. Compare also Psalm lxv. 7: "Who stilleth the raging of the sea: and the noise of his waves, and the madness of the people." And Shakspeare, *Coriolanus*, Act III. Scene 1:—

——Will you hence
Before the tag return? whose rage doth rend
Like interrupted waters, and o'erbear
What they are used to bear.

[2] See ante, p. 130.

sible for him to accomplish any of his objects, or he must commit falsehood and perjury, and have all men, Greeks and barbarians, witnesses of his baseness. For should he accept the Phocians as allies, and take the oaths to them in conjunction with you, it became necessary at once to break his oaths to the Thessalians and Thebans, the latter of whom he had sworn to assist in subjugating Bœotia, the former in restoring the Pylæan congress. Should he refuse to accept them, (as in fact he did refuse,) he thought you would not suffer him to pass, but would send forces to Thermopylæ, as, but for being overreached, you would have done, and in that case he reckoned it would be impossible to pass. This indeed there was no need for him to be informed by others; he had his own testimony to the fact: for the first time when he vanquished the Phocians, and overthrew their mercenary troops and their chieftain and general Onomarchus, when no people in the world, Greek or barbarian, succored the Phocians but you, so far from passing the strait or accomplishing any of his objects by the passage, he could not even approach it. He was certain therefore, I take it, that now when Thessaly was quarreling with him,—the Pheræans for example refused to join his march,—when the Thebans were getting the worst and had lost a battle, and a trophy had been erected over them, it was impossible to pass, if you sent forces, or to attempt it with impunity, unless he had recourse to some artifice. "How then shall I escape open falsehood, and effect all my objects without the imputation of perjury? How? In this way—if I can find some Athenian citizens to deceive the Athenians; for that disgrace will not devolve upon me." Therefore his embassadors gave you notice, that Philip would not accept the Phocians for allies; but these men explained it to the people thus—that it was not proper for Philip openly to accept the Phocians for allies, on account of the Thebans and Thessalians; but if he got things into his hands and obtained the peace, he would then do exactly what we should now desire him to agree to. By such promises and lures he obtained peace from you, excluding the Phocians; but he had next to prevent your sending succor to Thermopylæ, for the chance of which even then your fifty galleys were lying at anchor, so that, if Philip advanced, you might oppose him. "Well? what contrivance shall I have again about this?"

To deprive you of your opportunities, and bring matters suddenly upon you,[1] so that, even if you wished, you should not be able to march from home. It was managed by these men accordingly, it appears. I, as you have heard several times, was unable to depart earlier, and though I hired a vessel, I was prevented from setting sail. But it was necessary also that the Phocians should put confidence in Philip, and voluntarily surrender themselves, so that no delay might intervene, and no hostile decree come from you. "Well then; it shall be reported by the Athenian embassadors, that the Phocians are to be saved, so that even those who mistrust me will deliver themselves up, relying on the embassadors: the Athenians themselves I will send for, that they, believing all their objects to be secured, may pass no adverse vote; and these men shall carry such reports and assurances from me, that under no circumstances will they be induced to stir."

In this manner and by such contrivances, through men doomed themselves to destruction, was every thing brought to ruin; for immediately, instead of seeing Thespiæ and Platæa re-established, you heard that Orchomenus and Coronea were enslaved; instead of Thebes being humbled and her pride and insolence abated, the fortifications of your allies the Phocians were being razed to the ground, the persons razing them were the Thebans, who by Æschines in his speech had been scattered into villages. Instead of Eubœa being given to you as a compensation for Amphipolis, Philip is even establishing places in Eubœa to attack you from, and is continually forming designs upon Geræstus and Megara. Instead

[1] So it is well explained by Reiske in his Index, under ἐφιστάναι,—"repente admovere, immittere, ut copias, quibus eum opprimas." Ἀγαγόντας refers not to any particular persons, as the Athenian embassadors, but generally to Philip and all his party—"that they should bring," &c.; as Pabst has it: *Man wird machen müssen, dass Ihr zum Handeln keine Zeit mehr findet, und die Sache so leiten müssen dass er plötzlich Euch über den Hals kommt;* in which version however the last clause deviates a little from the original. Schaefer properly says the sentence is resolvable into ἀγαγεῖν ἄφνω τὰ πράγματα καὶ ἐπιστῆσαι. Shilleto is wrong in supposing that Φίλιππον could be understood after ἐπιστῆσαι. He translates the passage—"that they (the Athenian envoys) should rob you of your times and opportunities of action, and all on a sudden bring on affairs, and place Philip at their head." Francis had fallen into a similar error, rendering it, "and proper persons must be appointed to conduct and suddenly bring it to such a conclusion," &c.

of Oropus being restored to us, we are marching out with arms to fight for Drymus and the country by Panactus,[1] which we never did while the Phocians were in safety. Instead of the ancient rites in the temple being restored, and his treasures being recovered for the god, the genuine Amphictyons are exiled and expelled, and their country has been laid desolate; they that never were Amphictyons in the olden time, Macedonians and barbarians, are now thrusting themselves into the council; whoever makes mention of the holy treasures is thrown down the precipice, and Athens has been deprived of her preaudience at Delphi.[2] The whole business has been a sort of enigma to the state. Philip has been disappointed in nothing, and has accomplished every one of his purposes; you, after expecting all that you could wish, have seen the reverse come to pass, and, while you appear to be at peace, have suffered greater calamities than if you were at war; and these men have their wages for it, and up to the present day have not been brought to justice.

That they have been bribed outright for all this, and have received the price of it, has in many ways, I imagine, been apparent to you for some time; and I fear I am doing the reverse of what I intend—I have been annoying you all this

[1] Panactus is on the confines of Attica and Bœotia, and so is Drymus, according to Suidas. What gave rise to this particular expedition of which Demosthenes speaks, we have no certain information; but there can hardly be a doubt, mentioned as it is in connection with Oropus, that it related to a quarrel between Thebes and Athens, and not, as Winiewski supposed, to Philip's designs on Megara. Thirlwall, in a note on the passage already quoted (ante, p. 210), writes as follows:—

"The language of Demosthenes would rather incline one to suppose that the expedition was sent to resist some aggressions of the Thebans on the debatable frontier. Both Winiewski, (p. 146,) and Voemel, (in Orat. de Halonneso, p. 46,)—who also believes that these forces were sent to oppose the passage of Philip's troops to Megara,—conceive that this Drymus lay on the confines, not of Attica and Bœotia, like Panactus, but of Phocis and Doris. Their only reason for this opinion seems to be the accent. *Δρύμος* is mentioned by Herodotus, viii. 33, as a Phocian town on the Cephisus. Whether a town of that name existed there in the time of Demosthenes is doubtful. The place seems then to have been called *Δρυμαία*. Paus. x. 3. 2. But Harpocration has *Δρυμὸς, πόλις μεταξὺ τῆς Βοιωτίας καὶ τῆς, Αττικῆς*. Even independently of this authority, it seems hard to believe that Demosthenes would have coupled the name of a place in Phocis with that of one on the Attic frontier, as Winiewski and Voemel suppose him to have done."

[2] See Appendix I.

time in striving to make out a complete demonstration of what you knew yourselves. However, do let me add one thing more: Is there any of the embassadors sent by Philip to whom you, men of the jury, would erect a brazen statue in the market-place? Nay: would you give dinner in the city-hall, or any other of those rewards which you honor your benefactors with? I should think not. Why? You are certainly neither ungrateful nor unjust nor bad men. It is, you would say, and with truth and justice, because they did every thing for Philip and not a thing for you. Think ye then that your sentiments are such, and Philip's are different, —that he confers upon these men presents of such number and value, because on their embassy they acted well and faithfully for you? Impossible. You see how he received Hegesippus and his co-embassadors. I pass by the rest; but he banished our poet Xenoclides for entertaining them, his fellow-countrymen. Such is the way he behaves to those who honestly speak their opinions on your behalf, while to those who have sold themselves he behaves as he does to these men. Are witnesses required for this? Are any stronger proofs wanted for this? Can any one get this away from you?

A person however came up to me just before the opening of the court,[1] and told me the strangest thing,[2]—that he was prepared to accuse Chares,[3] and expected, by taking that course and talking in that style, to impose on you. Now I will not strongly insist upon this fact, that Chares (howsoever brought to trial) has been found to have acted faithfully and loyally, as far as lay in his power, for your interests, though he has incurred many failures through persons who from corrupt motives ruin every thing; but I will make a large concession. Let me grant that the defendant will speak nothing about him but the truth: even then, I say, it is a perfect mockery for the defendant to accuse him; for I charge not Æschines with any of the transactions in the war, (for them the generals are accountable,) nor with the state's having concluded peace: but thus far I acquit him entirely. What

[1] I have followed Schaefer's interpretation of *πρὸ τοῦ δικαστηρίου.* Pabst makes it refer to place.

[2] Pabst incorrectly renders these words: *und sagte mir als eine unerhörte Neuigkeit.*

[3] See Appendix II.

then do I say, and from what do my charges take their rise? From his speaking, when the state was concluding peace, on the side of Philocrates, and not on theirs who moved for the good of the country; and from his having taken bribes; from his afterward on the second embassy wasting the times, and performing none of your instructions; from his tricking the state, and, after giving us to expect that Philip would do all we desired, having utterly ruined our affairs; from his afterward, when others warned you to beware of a man who had done so many wrongs,[1] appearing as that man's advocate. These are my charges; keep these in remembrance: for a just and equitable peace, and men who had betrayed nothing and not afterward told lies, I would even have commended, and advised you to honor them with a crown. But if any general has injured you, it has nothing to do with the present inquiry. For what general has lost Halus, or who has destroyed the Phocians? who Doriscus? who Cersobleptes? who the Sacred Mountain? who Thermopylæ? who has given to Philip a road all the way to Attica through the territory of friends and allies? who has alienated Coronea, Orchomenus, Eubœa? who nearly Megara lately? who has made the Thebans powerful? Of all these important matters none was lost through the generals; none has Philip had yielded to him at the peace with your consent: they have been lost through these men and their venality. If therefore he shirks these points, if, to lead you astray, he will talk of any thing sooner than them: meet him as I suggest—"We are not sitting in judgment upon a general; you are not tried upon those charges. Don't tell us who else has caused the destruction of the Phocians, but show that you are not the cause. Why, if Demosthenes did any wrong, do you mention it now, but did not accuse him when he rendered his account? For this very reason you have deserved to perish. Don't tell us that peace is a fine thing or an advantageous thing, for no one charges you with the state's having concluded peace; but that the peace is not a shameful and ignominious one—that we have not been cheated in many ways and all was not lost after it—this you may tell us.

[1] Philip; in whose favor Æschines spoke when the Macedonian embassadors came to Athens, and required the Athenians to acknowledge his title as member of the Amphictyonic Council.

For all these consequences are proved to have been brought upon us by you; and how is it that up to this very day you praise the author of such things?" If you keep watch upon him thus, he will have nothing to say, but will raise his voice here and have exercised himself in spouting all to no purpose.[1]

About his voice too it may be necessary to say something; for I hear that upon this also he very confidently relies, as if he can overpower you by his acting. I think however, you would be committing a gross absurdity, if, when he played the miseries of Thyestes and the men at Troy, you drove and hissed him off the boards, and nearly stoned him to death, so that at last he desisted from his playing of third-rate parts, yet now that, not upon the stage, but in public and most important affairs of state, he has wrought infinity of evil, you should pay regard to him as a fine speaker. Heaven forbid! Do not you be guilty of any folly, but consider: if you are making trial of a herald, you should see that he has a good voice, but if of an embassador and undertaker of public duties, that he is honest, that he demeans himself with spirit as your representative, like a fellow-citizen toward you;[2] as I (for example) had no respect for Philip, but respected the prisoners, delivered them, and never flinched; whereas the defendant crouched before him, and sang the pæans, but you he disregarded. Further, when you see eloquence or a fine voice or any other such accomplishment in a man of probity and honorable ambition, you should all rejoice at it and encourage its display; for it is a common advantage to you all: but when you see the like in a corrupt and base man, who yields to every temptation of gain, you should discourage and hear him with enmity and aversion; as knavery, getting from you the reputation of power, is an engine against the state. You see what mighty troubles have fallen upon the state from what the defendant has got renown by. And

[1] Auger, not badly: "Inutilement alors fera-t-il éclater cette belle voix qu'il aura bien exercée." Schaefer: "Incassum hic tollet vocem ad hoc ipsum prius exercitam."

Demosthenes by his frequent sneers at the fine voice of his adversary betrays his fear of that which he affects to undervalue.

[2] Auger: "doit avoir de la fierté quand il agit pour vous, de la douceur quand il vit avec vous."

other powers are tolerably independent; but that of speaking is crippled, if you the hearers are unfavorable. Listen then to this man as to a venal knave, who will not speak a syllable of truth.

Observe now, that not only in other respects, but in relation to your dealings with Philip, it is in every way expedient for the defendant to be convicted. For, on the one hand, should he ever arrive at the necessity of doing justice to Athens, he will alter his plan;—now he has determined to cheat the many and court the few; but if he hear that these men are destroyed, he will choose hereafter to serve you the many and masters of all. On the other hand, should he continue in the same position of power and pride, the persons who are ready to do any thing for him you will have removed from the country, if you remove these. How think ye?—men that acted so, believing they should be called to account—what will they do if they have your license for their acts? What Euthycrates, what Lasthenes, what traitor will they not surpass? And which of all the rest will not be a worse member of the commonwealth, seeing that those who have sold your interests obtain riches, credit, a capital in Philip's friendship, while those who behave themselves like honest men and have spent money of their own get annoyance, enmity, ill-will from a certain class of people? Never let it come to this! Neither for your honor, nor for your religion, nor for your safety, nor in any other point of view, is it desirable to acquit the defendant. You must avenge yourselves, and make him an example to all, both to your fellow-citizens and to the rest of the Greeks.

APPENDIX I.

THE SACRED WAR.

JUSTIN commences the chapter, in which the subject of this war is introduced, with the following passage:[1]

"Græciæ civitates, cum imperare singulæ cupiunt, imperium omnes perdiderunt." And he attributes the destruction of Greek liberty to the ambition of the Thebans, and the impolitic measures which they took to secure their own predominance. It was indeed the weakness to which they had been reduced by the long continuance of a war provoked by themselves, together with the distractions of Thessaly, and the necessity which there seemed to be for some controlling power, which caused Philip of Macedon to be put at the head of the Amphictyonic League, gave him a victorious inroad into southern Greece, and made him the arbiter of her destinies.

Phocis,[2] the principal seat of this war, is a country bounded on the east by Bœotia, on the south by the Corinthian bay, on the west by the Ozolian Locrians and a part of Ætolia. To the north-west is the little triangular district called Doris, anciently occupied by the Dryopes, but wrested from them by the more warlike tribe of Dorians, who afterwards became so powerful a part of the Hellenic body, and issued from this very district to effect the conquest of Peloponnesus. North and north-east are the Epicnemidian Locrians and the Opuntian Locrians. The rugged ridges of Mount Œta stretch across the northern frontiers of Doris, Phocis, and Epicnemidian Locris, and separate them from Thessaly. This chain of mountains, forming the principal barrier of southern Greece, is terminated by the sea at the extremity of the Malian bay. Here was the pass of Thermopylæ, which extended more than a mile in

[1] Lib. viii. c. 1.

[2] The ninth book of Strabo, chapter 3, contains a description of Phocis. The tenth book of Pausanias is on the same subject, the greater part being devoted to Delphi.

length between the cliffs of Œta[1] and a marshy tract close to the shore of the bay, and opened by a narrow pass into the territory of Epicnemidian Locris. In early times it belonged to the Phocians, who carried a wall across the western end of the pass, to check the incursions of the Thessalians. The Phocian territory then extended as far as the Eubœan strait, and there was a Phocian town on the coast called Daphnus. A Locrian tribe afterwards got possession of this district as far as the sea-coast, and Phocis was separated from them by the mountains of Cnemis, from which that tribe took its name.[2]

The river Cephissus, rising in the Dorian hills near the town of Lilæa, flows through the northern part of Phocis, and empties itself into the Copaic Lake in Bœotia.[3] On a slight eminence between the valley of this river and Mount Cnemis stood Elatea, the second city of Phocis; and some miles eastward a road by the mountains led to the city of Abæ, where there was an ancient oracular temple of Apollo destroyed by Xerxes, the ruins of which were long preserved by the Greeks as a memorial.[4]

The far-famed mountain of Parnassus rises a little above the centre of Phocis, its highest summit being nearly 8,000 feet above the level of the sea. On a slope of the mountain, about seven or eight miles below the summit, and itself 2,000 feet above the level of the sea, stood the ancient Pytho, afterwards Delphi, the capital city of Phocis, and seat of the famous oracle of Apollo. Homer calls it the rocky Pytho.[5] Seven miles and a half to the south, at the head of the Crissæan bay, was Cirrha, anciently called Crissa. A mountain called Cirphis overhung the town, and the river Plistus, rising in the Parnassian hills, flowed through it into the bay. This afterwards, as we shall see, became the port of Delphi.[6]

Under the eastern declivity of Parnassus, two or three miles from the Bœotian frontier, was Daulis, whose people are said by Pausa-

[1] At that point the mountain took the name of Callidromus. Strabo, ix. 428.

[2] Strabo, ix. 416, 424, 425. Daphnus for some time divided the territory of the Epicnemidian Locrians from that of the Opuntian Locrians; then it became a Locrian town, but was at length destroyed. There was an ancient monument here to Schedius, the Homeric leader of the Phocians.

[3] Lilæa, near to its source, is mentioned as a Phocian town by Homer; Iliad, ii. 523.

[4] Pausanias, x. 34, 35. Sophocles, Œdipus Rex, 899.

[5] *Πυθῶνά τε πετρήεσσαν.* Iliad, ii. 519.

[6] Pausanias, x. 1, 37. But Strabo, ix. 418, represents Crissa and Cirrha to have been different towns. Grote has adopted this view, though he rejects Strabo's account of the two wars, one in which Cirrha was destroyed by the Crissæans, the other in which Crissa was destroyed by the Amphictyons. (History of Greece, iv. 82.)

nias to have been the most warlike of the Phocians.[1] The town of Anticyra stood at the head of a gulf bearing the same name, to the east of the Crissæan gulf, and is said to have been the same town which Homer in the catalogue of warriors calls Cyparissus.[2]

Other Phocian towns were Charadra and Amphiclea (called Amphicæa by Herodotus) on the borders of Doris; Hyampolis on the confines of Opuntian Locris; Ledon (the birth-place of Philomelus) and Parapotamii, situated in the vale of the Cephisus, the most fertile part of Phocis: Neon, to the north-west of Mount Parnassus; Anemorea, the most central town; Panopeus and Ambrysus, on the Bœotian frontier, the last of which became of importance in the war of Thebes and Athens against Philip.[3]

Altogether Phocis comprised from twenty to thirty small cities or communities, which were federally united. A general congress was held at a place on the road from Daulis to Delphi, where there was a large national building called Phocicum, to which deputies were sent by each of the communities.[4] Delphi, however, notwithstanding its local position, had from an early period separated itself from the Phocian confederacy, and the inhabitants did not even like to be called Phocians.[5] The government was in the hands of a few noble families, who traced their descent from Deucalion, and from whom were chosen a council of five, to manage the affairs of the temple. The members of this council held their offices for life, and were called "The Sacred ones."[6]

The Delphian oracle was the most celebrated of all in the Grecian

[1] Pausanias, x. 4. It was here that the metamorphosis of Philomela took place according to the fable, whence the nightingale is called *Daulias ales.* Ovid, Epist. Sappho, 154. Thucydides, ii. 29. Strabo, ix. 423.

[2] Homer, Iliad, ii. 519, and Heyne's notes on the passage. Pausanias, x. 36. This, like the Thessalian Anticyra, was celebrated for its hellebore. Strabo, ix. 418.

[3] Pausanias, x. 33, &c.

[4] Pausanias, x. 5, 1.

[5] Pausanias, iv. 34, 11. Thirlwall thinks that the Delphians were of Dorian extraction, and that this may account for their generally favoring the cause of the Spartans and their Dorian allies. (History of Greece, i. 377.) It is probable enough that as Delphi, from a mere village, grew by degrees into a large and flourishing city, enriched and embellished by the tribute of visitors from all parts, the Delphians chose to consider it as belonging to the whole Hellenic nation, rather than to any local community, and on such grounds asserted their independence; in which they found themselves supported by some of the stronger states of Greece.

[6] Plutarch, Gr. Quæst. 9. In Euripides, Ion, 416, they are called *Δελφῶν ἀριστεῖς, οὓς ἐκλήρωσεν πάλος.* Herodotus, viii. 36, speaks of *τοῦ προφήτεω.* Was he the chief member of the council?

world, and held from the earliest times in the highest veneration. It was consulted on the most important occasions, both for political purposes, as on questions of war and peace, the establishment of laws, the institution of religious ceremonies, the founding of colonies, and the like, and also for advice in the concerns of private life.[1] Its origin is necessarily obscure. It is said that a vapor, issuing from the well of Cassotis, intoxicated those that approached it, and threw them into delirium. The discovery was made by some shepherds, whose flocks straying near the spot had been seized with convulsions. It was then found that human beings were similarly affected, and that, while the fit was on them, they received a miraculous power of prophetic vision and speech. This led to the idea of securing the benefit of the divine agency, which produced such miraculous effects, by establishing a permanent oracle on the spot. A temple was built accordingly: the chasm from which the vapor ascended was exactly in the centre: a tripod was placed over it; on this sat the priestess and inhaled the sacred smoke, under whose influence she poured forth the supernatural sounds inspired by Apollo.[2]

[1] Colonies were rarely founded without the sanction of Apollo. Callimachus says, in his hymn:—

Φοῖβος γὰρ ἀεὶ πολίεσσι φιληδεῖ
Κτιζομέναις, αὐτὸς δὲ θεμείλια φοῖβος ὑφαίνει.

Instances of consulting the oracle before making war, or taking other decisive measures, abound in Herodotus, Thucydides, and other ancient historians. The cases of Lycurgus and Crœsus are familiar. The Corcyræans offer to refer their dispute about Epidamnus to the arbitration of the Delphian oracle. (Thucydides, i. 28.) Apollo commands the Lacedæmonians to remove the sepulchre of Pausanias, and erect statues to him in the temple of Pallas. (Thucydides, i. 134.) Many examples occur of private men consulting the god. To consult him however for a wicked purpose was a dangerous experiment. The general belief on that subject is illustrated by the story of the Spartan Glaucus, who inquired whether it would be safe to refuse restoration of a deposit, and was punished by extirpation of his race. Herodotus, vi. 86. Juvenal, Sat. xiii. 199.

Spartano cuidam respondit Pythia vates,
Haud impunitum quondam fore, quod dubitaret
Depositum retinere, et fraudem jure tueri
Jurando: quærebat enim quæ numinis esset
Mens, et an hoc illi facinus suaderet Apollo.
Reddidit ergo metu, non moribus, et tamen omnem
Vocem adyti dignam templo veramque probavit,
Extinctus totâ pariter cum gente domoque,
Et quamvis longâ deductis gente propinquis.

[2] Pausanias, x. 24, 7. Strabo, ix. 419. Diodorus, xvi. 26. As to the ancient legend of Apollo, his choice of the oracular seat, his killing of

The priestess, or Pythia, as she was called, was a native of Delphi, and chosen from a humble family. She was anciently a girl; but one having been seduced by a young Thessalian, it was determined by the Delphians that, for the future, no priestess should be appointed under the age of fifty, though she was always to be dressed in the garb of a maiden. As the importance of the oracle increased, it became necessary to appoint two and even three women to perform the prophetic functions. For these they were duly prepared by a three days' fast, by bathing in the holy spring of Castaly, and other religious rites. The due observance of such rites was seen to by the Delphian managers, to whom the business of the oracle was confided. It has been supposed, that the priestess frequently acted under their dictation in delivering the responses; in later times, when powerful states made a tool of the oracle, this was very frequently the case; but to suppose that it was an ordinary occurrence in the early times, would be inconsistent with the received traditions of history, as well as with probability. In the great multitude of instances in which the god was consulted, the Delphians had no interest in practicing deception; while they had an interest, which in the early ages must generally have been paramount to all other motives, in maintaining the reputation of the oracle for truth and wisdom. The priestess was usually, from either physical or mental causes, or both, excited to a species of frenzy; and sometimes even died in convulsions after her prophetic labors. We can hardly believe that her madness was habitually feigned, and it is not compatible with a system of craft on the part of the Pythia or her employers.[1]

the serpent that guarded it, the origin of the names Pytho and Delphi, &c.; see the Homeric Hymn to Apollo, and also Pausanias, x. 6, 3. Compare Strabo, ix. 422.

[1] Plutarch, de Defectu Oracul. 51. The general respect in which the Delphian oracle was held by the Grecian world inclines one to believe in some superhuman agency, whether of a divine or of an evil spirit. Many of the responses were (no doubt) expressed with designed ambiguity; but the well attested truthfulness of others can not be set down to chance. Strabo agrees with Herodotus as to the character of the oracle. He calls it *ἀψευδέστατον τῶν πάντον*, (ix. 419, 422.) Cicero in his first book de Divinatione (c. 19) urges in favor of the oracle, that it never could have been so celebrated but for its veracity. Admitting its decline in later times, he says, "Ut igitur nunc minori gloriâ est, quia minus oraculorum veritas excellit, sic tum, nisi summâ veritate, in tantâ gloriâ non fuisset." He suggests as a possible cause of its decline, that the inspiring vapor may have disappeared: "Potest vis illa terræ, quæ mentem Pythiæ divino afflatu concitabat, evanuisse vetustate, ut quosdam exaruisse amnes aut in alium cursum contortos et deflexos videmus." The decline of the oracle after the Christian era, which Milton has so beautifully touched upon in his Christmas hymn, favors the no-

Certain days in every month were appointed for consulting the oracle, to which people came from every state of Greece. The Delphians regulated the order of consultation, which was generally determined by lot; but sometimes, as a mark of honor or favor, they granted precedency to particular states, as for example, to Crœsus, to Sparta, to Athens, and afterwards to Philip of Macedon. Sometimes also they granted exemption from payment of the usual fees.[1]

Delphi stood pretty nearly in the centre of Greece, a position highly favorable for the oracle.[2] The temple was built on rising ground in the highest part of the city, the front (after its reconstruction, B.C. 548) being of Parian marble. The sacred precinct was adorned with a multitude of beautiful statues and sculptures, presented by the different states of Greece.[3] Gifts of all kinds, ingots of gold and silver, vases, bowls, statues, shields, and other ornaments, were sent by kings and people, as well as by private individuals, from Greece, Italy, Sicily, Sardinia, the Ægæan isles, and Asia Minor; particular cells or compartments being appropriated for their reception.[4] Even in Homer's time Delphi was celebrated for its riches.[5]

These were continually augmented till the period of the second Persian invasion, when Xerxes, having received accurate intelligence of the accumulated treasures, marched to Delphi for the ex-

tion of demoniacal agency. Lucan expresses the feelings of the most pious heathens, when he says:—

> Non ullo sæcula dono
> Nostra carent majore Deûm, quam Delphica sedes
> Quod siluit.

[1] Euripides, Ion, 421. Æschylus, Eumenid. 32. Demosthenes, 3 Philipp. 119. De Fals. Leg. 446. Herodotus, i. 54, and Schweighæuser's note. Plutarch in Vit. Pericl. 21, Vit. Alexand. 14. Alexander, when the priestess demurred about the time of consultation, dragged her by force into the temple; upon which she exclaimed, "My son, thou art invincible:" and he said there was no further need to question the god.

[2] Hence called *γῆς ὀμφαλός*. Strabo, ix. 419. The allusion to this by the poets are frequent. Ex. gr. Euripides, Orest. 591.

> *'Ορᾷς ; 'Απόλλων, ὃς μεσομφάλους ἕδρας*
> *ναίων βροτοῖσι στόμα νέμει σαφέστατον.*

[3] Pausanias, x. 8, 9. The following chapters contain a long enumeration of what he had seen. Herodotus, v. 62.

[4] Herodotus, i. 14, 50, 51. Strabo, ix. 421.

[5] Iliad, ix. 404.

> *Οὐδ' ὅσα λάϊνος οὐδὸς ἀφήτορος ἐντὸς ἐέργει*
> *Φοίβου 'Απόλλωνος Πυθοῖ ἔνι πετρηέσσῃ,*

Sophocles calls it *πολυχρύσου Πυθῶνος*. Œdipus Tyr. 151.

press purpose of pillage.[1] After his defeat Apollo shared with the other gods in the spoil of the invader.[2]

The importance of Delphi was yet further increased by the institution of the Pythian games, and by its having been at a still earlier period chosen as one of the seats of the Amphictyonic council. The nature and functions of this council are so intimately connected with the subject before us, that I must stop to explain them.

It is related by ancient historians, that Amphictyon, the son of Deucalion, founded the institution which bears his name, and the importance of which was in course of time so greatly enlarged as to have been called a general council or diet of all Greece.[3] Modern writers consider Amphictyon to be a fictitious personage, invented by mythologists, and deriving his name from the very council which he is supposed to have founded, and which really signifies (according to the etymology of the word)[4] an association of neighboring people for some common purpose, whether of mutual defense, intercourse, or sacrifice. The habits of the ancient Greeks inclined them to form associations of this kind, especially those of a religious character; and that many such existed, and were called Amphictyones, we are distinctly informed; for example, one in the island Calauria, one at Onchestus in Bœotia, and the more celebrated one of Delos. But that which held its meetings at Delphi and Thermopylæ acquired so much greater a celebrity than all the rest, as to be specially called the Amphictyonic assembly.[5]

Twelve different people or tribes united to form this association; Bœotians, Dorians, Ionians, Thessalians, Perrhæbians, Magnetes, Œtæans, Phthiots, Malians, Locrians, Phocians, Dolopians.[6] Such, gathered from the somewhat varying accounts of different authors, is considered to be the most probable enumeration of its members.

[1] Herodotus, vii. 35.

[2] Herodotus, viii. 121; ix. 81. Delphi, like other temples, was greatly enriched by the spoils of war, as appears from a multitude of cases mentioned by ancient authors. Compare Herodotus, vii. 132; viii. 27. Thucydides, ii. 84; iv. 134. Xenophon, Hellen. iii. c. 3, s. 1. Diodorus, xii. 29; xiv. 93, where it is mentioned that the Romans sent to Delphi a tithe of the spoils of Veii.

[3] So Cicero calls it, De Inventione, ii. 23. "Accusantur apud Amphictyonas, id est, apud commune Græciæ concilium." In the Amphictyonic decree cited in Demosthenes de Coron. 198, it is called *τὸ κοινὸν τῶν Ἑλλήνων συνέδριον*.

[4] *Ἀμφικτίονες*. See Pindar, Isthm. iv. 13. How the vowel came to be changed, we can not tell.

[5] Pausanias, x. 8. Strabo, ix. 429. Herodotus, vii. 200. Thirlwall, Gr. Hist. i. 373. Grote, ii. 321. Archæological Dictionary, Title *Amphictyones.*

[6] Thirlwall, (i. 377,) thinks that the Dolopians were finally supplanted by the Delphians, who appear in another list.

They met twice a year; in the spring at Delphi, in the autumn at the temple of Ceres in Thermopylæ, near to the town of Anthela. Each tribe sent deputies to the congress, called *Pylagoræ* and *Hieromnemones*. The former attended and spoke in the debates, and voted for their respective tribes, each of whom had two votes. The latter were persons of a sacerdotal character, whose functions were principally executive, and related to the sacrifices and religious observances, though they seem also to have attended the debates and assisted the Pylagoræ, but without the right of voting. From Athens there were sent three Pylagoræ, annually elected by the people, and one Hieromnemon, chosen by lot.[1] It appears both from Æschines and Demosthenes, that besides the ordinary congress of deputies, which sat in the temple or sacred building, there was occasionally convened a sort of popular Amphictyonic assembly, composed not only of the Pylagoræ and Hieromnemons, but also of the inhabitants of the place, and such strangers as had come to worship or consult the Deity.[2]

The list of tribes indicates that it was anciently a local rather than a national confederacy. Peloponnesus was altogether excluded; for the Dorians, at the institution of the council, were simply the Dorians under Mount Œta, not the conquering race who at a later period comprised the most warlike states of Greece. These states afterwards became Amphictyonic, by virtue of their Dorian origin, as Athens did by virtue of its Ionic. Arcadia, Elis, and Achaia, however, at no time belonged to the confederacy; neither did Ætolia, or Acarnania.

Another thing to be remarked is the preponderance of Greeks north of Thermopylæ, and the power thereby given to the Thessalians; a circumstance which became of great moment in the struggle with Philip of Macedon. Thessaly,[3] in its widest sense included the whole district bounded on the north by Olympus and the Cambunian range of mountains, on the east by the Ægæan sea, on the south and west by Mounts Œta and Pindus. Thus considered, it

[1] Aristophanes, Nubes, 624. The office of Hieromnemon was deemed a very honorable one (See Demosthenes cont. Timocr. 747), and the better opinion is, that it was held for a longer period than one year, and perhaps for life. See the Archæol. Dict. title *Amphictyones*.

[2] Æschines, cont. Ctesiph. 71. De Fals. Leg. 48. Demosthenes, de Coron. 278. Who are the *σύνεδροι*, mentioned in the Amphictyonic decrees in Demosthenes, is uncertain; but perhaps it means the Hieromnemons, who sat as assessors with the Pylagoræ, to suggest and advise, (see p. 276), and are said even in a loose way (p. 277) *ψηφίσασθαι*. By the decree it was resolved, *ἐπελθεῖν τοὺς πυλαγόρους καὶ τοὺς συνέδρους*, and by the showing of Demosthenes, the Hieromnemons did walk over the district in question.

[3] The description of Thessaly occupies the fifth chapter of the ninth book of Strabo.

comprehends half of the Amphictyonic tribes; but the Thessalians, strictly so called, occupied only a portion of this district, the remainder being held by other races, more or less subject or subordinate to them. The Perrhæbians dwelt between the river Peneus and Mount Olympus. The Magnetes on the coast of the Ægæan, under Mounts Ossa and Pelion: their country was called Magnesia. The Achæan Phthiots occupied the plain beneath Mount Othrys, stretching from thence in a south-easterly direction as far as the Pagasæan bay, upon which was the town of Halus. The Malians were between Phthiotis and Thermopylæ, giving name to the Malian bay; in their country were the cities of Anticyra and Trachis; and afterwards Heraclea was founded by the Lacedæmonians.[1] West of the Malians were the Œtæans, occupying the northern slopes of Mount Œta: they included the Ænianes, whom Pausanias enumerates as one of the Amphictyonic people. Dolopia was to the north-east of Mount Othrys, and stretched beyond Pindus as far as the river Achelous.

The people strictly called Thessali inhabited chiefly the central plain between Mounts Pindus, Olympus, Ossa, Pelion, and Othrys. Their chief cities were Larissa, Pharsalus, Crannon, and Pheræ. Originally they came from Thesprotia in Epirus, and after subduing a Pelasgic or Æolian race, whom they found in occupation, they established themselves in their new country as a sort of dominant aristocracy. The conquered people were reduced to the condition of serfs, and were called Penestæ;[2] being bound to cultivate the land, and follow their masters to battle when required. The Thessalians gradually extended their power over the circumjacent tribes; and, could they have been united and under a firm government, would have become formidable to the southern states of Greece: but they had no organized system of government, and the feuds between the great families prevented any union taking place, except on particular occasions, and for short periods. The ancient quadruple division of Thessaly, which Philip revived for his own purposes, was probably established at a time when the Thessalians had arrived at a considerable height of power. The four districts were called Thessaliotis, Histiæotis, Pelasgiotis, and Phthiotis; of which the first comprised the central plain, the second the territory of the Perrhæbians and the north-western parts, the third the east-

[1] Thucydides, ii. 92. They hoped that it would give them the command of Thermopylæ, and the means of making a descent upon the northern coast of Eubœa.

[2] The word is either derived from πενία, *poverty*; or, according to another account, is a corruption of μένεσται, from μένω, because they were permanently attached to the soil, and could not, like slaves, be sold or sent away. Dionysius, Antiq. Rom. ii. 9. Athenæus, vi. 264.

ern coast, and the fourth the country of the Achæan Phthiots already described.[1]

Another thing to be noticed is, that Amphictyonic membership belonged not to cities, but to tribes or races, each of whom had the same number of votes, however great, or however small; so that, after the great expansion of the Ionic and Doric races, the right of representation in the Amphictyonic congress was shared by Athens and Sparta with the numerous communities which had sprung out of those races respectively. It is supposed that the different cities of one tribe took their turns of sending representatives, according to some arrangement of which we have no particular information. It is probable that a leading and powerful state would gradually assume to itself the rights of the whole tribe; yet still its constitutional power in the congress would be limited to the original number of votes; and Athens or Sparta could only acquire a preponderating weight among the Amphictyons through the influence which they exerted over the other constituent tribes. To such influence is partly to be ascribed the increasing importance of the Amphictyonic body, and its growth from a mere local association into the semblance of an Hellenic diet. The sanctity of the Delphian temple gave an additional lustre to its meetings.[2]

The oath anciently taken by the members of the league was to the following effect:—"That they would not destroy any city of the Amphictyonic tribes; that they would not cut of their springs of water either in peace or war; that they would turn their arms against any people who did such things, and destroy their cities; that, if any one committed sacrilege against the god, or formed, or was privy to, any design to injure the temple, they would exert themselves with hand, foot, tongue, and all their might, to punish him."[3]

History furnishes us with a few examples in which the Amphictyons at an early period interposed in the affairs of Greece, to vindicate national rights or public justice, or to maintain the honor of Apollo. Thus, when the conductors of a procession to Delphi were insulted by some Megarians, the Amphictyons passed sentence on the offenders.[4] When the Dolopians Scyrus, who had long been addicted to piracy, seized and imprisoned some Thessalian merchants who put into their port, and the merchants escaping preferred their complaint to the Amphictyons, they condemned the islanders

[1] Strabo, ix. 430. Diodorus, iv. 67. Herodotus, vii. 129, 176. Thucydides, i. 2; ii. 22; iv. 78. Xenophon, Hellen. vi. c. 1. Grote's History of Greece, ii. 367.

[2] The meeting at Delphi, as well as that at Thermopylæ, was called ἡ Πυλαία, *the Pylæan meeting*, a circumstance tending to show the greater antiquity of the latter. See Grote, ii. 328.

[3] Æschines, De Fals. Leg. 43.

[4] Plutarch, Gr. Quæst. 59.

to pay a fine. The guilty people, rather than pay the fine, chose to surrender the island to Cimon, who took advantage of the occasion to annex it to the dominion of Athens.[1] At the close of the Persian war, the Amphictyons offered a reward for Ephialtes who betrayed the pass over the mountains to Xerxes.[2] They erected a monument to Leonidas.[3] After the burning of the Delphian temple, B.C. 548, we find them intrusted with the task of rebuilding it, and the Alcmæonids taking the contract from them for three hundred talents.[4] They claimed the right, supposed to be derived from their earliest institution, of sitting in judgment upon disputes between Amphictyonic cities; a right which it must have been difficult to exercise, except over the less powerful of their members. Traces of such a jurisdiction however are to be found.[5]

The most memorable instance of Amphictyonic action in the early times is that known by the name of the first Sacred war, which terminated in the destruction of the city of Crissa, and afforded a precedent for the punishment of the Phocians and Locrians two or three centuries after. The Crissæans were charged with taking extortionate tolls from the visitors who came to Delphi by sea from the western parts of Greece, or from Italy and Sicily, and who came across the Corinthian gulf into the Crissæan harbor. They were charged (according to another account) with having encroached upon the land of Apollo, and with having committed outrages upon some Phocian and Argive women returning from the temple. Perhaps all these charges were mixed together.[6] War was declared by the Amphictyons, at the instigation (according to Plutarch)[7] of Solon the Athenian. Clisthenes, king of Sicyon, was chosen to conduct the war, in which the Athenians took an active part, under the command either of Solon himself or of Alcmæon, and the Thessalians under Eurylochus. The Crissæans were besieged, but they made an obstinate resistance, and the war, like that of Troy, is said to have lasted ten years. It was declared by the oracle, that Crissa would never be taken, until the waves washed the territories of

1 Plutarch in Vit. Cimon. 8. Thucydides, i. 98.

2 Herodotus, vii. 213.

3 Herodotus, 228.

4 Herodotus, ii. 180; v. 62; Strabo, ix. 421; Pausanias, x. 5. The temple built by the Amphictyons was said to be the third.

5 Strabo, ix. 420. Demosthenes de Coron. 271. The suit there referred to was probably an Amphictyonic suit. Compare the same oration, p. 277.

6 They are stated with vague generality by Æschines, Cont. Ctes. 68. It is probable, that the Delphians, who owed their prosperity to the donations of visitors, were jealous of any thing which diverted that source of profit into another channel.

7 In the life of Solon. He professes to follow Aristotle's treatise on the victors at the Pythian games.

Delphi. Solon advised, that the way to fulfill the oracle was to consecrate to Apollo all the land of the Crissæans. This was done; the besiegers solemnly vowed that the Crissæan land should be given to Apollo, and should for ever lie waste: soon after this the city was taken by stratagem. Solon diverted the stream of the Plistus, and after poisoning the waters with the roots of hellebore, suffered them to return to their former channel; the besieged drank them with avidity and miserably perished. Thus Crissa fell, in the year B.C. 585. The victors performed their vow, and after razing the city to the ground, turned the whole of its domain into a wilderness. The harbor was given to the Delphians, who now became masters of the whole plain from Parnassus to the sea.[1]

To commemorate this victory, the Amphictyons, enriched by the spoil of the conquered city, established the Pythian games, which thenceforth were celebrated quadriennially in the third year of every Olympic period. There had been anciently, established by the Delphians themselves, an octennial musical festival, in one of which it was said the poet Thamyris had obtained the prize. This was enlarged into a more comprehensive one, including not only competition in music and poetry, exhibitions of art in painting and sculpture, but also gymnastic contests, with foot, horse, and chariot races, after the model of the Olympic. These were not indeed established all at once, but with additions in successive periods: the chariot race was introduced in the second Pythiad, when Clisthenes of Sicyon was the victor: a part of the Crissæan plain was converted into the race-course. At the same time the prizes (which were at first awarded as in the old musical contests) were abolished, and the victor's meed was thenceforth a simple wreath of laurel; no less efficacious than the Olympian olive to excite the emulation of competitors, striving for glory before the eyes of assembled Greece. The games were under the immediate superintendence of the Amphictyonic deputies.[2]

[1] Pausanias, x. 37. Strabo, ix. 418. Æschines, Cont. Ctes. 69. Atheuæus, xiii. 560. Polyænus, vi. 13.

[2] Pausanias, x. 7, 33. Strabo, ix. 421. Archæological Dictionary, title *Pythia*. The course is called the Crissæan Plain by Sophocles, Electra, 729.

πᾶν δ' ἐπίμπλατο
Ναυαγίων Κρισᾶιον ἱππικῶν πέδον.

The Pythian games were open to all the Greeks, not only to the members of the Amphictyonic association: an Ætolian is mentioned in the same passage as one of the competitors, v. 704.

Whether the games were celebrated in the spring or the autumn, has been a contested point. Boeckh is for the spring: Clinton and Grote are for the autumn. See Grote's History of Greece, iv. 86.

The surprise of the Persian on hearing that the Greek athletes contended for an olive garland is well described by Herodotus, viii. 26.

Of the history of the Phocians little is known till just before the second Persian invasion. We learn that they had much difficulty in maintaining their independence against the Thessalians, who, after subduing most of the tribes north of Mount Œta, endeavored to push their conquests southward. To check their incursions, the Phocians had anciently, at a time when Thermopylæ belonged to them, closed up its western entrance with a wall, which, when properly guarded, was deemed a complete barrier against an enemy advancing from the Malian side. The pass had two gates or openings; one where the wall was built, which opened into the road from Anthela to Trachis, giving room for a single wagon only to enter; another, equally narrow, which opened about a mile to the east just above the town of Alpeni. The space between the two gates was considerably wider, and contained hot springs, salt or sulphurous, which gave to the pass the name of Thermopylæ, or *Hot Gates.*[1] The Phocians, besides blocking up the entrance, endeavored to make the road impassable by turning into it the water of the mineral springs. These precautions however were rendered of no avail by the discovery of a new road; which, commencing near Trachis, and taking a westerly course up the gorge of the river Asopus, ascended the mountain by a track called Anopæa, then turned eastward and descended to Alpeni. The Trachinians having revealed this road to the Thessalians, the pass ceased to be an invincible barrier, and the wall soon afterwards was neglected or abandoned. It was probably owing to this, that the Phocians lost the territory, which was afterwards acquired by the Epicnemidian Locrians. Certain it is, that they became exposed to invasion from the north, and were reduced to rely on their own valor for their safety.[2] We have no particulars of the wars carried on between them and the Thessalians, until not many years before the Persian invasion, when a Thessalian army crossed the Locrian frontier, and were defeated by a stratagem at Hyampolis. The Phocians, dreading their superiority in cavalry, put into the ground a quantity of pots covered with loose earth; the horses charging over these were lamed, and their riders overthrown and slaughtered. To avenge this disaster, the Thessalians entered Phocis with an immense force collected from all their confederate cities. The Phocians terrified by their numbers, and further disheartened by the loss of a detachment whom they had sent to reconnoitre the enemy, made a huge funeral pile, and bringing together all their women and children, their gold, silver, and other valuables, and the images of their gods, gave them in charge to thirty of their countrymen, with orders, in case they should be defeated, to kill the

[1] Thermopylæ was the name given by the Greeks in general; Pylæ, by the neighbors and surrounding people. Herodotus, vii. 201. Strabo, ix. 428.

[2] Herodotus, vii. 176, 199, 200, 215, 216.

women and children, and burn their bodies together with all the property on the funeral pile, then to kill themselves or rush upon the swords of the enemy. Having given such order, they marched to meet the Thessalians, and fought with such desperation, that they gained a great victory and delivered their country. From this Phocian desperation became a proverb.[1]

Herodotus and Pausanias, from whom we pick up these scraps of history, mention also a successful night-attack made upon the Thessalian camp by a select body of Phocians, having first whitened their faces and shields with chalk, to distinguish them from the enemy. According to Herodotus, the Phocians had first been driven to the fastnessess of Parnassus. Pausanias relates, that the Phocians in their alarm consulted the Delphian oracle, which returned a mysterious answer, that Apollo would cause a mortal to encounter an immortal, that he would give victory to both, but more complete victory to the mortal. This was understood to be fulfilled after the final battle, in which the Thessalians chose for their watchword Itonian Pallas, the Phocians their Eponymous hero, Phocus. To show their gratitude, the Phocians sent to Delphi statues of Apollo and their own commanders, including the prophet Tellias of Elis, under whose counsel they had acted.

After the battle of Thermopylæ the Thessalians had their revenge. They were at first opposed to Xerxes, notwithstanding that the Aleuadæ had invited him into Greece; and, while he was preparing to cross the Hellespont, they sent envoys to Peloponnesus, urging that troops should be brought to guard the passes of Olympus, and proffering their assistance. Themistocles and Euænetus sailed with this force to Halus, from whence they marched across Thessaly, and joined by the Thessalian cavalry occupied the defiles of Tempe: being informed however, that their position could easily be turned by the enemy, they re-embarked their troops and sailed home. The Thessalians then, finding that they could have no support from the southern Greeks, tendered their submission to Xerxes, in which they were followed by the Perrhæbians, Magnetes, and other northern tribes, and also by the Dorians, Locrians, and Bœotians excepting Thespiæ and Platæa. The Greeks determined on defending Thermopylæ, which Leonidas with an advanced body was sent to occupy, whilst the fleet sailed to Artemisium, on the north of the Eubœan channel, from which point they could freely communicate with Leonidas, and prevent the Persians landing troops in his rear.[2]

Leonidas, arriving at Thermopylæ, invited the Phocians and the Opuntian Locrians to join him. They both complied; the Phocians joining him with a thousand men, the Opuntian Locrians with their

[1] Herodotus, viii. 27, 28. Pausanias, x 1.
[2] Herodotus, vii. 6, 172, 173, 174, 175.

whole force.[1] He set to work immediately to repair the ancient wall; but hearing now for the first time, that there was another road over the mountains, he sent the Phocians, at their own request, to defend it, while with the remainder of his forces he kept his station in the pass. Most of the Greeks were struck with terror at the approaching multitudes of the enemy, and desired to retreat to the isthmus; it was with some difficulty, and chiefly owing to the remonstrances of the Phocians and Locrians, anxious for the safety of their own countries, that they were induced to remain at Thermopylæ. Xerxes, having marched through Macedonia and Thessaly, arrived in the Malian territory, and encamped at Trachis, two miles from the pass. After two days fighting, in which the Persians suffered prodigious loss, Xerxes learned from the Trachinians the existence of the mountain road, and dispatched Hydarnes with a body of Persians (who were called the Immortals) to march by night over the cliff and fall upon the rear of Leonidas. The Persians, under the guidance of Ephialtes the Trachinian, marched all night, and at daybreak had mounted to the highest part of the rocky road, and were heard by the Phocians, who grasped their arms and prepared for battle; but soon, overwhelmed by the arrows of so numerous a host, they fled to the brow of the cliff, where they awaited the enemy with the intention of selling their lives dearly. Hydarnes, not caring to attack the Phocians, pursued his march and descended the mountain. The Greeks, hearing of his advance, had just time to retire from their perilous situation, where Leonidas and his devoted band preferred to remain and sacrifice themselves for the honor of their country.[2]

Xerxes, advancing from Thermopylæ, was reinforced by an addition of Greek auxiliaries, the Malians, Dorians, Locrians, and Bœotians, who now joined him with all their troops, excepting (as before) the people of Thespiæ and Platæa.[3] The Locrians would probably have joined him at Thermopylæ, for they had engaged to seize the pass for him, but had been prevented by the arrival of Leonidas.[4] The Phocians, notwithstanding the advance of so numerous an army, still refused submission. A message of a singular kind was sent to them by the Thessalians, stating that they (the Thessalians) had great influence with Xerxes, and that it depended on them whether the Phocians should be reduced to slavery or otherwise; that they were willing to forget past injuries, and, if the Phocians would give them fifty talents, they would undertake to

[1] Πανστρατιῇ. (Herodotus, vii. 203.) This means their whole force of heavy armed troops. The Opuntian Locrians, as well as the Phocians, were armed in this fashion. Pausanias, i. 23.

[2] Herodotus, vii. 201, 207, 208, 211, 213—23.

[3] Herodotus, viii. 66.

[4] Diodorus, xi. 4.

avert the tempest that was about to fall upon them. The Phocians spurned this proposal. Herodotus says, they sided with the Greeks purely out of hatred to the Thessalians; that, if the Thessalians had been on the other side, the Phocians would have been with the Mede. There seems however scarcely any ground for attributing their conduct to such a motive. The answer which the Phocians returned was, that they would give no money, that they were at liberty to Medise as well as the Thessalians, if they chose; but they would not consent to betray the cause of Greece.[1]

The Thessalians, on receiving this answer, conducted the barbarian army into Phocis, entering it from the north by a narrow strip of Doris which separates it from Mount Œta, and commenced ravaging the rich valley of the Cephisus. The Phocian people every where fled before them. Some took refuge in the heights of Parnassus, on a ridge of rocks called the Tithorea, above the city of Neon. The greater part found shelter at Amphissa in Ozolian Locris. Meanwhile the Persians laid waste the whole country, plundering and destroying all in their way, and setting fire to the cities and the temples. Fifteen of the principal cities, including Drymus, Charadra, Tethronium, Amphicæa, Neon, Elatea, Hyampolis, Parapotamii, Abæ with its oracular temple, and Panopeus, were burned to the ground.[2]

A division of the army was sent to Delphi, with special orders to seize the treasures of the temple. The Delphians in alarm inquired of the oracle, whether they should bury their treasures, or carry them away into another land; Apollo assured them, that he was able to defend his own without their assistance. They then left their city, seeking refuge on the mountains, in the Corycian cave, or at Amphissa; their wives and children they sent over to Achaia. Sixty men only remained, with the chief-priest[3] Aceratus. The barbarians advanced, but hardly had they reached the temple of Pallas, which stood in front of the Phœbean sanctuary, when their progress was arrested by dreadful prodigies; a burst of thunder, the rolling of two immense crags from Parnassus, which struck down several of their host, and a war-cry issuing from the shrine of Pallas. Smitten with sudden panic, they turned and fled; the Delphians at that moment rushed upon them and completed the rout, assisted (as the surviving Persians themselves reported) by two superhuman figures in panoply, who never ceased pursuing and slaughtering them till they reached Bœotia. The Delphians declared these to be their own native heroes, Phylacus and Autonous, who had portions of ground consecrated to them in the neighborhood of the temple.

[1] Herodotus, viii. 29, 30.
[2] Herodotus, viii. 31, 32, 33, 35.
[3] See ante, page 225, note 4.

Thus did Apollo fulfill his promise, and vindicate the sanctity of the oracle.[1]

After this, it appears, a part of the Phocian people, those probably whose cities had been spared, submitted with reluctance to Xerxes; the rest maintained themselves in the mountains, from which they made incursions from time to time against the Persian army. A thousand Phocians however were sent to join Mardonius. They came so tardily, that Mardonius, to mark his displeasure, or to intimidate them for the future, or perhaps at first with a more serious intention, ordered their troop to be drawn up in a plain, and surrounded them with his numerous cavalry. The Phocians, supposing they were doomed to destruction, formed in a square, and with firm countenance awaited the attack. The horsemen rode up with lifted javelins, making a feint to charge, but as suddenly they wheeled round and retreated. Mardonius applauded the Phocians for the courage which they had shown, and assured them, if they behaved themselves well in the ensuing campaign, they would be rewarded by the king. At Platæa they were stationed with the Thebans and other Greek allies of Xerxes, and in the battle were opposed to the Athenians; but all, except the Thebans, fled without striking a blow, and Pausanias indeed states, that the Phocians deserted in battle to the Greeks.[2]

Of the spoils of the battle of Salamis the choicest part was sent to Delphi, and devoted to the construction of a colossal statue. The united Greeks inquired of the god, whether he was content with their offerings; and he replied, that he was satisfied with those of the other Greeks, but looked for a special gift from the Æginetans, to whom the palm of valor had been awarded; they sent him accordingly three golden stars fixed on a brazen mast.[3] At the close of the war a tithe of the spoil was given to Apollo, and out of it was made a golden tripod, placed by the Delphians on a three-headed brazen serpent, which endured to the time of Pausanias. Shares were assigned also to the Olympian Jupiter and Isthmian Neptune.[4] A circumstance is related by Plutarch in the life of Aristides, which proves the peculiar veneration in which the Delphian sanctuary was held by the Greeks. Soon after the battle of Platæa the oracle directed that an altar should be raised on the Platæan ground to Jupiter the Deliverer; but, as the fires in the country had been polluted by the barbarians, it commanded them to be extinguished,

[1] Herodotus, viii. 36—39; who represents that the two crags were shown to him in the sacred grove of Pallas Pronæa. Compare Pausanias, x. 23.

[2] Herodotus, ix. 17, 31, 67. Pausanias, x. 2.

[3] Herodotus, viii. 121, 122.

[4] Herodotus, ix. 81. Pausanias, x. 13. Diodorus, xi. 33. Thucydides, iii. 57.

and no sacrifice to be offered, till fire was brought from the hearth of Apollo. To comply with this injunction, Euchidas, a Platæan, ran in one day from Platæa to Delphi and back, carrying with him the sacred fire, and at the moment of his return dropped down dead with exhaustion. He was rewarded for his act of piety with a monument in the temple of Diana.[1]

A congress of the Amphictyons was held somewhere about this time, at which divers resolutions were passed touching the events of the war; among others, to offer a reward for Ephialtes, and decree a monument to Leonidas, as I have already mentioned. It was moved by the Lacedæmonians, that the Greeks who had joined Xerxes should be expelled from the Amphictyonic council; but this proposal was rejected by the deputies, under the advice of Themistocles, who feared that, if the Thessalians, Thebans, and so many other members were removed from the council, it would fall entirely under the influence of Sparta.[2]

In the long period which elapsed between the Persian and the second Sacred War the Phocians interfered but little in the general affairs of Greece; they were forced from time to time into alliances with the more powerful states, Athens, Sparta, or Thebes, in whose wars they played but a subordinate part. To recover their power at Delphi; was a thing which they still aimed at, but were never able fully to accomplish, owing to the interference of Sparta. In the year 457 B.C. they invaded the country of the Dorians, and took one or two of their cities; but the Lacedæmonians marching against them with a large Peloponnesian force defeated them in battle, and compelled them to restore their conquest.[3] After the victory of Œnophyta, won in the following year by the Athenians under Myronides over the Bœotians, not only the whole of Bœotia, but Phocis also and Opuntian Locris, fell into the power of the Athenians, and furnished them with auxiliary troops in an expedition which they made against Pharsalus in Thessaly.[4]

Just at this period Athens had acquired a vast accession of strength as a land as well as a naval power, and the Phocians by their connection with her were enabled, it seems, to become masters of Delphi; for, in the year 448 B.C. it became necessary for the Lacedæmonians to send an army into Phocis, to commence a sort of sacred war, in which they got possession of the temple and delivered it up to the Delphians; but no sooner had they retired, than the Athenians marched into the country and restored the temple to the Phocians.[5] This state of things however was of short duration; for

[1] Plutarch, in Vit. Aristid. 20.
[2] Plutarch, in Vit. Themistocl. 20.
[3] Thucydides, i. 107. Diodorus, xi. 79.
[4] Thucydides, i. 108, 111. Diodorus, xi. 81, 82, 83.
[5] Thucydides, i. 112.

in the next year the Athenians suffered the calamitous defeat at Coronea, by which they lost Bœotia and the whole of their power in the northern parts of Greece; and in two years after the thirty years truce was concluded between them and the Lacedæmonians.[1] Nine years later we find the Lacedæmonians consulting the Delphian oracle, as to the prospect of success in a war with Athens, and the god replying, that, if they carried it on with all their might, they would get the victory, and he would himself assist them: which may seem to indicate that Spartan influence was then re-established at Delphi.[2] The Corinthian speaker in the congress of allies at Sparta suggests, that for the purpose of equipping a fleet they could borrow money from Delphi and Olympia.[3] At the breaking out of the war, the Phocians are in alliance with the Peloponnesians, and together with the Bœotians and Locrians furnish a contingent of cavalry.[4] Their old enemies the Thessalians are not classed among the regular allies of Athens, though the great mass of the people were friendly to her, and succors of Thessalian horse were occasionally sent to the Athenians; but many of the nobles in Thessaly favored the Lacedæmonians, and they furnished assistance to Brasidas upon his march to Thrace.[5]

At the truce for a year concluded between the Spartans and Athenians, in the ninth year of the Peloponnesian war, the first articles of their convention were the following:[6]

[1] Thucydides, i. 113, 115. Diodorus, xii. 6, 7.

[2] Thucydides, i. 118.

[3] Thucydides, i. 121.

[4] Thucydides, ii. 9. Diodorus, xii. 42. But the Ozolian Locrians were allied with Athens. Thucydides, iii. 95, 101.

[5] Thucydides, ii. 22; iv. 78; v. 13. Compare Demosthenes, Περὶ Συντάξεως, 173. The division of parties among the Thessalians may account for their so often changing sides even in battle. Thucydides, i. 107. Diodorus, xv. 11; xviii. 12.

[6] Thucydides, iv. 118, where Haack correctly observes, that the first clause refers solely to the Lacedæmonians and their allies, by whom the privilege of access to Delphi was a concession made to Athens. The Athenians were by the war excluded generally from the continent of Greece, and unable either to consult the oracle, or attend the Pythian games. This they sorely felt, and therefore in the peace that followed, we find them expressly stipulating for liberty to all to attend the public games. The grand display made by the Athenians, especially Alcibiades, at the Olympic festival, which was celebrated in the eleventh year of the war, is particularly noticed by Plutarch in his life of that extraordinary man. Compare Thucydides, vi. 16. Grote's History of Greece, vii. 74, note.

Whether any particular offenders are alluded to by the τοὺς ἀδικοῦντας in the clause of the truce, has been a subject of question. It is not improbable that the Athenians may have charged their adversaries with

"With respect to the temple and oracle of the Pythian Apollo, we are content that all people who please may use them safely and fearlessly, according to the national customs. The Lacedæmonians and their allies who are present consent to this, and declare that they will send heralds and persuade the Bœotians and Phocians, if they can. With respect to the treasures of the god, we will take measures for the discovery of all offenders, both we and you, righteously and honestly, according to the customs of our countries, and the rest who agree, according to the customs of their countries respectively."

At the peace of Nicias, concluded in the ensuing year, the first articles were as follows:[1]

"With respect to the national temples, it is agreed that all people who please may sacrifice, and visit them, and consult the oracle, and attend the festivals, according to the customs of their country, traveling fearlessly both by sea and land. The temple and sanctuary of the Delphian Apollo, and Delphi, shall be subject to their own laws, their own taxation, and their own judicature, in regard both to persons and land belonging to them, according to their ancient customs."

From the above clauses we may perceive the great importance attached by the leading states of Greece to Delphi and its oracle, to the Pythian and other national festivals, and their anxiety to secure free access to them for all the Greeks.

We may notice also, that at this period every thing is done by Athens or Lacedæmon; the rest are all absorbed into the alliance of one or other of those cities; no national congress decides any thing; the Amphictyons are never even mentioned.

Diodorus relates that in the year B.C. 418, during the interval of the general peace, a war broke out between the Phocians and Locrians, and that a battle was fought in which more than a thousand of the Locrians were slain;[2] this is not mentioned by Thucydides, but the fact is not therefore to be doubted. That there was a feud between the Phocians and the Opuntian as well as Ozolian Locrians, which led at a later period to important consequences, is abundantly clear. Jealousies between neighbors in Greece, about some disputed

taking some of the sacred property, and that this clause was inserted to quiet them.

[1] Thucydides, v. 18. It is scarcely possible to translate accurately the word ἱερὸν, which signifies not only the sacred edifice, but all the precinct and ground consecrated to the god, including often an extensive walk or grove. Ναὸς is the building only. See Valckanaer and Schweighæuser ad Herod. vi. 19. The Delphians had their boundaries fixed, when they were definitely separated from the Phocians. (Strabo, ix. 423.)

[2] Diodorus, xii. 80. He does not say which Locrians.

territory, or for other causes, were only too common: thus the Phocians hated not only the Locrians, but the Bœotians; while towards the Athenians they had friendly feelings, and were drawn into the Peloponnesian alliance by compulsion.[1] During the blockade of Athens, when the allies debated whether mercy should be shown to the vanquished, and many, especially the Corinthians and Thebans, pressed for their destruction, the Phocians voted on the merciful side of the question, which was carried, the Lacedæmonians having strongly pronounced themselves in its favor.[2]

In the year B.C. 359, a new combination was formed among the states of Greece. Athens, Thebes, Corinth, and Argos were at the head of a league against Lacedæmon; contrived originally by the satrap Tithraustes, who sent money to Greece, in order to excite a war and withdraw Agesilaus from Asia. Certain leading men in Thebes, Corinth, and Argos, accepted the Persian gold, and proceeded at once to perform the required service, in which they found not much difficulty; for even at Thebes and Corinth the ancient feeling of attachment to Sparta had for some time past been exchanged for one of distrust and jealousy.[3] The immediate cause of war was a proceeding of the Theban statesmen, Androclidas, Ismenias, and Galaxidorus, who, wishing to throw the odium of breaking peace upon the Lacedæmonians, contrived to raise a quarrel between the Phocians and Opuntian[4] Locrians, which they expected would lead to Spartan interference. They persuaded the Locrians to commit a trespass upon some land which was the subject of dispute between them and their neighbors. To punish this, the Phocians invaded Locris, and carried off a large quantity of plunder. Androclidas and his party then urged their contrymen to assist the Locrians; and accordingly the Thebans marched into Phocis, and ravaged the country. The Phocians sent to Sparta for succor, which was readily granted; and Lysander was sent to Phocis, with orders to assemble the forces of all the allies in that neighborhood, namely, the Phocians, Œtæans, Heracleots, Malians, and Ænianians, and lead them to Haliartus in Bœotia, where the king Pausanias, who was to follow with the Peloponnesian troops and take the chief command, appointed to meet him on a given day. Lysander assembled the allies and marched into Bœotia, where he rendered an

[1] Thucydides, iii. 95, 101. Xenophon, Hellen. iii. c. 5, s. 3.

[2] Demosthenes, De Fals. Leg. 361. He mentions this as a current report at Athens. Nor is it at all inconsistent with the account of Xenophon, Hellen. ii. c. 2, s. 19, 20, though he does not state that the question was formally put to the vote.

[3] Xenophon, Hellen. iii. c. 5, ss. 1, 2. Plutarch, in Vit. Lysand. 27; in Vit. Artaxerx. 20.

[4] Pausanias, iii. 9, says it was the Amphissian Locrians; but probably he confounds this with subsequent events.

important service by detaching Orchomenus from the Theban confederacy, but afterwards, making a rash attack upon Haliartus before the arrival of Pausanias, he was defeated and slain. The Phocian and other allies dispersed. Pausanias arrived soon after; but the Thebans being reinforced by an Athenian army under Thrasybulus, he entered into a convention and returned home; for which act he was banished from Sparta, and died in exile.[1]

Soon after this a congress was held at Corinth, to consider what measures should be taken against Sparta, and it was determined to send embassies to the different states of Greece, to excite them against her. A message came to them from Medius, chief of the Alcuadæ of Larissa, requesting their aid against Lycophron, the despot of Pheræ, who was supported by the Lacedæmonians. Two thousand of the allies under the command of the Theban Ismenias were sent into Thessaly; with whose assistance Medius took the city of Pharsalus, then held by a Lacedæmonian garrison; after which Ismenias with a force of Bœotians and Argives surprised the Trachinian Heraclea,[2] and, after putting to the sword the Lacedæmonians whom he found in that city, delivered it up to the ancient inhabitants, whom he brought back from exile, strengthening them with a garrison of Argives. He then persuaded the Ænianians and Athamanians to change sides, and collecting an army of about six thousand men, prepared to take revenge on the Phocians. They, under the conduct of Lacisthenes a Laconian, marched into Locris to meet him, but were defeated with a loss of nearly a thousand men: Ismenias himself lost half that number; and the Phocians returned home without further molestation.[3]

The aspect of things was changed upon the return of Agesilaus from Asia. That general, having crossed the Hellespont, marched

[1] Xenophon, Hellen. iii. c. 5, ss. 3—7, 17—25. The Thebans, expecting the Spartan invasion, send to Athens for succor. The speech of the Theban embassador, and the reply made, occur in sections 8—16. Compare Diodorus, xiv. 81.

[2] This city, though a pet colony of Lacedæmon, had never prospered. The Thessalians and mountaineers of Œta, who considered it was fortified against them, continually annoyed and made war upon the new settlers, till they reduced it to a very scanty population. The misgovernment of the Lacedæmonian officers contributed to its ruin. In the twelfth year of the Peloponnesian war, it was in such a state of weakness, that the Bœotians took possession of it, for fear the Athenians might do the same, and they dismissed the Lacedæmonian governor. This however gave great offense at Sparta. (See Thucydides, iii. 92, 93, 100; v. 51, 52.) In the year B.C. 399, the Lacedæmonians had taken strong measures to re-establish their power at Heraclea, and driven from their homes large numbers of the mountaineers who were opposed to them. (Diodorus, xiv. 38.)

[3] Diodorus, xiv. 82.

through Thrace and Macedonia into Thessaly. There he encountered a large body of Thessalian horse, chiefly those of Larissa, Crannon, Scotussa, and Pharsalus, who, being in close alliance with the Bœotians, gathered round him to dispute his passage. Unsupported by infantry, they would not venture to join in close combat with the heavy-armed veterans of the Spartan, but hovered on his rear, and distressed him by frequent charges, till at length Agesilaus by a successful manœuvre attacked and put them to the rout. He then pursued his march through Phthiotis, and passed the strait of Thermopylæ.[1] Joined hy the troops of Phocis and Orchomenus, and by a reinforcement from Peloponnesus, he met the united army of his opponents, consisting of Bœotians, Athenians, Argives, Corinthians, Ænianians, Eubœans, and Locrians, at Coronea. The victory won in this field was purchased with hard fighting. Agesilaus severely wounded withdrew to Delphi, where he offered up a tithe of his spoils (being no less than a hundred talents) to Apollo: meanwhile his lieutenant Gylis made an irruption into Locris, and plundered the country without opposition till towards the evening, when the Locrians, occupying some high ground by which the enemy had to return, fell upon their rear, and assailing them with missiles from the heights, slew both Gylis himself and many of his officers and soldiers. The army of Agesilaus was soon afterwards disbanded, and he sailed to Sparta.[2]

The scene of war was afterwards removed to Peloponnesus, and the Lacedæmonians, being occupied nearer home, had not leisure to invade Bœotia or Attica.[3] The war continued eight years, from B.C. 395 to B.C. 387, and was terminated by the peace of Antalcidas.[4] By this it was stipulated that the Greek states should be independent; an arrangement which virtually secured the leadership to Sparta; for she was constituted guardian of the peace, and remained at the head of a great alliance, keeping also her governors, or Harmostæ, in a great number of cities, while Athens had no subjects left her but the small islands of Lemnos, Imbrus, and Sycrus; and Thebes was entirely deprived of her sovereignty over the Bœotian cities. At first the Thebans demurred to accept the peace with that condition, and insisted on taking the oath in the name of all the Bœotians; but the threat of a war, in which they would be isolated from all their allies, compelled them to accept the terms dictated by Sparta and the Persian king. The Spartans were especially rejoiced at the humiliation of Thebes, their views with respect to

[1] Xenophon, Hellen. iv. c. 3, ss. 1—9. Diodorus, xiv. 83. Plutarch, in Vit. Agesil. 16.

[2] Xenophon, Hellen. iv. c. 3, ss. 15—23; c. iv. s. 1. Diodorus, xiv. 84. Plutarch, in Vit. Agesil. 19.

[3] Xenophon, Hellen. iv. c. 7, s. 2.

[4] Diodorus, xiv. 86.

that city having been entirely changed since the end of the Peloponnesian war.[1]

The Spartans were the first to violate the conditions of that very peace which they so earnestly promoted, by their attack upon Mantinea, whose walls they demolished, and whose citizens they dispersed into villages.[2] But their most signal violation of the treaty, as well as of international faith and law, was the seizure of the Cadmea in the year B.C. 382, which brought a speedy retribution upon themselves, and led to a total change in the position and prospects of the other Greek states.[3] Of the events which followed I can make but cursory mention. The Thebans three years afterwards expel the Spartan garrison, and Sparta declares war, which however she does not prosecute with her accustomed activity. The Athenians, with the instinctive impulse which prompted them so often to assist the weak against the strong (an impulse both of policy and generosity), support their neighbors in the apparently unequal contest; until, after a seven years' war, the Thebans not only succeed in repulsing the invader, but become strong enough to reconquer the Bœotian towns, two of which, Thespiæ and Platæa, they raze to the ground, and expel the inhabitants. Immediately after this, the Athenians make peace on liberal terms with Sparta, and Thebes is left to fight single-handed. The battle of Leucta proved, contrary to the previous opinion of the Greeks, that Thebes was a match, or more than a match, for her rival in military prowess, and transferred to her that pre-eminence as a land power which had so long exclusively belonged to Sparta. The breaking np of the old Peloponnesian alliance, the Theban invasion of Laconia, the foundation of Messene and Megalopolis, were the rapid and most important consequences of this victory.[4]

This period was marked not only by the display of an extraordinary martial spirit and energy on the part of the Thebans, but by a great improvement in military tactics and organization, due to the genius of Epaminondas. His chief aim in battle seems to have been that which has been pursued with success by generals in modern times; namely, to concentrate his efforts upon some vital and decisive point, and at that point to make his attack with a numerous force of the choicest troops; a system which often gives the advan-

[1] Xenophon, Hellen. v. c. 1, ss. 31—36. Sixteen years after, the Thebans preferred fighting Sparta and her allies alone to accepting such terms; but then Epaminondas was their counselor.

[2] Xenophon, Hellen. v. c. 2, ss. 1—7. Diodorus, xv. 12.

[3] Xenophon, Hellen. v. c. 4, s. 1. Diodorus, xv. 1, 20.

[4] See my observations in the argument to the oration for the Megalopolitans, i. 204. Compare Xenophon, Hellen. vi. c. 3, 4. Diodorus, xv. 56, 59, 62. Pausanias, vi. 12; viii. 27; ix. 13, 14. Dinarchus, c. Dem. 99.

tage of superior numbers to an army less numerous on the whole than the adversary. The institution of the Sacred Band—a select body of three hundred men of the best families, intimately connected by ties of friendship, animated by the same spirit, and trained to act together as one man in battle—had a good effect in exciting emulation and setting an example to the rest of the army. This band was maintained in the Cadmea at the public cost. The whole body of citizens composing the army were by constant exercises inured to the discipline of war; and their fine appearance and martial bearing, both in the camp and in the field, excited general admiration. The leadership of Greece, thus transferred from Sparta to Thebes, may be considered to have been held by her for about ten years, from the battle of Leuctra to that of Mantinea, after which she declined.[1]

Meanwhile Athens had profited by the rupture between Sparta and Thebes, and by the dissatisfaction which the harsh measures of Sparta had excited in Greece, to put herself at the head of a new confederacy, including a great number of her old allies. Chios and Byzantium, Rhodes and Mitylene, were the first to join her; others soon followed: the alliance was formed upon an equitable basis; each member of it was to be independent, and have an equal vote in the congress, which was held at Athens. The Athenians applied themselves vigorously to the augmentation of their navy, and the battle of Naxos, B.C. 376, made her again mistress of the sea. The Lacedæmonians, making peace with Athens, B.C. 371, were content to withdraw their governors from the towns which they had so long kept in subjection, and to grant to the Greek states in reality that independence of which the peace of Antalcidas had given them but the name.[2]

The further humiliation of Sparta, consequent upon the battle of Leuctra, revived in the minds of the Athenians their ancient jealousies of Thebes, and alarmed them also, for fear the balance of power should incline too much in her favor. This again brought them into connection with Lacedæmon, and they conceived at one time the idea that they might step into her place as protectors of the

[1] Xenophon, Hellen. vi. c. 4, s. 12; vii. c. 5, ss. 12, 23, 24. Diodorus, xv. 55, 85, 88. Plutarch, in Vit. Pelopid. 18, 19. He states that Gorgidas, who first established the Sacred Band, distributed them among the different ranks; but Pelopidas, who proved their valor at Tegyra, where they fought together, ever afterwards kept them united, and charged at their head in the most difficult and dangerous enterprises. This battle of Tegyra, he says, taught the Spartans, that it was not the Eurotas that made men brave, but bravery was the produce of all countries.

[2] Diodorus, xv. 28, 29, 34. Xenophon, Hellen. v. c. 4, ss. 61—66; vi. c. 3, s. 18.

Peloponnesian allies; a scheme not destined to be realized. The junction of these two states however greatly contributed to check the ambitious efforts of the Thebans, who, after the battle of Mantinea, and the irreparable loss of their great general and statesman, Epaminondas, found that they had only depressed their enemies without being able to maintain their own position as the chiefs of a great Hellenic confederacy. Athens, with her naval strength, her insular alliance, and increasing commercial resources, was after the battle of Mantinea unquestionably the first city in Greece.[1]

The Phocians, during the first eight years of the war with Thebes, remained faithful to the Spartan alliance. They accompanied the Lacedæmonian armies in the campaigns of Agesilaus and Cleombrotus, and fought for them at Leuctra. In the year following the battle of Tegyra, that is, B.C. 374, the Thebans, having reduced the Bœotian towns, carried their arms into Phocis; a measure which (according to Xenophon) caused offence to Athens, on account of her ancient connection with that country. Cleombrotus arrived with succors, and for the time the Thebans retreated; but after the battle of Leuctra they were in a condition to persuade or compel almost all their neighbors, except the Athenians, to join them. Xenophon says, the Phocians became their subjects; Diodorus, their friends. These different terms may perhaps represent the same thing; or it may be, the mild and liberal policy of Epaminondas had prevailed upon the Phocians to fall into his views. At all events they, with the Eubœans, Locrians, Acarnanians, Heracleots, Malians, and Thessalians, formed a part of the army with which that general for the first time invaded Laconia, B.C. 369. Yet on his last expedition, before the battle of Mantinea, B.C. 362, the Phocians refused to follow him, alleging that by the terms of their treaty they were bound to defend the Thebans, if attacked, but not to join them in offensive war.[2]

The Thessalians had made but little advance, either in power or in general estimation, among the Greeks, owing chiefly to their irregular government and want of union. Unfaithful to their foreign alliances, they were not more steady among themselves. A licentious aristocracy, devoted to the pleasures of the table and riotous amusements, took no thought to improve the condition of their own dependents, much less to promote the welfare of their own common country.[3]

[1] Xenophon, Hellen. vi. c. 4, ss. 19, 20; c. 5, ss. 2, 3, 33—49. Demosthenes, Olynth. iii. 36.

[2] Xenophon, Hellen. vi. c. 1, s. 1; c. 2, s. 1; c. 3, s. 1; c. 5, s. 23; vii. c. 5, s. 4. Diodorus, xv. 31, 53, 58, 85.

[3] Isocrates, Epist. ad Philipp. ii. 410. Athenæus, vi. p. 260. Demosthenes, Olynth. i. 15, says they were *ἄπιστα φύσει καὶ ἀεὶ πᾶσιν ἀνθρώποις*. Again, De Coron. 240, *οἱ κατάπτυστοι Θετταλοὶ καὶ ἀναίσθητοι Θηβαῖοι*. The Aleuadæ were the most intelligent and refined. They

Commanding their various hordes of retainers,[1] they broke out from time to time into dissension and war with each other. A few great families, such as the Aleuadæ of Larissa, the Scopadæ of Pharsalus and Crannon, obtained by their wealth and influence a political power, which extended itself more or less over the adjacent people. Occasionally some eminent man among these families was, either with their consent, or by some other means, invested with a sort of despotic authority under the title of *Tagus.* Thus, we have seen, Medius was the chief of the Aleuadæ at Larissa.[2] In early times, as we gather from the speech (to be noticed presently) of Polydamas, a Tagus was appointed for the whole of united Thessaly, who, having a large army and national revenue at his disposal, became a very formidable potentate. The jealousy of the nobles, and their love of rude independence, prevented any such authority being permanently established. At Pheræ we find that *a tyranny*, that is, an unconstitutional sovereignty assumed without the consent of the people, prevailed for a considerable time. At the close of the Peloponnesian war that city was governed by Lycophron, who formed the design of reducing all Thessaly under his dominion, and defeated with great slaughter the Larissæans and other Thessalians who opposed him.[3] This is the same Lycophron who was the ally of Sparta, and against whom the Bœotians and their allies sent succors to Medius, as before mentioned. Xenophon relates, that Aristippus of Larissa, being a

take the lead in putting down the tyranny at Pheræ Diodorus, xvi. 14. Plato, in the beginning of the Meno, speaks of them as having been instructed by the Sophist Gorgias. He was also entertained by Jason. See Pausanias, vi. 17; and compare Isocrates, Περὶ Ἀντιδόσεως, 166; Cicero, Orator. 52. The Pharsalians were the most luxurious and idle people in Thessaly, according to Theopompus, apud Athenæum, xii. 527.

[1] The Penestæ. See ante, p. 231. They sometimes revolted, like the Helots of Laconia. See Xenophon, Hellen. ii. c. 3, s. 36. Memorab. i. c. 2, s. 24.

[2] Diodorus, xiv. 82. He makes a distinction between the constitutional authority of Medius *δυναστεύοντος τῆς Λαοίσσης*, and that of Lycrophon *τὸν φερῶν τόραννον.* Herodotus calls the Aleuadæ *Θεσσαλίης βασιλῆες.* (vii. 6.) Orestes, whom the Athenians endeavored to restore, is called Βασιλεύς. (Thucydides, i. 111.) The term is used vaguely to denote the quasi-regal power exercised by the members of these noble families, either jointly or singly, in those parts of Thessaly which acknowledged their sway. Compare Pindar, Pyth. x. 8. Theocritus, Idyll. xvi. 34. The Aleuadæ had complete ascendency in Thessaly, after the second Persian invasion. Leotychidas the Spartan was sent to punish them for the assistance they had rendered to Xerxes, but was bribed by them to withdraw his troops, when he had the opportunity of conquering the whole country. (Herodotus, vi. 72. Pausanias, iii. 7.) The word *Tagus* signified *Marshal* or *Director*, and was perhaps a military title.

[3] Xenophon, Hellen. ii. c. 3, s. 4, with Schneider's note.

friend of Cyrus, obtained from him the loan of four thousand soldiers with pay for six months, to assist him against an opposing faction in his own city, and that Cyrus requested him not to make up his quarrel without first consulting him. A portion of these soldiers, under the command of Meno, were sent back to Cyrus, and marched with him against his brother Artaxerxes.[1] Whether the disturbances which Aristippus desired to quell were, as Schneider thinks, connected with the designs of Lycophron, or arose merely out of the domestic quarrels of Larissa, we can not determine.

Lycophron was succeeded by his son Jason, a man whose history deserves particular attention. Inheriting his father's ambition, but with greater vigor and capacity, he was enabled to accomplish the scheme, which Lycophron had formed, of uniting all Thessaly under his dominion. Connecting himself with Amyntas, king of Macedonia, and Alcetas, king of Epirus, he conceived the idea, (at least after the battle of Leuctra,) of seizing the vacant leadership of Greece, with he considered that the Lacedæmonians had irretrievably lost, the Thebans were not competent to hold, and no other power was prepared to strive for. The character of his designs, and the circumstances which favored them, are so vividly set forth in the statement of Polydamas at Sparta, related by Xenophon, that I can not do better than give it in the words of that historian.[2]

In the year B.C. 374, about two years before the battle of Leuctra, Polydamas of Pharsalus presented himself to the authorities at Sparta, and requested an audience. He was a man of high reputation throughout all Thessaly, and so esteemed by the Pharsalians for his honor and integrity, that in a time of civil broil they put their citadel into his keeping, and intrusted him with the receipt of their revenues, out of which he was to expend a fixed sum upon the public worship and the general administration. This duty he faithfully discharged, maintaining a garrison in the citadel, defraying all the expenses of government, and accounting every year for what moneys he received. If there was a deficiency, he made it up out of his own private purse, and repaid himself when there was a surplus. He was in general given to hospitality and magnificence in the Thessalian fashion. Introduced to the Lacedæmonian assembly, he addressed them thus:—

"Men of Lacedæmon, I have been your state-friend and benefactor, as my ancestors have been from time immemorial; and I deem it proper to apply to you if I am in any difficulty, and to give you notice if any scheme adverse to your interests is formed in Thessaly. You must have heard the name of Jason; for he is a man of

[1] Xenophon, Anabasis, i. c. 1, s. 10; c. 2, ss. 1, 6. Meno's character, as described by Xenophon, is a pretty good specimen of Thessalian perfidy. See Lib. ii. c. 6, ss. 21—29.

[2] Xenophon, Hellen. vi. c. 1. Compare Diodorus, xv. 57, 60.

great power and celebrity. This Jason made a truce with me, obtained an interview, and spoke as follows:—'Polydamas,' he said, 'that I could force your city of Pharsalus to submission, you may infer from what I am about to say. I have most of the Thessalian cities, and those of the greatest importance, allied to me; I brought them into subjection, notwithstanding that you fought on their side against me. You know, of course, that I have soldiers in my pay to the number of six thousand, whom, I imagine, no city could easily resist. A force equally numerous may be turned out elsewhere; but the state armies have some men advanced in age, others not yet in their prime; and very few in any city undergo bodily training; whereas no one is in my pay who is not able to toil equally with myself.' Jason (I must tell you the truth) has great personal strength, is generally fond of labor, and makes a trial of his followers every day. For he leads them with arms in hand both in their exercises and on their marches; and whomsoever he sees fond of the toils and perils of war, he rewards with double, treble, and quadruple pay, besides other presents, and also with medical attendance in sickness, and with a distinguished funeral; so that all his soldiers are sure that merit in war procures for them a life of the greatest honor and abundance. He showed me also (what I knew before), that the Maracians[1] and Dolopians were subject to him, and Alcetas, the governor of Epirus. 'Therefore,' said he, 'why should I have any doubt of being able to subdue you easily? A person unacquainted with me might say—Why then do you delay, and not march directly against the Pharsalians? Because I deem it infinitely better to gain you for willing than for unwilling allies. For, were you forced into subjection, you would be plotting all the mischief you could against me, and I should desire you to be as weak as possible; whereas, if you are persuaded to join me, it is plain we should do our utmost to strengthen each other. I perceive, Polydamas, that your country looks on you with respect. If now you will bring it into friendly relations with me, I promise you, that I will make you the greatest man in Greece next to myself. What it is that I offer you the second place in, I beg you to hear; and don't believe any thing I say, unless on reflection you judge it to be true. Well; this is evident, that by the accession of Pharsalus and the cities dependent on you, I should easily become Tagus of all the Thessalians: it is certain also, that, when Thessaly is under a Tagus, her cavalry amount to six thousand men, and her heavy-armed infantry are more than ten thousand. Looking at their strength and spirit, I think, if they were well taken care of, there is not a nation to which the Thessalians would endure to be subject. Vast as is the breadth of Thessaly, all the surrounding tribes are her subjects,

[1] An Ætolian people, adjacent to the Dolopians. See Schneider's note.

when a Tagus is appointed here; and nearly all the people in these parts are armed with the javelin, so that probably we should have an overpowering force of Peltastæ. Further, the Bœotians and all now at war with Lacedæmon are my allies; and they are content to follow me, if I will only deliver them from the Lacedæmonians. Even the Athenians, I know, would do any thing to obtain my alliance; but I am not inclined to be connected with them, for I think I could get the empire of the sea still more easily than that of the land. Consider if this again be a reasonable calculation. Having possession of Macedonia, from which the Athenians import their timber, surely we shall be able to build more ships than they will; and for manning them, which do you think would have more facilities—the Athenians, or we, with so many valuable retainers? For the maintenance of seamen which would be the better provided, we, who have such an abundance of corn that we export it elsewhere, or the Athenians, who have not sufficient for themselves without buying it? And in all probability, I take it, we should have a more abundant supply of money, when we should not be dependent on little islands, but enjoy the produce of continental countries; for it is certain that all the people round pay tribute, when Thessaly is under a Tagus. You know of course that the Persian king, who is the richest of men, derives his revenue not from islands, but from the continent. Him I believe I could conquer still more easily than Greece; for I know that all people there but one are more addicted to servitude than to fighting; and I know what a force marching up with Cyrus, and what a force with Agesilaus, reduced the king to extremities.' To this I replied, that every thing which he had said was worthy of consideration; but as we were the friends of Lacedæmon, it was impossible, I thought, to go over to their enemies, without having any ground of complaint. He commended me, and said that my friendship was the more to be desired for my fidelity; and he gave me leave to come and declare to you the truth, that he intended to attack the Pharsalians, if we complied not with his request. He bade me apply to you for assistance: 'and if they give it you,' said he, 'that is, if you can persuade them to send sufficient succors to carry on war with me, let us then abide the issue of the war, whatever it may be; but if their aid be not in your opinion sufficient, your country may have cause to complain of you—that country in which you are honored and enjoy the highest prosperity.' Upon this matter, therefore, I am come to you, and I tell you all that I see myself in that country, and all that I have heard from him. And, men of Lacedæmon, the state of things I conceive to be this:—If you will send a force that, not only in my judgment, but in that of the Thessalians in general, is adequate to maintain a war with Jason, the cities will revolt from him; for they are all watching with alarm the progress of his power. If you suppose, however, that your emancipated Helots and a man of private station will be sufficient, I advise you to keep quiet. For be assured, that the war will be against a formidable array of strength, and against a man who is so prudent a general, that whatever he attempts, whether in the way of stratagem, or surprise, or open attack, he hardly ever fails. He can make the same use of the night as of the day, and on occasions of haste he can work while he is taking his meals. He thinks it time to rest, when he has returned to the place from which he started and transacted his business. And his followers he has inured to the same habits. When the soldiers have, by their exertions achieved a good piece of success, he knows how to excite their imaginations; so that his men are taught this, that relaxation is procured by toil. Moreover, in regard to sensual pleasures, he is the most temperate man I know; so that nothing of this kind keeps him from the regular performance of his duty. Consider then, and tell me, as is but fair, what you will be able and what you intend to do."

For the particulars of this remarkable speech we can rely on the account of Xenophon, who had good opportunities of learning them at Sparta. It is interesting in one point of view especially, as showing that the divisions of the Greek states had even at this time excited in the breast of one ambitious man the hope of conquering them all. The grounds upon which Jason founded his hopes were pretty nearly the same as those which formed the basis of Philip's calculations, when he strove for the mastery of Greece. The circumstances were indeed much more favorable to Philip than to Jason. We can scarcely help charging the latter with exaggeration in his estimates, and perhaps with some degree of ignorance and presumption, if we suppose him to have spoken his real opinions to Polydamas. He seems to have overrated the quality of his own infantry, as compared with those of the Greek states; certainly he overrated his chances of obtaining maritime ascendency. The facility with which Alexander was afterwards overpowered by the Thebans shows in some degree the precarious character of the force on which Jason depended. Philip held a constitutional monarchy, inherited from his ancestors, and had brought his army to a high state of discipline, the efficiency of which he had tried in many bloody encounters with his warlike neighbors, before he ventured to attack the southern Greeks: even then he proceeded with the utmost caution. He never in his life established a navy which was able to cope with the Athenian; and when he attacked the Greeks, they were far weaker and more divided than at the time of the battle of Leuctra. It is next to certain, that Jason would havs failed in the attempt in which Philip succeeded. The characters of the two men, however, were very similar.[1]

[1] See the observations of Isocrates, Philipp. p. 106. Cicero compares Jason, as a crafty politician, with Themistocles. (De Officiis, i. 30.)

The Lacedæmonians took two days to consider their reply to Polydamas, and on the third day, seeing how many of their troops were employed in the war with Thebes and Athens, they informed him that for the present they were unable to send out any adequate succors, and advised him to return and do the best that he could for himself and his city. He thanked them for their straight-forward answer, and left them. On his return, he begged Jason not to compel him to give up the citadel, which had been intrusted to his keeping; but gave his own sons as hostages, and promised that he would bring his country over to Jason's alliance, and help to make him Tagus. Both these things were accomplished. The Pharsalians entered into a treaty with Jason, and he was appointed Tagus of all Thessaly. He then arranged the contingents which every city was to furnish of cavalry and heavy-armed infantry; and it was found that the cavalry of the Thessalians and their allies numbered more than eight thousand, their heavy-armed infantry as many as twenty thousand, besides an immense force of Peltastæ.

In the following year, B. C. 373, Jason came with Alcetas of Epirus to Athens, to intercede with the people on behalf of Timotheus, who was brought to trial for his delay in carrying succors to Corcyra. Timotheus was at that time so poor, that to entertain his illustrious visitors, who lodged in his house in the Piræus, he was obliged to borrow some articles of dress and furniture, two silver cups, and a mina in money. Their intercession prevailed, but he was removed from his command.[1]

After the battle of Leuctra the Thebans sent to Jason for assistance, wishing to complete the rout of the defeated army, and fearing the arrival of reinforcements from Peloponnesus. Jason, intending to march through Phocis, gave orders to prepare a fleet, as if he was going by sea; then with a small body of troops, before the Phocians had time to assemble, he passed rapidly through their territory and joined the Bœotian army. The Thebans wished him to fall upon the rear of the Peloponnesians, who were still encamped in Bœotia, while they attacked them in front; but Jason advised, that it was better to let them quit the country than to risk the chance of another battle, in which the desperation of the enemy might give them the

Aristotle mentions a saying of his, "that it is lawful to do some evil, in order to effect great good." (Rhetoric, i. 12, 31.) Compare the anecdotes of Polyænus, Strateg. vi. 1.

[1] Demosthenes, cont. Timoth. 1187, 1190, 1191. Xenophon, Hellen. vi. c. 2, s. 13. Cornelius Nepos, in Vit. Timoth. 75. Alcetas assisted in the transportation of Athenian troops to Corcyra. Xenophon, ibid. s. 11. Jason was on friendly terms with the Thebans and Athenians, but not in active alliance with them. His intimacy with Timotheus made him of course acquainted with Isocrates. There is an extant epistle of Isocrates to the sons of Jason, in which he declines an invitation to Pheræ.

victory. He then went to the adversary's camp, (for notwithstanding his alliance with Thebes, he still kept up his hereditary connection with Sparta,) and he represented to the Lacedæmonians, how dangerous it might be for them to stay in Bœotia in the presence of a victorious army, with allies not hearty in their cause, and who were thinking even of treating with the enemy. His counsels prevailed, and the Lacedæmonians, after concluding an armistice, retreated. Jason gained his object, which was, to attach both parties to himself, and let neither obtain any decisive advantage. He then returned by Phocis, attacking Hyampolis on his road, and doing considerable damage to its town and territory; after which, passing by Heraclea, he razed the walls, to prevent it being used as a fortress against him when he marched southward.[1]

In the following year Jason took steps which opened the eyes of Greece yet more clearly to his designs. The Pythian festival was coming on. He ordered preparations to be made on a great scale for the sacrifice; each city in his dominion was required to furnish a certain number of oxen, sheep, goats, and swine; the total of which, without any city being heavily charged, amounted to a thousand oxen, and ten thousand of the smaller animals: and he offered the reward of a golden crown to the city which produced the finest ox. He gave notice to the Thessalians to prepare themselves for a military expedition by the time of the festival: it was supposed that he intended to hold the games under his own presidency, and there were misgivings as to his designs on the Delphian treasures. The Delphians asked the oracle, what was to be done if he laid his hands upon them; and Apollo replied, that he would see to it. Whatever his schemes may have been, they were brought to a sudden termination. One day, after he had held a review of his cavalry at Pheræ, he sat in his chair of state to give audience to his subjects, when seven youths, under the pretense of asking his judgment upon some private quarrel, advanced close up to him, and, before his guards had time to interpose, savagely attacked and murdered him. One of them was slain in the act of striking; a second was taken and instantly put to death; the other five jumped on horses that were ready for them, and effected their escape. In every Greek city, through which they passed, honors were conferred upon the assassins; a proof how great had been the terror excited by the enterprises of this man.[2]

Jason was succeeded by his brothers Polydorus and Polyphron; the former of whom came to a sudden death, not without suspicion of foul play. Polyphron, on whom suspicion fell, confirmed the bad

[1] Xenophon, Hellen. vi. c. 4, ss. 20—27. The account which Diodorus gives of these proceedings is somewhat different, and not so probable. See Thirlwall, Hist. of Greece, v. 78.

[2] Xenophon, Hellen. vi. c. 4, ss. 28—32. Diodorus, xv. 60.

opinion of his subjects by various tyrannical acts. He put to death Polydamas and eight other of the principal citizens of Pharsalus; and drove many from Larissa into exile. After governing Thessaly for one year, he was murdered by his nephew Alexander, who surpassed him in vice and cruelty, and in a short time drove the Thessalians to solicit foreign aid. This brought back Thessaly to a state of disunion and weakness. Alexander, notwithstanding the combination against him, maintained his power in Pheræ and the adjacent towns, and reigned altogether about eleven years, siding alternately with Thebes and Athens, and doing no little mischief to both.[1]

The Aleuads of Larissa made the first effort for the deliverance of their country, by inviting to their assistance Alexander king of Macedon. The young king, who had just succeeded his father Amyntas, came promptly at their request, and while the tyrant of Pheræ was preparing to carry the war into Macedonia, took by surprise the cities of Larissa and Crannon, and put garrisons in both.[2] But he was soon recalled to his own kingdom, probably by the intrigues of his mother Eurydice and Ptolemy of Alorus; and the Thessalians, again pressed by the tyrant, invoked the aid of Thebes. Pelopidas was sent with an army, and with orders to settle the affairs of Thessaly in the best manner for Theban interests. Having advanced to Larissa, which was surrendered to him, he had an interview with Alexander of Pheræ, and reproached him so severely for his conduct, that Alexander, in alarm for his safety, retired to Pheræ, leaving the Theban general to settle matters as he chose with his allies in Thessaly. Pelopidas made such arrangements for the future government of Thessaly as were generally acceptable to his allies, and in accordance with his instructions from home. He proceeded also to Macedonia, where he strengthened his country's cause by an alliance which he concluded with king Alexander, receiving from him (according to Diodorus) his brother Philip, then fifteen years old, as a hostage;[3] after which he returned into Bœo-

[1] Xenophon, Hellen. vi. c. 4, ss. 33—35. Diodorus, xv. 61, differs from him in some particulars. Plutarch (in Vit. Pelopid. 29) agrees with Xenophon in making Alexander the nephew, not the brother of Polydorus. See Schneider and Wesseling's notes.

[2] Diodorus, xv. 61.

[3] Diodorus, xv. 67. Compare section 61; according to which, Alexander intended to hold Larissa and Crannon for himself. Pelopidas, therefore, thought it necessary to secure his fidelity. Diodorus, however, gives a different account of the manner in which Philip came to be sent to Thebes, Lib. xvi. 2. Plutarch (in Vit. Pelopid. 26 et seqq.) states that Pelopidas was invited to Macedonia, to settle the disputes between Alexander and Ptolemy; and also that he went upon a second occasion, after the murder of Alexander, and compelled Ptolemy to give hostages to insure his proper administration as regent. See Grote's

tia, leaving Thessaly, through which he again passed, apparently tranquil. The year however had scarcely passed, when Theban interference was again solicited, on account of some new oppressions from Pheræ. Pelopidas and Ismenias were sent, but without troops, in the character of embassadors; for it was thought, that their name and presence would be sufficient to overawe the tyrant. This expectation was futile. Alexander came with an army to Pharsalus, where a conference was appointed to be held between him and the Theban generals; and they imprudently put both the city and themselves into the power of a man who was totally regardless of good faith and honor. He seized their persons, carried them prisoners to Pheræ, and treated them with the utmost indignity. To avenge this insult, the Thebans sent Hypatus and Cleomenes into Thessaly, with an army of eight thousand foot and six hundred horse; to oppose which, Alexander, not trusting entirely to his own forces, applied to the Athenians, who dispatched to his assistance a fleet of thirty sail and a thousand soldiers, under the command of Autocles. The Thebans approaching Pheræ were met by Alexander with a force greatly superior in cavalry, notwithstanding which, they desired to attack him; but before they could join battle, their Thessalian allies deserted; Alexander was reinforced by the troops of Athens and other auxiliaries, and the Thebans, distressed for provisions, found it necessary to retreat. Their march was through an open plain; Alexander assailed their rear with his cavalry and javelin-men, who did such execution, that the whole of the Theban army was in peril. The soldiers, almost in despair, called upon Epaminondas, who was serving among them as a volunteer,[1] to take the command. He quickly restored confidence; forming a rear-guard with his horse and light troops, he repulsed the pursuing enemy, and effected his retreat in safety.[2]

The Thebans fined Hypatus and Cleomenes on their return for misconduct, and chose Epaminondas for their general, to retrieve the fortune of the war. He proceeded early in the year B.C. 367 to execute his commission; but Alexander, fearing to encounter a Theban army under such a general, and perhaps disappointed of some expected aid from Athens, thought proper to come to terms,

views as to the different expeditions of Pelopidas into Thessaly. (History of Greece, x. 361.)

[1] He had been deposed from his office of Bœotarch, on a charge of having shown undue favor to the Lacedæmonians in the last Peleponnesian campaign, by not pushing the advantage which he had gained in the battle at the Isthmus. Diodorus, xv. 72.

[2] Diodorus, xv. 71. Cornelius Nepos, in Vit. Pelopid. 101. Pausanias, ix. 15; who represents Alexander to have laid an ambush for the Thebans, soon after they had passed Thermopylæ. He also states, that Alexander released Pelopidas on this first expedition.

[3] The Athenians advised that certain succors, which Dionysius had sent

and consented to release his prisoners. Epaminondas, having accomplished the main objects of the expedition, withdrew his army.[1]

During three years that followed, the Thebans, as it appears, had no leisure to attend to the affairs of Thessaly; and Alexander used the opportunity thus afforded him for exercising his cruelty and extending his power. He occupied with garrisons the districts of Magnesia and Phthiotis. In Melibœa and Scotussa he perpetrated frightful massacres. The citizens in each of these were summoned to a general assembly, to answer some complaints which he had against them: he then surrounded them with his guards, who speared them all, and cast their bodies into the town-moat. The cities were given up to plunder, and the women and children sold for slaves.[2]

In the year B.C. 364 the Thebans were again solicited to chastise the tyrant, and they determined to send seven thousand men under the command of Pelopidas. It so happened, before the Theban troops set out, there was an eclipse of the sun, an event which was considered an unlucky omen among the Greeks. The expedition was postponed: but Pelopidas with a small band of volunteers proceeded to Pharsalus, and putting himself at the head of his Thessalian confederates, did not fear to meet Alexander with an army double his own number. They fought at Cynoscepalæ, and Alexander was defeated; but unfortunately Pelopidas, pressing rashly forward and challenging the tyrant to personal combat, was overpowered by numbers and slain. He was honored with a splendid funeral by the Thessalians, who requested as a special favor of the Thebans, that he might be buried in their country.[3] The war was vigorously prosecuted; the Theban reinforcements arriving, defeated

that year to Peloponnesus, should be carried into Thessaly, to oppose the Thebans. But the Lacedæmonians said they were wanted in Laconia. Xenophon, Hellen. vii. c. 1, s. 28. Alexander, by his imprisonment of Pelopidas, and liberal promises to the Athenians, was in high favor among them at this time. Demosthenes, contr. Aristoc. 660.

[1] Plutarch, in Vit. Pelopid. 29. Diodorus, xv. 75, puts the liberation of Pelopidas a year later, and says nothing of Epaminondas.

[2] Diodorus, xv. 75. Pausanias, vi. 5.

[3] Pelopidas was as able an officer, as Epaminondas was a general. The victory at Leuctra was as much owing to his prompt and timely charge with the Sacred Band, as to the main design of the battle by his colleague. In other respects, Pelopidas was one of the best characters of antiquity: a true patriot, brave, generous, unselfish. These qualities were perhaps not sufficiently tempered with prudence. His rashness in battle (for which Plutarch blames him) cost him his life. He is compared by the biographer with Marcellus, who owed his death to a similar and less excusable want of caution. Compare Polybius, viii. 1. Diodorus, xv. 81.

Alexander in a second and more decisive battle, and constrained him to accept a peace, by the terms of which he was to withdraw his garrisons from Magnesia and Phthiotis, confine himself to his hereditary dominion of Pheræ, and also become a subject ally of Thebes. Troops both of Alexander and the independent Thessalians served under Epaminondas in the campaign of Mantinea.[1]

Peace with Thebes had severed Alexander from the alliance of Athens; and he turned his attention to the equipment of a navy, chiefly with a view to enrich himself by piracy. Pagasæ, the port of Pheræ, was conveniently situated for an outlet into the Ægæan sea, and the small islands off the coast of Thessaly, then belonging to Athens, were exposed to his attack. In the year B.C. 361 he took the island of Tenus, and made slaves of the inhabitants. The next year he took or pillaged several other of the Cyclad isles, and made a descent on Peparethus; he even defeated an Athenian fleet, captured six vessels and a large number of prisoners, and then suddenly sailed into Piræus, landed on the quay, and carried off considerable plunder. The Athenians were so incensed with their commander Leosthenes, for his negligence in permitting such disasters, that they sentenced him to death.[2]

We now approach the period of the Sacred War, the causes of which could not easily be explained without first presenting before the reader a general view of Grecian affairs, and of the relation in which the various parties stood to each other at the time when the war broke out.

After the general peace which followed the battle of Mantinea, the Thebans found that their influence among the Greek states was considerably diminished. This may have been owing partly to the severity of their proceedings against the Bœotian cities, which offended the feelings of the Greeks, partly to the fears and jealousies of the independent states. Theban headship was a thing which they had not been accustomed to, and which they could hardly reconcile to sentiments of Hellenic patriotism.[3] Accordingly, though alliance of the most friendly kind subsisted between the Thebans and the Argives, Megalopolitans, and Messenians, the last of whom owed their very existence as a nation to Epaminondas, the Thebans could no longer sway the counsels of these confederates, so as to

[1] Diodorus, xv. 80, 85. Xenophon, Hellen. vii. c. 5, s. 4. Plutarch, in Vit. Pelopid. 32.

[2] Diodorus, xv. 95. Demosthenes, contr. Polyd. 1207. De Coron. Trierarch. 1230. Polyænus, Strateg. vi. 2. I have already noticed the proceedings against some of the Trierarchs, who delegated their command on this occasion. Vol. i. appendix v. p. 316.

[3] Diodorus, xv. 60, represents Jason as asserting, *Θηβαίους τῶν πρωτείων μὴ ἀξίους εἶναι.* Compare Demosthenes, De Coron. 231. Isocrates, De Pace, 162, 171. Philipp. 93.

make them subservient to ambitious views of their own. In the north, they were in friendly connection with the Locrians and Thessalians; while towards the Phocians they had entertained feelings of anger and hostility, ever since that people had refused to join them in their last expedition to Peloponnesus. But the principal check to the ambition of Thebes was Athens, who by her maritime situation and resources was secure against attack, and could offer protection to her weaker neighbors against Theban encroachment. Epaminondas had seen, that his country would never retain her ascendency in Greece, unless she applied herself to maritime affairs, and strove to compete with Athens for the dominion of the sea. The year before his death he made an exciting speech before the people, encouraging them to aim at naval supremacy, and boldly declaring that the Propylæa of the Athenian Acropolis should be transferred to the Cadmea. A decree was passed at his suggestion for the construction of an arsenal and a hundred vessels of war; and Epaminondas was actually sent with an armament to the Ægæan and the Propontis, to excite revolt among the Athenian allies. He succeeded so far as to drive an Athenian squadron from the sea, and obtain promises of alliance from Chios, Rhodes, and Byzantium, the same states which, a few years later, took the lead in the Social War against Athens.[1] These naval projects however, died with Epaminondas; nor indeed was Thebes favorably situated for becoming a maritime power, unless she had possession of Eubœa. Here again was a fruitful subject of contention with Athens, to whom the dominion, or at least the friendship, of Eubœa was of immense importance in more than one point of view. The people of that island had most of them joined the Attic and Theban confederacy against Sparta, with the exception of the Orites, who resisted all the efforts of Chabrias to make himself master of their city.[2] When Athens went over to Sparta, the Theban interest seems to have prevailed in the island; for Eubœans are numbered among the troops that followed Epaminondas to Peloponnesus. Eubœa itself, however, was much divided. Tyrants sprang up in some of the cities, who were ready to side with either Athens or Thebes, according as it suited their views. Such were Mnescharchus of Chalcis and Themison of Eretria.[3] The latter had in the year B.C. 366 inflicted a great blow upon Athens, by causing her to lose Oropus. He assisted some exiles, sallying from Eubœa to get possession of it; and the Athenians, after sending forces for its recovery, were persuaded to enter into an arrangement, by which the

[1] Diodorus, xv. 78, 79; who asserts that, if Epaminondas had lived longer, the Thebans would undoubtedly have acquired the empire of the sea. Compare Æschines, De Fals. Leg. 42. Isocrates, Philipp. 93.

[2] Diodorus, xv. 30.

[3] Æschines, contr. Ctesiph. 65.

Thebans were to hold the city in trust, until the claims of the contending parties could be decided. Instead of this ever being done, the Thebans, not liking to part with a place so desirable for the command of Eubœa, kept it in their own hands, nor was it restored even at the general peace.[1]

In the year B.C. 358 or 357, Eubœa was the scene of a short but fierce contest between the Athenians and Thebans. It was brought about by some internal disputes in the island, in which the aid of Thebes was invoked against the despots Menesarchus and Themison. The Thebans, to support their partisans and maintain their supremacy in Eubœa, sent over a large force; while their opponents applied for succor to the Athenians. At this time hardly a city in Eubœa was connected with the Athenians, except Orcus perhaps, which the Spartan alliance may have brought over to them. A good opportunity now presented itself to recover their power in the island. Still they hesitated, either doubting their chance of success, or suspecting the sincerity of the parties who invited them: a debate was held on the question, when Timotheus starting up made that forcible appeal to his countrymen, which is related by Demosthenes in the Oration on the Chersonese—"Are you deliberating what to do, when you have the Thebans in the island? Will you not cover the sea with galleys? Will you not rush to the Piræus immediately and launch your ships?"—The people, roused by this language, voted war on the instant; and such was their zeal, aided by the patriotism of many wealthy citizens who volunteered to serve the office of trierarch, (among them Demosthenes himself,) that the whole armament was equipped and sent off within five days. The campaign lasted about a month, during which there was no decisive action, but a great deal of fighting and much loss of life on both sides. The general result was to the advantage of the Athenians, who forced their adversaries into a convention, by which they agreed to evacuate the island; and having freed it from the presence of the Theban army, and withdrawing themselves from further interference, were regarded as benefactors, and honored with a golden crown. The Eubœan cities, left to their own domestic governments, were re-annexed to the Athenian confederacy, and severed entirely from the dominion of Thebes.[2]

Such was the positiou of affairs, when the Thebans in an evil hour for Grecian liberty determined on taking a step, by which, while they gratified their revengeful feelings against their enemies, they hoped possibly to exalt themselves at their expense. This

Xenophon, Hellen. vii. c. 4, s. 1; where see the note of Schneider: and compare the Oration for the Megalopolitans, vol. i. p. 210, note 1.

[2] Diodorus, xvi. 7. Æschines, contr. Ctesiph. 65, 67. Demosthenes, De Cherson. 108; Pro Megalopol. 205; De Coron. 259; Contr. Mid. 566, 570; Contr. Androt. 597, 616; Contr. Timocr. 756.

was to invoke upon them the sentence of an Amphictyonic assembly. It was a long time since the Amphictyons had taken any active part in Grecian politics. Their periodical meetings had been regularly held as usual, in the spring at Delphi, in the autumn at Thermopylæ; but their attention had been confined wholly to religious ceremonies and local business, without meddling in the more momentous questions of war and peace or other international concerns. The Thebans, on friendly terms with the majority of the Amphictyonic tribes, deemed it a good opportunity to revive the dormant functions of the council, and make it a political engine for their own purposes. This, under existing circumstances, might afford an easier and cheaper means of accomplishing their ends than either war or diplomacy. Accordingly they preferred a complaint against the Lacedæmonians for their perfidious seizure of the Cadmea, and induced the Amphictyons to impose on them a fine of five hundred talents. The exact time when this sentence was passed does not appear, but it was probably soon after the battle of Mantinea.[1] The fine not having been paid was doubled; but the Lacedæmonians took no notice either of one sentence or the other. In the year B.C. 357 or 356, the Thebans preferred a charge against the Phocians for having cultivated a portion of the Cirrhæan plain, which had been condemned to lie waste ever since the first Sacred War. It is probable enough, that both the Phocians and the Amphissian Locrians had committed trespasses upon this land, tilling or inclosing from the waste portions which were of no value either to the temple or to the Pythian festival; and it might be these very encroachments which formed the debateable land of which Pausanias speaks.[2] None but those in the neighborhood would care really about the matter; but it made a good pretext for complaint against people who were obnoxious on other grounds, and with such view was eagerly taken up by the Thebans, and perhaps the Thessalians. A decree passed against the Phocians, condemning them to a fine of many talents; which not being paid, the Hieromnemons brought the case again before the council, and demanded judgment against them for their contumacy; stating that there were others too whose penalties ought to be enforced, to wit, the Lacedæmonians, and that the defaulters merited public execration. Judgment was passed, that the land of the Phocians should be consecrated to Apollo.[3] Diodorus, who always takes what he

[1] Where Diodorus (xvi. 23) narrates the charges preferred against the Lacedæmonians and the Phocians, he is speaking of past events, not referable to the year with which he prefaces the chapter. The narrative of the current year commences with the acts of Philomelus.

[2] Pausanias, iii. 9.

[3] Diodorus, xvi. 23, 29. Justin. viii. 1, states the charge against the Phocians to have been, that they had ravaged the Bœotian territory.

considered the religious view of the question, says that the sentence of the Amphictyons was greatly approved by the Greeks. He seems to forget that the Thebans, for having razed to the ground Platæ, Thespiæ, and Orchomenus, were equally liable to Amphictyonic censure; and also that the motives of the parties concerned in these proceedings were not the purest in the world. In asserting that they were generally sanctioned by public opinion, he most likely confounds the time when the sentence was passed with a subsequent period, when the proceedings of the Phocians at Delphi excited disapprobation even among those who were not well inclined to their enemies.[1]

While this sentence impended over the Phocians, and they were in alarm lest it should be immediately put in force, Philomelus, a native of Ledon, and a man of high reputation among his countrymen, addressed them in a tone of encouragement, urging that it was impossible to pay the fine on account of its magnitude, and that to allow their land to be taken as forfeit would not only be cowardice on their part, but absolute and certain ruin. He showed the injustice of the sentence, and its disproportion to the alleged crime; and then advised them to procure its reversal, which they might easily do, if they would assert their ancient title to the possession of Delphi and the presidency of the oracle; in support of which he cited the well-known lines from the catalogue of the ships in Homer.[2] If they would only make him their general with full powers, he offered to guarantee their success.[3]

The Phocians, stimulated by their fears, elected Philomelus to be their general, and invested him with absolute powers.[4] He pro-

If this be well founded, it must have referred to the part they took in the campaigns of Agesilaus and Cleombrotus; and this would lead us to suppose, that the charge was preferred soon after the battle of Leuctra; for it would have been absurd to revive it at a later period, after the Phocians had been admitted to the Theban alliance. But this was hardly the kind of offense to be a fit subject for Amphictyonic cognizance. I could rather believe the story cited from Duris by Athenæus (xiii. 560), that an outrage committed by some Phocian upon a Theban lady was the cause of the war. Pausanias (x. 2) says he has not been able to discover, whether the fine was imposed on the Phocians for any real offense, or whether it was owing to the malice of their old enemies, the Thessalians.

[1] Demosthenes (De Coron. 231) intimates distinctly, that the Athenians, though they wished well to the Phocians in the war, disapproved of their proceedings, by which he refers to their seizure of Delphi and its treasures.

[2] Αὐτὰρ φωκήων Σχέδιος καὶ Ἐπίστροφος ἦρχον,
Οἳ Κυπάρισσον ἔχον Πυθῶνά τε πετρήεσσαν.

[3] Diodorus, xvi. 23. Pausanias, x. 2.

[4] The Phocian generals were civil as well as military despots, during

ceeded immediately to Sparta, and revealed his plans in confidence to King Archidamus; saying, that it was the interest of Sparta no less than of his own country, to rescind the illegal decrees of the Amphictyons; that he had determined to seize upon Delphi for that purpose, and the Spartans ought to make common cause with him. Archidamus approved of his resolution; and declared that, although he could not openly co-operate with him for the present, he would render him secretly all the assistance in his power. He supplied him for immediate exigencies with a loan of fifteen talents and some mercenary troops.[1]

If Theopompus is to be believed, the Spartan king was induced to espouse the Phocian cause by bribes given to himself and his queen, Deinicha; and a similar charge was made against the Ephors and senate. Their hostility to Thebes, and the identity of Spartan and Phocian interests, are sufficient of themselves to account for the side which they chose; though it is likely enough that some of the Delphic money was afterwards distributed at Sparta, as it was among the influential men of other states.[2]

The subsidy furnished by Archidamus, together with an equal sum advanced out of his own private purse, enabled the Phocian general to raise a considerable body of mercenaries. With these and a thousand Phocian targeteers he marched suddenly upon Delphi, and took possession of the temple; the Thracidæ, one of the five families connected with the oracle, who attempted to oppose him, he put to death, and confiscated their property; then, seeing that this had excited general alarm, he assured the Delphians, that, if they would keep quiet, they had nothing to fear.[3] The news was however quickly carried round. The nearest neighbors were the Amphissian Locrians, who no sooner heard of the seizure of Delphi, than they marched against the aggressor. A battle took place in the outskirts of the city; and the Locrians, after losing a large number of men, were put to flight. Philomelus, emboldened by his victory, effaced the pillars on which

the period of their command, and are designated as *τύφαννοι, δυνασταί*. Pausanias, iii. 10; iv. 5. Æschines, De Fals. Leg. 45, 46. Athenæus, xiii. 605. Polyænus, Strateg. v. 45.

[1] Diodorus, xvi. 24.

[2] Pausanias, iii. 10; iv. 5. Philomelus was not in a condition to give bribes at this time. Whether he made promises, is another question. It is impossible to known for certain, either what the original intentions of Philomelus were, or how far he opened his mind to the Spartan king. After the spoliation of the temple had actually occurred, it was natural that all kinds of reports should be circulated.

[3] Pausanias (iii. 10) mentions a story, that the Delphians were saved from a general massacre, and the women and children from slavery, by the intercession of Archidamus.

the Amphictyonic decrees were inscribed, and destroyed every record of them; at the same time he gave out, that he had no intention of plundering the temple or committing any illegal outrage; his object was only to rescind an unjust sentence against his countrymen, and to assert their ancient right to be administrators and guardians of the sanctuary.[1]

The intelligence having reached Thebes, an assembly of the people was held, and a resolution passed to take arms in the sacred cause.[2] While they were yet considering in what way they should proceed to punish the offenders, Philomelus was busy fortifying Delphi with a wall, and making a general levy among all the Phocians who were fit for military service. He gathered round him fresh bodies of mercenaries, by promising half as much again as the usual pay; and boldly pitching his camp before the city, appeared to bid defiance to his enemies. The number of his troops (reckoning only the regular infantry) was about five thousand. Seeing the advantage of bringing them speedily to action and striking a blow before all his enemies were united, and with the further object of enriching himself by plunder, he invaded and ravaged the country of the Amphissian Locrians. In an attack upon a strong fortress he received a check, and afterwards in a skirmish with the Locrians lost twenty of his men. Having applied by a herald for permission to bury them, he was refused, the Locrians answering, that it was the universal custom of the Greeks to cast away without sepulture the bodies of men guilty of sacrilege. In a subsequent skirmish the Phocians were left masters of the field, and the Locrians, being compelled to ask permission to bury their own dead, were glad to make an exchange. Philomelus, not able to bring the enemy to a general battle, continued for some time to ravage the country, and then returned home laden with spoil.[3]

His next proceeding was to obtain the sanction of the oracle for his cause. He commanded the priestess to deliver her prophecy from the tripod according to ancient custom. She demurred at first, saying that he sought to violate the ancient custom; but on his threatening her, she mounted the tripod, and pronounced that it was lawful for him to do what he pleased. This response, which he declared to be perfectly satisfactory, he reduced to writing, and exposed to public view in the city of Delphi; he called an assembly for the

[1] Diodorus, xvi. 24.

[2] Diodorns (xvi. 25) says, *παραχρῆμα στρατιώτας ἐξέπεμψαν.* But of the destination or proceedings of these troops we hear nothing further. The Thebans were not yet decided as to their course of action, and perhaps recalled the troops whom in the first burst of anger they had sent out.

[3] Diodorus, xvi. 25.

special purpose of announcing it, and congratulated his friends on the encouragement which Apollo had given them. A slight thing which happened about the same time was hailed as a favorable omen. An eagle, flying over the altar, snatched up some of the tame doves that were kept in the temple;[1] which was interpreted as a sign, that Philomelus would be the master of Delphi. Elated now with hope, yet impressed with the necessity of conciliating the Greeks, and averting the suspicion which some of his acts were likely to inspire, he dispatched select envoys to the principal cities of Greece, not excepting even Thebes, to justify and explain his conduct; in particular to show, that, while he asserted the claims of his country to the guardianship of the Delphic temple, he had no design to plunder it of its treasures; that he was willing to render an account of them to all the Greeks; and that any who chose might come and examine the sacred offerings, to see that their weight and number were correct.[2] To those people who had ancient feuds with his countrymen, he urged the injustice of making war upon a false pretext, to gratify private enmity; praying that, if they would not assist him, they would at least be neutral. At Thebes and in Locris these remonstrances produced no effect, but were answered by a declaration of war. Athens, Sparta, and some other cities concluded alliance with the Phocians, and gave them promises of assistance.[3] Such were the events of the first year of the war, B. C. 355.

To meet the exigencies of the ensuing campaign, Philomelus made new levies of soldiers, and to provide pay for them, exacted heavy

[1] Such an occurrence was likely enough. The number of birds that flocked round the temple is noticed in Euripides, Ion. 106, 171.

[2] Grote, in his History of Greece, xi. 350, has the following note upon the subject of these treasures:—"In reference to the engagement taken by Philomelus, that he would exhibit and verify, before any general Hellenic examiners, all the valuable property in the Delphian temple, by weight and number of articles, the reader will find interesting matter of comparison in the Attic inscriptions, No. 137—142, vol. i. of Boeckh's Corpus Inscript. Græcarum, with Boeckh's valuable commentary. These are the records of the numerous gold and silver donatives, preserved in the Parthenon, handed over by the treasurers of the goddess annually appointed to their successors at the end of the year, from one Panathenaic festival to the next. The weight of each article is formally recorded, and the new articles received each year (ἐπέτεια) are specified. Where an article is transferred without being weighed (ἄσταθμον), the fact is noticed. That the precious donatives in the Delphian temple also were carefully weighed, we may judge from the statement of Herodotus, that the golden lion dedicated by Crœsus had lost a fraction of its weight in the conflagration of the building. (Herod. i. 50.)" Compare the note in the same volume, p. 354.

[3] Diodorus, xvi. 27. Demosthenes (De Fals. Leg. 360) reads to the jury the articles of treaty between the Athenians and Phocians.

contributions from the wealthy citizens of Delphi. Collecting all his troops together, he reviewed them, and made an imposing show of strength; but if he hoped to deter his enemies from attacking him, he was quickly disappointed. The Locrians, eager to revenge their former defeat, without waiting for any auxiliaries, advanced against him, and gave battle at the Phædriad cliffs near Delphi. Philomelus was again victorious, killing great numbers of the enemy, and taking a multitude of prisoners: the Locrians, seeing that they were not a match for the Phocians by themselves, sent to Thebes for succor. We have no explanation why the Thebans did not at an earlier period enter actively into the war; but in this as in other parts of their conduct we perceive a want of that vigorous energy, which they displayed in the time of Epaminondas. It is possible that they delayed commencing hostilities till Philomelus had put himself more completely in the wrong; and they were anxious to procure a solemn vote of the Amphictyons, appointing them to conduct a holy war as champions of the god. With such view apparently, and to counteract the efforts of the Phocian agents, they dispatched embassies to the various Amphictyonic states, calling upon them to unite in the cause of religion against the Phocians. The majority complied, including the Locrians, Dorians, Thessalians, Perrhæbians, Magnetes, Dolopians, Athamanians, Phthiots, and Ænianians; while Athens, Lacedæmon, and some other states of Peloponnesus, adhered to the Phocian cause. It may be inferred from the words of Diodorus, that a formal declaration of war was passed at a congress of Amphictyons (which must have been held at Thermopylæ); and severe sentences were passed not only upon the whole Phocian people, as impious and sacrilegious criminals, but specially upon Philomelus and the most prominent leaders of his party, who were condemned to heavy fines. It does not appear, however, that the Thebans were chosen to command the united force of the league, nor that any plan was agreed upon for carrying on the war with effect.[1]

The remissness of his adversaries gave time to Philomelus for preparation. Seeing the necessity of greatly augmenting his numbers, and of providing pay for them by extraordinary means, he now openly laid his hands upon the Delphic treasures, and giving notice that the pay of his soldiers would be half as much again as before, he invited the mercenaries, with whom Greece then abounded, to enlist under his banners. No sooner were his intentions made publicly known, than a multitude of adventurers, chiefly men of desperate fortune and character, flocked from all quarters to his camp, eager to share in the plunder that was promised them. Finding himself at the head of a considerable army, he anticipated the enemy's attack by a rapid march into Epicnemidian Locris, where

[1] Diodorus, xvi. 28, 29, 32.

he met the native troops joined by a small detachment of the Bœotians; and having defeated them in a cavalry action, fell suddenly upon a body of six thousand Thessalians advancing from the north, and defeated them separately on a cliff (forming one of the Locrian range of hills) called Argolas. But now the main army of the Bœotians, thirteen thousand strong, advanced into Locris, and pitching their camp opposite to the Phocian general, offered him battle. Philomelus was reinforced by fifteen hundred Achæans; yet, as his whole army did not much exceed eleven thousand, he thought it more prudent to decline a general engagement. The foraging parties, however, met in frequent skirmishes; and the Bœotians, having taken some prisoners, caused them to be led out in front of the camp and executed as malefactors, declaring that such was the judgment pronounced on them by the Amphictyons. The soldiers of Philomelus, enraged at this savage conduct, insisted that he should retaliate; and exerting themselves to take alive as many as they possibly could of the enemy, they soon put him in a condition to do so. Philomelus without hesitation put all his prisoners to death. This led to a mutual abandonment of a barbarous practice, which was not sanctioned by the general usages of Grecian warfare. While the armies remained in this position, no action occurred worthy of notice; and at length Philomelus found it necessary to retreat into his own country. He was followed by the enemy, whom he drew into the mountainous and woody regions of Parnassus, hoping to obtain advantage over them by his better knowledge of the locality. After some marching and counter-marching, he was surprised by the Bœotians near the city of Neon, and compelled to fight a battle with one division of his forces against greatly superior numbers. Here his troops were totally routed; he himself fighting bravely to the last was driven to the edge of a precipice, from which, rather than be taken alive, he threw himself headlong down, and met the very death to which sacrilegious criminals were doomed by Hellenic law; a sign, as Diodorus thinks, that the vengeance of the gods had overtaken him. Onomarchus, his brother, succeeding to the command, rallied the fugitives, and led them back to Delphi.[1]

It might have been expected that the Thebans would have followed up their victory, by marching instantly to the holy city, scattering the remnant of their vanquished foes, and rescuing the temple from further pillage. Instead of this, they relieved the beaten Phocians from any immediate apprehension of danger, by retreating themselves into Bœotia. The explanation which Diodorus gives of their conduct is, that they considered the main objects of the war were accomplished by the death of Philomelus; that the Phocians, seeing him, the author of their calamities, to have been signally

[1] Diodorus, xvi. 30, 31. Pausanias, x. 2. The death of Philomelus occurred B.C. 354.

punished by gods and men, would repent of their folly and turn to wiser counsels. If this were so, it is one among many proofs, that the Thebans had among them at that time no able adviser. I am more disposed however to take Thirlwall's view, that the retreat of the Thebans was owing to strategic causes, the victory of Neon not having been so decisive as to encourage them to pursue the enemy, much less to undertake a siege of Delphi.

The proceedings in that city after the battle show what important results might have been accomplished by the rapid advance of a victorious army. Among the national troops and counselors of the Phocians there was a moderate party, who were desirous of peace, dreading the consequences of opposition to so large a body of the Greeks, and seeing how feebly they had been supported by their professed allies. Some had religious scruples, and were shocked at a state of things, under which they were as a nation excommunicated from Hellenic society and brotherhood: others were jealous of the despotic power exercised by the general, or disgusted with the licentiousness of his mercenary camp. Onomarchus, on the other hand, felt that the only chance of honor and distinction for himself and his family lay in the continuance of the war; his very safety depended upon it, as he was personally implicated in the charges preferred by the Amphictyons, and sentenced by them to the penalties of sacrilege. On his side were the more bold and unscrupulous part of the Phocians, and the whole body of mercenaries, who saw their advantage in the prospect of pay and plunder. An assembly or council of war was convened, and Onomarchus in a powerful and well-prepared speech urged the necessity of resisting the enemy, and persevering in the manly course begun by Philomelus. His eloquence, backed by the support of the army, carried the day; and he was elected to fill the office of general with the same absolute powers which had been conferred upon his predecessor. His first care was to fill up the places of the soldiers who had fallen in battle, to make new levies of mercenaries, and provide himself with an immense quantity of arms and military stores. The work of spoliation was now commenced on a larger scale than before. Whatever donatives of brass and iron manufacture he found in the temple, he converted into arms; the gold and silver he melted down for coinage, employing it not only for the maintenance of his own troops, but for distribution among the leading statesmen of Athens, Sparta, and other cities in alliance with him. Experience had shown that little was to be expected from the voluntary exertions of these allies, occupied as they were by their own affairs, or distracted by their own troubles. It was necessary to stimulate their zeal by some extraordinary means, and gold was profusely lavished for this purpose. But Onomarchus did not stop here. He employed the ample means of corruption which he had at his command to purchase peace from his enemies; some of whom he gained over to his side, others he persuaded to be neutral. Among these were the Thessalians.[1]

The feelings of pious men were further outraged, by seeing the riches of the temple not only applied to purposes of war and administration, but lavished on amusement and vanity. Onomarchus was vicious in his pleasures. Precious ornaments, hallowed by their antiquity and the memories associated with them, were taken from the custody of Apollo, to hang on the necks or encircle the brows of his mistresses and favorites. Philomenus had occasionally been generous in this way at the expense of the god; yet there were bounds to his liberality, which the extravagance of his successor disregarded. Philomelus had been mild in his domestic goverment, and gained a well-merited popularity, which had helped to secure the succession to his brother. Onomarchus, irritable in his temper, and intolerant of opposition, seized the principal Phocians who had either resisted his election, or whom he considered to be forming a party against him in the state, and condemned them to lose their lives and property. With all this, he was not free from the superstition of the age. He was encouraged by a dream, in which a colossal statue, one of the ornaments of the temple, seemed to grow under his hands in height and bulk; which portended, as he thought, an increase of glory under his own generalship; whereas, in the historian's view, it signified that he would be an instrument for increasing the penalties to which his countrymen were doomed.[2]

Having now raised by his exertions a numerous and well-appointed army, he lost no time in making the best use of it. The Amphissian Locrians, terrified by his approach, and isolated from their confederates, had no resource but in submission. Entering the territory of the Dorians, who were equally remote from all assistance, he ravaged and plundered it with impunity. He overran Epicnemidian Locris, taking and occupying with a garrison the city of Thronium, the inhabitants of which he sold into slavery.

Whether it was at this time, as Grote thinks, or a little later that he took Nicæa and Alponus, is not clear. Certain it is, that he was shortly afterwards master of the pass of Thermopylæ, the access to which those fortresses commanded. From the hills of Cnemis he descended into Bœotia, approaching the north-western bank of the Lake Copias, where stood the ruins of Orchomenus, once the first of Bœotian cities. It had been destroyed by the Thebans, who cherished a bitter hatred against the city for having sided with Lacedæmon, and after the battle of Leuctra were only restrained from wreaking their vengeance upon it by the entreaties of Epaminondas; but in the year B.C. 364, having discovered a conspiracy of the

[1] Diodorus, xvi. 32, 33, 57. Athenæus, xii. 532. As to the bribery at Sparta, see ante, p. 264.

[2] Diodorus, xvi. 33, 64. Athenæus, xiii. 605.

Orchomenian knights and certain of their own exiles to overthrow the government, they seized the occasion, during the absence of Epaminondas, to punish the crime of a few citizens by the extirpation of the whole people, whom they massacred in cold blood, sell- the women and children for slaves.[1] Onomarchus took possession of the ruined city, intending to establish it as a fortress and sallying place against the enemy. There may have been a village population in Orchomenus at this time; but there is no doubt that he left a garrison in it, and repaired the fortifications; for it continued to be occupied by the Phocians till the end of the war. He next laid siege to Chæronea; but the Thebans coming to its relief, and his army being weakened by the garrisons which he had detached, he was driven with some loss from the walls of that city, and returned into Phocis.[2]

The inaction of the Thebans at this period is attributable to several causes; chiefly to the disunion sown among their allies by the craft of their opponent, and the great advantage which he had over them in recruiting his military resources. They had vainly imagined that they could maintain an army at their own cost, which would overcome any mercenary force provided by the pillage of Delphi, and they had found their mistake.[3] The want of money now compelled them to send five thousand men under Pammenes to assist the satrap Artabazus, who had revolted against the Persian king.[4] But such a number could be ill spared from a war, in which they had to contend against a power growing every day more formidable. Onomarchus, in the year B.C. 353, commanded the largest standing army in Greece, and was seemingly supported by the strongest alliances. There was but one man able to cope with him, and that was Philip of Macedon; with whom a series of events, which must now be adverted to, brought him into conflict.

Alexander of Pheræ, after a reign of eleven years, in which he had shown some vigor and aptitude for command, mingled with the most inhuman and savage ferocity, was murdered in his bed by the contrivance of his wife Thebe, assisted by her brothers Tisiphonus and Lycophron.[5] Tisiphonus, either alone or jointly with his

[1] Diodorus, xv. 57, 79. Pausanias, ix. 15. Demosthenes, contr. Leptin. 490.

[2] Diodorus, xvi. 33. Demosthenes, De Fals. Leg. 387. Æschines, De Fals. Leg. 45. Grote's History of Greece, xi. 360.

[3] Isocrates, Philipp. 93.

[4] Diodorus, xvi. 34.

[5] Xenophon, Hellen. vi. c. 4, ss. 35—37. Plutarch, in Vit. Pelopid. 35. Diodorus, xvi. 14. The romantic incidents of this murder are familiar to most readers—how Thebe removed the fierce dog that usually guarded the chamber—how she laid wool upon the stairs, that

brother, was raised to the supreme power, and having delivered their country from an odious tyrant, they were at first highly popular, but in course of time, as they became despotic, and rested their support upon the mercenary troops, they excited an opposition, which could only be put down by measures of violence. Tisiphonus survived but a few years, and at the time to which we are drawing attention Lycophron had the sole sway. When Onomarchus opened his negotiations in Thessaly, Lycophron joined alliance with him. Common sympathies attracted these two potentates to each other; and it is likely enough that they entered into a compact for mutual support in their schemes of ambition. Lycophron recommenced that system of encroachment upon the Thessalian body, which had caused them in Alexander's reign to invite foreign assistance. The exact time when dissensions broke out between them and the ruler of Pheræ can not, in the absence of historical information, be clearly ascertained. There is evidence to warrant the conjecture, that he had enlarged his dominions at their expense, and got possession of some of their fortresses, as early as the year 355 B.C., and that the Thessalians were then in a distressed and impoverished condition: but it does not appear that any foreign aid was called in before the year 353 B.C. It was then useless to apply to Thebes, cut off as she was from communication with the north, and scarcely able to defend herself at home. The Aleuads therefore turned their eyes to Philip of Macedon, who, still carrying on war against Athens and her dependencies, had advanced to besiege Methone, the last remaining possession of the Athenians on the Macedonian coast.[1]

Methone fell after a long siege; and Philip, at the invitation to the Aleuads, marched into Thessaly. The course of his operations is not clear. It is probable that one of the earliest was against Pagasæ, which he would be anxious to take before the Athenians could send relief to it by sea. They did send a fleet, which, as usual, arrived too late, and Pagasæ fell into his hands.[2] Lycophron

the steps of her brothers might not be heard—how, when they hesitated at the last moment, she threatened them with discovery, if they did not mount the staircase—and how she herself held the bolt of the door, while they completed the murderous task. Plutarch mentions the third brother, Pytholaus, as joining in it.

[1] Isocrates, De Pace, 183. Diodorus, xvi. 14, 34, 35. Thirlwall (History of Greece, v. 280, note 2) rightly considers that Diodorus, in the first of the above-cited chapters, is only giving a general view of the course of events in Thessaly, and not speaking of any interference by Philip soon after Alexander's death.

[2] Demosthenes, Olynth. i. 11. Philipp. i. 50. Diodorus, xvi. 31. Παγὰς in this passage ought to be Παγασάς, though the date is wrong, for Philip never could have attacked Pagasæ before his expedition into Thessaly, B. C. 353. Diodorus rightly makes the siege of Pagasæ follow

meanwhile had applied for succor to the Phocian general, who sent seven thousand men under the command of his brother Phayllus; but he was beaten by Philip, and driven back from Thessaly; upon which Onomarchus, seeing the great importance of repelling so dangerous an adversary, mustered all his forces together, and hastened in person to the scene of action. Twice did these two generals, the ablest then in Greece, encounter each other in battle; and twice was Philip worsted. In the first engagement Onomarchus, not trusting entirely to superior numbers, resorted to a stratagem difficult and dangerous to practice except with experienced troops. He had occupied some rising ground under a semicircular ridge of hills. On the high cliffs which flanked him on either side he placed a heap of loose rocks and a body of men in concealment, then descended into the plain to meet the enemy. They instantly attacked him, the light troops discharging their missiles, and he by a pretended flight drew them after him into the concavity of the hills. As the Macedonians rushed tumultuously forward, their progress was suddenly arrested by crushing masses of rock hurled down among them from the cliffs: at that moment Onomarchus gave the signal, and the Phocians charging their disordered ranks drove them back with slaughter to their camp. In the midst of the flight Philip lost not his presence of mind, but coolly observed to those about him, that he was retiring like a battering-ram, only to be more terrible in the reaction.[1] Notwithstanding this vaunt, he was again defeated, and the second time so severely, that he escaped with some difficulty from the field, his soldiers deserting him, or breaking into open mutiny. Using all his powers of persuasion to keep the discouraged remnant in obedience, he led them back to his own kingdom. He was not however pursued, events

that of Methone; but he has evidently committed some mistake, for he mentions the siege of Methone twice, the right place being in chapter 34. See Leland's Life of Philip, i. p. 213. Grote's History of Greece, xi. 365, 412. Grote thinks that Pagasæ was not taken till after Pheræ. But against this we may observe, that there actually was a siege of Pagasæ, as we learn from Demosthenes; but there could have been no occasion for it after Pheræ had been surrendered. Again, had there been a siege of Pagasæ at that time, there was an Athenian fleet on the coast to relieve it, and Demosthenes would hardly have imputed its fall to the dilatoriness of Athens.

[1] Polyænus, Strateg. ii. 38. Thirlwall (History of Greece, v. 281) thinks this anecdote should be referred to the second battle. It seems to me that the words of Philip are more applicable to a partial defeat, after which he might contemplate another immediate attack, than to the severe defeat which followed, and which drove him for the time from Thessaly. He said these words to cheer his soldiers *ἐν αὐτῇ τῇ φυγῇ*.

having happened which required the presence of Onomarchus in Bœotia.[1]

The diversion made by Philip in Thessaly had encouraged the Thebans again to try the fortune of war. They had taken the field, with the intention perhaps of recovering Orchomenus; but whatever their plans were, they were disconcerted by the rapidity of the Phocian general, who with his victorious army appearing suddenly in Bœotia overcame them in battle, and then besieged and took Coronea. This city was near the south-western shore of Lake Copais, and about twenty miles from Thebes. The loss of such a place must have been a great blow to the Thebans, and proves how incapable they were at this time to defend themselves against the superior force of the enemy. It is not unlikely, the population of Coronea were unfriendly to Thebes, and surrendered their city without much reluctance: for it remained in possession of the Phocians until the end of the war, and met then with the same severe punishment which was inflicted upon Orchomenus.[2] The campaign might further have been prolonged, with still more disastrous issues to the Thebans; but, fortunately for them, Onomarchus was recalled by the alarming intelligence, that Philip had again raised his standard in Thessaly.[3]

That indefatigable prince, having repaired the strength and discipline of his army in Macedonia, returned with the resolute determination to accomplish his original purpose. Unless he could retrieve his honor and establish his ascendency in Thessaly, it was all over with ulterior projects of empire. He therefore strenuously exerted himself to levy troops among his allies. To stimulate their zeal, he proclaimed that he was come not only to deliver them from the Pheræan tyranny, but to subdue the sacrilegious Phocians, and restore to the Amphictyons their Pylæan synod.[4] The Aleuads seconded his efforts, and in a short time his army, reinforced by the Thessalians, amounted to above twenty thousand foot and three thousand horse. He ordered his men to wear wreaths of laurel, as soldiers in the cause of Apollo;[5] and having raised their ardor and courage to the highest pitch, he led them against the enemy. Onomarchus had come promptly to the aid of Lycophron, and was already in the Pheræan territory with a force of twenty thousand foot and four hundred horse. The two armies met on the shore of the Pagasæan gulf, not far from Pagasæ, and within sight of an Athenian squadron under Chares, which was cruising off the coast. It was now to be decided, whether Philip or Onomarchus should be

[1] Diodorus, xvi. 35.
[2] Demosthenes, De Pace, 62. De Fals. Leg. 375, 387, 445.
[3] Diodorus, xvi. 35.
[4] Demosthenes, De Chersoneso, 105. De Fals. Leg. 443.
[5] Justin, viii. 2.

the future lord of Thessaly, and perhaps of Greece. The battle was long and obstinate, but the fortune of Philip prevailed, owing chiefly to the numbers and valor of his Thessalian cavalry. The Phocians, broken on all sides, fled to the beach; many plunging into the waves, in the vain attempt to swim to the Athenian ships, were either drowned or cut to pieces by pursuing horsemen. Among these was Onomarchus himself. Six thousand of his troops were slain; three thousand prisoners were drowned in the sea as criminals by the command of the conqueror. The body of Onomarchus was nailed to a cross.[1] Thus perished, in the fourth year of the Sacred War, the only general who had ability enough to compete with the king of Macedon.[2]

Phayllus, succeeding to the command, applied himself without delay to repair the dreadful loss which his country had sustained, and to put her in a posture of defense. The flower of the Phocian army had been destroyed. Scarce a third part of the force which had marched into Thessaly could have returned to their standards. To obtain speedy succor was indispensable. Phocis might be attacked by all her enemies at once. The Macedonians might penetrate the straits of Thermopylæ, while the Thebans and Locrians invaded the eastern frontier. Phayllus, to recruit his army, could employ the same means which his predecessors had done, and those he did not neglect: but for new levies of soldiers some time would be required, and every moment was of importance. He therefore sent pressing messages to Athens, to Sparta, and to his other allies, representing the urgency of the peril, and imploring immediate succor.[3]

The Athenians, in the beginning of the war, notwithstanding their treaty of alliance with the Phocians, had lent them no military aid. They had been themselves impoverished and weakened by the

[1] Diodorus, xvi. 35. Pausanias, x. 2, states that Onomarchus was killed by his own soldiers, attributing the defeat to his cowardice and incapacity. As to this, and as to the punishment of criminals by drowning, see Wesselng's notes on the passage in Diodorus.

[2] The ability of Onomarchus is sufficiently proved by his acts. The loss of the battle is attributed by Diodorus to his inferiority in cavalry. It would seem, that he had acquired experience as a commander in the Leuctric war. Polyænus (ii. 38) relates a stratagem of his, which must have occurred at that period. The Thebans, under Pelopidas, were besieging Elatea. Onomarchus opened the gates of the city, brought out the old men, woman, and children, and in front of them drew up the whole force of the heavy-armed. Pelopidas, fearing to drive the Phocians to despair, withdrew his army.—This reminds one of the old tale of Phocian desperation, already cited from Pausanias (ante, p. 236).

[3] Diodorus, xvi. 36.

Social War,[1] and were still engaged in a harassing contest with Macedonia. Their interest in the Phocian quarrel was remote; and that any danger to the liberty of Greece was to be apprehended from it, was a thing which the most acute politician could not have dreamed of. It appeared in a short time, that the Phocians, so far from needing foreign assistance, were more than a match for their adversaries. We may be surprised that after the successes of Onomarchus, when the Thebans were so enfeebled as not to be able to defend their own territory, the Athenians should not have taken advantage of the occasion to attempt the recovery of Oropus. This may serve to show both the military weakness of Athens, and the supineness of her people. The siege of Pagasæ, so soon following the capture of Methone, alarmed them a little on their own account, and they sent a fleet to relieve it, which, as already mentioned, arrived too late. Now however, when Philip, having destroyed the army of Onomarchus, was ready to march with an overpowering force to Thermopylæ, the magnitude of the crisis became apparent; and it needed not the urgent appeal of Phayllus to convince the Athenians, that they themselves were deeply concerned in checking Philip's further progress. Should he succeed in passing the barrier of southern Greece, the road was open not merely to Phocis but to Athens. Their own sailors, eye-witnesses of the battle, must have brought them the earliest intelligence. From the Phocian envoys they would learn, that Phayllus was unable to hold the pass unassisted. Roused at once from their lethargy, the Athenians voted the required succors, and shipped them off with the utmost expedition for the straits of Thermopylæ. The land force consisted of five thousand infantry and four hundred horse, commanded by Nausicles. These, properly supported by the Phocians, would be sufficient to guard the pass, so long as the fleet, keeping command of the sea, prevented Philip landing troops in their rear. Succors came also from Peloponnesus; a thousand Lacedæmonians, and two thousand Achæans.[2]

Philip immediately after his victory proceeded to the reduction of Pheræ. This was expected of him by the Thessalians, as the prime object of the expedition. Pheræ, garrisoned by the troops of Lycophron, would be capable of holding out for some time; and it might be policy in the tyrant to make some show of vigorous defence, if it were merely for the sake of obtaining better terms. There could

[1] Isocrates, De Pace, 163. This oration was composed at the close of the Social War.

[2] Diodorus, xvi. 37. The cost of the Athenian armament (according to Demosthenes, De Fals. Leg. 367) was more than two hundred talents, reckoning the private outlay of individuals as well as the public. We can not doubt however that the Athenians received money from Phayllus.

be no chance for him however of ultimate success, cut off as he was from all hope of assistance: he therefore capitulated, receiving permission for himself and his brother Pitholaus to retire with their mercenaries from Thessaly. Two thousand soldiers were carried over by them to the Phocians. Pheræ was surrendered to Philip, who abolished the dynasty to which it had so long been subject, and established a free or popular government. After this he marched to Thermopylæ; but finding on his arrival that it was strongly guarded by Athenian troops, he retreated without making any attempt to force the pass. Thus did the Athenians by a prudent and timely effort (more than once made the subject of eulogy by Demosthenes, and cited by him as an axample for imitation), avert from themselves apparently a very serious danger.[1]

Thirwall, in his History of Greece, expresses a doubt whether the retreat of Philip from Thermopylæ was owing to any fear of the Athenians; suggesting that perhaps he was not desirous of terminating the war so soon; had this been so, he would have followed up his victory more rapidly: it was to his advantage that the Sacred War, which was wasting the strength of the Greeks, should be kept up some time longer; he advanced perhaps at the request of the Thessalians, and was glad to find a pretext for retiring from Thermopylæ.[2] There are, as it appears to me, very fair grounds for the suspicion of the learned historian; though I am less inclined to consider that Philip could have forced the pass against the Athenians, than that he purposely delayed his own advance, deeming it premature at that moment to carry his arms southward. The motives of his conduct are to be looked for in the affairs of Thessaly, and in his relations with the people of that country.

The proceedings of Philip in Thessaly are but imperfectly known to us. That he ultimately acquired such a preponderance in that country as to be a sort of Tagus, exercising both a military and a political authority, is certain: the steps by which he arrived at that power are not so clearly revealed. On the one hand, we learn from Diodorus, that Philip, by his generous services to the Thessalians in putting down the tyrants and restoring the freedom of their cities, secured their grateful co-operation in his own wars.[3] Theopompus attributes much of the popularity of Philip to his good companionship. Knowing (he says) that the Thessalians were addicted to intemperance and debauchery, he followed the bent of their humor, which indeed was quite natural to him, as he was himself a hard

[1] Demosthenes, Philipp. i. 44. De Coron. 236. De Fals. Leg. 367, 397, 443.

[2] Thirlwall, History of Greece, v. 283.

[3] Diodorus, xvi. 14. *Κατεπολέμησε τοὺς τυράννους, καὶ ταῖς πόλεσιν ἀνακτησάμενος τὴν ἐλευθερίαν, μεγάλην εὔνοιαν εἰς τοὺς Θετταλοὺς ἐνεδείξατο· διόπερ ἐν ταῖς μετὰ ταῦτα πράξεσιν ἀεὶ συναγωνιστὰς ἔσχεν.*

drinker, fond of loose pleasures, coarse wit, and buffoonery; he therefore lived among them freely, and by thus making himself agreeable he attached them to him more strongly than by his profuse liberality.[1] Isocrates, writing at the end of the Sacred War, tells us that the Thessalians had become so attached to Philip as to put more confidence in him than in their own countrymen.[2] Demosthenes, having reference to the issue of that war, says they regarded him as a saviour and benefactor:[3] and we know that they afterwards assisted him in Thrace; they chose him for their general in the Amphissian war, and followed him to Chæronea; and their embassadors supported the Macedonian at Thebes against Demosthenes.[4] On the other hand, we are told by Justin, that Philip after the victory of Pagasæ requited his Thessalian allies with the most atrocious perfidy; that he took hostile possession of the very cities which had furnished him with auxiliaries; that he sold their women and children by public auction, and spared not even the temples or the houses in which he had been hospitably entertained.[5] This statement, which may be regarded as an exaggeration, coincides in some measure with an anecdote of Polyænus, who relates, that Philip came to Larissa to destroy the houses of the Aleuads; that he sought by a pretended sickness to entice them to visit him, and then to seize their persons; and that the plot failed by the discovery of one Bœscus:[6] some additional confirmation is afforded by another passage of the same author, in which he gives an account of Philip's general policy towards the Thessalians; stating that he contrived a means to subdue them without making any open war; that, finding they were divided among themselves and the different cities continually quarreling,—for example, Pelinna with Pharsalus, Larissa with Pheræ,—he interfered from time to time on behalf of those who solicited his aid, but when he overcame their adversaries, he never pursued them to destruction, nor deprived them of their arms or fortifications; his plan was always to take the part of the weak against the strong, to support the lower against the higher classes, and to encourage the demagogues: by such arts he got the dominion of all Thessaly.[7] Light is thrown on this by the war which undoubtedly broke out between Pharsalus and Halus, B.C. 347—346, in which Philip espoused the cause of the

[1] Theopompus, apud Athenæum, vi. 260. Compare iv. 167; x. 435. Polybius censures Theopompus for his injustice to Philip. Lib. viii. 11, 12.

[2] Isocrates, Philipp. 86.

[3] Demosthenes, De Coron. 240.

[4] Demosthenes, De Cherson. 93. De Coron. 237, 246, 277, 298. Isocrates, Philipp. 97.

[5] Justin, viii. 3.

[6] Polyænus, Strateg. iv. c. 2, s. 11.

[7] Polyænus, Strateg. iv. c. 2, s. 19.

Pharsalians, and gave them the city after its capture.[1] And it appears also, from divers passages of Demosthenes, that some of Philip's acts were unpopular among the Thessalians, or at least excited murmurs and complaints; for instance, his garrisoning of their towns, and his appropriation of their public revenues; that during the first few years of his connection with them he had some little difficulty in keeping them under his command, and resorted occasionally to harsh measures; and that at last he divided the country into tetrarchies, placing his own creatures in the chief towns, to insure their dependence on himself.[2]

From these various statements, if we distinguish the different times and circumstances to which they have reference, and make due allowance for high coloring and exaggeration, we may gather, not indeed an exact series of historical events, but a probable view of the course of things.

Philip, when he entered Thessaly, never meant to put down the tyrants of Pheræ and then quietly go away; nor to set up the Aleuads or any other aristocratical family in the place which that dynasty had usurped. He intended to conquer Thessaly for himself, and to use it as an instrument for ulterior purposes. But such conquest was not achieved by the defeat of Onomarchus, nor yet by the capture of Pheræ and Pagasæ. It was not even certain that, if he advanced into Phocis and put an end to the Sacred War, the Thessalians would afterwards follow him into Attica, or assist him in any other aggressive movement of his own.[3] There was not much reliance to be placed on the friendship or gratitude of that people.[4] It was necessary to bring them entirely under his rule, before he made any attempt against the Greeks south of Thermopylæ. How was this to be accomplished? Partly by conciliation and persuasion, partly by coercion and force. He must make the Thessalians understand that Macedonian protection was indispensable to them. With such view it was good policy to let the

[1] Demosthenes, Orat. ad. Epist. 152. De Fals. Leg. 352, 353, 391, 392. He says of the Halians, *'Εξελήλανται καὶ ἀνάστατος ἡ πόλις αὐτῶν γέγονε.* Isocrates says, Philipp. 86, *Τῶν πόλεων τῶν περὶ τὸν τόπον ἐκεῖνον τὰς μὲν ταῖς εὐεργεσίαις πρὸς τὴν αὐτοῦ συμμαχίαν προσῆκται, τὰς δὲ σφόδρα λυπούσας αὐτὸν ἀναστάτους πεποίηκεν.*

[2] Demosthenes, Olynth. i. 15; ii. 21, 22. De Cherson. 105. Philipp. ii. 71; iii. 117, 119; iv. 148, 149. Orat. ad Epist. 153. De Coron. 241, 324. De Fals. Leg. 424, 444. Athenæus, vi. 249. Harpocration, sub. v. *δεκαδαρχία.*

[3] Demosthenes, De Pace, 60. De Coron. 276. De Fals. Leg. 444. *'Εστασίαζε μὲν αὐτῷ τὰ Θετταλῶν, καὶ Φεραῖοι πρῶτον οὐ συνηκολούθουν.* The Pheræans were unwilling to follow him even against the Phocians, to put an end to the Sacred War. Much more would they have been reluctant to assist him in a private war of his own.

[4] Demosthenes, contr. Aristocr. 657.

Phocians gather new strength; and it was better also to let Lycophron and Pitholaus retire with their adherents to a place of safety, than entirely to uproot the regnant house and remove all fear of their return. He knew again, that the same nobles who had invited him to expel the tyrant would be dissatisfied with his own assumption of power, though to the mass of the people it might not be so unacceptable. He therefore made it his business to court favor with the less wealthy classes, even with the Penestæ,[1] who formed part of the army; and strove to elevate them at the expense of the nobility. The expression of Diodorus, that Philip restored freedom to Pheræ, may be literally true;[2] and he may have established in that city a species of democracy. The Aleuads, who expected that Pheræ would be given up either to themselves or to parties in connection with them, were indignant at Philip's conduct; and gave utterance to their resentment in complaints and threats, the more loud and vehement, as they were able with some justice to urge, that, while he was meddling with the internal affairs of Thessaly, he was neglecting his engagement to prosecute the Phocian war. A party was formed against Philip, and it became necessary for him either to intimidate his opponents, or to destroy their power and influence. Strong measures were immediately adopted, such as those indicated by Justin and Polyænus. Larissa was the stronghold of the Aleuads; and Philip, while he insulted and degraded the members of that ancient house, would take care not to leave so important a city under their control. Of the manner in which he proceeded to foment the divisions among the different cities of Thessaly, we have no further particulars than those which have been already stated. His operations at Pagasæ must have been among the earliest at this period. He there took possession of the shipping and naval stores, and speedily turned them to account against the Athenians, sending out cruisers to plunder their allies and seize the merchant vessels in the Ægean. A Macedonian squadron made a descent on Lemnos and Imbrus, and took some Athenian citizens prisoners: another made a valuable prize of some merchantmen off the southern coast of Eubœa, and afterwards entered the bay of Marathon and carried off the sacred galley. The Athenians now discovered that not only their distant possessions, but those near home, were in danger. Philip had for seven or eight years been attacking them in Macedonia and Thrace; now he was threatening even Attica itself. Demosthenes, in an assembly held at the close of the year 352 B.C., delivered his first Philippic, in which he

[1] Theopompus mentions one Agathocles (a Penest) who amused Philip by his flattery and jesting powers, and was employed by him to corrupt the Perrhæbians, and manage his affairs in their country. Athenæus, vi. 260.

[2] Τῇ πόλει τὴν ἐλευθερίαν ἀποδούς. Diodorus, xvi. 38.

specially notices these piratical excursions of Philip, and the damage which they had done to Athens.[1] He makes, however, no allusion to the place in which such expeditions were prepared; and it is likely enough, that the proceedings of Philip in Thessaly were at this time wholly unknown to him. One of the advantages resulting to Philip from his occupation of the gulf of Pagasæ was, that it excluded the Athenians from communication with Thessaly by sea, while it enabled him to carry on his intrigues in Eubœa, and to menace the neighboring islands, Sciathus, Halonnesus, and Peparethus.[2] He also gathered a considerable revenue from the customs and harbor-dues of Pagasæ, which he took into his own hands under the pretense at first of reimbursing himself for the expenses of the war, and afterwards of maintaining a sufficient war establishment for the defense of the country. To secure these advantages to himself, he kept the city strongly fortified, and occupied it with a Macedonian garrison. Having settled the affairs of the Phærean kingdom, he turned his arms against the Magnetes and Perrhæbians.[3] Those tribes had perhaps asserted their independence of the Thessalians, and refused to lend any assistance in the war against Lycophron. Philip subdued them under the pretense of augmenting the security of Thessaly, but in reality for the purpose of strengthening his own dominion. The city of Magnesia, which he fortified and kept in his own possession, was conveniently situated on the Ægean coast above the bay of Pagasæ.[4] The Perrhæbians commanded the passes of Mount Olympus, and by their conquest an entrance to Thessaly was secured.[5] These proceedings occupied Philip until the autumn of the year B.C. 352, when he entered upon a Thracian expedition, which kept him actively engaged for about a twelve-month; at the end of which time he fell ill, and was obliged to return to his own kingdom.[6] During his absence the aristocratical parties began again to make head in Thessaly, and to intrigue

[1] Demosthenes, Philipp. i. 49, 50.

[2] Strabo, ix. 436, 437. Demosthenes recommends these islands as winter quarters for the standing force which he proposed to establish for the annoyance of Philip's coast. (Philipp. i. 49.) The importance which Philip attached to this position partly appears from the complaints in his letter. (Epist. Philipp. 159.) Compare Demosthenes, Philipp. iii. 120; iv. 133.

[3] Isocrates, Philipp. 86. *Μάγνητας δὲ καὶ Περῤαιβοιους καὶ Παίονας κατέστραπται, καὶ πάντας ὑπηκόους αὐτοὺς εἴληφεν.*

[4] Grote thinks there was no city called Magnesia, but that this name denotes the region only. (History of Greece, xi. p. 425, note 3.) It looks as if a city were spoken of in Demosthenes, Olynth. i. 13; *Φερὰς, Παγασὰς, Μαγνησίαν, πάνθ' ὃν ἐβούλετο εὐτρεπίσας τρόπον.* And also in Polyænus, Strateg. vi. 2.

[5] Herodotus, vii. 128, 172.

[6] Demosthenes, Olynth. i. 13; iii. 29.

against him. Exciting topics easily presented themselves—his retention of their cities and revenues, his arbitrary innovations, and his intention to set himself up as a tyrant (no better than those of Pheræ) under the mask of a protector. Philip's partisans on the other hand were not idle: they reminded the people of his past services, and promised that he would take the earliest opportunity of chastising the Phocians and restoring the Pylæan congress. Notwithstanding all their efforts, however, the opposite party obtained a partial success, and adverse votes were passed in some of the cities, asserting their own independence, calling upon Philip to abandon his fortification of Magnesia, to make restitution of Pagasæ, and the like.[1] Things had taken such a turn, that the presence of Philip was required to overawe the malcontents, and restore confidence to his party. It happened fortunately for him at this crisis, that an attempt was made by the exiled Pytholaus to recover his power in Pheræ. Philip's adherents seized upon this as a pretext for calling him into the country. Accordingly, about the middle of the year B.C. 350 he re-entered Thessaly: his mere approach was sufficient to frighten away the intruder; and all that remained for him to do was, by liberal promises and politic measures to consolidate his power and popularity.[2] He was then preparing for the Olynthian war, on the issue of which hung such important consequences; and he was glad to enlist under his standard the horsemen of Thessaly. Many of them he kept permanently in his pay; and, as victory and reward attached them to their commander, they answered the double purpose of strengthening his army, and securing his ascendency in their native land.[3]

[1] Demosthenes, Olynth. i. 15. *Παγασὰς ἀπειτεῖν αὐτόν εἰσιν ἐψηφισμένοι, καὶ Μαγνησίαν κεκωλύκασι τειχίζειν.* The verb *κεκωλύκασι* has reference to intention only. The Thessalians endeavored to prevent him by remonstrance. Compare Olynth. ii. 20, 21. In the first of these passages he calls the Thessalians *δεδουλωμένοι.* In drawing our inferences from what Demosthenes says, we must make allowance for the inaccuracy of his information, as well as for other things. That there were meetings and debates in Thessaly, is indicated by the passages, De Cherson. 105; Philipp. iv. 149: *Οὐκ ἦν ἀσφαλὲς λέγειν ἐν Θετταλίᾳ τὰ Φιλίππου, μὴ συνευπεπονθότος τοῦ πλήθους τοῦ Θετταλῶν τῷ τοὺς τυράννους ἐκβαλεῖν Φίλιππον αὐτοῖς καὶ τὴν Πυλαίαν ἀποδοῦναι.* Here there is no doubt an exaggeration of the truth, for the sake of an antithesis with what follows.

[2] Diodorus, xvi. 52. The attempt of Pitholaus was so opportune for Philip, that Thirlwall suspects him of having connived at it. (History of Greece, v. 307.) Pitholaus however may have had a powerful party in Pheræ, who thought the occasion favorable for their *coup d'état.* We have seen that the Pheræans showed reluctance to follow Philip to the Sacred War. Demosthenes, De Fals. Leg. 444.

[3] Theopompus, apud Athen. iv. 167. *Οἱ ἑταῖροι αὐτοῦ ἐκ πολλῶν τό-*

I have carried the reader a little out of chronological order, to give a clearer view of Thessalian affairs; and now return to the more direct transactions of the Sacred War.

Phayllus, relieved by his allies from the pressure of immediate danger, spared neither trouble nor expense to re-establish his own military force. Drawing from the resources of the temple no less profusely than Onomarchus had done, he now melted down the golden ingots of Crœsus, a hundred and seventeen in number, and weighing two talents each or nearly; also the female statue and golden lion, and three hundred and sixty golden beakers, which together weighed thirty talents. All these were converted into coin.[1] The produce enabled him to make speedy levies of troops, and he was soon strong enough to take the field in Bœotia. He was there defeated in a severe engagement with the Thebans near Orchomenus, in another on the banks of the Cephisus, and in a third by Coronea. It is not unlikely that the Thebans had advanced to besiege one or both of these cities, and that Phayllus had come to their relief. His army, beaten in open field, took refuge within the walls, and the Thebans, unable to follow up their victory, retired. Shortly afterwards Phayllus made an incursion into Epicnemidian Locris, and reduced all the cities into his power, except Aryca or Naryx, from which, after it had been betrayed to him in the night time, he was driven out again with some loss. Leaving a force before it to carry on the siege, he retreated into Phocis, but, while he was encamped near Abæ, he was surprised by the Thebans, who attacked him in the night and killed a considerable number of his troops. Elated with this success, they advanced further into the Phocian territory, ravaged a large tract of it, and carried off a heap of plunder: returning however through Locris to raise the siege of Aryca, they were suddenly attacked and put to the rout by Phayllus; after which he took the city by storm, and razed it to the ground. Thus had he brought to a creditable issue a campaign checkered with many reverses, when he was overtaken by a consumptive disease, which, after long and painful suffering, terminated fatally B.C. 351. In the manner of his death the ancient historian sees the visitation of heaven. He was succeeded as general-in-chief by Phalæcus, son of his brother Onomarchus, who, being a minor, was put under the guardianship of Mnaseas, a friend of the family.[2]

During these last occurrences both the Thebans and the Phocians

πων ἦσαν συνεῤῥυηκότες· οἱ μὲν γὰρ ἐξ αὐτῆς τῆς χώρας, οἱ δ' ἐκ Θετταλίας, οἱ δὲ ἐκ τῆς ἄλλης 'Ελλάδος.

[1] Diodorus, xvi. 56, and Wesseling's notes. Herodotus, i. 50, 51.

[2] Diodorus, xvi. 38. Pausanias, x. 2; who says the disease of Phayllus was the fulfillment of a dream, in which he fancied himself to be like a certain skeleton statue, which had been presented to Apollo by Hippocrates the physician.

sent succors to their respective allies in Peloponnesus, where the Lacedæmonians had commenced war against Megalopolis and Messene. The details of this I have given in another appendix.

The war was renewed by Mnaseas in Bœotia; but he having been killed in a night-combat by the Thebans, Phalæcus himself took the command. A cavalry action occurred near Chæronea, in which the Phocians were worsted; yet still they kept the field in the enemy's country, and at one time had succeeded in taking Chæronea, but were again driven out by the Thebans, who now, reinforced by their troops returned from Peloponnesus, resolved on attempting a diversion, by which, if they could not free their own country from the presence of hostile garrisons, they would at least retaliate the miseries of war upon their opponents. Accordingly they invaded Phocis, and meeting with no resistance, laid waste the greater part of it with fire and sword. One of the smaller towns they captured, and returned laden with spoil into Bœotia.[1]

Notwithstanding all the efforts of the Thebans, they were unable to dislodge their enemies from the Bœotian fortresses, from which they made continual incursions, and threatened them with further conquest. It is probable that the mercenaries were employed in this foreign service, while the native Phocians remained to defend their homes. The Theban troops, consisting chiefly of heavy-armed infantry, were superior in close combat to the mercenaries, who were for the most part peltastæ; this may account for the number of Theban victories in the field: but the mercenaries were quicker in their movements, easily rallied, and more efficient in desultory fighting. Besides, the Theban army being composed of citizens, their losses were not easily repaired; while the Phocian general was continually recruiting his numbers, as all the fighting men in Greece, who could find no better way to employ themselves, repaired to his camp for enlistment. Thus did the Thebans become every year more and more embarrassed by the war, which at the end of five years, instead of having accomplished the deliverance of Delphi, had reduced them to contend with their neighbors for supremacy in Bœotia. About 350 or 349 B. C., such was the low condition of their finances, that they applied to the Persian monarch for a subsidy, and received from him a present of three hundred talents, which they shortly afterwards requited by sending a thousand men under Lacrates to assist him in the re-conquest of Egypt. Yet even this assistance did not enable them to achieve any important advantage over their enemies; and the war was kept up only by a repetition of petty skirmishes and mutual predatory incursions. In the annals of Diodorus three consecutive years following the Persian loan present a perfect blank; but his silence will not warrant us in assuming that there was an entire cessation

[1] Diodorus, xvi. 38, 39.

[2] Diodorus, xvi. 40, 44.

of all warlike operations. We know that before the close of the war the Phocians had taken Corsiæ, a city in the north-eastern part of Bœotia,[1] and also the fortress of Tilphossæum.[2] And yet Diodorus never mentions the taking of either of these places, though he casually alludes to the former as being in the possession of the Phocians.[3] We collect also from other sources, that the war was carried on both in Phocis and Bœotia; nor is it at all likely, either that Phalæcus would keep his paid soldiers inactive in their quarters, instead of employing them to annoy the enemy and gather plunder, or that the Thebans would sit contentedly at home while their territories were overrun and pillaged by the Phocian general. The progress of the war was altogether to the disadvantage of the Thebans.[4]

In the summer of 348 B.C., the Thebans opened the campaign with an invasion of Phocis, and gained a victory of no great importance at Hyampolis. Returning home by Coronea, they encountered the army of Phalæcus, and were defeated with considerable loss. Not discouraged by this failure, they again entered and ravaged the enemy's country, and again on their return suffered defeat.[5] We see by their style of warfare, that the Thebans knew but little of the improved method of besieging fortresses, which Philip had so successfully employed; or they were destitute of the means of carrying on such operations. Annoyed and harassed though they were by hostile garrisons in Bœotian cities, they make no vigorous attempt to recapture them; but can only resort to the old system of ravaging the land of their adversaries.

But while Phalæcus kept his ground in Bœotia, and conducted the war there with success, his power was undermined by an adverse party at home, who excited the people against him. It seems that, as the spoliation of the temple was regularly continued, and

[1] Pausanias, ix. 24.

[2] Situated on a mountain of the same name, a little to the east of Coronea. It was called also Tilphossium, or Tilphosium. There was a fountain issuing from it, called Tilphosa, and near it the tomb of the prophet Tiresias, who died after drinking its waters. Strabo, ix. 411, 413. Pausanias, ix. 33.

[3] Diodorus, xvi. 58. In the same way he makes no mention of the taking of Nicæa and Alponus.

[4] Isocrates, Philipp. 93. Æschines, contra Ctesiph. 73, 74. Demosthenes, De Coron. 231. De Fals. Leg. 385, 387. *Εἰχόν γε Ὀρχομενὸν καὶ Κορώνειαν καὶ τὸ Τιλφωσσαῖον, καὶ τοὺς ἐν Νέωσιν ἀπειλήφεσαν αὐτῶν, καὶ ἑβδομήκοντα καὶ διακοσίους ἀπεκτόνεσαν ἐπὶ τῷ Ἡδυλείῳ, καὶ τρόπαιον εἱστήκει, καὶ ἱπποκράτουν, καὶ κακῶν Ἰλιὰς περιειστήκει Θηβαίους.* We have no further historical information concerning the capture of Tilphossæum and the affairs at Neon and Hedyleum, which Demosthenes alludes to as incidents well known at Athens.

[5] Diodorus, xvi. 56.

the treasures every year more and more sensibly diminished, the moderate Phocian statesmen and the bulk of the people viewed the affair with increased displeasure and alarm. The former generals had given great offense by appareling their wives, mistresses, or favorites, in some of the choicest ornaments of the temple, such as the celebrated necklaces of Helen and Eriphyle.[1] Phayllus had bestowed a golden ivy-wreath, a present of the Peparethians to Apollo, upon some favorite girl, a flute-player; and he introduced her with this wreath to play the flute at the Pythian games; but the audience would not permit her to appear.[2] The Phocians were a simple people of primitive habits and tastes, insomuch that even the better classes used to keep no servants in their houses, but the younger members of a family waited upon the elder. They were therefore a little scandalized, when the wife of Philomelus had two female domestics to attend upon her; and far more so at the number of slaves soon afterwards brought into the country, who could only subsist (it was thought) by eating the bread of the poorer citizens.[3] Yet with all their luxury and extravagance, and with all the shock which it gave to Phocian prejudices, the generals by means of their military power, and by the success which usually attended their arms, had silenced the murmurs of the people. But at length it became obvious to every eye, that the fund which had supplied their prodigality would in no very long time become exhausted;[4] and the Phocians in alarm began to ask themselves—"What will the Greeks say, when all the Delphian treasures are actually gone? and what means of defending ourselves shall we have then?"—Fear thus drove them into a condemnation of measures which they had so long either sanctioned or tolerated. Phalæcus, at the suggestion of one of his followers, had dug for a concealed treasure in the very centre of the temple, under the ground of the prophetic tripod. There was a traditional belief, founded upon two verses in Homer,[5] that immense riches lay under the stone floor of Apollo; and here they expected to find them. The soldiers however, who began to excavate the ground, were stopped by an earthquake,

[1] Diodorus, xvi. 64. Athenæus, vi. 231, 232.

[2] Athenæs, xiii. 605; where other instances are quoted from Theopompus.

[3] Athenæus, vi. 264.

[4] Demosthenes, so early as 349 B.C., speaks of the Delphic fund as beginning to be exhausted: *'Απειρηκότων χρήμασι Φωκέων.* Olynth. iii. 30. Compare Olynth. i. 16. Æschines (De Fals. Leg. 45) partly attributes the ruin of the Phocians to the failure of money to pay their troops: *Κατελύθησαν ἀπορίᾳ χρημάτων, ἐπειδὴ κατεμισθοφόρησαν τὰ ὑπάρχοντα.*

[5] Iliad, ix. 404:

Οὐδ' ὅσα λάϊνος οὐδὸς ἀφήτορος ἐντὸς ἐέργει
Φοίβου 'Απόλλωνος Πυθοῖ ἐνὶ πετρηέσσῃ.

which terrified all present: it seemed as if Apollo had given a solemn warning, that the violators of his sanctuary would soon be punished. The enemies of Phalæcus were encouraged to try an impeachment against him; and they accused him before the people of having embezzled the sacred treasures. To have charged him with expending them in the prosecution of the war would have been palpably unjust. A distinction therefore was drawn between their application to public and to private purposes. The people, considering that Phalæcus had wasted the funds on objects of personal ambition and vanity, passed a vote of condemnation, and deposed him from his office. Three generals were elected in his room, Dinocrates, Callias, and Sophanes, with instructions to make a searching inquiry into the misapplication of the sacred fund. An account was demanded of the persons through whose hands it had passed. The chief manager was one Philo, who, not being able to render any account, was convicted of embezzlement, and after suffering the torture, betrayed his accomplices. They were all put to death; the plunder which they had taken, at least what remained of it, was restored, and brought into the public exchequer. It was computed, that the aggregate of treasure, which had been taken from the Delphic temple since the beginning of the war, amounted in value to more than ten thousand talents.[1]

There could be little doubt, that such a wholesale destruction of a property not only sacred in general estimation, but in some sort national, would, as soon as its extent was fully known, raise a new outcry against the Phocians in Greece. No one had ever been known before to lay sacrilegious hands upon the Delphian temple. The penalty which Xerxes paid for the attempt was a well-known matter of history.[2] The proposal of the Corinthian envoy at Sparta, to borrow money from Delphi and Olympia for equipping a fleet, had never been acted upon, though it may have given rise to that clause in the treaty of peace, which provided for the security of the sacred treasures.[3] Jason, as we have seen, was suspected of designs upon Delphi, and his death was hailed with joy by the cities of Greece.[4] A scheme is attributed to Dionysius, of penetrating through Epirus into Phocis, and seizing upon the temple; and it is

[1] Diodorus, xvi. 56. Pausanias, x. 2.

[2] Ante, p. 238.

[3] Ante, p. 242. Compare Thucydides i. 143; ii. 13. A borrowing of the sacred moneys, with the intention of returning them, might upon an occasion of necessity be unobjectionable and even proper. Thus the Amphictyons made a loan to Clisthenes. (Isocrates, περὶ Ἀντιδόσεως, s. 248. The advice of Hecatæus to the Milesians (which they rejected) to take the treasures at Branchidæ, more resembles the proceedings of the Phocian generals. (Herodotus, v. 36.)

[4] Ante, p. 255.

related that, in order to get a footing on the Epirotic coast, he entered into an alliance with the Illyrians, and assisted them to restore Alcetas the Molossian to his kingdom; but the project was not carried any further.[1] Now, however, the whole accumulated wealth of the sanctuary had been swept away by a people who ought most especially to have been its guardians and protectors. Such were the reflections likely to be made in Greece; and the Phocians were filled with gloomy forebodings at the prospect before them.

Their fears were soon to be increased by more alarming intelligence. The Thebans, worn out by a calamitous contest which there seemed no hope of terminating by their own unaided efforts, determined to apply for succor to the king of Macedon. This fatal step was taken in the year B.C. 347. Until then it does not appear that the Thebans had ever desired his interference: fear or pride may have prevented them from seeking it. But the continued encroachment on their territories; the insults to which they were daily exposed by marauding incursions, which not only weakened their sway over the cities yet subject to them in Bœotia, but rendered it unsafe to leave their home except with an armed force; again, the shame of yielding to an adversary whom they once despised, and a burning desire of revenge, overcame every other feeling. It was just what Philip himself had most anxiously looked for. The Thessalians had been long pressing him to take arms in the cause of the Amphictyons; but the united petition of the Thessalians and Thebans would invest him with a still more august character, and enable him to terminate the war more easily. It excluded also the probable contingency of a junction between Thebes and Athens, leading to some peaceful settlement of the Phocian question.[2] He did not hesitate, therefore, a moment in accepting the invitation of the Thebans; and a solemn engagement was entered into between them, and ratified by their mutual oaths, by which Philip bound himself, with due support from his allies, to accomplish the deliverance of Delphi, the punishment of the impious Phocians, and the restitution of the Amphictyonic congress.[3] Diodorus says, that he sent a small body of troops immediately into Bœotia, as an earnest that he was sincere in the cause.[4] It is certain that Parmenio led

[1] Diodorus, xv. 13. Other acts of sacrilege perhaps caused him to be suspected of a design on Delphi; for example, his plunder of the temple at Agylla, *ibid.* 14. Ælian Var. Hist. i. 20. He may, notwithstanding this, have been impudent enough to rebuke the Athenians in the manner related by Diodorus, xvi. 57.

[2] Demosthenes, De Coron. 231.

[3] Demosthenes, De Fals. Leg. 443. De Pace, 62.

[4] Thirlwall (History of Greece, v. 340) says, the total silence of the orators renders this statement of Diodorus suspicious; and that such an

an army this year into Thessaly, and proceeded at the request of the Pharsalians to besiege Halus. He may have sent a few troops across the gulf of Pagasæ to Eubœa, and thence to Bœotia. Their presence may have encouraged the Thebans to try another invasion of Phocis, in which they inflicted some loss upon the enemy, surprising and dispersing a large body of them who were engaged in erecting a fortress near Abæ. The greater part of the Phocians escaped; but five hundred, who fled for refuge into the temple, perished by an accidental fire which consumed the sacred edifice.[1]

Rumors of Philip's hostile intentions having reached the Phocian government, embassies were sent instantly both to Athens and to Lacedæmon, praying for assistance. The most effectual means of averting the threatened danger was to hold the pass of Thermopylæ, as before, which could not be done without the aid of a powerful naval force. The Phocian envoys offered to put the Athenians in possession of the three fortresses, Alponus, Thronium, and Nicæa, which commanded the entrance to Thermopylæ. A decree was passed by the Athenians, empowering their general Proxenus to receive those places from the Phocians, and ordering an equipment of fifty galleys and a muster of all their citizens fit for service under thirty years of age. Proxenus, sailing with the Phocian envoys to the Malian gulf, applied to the commanders of the fortresses, requesting them to be delivered up to him according to promise. Unfortunately, however, the revolution which had taken place in Phocis prevented the completion of this arrangement. It seems that Phalæcus, after his deposition from office, still retained his command over the mercenaries, whose confidence he possessed; and retiring from Phocis, (if indeed he was not abroad when the revolution happened,) took up his quarters, as before, with the troops in Bœotia. The commanders of the fortresses in Locris, as well as Bœotia were his officers, and devoted to his cause. When the order came from home, to deliver up the Locrian cities to the Athenians, Phalæcus regarded it as an act of hostility to himself, rather than a measure of defense against the common enemy; and so much did he resent it, that he not only refused compliance with the order, but threw the

indication of Philip's design must have excited attention at Athens. On the other hand I may observe, that Philip from the first held himself out as the professed enemy of the Phocians, and would not allow them to be included in the treaty. It was only suggested by Æschines, that he would turn out to be their friend at the last. Moreover, it is likely that Philip would be eager to secure the Thebans to his alliance by some early demonstration of his good will. The words of Diodorus are: 'Ο *δὲ βασιλεὺς ἡδέως ὁρῶν τὴν ταπείνωσιν αὐτῶν, καὶ βουλόμενος τὰ* Λευκ*τρικὰ φρονήματα συστεῖλαι τῶν* Βοιωτῶν, *οὐκ ὀλίγους ἀπέστειλε στρατιώτας, αὐτὸ μόνον φυλαττόμενος τὸ δοκεῖν μὴ περιορᾷν τὸ μαντεῖον σεσυλημένον*. I agree with Thirlwall, that the *οὐκ* should be omitted.

[1] Diodorus, xvi. 58. Demosthenes, De Fals. Leg. 391, 392, 395.

Phocian envoys into prison, and insulted the Athenian heralds who announced the truce of the Eleusinian myteries. This happened in the month of Boedromion (September), 347 B.C. Soon afterwards Archidamus arrived with a thousand Lacedæmonians, and offered to guard the fortresses; but Phalæcus declined the offer, telling him to mind his own business, and not trouble himself with that of the Phocians.[1] Notwithstanding this answer, the Spartan king remained for some time with his allies; and the Athenian fleet, which had been sent to the straits, was kept stationed at Oreus, to act as occasion might require.[2]

Thus, by the dissensions of the Phocian people, happening unfortunately at a most critical time, the Athenians were prevented from occupying Thermopylæ, the only measure which could prevent the destructive inroad of Philip. There was time enough, however, to rectify this false step. The pass might yet be defended: the Phocian native troops and mercenaries united could form an army of twenty thousand men; and, if well supported by their allies, would not be vanquished very easily. Philip was aware of this, and with his usual prudence studied how he could smooth his way to a certain and easy conquest. His plan was to withdraw the Athenians from the Phocian alliance, by concluding a separate peace with them; and lest before the termination of the war they should change their minds, he resolved to amuse them by deceitful promises, and lead them into a false security, till it should be too late to save the Phocians from ruin. That this was the general scheme of Philip, and that it was ably and artfully accomplished by him, is certain. As to the details of its execution—and how far he was assisted by the treason or by the culpable negligence of Athenian statesmen—there is some degree of uncertainty, owing to the want of historical information.[3]

Already had Philip, even early in the year 347 B.C., caused it to

[1] Æschines, De Fals. Leg. 45. The τύραννοι there mentioned are the officers of Phalæcus. As to the whole of this passage, the reader may profitably consult Thirlwall's History of Greece, v. 367. Grote, xi. 522, 523. Compare also Æschines, De Fals. Leg. 33. Demosthenes, De Fals. Leg. 364.

[2] Demosthenes, De Fals. Leg. 365, 389, 444. Diodorus, xvi. 59.

[3] The materials for the history of these proceedings are chiefly derived from the speeches of Demosthenes and Æschines on the Embassy and the Crown, in which the orators not only frequently contradict each other, but are not always consistent with themselves. We can not therefore safely assume as true any one-sided statement in any of these speeches, which is not supported by some collateral proof or strong probability. There are many points of contention between them, rather of a private and personal than of a political or historical bearing. These I have generally passed over, confining myself to the prominent and most important features of the embassies and negotiations.

be indirectly communicated at Athens, that he was desirous of peace. According to Æschines, the intimation was first made by some Eubœan envoys, who came to Athens to settle terms of peace on their own account.[1] But not much attention was paid to them. After the capture of Olynthus, the Athenians, exasperated against Philip and terrified by his successes, passed vehement resolutions against him in the assembly, and sent envoys to Peloponnesus and elsewhere to warn the Greeks of the danger which threatened them from his ambition. This was the occasion upon which Æschines went to Arcadia, and addressed a violent Phillipic to the Ten Thousand at Megalopolis.[2] About the same time Timarchus made his motion, prohibiting, on pain of death, the carrying of arms or naval stores to Philip.[3] Eubulus and his friends, who represented the peace party at Athens, beginning now to see danger from Macedonia, looked to a reconciliation with Thebes as their best security, and would gladly have taken measures to bring it about. Unhappily the feelings of the two people were so embittered against each other, that an amicable adjustment at this time was impossible,[4] and it was soon discovered that there were no better hopes from the rest of the Greeks, who could not be made to understand, that the cause of Athens against Macedonia was one in which they were much interested themselves.[5] Under these circumstances, a renewal of Philip's pacific overtures met with a more favorable reception. He so contrived it, that they came through the mouth of Athenian citizens. One Phrynon, complaining at Athens that he had been taken by a Macedonian privateer during the Olympian truce, got himself to be sent to Philip in the quality of an embassador, to recover the ransom which he had been compelled to pay.[6] Ctesiphon was sent with him, and brought back a report, not only that the ransom had been restored, but that Philip professed the greatest good will towards Athens, that he had reluctantly engaged in hostilities with her, and was anxious to put an end to them. This report having been well received by the people, Philocrates moved that Philip should have permission to send a herald and embassadors to treat for peace. The motion was carried without opposition: but the war party were

[1] Æschines, De Fals. Leg. 29.

[2] Demosthenes, De Fals. Leg. 344, 426, 427, 438, 439. Æschines, De Fals. Leg. 38.

[3] Demosthenes, De Fals. Leg. 433.

[4] Æschines, Contr. Ctesiph. 73. Demosth. De Coron. 237. Demosthenes himself was inclined to the same policy. Æschines, De Fals. Leg. 42, 46, 47. Demosth. De Coron. 281.

[5] Æschines, De Fals. Leg. 38. Demosthenes, De Coron. 231, 233.

[6] There is a difficulty about the Olympic truce spoken of in the passage of Æschines, De Fals. Leg. 29. It has been conjectured that it may refer to Philip's Olympic festival at Dium. Thirlwall is inclined to that opinion. But see Grote, History of Greece, xi. 513, note 3.

still determined to try their strength, and they preferred an indictment against Philocrates, charging him with having passed a measure contrary to the spirit of the Athenian laws. He was defended by Demosthenes, and acquitted, the accuser not obtaining a fifth part of the votes.[1] It was evident that the current of feeling at Athens was now for peace. The war, besides stripping them of numerous possessions, had entailed on the Athenians a loss of fifteen hundred talents; and the late conquest of Chalcidice had imperiled their dominions in the Chersonese.[2] Athenian prisoners too had been taken in Olynthus; among them Iatrocles, who was afterwards embassador. The friends of these men, taking advantage of the general feeling, presented a petition to the assembly, requesting that their case might be considered. The appeal had its effect; and the people consented that Aristodemus the actor might be sent to Macedonia, to see what could be done on behalf of the prisoners, and to ascertain what Philip's intentions were on the subject of peace. The commission was somewhat irregular, but the professional character and celebrity of Aristodemus rendered him a sort of privileged person.[3] He was absent for some time, engaged very likely (together with Neoptolemus the actor, who obtained similar leave of absence) in the Olympic festivities of Dium. His report was, that Philip had the most friendly disposition towards Athens, and wished to become her ally. Neoptolemus came back with the same story: the appearance of Iatrocles, who had been liberated without ransom, tended to confirm their statements.[4]

Yet, notwithstanding these assurances of Philip's desire for

[1] Æschines, De Fals. Leg. 29, 30. Contr. Ctesiph. 62. This statement is made by Æschines alone, but it is abundantly clear that Demosthenes was at this time in favor of peace, having been disheartened by the result of the Olynthian war.

[2] Æschines, De Fals. Leg. 37. Demosthenes, Olynth. iii. 36. Philipp. i. 52. De Syntax. 174.

[3] Argumentum ii. ad Demosthenes, De Fals. Leg. 335.

[4] Æschines, De Fals. Leg. 30. The order of these events is taken from Æschines, and may perhaps be correct. Demosthenes appears to differ from him in this only, that he makes Aristodemus to have first mentioned the subject of peace. (De Coron. 232.) This indeed is not absolutely inconsistent with the account of Æschines; and it is not clear that either of them pretends to give accurate details of the whole proceeding. Compare Demosthenes, De Fals. Leg. 344, 371, 443. From the statements of the two orators one is strongly induced to suspect, that some at least of these men, Phrynon, Ctesiphon, Aristodemus, Iatrocles, and Neoptolemus, were from the first acting in corrupt concert with Philip. Phrynon, if we can believe Demosthenes, was a man steeped in infamy. (De Fals. Leg. 412.) Neoptolemus, after the peace, sold all his property in Athens, and went to live in Macedonia. Demosth. De Pace, 58, 59. Diodorus, xvi. 92.

peace, the time passed on without his making any direct overture, or sending any herald or minister to Athens. The Athenians, having once entertained the hope of peace, became impatient for its consummation; and their anxiety was still further increased by the suspicious conduct of Phalæcus, and the apparent weakness of the Phocian government. At length, upon the motion of Philocrates, a decree was passed, that ten embassadors should be sent to Macedonia, to open a treaty of peace, and discuss the terms with Philip. Thus was accomplished, by the agency of the same Philocrates, who continues henceforth to take the lead in every step of this negotiation, the very thing which Philip had been contriving, viz. that the first formal proposal for peace should come from the Athenians. Ten embassadors were chosen accordingly—Demosthenes, Æschines, Aristodemus, Ctesiphon, Phrynon, Iatrocles, Philocrates, Dercyllus, Cimon, and Nausicles—to whom was added Aglacreon of Tenedos, as representative of the allies. Their instructions were, to ascertain positively whether Philip was desirous of peace; and if he were, to bring embassadors from him with power to conclude it.[1]

A herald was sent before the embassadors, to procure them a safe conduct. They did not wait however for his return, but, having sailed to Oreus in Eubœa, they crossed over to Halus, then besieged by Parmenio, and obtained permission to pass through his lines to Pagasæ, from which they pursued their journey to Larissa, and there meeting the herald, proceeded with all the speed they could to the Macedonian capital, and obtained an interview with the king. This was early in the year 346 B.C. The transactions of the embassy are chiefly gathered from Æschines, who entertains us with a good deal of gossip about the journey, and what passed among the embassadors in private, but omits much that we should have liked to know about more important matters. We are told about the offensive conduct of Demosthenes towards his colleagues, and his entire failure and breaking down in the attempt to address Philip: we have an account also of the speech made by Æschines himself on the same occasion, in which he enlarged upon the ancient connection between Amýntas, Philip's father, and the Athenians, and the grounds upon which his countrymen maintained

[1] Argumentum ii. Demosth. De Fals. Leg. *Πέμπουσι δὲ τούτους εἰς Μακεδονίαν, ἵνα μάθωσιν εἰ μετ' ἀληθείας βούλεται εἰρήνην ἄγειν ὁ Φίλιππος· καὶ εἰ ἀληθές ἐστιν, ἐνέγκαι παρ' αὐτοῦ πρέσβεις τοὺς ληψομένους τοὺς ὅρκους.* Æschines states, that Demosthenes was proposed by Philocrates; and that to obtain the services of Aristodemus on the embassy, he being under an engagement to appear on the stage in certain Greek cities, Demosthenes moved in the council, that envoys should be sent to procure his release from the penalties. De Fals. Leg. 30.

their right to Amphipolis.[1] Of the reply which Philip made to the embassadors we learn nothing more, than that it was addressed mainly to the arguments of Æschines; though we are assured that he astonished them all by his good memory and powers of speech; and still further charmed them by his hospitality and politeness at the banquet. The end of it was, the embassadors brought back a letter from Philip to the Athenians, in which he assured them that he was desirous both of peace and alliance with Athens, that he was inclined to be her friend, and he would have stated expressly what service he meant to render her, if he could have been sure of being her ally. The terms of peace which he offered were, that both parties should retain what they possessed; which of course secured to Philip all his previous conquests, and, owing to a want of firmness on the part of the Athenian envoys, enabled him to retain conquests which he made between that time and the conclusion of the treaty. Philip gave them to understand before they left him, that he was about to march against Cersobleptes; yet no stipulation was made on behalf of that prince, though he was an ally of Athens: Philip only promised, that pending the negotiations for peace, he would not attack the Chersonese. Whether any thing passed between them on the subject of Phocis and the Sacred War, we are not informed. The embassadors returned home with a Macedonian herald about the first of Elaphebolion (March). Philip's envoys were to follow shortly, to settle the terms of peace at Athens.[2]

A formal report of their proceedings was made by the embassadors, in the manner required by Athenian law, first to the council and afterwards to the popular assembly. Demosthenes, rising after his colleagues, moved the formal grant of safe conduct and hospitality to the Macedonian herald and embassadors; and further, that the presidents of the council should, as soon as the embassadors arrived, appoint two consecutive days for holding an assembly to deliberate on the questions both of peace and alliance. He moved also, as he had already done in the council, for the usual compliments to the Athenian embassadors—a vote of thanks, and invitation to dinner in the Prytaneum. The ministers of Philip, three men of high distinction in their own country—Antipater, Parmenio, and Eurylochus—arrived a few days after; and the eighteenth and

[1] See as to all these particulars Thirlwall, History of Greece, v. 342. Grote, xi. 529. Leland's Life of Philip, ii. 58.

[2] Demosthenes, De Fals. Leg. 353, 354, 392, 421. De Halonn. 83, 85. Æschines, De Fals. Leg. 31, 32, 33, 39. Contr. Ctesiph. 63. Demosthenes not only denies that Æschines spoke to Philip about Amphipolis, but says he betrayed his country's interests by not doing so. Here his enmity somewhat perverts his judgment; for he must have known, that Philip would never restore Amphipolis to Athens.

nineteenth days of Elaphebolion were, on the motion of Demosthenes, appointed for discussing the questions of peace and alliance with Philip. Demosthenes himself paid marked attention to the Macedonian envoys, entertaining them handsomely at his own house, and taking care that suitable places and comfortable seats were provided for them at the Dionysian festival.[1]

At the time when the embassy returned, there were assembled at Athens the deputies of the Athenian confederacy, who had probably been sent for on the occasion. To them Aglacreon of Tenedos made his report; and they on behalf of their constituents passed a resolution, which, though it was not binding on the Athenians, it behoved them, having regard to the interests of their whole empire, duly to weigh and consider. Two clauses only of this resolution are preserved to us, by quotation in the speeches of Æschines. One declared[2]—"that, whereas the people of Athens were deliberating on the question of peace with Philip, and the embassadors were not yet returned, whom the people had sent into Greece to rouse the states in defense of Grecian liberty, it was the advice of the confederates, that, after the embassadors had arrived and made their report, the presidents should appoint two assemblies to be held according to the laws for debating on the question of peace: and whatever the people should decide, that should be agreed to by the confederates." The other clause recommended[3]—"that any of the Greek states should be at liberty within three months to become parties to the treaty, by inscribing their names on the pillar of record and taking the oaths." These clauses are made by Æschines the foundation of grave charges against Demosthenes—namely, that by fixing an early day for the assembly, for which it was impossible the Athenian envoys could return in time, he ex-

[1] Æschines, De Fals. Leg. 34, 35, 36, 42. Contr. Ctesiph. 62, 63, 64. Demosthenes, De Fals. Leg. 414. De Coron. 234. Æschines says, Demosthenes played a practical joke upon him and his colleagues. On the journey home he challenged them to speak, if they dared, in praise of Philip to the people. Ctesiphon and himself accepted the challenge, and in making their report talked about the good looks and agreeable manners and pleasant companionship of Philip; Demosthenes then got up, and reproved them for wasting the time of the assembly with idle chit-chat. Æschines in the later speech, but not in the former, says, that Demosthenes moved for an assembly to be held on the eighth of Elaphebolian, a day sacred to Æsculapius, and usually kept as a holiday. His object is to prove the great anxiety of Demosthenes to hurry on the peace. It is very possible that such a day may have been proposed, in the expectation that the embassadors would arrive in time for it. There is no doubt that Demosthenes was anxious for a speedy conclusion of the peace.

[2] Æschines, De Fals. Leg. 35.

[3] Æschines Contra Ctesiph. 63.

cluded all chance of benefit from their mission to the Greek states; and further, that, by opposing the last clause of the resolution, he prevented his countrymen acting in concert with the Greeks, which would have been attended with this great advantage, that, if Philip afterwards violated the treaty, they must have made common cause with Athens. Demosthenes in answer to the charge asserts,[1] that there was no embassy at this time to the Greek states, for the Greeks had all been tried long ago; and it would have been disgraceful to invite the Greeks to make war, when they were treating with Philip for peace: and he puts the following dilemma—"For what purpose could you have been sending for the Greeks at that crisis? To make peace? But they all had peace. To make war? But you were yourselves deliberating about peace." The dilemma is a bad one for this reason, that the embassy had been sent to the Greeks before any negotiation for peace was opened with Philip. Yet the answer of Demosthenes was, I believe, substantially true: for the embassies to rouse the Greeks against Philip had been dispatched six or eight months before, that of Æschines to Peloponnesus perhaps even earlier; and although it is possible that some of the envoys had not returned by the month of Elaphebolion, it had been pretty well ascertained, by the reports of those that had returned, and from other sources, that no assistance was to be expected from the Greeks; in fact, all thoughts of it had been dropped at Athens, and the people had, partly on that very account, been driven to seek for peace. This does not rest upon the assertion of Demosthenes alone. Æschines justifies his own conversion, from a strenuous opponent of Philip to a warm advocate of peace, upon the ground that none of the Grecian states would help Athens in her unequal war—that they were all either on Philip's side, or indifferent as to the issue of the contest.[2] Under these circumstances, although the synod of allies might think proper to revive this somewhat stale question of a Greek combination, and to notice the possible contingency of some good result turning up from the embassies, it can not surprise us that little attention was paid to it by the Athenians. Demosthenes, in naming a day for the discussion of the peace, fixed it without any reference to a resolution which would have postponed it indefinitely; and no objection was raised by any one. The embassadors had very likely arranged with Philip at Pella, that an early day should be appointed for the conference with his ministers: and Demosthenes was desirous that the treaty should be concluded as soon as pos-

[1] Demosthenes, De Coron. 233. *Οὔτε γὰρ ἦν πρεσβεία πρὸς οὐδένας ἀπεσταλμένη τότε τῶν Ἑλλήνων.* We must take notice of the word *τότε.* There was no negotiation then on foot, no embassy whose return was looked for.

[2] Æschines, De Fals. Leg. 38.

sible, in order that Philip might have no time for making further conquests.

The first assembly was held on the appointed day, the eighteenth of Elaphebolion. Antipater and his colleagues attended, and were introduced to the people in due form. The questions for discussion, as prepared by the presidents of the council, were read: so was the resolution of the confederacy. A motion was made by Philocrates, embodying the terms of peace which Philip was willing to grant. In the debate which followed, many points were hotly contested between the different speakers. One was, whether there should be peace only, or peace and alliance with Philip. Another was, whether the Phocians and Halians should be included in the treaty. Philocrates in his decree had inserted a special clause for their exclusion, which he knew to be desired by Philip; but the sense of the meeting was against him, and Æschines as well as Demosthenes opposed the clause.[1] A discussion arose also upon that recommendation of the allies, by which the Greek states were to have the option of becoming parties to the treaty. According to Æschines, all the speakers (including himself) were in favor of it; and it was the general opinion, that the alliance with Philip should be postponed until the Greeks had an opportunity of declaring themselves.[2] Many objections were raised to the terms offered by Philip, which, it was said, involved concessions disgraceful to Athens, such as the relinquishment of Amphipolis, Cardia, and other places of right belonging to her. Eubulus told the people what he considered the plain truth, that they must either go down to the Piræus immediately, pay a property-tax, and convert the theatric fund into a military one, or vote for the decree of Philocrates.[3] Notwithstanding his admonition, the vehemence of anti-Macedonian orators made an impression on the assembly.

The next day Demosthenes endeavored to allay the ferment which had been excited. He advised the people to accept the proffered alliance of Philip, pointing out to them the true position of things; that it would be imprudent as well as inconvenient to postpone the question—that it was one which concerned them and their allies only, not the whole body of the Greeks—and that there was no necessity for people who were not at war with Philip to enter into a treaty of peace with him.[4] At the same time he insisted that all the

[1] That Æschines opposed the decree of Philocrates on the first day, is stated by Demosthenes, De Fals. Leg. 345; and this was probably the chief ground of his opposition. Grote however thinks differently. See his reasons, History of Greece, xi. 546.

[2] Æschines, Contr. Ctesiph. 63.

[3] Æschines, Contr. Ctesiph. 37, 38. Demosth. De Pace, 63. De Fals. Leg. 434.

[4] Demosthenes asserts (De Fals. Leg. 345, 385), that he supported the

allies of Athens should be comprehended in the treaty, condemning as unjust and impolitic the proposal of Philocrates to exclude the Phocians and Halians. Æschines spoke to the same effect, but still more strongly, and in the strain of Eubulus, showing the folly and danger of carrying on war without adequate means—reproving those speakers who by unseasonable counsel would hurry on the people to their ruin—and reminding them that, although the peace offered by Philip might not be the most honorable in the world, it was not more disgraceful than the war had been. The result was, that an amended decree was carried, omitting the obnoxious article which excluded the Phocians and Halians, but in other respects coinciding with the original motion of Philocrates. It established peace and alliance between Philip and the Athenians and their respective allies, and secured to each party all such territory and dominion, whether acquired by conquest or otherwise, as each actually possessed at the time.[1]

To give any thing like a history of what passed in these assemblies, one has to choose between the conflicting statements of the rival orators. I reject as entirely false the assertion of Æschines,[2] that there was no debate on the second day, notwithstanding the evidence which he produces of a decree of Demosthenes, which restricted the business of that day to taking the votes. In the first place, the proof offered is suspicious and doubtful; and in the next

resolution of the allies. If by this he meant the clauses quoted by Æschines, the assertion is not credible, since by his own showing (De Coron. 233) there could have been no use in supporting them; nor does he pretend in the later speech, where he replies to Æschines, that he did support them. It is possible however, that he refers to some other suggestion in the decree which is not preserved, or to some general words recommending a fair and equitable peace. In the first passage, *ἐμοῦ τῷ τῶν συμμάχων σὺνηγοροῦντος δόγματι καὶ τὴν εἰρήνην ὅπως ἴση καὶ δικαία γένηται πράττοντος*, the latter clause is explanatory of the former; so that it signifies, "when I, in conformity with the resolution of the allies, labored to make the peace equitable and just." In what particular equitable and just, he does not say: he may refer either to the question of including the Phocians, or to some other which is not mentioned. We gather nothing definite from it. Nearly as vague is the assertion at page 385. He affects however to disclaim all participation in the decree of Philocrates, which is too improbable to be believed. Common experience shows how easy a thing it is, to misreport what a man has said some time ago.

[1] Æschines, De Fals. Leg. 36—38. Contr. Timarch. 24. Contr. Ctesiph. 63, 64. Demosthenes, De Halonn. 82, 83. De Coron. 234. De Fals. Leg. 354, 385. That an attempt was afterwards made to bring all the Greek states within the protection of the treaty, appears from the oration De Halonn. 34.

[2] De Fals. Leg. 36.

place, the fact is inconsistent with other statements of his own. Let us see how the matter stands. Demosthenes accuses him of having spoken against Philocrates on the first day, and in his support on the second day. Æschines says: he could not have been guilty of this, because there was no speaking allowed on the second day, by reason of the decree which he produced. Now, supposing that there was a decree which prohibited speaking, it is still very possible that the irregularity might be committed, perhaps encouraged by the people, or at least not objected to. Æschines should have produced a witness to prove that there actually was no speaking, rather than a documentary piece of evidence which only shows that there ought to have been none, and is but an argumentative denial of the fact. It appears that he came prepared to meet the charge, and therefore we might expect better proof. But further; according to his own statement, it is certain that this decree was not acted upon: and next to certain, that there was a debate on the second day, in which Æschines spoke more strongly in favor of the motion of Philocrates than he had spoken on the first day. He says in the speech against Ctesiphon,[1] that on the first day all the orators (including himself) supported the recommendation of the allies, to bring the Greek states into the treaty; that, when the assembly broke up, the general opinion was, that it was not advisable to conclude an alliance with Philip, till it could be done in conjunction with the Greek body. If so, what caused the people to change their opinion the next morning? How came they to pass the decree for alliance as well as peace? There must have been another debate; and that there was one, is clear from Æschines himself, who says that Demosthenes addressed the assembly. He says indeed, that Demosthenes cut the matter very short; by simply telling the people that Philip would not have peace without alliance,[2] and appealing to Antipater (with whom he was in concert) in support of his assertion, he forced the assembly to pass the decree of Philocrates. To suppose however that Demosthenes could have carried his point in this off-hand way, is out of the question. The additions we may set down as rhetorical exaggeration. The fact remains, that Demosthenes did address the people, overthrowing the argument that no one could have done so; and the change of opinion to which they were brought is a strong circumstance to prove that there was a regular debate. But again, Æschines says,[3] he sided on the first day with all the speakers who

[1] Contr. Ctesiph. 63.

[2] Demosthenes said, "they must not dissever the alliance from the peace." *Οὐ γὰρ ἔφη δεῖν ἀποῤῥῆξαι τῆς εἰρήνης τὴν συμμαχίαν.* Æschines says, he remembers his using these words, on account of the harshness both of the phrase and the manner.

[3] Cont. Ctesiph. 63. *Τούτῳ τῷ δόγματι συνειπεῖν ὁμολογῶ.*

advised postponement of the alliance with Philip. He says also,[1] that he advised the measure which was ultimately carried. These two statements are irreconcilable, except on the supposition that he spoke on both of the assembly days; for on the first he was (by his own admission) a dissentient to one of the most important articles, and, as this ultimately passed, he must have supported it on the second day. Thus by his own showing Æschines stands convicted of paltering with the truth. I do not hesitate therefore in accepting the statement of Demosthenes to this extent, that Æschines, in the assembly held on the nineteenth of Elaphebolion, spoke decidedly and strongly in favor of the amended decree.

On the other hand, it appears to me that Demosthenes, when he accuses Æschines of having entirely shifted his ground on the second day and given disgraceful advice to the Athenians, deals unfairly with his adversary, and misrepresents the import of what he really said.[2] The position of things at the beginning of that day has already been stated. In the previous debate the more violent orators of the war party had talked about Marathon and Salamis, and the great deeds of their ancestors, and the duty of upholding Grecian liberty; themes proper and pertinent enough on some occasions, but so often enlarged upon and misapplied by third-rate speakers on the Athenian platform, that sober-minded statesmen must have been heartily sick of them. Æschines, rising to combat the arguments of these men, told the people that this was not the time for empty

[1] Æschines, De Fals. Leg. 38. *'Ομολογῶ συμβουλεῦσαι τῷ δήμῳ διαλύσασθαι πρὸς Φίλιππον καὶ τὴν εἰρήνην συνθέσθαι, ἣν σὺ νῦν αἰσχρὰν νομίζεις οὐδεπώποθ' ἁψάμενος ὅπλων, ἐγὼ δὲ ταύτην εἶναι πολλῷ φημὶ καλλίω τοῦ πολέμου.* Compare the same Oration, p. 49; and Contr. Timarch. 24.

[2] Demosthenes, De Fals. Leg. 345, 346, 439. The assertion that Æschines gave this disgraceful advice in the presence of the Greek envoys is an aggravation of the charge, which is not very material in itself, but has given rise to some difficulty; since Æschines positively denies that any Greek envoys had arrived in Athens, and boldly challenges Demosthenes to name them; and it has been thought to be inconsistent with the denial, given by Demosthenes himself, to the fact of their being any negotiation with the Greek cities. (See ante, p. 296.) It does not seem to me, that the presence of some Greek envoys at Athens is inconsistent with that denial. They may have brought refusals to co-operate with Athens; or they may have been sent merely to watch the proceedings there; or there may have been Greeks present at the assembly, without any special mission from their own countries, whom Demosthenes incorrectly dignifies with the title of envoys. The suggestion of Thirlwall, (History of Greece, v. 350,) that by these envoys Demosthenes may have meant the deputies of the allies then present in Athens, does not agree with the words: *οὓς ἀπὸ τῶν 'Ελλήνων μετεπέμψασθε ὑπὸ τούτου πεισθέντες.* See Grote's learned note on this subject: History of Greece, xi. 539.

declamation about ancient trophies and glories, when the question before them was, how to get rid of a war which they had been waging many years without either glory or advantage; that the Greeks during all those years had rendered them no assistance, and they were not bound to fight the battle of Greece by themselves without any reasonable chance of success. He advised them therefore to retire from the contest while they had the opportunity, before any irretrievable disaster had fallen upon the republic; warning them emphatically against those hazardous and desperate courses, into which evil counsels had plunged the Athenians in former times, referring more particularly to the Sicilian expedition, and to their refusal to accept the peace offered by Sparta before the end of the Peloponnesian war.[1]

Such is the account which Æschines gives of his own speech, not only highly probable in itself, but exactly agreeing with what Demosthenes says in the Oration on the Crown,[2] viz., that the Athenians were driven to make peace with Philip by the conduct of the rest of the Greeks, who, out of cowardice or ignorance, refused to lend any help in the common cause. Demosthenes, however, tortures the language of his opponent into something very different; as if he had counseled the Athenians to forget their ancestors altogether, to shut their ears against all mention of the trophies of olden time, and never to succor any people who had not previously succored them. Language of this sort would indeed have been too absurd for any Athenian to utter in the assembly. Yet we may observe how easily, by a little exaggeration or omission, what Æschines really said is converted into what Demosthenes reports him to have said. Æschines advises the Athenians "not to listen to men who talk about ancient glories idly and unseasonably." Repeated by the adversary, this becomes advice "not to listen to them at all, or under any circumstances." Thus do the two orators, in their mutual charges and recriminations, pervert and misrepresent the words and acts of one another. Æschines ransacks the public archives for documents to prove a case against Demosthenes, which he knew to be contrary to the generally received opinion of his countrymen; that throughout these proceedings he had acted with corrupt purpose in concert with Philocrates to serve the interests of Philip.[3] Demosthenes, over-anxious to disconnect himself from

[1] Æschines, De Fals. Leg. 37, 38.

[2] Demosthenes, De Coron. 231. 'Η τῶν ἄλλων 'Ελλήνων εἴτε χρὴ κακίαν εἴτ' ἄγνοιαν εἴτε καὶ ἀμφότερα ταῦτ' εἰπεῖν, οἳ πόλεμον συνεχῆ καὶ μακρὸν πολεμούντων ὑμῶν, καὶ τοῦτον ὑπὲρ τῶν πᾶσι συμφερόντων, ὡς ἔργῳ φανερὸν γέγονεν, οὔτε χρήμασιν οὔτε σώμασιν οὔτ' ἄλλῳ οὐδενὶ τῶν ἁπάντων συνελάμβανον ὑμῖν· οἷς καὶ δικαίως· καὶ προσηκόντως ὀργιζόμενοι ἑτοίμως ὑπηκούσατε Φιλίππῳ.

[3] Æschines, Contr. Ctesiph. 62, 65.

Philocrates, with whom there is no doubt that up to a certain period he had unsuspiciously co-operated, strives to conceal the part which he took in the first instance as a joint promoter of the peace, and lays to the charge of Æschines many things for which he is himself at least equally responsible.[1]

The terms of peace having been agreed upon, it remained that the oaths of ratification should be sworn by both parties, by Philip and his allies on the one side, and the Athenians and their allies on the other. In order to administer the oath to Philip and his allies, it was necessary for the Athenians to appoint another embassy; and within a day or two after the nineteenth[2] they elected the same ten embassadors as before. The Athenians and their allies were to have the oaths administered to them at Athens by the Macedonian envoys, and an assembly was held on the twenty-third, to make the necessary arrangements.[3] Here a question arose; what allies of the Athenians were entitled to take the oaths? It principally concerned the Phocians. Philocrates had already informed his countrymen that Philip would not accept them as parties to the treaty, and had on this ground moved the clause for their exclusion. The rejection of that clause by the Athenians was a virtual declaration that they regarded the Phocians as comprehended under the name of allies. Antipater and his colleagues, having positive instructions from Philip not to enter into any terms of peace with the Phocians, were compelled to speak out, and accordingly they gave formal notice to the Athenian people of their master's determination upon this point. The assembly was adjourned to the next day for further consideration.[4]

Meanwhile Philocrates and his associates concerted their scheme of operations. It has already been mentioned what impression had

[1] Demosthenes says as little as possible in either of his speeches about the proceedings between the first opening of the negotiations with Philip and the debates on the treaty; nor does he seek to give any clear account of his own share in the transactions of that period. He answers Æschines by vague generalities, denying that he had any thing to do with Philocrates, or was in any way accountable for the mischievous diplomacy of him and his associates. (De Coron. 232.)

[2] All that we can gather from Æschines is, that the election took place before the twenty-third. (De Fals. Leg. 39.)

[3] It seems to have been necessary to pass a distinct decree, fixing the time and manner of taking the oaths. See Æschines, Contr. Ctesiph. 64.

[4] From the statements of Æschines, (De Fals. Leg. 39, 40; Contr. Ctesiph. 64,) though they are confused, we may perhaps collect, that there were two assemblies. The first may not have been well attended, as only formal business was expected; but when questions arose about the Phocians and Cersobleptes, it became desirable to have another assembly.

been made on the Athenians by the reports which Aristodemus and others brought from Macedonia, of Philip's good will and friendly feelings to Athens. His own letter, brought by the embassadors, spoke mysteriously of the benefits which he designed for them in the event of becoming their ally. Assurances to the same effect were repeated by his envoys, and studiously disseminated among the Athenians by his partisans and agents. To those who inquired what Philip could mean by such mysterious promises, hints were given about Eubœa, Oropus, Thespiæ, Platæa, the settlement of the Phocian question, and the humiliation of Thebes. Now, however, when Philip's ministers had announced that the Phocians must be excluded from the general peace, it became necessary, in order to disarm suspicion of his intentions, that some explanation, resting on better authority than mere rumor, should be given to the Athenian public. Accordingly, on the day of the assembly, Philocrates came forward, and in the presence of the Macedonian envoys boldly proclaimed to the Athenians, that it was impossible for Philip, with any regard to honor or decency, to accept the Phocians openly for his allies, because he was bound by solemn engagement with the Thebans and Thessalians to prosecute the Sacred War; he must, therefore, ostensibly treat the Phocians as enemies for the present; but let him once bring the war to an issue, and get the power into his own hands, he would settle matters exactly as the Athenians desired; the Phocians would be no sufferers by it, the Thebans would be no gainers, and Philip would prove himself the friend and benefactor of Athens, as he had promised in his letter. The Macedonians stood by, and apparently assented to all this. Philocrates pretended to speak from his own knowledge and information, as the confidante of Philip's views and plans; appealed, perhaps, to some of his colleagues in the embassy, who confirmed his statements. No one stood up to contradict him. What were the Athenians to do? The Phocian question was altogether complex and difficult. On the one hand, the seizure and pillage of Delphi, the exclusion of Amphictyonic Greeks from the Pythian festival and synod, the occupation of Locris and a part of Bœotia by the Phocian army, were things not to be defended. There was a general expectation that, as the Delphic fund was beginning to fail, the Phocians could not much longer maintain their position; and the inclination of the Athenians to assist them had been greatly cooled by the late offensive conduct of Phalæcus. On the other hand, it would not be very honorable to abandon allies with whom they were connected by treaty, and to whom they had for so many years given a moral, if not an active support. There would be danger attending the prostration of an independent people, whose existence formed one of the safeguards of southern Greece; and still greater peril, if Thermopylæ should fall into the hands of a powerful enemy. But how, if the solution of all these difficulties was now before them?—if Philip really intended to act as equitable mediator in the Sacred War, and fulfill the promises which had been made in his name? The Phocians would have no reason to complain, if they were really benefited even against their will. The only doubt was, could Philip be trusted? But there was not much time for deliberation: the Macedonian envoys were about to quit Athens immediately. Unless their demands were complied with, there was an end of the peace, which the Athenians had made up their minds to have, and enjoyed by anticipation already. If they wavered for a moment, their wishes turned the scale. It does not appear that there were any Phocian envoys to protest against this sacrifice of their country; or that a single warning voice was heard from any leading orator or statesman. The Athenians were prevailed on by delusive promises, encouraging their natural indolence, to swear to the treaty of peace without the Phocians.[1]

A question had also arisen about Cersobleptes. One Aristobulus of Lampsacus appeared as his representative, and demanded to take the oath in his name as one of the allies of Athens. An objection was made, as Æschines states by Demosthenes, and, being referred to the assembly, was overruled. Notwithstanding the decision of the people, Æschines asserts in his later speech, that Cersobleptes was excluded ultimately, but upon another ground, by the contrivance of Demosthenes. It is impossible to determine what really took place.[2]

[1] Demosthenes, De Fals. Leg. 371, 387, 388, 391, 409, 444. There is nothing to show that Æschines spoke in support of Philocrates in this matter. The use of the plural *οὗτοι*, in the passage last cited, is no proof that more than one person spoke; and it rather tends to prove that Æschines did not. For if he had, Demosthenes would have mentioned him specially, as he does at p 347, in reference to his reports after the second embassy. It is probable that both Æschines and Demosthenes were passive on this occasion. Neither of them gives us any particulars of what passed; and each had his reasons for silence. The decree perhaps contained the words mentioned in Æschines, Contr. Ctesiph. 64, requiring the oaths to be taken by the deputies of the Athenian allies; and possibly it was so drawn up for the very purpose of shuffling over the difficulty about the Phocians, who, having no deputy representing them at Athens, like the tributary allies, would not be competent to swear to the treaty under a decree in such form. It then may have accidentally created the question about Cersobleptes, which Æschines represents as designedly raised by Demosthenes, in order to shut him out from the treaty.

[2] Æschines, De Fals. Leg. 39, 40. Contr. Ctesiph. 64. Demosthenes, De Fals. Leg. 395, 398. Philipp. Epist. 160. And see the last note. It seems, by comparison of all the passages, that Cersobleptes was excluded from taking the oath; but on what ground, or through whose opposition, is uncertain. Thirlwall's conjecture is by no means improb-

The oaths were administered to the Athenians and their allies in the board-room of the generals, on the same day that the assembly passed their last decree. The Macedonian envoys then took their departure, Demosthenes accompanying them, as a mark of respect, a part of the way on their road to Thebes.[1] For this, as well as for the other attentions which he paid them, he is reproached by Æschines unjustly. The fact however is significant, as tending to show, that up to that moment Demosthenes was not in opposition to the promoters of the peace. It suited him at a later period to represent, that he was disgusted with his colleagues before the second embassy to Macedonia, and that he would not have accepted the appointment, if he had not promised some of the Athenian prisoners to bring money for their ransom.[2] But there is no evidence of any act by which he testified displeasure against his colleagues or dissatisfaction with the treaty before his second appointment. He felt indeed, in common with the rest of his countrymen, that the peace was not honorable to Athens; nor was it to be expected, when she had fared so badly in the war: yet still it drew with it certain advantages, such as financial relief, security for her remaining possessions, restoration of her captives: and as to other matters, he shared to some extent in the general delusion.[3]

It was deemed however a point of great moment by Demosthenes, that the peace should be ratified by Philip immediately and commenced in earnest. The Athenians, having once abandoned themselves to the idea of peace, had from that moment discontinued all warlike preparations; whereas Philip was still carrying on war in Thrace. In order to put a stop to any further conquests, it was important to give Philip speedy notice of the treaty having been concluded; and Demosthenes pressed his colleagues to set off without delay. They however were in no humor to leave Athens so soon, and refused to comply with his entreaties. About this time there arrived a letter from Chares, who commanded an Athenian fleet in the Hellespont, announcing the defeat of Cersobleptes and the capture of the Sacred Mountain by Philip. The case seeming urgent, Demosthenes on the third of Munychion (April) applied to the council, (of which he was a member, and which had a special authority for such purpose from the assembly,) and procured an order, commanding the embassadors to take their departure instantly, and requiring Proxenus to convey them wherever he could ascer-

able; that an objection was raised by the Macedonians, and that it was reserved by mutual consent to be discussed in a conference with Philip. (History of Greece, v. 356.)

[1] Æschines, Contr. Ctesiph. 64.

[2] Demosthenes, De Fals. Leg. 394, 395. He felt the weakness of that part of his case, and anticipates the adversary's objection.

[3] Demosthenes, De Fals. Leg. 387, 388.

tain Philip to be. The embassadors, thus compelled, sailed to Oreus, where Proxenus was stationed with his squadron; but instead of his conveying them to the Hellespont or the coast of Thrace, which they might have reached easily in six or eight days, they were carried to the coast either of Thessaly or Macedonia, and thence pursued their journey to Pella, consuming three-and-twenty days. At Pella they had to wait till Philip returned from his campaign, which did not happen till the fiftieth day after they had left Athens.[1]

The variance between Demosthenes and his colleagues began upon this journey. He told them plainly that they were bound to obey the order of the council; first he reasoned with them, then he remonstrated more strongly, at last he reproached them for their conduct in no lenient terms. All this only excited their anger. The whole body were against him, and refused either to take their meals with him, or to put up at the same inn. Æschines says this refusal was owing to the misbehavior of Demosthenes on the former embassy; and he defends the journey to Pella, by alleging that they were not ordered to go to Thrace, and that it would have been of no use to go there, when Cersobleptes had lost his kingdom before they left Athens. It is manifest however, that the order of council was disobeyed both in the letter and spirit; and, as Æschines can suggest no better excuse, the complaint of Demosthenes on this head must be taken as well founded. The event proved that Philip's Thracian campaign was not terminated when the embassadors quitted Athens: it continued for five or six weeks after; and during that time many important places were captured by him. The son of Cersobleptes he brought with him as a hostage to Pella.[2]

There he found not only the Athenian embassadors awaiting his arrival, but others also from various parts of Greece; from Thebes, Thessaly, Sparta, Phocis, and Eubœa. An immense army was assembled: it was notorious to all that Philip was about to march to Thermopylæ: what he intended to do was not certainly known to any of the parties present; but all were deeply interested in the result, and agitated by various hopes and fears.[3]

The duty of the Athenian embassadors was by no means clear. It might be argued, that they had nothing to do but to administer the

[1] Demosthenes, De Coron, 233—235. De Fals Leg. 388—390. Æschines, De Fals. Leg. 40.

[2] Demosthenes, De Fals. Leg. 390, 397. Philipp. iv. 133. De Halonn. 85. Æschines, De Fals. Leg. 38, 40, 41. As regards Cersobleptes, the amount of blame with which the embassadors are chargeable depends much upon the question, whether he was an ally included in the treaty. See ante, p. 304.

[3] Demosthenes, De Fals. Leg. 384. Æschines, De Fals. Leg. 41. Justin, viii. 4.

oath to Philip and his allies, and then return to Athens and make their report. As however the treaty had been concluded without settling the question of the Sacred War; as Philip was virtually left at liberty to deal with it as he pleased, subject only to a loose promise that he would do what was right and promote the interests of Athens; it might seem to be proper, when the embassadors were in the presence of Philip, that they should come to some positive understanding with him on the subject, and ascertain what he really meant to do. By such means they would be enabled, on their return, to furnish such a report as might guide the Athenians in their future counsels. True, there could be no guarantee that Philip would perform any engagement which he made to the embassadors. That however would not be the fault of the embassadors, but of the Athenians themselves, who suffered the Phocian question to go off upon vague assurances, instead of insisting upon the Phocians being comprehended in the treaty. They had committed the grave error of making peace, without settling the most important matter in the war; so that in effect the war remained an open question, unless they chose to leave the Phocians and all their own interests connected with them entirely to the mercy of Philip. In the instructions to the embassadors there was, besides the special clauses, a general one, requiring them to do whatever else they could for the service of the commonwealth; which, under the circumstances, might be construed as imposing an obligation to discuss with Philip the affairs of the Sacred War, and bring him over, if possible, to the side of Athens.

Such was the view taken apparently by Æschines, who states that at a conference with his colleagues he urged upon them the necessity of performing this part of their instructions, and exhorting Philip to chastise the Thebans and restore the Bœotian cities. Though there was no express order to this effect, (for such matters could not be mentioned openly in a state paper,) yet it was clearly, he said, the true intent and meaning of their countrymen. Demosthenes took a different view; and after some discussion it was agreed, that each of the embassadors should address Philip as he thought fit.[1]

Of the audience which the Athenian embassadors had with the king, Æschines gives the following account—That Demosthenes made an offensive speech in disparagement of his colleagues and praise of himself, recounting the services which he had rendered Philip in promoting the peace, and the attention which he had paid to his ministers at Athens, and endeavoring to ingratiate himself with him by fulsome and coarse flattery: after which he (Æschines) commenced his address; first rebuking Demosthenes for his personalities, then briefly touching upon the subject of the oaths and other formal matters, lastly, entering upon the topic paramount to all, viz. the

[1] Æschines, De Fals. Leg. 41, 42.

march to Thermopylæ, and the affairs of Delphi and the Amphictyons. He entreated Philip to decide the quarrel by judicial sentence, and not by arms; but if that were impossible, (as the military preparations seemed to indicate,) then, said Æschines, it behoved the champion of Hellenic religion to consider what his sacred office required of him, and to listen to those who could instruct him on the subject of their ancient institutions. Upon which he explained to the king all that he knew about the foundation of the temple, the origin of the Amphictyonic league, the tribes that composed it, their oath and obligations. He argued that, the Bœotian cities being Amphictyonic, Philip could not justly allow them to be destroyed. The object of his expedition was holy and just; but when the Amphictyons were restored to their rights, punishment should be inflicted upon the guilty parties only, upon those who actually seized the temple or who advised it, not upon their countries, if they would deliver up the offenders for judgment. Should Philip make use of his power to confirm the iniquitous acts of the Thebans, he would not insure their gratitude, (for they had been ungrateful to the Athenians, who had done them still greater services,) and he would make enemies of the people whom he betrayed.[1]

What answer Philip made to this address, Æschines does not say. It is not pretended that he gave to the collective body of embassadors the promises which were afterwards reported at Athens. Yet that did not prevent him from sending indirect communications to some of them, whom he thought likely to become his instruments. He was playing a profoundly artful game. While Æschines was flattering himself with the impression made by his own harangue, the Thebans and Thessalians were urging Philip to march against their common enemy. To them be could speak more openly of his intentions; yet they were not free from uneasiness, seeing that intrigues were still going on, that private conferences were held not only with the Athenians, but with the Spartans and Phocians, and that they were apparently not dissatisfied with their reception. The betrayal of any fears or misgivings on the part of his own intimate allies favored the illusion which Philip was keeping up. It was important for him to amuse with hope those parties from whom he most feared opposition. Phalæcus held the pass of Thermopylæ; Archidamus with a thousand Spartans was yet in Phocis; an Athenian fleet was ready to occupy the straits, if the people should take it in their heads to give the order. To prevent the combination of these forces, which was a very possible contingency, if his designs should be seen through; to contrive things so that, when he arrived at the pass, all resistance should be hopeless; these were points to be accomplished by a tissue of artifice and deceit. Æschines declares that it was the universal expectation at Pella, that Philip would

[1] Æschines, De Fals. Leg. 42, 43.

humble Thebes; that the Spartan envoys were quarreling with the Theban, and openly threatening them; that the Thebans were in distress and alarm; that the Thessalians laughed at all the rest, and said the expedition was for their own benefit; while some of Philip's officers told some of the Athenian embassadors, that he meant to re-establish the Bœotian cities. This may be taken as no great exaggeration of what really occurred[1]

Demosthenes states, that during all the time they were at Pella he was in opposition to his colleagues; he offered them honest and sound advice, but every opinion of his was overruled by the majority. All the service that he could do was, to seek out his captive fellow-citizens and procure their release, ransoming some of them with his own money, and prevailing on Philip to redeem the others. Philip tried to corrupt the embassadors, first separately, and then jointly. Demosthenes refused a large present of gold that was sent him. Another was offered to the whole body, under the pretense of hospitality. It was of course a bribe in disguise. As Demosthenes would accept no share, his colleagues divided it among themselves: he requested Philip to apply the money that he would have bestowed in presents towards redeeming the Athenian captives, and Philip was prevailed upon to promise that they should be sent home by the Panathenæan festival.[2]

All this time the embassadors never demanded that Philip should swear the oath, nor said a word about the restoration of the places captured since the peace, nor sent home any intelligence of the preparations going on at Pella. They loitered there without any other reason than the request of Philip himself, who told them he wanted their mediation to settle the quarrel between the Pharsalians and Halians; a quarrel which he himself not long afterwards very summarily decided, by taking the city of Halus and expelling the population. When all things were ready for his march, Philip set out, and carried the Athenian embassadors with him as far as Pheræ, where at length they administered the oaths to him and his allies. But here they are charged with two further acts of disobedience to their instructions. They were commanded to administer the oaths to the magistrates of the cities allied to Philip. Instead of this, they accepted any persons whom Philip chose to send as accredited agents for that purpose. Secondly, they allowed Philip and his allies, on swearing the oaths, to except the Phocians, the Halians, and Cersobleptes; thereby, it was said, overruling the decree of the Athenian people, who had refused to admit a clause to that effect in the treaty. The charge however (as far as regards

[1] Æschines, De Fals. Leg. 46. Demosthenes, Philipp. iii. 113. De Fals. Leg. 365, 384, 445. Justin, viii. 4.

[2] Demosthenes, De Fals. Leg. 393—395. As to the captives, see the reply of Æschines, De Fals. Leg. 41.

the Phocians at least) appears to be unfairly urged against the embassadors. The Athenians, having consented on their side to ratify the treaty without the Phocians, could not expect that Philip would bind himself to any engagement with them. Indeed the understanding was quite the contrary. If then the words of the treaty left an ambiguity, it became necessary for Philip to protest against a construction that would have been opposite to his declared intentions. Such a protest was doubtless made. The Athenian embassadors were informed distinctly, that Philip and his allies would not swear to the treaty, except upon the condition of excludiug the Phocians. What then was to be done? The embassadors were in an unavoidable dilemma. Either they must decline to administer the oaths altogether, or they must accept the qualification which Philip and his allies insisted upon. But for what had passed at Athens, the former would have been the proper course: under existing circumstances, the latter was perhaps more prudent; otherwise they must have taken upon themselves the responsibility of renewing the war.[1]

The chief grounds of complaint against the embassadors were, their dilatoriness in dispatching the business for which they were sent out, and their neglect to send or carry home correct information of what was going on. If they acted thus from corrupt motives, they were of course guilty of treason. Demosthenes, from what he had seen before, had formed no good opinion of Philip's designs, and at Pheræ, observing what course things were taking, and being alarmed both at the danger which threatened his country, and for fear lest he should himself be implicated in the misconduct of others, wrote a letter to the Athenians, which gave them full information of every thing. His colleagues, he alleges, would not allow this to be sent, but themselves dispatched another, containing false intelligence; a charge in great measure borne out by the reports which they afterwards made at Athens. He says that he had resolved to return home alone, and actually hired a vessel for his conveyance, but was prevented from sailing by Philip. He observed that Æschines had numerous private interviews with Philip —a thing specially prohibited by a clause in their instructions;— that one night in particular he was watched coming out of Philip's tent at Pheræ; and that he stayed for a day with Philip after the

[1] Demosthenes, De Coron. 236. De Fals. Leg. 352, 353, 390, 391, 395, 430. It appears by the quotation from Philip's letter in Æschines, (De Fals. Leg. 45,) that he furnished the Athenians with the names of those parties who had taken the oaths, promising to send to Athens a few who had not come in time. One of the charges of Demosthenes is, that the Cardians were allowed to appear as allies of Philip. For this however the embassadors were not to blame; the Cardians having been excepted from the treaty by which the Chersonese was ceded to Athens.

others had gone. Æschines produced evidence in the nature of an alibi, to disprove that he ever visited Philip by night, yet apparently does not deny that he had interviews with him alone in the daytime.[1]

Philip, having detained the embassadors until he was ready to march to Thermopylæ, dismissed them with a letter to the Athenians, in which he formally notified to them the ratification of the treaty, and apologized for the manner in which their embassadors had administered the oaths, stating that they would have gone round to the different cities, but that he had prevented them, as he wanted their mediation between the Pharsalians and Halians. In terms the letter was polite and gracious, but it contained not a word about the Phocians, or about the promises which were made in his name.[2]

The embassadors arrived in Athens on the thirteenth of Scirophorion (June), and presented themselves before the council, as the law required. Here Demosthenes, being a member of the council, took the initiative, and gave a full report of all that had taken place, denouncing the treachery of his colleagues, showing into what peril they had brought the people, and urging that measures should be taken, before it was too late, to save the Phocians and Thermopylæ. His words produced such an effect upon the council, that in the order which was drawn up, for bringing the matter before the assembly, they withheld the vote of thanks and invitation to the public dining-hall, which embassadors never failed to receive on other occasions.[3]

The assembly was held on the sixteenth; and here Æschines got the first hearing. The people, alarmed by the rumor of Philip's march, were so eager for the report of the envoys, that they waited not for the order of council, introducing the business of the day, to be read. Æschines assured them that they had nothing to fear; that he had persuaded Philip to gratify their wishes in every particular, both on the Amphictyonic question and others;—(he re-

[1] Demosthenes, De Fals. Leg. 352, 357, 396, 397, 419, 446. Æschines, De Fals. Leg. 44. There is a further charge that Æschines wrote Philip's letter, to which he alludes. See the remarks in this volume, p. 170.

[2] See the forcible remarks of Demosthenes upon this letter. (De Fals. Leg. 352, 353, 355.) It was a juggle, he argues, between Philip and the embassadors. Philip took on him the blame of their neglect, and left to them the responsibility of making false promises in his name. And, although he had promised, if the Athenians would become his allies, to declare what he meant to do for them, now, when they had become his allies, he said he knew not what he could do to oblige them; but if they would tell him, he would do any thing that was not dishonorable.

[3] Demosthenes, De Fals. Leg. 346, 350, 351.

peated the heads of the speech which he had made against the Thebans;)—they need only remain quiet; in two or three days they would hear the most satisfactory results;—the Phocians would be preserved by Philip; Thebes would be besieged and broken up into villages, Thespiæ and Platæa re-established, and compensation exacted for the pillage of Delphi, not from the Phocians, but from the Thebans, who had originally planned it: he himself had convinced Philip that the first designers were more guilty than the perpetrators;[1] and for giving such counsel, the Thebans had set a price upon his head. Further, he had heard from some of the Eubœan envoys as a current report, that their own island was to be given up to the Athenians instead of Amphipolis; and there was yet another thing which his diplomacy had obtained for them, which he would not mention at present, because some of his colleagues were jealous of him. He was understood to mean Oropos.[2]

These assurances, confidently made by an envoy who had had official communication with Philip, agreeing also with what they had before heard from Philocrates, relieved the people from their anxiety. The letter of Philip was produced and read. The Athenians, charmed by its general professions of amity and good will, did not detect their hollowness and insincerity. Demosthenes rose to tell the plain realities of the case, as he had done in the council; but the people, dazzled by their bright prospects, refused to be undeceived, and he found it impossible to obtain a fair hearing. Æschines and Philocrates hooted and interrupted him continually, and were encouraged by the assembly. He could only get in a few words. He protested his entire ignorance of what Æschines had told them, and declared that he did not believe it. At this the people showed signs of anger. "Remember," cried Demosthenes, "I am not responsible for any of this." "By and by," said Æschines, "he'll want to have the credit of it." "No wonder," said Philocrates, "that there is a difference of opinion between Demosthenes and me; for he drinks water, and I drink wine:" at which the Athenians laughed.[3]

A decree was then carried, on the motion of Philocrates, thanking Philip in the warmest terms for his liberality to the republic, and extending the treaty of peace and alliance to his posterity. It

[1] For this insinuation, made by their enemies apparently against the Thebans, there seems to have been no foundation whatever.

[2] Demosthenes, De Pace, 59. Philipp. ii. 72, 73. De Coron. 236, 237. De Fals. Leg. 347, 348, 351, 352. Æschines says in reply, that he only reported what he heard; he made no promises: (τοῦτο οὐκ ἀπαγγεῖλαι ἀλλ' ὑποσχέσθαι:) and that what he reported was generally believed by others. (De Fals. Leg. 43, 44, 46.) This reply is beside the mark. He was charged with misleading the Athenians by wilfully false reports.

[3] Demosthenes, De Pace, 59. De Fals. Leg. 348, 352, 355.

declared also, that, unless the Phocians did what was right and delivered up the temple of Delphi to the Amphictyons, the people of Athens would enforce their wishes by arms. This decree, says Demosthenes, in effect delivered the Phocians over to their enemies, with their hands tied behind them.[1]

There was time to have succored the Phocians and defended Thermopylæ, had the Athenians acted promptly after the return of their embassadors. Phalæcus, who (it seems) had been reinstated in his command, and still held the Locrian fortresses with his garrisons, could have maintained the pass alone against a greatly superior force, if the enemy were prevented from landing troops in his rear. His safety depended on a continued maritime blockade, and for this purpose the co-operation of the Athenians was indispensable. But he had some reason to doubt their friendly disposition towards his countrymen, much more towards himself; and there was no time to be lost. He sent chosen messengers to Athens, with orders to learn the state of things, and bring him intelligence immediately. These messengers were present at the assembly held on the sixteenth of Scirophorion, and listening with anxiety to the speeches and all the proceedings. Philip in the meantime, approaching Thermopylæ, invited the Phocians to surrender, representing to them that there was no hope of succor from Athens, who had become his ally, and that they might safely throw themselves upon his generosity. We may presume, that he had already made this communication to them, before he began his march from Pheræ; and perhaps their own envoys, who accompanied him from Pella, brought home a tale of their kind reception by Philip, and his favorable intentions towards their country.[2] The Phocians gave little credit to it: they were not disposed to trust Philip, and they could hardly believe that the Athenians, their old allies, would abandon them: Phalæcus at all events would send no positive answer to Philip, until he knew what the intentions of the Athenians were. When however his messengers returned from Athens, bringing news of what had passed in the assembly—of the announcements of Æschines, the implicit faith put in them by the Athenians, their abandonment of every thing to Philip, and the menacing resolutions

[1] Demosthenes, De Fals. Leg. 356, 358. Philipp. ii. 73.

[2] Phalæcus must have sent his messengers to Athens before Philip commenced his march from Pheræ; or they could not have arrived in time for the assembly on the sixteenth. If the Phocians could have been induced to have submitted at once, before the Athenians had time for consideration, Philip's object was more surely gained. The Phocian envoys had been amused with promises to the last. Demosthenes, Philipp. iii. 112. *Εἰς Φωκέας ὡς πρὸς συμμάχους ἐπορεύετο, καὶ πρέσβεις Φωκέων ἦσαν οἳ παρηκολούθουν αὐτῷ πορευομένῳ καὶ παρ' ἡμῖν ἤριζον πολλοὶ Θηβαίοις οὐ λυσιτελήσειν τὴν ἐκείνου πάροδον.*

which they had passed against the Phocians—he perceived that resistance was hopeless; that neither himself nor his countrymen had any choice left but to make the best terms they could with the all-powerful king of Macedon.

Accordingly on the twenty-third of Scirophorion, while two or three days after he had received the news from Athens, he entered into a convention with Philip, agreeing to surrender the fortresses which he held in Locris and Bœotia, on condition only that he might retire where he pleased with his troops. It was carried into effect immediately. Philip entered the pass, and took possession of Alponus, Thronium, and Nicæa, while Phalæcus, with eight thousand mercenaries and such of the native soldiers as liked to follow him, passed over to Peloponnesus. Archidamus with his thousand Spartans had withdrawn shortly before, seeing the double game that was played by his allies, and considering his position dangerous. The Thebans marched out with all their forces to join Philip, who now, proclaiming openly that he had come as the ally of the Thebans and Thessalians and the champion of the god, marched with an overpowering army into Phocis, to terminate the Sacred War. The cities generally submitted to his arms; a few that offered a feeble resistance were taken by storm and razed to the ground. He then took possession of Delphi, and proceeded forthwith to hold an Amphictyonic council, to pronounce judgment upon the violators of the temple, and determine the various questions which the war had given rise to.[1]

The Athenians remained perfectly quiescent, expecting the accomplishment of all the good things which Philip had promised them, until the twenty-seventh day of the month. They had appointed an embassy to notify to Philip the decree which they passed in his favor. It consisted mostly of the same ten who served on the former embassies. Demosthenes, not wishing to go, swore an affidavit, as the law permitted, and excused himself. Æschines stayed behind on a plea of illness; a mere pretense, as Demosthenes alleges, in order that he might be at home to prevent the adoption of any measures adverse to Philip. The envoys had not long departed, when there came a letter from Philip to the Athenians, followed soon afterwards by another,[2] inviting them to join him with all their forces.

[1] Diodorus, xvi. 59. Demosthenes, De Coron. 238, 239: De Fals. Leg. 356, 358, 359, 360, 365. Æschines, De Fals. Leg. 45, 46.

[2] Æschines mentions only one letter: Demosthenes, two. The second may have come soon after the first; or it may have been dispatched after the capitulation of Phalæcus. For there was yet a possibility that the Phocians might resist, and give some trouble to Philip, if the Athenians gave them any hope of support: though I can not credit the assertion of Demosthenes (De Fals. Leg. 379) that the Phocians might

He must have sent the first of these letters immediately after Phalæcus had refused to surrender, while he was yet in doubt what course things might take. According to the terms of his alliance, as they had been interpreted and acted upon, he was entitled to make this demand of the Athenians; though we can hardly imagine that he either expected or desired their compliance. All that he really wished was their neutrality; and this his letter, assuming a tone of friendship, was calculated to secure. It was laid before the assembly; but no one moved that Philip's request should be granted. Demosthenes observed, that, if any troops were sent, they would be hostages in Philip's hands; and the matter was dropped. Æschines afterwards asserted, that, if an Athenian force had been present, it might have counteracted the influence of the Thebans and Thessalians, who, as it was, compelled Philip to adopt their own violent counsels. But if he thought so, why, it may be asked, did he not propose the measure to the people, especially as it was in accordance with their own decree? Perhaps he could not easily have prevailed upon them: for, besides a lurking fear that Demosthenes was right, they must have been somewhat ashamed of themselves for the attitude of hostility which they had already assumed towards the Phocians. But the punishment of their folly was at hand. On the twenty-seventh day of the month the envoys, who had gone as far as Chalcis in Eubœa, returned suddenly with the intelligence, that Philip had declared himself the ally of the Thebans, and had given up every thing into their hands. The Athenians, who happened to be in assembly at Piræus when these tidings were brought, in the alarm of the moment passed a vote to bring in all their women and children from the country, to repair their forts, to fortify Piræus, and perform their sacrifice to Hercules in the city. This decree was actually carried into effect; but the envoys were nevertheless sent to Philip, and traveled by land through Bœotia, Æschines this time going with them. The fears of the people were soon allayed by finding that the allied powers had no thought of coming near Attica; though perhaps their ill humor was increased by a letter which came from Philip, calmly informing them of what he had done, and reproving them for their demonstration of hostility.[1]

The Amphictyonic council, composed of the Thebans, Thessalians, and their allies, proceeded to sit in judgment upon the Phocians.

in that event have been saved, owing to the impossibility of Philip's finding subsistence in their territory.

[1] Demosthenes, De Coron. 237—239: De Fals. Leg. 357, 359, 360, 378—381: Philipp. ii. 69. Æschines, De Fals. Leg. 40, 46. That Æschines should have gone upon this embassy after his plea of illness, and that he should have passed through Thebes, after saying that the Thebans had set a price upon his head, are urged as proofs of crime by Demosthenes.

Their first act was one of gratitude as well as justice. They deprived the conquered people of their seat and votes in the council, and transferred them to the king of Macedon and his descendants. Their further sentence was, that the Phocian cities should be razed to the ground, and the population of each dispersed into villages, containing not more than fifty dwelling-houses, and at the distance of not less than a furlong from each other. The Phocians were to have no access to the temple of Delphi, and to possess neither arms nor horses, but to be allowed to cultivate their land and take the produce thereof, paying every year a tribute of sixty talents to Apollo, until the whole of their plunder, estimated in value at ten thousand talents, should be restored. Any guilty parties, whether Phocians or auxiliaries, who had fled from justice, were declared to be outlaws. All arms which had been used by the troops were to be broken and destroyed; their horses to be sold. Regulations were made for the future management of the oracle, for the establishment of peace and amity among the Greek states, and the maintenance of their common religion. The Spartans were excommunicated from Amphictyonic privileges: and it was determined that Philip should preside over the Pythian games in conjunction with the Thebans and Thessalians.[1]

Thus were the Phocians not only degraded from their rank as one of the Amphictyonic communities, but reduced to become a mere rural population, little better than the serfs of Thessaly. Their rank they did not regain till many years after, when, by their valor in repelling the Celtic invasion, they expiated the memory of their former crime. One part of the sentence appears to have been in violation of the engagement made by Philip with Phalæcus; yet they had enemies in the council, who would have inflicted on them a still heavier punishment. Æschines says, the Œtæans proposed to cast all the adult males down the precipice, and that he himself pleaded on their behalf and saved them. The sentence, however, was rigorously executed. Of twenty-one cities enumerated by Pausanias, Abæ alone was spared, as having taken no part in the sacrilege: the rest were destroyed; their walls at least and principal buildings were razed to the ground, and the inhabitants driven to seek homes elsewhere, according to the terms of the judgment.

[1] Diodorus, xvi. 60. Pausanias, x. 3. In the words of Diodorus, *τῶν δ' ἐν Φωκεῦσι τριῶν πόλεων περιελεῖν τὰ τείχη*, it would seem that *τριῶν* should be omitted; and even then there remains a tautology, when he says afterwards, *τὰς δὲ πόλεις ἁπάσας τῶν Φωκέων κατασκάψαι.* Leland, in his Dissertation on the Amphictyonic Council, prefixed to the Life of Philip, (page 40,) tries to explain this, by suggesting that there were three Amphictyonic cities in Phocis; and as they could not be entirely demolished consistently with the oath of the Amphictyons, their walls only were sentenced to be razed. See also Wesseling's note.

That the expulsion from their ancient dwellings, the separation of friends, neighbors, and relatives, must necessarily have been attended with great hardship and suffering, is manifest. But the evil was aggravated by the presence of an insulting and vindictive enemy. The work of destruction was committed to the Thebans, who, occupying the country with their army, in the license of military power committed excesses of cruelty, against which it was impossible to obtain redress, and useless to murmur. Large numbers of the people, chiefly men in the prime and vigor of their life, emigrated to other lands. Demosthenes, traveling through Phocis two or three years after, describes what he saw with his own eyes; a dreadful scene of desolation; cities lying in ruin, hardly any grown men in the country, a population consisting almost entirely of the old and infirm, women and children. Most of the spoil that could be collected became the prize of Philip. But the Thebans were permitted to annex some portion of the Phocian territory to their own dominion. The Bœotian towns, Orchomenus, Coronea, and Corsiæ, were delivered up to them; and the two former they punished by enslaving the inhabitants. Yet the majority of these avoided their doom by flight, and, together with a large number of Phocian exiles, found refuge in Athens.[1]

The allies of Philip thoughtlessly exulted in the vengeance which they had inflicted on their enemies, and the advantages which they had acquired for themselves. The Thessalians, pleased with the restoration of the Pylæan synod and the festival, little heeded that they had found a new master. The Thebans, having recovered their lost dominion in Bœotia and got an accession of territory, thought not for the moment that it was at the expense of their honor and credit, that their acquisitions were the gift of the king of Macedon, and that they were to see a Macedonian garrison established at Nicæa, a monument of his power and their own weakness. In fact, the real advantages were Philip's, who had obtained an immense increase both of power and reputation. His kingdom, but lately regarded as semi-barbarous, now took her rank among the Amphictyonic communities. He was further honored by the Delphians with precedency in the consultation of the oracle—a distinction formerly conferred upon Athens and Lacedæmon. But, what was far more important, he had extended his alliances, enlarged the sphere of his influence, and got the command of Thermopylæ, which gave him at any time an entrance to southern Greece. The Athenians, when all the mischief had been done, opened their eyes, and saw how they had been duped and cheated. They made empty protests and passed idle votes about the intrusion of barbarians into the Amphictyonic council: they resolved to take no part in its proceed-

[1] Pausanias, x. 3, 8. Justin, viii. 5. Æschines, De Fals. Leg. 47. Demosthenes, De Pace, 61, 62: De Fals. Leg. 361, 385, 445.

ings, and send no deputies to the Pythian games. Yet all this had no other effect than to exhibit their ill humor, and irritate the rest of the Amphictyons; and when that body sent an embassy to Athens, requiring them to accept the acts of the congress as legal, they dared not refuse compliance.[1]

Phalæcus, having carried away what remained of the Delphian plunder, maintained his troops for a while in Peloponnesus; at length, hiring a sufficient number of transports at Corinth, he embarked and sailed for the Ionian sea, intending to cross over to Italy or Sicily. There he hoped either to get possession of some city, or to find military employment; for he had heard there was a war between the Lucanians and the Tarentines; and he gave out that he had been invited to go over by the natives. His soldiers, however, when they got into the open sea, observing that there was no envoy on board from any foreign state, suspected that he was playing them false, and mutinied; the principal officers came with drawn swords to him and his pilot, and insisted that he should sail back to Peloponnesus. He returned accordingly, and landed at Malea, the southern promontory of Laconia; where he found an embassy from the Cnossians of Crete, who had come to enlist troops for a war against the Lyctians. Phalæcus, receiving a large sum of money in advance, consented to enter their service, and sailing with them to Crete, he attacked and took the city of Lyctus. Just at this time there came an unexpected auxiliary to the Lyctians, no less a person than Archidamus, king of Sparta. It so happened, the people of Tarentum had applied for succor to the Spartans, who, collecting a large force for the defense of their ancient colony, gave the command to Archidamus; but, before he had set sail, envoys arrived from Lyctus, and prevailed on the Spartans to assist them first. Archidamus, therefore, was sent to Crete, and, strangely enough, found himself opposed to his old ally, Phalæcus, whom he defeated in battle, and drove out of the city of Lyctus. He then hastened to the relief of the Tarentines, in whose cause some time afterwards he perished with his whole army, fighting valiantly against the Lucanians. Phalæcus, dispossessed of his former conquest, made an attempt on the city of Cydonia, and brought up his battering engines; but ere they could be applied, they were struck by lightning, and he himself and a considerable number of the besiegers were consumed in the flames. According to another account, Phalæcus was killed by one of his own soldiers, whom he had offended. The relics of his army were transported by some Elean exiles to Peloponnesus, where, in an invasion of Elis, they

[1] Demosthenes, De Fals. Leg. 380, 381, 446: Philipp. ii 74; iii. 119; iv. 148: Ad. Epist. 153: De Coron. 240: and the whole of the Argument and the Oration on the Peace. Compare Æschines, Contr. Ctesiph. 73.

were signally defeated, and four thousand of them taken prisoners. The Elean government divided the captives between themselves and their Arcadian allies. Those allotted to the Arcadians were sold into slavery; the Eleans put theirs to death.[1]

Thus, says Diodorus, all parties who had been concerned in the plunder of Delphi met with signal retribution from heaven. Even the women, who had worn any of the sacred ornaments, came to a miserable and shameful end. To the same cause he attributes the calamities that afterwards fell upon Athens and Lacedæmon. Philip, who vindicated the oracular temple of Apollo, continued (he says) from that time forth to prosper more and more, till at length, as the reward of his piety, he was elected generalissimo of the Greeks, and established the greatest monarchy in Europe.[2] Such was the strain in which the fanatics and parasites of the day extolled the king of Macedon. Æschines chimes in with it, discordant as it was with the true interests of his country, and with the feelings which should have animated every well-wisher of the Hellenic happiness and freedom.[3]

APPENDIX II.

ORATORS AND STATESMEN.

ÆSCHINES.

Æschines, the second in reputation of Athenian orators, was born in the year B.C. 389, four years before Demosthenes. As to the rank and character of his parents, different statements are made by himself and by his opponent. According to his own account, his father Atrometus was an honorable citizen, connected by birth with the illustrious priestly house of the Eteobutadæ, who lost his property in the Peloponnesian war; and, having been forced to quit Athens during the government of the Thirty, served for a time as a mercenary soldier in Asia, and on his return lived in reduced circum-

[1] Diodorus, xvi. 61—63. Strabo, vi. 280. Pausanias, x. 2.

[2] Diodorus, xvi. 64. He should have gone on to say, "And two years afterwards this same Philip perished by the hand of an assassin; an inadequate punishment for his crimes, and for all the mischief he had done to Greece."

[3] Æschines, Contr. Ctesiph. 72. *Καὶ τοὺς αὐτοὺς ὁρῶμεν τῆς τε δόξης ταύτης καὶ τῆς ἐπὶ τὸν Πέρσην ἡγεμονίας ἠξιωμένους, οἳ καὶ τὸ ἐν Δελφοῖς ἱερὸν ἠλευθέρωσαν.* Compare De Fals. Leg. 50.

stances. His mother, Glaucothea, was the daughter of a respectable Athenian citizen. The account which Demosthenes gives of the parents and early life of Æschines may be regarded in some measure as a caricature;[1] yet it is not improbable, that the poverty to which Æschines himself admits his parents to have been reduced, compelled them to earn their livelihood by somewhat mean occupations. Notwithstanding the disadvantage of early poverty, their three sons all raised themselves to honor and dignity at Athens.[2] That Æschines must have received a good education, is attested by the works which he has left behind him; and it is possible that he may have owed this to the very school which his father is said to have kept. While he was yet very young, he obtained the situation of clerk to Aristophon, one of the leading statesmen of Athens; afterwards he went into the service of Eubulus, with whom he continued to be connected for the rest of his life as a politician and a friend. Being gifted with a handsome person and sonorous voice, he tried his fortune as an actor; but in this profession, which was by no means dishonorable at Athens, he appears, for some cause or other, not to have succeeded.[3] Like other Athenian citizens, he was called upon to perform military service for his country, and he acquitted himself with honor in several campaigns; more particularly at Phlius, at Mantinea, and at Tamynæ. In this last battle he displayed such signal courage, that he was chosen to carry home the news of the victory, and rewarded by the Athenians with a crown. Phocion, who had witnessed his bravery, not only praised him on the spot, but honored and esteemed him ever afterwards. But the laurels which he earned as a speaker soon threw into the shade those of the battle-field. His connection with Eubulus procured for him the situation of clerk to the popular assembly, through which he got an intimate acquaintance with the laws, the politics, and the public business of his country. This he found of immense advantage, when he came himself to take a part in the debates; and it is no wonder, that with his powerful voice and delivery, his literary acquirements, and great command of words, he quickly obtained a prominent place among the orators of the day.

The capture of Olynthus caused Æschines to come forward as a strong advocate of warlike measures against Philip. The statements of Demosthenes upon this subject—how he introduced Ischander to the council; how he proposed the sending of embassies to rouse the Greeks, and invite them to a congress at Athens; how he himself undertook the mission to Arcadia, and discharged that duty with zeal and ability—all are fully admitted by Æschines. How he came

[1] See this translation, ante, pp. 54, 55, 94—97, 193.

[2] See ante, p. 189.

[3] The sneers of Demosthenes are at the failure of Æschines, not at the profession itself.

to change his opinion, and to see the necessity of making peace with Philip at that crisis, he himself gives a not unreasonable explanation: as to which, and as to the part which he took in the embassy to Philip and the negotiation for peace, the reader is referred to the preceding history of the Sacred War.[1]

The circumstances attending the conclusion of this peace first created hostility between Æschines and Demosthenes. The accusation preferred by the latter against his rival brought them into an antagonism, both political and personal, which never ceased till Æschines finally quitted his native land. The peace had been so signally discreditable to Athens, and so manifestly injurious in its consequences, that in a very short time there was a strong reaction in the feelings of the Athenian people, and the war-party recovered their strength and popularity. Demosthenes stood forward as the exponent of their views, and raised himself to the position, which he had never occupied before, of a leading orator and governing statesman; while Æschines, having with difficulty obtained his acquittal on the charge of treason, notwithstanding the influence of his friends Eubulus and Phocion, withdrew for a considerable time from the strife of politics, and was rarely to be seen on the platform of the assembly. Besides other grounds of suspicion against him, the affair of Antiphon, in which he was charged with being an accomplice, left a stain upon his character; and he must have felt it as a deep disgrace, when the court of Areopagus took upon itself to deprive him of an honorable office, to which the people had elected him.[2]

In the year B.C. 340 he appears again on the scene of public life, as one of the Pylagoræ, representing his countrymen in the Amphictyonic congress. His conduct upon this occasion (whether by accident or design, it is impossible to say) contributed to kindle a third Sacred War, and bring on the fatal campaign of Chæronea. The details of this are given in Appendix IX.

Having on the trial of Ctesiphon[3] failed to obtain a fifth part of the votes, he quitted Athens, and lived in exile in Asia Minor, earning his livelihood by teaching rhetoric. During the lifetime of Alexander he cherished hopes of returning to Greece. Upon the death of that monarch he settled at Rhodes, where he lived peaceably for nine years, and founded a school of eloquence, which afterwards, under the name of the Asiatic, acquired considerable celebrity. It was there that his scholars, hearing him recite his own oration against Ctesiphon, expressed their astonishment at his having failed to get the verdict. "You will cease to wonder," said he, "when

[1] See especially pages 291, 293—312.

[2] See ante, p. 56. And see the Argument to the Oration on the Embassy.

[3] See the Argument to the Oration on the Crown.

you have heard the speech of my adversary." On another occasion, having read both of the speeches to a Rhodian assembly, and that of Demosthenes, which he delivered with great energy, having excited the admiration of all—" What would you have thought," said Æschines, " if you had heard the man himself!" Cicero tells this story, to illustrate the importance of manner and address in speaking. " Actio in dicendo una dominatur. Sine hâc summus orator esse in numero nullo potest; mediocris, hâc instructus, summos sæpe superare. Huic primas dedisse Demosthenes dicitur, cùm rogaretur quid in dicendo esset primum; huic secundas, huic tertias."

Of Æschines and his contemporaries Cicero, in his treatises on Oratory, speaks as follows :—

" Si qui se ad causas contulerunt, ut Demosthenes, Hyperides, Lycurgus, Æschines, Dinarchus, aliique complures, etsi inter se pares non fuerunt, tamen sunt omnes in eodum veritatis imitandæ genere versati; quorum quamdiu mansit imitatio, tamdiu genus illud dicendi studiumque vixit: posteaquam, extinctis his, omnis eorum memoria sensim obscurata est et evanuit, alia quædam dicendi molliora ac remissiora genera viguerunt."

"Suavitatem Isocrates, subtilitatem Lysias, acumen Hyperides, sonitum Æschines, vim Demosthenes habuit. Quis eorum non egregius? Tamen quis cujusquam nisi sui similis?"

"Nihil Lysiæ subtilitate cedit; nihil argutiis et acumine Hyperidi; nihil lenitate Æschini et splendore verborum."

Leland describes him thus:—

"Æschines was an orator whose style was full, diffusive, and sonorous. He was a stranger to the glowing expressions and daring figures of Demosthenes, which he treats with contempt and ridicule. But, though more simple, he is less affecting; and, by being less contracted, has not so much strength and energy. Or, as Quintilian expresses it, 'carnis plus habet, lacertorum minns.' But, if we would view his abilities to the greatest advantage, we must not compare them with those of his rival. Then will his figures appear to want neither beauty nor grandeur. His easy and natural manner will then be thought highly pleasing; and a just attention will discover a good degree of force and energy in his style, which at first appears only flowing and harmonious."

ARISTOPHON.

There are two persons of this name referred to in the orators: Aristophon of Colyttus, and Aristophon of Azenia: though Reiske is inclined to think they were the same person.

The former has been already mentioned as having taken Æschines into his service as clerk. He was a friend of Eubulus, and a politician of the same party. Demosthenes mentions them in connection, as both desiring the Theban alliance.[1]

Aristophon of Azenia was an older statesman, who took an active part in Athenian politics for about half a century after the end of the Peloponnesian war. He was an able speaker, and the author of many new laws. One of them, passed soon after the expulsion of the Thirty Tyrants, enacted, that no child should be deemed legitimate whose mother was not a citizen. Æschines in the oration against Ctesiphon says, that he was seventy-five times indicted for passing illegal measures, and every time acquitted. He conducted the prosecution, instituted by Chares, against Iphicrates and Timotheus, and procured the condemnation of the latter. One of his last political acts was the defence of the law of Leptines, B.C. 355.

CALLISTRATUS.

An eminent orator and statesman during the early life of Demosthenes. He was employed in various commands with Chabrias, Iphicrates, and Timotheus, during the war with Sparta. In the year B.C. 373 he joined Iphicrates in the prosecution of Timotheus, but failed to procure a conviction.[2] He was inclined to favor the Spartan connection, and, having accompanied the envoys who negotiated the peace of B.C. 371, he made a speech before the Peloponnesian congress, which is reported at some length by Xenophon, and which appears to have been much approved.

Two years afterwards, he supported the motion for assisting the Spartans, when Epaminondas invaded Laconia. He was ruined by the unfortunate affair of Oropus, having advised that it should be put into the hands of the Thebans.[3] For this both he and Chabrias were brought to trial, B.C. 366. Callistratus made a splendid speech, which was heard by Demosthenes, and is said to have kindled in his youthful breast the desire to become an orator. It was successful; and Callistratus was acquitted. But the loss of Oropus rankled in the minds of the Athenians; and five years afterwards he was tried again, and capitally convicted. Notwithstanding the sentence, he was allowed to withdraw into exile; and for some years he lived in Macedonia or Thrace; but choosing to return to Athens without permission from the people, he was arrested, dragged even from an altar, and suffered the penalty of the law.[4]

[1] Ante, p. 65; and see pp. 32, 33.

[2] Ante, p. 254.

[3] Ante, p. 260.

[4] On the history of Callistratus, there is a learned note and excursus of Schneider, Ad Xenoph. Hellen. vi. c. 3, s. 3.

CHARES.

A general, contemporary with Demosthenes, whom during a period of thirty years we find on various occasions commanding the Athenian armies, more often to the disadvantage than the advantage of his country. His first command was at Phlius, B.C. 367—366, when he successfully defended that city against the Argives. In 361 B.C., after Leosthenes had been defeated by Alexander of Pheræ, Chares was appointed admiral in his room; but he soon did much greater mischief than his predecessor; for, sailing to Corcyra, he lent his aid to a faction which overthrew the democracy, and which a few years afterwards seized the opportunity, when the Athenians were distressed by the Social War, to sever the island from their alliance. In the campaign against the Thebans in Eubœa Chares held some command, and was immediately afterwards sent to the Hellespont, where he compelled Charidemus to surrender the Chersonese according to treaty.[1] Having thus acquired some credit, he was chosen to command in the Social War. This was a series of disasters. He was defeated in the attack upon Chios, where fell the gallant Chabrias. In the second year of the war Iphicrates and Timotheus were associated with him in the command; but they were unable to obtain any success against the allies, who with a superior fleet ravaged Lemnos, Imbrus, and Samos, and levied contributions from the other subject islands. To relieve Byzantium, which was besieged by the Athenians, the allies advanced into the Propontis, and the two fleets met; but a storm arising, the two elder generals thought it not prudent to risk an engagement: Chares, eager for battle, violently reproached them, and afterwards wrote a letter to the people, accusing them of cowardice and treachery. Iphicrates and Timotheus were recalled, and afterwards brought to trial. Iphicrates with his son Menestheus was acquitted; Timotheus was condemned to a fine of a hundred talents, and retiring to Chalcis died in exile. The management of the war was left to Chares; who, though no longer restrained by the presence of his colleagues, never ventured to attack the enemy—(perhaps indeed they gave him no opportunity)—but carried his troops over to Asia Minor, to assist the satrap Artabazus in his rebellion against the Persian king. Having vanquished the royal forces, he received his promised reward, a sum of money which enabled him to maintain his army. But Artaxerxes having sent a wrathful message to Athens, complaining of this attack upon his kingdom, the Athenians, who at first had not been displeased at the assistance rendered to Artabazus, ordered Chares to quit his service; and not long afterwards, hearing that Artaxerxes was fitting out an armament of three hundred galleys, and being quite unprepared for

[1] See Vol. I. Appendix III. pp. 280, 281.

a contest against such formidable odds, they concluded peace with the revolted allies, and acknowledged their independence.

Chares still commanded in the Hellespont, where it was necessary for the Athenians to have a fleet constantly stationed, for the protection of their Thracian settlements and of the corn-trade. In the year 355 B.C. he took Sestus. Polyænus relates a stratagem by which Philip, having some transports to carry along the coast from Maronea, contrived to elude the pursuit of Chares, who with a squadron of twenty ships was lying in watch at Neapolis. Of his sorry performances in the Olynthian war, and the inefficiency of his operations in 346 B.C., when Philip was attacking Thrace, I have spoken in the preceding volume.[1] We may presume indeed, that during all this time he did some service by keeping Philip's squadrons at a distance, by blockading his coast and intercepting his commerce.

That Philip suffered injury in this way from the war, is asserted by Demosthenes, and is probable enough. But the cruisers of Chares were no less formidable to neutral and even friendly states than to the enemy; and this from the same cause which took him away from his duty to serve Artabazus, viz. the want of proper supplies from home. His troops were chiefly mercenaries, levied partly by his own exertions; and, in order to keep them together, he was obliged to provide pay in the best manner that he could, which was too often by forced contributions from the merchants, the Ægean islands, and the cities of Asia Minor.[2] This practice, which in effect was a species of piracy, suited the views of a man like Chares, for it gave him a more absolute command over his troops, and made him in some measure independent of his country; while the Athenians connived at it, because it relieved them from taxes and contributions. Chares resided chiefly at Sigeum, while he kept up his influence at Athens by means of the orators of his party, and by lavish distributions of money.

For his reception at Byzantium in the war of 340 B.C. I refer to the last volume;[3] and for his performances in the campaign of Chæronea, to Appendix IX. of this volume. Chares was one of the Athenians whom Alexander required to be surrendered with Demosthenes. When Alexander crossed over to Asia, Chares was living at Sigeum, and came to meet him at Ilium. Afterwards we read of his seizing Mitylene, apparently on behalf of Darius; from which he was expelled by Hegelochus the Macedonian general.

The character of the man appears from the history of his public life. He was a vain, dashing officer, with a good deal of personal

[1] See pp. 248—251, 288, 289.

[2] One writer attributes the origin of the Social War to these very practices of Chares. See Thirlwall's History of Greece, v. 213, 229.

[3] Vol. I. Appendix III. p. 303.

bravery, but little strategic skill. He was too fond of luxury and ease to perform his military duties properly. He used to carry about with him on his expeditions music-girls and dancers and other ministers of his pleasure. Funds which he received for war-like purposes he scrupled not to dissipate on idle amusement, or spend in bribing the orators and jurymen at Athens. Such is the account of Theopompus, perhaps a little overcharged; yet that it is true in the main appears from other sources. According to Suidas, his bad faith was so notorious, that the "promises of Chares" passed into a proverb. The influence which such a man acquired at Athens was owing partly to the absence of able competitors, partly to the vice and corruption of the day. Statesman and general were not united in the same person, as in the time of Pericles. The general serving abroad was connected with the orator who stayed at home; and they gave to each other a mutual support. Thus might an indifferent commander be kept in his employment by party influence. Aristophon was for some time the fighting orator who supported Chares at Athens. We find Demosthenes in the second Olynthian censuring this as a vicious practice, and pointing seemingly to Chares, though not by name. After the peace Chares and his party joined Demosthenes, who was then confessedly the best orator of the day, and had got the ear and confidence of the assembly. In the oration on the Chersonese, Demosthenes somewhat excuses the irregular practices of the generals abroad, and speaks indulgently both of Chares and Aristophon. Yet of the faults of Chares we can not doubt that he was fully conscious, though friendship may have tied his tongue. He speaks with extreme caution, where he defends him against Æschines in the Oration on the Embassy.[1]

DEMADES.

A clever but profligate orator, who first becomes known to us in the debate of 349 B. C., when he opposed the sending of succors to Olynthus. From this time he attached himself wholly to the Macedonian party at Athens, and received the pay first of Philip, and then of Alexander. As a necessary consequence, he was an enemy of Demosthenes, with whom he came into frequent collision in the popular assembly. His politics were not more opposite to those of Demosthenes than was the style of his eloquence. Demades was an off-hand and facetious speaker, without art and cultivation, but with great natural powers, pleasing often by his coarse wit and vulgarity more than others did by their studied rhetoric. If the people chanced to be in the humor for his sallies, which was no rare occurrence, he was a match even for Demosthenes himself.

It would appear, from the character given of him by Theophrastus

[1] Ante, p. 219.

and Cicero, and by divers anecdotes which are related of him, that Demades was capable of something better than levity and joking, when he chose to exert himself; but his inordinate love of money and pleasure rendered it impossible for him to be an honest man or a good citizen.

Among the sayings ascribed to him are the following:—

Being told that his politics were unworthy of Athens, he said, "he ought to be excused, for he steered but the wreck of the commonwealth." Being reproached for changing sides, he declared that "he often spoke against himself, but never against the state."

When the news of Alexander's death was brought to Athens, he said, "he did not believe it; for if it were true, the whole world must by that time have smelt his carcass."

Diodorus relates, that after the battle of Chæronea Philip in a fit of intoxication insulted his prisoners, and was rebuked by Demades in the following terms: "Fortune, O king, has placed you in the position of Agamemnon; are you not ashamed to act the part of Thersites?"—that he took the reproof well, and even honored Demades for his freedom; held friendly converse with him, and at his persuasion released the Athenian prisoners without ransom. We learn from Demosthenes, that he negotiated the terms of peace with Philip.[1]

When Alexander demanded the anti-Macedonian orators, Demades, for a bribe of five talents, undertook to save them. An assembly being held to consider the question of delivering them up, Demades moved an artful decree, by which the people, while they excused the orators, promised to punish them according to the laws if they deserved it. The Athenians passed the decree, and chose Demades to be the bearer of it to Alexander. He took Phocion with him, and by their persuasion Alexander was induced not only to grant the required pardon, but to allow the Theban exiles to be received at Athens.

By the ascendency of Macedonia Demades acquired influence at Athens, notwithstanding his notorious corruption, of which he made no secret, while he squandered his wealth as infamously as he got it. He succeeded Demosthenes as treasurer of the theoric fund, and held the appointment for twelve years. It is related by Plutarch, that succors would have been sent to the Lacedæmonians against Antipater, if Demades had not told the people, that they must then forego the sum which he was about to distribute among them for a festival. When Alexander claimed to receive divine honors from the Greek states, Demades moved at Athens that the king's demand be complied with, and meeting some opposition, bade the people mind that they did not lose earth, while they contested the possession of heaven. His motion was carried; but, after the revolution which followed Alexander's death, he was sentenced to a fine of ten talents

[1] See ante, p. 103.

for being the author of so base a decree. In the affair of Harpalus, we find Demades coming in for his share of the plunder, and confessing it without scruple; his maxim being, never to refuse what was offered him.

During the Lamian war Demades was in disgrace; but when Antipater was marching upon Athens, he was again employed to mediate for the people. Yet with all his powers of persuasion, assisted by Phocion and Xenocrates, he could only obtain peace for Athens, on the terms of her receiving a Macedonian garrison and a new constitution, paying the cost of the war, and giving up Demosthenes and other obnoxious orators. To the last condition we may presume Demades offered no objection; for he immediately afterwards moved the decree which sentenced those men to death.

After this disgraceful peace, Phocion and Demades were the two leading citizens of Athens; the real governor being Antipater's lieutenant Menyllus. Phocion preserved a moral, if not a political independence; while Demades was in every respect subservient to his foreign patron. Antipater used to say, that of his two Athenian friends, he could not get Phocion to accept any presents, and to Demades he could never give enough. Demades boasted of the source from which he got his supplies; and when he celebrated the marriage of his son, observed that the wedding-feast was furnished by princes. Yet all the liberality of Antipater did not satisfy him, and he at length brought about his ruin by his own treachery. He wrote a letter to Perdiccas, urging him to come and deliver Greece, which he said was "hanging by an old rotten thread." The letter fell into the hands of Antipater. It so happened, that Demades was shortly after sent by the Athenians to Macedonia, to petition for the withdrawal of the garrison from Athens. Antipater, then in his last illness, admitted him to an audience, and produced the letter. Demades, having not a word to say in his defense, was led away to execution.

HEGESIPPUS.

An orator of the war-party at Athens. He supported the Phocian alliance. He defended Timarchus, and seems to have been greatly disliked by Æschines and his friends, who gave him the nickname of Crobylus, from the manner in which he braided his hair.[1] He was sent on the embassy to Philip, in 343, B.C., to negotiate about the restitution of Halonnesus, the amendment of the peace, and other matters; on which occasion he gave such offense by his demands, that Philip banished the poet Xenoclides from Pella for showing him hospitality. He afterwards denounced Philip's conduct at Athens. The extant oration on Halonnesus is generally attributed to him.

[1] Perhaps in the fashion mentioned by Thucydides, i. 6.

HYPERIDES.

One of the most distinguished Athenians who flourished in the time of Demosthenes; with whom he was intimately connected, and whom he supported in all his efforts to support the sinking cause of Athens and of Greece against the king of Macedon. Though an honest and generous politician, in his private character he was not free from vice; and he was apt to display the violence of his passions both in the assembly and elsewhere. In early life he received a good education, having studied under Isocrates and Plato. Like Demosthenes, he prepared forensic speeches for other men; and he spoke and published many excellent orations, of which but a few fragments have come down to us. In style he was subtle and argumentative; occasionally bold and striking in his figures; yet, as Cicero says, very unlike Demosthenes. His delivery wanted animation.

Hyperides was one of the patriotic citizens who equipped galleys at their own expense, to carry troops to Eubœa, when the Thebans invaded the island. We have seen that he impeached Philocrates for his treasonable conduct on the embassy. After the battle of Chæronea he exerted himself with Demosthenes to put the city in a condition of defense, and moved a decree to restore the exiles and the disfranchised, to enfranchise aliens, and give liberty to slaves who fought in defense of Athens. For this he was indicted by Aristogiton, and acquitted. A fragment of his speech is preserved:—

"What is it you reproach me with? Proposing to give slaves their freedom? I did so to save freemen from slavery. Restoring exiles to their country? I restored them that no man might become an exile. Not reading the laws which forbade the measure? I could not read them; for the arms of the Macedonians took away my eyesight."

He was one of the obnoxious statesmen whom Alexander demanded to be given up to him with Demosthenes and Chares. The affair of Harpalus caused a rupture between him and Demosthenes, against whom he appeared as an accuser. When Demosthenes had gone into exile, Hyperides was the leader of the anti-Macedonian party at Athens; and after Alexander's death, he and Polyeuctus proposed the warlike measures that were undertaken for the liberation of Greece. When envoys came from Antipater, and praised the mildness of his disposition, Hyperides answered, "We do not want a mild master." Upon the death of Leosthenes, who was killed in a sally from Lamia, Hyperides spoke the funeral oration in honor of the slain; of which the following remarkable sentence is preserved:—

"If death is like the state of the unborn, these departed ones are released from disease, and sorrow, and all the casualties to which humanity is subject. But if, as we believe, there still remains in the invisible world a sense of the divine goodness, none surely can deserve it so well as those who have vindicated the profaned sanctity of the gods."

The end of Hyperides is invested with the same melancholy interest as that of Demosthenes. After the submission to Antipater, they were both, on the motion of Demades, sentenced to death; but they had previously escaped to Ægina. Here Hyperides entreated his old friend to forgive him for his unkindness. They then took a last farewell; Demosthenes retiring to the island of Calauria, Hyperides to Hermione, where he sought refuge in the temple of Ceres. Both were soon to be hunted down by the bloodhounds of the victor. Hyperides, dragged from his sanctuary, was carried to Antipater, who ordered his tongue to be cut out, and his body to be thrown to the dogs. His bones were afterwards obtained by one of his kinsmen, and carried to Athens to be buried.

LYCURGUS.

An eminent statesman and orator, chiefly known to us as the author of the speech against Leocrates, whom he prosecuted as a traitor for having deserted his country after the battle of Chæronea. The case is remarkable, as showing what sort of offenses might be construed as treasonable at Athens; and the whole speech deserves to be read.[1] Leocrates was a man of some wealth, who, on hearing of the signal defeat at Chæronea, packed up all his effects, and sailed away to Rhodes, where he spread a report that Athens was taken by Philip. After staying abroad for seven years he returned home, and resumed his post as a citizen, but was immediately impeached by Lycurgus, brought to trial, and convicted. Thirwall, in the seventh book of his history, where this circumstance is recorded, gives an admirable description of the life and character of Lycurgus, which I present, somewhat abridged, to my reader:—

"Lycurgus, the prosecutor, was one of the few men then living at Athens who could undertake such a task with dignity, as conscious of a life irreproachably spent in the service of his country. There are few Athenian statesmen of any age who can bear a comparison with him. Phocion equalled him in honesty and disinterestedness; but in his general character, and in his political conduct, seems to fall far below him. He was a genuine Athenian, his family being one of the oldest and most illustrious in Athens. He traced the origin of his house (the Eteobutads) to the hero Erechtheus. By virtue of this descent his family possessed an hereditary priesthood of Poseidon. In the Erechtheum, the temple dedicated in common to the hero and the god, the portraits of his ancestors who had held that office were painted on the walls. Lycophron, his grandfather, had been put to death by the Thirty, and both he and

[1] See my article Προδοσία, in the Archæological Dictionary.

Lycomedes, another of the orator's progenitors, had been honored with a public funeral. Lycurgus had studied in the schools both of Plato and Isocrates; but had not learned from the one to withdraw from active life into a visionary world, nor from the other to cultivate empty rhetoric at the expense of truth and of his country. His manly eloquence breathes a deep love and reverence for what was truly venerable in antiquity. His speech against Leocrates, which is still extant, shows that he dwelt with a fondness becoming his birth and station on the stirring legends of older times; but his admiration for them had not made him indifferent or unjust towards those in which he lived. He possessed an ample hereditary fortune; but he lived, like Phocion, with Spartan simplicity. In an age of growing luxury he wore the same garments through summer and winter, and, like Socrates, was only seen with sandals on extraordinary occasions. Yet he had to struggle against the aristocratical habits and prejudices of his family. He was the author of a law, to restrain the wealthier women from shaming their poorer neighbors by the costliness of their equipages in the festive procession to Eleusis; but his own wife was the first to break it. His frugality, however, did not arise from parsimony, and was confined to his personal wants. He was reproached with the liberality which he displayed toward the various masters of learning whom he employed, and declared that, if he could find any that would make his sons better men, he would gladly pay them with half his fortune. He devoted himself to public life in a career of quiet, unostentatious, but useful activity. He was a powerful, but not a ready speaker: like Pericles and Demosthenes, he never willingly mounted the bema without elaborate preparation; and his writing instruments were constantly placed by the side of the simple couch on which he rested, and from which he frequently rose in the night to pursue his labors. But to shine in the popular assembly was not the object of his studies; he seems only to have appeared there on necessary or important occasions. His genius was peculiarly formed for the management of financial affairs; and the economy of the state was the business of a large portion of his public life. In the latter part of Philip's reign he was placed at the head of the treasury. The duties of his office embraced not only the collection, but the ordinary expenditure of the Athenian revenues, so far as they were not appropriated to particular purposes. On the administration of the person who filled it depended both the resources of the state and the manner in which they were regularly applied. The office was tenable for four years; a law dictated by republican jealousy, and (it seems) proposed by Lycurgus himself, forbade it to remain longer in the same hands. Yet Lycurgus was permitted to exercise its functions during twelve successive years, selecting some of his friends for the last two terms to bear the title. In the course of this period nearly 19,000 talents passed through his hands. He is said to have raised the ordinary revenue from 600 to 1,200 talents. We hear of no expedients but unwearied diligence by which he effected this increase. It is only as to the application that we are more fully informed. It seems that the amount and the nature of the domestic expenditure were committed in a great degree to his discretion. As the surplus not required for war fell into the theoric fund, which was devoted to the transient gratification of the people, it required all the influence of the treasurer to apply as large a sum as possible to objects permanently useful. The administration of Lycurgus was distinguished above every other since Pericles by the number of public buildings which he erected or completed. Among his monuments were an arsenal, an armory, a theatre, a gymnasium, a palæstra, a stadium. After the example of Pericles, he laid up a considerable treasure in the citadel, in images, vessels, and ornaments of gold and silver, which at the same time served to heighten the splendor of the sacred festivals. It was in a different capacity, under a special commission, that he also built four hundred galleys, and formed a great magazine of arms. He seems likewise to have taken Pericles for his model in a continual endeavor to raise the character and to refine the taste of the people. We find his attention directed to important branches of art and literature. He was the author of a regulation for the better management of the comic drama. But he conferred a more lasting benefit on his country, and on all posterity, by another measure designed to preserve the works of the three great tragic poets of Athens. The dramas of Sophocles and Euripides, if not of Æschylus, were still frequently exhibited: they were acknowledged as the most perfect models of dramatic poetry; but this did not prevent them from undergoing a fate similar to that which has so often befallen the works of our early dramatists: they were frequently interpolated and mutilated by the actors. Before the invention of the press this was a serious evil, as it endangered the very existence of the original works. To remedy it, Lycurgus caused a new transcript or edition to be made of them by public authority, in many cases probably from the manuscripts of the authors, and to be deposited in the state archives. The value of this edition was proved by its fate. It was afterwards borrowed by one of the Ptolemies to be copied for the Alexandrian library, and fifteen talents were left at Athens as a pledge for its restitution. The king however sent back the copy instead of the original, and forfeited his pledge. By the decree of Lycurgus it was directed, that the players should conform in their representations to this authentic edition.

"All these works attest the influence of Lycurgus, while they show the spirit in which it was exerted. As the state intrusted him with its revenues, so private persons deposited their property in his custody. When a piece of ground was required for his new stadium, Dinias, its owner, made a present of it to the people, with the extraordinary declaration, that he gave it for the sake of Lycurgus. His testimony was sought as the most efficacious aid in the courts of justice. He was once summoned by an adversary of Demosthenes. Demosthenes said he should only ask, whether Lycurgus would consent to be thought like the man whom he befriended. He could venture sharply to rebuke the assembled people, when he was interrupted in a speech by clamors of disapprobation. We hear but of one case in which he may seem to have courted popular favor by a deviation from his principles in the management of the public funds. He had convicted a wealthy man of a gross fraud on the state in the working of the mines at Laurium. The offender was put to death, and his whole estate confiscated, and Lycurgus consented to distribute the sum which it brought into the treasury among the people, as the whole produce of the mines had been distributed before the time of Themistocles. The general tendency of his measures, and the impression produced by his character, were rather of an opposite kind. He inspired a feeling approaching to awe by his antique Spartan-like austerity, as he publicly avowed his admiration of the old Spartan manners. When he was appointed to superintend the police of the city, the measures by which he cleared it of rogues and vagrants were deemed so rigorous, as to be compared with the laws of Draco. On the other hand, one of his celebrated enactments was a provision against one of the grosser abuses of the slave-trade, by which it sometimes happened that free persons were sold under false pretexts in the Athenian market.

"The account, to which every Athenian magistrate was liable, was rigidly exacted from one who filled such an office as Lycurgus discharged for twelve years in succession. He rendered one at the end of each quadriennial period, either in his own name, or in that of the titular minister for whom he acted. No flaw was ever detected in his reckonings, and it appeared that he had on various occasions borrowed between 600 and 700 talents for the public service. Still he himself was not satisfied with the ordinary inspection to which his accounts were liable; he justly considered them as one of his fairest titles to gratitude and esteem, and he therefore caused them to be inscribed on a monument which he erected in the palæstra founded by himself: and it appears that a considerable part of this inscription has been preserved to our day. A short time before his death, which seems to have a little preceded Alexander's, he directed himself to be carried to the council-chamber, and challenged a fresh scrutiny of his whole administration. The only person who came forward to lay any thing to his charge was one Menesæchmus, whom he had prosecuted, and he now refuted all his cavils.

"Crowns, statues, and a seat at the table of the Prytanes, had been bestowed on him in his life. After his death he was honored with a public funeral, and with a bronze statue near the ten heroes of the tribes, and the distinction he had enjoyed as a guest of the state was made hereditary in his family."

PHOCION.

Phocion is one of the heroes of Plutarch, who has written a very interesting life of him, in which, however, he greatly overrates his merits as a politician. He was born of humble parents in the year 402 B.C., and lived to the age of eighty. During all this time he was remarkable not only for an inflexible integrity of conduct, but for an austere virtue and simplicity, exemplified in his manners, his dress, and his whole style of living. His early habits had accustomed him to the endurance of hardships; and the precepts of philosophy, which he imbibed from Plato and Xenocrates, under whom he afterwards studied, taught him to despise riches and other external advantages. Partly on such account, partly by his valor in the field, and by means of a fluent and natural eloquence, he became a favorite with the people, and was forty-five times elected to the office of general, and on five occasions at least intrusted with important commands, in all of which he was successful.

At the battle of Naxos he served under Chabrias, and greatly distinguished himself. Chabrias observed, that his courage was tempered with prudence, a quality in which he himself was somewhat deficient, and for want of which he lost his life afterwards in the action at Chios. He selected Phocion to execute an important commission, that of collecting contributions from the islands, and offered him a guard of twenty sail. Phocion said, if he was sent to enemies, the force was not large enough; if to friends, one vessel was sufficient. Accordingly he took a single ship, and managed things so well, that he gathered all the arrears due from the allies. After the death of Chabrias, Phocion, in requital of his kindness, took the utmost pains to reform the morals of his son Ctesippus, but found him incorrigible.

His first important command was in Eubœa, when he carried succors to Plutarch of Eretria against Callias of Chalcis, who had received assistance from Macedonia. He found that Plutarch had deceived the Athenians with respect to the amount of support which he could offer. His own force was small, and through the negligence or treachery of his ally he was brought into a perilous position in the plain of Tamynæ, where he was exposed to an attack by superior numbers. He chose some rising ground, and fortified his camp. Some of his men being mutinous, and straggling from the camp, he told his officers not to mind them, as they would do him more harm than good. When Callias advanced with his Macedonian auxiliaries, some of the Athenians were eager to charge: he told them to wait till he had offered sacrifice; notwithstanding which, his cavalry and the Eubœans rushed impetuously forward, but were speedily routed, Plutarch being the first to fly. Callias, thinking the battle won, led his troops in some confusion up to the Athenian lines, when Phocion, informing his men that the sacrifices were propitious, gave the order for attack; and his small band of infantry, falling with fury upon their enemies, after an obstinate fight won the victory. Phocion afterwards expelled Plutarch from Eretria, in which he established popular government, and secured it by a fort called Zaratra, which he occupied, on a neck of land projecting into the channel. His successor Molossus managed things so ill, that he was taken prisoner by the enemy; and Eretria was lost to Athens. It fell soon under the tyranny of Clitarchus, a creature of Philip.

In the year 351 B.C., Phocion went to assist Evagoras in the expedition for the reduction of Cyprus, which in the following year was re-annexed to the Persian empire. In 343, B.C., his services were required to secure Megara against the intrigues of Philip. He marched rapidly to the city with a large body of Athenians, and being welcomed by the Megarian people, he proceeded to fortify the harbor of Nisæa and complete the long walls, thus bringing it under the protection of Athens, and defeating the plot of Ptœodorus to introduce Macedonian troops. In 341, B.C., he restored Eubœa to his country, driving out the tyrants and the Macedonian garrisons from Eretria and Oreus. And in the following year he achieved the signal successes which preserved Byzantium and the Chersonese.[1]

Seeing the warlike abilities displayed by Phocion, we can not help deeming it unfortunate that he was not oftener employed, and particularly in the critical campaigns of Olynthus and Chæronea. Had he been sent to assist Phalæcus in the defense of Thermopylæ, the destiny of Greece might have been changed. He does not appear to have been intrusted with any important command until he was forty-eight years of age. For the cause of this we must look partly to his own unambitious temper of mind, partly to the politics of the time. Phocion was not a party man; both in private and in public life, his views and his acts were independent: he did not command the political influence, and he would have disdained to use the arts which elevated such men as Chares to honors and dignities. He was generally opposed to the war-party; and it was but natural that, when they had the opportunity, they should select for the execution of their measures, the men who supported them. There is another thing also to be noticed.—Phocion was an orator as well as a general: he is said to have been the last of the Athenians in whom those two functions were united. He never made long speeches; yet he commanded as much attention as any of those who mounted the platform. He spoke with a pithy and sententious brevity, which comported well with the gravity of his demeanor, and had the more

[1] See ante, pp. 32, 35, 37, 109, 209: and see Vol. I. pp. 107, 119, 128, 303, 304.

effect on account of the esteem in which his character was held. Without being ill-natured or discourteous, he had a dry, caustic humor, which could administer very sharp reproof to those who, he thought, by their folly or presumption, or by the dangerous tendency of their argument, deserved it. Even Demosthenes feared him, and once, when Phocion rose to speak, whispered to a friend—"Here comes the chopper[1] of my harangues." Nor did he spare the people themselves more than his competitors, but was constantly rebuking them for their follies. He told them once, he had given them a great deal of good advice, but they had not the wit to follow it. Yet for all that he was a favorite with the assembly; for they respected his good qualities; and they always liked a man who threw life into their debates.

A great number of his sayings are preserved by Plutarch; among them the following:—

Chares rallied him in the assembly upon the gravity of his countenance: Phocion said, "My grave looks never hurt the Athenians; but your mirth has cost them many a tear."

Being asked, in the theatre, why he was looking so thoughtful? "I am considering," said he, "how to retrench something in a speech I am about making to the people."

Demosthenes said to him, "The Athenians will kill you some day in one of their mad fits:" "And you," said he, "if ever they come to their senses."

His speech having been received with applause in the assembly, he asked one of his friends, "if he had let drop any thing silly or impertinent."

Being reproached for defending an unworthy man, he said, "The innocent have no need of an advocate."

Aristogiton, a pettifogging orator, having been sentenced to a heavy fine, requested Phocion to come and speak with him in prison. His friends advising him not to go, Phocion said, "I know no place where I would rather meet Aristogiton."

He reproved the people for their rejoicing at Philip's death, saying, "Remember, the army that beat you at Chæronea is lessened only by one man."

When Demosthenes was inveighing against Alexander, then before the walls of Thebes, Phocion quoted the lines of Homer, in which the companions of Ulysses entreat him not to provoke Polyphemus:

[1] Κοπίς. This illustrates the passage in the Oration on the Embassy (p. 450): 'Η δὲ τοῦ λέγειν (δύναμις,) ἂν τὰ παρ' ὑπῶν τῶν ἀκουόντων ἀντιστῇ, διακόπτεται.

What boots the godless giant to provoke,
Whose arm may sink us at a single stroke?[1]

It is necessary however to advert to the political character of Phocion, as to which there is some difference of opinion. Mitford regards him as the best of Athenian statesmen. Plutarch takes but little notice of those faults which Thirlwall and Grote comment on with not more severity than justice. Phocion as a statesman neglected the duty, which as a general he would have been the first to acknowledge; that of defending his country; defending her by his foresight and his counsel; descrying the danger that was approaching her, and advising the proper measures to avert it. He either did not see the peril, or, when he did see it, he despaired of safety. He gave up the game, while there was yet a chance of winning it. This is proved even by the campaign of Chæronea, the issue of which was doubtful, and might have been different, if there had been abler commanders on the Athenian side. Phocion was keenly alive to the faults of his countrymen, but he did not strive to amend them: he was content to sneer and moralize, without endeavoring to instruct or improve. Athens, with all her faults, was the best governed of all the states in Greece, and secured the largest amount of rational happiness to her citizens. She was worth preserving for the sake of Greece and of the world. It was an injury to the cause of civilization and humanity, that such a state should be overthrown by the brute strength of a semi-barbarous power. Phocion should have co-operated with those who labored to save their country, and not have thrown difficulties in their way. What Athens wanted was the energy which animated her citizens of a former age, and the military training and organization which gives efficiency to an army. No man was better able than Phocion to advise the Athenians upon these subjects; yet we no where find him exhorting them to rouse from indolence and prepare for a struggle that was inevitable. Tamynæ might have shown him that they were capable of doing something if properly directed. Still he persisted in looking at the dark instead of the bright side of things; and though he always did his duty in the field, he damped the spirits of his countrymen and fostered their apathy and idleness at

[1] Pope's translation of the Odyssey, ix. 494, where the companions of Ulysses entreat him not to provoke Polyphemus:—

Σχέτλιε, τίπτ' ἐθέλεις ἐρεθιζέμεν ἄγριον ἄνδρα;
Ὃς καὶ νῦν πόντονδε βαλὼν βέλος, ἤγαγε νῆα
Αὖτις ἐς ἤπειρον, καὶ δὴ φάμεν αὐτόθ' ὀλέσθαι.

Phocion was probably right in his counsel here. Yet Demosthenes might have rejoined, that Ulysses was not convinced by his companions, and quoted his words:

Ὣς φάσαν· ἀλλ' οὐ πεῖθον ἐμὸν μεγαλήτορα θυμόν.

home. His philosophy was one-sided, not teaching him to be a good patriot as well as a good man. Even in his sayings we may discover an inclination to be smart rather than just, to sacrifice truth occasionally to repartee. When Demosthenes advised that Philip should be engaged in war as far as possible away from Attica, Phocion said, "Let us not be so careful about the place where we fight, as how to get the victory." Here, as it appears to me, Demosthenes gave sound advice, and Phocion's answer was not to the point. Demosthenes might have said, "Yes; I am also for taking every possible means to secure the victory; but still I think it safer to fight Philip abroad than at home. Let us do this, and not leave the other undone." Phocion censured the measures of Leosthenes which led to the Lamian war; and being asked by Hyperides, when he would advise the Athenians to declare war, answered, "When I see the young observant of discipline, the rich ready to contribute, and the orators abstaining from plunder." This was ill-timed.

Phocion seems to have thought, like Isocrates, that Macedonian ascendency was not inconsistent with the freedom of the Greek states. Chæronea soon undeceived him. When Philip invited a general congress to meet at Corinth, and Demades proposed that the Athenians should join it, Phocion advised them to wait until they knew what Philip would demand. Afterwards, when it was found that Philip demanded of them a contingent of cavalry and ships, the Athenians (says Plutarch) repented that they had not followed Phocion's advice. Yet it may be doubted, whether they would have done any good by merely absenting themselves from the congress.

In the debate upon Alexander's demand of the orators, Phocion advised the people to surrender them, and urged the orators to yield themselves up for the public good. We may credit the declaration which Plutarch puts into his mouth, that he would have been equally willing to resign his own life to insure the safety of his country; and yet it is painful to see Phocion recommending the sacrifice of these distinguished men to his country's enemy. Of the relations which existed between Phocion and Demosthenes we know but little. They were opposed in politics; yet it does not appear that they were enemies in private: not a word is ever uttered by Demosthenes in disparagement of Phocion;[1] and it is observable that three important commands (upon the expeditions to Megara, to Eubœa, and to Byzantium) were conferred upon him after Demosthenes had acquired political power. While we lament

[1] Phocion appeared to support Æschines on his trial: he was, as we should say, a witness to character. Demosthenes, where he alludes to his adversary's supporters, does not name Phocion, though he addresses Eubulus in language of strong reproof. See ante, pp. 189, 207, 208.

Phocion's mistaken views of duty, we can not suppose that he acted from any ill will towards Demosthenes or his friends. He went with Demades on the deprecatory mission to Alexander,[1] and was most favorably received by that prince, who is reported on that occasion to have said, "The Athenians must keep their eyes open; for, if any thing should happen to me, they alone are worthy to command."

Alexander during the short time that he conversed with Phocion conceived a great regard for him, and, after he had gone to Asia, corresponded with him as a friend. In the letters which he wrote after his conquest of the Persian kingdom he omitted the word *Greeting* (the common form of salutation) to all persons whom he addressed except Antipater and Phocion. He could not however induce Phocion to accept any presents from him. To some officers who brought him a hundred talents Phocion said—"How comes it that among all the Athenians I alone am the object of Alexander's bounty?" and being told, that it was because Alexander esteemed him alone to be a man of honor and probity; "then," said he, "let him allow me to continue so." Craterus was ordered to offer Phocion his choice of four Asiatic cities: this also he refused. Alexander in some displeasure wrote to say, that he could not regard a man as his friend, who would accept no obligation from him; upon which Phocion requested him to pardon four persons, who for some offense were in custody at Sardis; and accordingly they were set at liberty.

When Alexander sent for the ships which the Athenians had promised to furnish, and some opposition was made in the assembly, Phocion warned them to keep friendship with those in power, until they had greater power themselves. It does not appear what part he took upon the motion for deifying Alexander. When Harpalus came to Athens, Phocion rejected his bribes, but dissuaded the giving him up to Antipater. When the people were in excitement upon the first news of Alexander's death, some saying it was false, others crying out that it was true—"Well," said Phocion, "if it is true to-day, it will be true to-morrow and the next day; and we shall have time to deliberate about it at our leisure."

He opposed the Lamian war from the first, thinking the Athenians would not have the means to carry it on. In the midst of their successes in the first year he disheartened them by his gloomy forebodings. Those who judge by the event have praised him; yet the history of the war itself proves, in spite of all that Diodorus and others have said to the contrary, that there was a very good chance of success, and that the Athenians were fully justified in commencing it. Had Phocion not shown so despondent a temper, he

[1] See ante, p. 327.

would probably have been chosen to succeed Leosthenes as general of the allied army; and his military talents might have produced a different result. Once more only was he destined to lead his countrymen to victory. He had dissuaded them (perhaps prudently) from invading Bœotia, while the flower of their army was engaged in Thessaly. But when the Macedonian fleet, having been victorious at sea, made a descent at Rhamnus, and landed a large force which overran and ravaged the country, Phocion mustered all that were capable of bearing arms, and putting himself at their head, marched to the defence of Attica. Here again we find him, as in his younger days, checking the too forward eagerness of his soldiers, and exerting himself to keep them under command. Nor was this without effect. The Macedonians were routed, and their general Micion was slain. This was the last gleam of success which attended the Athenian arms.

When Antipater was approaching Athens with his victorious army, Phocion, as we have seen already, was sent with Demades and Xenocrates to appease him; but the only terms which he could obtain were such as annihilated his country's independence. Athens was deprived of the few insular possessions which Philip had left her. She was forced to accept a new constitution, by which nearly two-thirds of her citizens were disfranchised. Many of them emigrated to Thrace, where Antipater offered them an abode. Some of the upper class were banished from the city. A Macedonian garrison was established at Munychia, to overawe any malcontents that might remain.

Amidst all the calamities and disgraces which had fallen upon his country, Phocion preserved his serenity of mind. He had survived all that was great and noble in Athens. There however he lived, on friendly terms with the Macedonian governor, Menyllus, with whom he had been formerly acquainted: while he refrained from all opposition to the ruling power, which then would have been useless, he refused all the proffered favors of Antipater, as he had once refused Alexander's. The influence which he could exert at Athens was greater than at any former period, owing indeed as much to Menyllus as to himself. Yet even of this poor consolation he was soon to be deprived by the death of Antipater, which occasioned a new revolution.

Antipater, before he died, had nominated Polysperchon as his successor in the regency: Cassander, his son, prepared to contest this appointment, and, among other precautions which he took to secure his own power, sent his friend Nicanor to Athens, to receive from Menyllus the command of the garrison. Menyllus, ignorant of Antipater's death, resigned his charge immediately. Polysperchon, to counteract the efforts of Cassander, drew up an edict in the name of king Aridæus, Philip's son, making liberal promises in favor of the Greek cities; and wrote a conciliatory letter to Athens, proposing to restore the democracy. At the same time he sent troops under his son Alexander to expel Nicanor from Munychia, and prepared himself to follow with a larger force.

The Athenians, beguiled by the regent's letter, were eager to get rid of Nicanor and his garrison; and a plot was laid to seize him in the Piræus, where he was invited to attend a meeting of the council. Nicanor, who was secretly collecting reinforcements to maintain his position, attended the meeting, upon Phocion's undertaking to be answerable for his safety; but hastily withdrew, upon receiving a hint of his enemies' designs. Phocion was reproached by the Athenians for not having seized Nicanor's person, as he might have done. He asserted that there was no reason to suspect Nicanor of any hostile intention; but this only aggravated the displeasure of the people, when Nicanor, having received his reinforcements from Salamis, surprised Piræus in the night. He then offered to lead his countrymen against Nicanor, but they refused to follow him, and soon afterwards, when Alexander appeared with his troops before the walls, they deposed Phocion from his office of general.

The Athenians had imagined, that Alexander was come to liberate them from the garrison and to enforce the king's edict; but they soon found themselves mistaken. Alexander was observed to hold private conferences with Nicanor. It was suspected that they were concerting measures together, and that Phocion, who had himself had interviews with Alexander, was at the bottom of the scheme. A number of exiles, who had followed the march of the Macedonian army, had got admission to the city, and helped to inflame the people against Phocion. One Agnonides accused him of treason: upon which he with some of his friends fled to the Macedonian camp. Agnonides persuaded the Athenians to send embassadors with an accusation against him to Polysperchon. Phocion was sent by Alexander with a letter recommending him to his father's protection.

Notwithstanding this, Polysperchon, who had now advanced with an army into Phocis, received him with the utmost rudeness; and, when he was accused by the Athenian envoys, refused to hear any defense. An uproar being occasioned by many of the Athenians speaking at once, "Put us all into one cage," said Agnonides, "and send us to Athens to try our quarrel there." This strange request was after a while complied with; and Phocion and the other accused parties were put in a wagon, and sent in chains to Athens under the escort of Clitus.

They were carried to the theatre, where the assembly was to sit in judgment upon them. A vast crowd was gathered, consisting in part of exiles, foreigners, and slaves. The exiles were peculiarly exasperated against Phocion, because he had been the friend of Antipater. Clitus read a letter from the king, which declared that he believed all the prisoners guilty, but that he left their case to the free judgment of the Athenian people. The accusers charged Phocion with being the author of all the evils which had fallen upon them since the Lamian war; the overthrow of the democracy, the death and exile of so many citizens, the yoke of the Macedonian garrison. It was in vain that he attempted to speak. His voice was drowned by clamor. "Athenians"—at length he exclaimed:—"I myself plead guilty: but what have these my friends done?"—"It is enough"—cried the people—"that they are your accomplices." Agnonides moved, that they should decide at once, by show of hands, whether the prisoners were guilty; and if so, that they should be put to death. The sentence of condemnation was unanimous. Torture was proposed; but even Agnonides declared, he could never consent to treat Phocion in such a manner: and one honest voice was heard to exclaim—"You are right, Agnonides: for if we put Phocion to the torture, what may you not expect?"

Four of the condemned persons were carried with Phocion to execution. He was insulted as he passed along: one man spat in his face: he turned to the archons and said—"Will no one correct this fellow's rudeness?" He preserved his own calm composure to the last, and endeavored to cheer his companions. Being asked, if he had any message to his son, he answered—"Yes: tell him to forget how the Athenians treated his father." Nicocles, who had been one of his dearest friends, entreated that he might drink the hemlock first. "Ah!" said Phocion; "of all the requests you ever made this is the most painful to me; but, as I never refused you any thing, I must grant this also." The executioner had not mixed hemlock enough for all, and asked twelve drachms for a fresh supply: "What?" said Phocion: "can't one die free of cost at Athens?"—and he requested one of his friends to give the man his fee.

Such was the end of Phocion. It was compared to that of Socrates. It reminds one also of Sir Thomas More.

APPENDIX III.

THE COUNCIL OF AREOPAGUS.

THIS council, so called from the Hill of Mars, where it held its sittings, near the Acropolis, was a judicial and deliberative body greatly esteemed at Athens. It was from time immemorial established as a court of criminal jurisdiction, to try cases of murder, maiming, and arson. It sat in the open air, to escape the pollution of being under the some roof with the guilty. In its proceedings the utmost solemnity was observed. Both parties were sworn to speak the truth; and the facts alone were inquired into, without appeals to the feelings or oratorical display.

The Areopagites used to be taken from the noble families of Attica. But Solon introduced a new law, that the Archons whose official conduct had been approved should be members of this council for life. At the same time he enlarged the power of the council, attaching to it political and censorial duties, in order that with the council of five hundred it might act as a check upon the democracy.

In their censorial character the Areopagites kept watch over the religion and morals of the city, maintained order and decency, looked to the education of the young, inquired how people got their living, and checked riotous excesses and debauchery. They had power to summon before them and punish offenders. They acted often from their own personal knowledge, without requiring testimonial evidence. We read of their entering houses on feast days, to see that the guests were not too numerous. Menedemus and Asclepiades, two poor young men, were called before the council, and asked how they could manage to live, when they spent all their days in idleness in company with philosophers: they proved that every night they earned two drachms by grinding at a mill; whereupon the council rewarded them with a present of two hundred drachms.

As a political body, it was their province to inquire into offenses against the state and report them to the people. If the public safety required it, or if there was not time to wait for the ordinary course of law, they could interfere summarily to avert threatened danger, to prevent the consummation of crime, or bring the offenders to speedy justice.

For example: after the battle of Chæronea, when it was expected that Athens would be besieged, the Areopagites caused certain men, who were preparing to leave their country, to be seized and put to death. So also, they put Antiphon to the torture and sentenced him to death, although he had been dismissed by the popular assembly; and they deprived Æschines, suspected of being his accomplice, of an office to which he had been elected by the people.[1]

Or the people might give a special commission to be executed by the Areopagites. Thus in the affair of Harpalus a decree was passed, directing them to investigate what had become of the treasure which that officer brought to Athens. They instituted a rigid inquiry, searching the houses of the suspected parties; and

[1] See ante, pp. 56, 118, 181; and Vol. I. p. 168, note 3.

then made a report, charging several persons with having received presents, and among them, Demades and Demosthenes.

Had not the council maintained a high character for justice, prudence, and moderation, it would have been impossible for such inquisitorial and summary powers to have been tolerated in a free state like Athens. That they were exercised generally to the advantage of the people, and that public opinion supported them, appears from the express testimony of Isocrates, Æschines, and other writers. Isocrates in his Areopagitic oration contrasts the loose morals of his own time with those of a former age, over which the Areopagus exercised a greater control: he says, that it was the most esteemed tribunal in Greece; that even bad men, when they became members of it, discarded their own nature, and conformed to the character of the institution.

In the time of Pericles the democratical party, of which that statesman was at the head, looked with jealousy upon the council of Areopagus, on account of the support which they thought it gave to the aristocratical or conservative interest: and they exerted themselves to bring it into discredit with the people, and to weaken its authority. The opposite party, headed by Cimon, resisted this attempt; and the poet Æschylus engaged his pen in the same cause. The tragedy of the Eumenides is said to have been composed for the express purpose of upholding the authority of the Areopagus. He there shows how it was established by the tutelary goddess of Athens; how its first sitting was appointed for the trial of Orestes, pursued by the vengeful Furies for shedding his mother's blood; how it pronounced his acquittal with the aid and sanction of the goddess; how Orestes vowed for himself and his country eternal alliance with Athens; and how Pallas declared that the court and council, composed of the best and worthiest Athenian citizens, revered for its wisdom and incorruptibility, should endure to all ages and be the safeguard of the country.[1] The inference was that,

[1] See the Eumenides, 465 :—

> *Κρίνασα δ' ἀστῶν τῶν ἐμῶν τὰ βέλτατα*
> *ἥξω, διαιρεῖν τοῦτο πρᾶγμ' ἐτητύμως,*
> *ὅρκον περῶντας μηδὲν ἔκδικον φρεσίν.*

And 651—670 :—

> *Κλύοιτ' ἂν ἤδη θεσμὸν, 'Αττικὸς λεως,*
> *πρώτας δίκας κρίνοντες αἵματος χυτοῦ.*
> *ἔσται δὲ καὶ τὸ λοιπὸν 'Αργείῳ στρατῷ*
> *ἀεὶ δικαστῶν τοῦτο βουλευτήριον.*
> * * * * *
> *τοιόνδε τοι ταρβοῦντες ἐνδίκως σέβας,*
> *ἔρυμά τε χώρας καὶ πόλεως σωτήριον*
> *ἔχοιτ' ἂν, οἷον οὔτις ἀνθρώπων ἔχει*
> *οὔτε Σκύθῃσιν, οὔτε Πέλοπος ἐν τόποις.*

instead of seeking to encroach upon the power of this solemn and awful tribunal, the people of Athens ought to regard it with veneration, and maintain it in all its integrity. However, notwithstanding this powerful appeal, and all the opposition of Cimon and his party, Ephialtes in the year B.C. 458 carried a decree, which to some extent abridged or limited the powers of the council. The exact nature of the change which he introduced is a matter of controversy. That the criminal jurisdiction of the court was not interfered with, appears from the testimony of Demosthenes, who in the oration against Aristocrates says, that neither tyrants nor people had ever deprived it of that jurisdiction, and that even the condemned had never complained of its verdicts. That it still continued to exercise large and undefined powers of an inquisitorial and political character, appears from the examples above mentioned, occurring in the age of Demosthenes. It is not unlikely, however, that some of the censorial functions of the Areopagus may have been taken away altogether. But what is still more probable is, that the Areopagites, as a political body, were made accountable to the people for the proper discharge of their duties. This would be a regulation perfectly just of itself, and in accordance with the spirit of the Athenian constitution, which did not permit the existence of any irresponsible functionaries. Under the check of such a law, they would be more cautious how they interfered on ordinary occasions with the rights and liberties of their fellow-citizens: but it would not prevent them from taking strong measures for the public safety or advantage, when necessity required it.[1]

APPENDIX IV.

THE COUNCIL OF FIVE HUNDRED.

THE council or senate of five hundred was an executive and deliberative body, appointed to manage various departments of the public business, more especially that which related to the popular assembly. As established by Solon, it consisted of four hundred members, a hundred from each of the four tribes into which the Athenians were then divided: but when the ten tribes were substi-

κερδῶν ἄθικτον τοῦτο βουλευτήριον,
αἰδοῖον, ὀξύθυμον, εὑδόντων ὕπερ
ἐγρηγορὸς φρούρημα γῆς καθίσταμαι.

[1] See Thirlwall's History of Greece, iii. 18, 22; and Whiston's article on the *Areopagus*, in the Archæological Dictionary.

tuted by Clisthenes for the four, the number of counselors was raised to five hundred, fifty being taken from each of the tribes. They were annually chosen by lot—in Solon's time from the three first classes only, but afterwards from the whole body of the people—with no other restriction than that they must be genuine citizens on both the father's and the mother's side, and of the age of thirty. To insure the legal qualification, the counselors elect underwent a scrutiny[1] before the existing council, and if any one was rejected, another was chosen in his room from the same tribe. Having passed the scrutiny, they took an oath to observe the laws and consult for the good of the commonwealth. At the expiration of their year of office they had, like all other functionaries, to render an account of their official conduct to the auditors: and during the term any one was liable to be expelled by his colleagues for misbehavior.

For the more convenient dispatch of business, the tribes apportioned the year among them, and took the duties in rotation. The council was thus divided into ten bodies of fifty men, who were called *Prytanes*, or Presidents, and who for the time represented the whole council. Their term of office was called a *Prytany*, or Presidency. As the lunar year at Athens consisted of 354 days, it was so arranged, that there were six *Prytanies* of thirty-five days each, and four of thirty-six, the supernumerary days being assigned to the four last *Prytanies*. This was a little modified in intercalated years. The turns were determined by lot. From the *Prytanes* again were taken for every seven days of their term of office an executive committee, called *Proedri*. They had an *Epistates*, or chairman, chosen for each of the seven days, by whom were kept the public records and seal.

Besides the committee thus taken from the presiding tribe, the chairman had to form a committee of nine counselors from the other tribes, choosing one from each by lot. This mixed commitee attended all the meetings of the council and the assembly, and nothing could be done without their sanction. The object of this regulation was, to give the other tribes a check upon the presiding tribe. And it appears that in later times the mixed committee performed the duties anciently appropriated to the committee of the single tribe; which was a better arrangement.[2]

The council was to be, according to Solon's design, a sort of directorial committee, to assist the people in their deliberations, and to guide and control their acts in assembly. It was their duty to discuss beforehand, and also to prepare and draw up in proper form, the measures that were to be submitted to the people, whether they emanated from themselves, or were proposed by any private indi-

[1] Δοκιμασία.

[2] Such is the explanation of Schömann. De Comitiis, p. 84. Antiquitates Juris Publici, p. 217.

viduals. This afforded some guarantee, that no ill-considered measures would be brought before the assembly. The proposition to be introduced, having received the sanction of the council, was called a *Probouleuma*, a decree or order of council, and when it was ratified by the assembly, it became a *Psephisma*,[1] or decree of the people. Thus, as we have seen, Ctesiphon's decree in honor of Demosthenes first passed the council, and afterwards the assembly. It would have been impossible however, in a democracy such as that of Athens became, to adhere to the ancient rule, which required every decree moved in the assembly to have been first approved by the council. This therefore was soon dispensed with. Amendments were proposed during the discussion of a bill, which the people could adopt if they pleased. And any citizen was at liberty to move a decree, upon first applying to the committee of council, and either getting them to prepare it for him, or obtaining their assent to it as prepared by himself. The form of the ancient practice was thus still preserved; for every motion was made through the council, though they might not actually have formed an opinion of its merits. And if it appeared to the committee of council, that any motion was objectionable, either in point of form or on more serious grounds, they might refuse to bring it before the assembly; for which refusal, if improper, they would of course be responsible to the people.

It was the business of the *Prytanes* in general to convene the popular assembly, and to give public notice of the business to be transacted. Their committee attended with the chairman and presided over it. They proposed the subject of discussion; caused to be read by the usher any bill which had been proposed; permitted the orators to speak; put the question to the assembly; and took the votes.[2]

Besides preparing questions for the general assembly, the council had a right to issue ordinances of their own, which, if not set aside by the people, remained in force for the year. And sometimes, for the sake of convenience, the people specially delegated to the Council of Five Hundred, as they did to the Areopagus, extraordinary powers, which they could not have ventured to exercise of their own authority. Of this we have seen an example in the case of the embassy to Philip, when the council issued that order, which Demosthenes complains of his colleagues for disobeying.[3]

The executive duties of the council were very numerous. The

[1] But the decree of the council was called sometimes *Ψήφισμα*.

[2] They were said—*χρηματίζειν* (to open the business of the assembly); *γνώμας προτιθέναι* (to give leave to address the assembly); *ἐπιψηφίζειν*, or *ἐπιχειροτονίαν διδόναι* (to put the question to the vote). De Schömann, De Comitiis, 89, 91, 120; Ant. Juris Publici, 221. For more on the subject of the Assembly, see the following Appendix.

[3] See ante, p. 306.

whole financial department of the administration was under their control. They superintended the letting of the public revenues.[1] They exacted payment from the lessees, and had power to send defaulters to prison. The collectors and receivers accounted to them for the public moneys. The treasurers of the revenue received the moneys handed over to them by their predecessors in the presence of some members of the council. In every *Prytany* an account of the revenue was laid by the council before the people.

They had the charge of building a certain number of galleys every year; and of rewarding those captains who had been most expeditious in the equipping and launching of their vessels. It was their peculiar duty to see that the horsemen whom the city maintained were properly trained and exercised, and their horses kept in good condition. And they attended in some measure to the musters of infantry and seamen.

We have seen that the counselors of the year examined the counselors elect as to their qualification for office. They had also to examine the archons elect, to see whether they were qualified by law, and worthy in all respects to undertake that important magistracy. Any citizen might come before them to show grounds of disqualification; and the council might hear arguments on both sides, and send the case, if they pleased, to be determined by a court of justice. The speech of Lysias against Evander is an example of a case of this kind heard before the council.

Impeachments[2] for any grave misdemeanors, which could not so well be dealt with by the ordinary processes of law, might be preferred to the council, who took cognizance of them in the first instance, and could themselves impose a penalty not exceeding five hundred drachms; but if the offense demanded a heavier punishment, they had to bring it before the popular assembly or a jury.

The council sat every day in the year, except holidays, for the transaction of business. To the multifarious character of their occupations Xenophon bears testimony in a remarkable passage in his treatise on the Athenian republic, as follows:

"I find some persons complain, that a man may wait a twelvemonth at Athens before he can get an audience of the council or the people. The fact is, they have so much to do at Athens, they are obliged to send away some without hearing them. How could it be otherwise, when they have more festivals to keep than any city in Greece, during which it is not easy to dispatch public business; and they have more lawsuits, prosecutions, and audits, than all the rest of the world? The council has a multitude of questions to consider, about war, about supplies of money, about the passing of laws, about

[1] A board of officers, called Πωλῆται, acted under their superintendence.

[2] Εἰσαγγελίαι.

the daily affairs of the city and those of their allies. They have also to receive tribute, and attend to the arsenals and the service of the temples. Is it at all wonderful, that, with so many occupations, they are not able to transact business with every body?"

The council-chamber was open to the public, and strangers sometimes attended to hear their consultations,[1] but might be directed to withdraw.

To assist them, the council had two secretaries; one[2] of whom was chosen for each presidency, whose business it was to keep the decrees and other records drawn up during that particular term; and another,[3] elected for the whole year, who had custody of the laws. There was also a checking-clerk,[4] whose especial duty it was to take an account of the moneys received by his employers. And these doubtless had under-clerks[5] to assist them.

The members received two drachms a day for their services, besides dinner at the public cost in the Prytaneum, or city-hall, which was close to the council-chamber.[6] During their year of office they were exempt from military service: and, as a further mark of distinction, principal places in the theatre were assigned to them. At their meetings they wore a wreath of myrtle; and at the end of the year, if they had given satisfaction, it was customary for the people to reward the whole body with a golden crown.

APPENDIX V.

THE POPULAR ASSEMBLY.

THE will of the sovereign people of Athens was expressed in the *Ecclesia*, or Assembly. Here were brought before them all matters which, as the supreme power of the state, they had to order or dispose of; questions of war and peace, treaties and alliances, levying of troops, raising of supplies, application of the revenue, religious ordinances, bestowing of citizenship and other honors, privileges, or rewards: likewise, the revision of the laws, the election of a great

[1] See an example, ante, p. 127.
[2] *Γραμματεὺς κατὰ Πρυτανείαν*. See, as to this officer and the others mentioned below, Schömann, De Comitiis, 319, 320.
[3] *Γραμματεὺς τῆς βουλῆς*.
[4] *'Αντιγραφεὺς τῆς βουλῆς*.
[5] *'Υπογραμματεῖς*.
[6] As to the Prytaneum, see ante, p. 130.

variety of magistrates and public functionaries, embassadors or other persons intrusted with special commissions; impeachments and informations for treason and high misdemeanors, which they either determined finally themselves, or sent before a judicial tribunal. Indeed, there was no question which could not ultimately be dealt with by the assembled people, if they chose to exert their plenary authority, though by the ordinary constitutional practice the duties of the Ecclesia were pretty well defined.

Anciently the people used to assemble once only in each Prytany, or ten times a year. After the democracy had grown stronger, and the business to be done by the whole people increased in magnitude and importance, they met four times in each Prytany. These were called the ordinary or regular assemblies.[1] On what days they were held, is not known; but it is thought they varied in the different terms.[2] The Athenians avoided meeting on holidays or unlucky[3] days. Assemblies, however, might be convened for other besides the regular days, if any emergency required it. These were called extraordinary.[4]

The Assembly used anciently to be held in the market-place. Afterwards it was transferred to the Pnyx,[5] and at a later period to the theatre of Bacchus. But it might be held any where, either in the city, or the Piræus, or elsewhere. The Pnyx, which was the common place of meeting in the time of Thucydides and Demosthenes, was an open semicircular piece of ground, opposite the Areopagus. It was naturally on an incline; but to make it level, the lower end was raised by a stone pavement.[6] Here was the entrance for the people.[7] The other end was skirted by a wall, from the centre of which projected the *Bema*, or speaker's platform, which was cut out of solid rock[8] ten feet from the ground, and to which there was

[1] *Κυρίαι*, or *νόμιμοι*.

[2] See Schömann, De Comitiis, chapters i. and ii.: Antiq. Juris Publici, p. 219.

[3] *Ἀποφράδες*. *Nefasti*, as the Romans would say.

[4] *Σύγκλητοι*.

[5] Hence the joke in the Knights of Aristophanes, where *Demus* (the impersonation of the Athenian people, like our John Bull) is called *Δῆμος Πυκνίτης*, *Demus of Pnyx*, as if the Pnyx were a township which gave him his legal addition.

[6] Hence the name of the Pnyx, according to Suidas, *παρὰ τὴν τῶν λίθων πυκνότητα* (on account of its being thickly paved with stones). Others have thought it took its name from the dense congregation of people.

[7] Hence the expression, *ἀναβαίνειν εἰς τὴν ἐκκλησίαν* (because they had to ascend). See ante, p. 68.

[8] Hence it is called, *the stone*, in Aristophanes, Pax, 680:

Ὅστις κρατεῖ νῦν τοῦ λίθου τοῦ 'ν τῇ Πνυκί.

an ascent by eight steps. There were stone seats for the people next the wall, and wooden benches in the middle.

The assemblies were usually convened by the presidents of the council, who published a notice four days before, specifying the day of meeting and the business to be transacted.[1] Extraordinary assemblies were called by the generals. All citizens of the age of twenty, who had been duly registered, were entitled to attend and vote. In early times it was considered by the greater number of them a burden rather than a privilege, as we may see by the regulations adopted to enforce attendance. A crier went round on the day to collect the citizens. Those who absented themselves were liable to a fine, which six officers called *Lexiarchs* were authorized to enforce. The police carried a rope stained with ruddle round the market and other public places; with this they drove the idlers to the assembly, or marked them if they would not go; at the same time blocking up the passages, to prevent their getting away.[3] To encourage the attendance of the poorer citizens, a regulation was introduced by Pericles, allowing a fee of an obol to those who came early. This was afterwards increased to three obols. A ticket was given to them on entrance, which entitled them afterwards to demand their fee from the Thesmothetæ. The Lexiarchs took care, after the business had begun, to keep the voters from coming out, and prevent the intrusion of strangers.

The assembly was presided over by the Proedri, that is, the committee of the tribe in office, assisted by the mixed committee, as before mentioned.[4] They sat on the steps before the speaker's platform, and maintained order among the people, with the assistance of the police, who were at hand to remove either from the platform or the seats any person who violated the prescribed rules, or offended against decency or propriety. They had power to impose on the instant a fine of fifty drachms: graver offences were referred to the council or the next assembly. At a later period a further regulation was adopted, owing to the outrageous conduct of Timarchus, who made an assault with his fists upon some of those about him. A special body of men was appointed for every assembly day, to sit in the front benches, and assist the presiding counselors in keeping order. Each tribe took its turn of making the appointment.[5]

[1] Hence the expressions, *προγράφειν ἐκκλησίαν*, *προτιθέναι ἐκκλησίαν*.

[2] Provided they were not under *ἀτιμία*. The age, Schömann thinks, was eighteen. (De Comitiis, 76.)

[3] Aristophanes, Acharn. 22:

Οἱ δ' ἐν ἀγορᾷ λαλοῦσι κἄνω καὶ κάτω
Τὸ σχοινίον φεύγουσι τὸ μεμιλτωμένον.

[4] See the last Appendix.

[5] Hence called, *ἡ προεδρεύουσα φυλή*. Schömann, De Comitiis, 88.

Before the business of the day commenced, a sacrifice of purification was offered. The lustral victims were young pigs, whose blood was carried round and sprinkled on the seats,[1] while at the same time incense was burned in a censer. The crier then pronounced a form of prayer and commination, of imploring the gods to bless and prosper the consultations of the people, and imprecating a curse upon all enemies and traitors.[2]

The chairman then opened the business of the day. If any bill had been prepared by the council, it was read by the crier or usher, and the people were asked if it met their approbation. If there was no opposition, it passed. Any citizen, however, might oppose it, or move an amendment. If the council had no decree framed by themselves, any citizen might propose one on the instant: it was necessary only that it should be in writing and in a proper form. He then delivered it to the presiding committee, to be read as a motion to the assembly; and if the committee saw nothing objectionable in it, they complied with his request. Cases occurred, where some one or more members of the committee opposed the reading of a motion, as being either illegal, or grossly improper, or irrelevant to the question before them. They were responsible, however, to the people, if they threw any vexatious impediment in the way of a citizen moving a decree; and sometimes the assembly itself would insist upon the question being put to them, notwithstanding the veto of the counselors. Æschines in his speech on the Embassy gives us an example. He says that Aleximachus moved a decree, authorizing the deputy of Cersobleptes to take the oath of peace to Philip; that the decree was delivered to the committee, and read to the assembly; that Demosthenes, being one of the committee, got up and declared he would not allow the question to be put; the people, however, were clamorous on the other side, and he was obliged to yield.[3]

Every member of the assembly was at liberty to speak, but only once in the debate. According to the institution of Solon, those who were above fifty years old were first called upon, and afterwards the younger men. But this custom fell into disuse. We find Demosthenes alluding to it in the opening of the first Philippic. Although all citizens had the right of speaking, the privilege was of course exercised by a few only, who felt themselves competent to the task; and in the time of Demosthenes, when rhetoric was studied as a science, the debates were mostly confined to a few practiced orators and statesmen, as they are generally elsewhere.[4]

[1] Young pigs were considered by the Athenians to have peculiarly expiatory powers.

[2] See ante, p. 102.

[3] See Schömann, De Comitiis, 119.

[4] Hence the *ῥήτορες* or *δημήγοροι* are distinguished from the *ἰδιῶται*, or general body of citizens, who took no part in the debates. They are

Whoever rose to speak, put on a wreath of myrtle, as a token that he was performing a public duty, and entitled on that account to respect. It was a breach of decorum to interrupt the speaker; yet one which it must have been impossible to prevent, except where it proceeded from a small number of persons. How Demosthenes was put down by the clamors of Philocrates and others, he himself describes.[1]

When the debate was ended, the chairman put the question to the vote. The method of voting was either by show of hands,[2] or by ballot.[3] Show of hands was the most common. The ballot was resorted to in a few cases, where it was expedient to ascertain the number of voters as accurately as possible, or to insure secrecy. These were chiefly cases of *privilegia*, such as ostracism and condemnation of state criminals, granting of citizenship or exemption from taxes, or restoration of the franchise. In all those cases the law required that there should be at least six thousand voters in favor of the motion. Generally speaking, however, the questions before the assembly were decided by a majority of votes. The chairman declared the numbers.[4]

When all the business was concluded, the crier by command of the presidents dismissed the assembly. If the business could not be finished in one day, it might be adjourned to the next day, or to the one after.[5] This happened sometimes on a sudden shower of rain or a thunder-storm. Any thing of this sort was considered as an unlucky omen among the Greeks.[6]

A decree having been carried by the votes of the people, it was copied on a tablet, and deposited by the secretary among other public records in the temple of Cybele.[7] Sometimes it was engraved on brass or stone, and set up in a conspicuous place, to be seen by

not to be confounded with the *συνήγοροι*, or public advocates; as to whom, see the seventh Appendix.

[1] See ante, p. 128.

[2] *Χειροτονία.*

[3] *Ψῆφος.*

[4] He was said, *ἀναγορεῦειν τὰς χειροτονίας.*

[5] Aristophanes, Acharn. 171:

> *τοὺς Θρᾴκας ἀπιέναι, παρεῖναι δ' εἰς ἕνην.*
> *οἱ γὰρ Πρυτάνεις λύουσι τὴν ἐκκλησίαν.*

[6] Such a phenomenon was called *διοσημία.* Any individual might call the attention of the presidents to the occurrence; as Dicæopolis does in the Acharnians, 168:

> *ἀλλ' ἀπαγορεύω μὴ ποιεῖν ἐκκλησίαν*
> *τοῖς Θρᾳξὶ περὶ μισθοῦ· λέγω δ' ὑμῖν ὅτι*
> *διοσημία 'στι, καὶ ῥανὶς βέβληκέ με.*

[7] *Τὸ Μητρῷον.*

all. As to the form in which decrees were drawn up, the reader may consult Schömann.[1] The mover's name was usually inserted, he being responsible for the measure, as we shall presently see.

We have to distinguish between decrees and laws,[2] in the Athenian sense. Decrees are measures of government, relating to particular matters or occasions; as for example, the election of magistrates, or the punishment of offenders; a declaration of war, or a resolution to make peace. They had indeed the force of laws for the time being, so far as regarded the obedience due to them. But by laws we are to understand the permanent institutions and ordinances of the commonwealth, by which every man knows how he is governed, and what are his franchises and rights. How these might be enacted and repealed at Athens, is explained in a following appendix.

APPENDIX VI.

THE OPINION OF POLYBIUS.

POLYBIUS, in the seventeenth book of his history, defends against the attack of Demosthenes those Greek statesmen, especially of Messene and Megalopolis, who took the Macedonian side in politics, and dissuaded their countrymen from taking arms against Philip.[3] The passage is as follows:—

"Demosthenes, deserving as he is of praise in many respects, must be condemned for the reckless and indiscriminate manner in which he reviles the most eminent Greek statesmen; saying, that in Arcadia, Cercidas and Hieronymus and Eucampidas were traitors to Greece, because they joined alliance with Philip; in Messene, the sons of Philiades, Neon and Thrasylochus; in Argos, Myrtis and Teledamus and Mnaseas: likewise in Thessaly, Daochus and Cineas, and among the Bœotians, Theogiton and Timolaus. And besides these, he has given a long list of others, with their names and countries. Now all the above-mentioned statesmen have good and ample grounds of justification for their conduct, but especially those of Arcadia and Messene. For they, having invited Philip into Peloponnesus and humbled the Lacedæmonians, gave repose and security to all the inhabitants of the Peninsula: further, by recovering the

[1] De Comitiis, c. 12.

[2] Ψηφίσματα and νόμοι.

[3] The principal passages of Demosthenes will be found ante, 23, 25, 29, 106, 109, 209.

territory and towns, which the Lacedæmonians in their days of prosperity had taken from the Messenians, Megalopolitans, Tegeans and Argives, they unquestionably promoted the welfare of their countries. So far therefore from going to war with Philip and the Macedonians, they were bound to use every exertion to increase their honor and glory. I grant, if at the same time they received a garrison in their countries from Philip, or overturned the laws and deprived their fellow-citizens of their rights and liberties, from motives of avarice or ambition, they deserved the reproach cast upon them. But if in the honest discharge of their duty as citizens they differed in judgment with Demosthenes, not considering the interests of Athens and of their own countries to be identical, surely he ought not to have called them traitors on that account. Measuring every thing by the interests of his own commonwealth, and thinking that all the Greeks should have looked up to the Athenians or else be stigmatized as traitors, it seems to me, he has taken a very wrong and mistaken view. My opinion is confirmed by the events that happened in Greece, which show that the true foresight was exercised, not by Demosthenes, but by Eucampidas and Hieronymus and Cercidas and the sons of Philiades. For the Athenians by their contest with Philip incurred signal disasters, being defeated in battle at Chæronea; and, but for the king's magnanimity and regard for his own honor, they would have suffered still more grievously than they did through the counsels of Demosthenes; whereas those other statesmen enabled the confederate Arcadians to enjoy perfect security against Lacedæmon, from which their respective countries reaped many important advantages."

If Demosthenes has been too severe upon the Greek statesmen, Polybius has not been quite just to Demosthenes. Polybius, looking at the state of Greece in his own time, argues as if the struggle against Philip was desperate, forgetting that it was rendered so by the very supineness and want of combination of which Demosthenes complains. Had the Athenians been assisted at Chæronea by such a force of Peloponnesians as afterwards battled with Antipater, Greece might have been saved. Again:—the facts of the case are not exactly as Polybius represents them. Messene and Megalopolis were capable of defending themselves against Sparta without Philip's protection. Even if it were not so, they but exchanged one master for another. Though they might not feel the weight of his yoke immediately, it was a yoke destined to gall them at no distant time. The humiliation of Sparta was a poor consolation to freemen who were humiliated themselves. The congress of Corinth and Philip's victorious progress through Peloponnesus, are evidences to the world that Grecian independence was gone. The Peloponnesians follow Alexander to his wars, as they had anciently followed Sparta, but less in the character of allies than of vassals. Alexander insults and terrifies them by his edicts. A tyranny is established in Messene. The Arcadians gain neither security nor repose by their fidelity to a foreign potentate. Two bloody wars, and Megalopolis twice besieged, first by Agis, and afterwards by Polysperchon, are the speedy and bitter fruits of Macedonian protection; disproving the foresight which Polybius claims for his countrymen.[1]

It is true, that grievous faults were committed both by Sparta and Athens. Sparta should have abandoned her pretensions to Messenia and her aggressive designs against her neighbors. Athens (not to speak of other errors) missed an excellent opportunity of gathering to her side a Peloponnesian confederacy, when the Megalopolitans solicited her aid against Sparta in the year B.C. 353. She should then have stood boldly forward, and declared that she would not permit Sparta to threaten the independence of her neighbors. This was what Demosthenes advised. The Athenians chose a timid course, which was not forgotten when she herself needed assistance. Unfortunately, the patriotism of the Greeks, in general, was too narrow, and their wisdom too short-sighted, to perceive that the cause of Athens against Philip was their own.

Polybius himself, in reference to the conduct of the Messenians at a later period, reasons more justly.[2] Censuring generally that policy which is determined to have peace at any sacrifice, he says the Messenians had been guilty of such an error; and the consequence was, that, although they escaped some trouble and danger for the time, they incurred still greater misfortunes in the end. Having two powerful people for their neighbors—the Lacedæmonians and the Arcadians; the former of whom nourished an implacable hostility against them, while the latter were their friends and well-wishers—the Messenians did not meet either the enmity of the one, or the friendship of the other, with a generous and brave spirit. When their neighbors were at war, the Messenians kept aloof, and, as their country lay out of the way, they were free from annoyance. But when the Lacedæmonians had nothing else to do, they attacked the Messenians, who had not the courage to resist by themselves, and through their system of neutrality were deprived of auxiliaries.

He goes on to declare that, if there should be a new revolution in Peloponnesus, the only chance of safety for the Messenians and Megalopolitans would be, to form an intimate union for mutual protection, according to the original design of Epaminondas, and to stand firmly and faithfully by one another in all difficulties and dangers.

Jacobs has expressed his opinion to the following effect, in the preface to his translation of Demosthenes:—

"The patriotic feelings which inspired Demosthenes were not

[1] Polybius was a Megalopolitan.

[2] Lib. iv. 32, 33.

equally felt by all the leading statesmen in Greece; but these feelings did not allow him always to be just towards men, who, being placed in different circumstances from himself, espoused a different line of politics. He frequently complains of the number of traitors, who sprang up like a crop of weeds in the states and cities of Greece, and attached themselves to the interests of Macedonia. If the words of the orator are to be taken in their literal sense, there must have been such a depth of corruption among the Greeks, that Heaven itself could not have saved them. There can be no doubt that Philip, in order to rule by division, availed himself of the party strife which prevailed as well at Athens as in most of the other states; and that he fomented it, both by his gold, and by the skillful manner in which he flattered the passions of the political antagonists. Even republican Greeks were not insensible to the favor of a crowned head, especially if polished speech and manner lent their influence to captivate them:[1] and it is probable enough, that many men of the best intentions were caught in this net, without being in the least degree conscious that their acts were treasonable. Where party spirit prevails, the judgments of men are necessarily one-sided. Every man thinks his own views alone are just, and looks upon one of different sentiments as an enemy to the good cause for which he is striving. That which at first is a contest of opinions becomes at length a contest of passions; which in their zeal for the cause which they espouse finds an excuse even for lawless violence. So in relation to Athens, it appears to me, that what Demosthenes so vehemently denounces as a crime, is, in regard to many of the accused parties, to be viewed in a milder light, as an error of party; and we would fain believe, for the honor of the Athenian people, that the greater number of the Philippising citizens intended to render the best service to their country. With reference to the friends of Philip in other states, especially the Peloponnesian, whom Demosthenes stigmatizes as traitors, the judgment of Polybius appears by no means unfair."

He then cites the following remarks of Valckenaer:—

"Proditorum atrum catalogum ex ingenio suo Demosthenes amplificavit: nam inter illos, quos Atticus orator turpi hôc nomine dehonestavit, fuisse credibile est, non pecuniâ sed humanitate regis captos, qui hujus imperium anteponerent speciosæ libertati quæ dice-

[1] Compare, Justin, ix. 8; who says of Philip—"Blandus pariter et insidiosus alloquio; qui plura promitteret quam præstaret; in seria et jocos artifex. Amicitias utilitate, non fide colebat. Gratiam fingere in odio, instruere in concordantes odia, apud utrumque gratiam quærere, solemnis illi consuetudo. Inter hæc eloquentia et insignis oratio, acuminis et solertiæ plena; ut nec oratui facilitas, nec facilitati inventionum deesset ornatus." And Cicero, De Officiis, i. 26—"Philippum rebus gestis et gloriâ superatum à filio, facilitate et humanitate video superiorem fuisse."

batur, et supurbis dominis, plebi, quique plebem ducerent concionatoribus."

This is but a sorry defense for traitorous correspondence with the enemy. Such arguments would justify any kind of treason. What the Philippising party gained by exchanging plebeian rule for Macedonian, is shown by the fate of Demades and Phocion.

APPENDIX VII.

REVISION OF LAWS.

THE enactment of laws (distinguished from decrees, as mentioned in Appendix V.) was not left by Solon to the people at large, but confided to a select body of them under an arrangement which has drawn praise from many modern critics and historians. That wise legislator was anxious to secure the stability of his institutions, knowing that laws which have been consecrated by long usage are more readily and cheerfully obeyed:[1] while on the other hand he foresaw, that the best constitution in the world might in course of time require amendment and adaptation to existing circumstances. Under the democracy which he created there would have been a danger of exposing the laws to perpetual change, had it been left to the multitude, upon the motion of any demagogue suddenly rising in the Assembly, to make and unmake statutes at their pleasure. He therefore so contrived matters, that, while his laws were subject to constant revision, a check should be put upon crude and hasty legislation.

There were annually chosen by lot six thousand citizens, of not less than thirty years of age, who formed a judicial court called Heliæa,[2] and whose functions corresponded in great measure with those of our jurymen. From them were taken not only the ordinary juries for the trial of civil and criminal causes, but also a select body of men called *Nomothetæ*, or law-revisors,[3] to whom the people referred

[1] This is a truth frequently enunciated both by ancient and modern philosophers. Compare Aristotle, Politic. ii.: *'Ο γὰρ νόμος ἰσχὺν οὐδεμίαν ἔχει πρὸς τὸ πείθεσθαι, πλὴν παρὰ τὸ ἔθος· τοῦτο δὲ οὐ γίνεται, εἰ μὴ διὰ χρόνου πλῆθος· ὥστε τὸ ῥᾳδίως μεταβάλλειν ἐκ τῶν νόμων εἰς ἑτέρους νόμους καινοὺς, ἀσθενῆ ποιεῖν ἐστὶ τὴν τοῦ νόμου δύναμιν.* And Thucydides, iii. 37: *Χείροσι νόμοις ἀκινήτοις χρωμένη πόλις κρείσσων ἐστὶν ἢ καλῶς ἔχουσιν ἀκύροις.*

[2] *'Ηλιαία* (an assembly). The whole body were called *Heliastæ.*

[3] The term *νομοθέτης* (legislator) was given *κατ' ἐξοχὴν* to Solon.

all questions of legislation that came before them. And further, if any new statute had been passed by these law-revisors, it might be impeached before a jury taken from the same Heliastic body, who had power to determine finally whether such statute should be abrogated or confirmed. The method of proceeding was as follows:—

It was a part of the business in the first ordinary assembly, which was held on the eleventh of Hecatombæon, to consider the state of the laws, and to receive proposals for their amendment. Any citizen was at liberty to make such proposal, having previously obtained leave from the council: but in order to insure a constant revision of the laws, the Thesmothetæ[1] of each year were directed to examine the whole code, and to see if there were any statutes contradictory, or useless, or improper to be retained. The people heard whatever proposal either these magistrates or any private citizen had to offer for an alteration in the law; and if they deemed it worthy of further consideration, they consented that it should be referred to a court of revisors, and they elected five advocates[2] to defend the old law against the new one. A fair copy of the new law was put up before the statues of the Heroes,[3] that every man might have an opportunity of seeing it: and to give it still further publicity, it was read aloud in every assembly before the revisors held their court. The third of the ordinary assemblies (towards the end of the month Hecatombæon (was appointed for the election of the revisors; of which notice was to be given by the presidents of the council; and the committee of council were directed (under severe penalties in case of neglect) to consult the people as to the number of persons to be elected, and as to their remuneration, duties, and term of office, which of course depended chiefly upon the amount of business to come before them. The number of the revisors was commonly about a thousand; but it might be more or less.

The various legislative questions referred by the people were tried on particular days appointed for each. The revisors were impaneled like a jury; though their court very much resembled a popular assembly, the presidents of the council being there as assessors, and the committee presiding with their chairman. Arguments were addressed to the court with the same formalities as upon a legal trial,

But it was applicable to any individual who moved the passing of a law; and clearly the whole legislative body might properly be so called. The court of the νομοθέται at Athens was peculiarly constituted, having no power of originating laws, and being judicial rather than legislative in our sense of the term; and there was, in effect, an appeal from them. They may aptly be styled revisors of the laws.

[1] As to this, see Schömann, De Comitiis, 259.

[2] Σύνδικοι, or συνήγοροι.

[3] Called Eponymi, Ἐπώνυμοι, because they gave name to the ten tribes. Their statues were in front of the council-chamber.

first by the supporters of the new law, next by the defenders of the old; and to prevent collusion, any one might appear as defender, besides the advocates specially chosen for that purpose. After hearing all that could be said on both sides, the question was put by the chairman, and the revisors decided by show of hands, whether the old law should stand, or the new be accepted. Their judgment was drawn up in the shape of a decree; and if the new law was passed, it became forthwith a binding statute, subject however to be impeached in the manner to be mentioned presently.

Thus we see, while all law-making orginated with the people, and the humblest citizens were at liberty to propose new enactments, the task of examining them at leisure, and considering all the questions to which they might give rise, was delegated to a superior tribunal, clothed with a judicial character, and more capable of exercising a calm and deliberate judgment on such matters than the full assembly of Athenian citizens.

That the general scheme was due to the genius of Solon we are expressly assured, though it is most probable that improvements were made in the details since his time. And here it may be observed, generally, with respect to the Attic laws, which are quoted by the orators and attributed by them to Solon, that we must not suppose all the extracts which they cite to be the actual words of the ancient law-giver: for not only did they receive additions and amendments from time to time, but it is very likely, as Schömann suggests,[1] that when the code was remodeled, after the expulsion of the Thirty Tyrants, or possibly upon some other occasion, the antiquated phraseology of Solon's time was translated into the language of the day. In a few years it would become difficult to distinguish what part of the code belonged to Solon, and what to a later period; and so the whole body of statutes were, both by orators and other persons, commonly spoken of as the laws of Solon.

Besides the regular time of holding the courts of revision, the people might, doubtless, if they pleased, appoint them to be held on extraordinary occasions. One such occasion happened after the expulsion of the Thirty Tyrants, who, having abolished many of Solon's laws, and corrupted them by interpolations, it was thought advisable to restore and remodel the ancient code; and a decree was passed authorizing the council to select a body of men to frame the necessary amendments, and send them afterwards to be considered by a court of revision in the usual way. We find Demosthenes, in his Olynthiac oration, recommending the appointment of revisors, for the special purpose of repealing the laws concerning the theoric fund.[2] One of the charges against Timocrates is, that he induced the people to appoint revisors out of the usual time. For thus the

[1] De Comitiis, 267.
[2] See Vol. I. p. 54; and Schömann, De Comitiis, 270, 271.

thing really stood:—It was competent for the people to pass a decree dispensing with the regular course of law; and it was impossible to call them to account for it. But, as in our own country, the maxim that the king can do no wrong does not shield from responsibility the minister who advises him, so at Athens, the author of an unconstitutional measure was not protected by the fiat of the sovereign people who decreed it. And this brings us to another important branch of the subject, viz., the proceeding by indictment against the movers of bad laws.[1]

As a further precaution against rash legislation, a power was given, after the passing of a law by the court of revision, to indict the author of it at any time within a year, and thus to procure both his punishment and the repeal of the law itself. The law might be impugned either for matter of form, as for the omission of some necessary step in the procedure; or upon the merits, as being inconsistent with some other law that was not repealed, or opposed to the general spirit of the Athenian laws, or for any cause whatever, mischievous in its tendency, or adverse to the interests of the commonwealth. Any citizen was at liberty to prefer an indictment against the author of a new law, alleging it to be bad in any of these respects. The case was then brought for trial before a jury, taken from the same Heliastic body, who reviewed the law once more, examining it in all its bearings upon the rest of the Athenian code, and the general welfare of the state. If they thought it open to the charges made against it, or any of them, they gave their verdict accordingly, pronouncing the law to be bad and void, and sentencing the author to such penalty as the nature of the case deserved. After the expiration of the year, although the author could not be punished, the law itself might still be impeached before a jury; but in such case the people appointed advocates to defend it. Of this the oration of Demosthenes against the law of Leptines is an example. The law, which prohibited all exemptions from public services, was repealed as being unjust and derogatory to the dignity of Athens; but Leptines himself was safe by the lapse of time.[2]

The same proceeding might be instituted to rescind illegal or improper decrees, which had been passed in the popular assembly, and to punish the movers of them. As there was a greater facility of procuring decrees than laws, so, it appears, the indictments preferred in these cases were much more numerous; and, in impugning a decree, every possible ground of objection might be taken, in regard either to legality or expediency. Very frequently, prosecution was but a method of trying the question over again, or perhaps of punishing the author for the evil consequences of his measure. We

[1] Γραφὴ παρανόμων.

[2] See Vol. I. Appendix V. p. 314. Schömann, De Comitiis, 278—280.

have seen that Aristophon was seventy-five times indicted for having moved improper decrees, and every time acquitted, Cephalus, on the other hand, boasted that he had never once been indicted.[1] To prevent vexatious prosecutions, the accuser, if he failed to obtain a fifth part of the votes, was liable to a fine of a thousand drachms, and was rendered incapable of bringing any such accusation in future.

Divers examples, illustrating this Athenian practice, are furnished by the orators.

Timocrates passed a law, allowing public debtors to be released on bail. Diodorus indicted him on these (among other) grounds—that he had not obtained the sanction of the council before he introduced his law to the people: that he had got the court of revision to be appointed for the twelfth of Hecatombæon, immediately after the first assembly, instead of waiting for the regular time, and that he had never put up his law in the usual way for public perusal: that it was contrary to other existing laws: and that it was bad on the merits. From the speech composed by Demosthenes in support of the prosecution we get most of our information upon the subject of the *Nomothetæ*. And here we find him complaining of a practice which had grown up, in contravention of Solon's regulation; whereby legislative measures were brought before the popular assembly out of the appointed time, and the people were persuaded to pass them in the shape of decrees. It is clear, as I have before observed, that the people could allow this to be done as often as they pleased: public opinion alone could effectually check it, by insuring the condemnation, in a court of justice, of the demagogue who misled the assembly.[2]

The case of Aristocrates, indicted for his decree in favor of Charidemus, is a memorable example; of which I have spoken elsewhere.[3] But the most familiar of all is the prosecution of Ctesiphon by Æschines; the grounds of which are fully explained in the argument to the Oration on the Crown, and in the last appendix to this volume.

[1] See ante, pp. 92, 323.

[2] Through this abuse (as Demosthenes says, Adv. Lept. 485,) ψηφισμάτων οὐδ' ὁτιοῦν διαφέρουσιν οἱ νόμοι. See Schömann, De Comitiis, 264, 265, 268, 269.

[3] Vol. I. Appendix III. pp. 282, 283.

APPENDIX VIII.

AFFAIRS OF PELOPONNESUS.

After the battle of Mantinea, Peloponnesus, as Demosthenes says, was divided.[1] Sparta could no longer domineer over her neighbors, as she had used to do; yet her enemies were unable to crush her entirely. The oligarchical states remained still attached to her—Corinth, Phlius, Epidaurus, Trœzen, Elis, and the Achaian cities, excepting Sicyon. But the powerful league originally formed under Theban protection, between the Messenians, Arcadians, and Argives, maintained the balance of power in the peninsula. The independence of Messene was acknowledged by the allies of Sparta at the general peace of B.C. 362. Sparta herself protested against it, refusing to accept as binding an arrangement by which she was humiliated and degraded. For not only was the fairest portion of her territory, which she had held for three centuries, taken away from her;[2] but she saw established on her confines a race of men whom she regarded as slaves and rebels, dangerous from the implacable hostility which they were sure to cherish against their late oppressors, and by the encouragement which they held out for further revolt among the Laconian Helots. But Sparta stood alone in her opposition, and could only protest and wait for better times.[3]

The feelings of the Spartan people upon this subject are pretty well described in the oration of Isocrates, entitled Archidamus; which was, in fact, a pamphlet published to vindicate the title of the Spartans to Messenia, but is in the form of a speech addressed by Archidamus, son of Agesilaus, to his countrymen, and seems to have been composed on the occasion when Corinth, Phlius, and

[1] Demosthenes, De Coron. 231.

[2] The fertility of Messenia, as contrasted with the Laconian soil, is described by the lines of Euripides, cited in Strabo, viii. 366. Of Laconia, he says :—

> πυλλὴν μὲν ἄροτον, ἐκπονεῖν δ' οὐ ῥᾴδιον·
> κοίλη γὰρ, ὄρεσι περίδρομος, τραχεῖά τε
> δυσείσβολός τε πολεμίοις.

Of Messenia :—

> καλλίκαρπον . . . . .
> κατάῤῥυτόν τε μυρίοισι νάμασι,
> καὶ βουσὶ καὶ ποίμναισιν εὐβοτωτάτην,
> οὔτ' ἐν πνοαῖσι χείματος δυσχείμερον,
> οὔτ' αὖ τεθρίπποις ἡλίου θερμὴν ἄγαν.

[3] Pausanias, iv. 27 ; viii. 27. Polybius, iv. 33. Diodorus, xv. 66, 89.

Epidaurus seceded from the Spartan alliance, and made a separate peace with the enemy, B.C. 366.[1] The substance of his advice is as follows:—

He contends that it would be disgraceful to let their revolted slaves retain possession of their land—the allies who urged them to abandon it had given both weak and dishonorable advice—their title to Messenia was unquestionable, being founded not only on length of time, but on a valid gift, confirmed (as he shows from history) by the Pythian oracle—the people who had been planted in Messene were not real Messenians, but Helots and vagabonds—their own cause was just, and they should defend it to the last—great things had been effected by individual Spartans in the defense of other cities, as by Brasidas at Amphipolis, and Gylippus at Syracuse; they should not then despair in the cause of their own country—the sympathies of the Greeks would probably be with them; even the democratized states of Peloponnesus would find they needed Spartan superintendence, for they had got nothing by their defection from Sparta but war, and anarchy, and intestine broils. Should their enemies insist on such hard terms as the emancipation of Messenia, and should the rest of the Greeks give their consent, then he advises his countrymen to remove their parents, wives, and children to Italy, or Sicily, or Cyrene, or some other place of safety, to sally forth from their home, as their ancestors had done in days of yore, to enter the land of their enemies as an invading army, and there to seize upon some stronghold, and commence a war of plunder and devastation, until their enemies would be only too glad to purchase peace by the restoration of Messenia. He argues that it would be impossible for peace to be maintained on the basis desired by their opponents—that the settlement of the Messenians on their confines would lead to perpetual quarrels and disturbances—that it would be such a degradation as Spartans, accustomed to pre-eminence in Greece, could never endure—that it might be well enough for Corinthians, Epidaurians, and Phliasians, to care only for life and safety, but for Spartans death was preferable to dishonor.[2] How could they go without shame to the Olympian and other national festivals: where formerly every individual Spartan was received with as much honor as the victors at the games, but now they would be looked upon with scorn; their revolted slaves would bring from the land which their fathers had bequeathed to them richer offerings than they did, and would insult them in revenge for their past sufferings? From such disgrace he calls upon them to rescue their country; to struggle through their present difficulties, as the Athenians and Thebans had out of theirs; and lastly, to remember that they had

[1] Isocrates, Archidamus, 135. Xenophon, Hellen. vii. c. 4, ss. 8—10.

[2] This passage reminds me of a similar one in Demosthenes, De Synt. 176.

never been defeated, when a king of his line had commanded them.

This singular pamphlet, which the renewal of friendship between Sparta and Athens encouraged Isocrates to publish, produced but little effect. It served as a manifesto to the Grecian world of the feeling, which for many years continued to animate the Spartans; but the coalition against them at this time was too strong to heed any of their threats, much less the desperate one contained in the pamphlet.

The emancipation of Messenia was not the only cause of discontent at Lacedæmon. The Arcadians from attached allies had been converted into jealous and hostile neighbors, and were the more likely to continue so on account of the political revolution which they had undergone. The aristocracies, which had maintained themselves in their respective cities by Spartan influence, and secured the connection of their country with Sparta, had been broken up or reduced to insignificance by the establishment of Megalopolis. To form this new city, designed to be the capital of the united Arcadians, and their barrier against the aggression of Sparta, a population was drawn from forty different communities, chiefly those bordering on Laconia. Of the smaller towns which contributed, some were deserted, others were reduced to villages. The larger cities were left in possession of their local governments, which for ordinary purposes they carried on as before, but they were required to send deputies to a federal congress held in the capital, which exercised a controlling power over all the concerns of the union, and represented the whole Arcadian body in their transactions with foreign states. Of the formation of this congress we know little more than that it was of a democratical character, consisting altogether of ten thousand members sent by the various constituents. From hence it took its name, and was called The Ten-thousand.[1] Heræa and Orchomenus were the only cities which refused to join the union. Tegea had at first opposed it, but through a revolution effected by the popular party she was brought over to the other side. This was a great blow to Sparta: for Tegea had been one of her warmest adherents, and was near to the north-eastern frontier of Laconia. Megalopolis was not far from the north-western: so that Sparta was cut off from her friends in both of those directions.[2]

In the year 363 B.C. dissensions arose in the Arcadian congress, chiefly through the mutual jealousies of the leading cities, though

[1] Οἱ μύριοι; and also τὸ κοινὸν τῶν Ἀρκάδων. Xenophon, Hellen. vii. c. 1, s. 38; c. 4, ss. 2, 35; c. 5, s. 1. Æschines, De Fals. Leg. 38. Demosthenes, De Fals. Leg. 344. Pausanias, vi. 12.

[2] Xenophon, Hellen. vi. c. 4, ss. 6—11, 22. Diodorus, xv. 59, 72. Pausanias, viii. 27; ix. 14.

the immediate cause of dispute was concerning the Olympian treasure which had been taken by the army. An aristocratical party sprang up, adverse both to the federal union and to the Theban alliance. The Mantineans, notwithstanding the zeal with which they had originally promoted the union, took the lead in a counter-movement which would have dissolved it, and sought to renew their connection with the Lacedæmonians, by whom their city had formerly been destroyed. It was owing to the measures taken by this party that Epaminondas led his army for the last time into Peloponnesus, the effect of which was to check the counter-revolution attempted in Arcadia, though the death of that great man prevented the completion of any further designs which he may have had for the settlement of Peloponnesian affairs.[1]

In the year following, however, the disturbances in Arcadia were renewed. Some of the families who had been settled in Megalopolis became dissatisfied with their change of residence; and taking advantage of a clause in the general peace, which ordered all parties to return to their respective countries, (a clause evidently framed with a different view,) they chose to migrate from the capital to their ancient towns. The Megalopolitan government insisted that they should come back: upon which they applied for aid to the Mantineans and other Peloponnesians who had assisted them in the late war. Theban intervention again became necessary; and Pammenes was sent with three thousand foot and three hundred horse to Arcadia. He reduced the malcontents to submission, but not till he had besieged and taken some of their towns; after which they returned quietly to Megalopolis, and the dissensions were appeased.[2]

In the last movement Sparta had not interfered. Her losses in the war with Thebes had greatly exhausted her. To recruit the finances of his country, Agesilaus at the age of eighty went over to Egypt, and engaged in the service first of Tachos, afterwards of Nectanabis, whom he established on the throne, and received a recompense of two hundred and thirty talents. On his return home he was taken ill and died on the coast of Africa.[3] The money was doubtless acceptable at Sparta: yet for the present she was not strong enough to attempt any hostile measures against her neigh-

[1] Xenophon, Hellen. viii. c. 4, ss. 33—40; c. 5, ss. 1—3; Pausanias, viii. 8.

[2] Diodorus, xv. 94. It scarcely needs argument to show that Ἀθηναίους in this passage is a mistake. See Vol. I. p. 209, note 2. Thirlwall, Hist. of Greece, v. 287. Grote, x. 494.

[3] Diodorus, xv. 93. Pausanias, iii. 10. Plutarch, Vit. Agesil. 40. Xenophon, Agesil. ii. 29, &c.; who says that one of the causes of his going to Egypt was, to punish the king of Persia for ordering that Messene should be free.

bors; nor did she receive the least encouragement to do so from her old allies, who were anxious only for neutrality and repose. For nine years after the battle of Mantinea the Peloponnesians enjoyed internal peace, disturbed only by events which happened beyond the peninsula, in which the Spartans alone had a direct interest. I allude to the proceedings of the Sacred War; in which, as we have seen, the only peninsular states that took an active part were the Spartans and Achæans, the latter partly influenced perhaps by their enmity to the Locrians.

Soon after the breaking out of the Sacred War the Spartans began to conceive that it might turn to their private advantage. Fear of the Thebans had in great measure restrained them from attempting to recover their lost dominion. Yet to the hope that they should be able to recover it at some future time they still most tenaciously clung.[1] Archidamus inherited all the courage and ambition of his father, and burned with the desire both to reconquer Messenia, and to break up the federal union, which made Arcadia independent of his country. A great point was gained, if the Thebans, by being employed elsewhere, could be kept away from Peloponnesus.[2] Yet even then Sparta would scarcely with her own force alone be able to accomplish her designs. It was desirable to rally round her as many as possible of her former allies, and attach them to her cause by the bonds of a common interest. To effect this, Archidamus conceived a scheme (which would be more or less attractive to all of them) for a general restitution of rights; by which Athens should recover Oropus, Elis the Triphylian towns, Phlius Tricaranum, and she herself Messene; and further that Orchomenus, Thespiæ, and Platæa, which the Thebans had destroyed, should be re-established, and the Arcadians who wished it restored to their ancient abodes.[3] The announcement of this project was made in the year B.C. 353, when the tide of success had turned so strongly against the Thebans, that they were unable to hold their ground in Bœotia, and it seemed almost impossible that they could spare any troops for the assistance of their friends in Peloponnesus. It soon became known, with what view the Spartans were canvassing their allies; nor could the warlike preparations in Laconia remain a secret. That very year indeed they commenced war against the Argives, whom they defeated, and took the town of Orneæ, probably with a view to cut off their communication with

[1] Xenophon, Hellen. vii. c. 4, s. 9. Polybius, iv. 32.

[2] Their fear of the Thebans is strongly stated by Isocrates, Philipp. 92: *Δεδιότες γὰρ διατελοῦσι μὴ Θηβαῖοι διαλυσάμενοι τὰ πρὸς Φωκέας πάλιν ἐπανελθόντες μείζοσιν αὐτοὺς συμφοραῖς περιβάλωσι τῶν πρότερον γεγενημένων.*

[3] Xenophon, Hellen. vii. c. 1, s. 26; c. 2, s. 1; c. 4, s. 11. Demosthenes, Pro Megalop. 203, 206, 208. And see ante, pp. 246, 261, 271.

Arcadia.[1] The Megalopolitans, alarmed at the danger which threatened them, and having at this time little hope of assistance from Thebes, sent an embassy to Athens, to solicit the protection of the Athenian people. They were supported by envoys from Argos and Messene, and opposed by a counter-embassy from Lacedæmon. A warm debate took place in the Athenian assembly: for an account of which, and especially of the view which Demosthenes took of the question, I may refer to the Oration for the Megalopolitans, and to the argument and notes in the first volume. The result was, that Athens determined to be neutral: a policy unfortunate in its results, as will hereafter appear.[2]

The Megalopolitans, being disappointed of Athenian aid, could only look to Thebes; but affairs took such a turn, that, when the time came, Thebes was able to assist them. The Lacedæmonians in their endeavor to negotiate an offensive alliance entirely failed, both at Athens and in Peloponnesus. This delayed their operations. They may have been promised assistance by Onomarchus, as soon as he could dispose of his enemies in the north. The battle of Pagasæ overthrew such hope, and rendered it necessary for them to send succor into Phocis. But soon afterwards the exertions of Phayllus, together with the support which he received from his allies, enabled him to renew the war in Bœotia. The Lacedæmonians readily seized this opportunity for commencing the long meditated attack upon their neighbors.

Archidamus opened the campaign by invading the Megalopolitan territory, which he ravaged for some time without opposition. The Megalopolitans sent for succor immediately to Argos, Sicyon, and Messene, and also to Thebes. From the three first-mentioned cities a large force was soon collected, and Thebes sent to their aid four thousand infantry and five hundred horse under the command of Cephision. Thus reinforced, they marched out and pitched their camp near the sources of the river Alpheus. Archidamus, instead of attacking them, led his troops off towards Mantinea, and took up a position near that city, which he may have hoped was still friendly to his cause. The allies advancing against him, he marched into Argolis, surprised Orneæ, which appears to have been retaken since his last expedition, and routed a body of Argives who were sent to its relief. But now the united force of the allies came up

[1] Diodorus, xvi. 34.

[2] Pausanias, iv. 28, states that the Athenians promised to assist the Messenians, if their country should be invaded, but declared they would not join them in any invasion of Laconia. If so, they made a distinction between them and the Megalopolitans, whom we know they did not assist. Compare however Demosthenes, Pro Megalop. 204; from which it would rather appear, that the engagement entered into with the Messenians took place before this occasion.

with him, and offered him battle. He had been reinforced by three thousand Phocian mercenaries and a hundred and fifty of the horsemen whom Lycophron had brought from Pheræ: yet his numbers were but half those of the enemy. An obstinate battle was fought, in which the Spartans by their superior discipline made up for the disparity of numbers: both sides, however, claimed the victory. The Argives and other Peloponnesian allies having returned to their homes, as was customary with citizen-troops in Greek warfare, Archidamus took advantage of their absence to renew his ravages in Arcadia, and take by storm the city of Helissus, with the spoils of which he returned to Sparta. Not long afterwards the Thebans and their allies, falling upon Anaxander, who commanded a Lacedæmonian division near Telphusa, defeated and made him prisoner. This battle was followed by two others, in which the Spartans were vanquished with much loss. In the next they gained a victory, which fairly retrieved their honor; but immediately afterwards they retreated to their own country. Archidamus, weary of a contest which promised him no advantage, and in which he had suffered no less damage than his adversaries, made overtures of peace, which the Megalopolitans accepted; and the foreign auxiliaries on both sides retired from Peloponnesus. The ill-advised project of Archidamus had no other effect, than to exhibit the unabated animosity of the Spartans against Megalopolis and Messene.[1]

Not many years after these events the Peloponnesians were apprised, that a more powerful enemy than Sparta was threatening the independence of Greece. Before the battle of Pagasæ they knew little of the king of Macedon besides his name. This brought him prominently before them as an able general, commanding troops formidable by their numbers and discipline. As yet however these troops had not been tried against the heavy-armed infantry of the leading states; and Philip was still looked upon as a mere northern potentate, protecting Thessaly, as his brother Alexander had done, and extending the frontiers of his own native kingdom, but with no thought of pushing his conquests south of Thermopylæ. Even the capture of Olynthus did not open the eyes of the Peloponnesians, although Athens sent her envoys round to their cities, and Æschines in his philippic at Megalopolis denounced the king of Macedon as a savage barbarian, who was rising up to be the plague of the Grecian world. They heard indeed that he had razed to the ground twenty or thirty Chalcidian cities, and they saw with their own eyes the Arcadian Atrestidas bringing to the slave-market a herd of Olynthian women and children. Yet all this, though it may have excited pity or indignation, did not convince them that Philip's progress was a thing to excite alarm. The

[1] Diodorus, xvi. 39. Pausanias. viii. 27.

conqueror of Olynthus had become a dangerous neighbor to the Athenian dominions in Thrace: they themselves were too far removed from the scene to have much interest in it. So they reasoned. Nor did there want orators to support these short-sighted views. One Hieronymus is said to have opposed Æschines and spoken on Philip's behalf in the Megalopolotan assembly. Æschines reported of the Arcadians, that they were glad to hear that Athens was bestirring herself: but whether this was true or not, they showed no desire to assist her.[1]

By the termination of the Sacred War Philip was raised to a position both novel and imposing, in which the magnitude of his power was apparent to all. He stepped forward into the midst of Greece as the elected general of the Amphictyons, the avenger of outraged religion, the arbiter of peace and war. He was at once king of Macedonia and Tagus of Thessaly: the mountain tribes of Olympus and Pindus, Othrys and Œta, were ready to flock to his standard: the Thebans and Locrians were his grateful and devoted allies. North of the Isthmus there were none to oppose him but the Athenians; and they by themselves could offer but feeble resistance to his power. Under these circumstances the Athenians turned their eyes to Peloponnesus, as the quarter from which they might reasonably hope to obtain support; it being now obvious that, if Athens should succumb to Philip, the Peloponnesians would have no barrier against him. Little was to be expected from the Lacedæmonians, disgusted with Athens for her weak and seemingly treacherous conduct in abandoning the Phocians. The best chance was with the other peninsular states, and to them the Athenians determined to apply, to form a league for mutual protection against Philip.

If the Athenians, however, imagined that Philip intended to leave the game of diplomacy in their hands, they were completely mistaken. Philip was no less active in negotiation than in war. Where he designed to extend his influence and power, his emissaries went like skirmishers before him, winning and seducing both statesmen and people to his side by every species of corruption and intrigue. It was soon found that he had been beforehand with the Athenians in Peloponnesus; and circumstances had happened which greatly favored his designs.

In a short time after the end of the Phocian war some territorial disputes arose between the Lacedæmonians and their neighbors. Pausanius says, that from early times it was the custom of the Lacedæmonians, when they had nothing to occupy them out of Peloponnesus, to raise a border quarrel with the Argives.[2] It was

[1] See ante, pp. 291, 292. The apathy of the Greeks is forcibly described by Demosthenes, in Philipp. iii. 119, 120.

[2] Pausanias, ii. 20.

not likely that the Messenians would fare much better with them. Philip having now established agents in these countries, they persuaded the people to solicit his support. There were plausible arguments for it. The Thebans, their former protectors, had been befriended by Philip; while the Athenians had rather displayed a sympathy with Sparta.[1] Philip eagerly availed himself of this favorable opportunity for putting himself at the head of the old Theban confederacy.[2] He sent a body of mercenaries and a supply of money to the Messenians and Argives, and promised to come in person, if necessary, to their assistance. At the same time he sent a peremptory message to the Spartans, requiring them (among other things) to abandon their pretensions to Messenia, and threatening them with war, in case of refusal. To this he received a laconic answer of defiance: yet his measures seemed to have had the desired effect of securing his allies against Spartan aggression, and establishing his own popularity not only at Argos and Messene, but also among their confederates in Arcadia. We read that shortly afterwards both the Arcadians and Argives erected statues to Philip, conferred crowns of honor upon him, and passed resolutions to receive him in their cities, if he came to Peloponnesus. Pausanias declares, that the hatred of the Arcadians to Sparta was one of the principal causes to which Philip and his kingdom owed their aggrandizement.[3]

These proceedings quickly excited attention at Athens. Demosthenes carried a decree for sending an embassy to Peloponnesus, and was himself put at its head.[4] He went to Argos and Messene, and in both of those cities made instructive speeches, setting forth the danger of their connection with Philip. He has given us in the second Philippic an extract from his speech to the Messenians, in which he bade them take warning by the example of Olynthus, which Philip first befriended and then destroyed, and also by that of Thessaly, which he had reduced to vassalage: he conjured them not to be deceived by the gifts or promises of Philip, not to trust a man of such notorious bad faith, and not to ally themselves with a despot, the natural enemy of republics.[5] This harangue was re-

[1] Demosthenes, De Pace, 61.

[2] Demosthenes, Orat. ad Epist. 153; from which it appears, that the Thebans were not well pleased at his interference with their allies.

[3] Pausanias, viii. 27. Demosthenes, Philipp. ii. 68, 69; De Fals. Leg. 424, 425. Thirlwall, History of Greece, vi. 8. Cicero, Tus. Qu. V. 14.

[4] Demosthenes, De Coron. 252: *Πρῶτον μὲν τὴν εἰς Πελοπόννησον πρεσβείαν ἔγραψα, ὅτε πρῶτον ἐκεῖνος εἰς Πελοπόννησον παρεδύετο.* This expression does not necessarily import, that Philip was coming in person to Peloponnesus, and therefore it may be referred to the occasion mentioned in the text.

[5] Demosthenes, Philipp. ii. 70.

ceived, as he tells us, with great applause; yet its effect was transient. The Peloponnesian allies of Philip could not be induced to break with him by any Athenian arguments. They had an advantage in Macedonian protection, which they doubted whether Athens was willing or able to afford.[1] The prospect of danger held out to them by Demosthenes was (in their view) remote: but there might be an immediate danger in offending Philip: as he was now a powerful friend, so he might be a powerful enemy. Things had already come about as Demosthenes feared they would. At first people could not imagine that Philip's power would ever be felt in southern Greece: all of a sudden he appears before them as a giant whom none can withstand: then the minor states are either desirous of his protection, or afraid to provoke his hostility. Such was his present influence over the Argives and Messenians, that he induced them to send embassadors in company with his own, to demand of the Athenians an explanation of their late embassy to Peloponnesus. A joint remonstrance was prepared, identifying the cause of Philip with that of his allies. The Athenians, it was alleged, had violated the treaty of peace by sending agents to stir up the Greeks against Philip; and at the same time they were encouraging the Spartans in their aggressive projects. Python of Byzantium was Philip's principal envoy, and it may perhaps have been on this occasion that he poured out that torrent of invective against Athens, which Demosthenes says he triumphantly answered, so as to vindicate his country from the calumnies of Philip. A reply was sent to the remonstrance, which left the dispute between Philip and the Athenians unsettled.[2]

Elis was next the theatre of intrigue. This city, formerly the best governed of any in Greece, was thrown into strife and disor-

[1] See what Demosthenes says about the selfish policy of the Argives, Messenians, and Arcadians, De Coron. 246.

[2] Argumentum ad Philipp. ii.: De Coron. 272. The occasion upon which this contest of eloquence took place between Python and Demosthenes is matter of controversy. Some assign it to a later period, when Python came to adjust disputes about the peace. Diodorus (xvi. 85) refers it to the debate at Thebes. In the passage cited from the Oration on the Crown, it is mentioned that Æschines spoke on Python's side; which indicates the debate to have taken place at Athens. It is mentioned also, that Philip's allies were present, and that, after hearing Demosthenes, they got up and admitted Philip to be in the wrong; which rather points to this occasion, when the Messenians and Argives accompanied the Macedonian embassadors. The second Philippic, it seems clear enough, was spoken in support of a motion for a reply to this embassy. (See Philipp. ii. 72. Dionysius, ad Ammæum, s. 10, p. 737.) It can not however have been the oration in which Demosthenes so triumphantly answered Python; for it contains no answer to him at all.

der by the corrupting arts of Philip. A Macedonian party got the upper hand, not without violence and bloodshed, and drove a large body of their opponents into exile. Elis was then transferred from the Lacedæmonian alliance to that of which Philip was at the head. The exiles afterwards, hiring the remnant of that mercenary band which had followed Phalæcus into Crete, invaded the country and were defeated, as I have already mentioned, by the Elean and Arcadian troops.[1] Demosthenes in the third Philippic speaks of Elis as being virtually in the power of Philip.[2]

It was Philip's design to surround with enemies both Sparta and Athens, so that, being cut off from support, they must ultimately yield to his demands. Sparta was already isolated; and so would Athens be, if Eubœa, Megara, Corinth, and Achaia were either subdued or gained over to his alliance. To make these acquisitions, Philip laid his plans in the year B.C. 343. The enterprises against Eubœa and Megara were left to his generals: that against Peloponnesus he resolved to conduct in person. It would have excited alarm, if he had marched by the ordinary route to the Isthmus, especially as he had no ostensible cause of war: he therefore purposed to take a westerly course through Epirus and Acarnania to the Corinthian gulf. The kingdom of Epirus seems at this time to have been divided between his uncle Arymbas and his brother-in-law Alexander.[3] Philip led his army to the Cassopian coast, and took by storm three cities, Elatea, Pandosia, and Bucheta, Elean colonies, which he annexed to the dominions of Alexander. He then advanced to the Ambracian gulf, meditating an attack upon the Corinthian colonies of Ambracia and Leucas; and it seems that he was negotiating an alliance with the Ætolians, to whom he promised to give Naupactus, as soon as he had taken it from the Achæans.[4] He would then have passed through Acarnania to join the Ætolians, and after taking the Achæan fortresses on the northern coast of the Corinthian gulf, might have transported his forces over to Achaia. It is not unlikely that the Achæans and Corinthians got information of these projects, and communicated them to Athens. The Athenians by unwonted exertions contrived to baffle Philip at this point, and arrest his further progress. An embassy, at the head of which were Demosthenes, Polyeuctus, Hegesippus, Clitomachus, and Lycurgus, was sent to Acarnania and Peloponnesus, where they

[1] Ante, p. 318.
[2] Demosthenes, Philipp. iii. 118; iv. 133: De Fals. Leg. 424, 435. Pausanias, iv 28; v. 4.
[3] See Thirlwall, History of Greece, vi. 16, note 3.
[4] The possession by the Achæans of Naupactus, Dyme, and Calydon, was an annoyance to the Ætolians. Epaminondas had expelled them. They regained possession after his death. See Diodorus, xv. 75. Xenophon, Hellen. iv. c. 6, s. 14.

succeeded in forming a league and organizing active measures for defense. Athenian troops were promptly sent into Acarnania. Megara also promised assistance, having been secured against Macedonian attack by the measures of Phocion, as already mentioned. Philip, either not being prepared, or not wishing to attack the Athenians at present, or failing in his negotiations with the Ætolians, desisted from his attempt and retired to Macedonia.[1]

No further movement occurred in Peloponnesus, until the campaign of Chæronea. Philip then invited his Peloponnesian allies to join him; but none of them came. The Achæans and Corinthians fought for Athens.[2] After the battle, having completed the subjugation of northern Greece, Philip led his army into the peninsula, to consolidate his power among the states, and enforce the submission of those which held out against him or wavered. He then designed to unite them all in a common league against Persia. None were inclined to dispute his will but the Lacedæmonians; and them he resolved to humble, both for the satisfaction of his allies, and as a measure of precaution against future disturbance. At the head of an overpowering force he entered Laconia, ravaging it on all sides, and pillaging or destroying some of the rural townships. The Spartans behaved worthily of their ancient reputation. Though not strong enough to encounter the enemy's whole force in open field, they still refused to capitulate. We read of one victory which they gained over a detached body of Macedonians at Gythium. Philip forbore to attack the capital. He sought to cripple the power of Sparta, not to crush her entirely; perhaps, as the Acarnanian envoy says in Polybius, he checked the more violent counsels of his Peloponnesian followers.[3] The end of it was, that he stripped Sparta of territory on every side, giving one portion of it to the Argives, another to the Tegeans, a third to the Megalopolitans, and a fourth to the Messenians.

[1] Demosthenes, Philipp. iii. 118—120, 129; iv. 133: De Halonn. 84: De Coron. 305, 306, 308. From the last of these passages, it would appear that Demosthenes had encountered Philip's agents at Ambracia. He justly boasts of his own zealous activity in executing, as well as designing and advising, these important missions (*ibid.* 301). Æschines (Contr. Ctesiph. 67) charges Demosthenes with giving a false account of his success on these expeditions. The charge is a mere calumny. That troops were sent into Acarnania, appears from the incidental mention of them in Demosthenes, Contr. Olympiodorum, 1173. And the harsh measures aftewards taken by Philip against the Ambraciots and Acarnanians, are evidence of their successful resistance before. (Diodorus, xvii. 3.)

[2] Pausanias, iv. 28; v. 4; viii. 27. And see the next Appendix.

[3] The Eleans, though they declined to aid him at Chæronea, are said to have followed him in this invasion from hatred of the Lacedæmonians. Pausanias, v. 4.

His acts were ratified afterwards by the Greek congress, though they were never acknowledged by the Lacedæmonians.[1]

On his return from Laconia, he visited some of the friendly states; making stay among the Arcadians, whom he wished to attach firmly to himself and draw entirely away from the cause of the Greeks. How well he succeeded, was fully proved by subsequent events: at this time it appeared in homage and flattery. At a village near Mantinea, where he pitched his camp, a spring received the name of Philip's spring. The Megalopolitans gave his name to a portico in their market-place. Similar compliments were paid him by the Eleans. He erected on the sacred ground at Olympia a circular building surrounded by a colonnade, which was named after him Philippeum.[2] The gracious and winning manners of the king helped doubtless to increase his popularity.[3]

He next proceeded to the Isthmus of Corinth, where he had invited a congress of all the Greeks to assemble. It was attended by deputies from all the chief cities, except Sparta. The dream of Isocrates was now about to be realized, though not exactly in the manner which that philosopher would have desired. Philip proposed to make war against the Persians, and take vengeance upon them for their profanation of the Greek temples in days of old. The deputies passed an unanimous vote in accordance with his desire. War was declared. Each state was ordered to furnish a contingent of ships or land force: and Philip was elected general of the national army.[4]

[1] Pausanias, ii. 20; iii. 24; vii. 11. Polybius, ix. 28, 33. Strabo, viii. 365.

[2] Pausanias, v. 17, 20; viii. 7, 30.

[3] As to this, see ante, p. 357, note 1.

[4] Diodorus, xvi. 89. Justin, ix. 5. "Compositis in Græciâ rebus, Philippus omnium civitatum legatos ad formandum rerum præsentium statum evocari Corinthum jubet. Ibi pacis legem universæ Græciæ pro meritis singularum civitatum statuit, conciliumque omnium, veluti unum senatum, ex omnibus legit. Soli Lacedæmonii et legem et regem contempserunt, servitutem, non pacem rati, quæ non ipsis civitatibus conveniret, sed a victore ferretur. Auxilia deinde singularum civitatum describuntur, sive adjuvandus eâ manu rex oppugnante aliquo foret, seu duce illo bellum inferendum. Neque enim dubium erat imperium Persarum his apparatibus peti."

APPENDIX IX.

CHÆRONEA.

Diodorus thus commences his narrative of the year 338 B.C.:[1]

"Philip, having won over the greater number of the Greeks to his alliance, was anxious to strike terror into the Athenians and hold without a rival the leadership of Greece. He therefore suddenly took possession of Elatea, and there gathering his forces resolved to attack the Athenians. As they were unprepared, by reason of the treaty of peace, he expected that he should easily conquer them: and such was the event."

Justin, after relating Philip's expedition into Scythia, his victory over Atheas the Scythian prince, and the bloody battle fought on his return with the Triballi, in which he was severely wounded, (the date of which event seems to be in the spring or early summer of 339 B.C.) continues thus:[2]

"Ubi vero ex vulnere primum convaluit, diu dissimulatum bellum Atheniensibus infert."

The treaty of peace referred to in the passage of Diodorus is that which he relates to have been concluded in the year B.C. 340, when Philip raised the siege of Byzantium.[3] This, as I have before mentioned,[4] has given rise to controversy among modern historians. The testimony of Diodorus, confirmed apparently by certain records cited in the oration on the Crown, has induced some writers to accept the peace as an historical fact. Others, who deem it irreconcilable with the language of Demosthenes, which represents the war of 340 B.C. as continuing long after the date of the supposed peace,[5] and who also consider the records in the oration on the Crown to be spurious, and the authority of Diodorus not sufficient of itself to prove a doubtful point—and swayed also by some other arguments—

[1] Diodorus, xvi. 84. Wesseling justly observes in his note, that the seizure of Elatea took place in the year 339 B.C. Diodorus has confused the dates, as well as the other circumstances of this war.

[2] Justin, ix. 3.

[3] Diodorus, xvi. 77: *Διόπερ Φίλιππος καταπλαγεὶς τῇ συνδρομῇ τῶν Ἑλλήνων, τὴν πολιορκίαν τῶν πόλεων ἔλυσε, καὶ πρὸς Ἀθηναίους καὶ τοὺς ἄλλους Ἕλληνας τοὺς ἐναντιουμένους συνέθετο τὴν εἰρήνην.*

[4] Ante, p. 17, note 1.

[5] Demosthenes, De Coron. 275, 276: *Οὐκ ἦν τοῦ πρὸς ὑμᾶς πολέμου πέρας οὐδ' ἀπαλλαγὴ Φιλίππῳ, εἰ μὴ Θηβαίους καὶ Θετταλοὺς ἐχθροὺς ποιήσειε τῇ πόλει·* &c. Compare p. 262, where he speaks of the successful results which attended his regulation of the trierarchy *during the whole of the war* (*πάντα τὸν πόλεμον*). Also, p. 304.

reject the peace altogether.[1] Grote takes a middle view of the question, supposing that Philip concluded peace with the Byzantines, Perinthians, and some other of the Greeks who had assisted them, but not with the Athenians and their more intimate allies.[2] This may seem to reconcile Diodorus with Demosthenes: yet it is hardly probable in itself, that the allies would consent to make such a distinction. Perhaps the simplest account of the matter is, that a mere armistice was concluded between the parties, leaving a more formal treaty of peace to be afterwards decided on; and that a naval war, chiefly of a privateering character, was irregularly carried on between Athens and Macedonia in spite of the armistice.[3]

The words of Justin (*diu dissimulatum bellum Atheniensibus infert*) throw no light on this question of the peace. They have reference to the long forbearance of Philip to attack the Athenians in their own country, which at length he determined to do.

It is further to be remarked, that neither Diodorus nor Justin makes the slightest mention of those extraordinary proceedings at Delphi in the year B.C. 339, which kindled a new Sacred War, and were, according to both of the Athenian orators, Demosthenes and Æschines, the immediate cause of Philip's march into Phocis and all the calamities that followed.

Demosthenes informs us (I give the sum of what he says):[4]—

That Philip was suffering greatly by the maritime blockade which the Athenians kept up around his coast, and by the depredations of their privateers: it therefore became desirable to carry the war into Attica; which could not well be done, unless the Thessalians were on his side, and the Thebans gave him a passage through their country. Neither of these people would have liked to assist him in a private quarrel; but if a new Sacred War could be stirred up, he might be chosen to conduct it as before, and so gather round his standard many of the Amphictyonic tribes. To accomplish this he engaged the services of Æschines; who, as the first step in the business, got himself appointed Amphictyonic deputy, no one at Athens in the least suspecting what his design was; then proceeding to the spring meeting at Delphi, and taking his place in the assembly, pre-

[1] See Thirlwall, History of Greece, vi. 59. The objections are there very clearly stated. Is it possible that Diodorus confounds this with the peace of 346 B. C.? It is remarkable that he gives no account of the latter.

[2] Grote, History of Greece, xi. 638.

[3] Chiefly perhaps to the advantage of the Athenians, as Demosthenes asserts; yet that Philip resorted to privateering, in order to recruit his finances, is related by Justin, ix. 1: "Igitur Philippus, longâ obsidionis morâ exhaustus, pecuniæ commercium de piraticâ mutuantur. Captis itaque centum septuaginta navibus mercibusque distractis, anhelantem inopiam paululum recreavit."

[4] Demosthenes, De Coron. 275—278.

ferred a charge of impiety against the Locrians of Amphissa, for cultivating a portion of the Cirrhæan ground. He made such an inflammatory speech, appealing to the religious feelings of the deputies, that they were persuaded to go in person and take a view of the sacred ground. The Locrians speedily came and drove them off, not abstaining from acts of violence. The council, resenting such an insult offered to its members, declared war against the Locrians, choosing Cottyphus for their general; but as it was found impossible by the voluntary exertions of the Amphictyonic states to get an army strong enough to enforce their authority, it was contrived by Philip's agents and partisans at the ensuing Pylæan congress, that he should be elected general. Philip then, collecting an army, and marching to Thermopylæ with the professed intention of chastising the Amphissians, suddenly took possession of Elatea.

If the statement of Demosthenes rested on his sole credit, one might be inclined to suspect that he had greatly magnified the importance of these transactions, or misrepresented the real truth. When, however, we find his statement confirmed in all its main features by Æschines, we can do no otherwise than accept it as historical evidence; and it proves to us, how little such writers as Diodorus and Justin are to be depended on for a correct outline of the events which they profess to relate.[1]

Æschines describes the scene at Delphi and the subsequent proceedings, in which he himself took an active part, with much greater prolixity of detail than Demosthenes. He gives a somewhat different color to the affair; yet, so far from denying that his own charge against the Locrians brought on a new Sacred War, he boasts of it; and contends that Athens might and ought to have put herself at the head of the movement, and that it was owing to the treacherous counsel of Demosthenes, that Philip was chosen to be Amphictyonic general. The bold manner in which Æschines launches into the history of this affair, denouncing his rival as the prime author of the whole mischief, gives the idea, as it was intended to do, that he himself brought the matter forward as an accuser only, and not because he felt the necessity of defending his own conduct. There is, however, no doubt, that his object was more to exculpate himself than to attack Demosthenes; and this, with all his craft, he can not help betraying. We have to bear in mind, that Æschines was not for the first time in the oration on the Crown charged by his opponent with having kindled the last Sacred War. That charge had been urged against him frequently before, both in public and in private; and Æschines knew perfectly well

[1] Plutarch, writing biography, not history, does not profess always to follow the course of events. He makes a passing allusion only to the Amphissian war. (Vit. Demosth. 18.)

what Demosthenes would have to say upon the subject in his reply.[1] For this very reason he prefers a counter-accusation, by which he hoped to beget a prejudice in his own favor; but which, as we shall see presently, is based upon little but the assertion of the accuser.

The account which Æschines gives of the whole proceeding is to the following effect:[2]—

That the Locrians of Amphissa were cultivating and turning to profane purposes the holy ground of Cirrha, notwithstanding the solemn oath sworn in the first Sacred War, which forbade it ever again to be appropriated to the use of man; that they had repaired the harbor of that ancient town, and built houses round it, and were taking tolls or duties of the visitors who landed there; that they had bribed some of the Amphictyonic deputies, among others Demosthenes, to say nothing about it; that Demosthenes had been paid a thousand drachms in the first instance, when he was sent as deputy from Athens, and they had engaged for the future to pay him twenty minas a year, if he would constantly support them at Athens.

That in the year 339 B. C. Midias, Thrasycles, and himself were elected to serve the office of Pylagoræ, and sent to Delphi, together with Diognetus the Hieromnemon. That soon after their arrival Diognetus and Midias were seized with a fever; the Amphictyons had already assembled, when a message was brought to Æschines, informing him that the Amphissians, to please their friends the Thebans, were about to move a resolution against the people of Athens; which was, to fine them fifty talents for having hung up in a new chapel, before it was finished, some golden shields with the following inscription:[3] "By the Athenians, out of spoil taken from

[1] That Æschines was all along anticipating an attack upon himself, that he well understood the course of argument which Demosthenes would pursue, and that he greatly feared the prejudice of the people in his opponent's favor, will appear from a careful perusal of the oration against Ctesiphon: see pp. 61, 62, where occurs the artful illustration which Demosthenes exposes, De Coron. 303: p. 71, where he anticipates the charge of having caused Philip's invasion: pp. 74, 77, where, from the words *ἆ πῶς ποθ' ὑμεῖς ὦ σιδήρεοι ἐκαρτερεῖτε ἀκροώμενοι*, one would imagine he perceived signs of disapprobation among the jury: p. 81, he forestalls the argument of Demosthenes, De Coron. 330, 331; (pp. 84, 85,) he betrays his dread of what Demosthenes will say about his political life: *οὕτω δὲ ταῖς αἰτίαις ἐνέφραξας τὰς κατὰ σαυτοῦ τιμωρίας, ὥστε τὸν κίνδυνον εἶναι μὴ σοὶ τῷ ἀδικήσαντι ἀλλὰ τοῖς ἐπεξιοῦσι, πολὺν μὲν τὸν 'Αλέξανδρον καὶ τὸν Φίλιππον ἐν ταῖς διαβολαῖς φερῶν.*

[2] Æschines, Contr. Ctesiph. 69—72.

[3] According to the words of Æschines (p. 70), the charges were two; one relating to the time or mode of presenting the shields, the other to the inscription. It would seem, that a new fane or chapel was in the course of erection at Delphi, and the Athenians had exhibited their of-

the Persians and Thebans when they fought against the Greeks." That Diognetus sent for him, and begged that he would go to the council, and defend his country before the Amphictyons. He did so; but scarcely had he begun to speak, when one of the Amphissians rudely interrupted him, crying out, "Men of Greece, if you were wise, you would not allow the name of the Athenians to be mentioned on these days, but would drive them from the temple as a people under a curse." At the same time he brought up the Phocian alliance and other matters of accusation against Athens; all which so enraged Æschines, that in the heat of the moment he retorted the charge of impiety against the Locrians, and reproached them with the use which they had made of the consecrated plain. The plain itself and the port of Cirrha were visible from the spot where they were assembled. Æschines pointed them out to the deputies. "Amphictyons!" he cried: "you behold yonder plain cultivated by the Amphissians, with the pottery works and farm-houses which they have built upon it. You see with your own eyes the fortifications of the devoted harbor. You know yourselves, and need no witnesses to tell you, that these men have taken tolls and are making profits from the sacred harbor." He then bade them read the oracle, the oath of their ancestors, and the solemn imprecation, (all which were before their eyes, inscribed on a tablet;) and having first declared his determination, on behalf of the people of Athens, himself, his children, and his family, to stand by the god and the sacred land, as that ancient oath required, he solemnly adjured the Amphictyons to do the same, and to free themselves from the curse that must otherwise hang over them as the abettors or tolerators of sacrilege.

The speech of Æschines—so he goes on to state—caused a great tumult and uproar in the council. All question of the shields was forgotten, and nothing thought of but the punishment of the Locrians. As the day was far advanced, a proclamation was made by the herald, commanding that all the Delphians of military age, both freemen and slaves, should assemble the next morning with spades and pickaxes at the place of sacrifice, and that the Hieromnemons and other deputies should be at the same place to assist in the cause of Apollo and the sacred land: and further announcing that, whatever

ferings before it was completely finished, or before some ceremony of consecration had been peformed. The inscription was necessarily offensive to the Thebans; and, although the Athenians had probably presented these shields in lieu of others similarly inscribed, which the Phocian generals had destroyed, it gave a handle for censure, that they should at this time have taken a step which would hurt the feelings of their neighbors. See Thirlwall, History of Greece, vi. 54. Grote, xi. 650; who gives a somewhat different explanation.

people failed to attend, would be excluded from the temple, and regarded as execrable and accursed.

At the time appointed, he says, the full multitude came together and went down to Cirrha, where they quickly demolished the harbor and set fire to the houses which had been erected: but a large body of Amphissians coming with arms to attack them, they took to their heels, and with difficulty escaped to Delphi. The next day Cottyphus, a Pharsalian citizen, who officiated as president of the congress, called a general assembly of Amphictyons, composed not only of the representative synod, but of all who came to take a part in the sacrifice or consult the oracle. Here, after much abuse of the Locrians and praise of Athens, a resolution was passed, that the deputies should assemble at Thermopylæ on a certain day before the next ordinary meeting, to pass sentence on the Locrians for their acts of sacrilege and insult to the Amphictyons."

When this resolution was first communicated to the Athenians, Æschines declares, they fully acquiesced in its propriety, and expressed their readiness to comply with it. Demosthenes raised some opposition, in pursuance of his engagement with the Locrians; but he (Æschines) completely set him down.[1] Upon which Demosthenes had recourse to a maneuvre: he got a degree first secretly passed by the council, and then carried in the assembly after the regular business was all over, and when hardly any citizens were present; which decree was to the effect:—"That the deputies of Athens should go regularly to Thermopylæ and to Delphi at the times appointed by their ancestors; and that they should take no part whatever in the extraordinary meeting about to be held at Thermopylæ." The consequence was, that Athens took no part in the ensuing measures of the Amphictyons. The special meeting was attended by representatives from all the other states except Thebes. War was declared against the Amphissian Locrians, and Cottyphus was elected general. The Amphictyonic army marched into Locris, but behaved with the utmost moderation, imposing a fine only on the people, to be paid on a given day, banishing the principal advisers of the sacrilege, and restoring the opponents who had been driven into exile. As the fine, however, was not paid, and the Amphissians reversed the acts of Cottyphus after his troops had been withdrawn, the second expedition against them took place after a long interval, when Philip had returned from Scythia. "And so," says Æschines, "when the gods had given the lead in this pious

[1] This quite agrees with what Demosthenes says (De Coron. 275): *Καὶ τότ' εὐθὺς ἐμοῦ διαμαρτυρομένου καὶ βοῶντος ἐν τῇ ἐκκλησίᾳ "πόλεμον εἰς τὴν 'Αττικὴν εἰσάγεις, Αἰσχίνη, πόλεμον 'Αμφικτυονικόν·" οἱ μὲν ἐκ παρακλήσεως συγκαθήμενοι οὐκ εἴων με λέγειν, οἱ δ' ἐθαύμαζον καὶ κενὴν αἰτίαν διὰ τὴν ἰδίαν ἔχθραν ἐπάγειν με ὑπελάμβανον αὐτῷ.*

enterprise to Athens, she was deprived of it by the corrupt act of Demosthenes."

Here Æschines breaks off, just at the time when we should have been glad to hear the rest of his narrative. Instead of giving any explanation about Philip's appointment and the circumstances attending it, he quits these matters of fact, and runs into a rhapsody of declamation, by which, as he had played upon the weak understandings of the Amphictyonic council, he might hope to excite the feelings of the Athenian people: but he had not the same success.[1]

The accounts of Demosthenes and Æschines, agreeing in their main outlines, and especially in the important result of Philip's election to conduct the new Sacred War, differ in the following particulars: 1. As to the Locrians having preferred a charge of impiety against the Athenians: 2. As to the motives which each of the two orators imputes to his rival: 3. As to some of the details of the first Amphictyonic campaign.

That the Locrian people should have brought a formal accusation against the Athenians, such as that mentioned by Æschines, is improbable, not merely for the reason assigned by Demosthenes, that no record is produced of a citation to answer the charge; but also because the alleged offense is not one which the Locrian people were likely to have cared about; and further, if (as Æschines says) they were conscious of being themselves trespassers upon the sacred land, this would naturally have deterred them from raising such questions against others. If it be said, that they were instigated by the Thebans, we may answer first, that there is no evidence of this; secondly, it is disproved by the conduct of the Thebans themselves, who showed pretty clearly by their keeping aloof from the special meeting at Thermopylæ, that they had had quite enough of Sacred Wars and Amphictyonic quarrels. It is very possible, however, that some individual Amphissian, either at Philip's instigation or from other motives, got up in the council to complain of what the Athenians had done; and this led to an angry debate, in which Æschines retorted the charge of impiety upon the countrymen of his opponent.

And what time the Amphissians began to take possession of the port and plain of Cirrha, Æschines does not inform us: and modern historians do not agree upon the subject. Grote says,[2] it appears both from Demosthenes and Æschines, that it was an ancient and established occupation. The passages which he cites however do not bear him out;[3] on the contrary, the whole narrative of Æschines

[1] The whole of the passage beginning at page 72, ἀλλ' οὐ προὔλεγον, and ending at page 73, ἐκ τῆς τούτου πολιτείας, is wretched affectation and bombast.

[2] History of Greece, xi. 648.

[3] Demosthenes, De Coron. 277. Æschines, Contr. Ctesiph. 69: Οἱ

tends to prove, that it was a recent intrusion of which the Amphissians were accused. Had it been otherwise, it would not have been easy to excite a tumult against them at Delphi: nor would there have been any color for the charge which Æschines brings against Demosthenes, of having received bribes from the Amphissian people. Though we may have no hesitation in rejecting the truth of that charge, it is difficult to suppose that it could have been advanced, unless the Amphissians had some assignable motive for offering a bribe. If what they were doing at Cirrha had been acquiesced in for so long a period, they could have had little to fear, and had no occasion to purchase the silence of the Amphictyonic deputies. If this usurpation had been recent, one can understand their motives in so doing. But further, it is distinctly asserted by Æschines, that the Amphictyons, when they invaded Locris, banished the principal authors of the sacrilege, and restored those who had been driven into exile for their piety, that is, for their opposition to the sacrilege: a statement which implies, as I conceive, that the alleged sacrilege had been recently committed and was the subject of contest among the Locrians themselves.[1]

That after the first Sacred War it became necessary to renovate in some degree the port and town of Cirrha, for the accommodation of visitors coming by sea to Delphi, we may with Grote very fairly assume: but I see no reason for supposing that the Amphissian Locrians took this duty upon them. It is more likely that the Delphians provided the convenience of a harbor for their guests, regarding it both as a duty and a privilege of their own. When the second Sacred War broke out, Cirrha fell into the hands of the Phocians; and we have no historical account of what they did with it. When however the Amphissian Locrians submitted to Onomarchus, it is very possible that he permitted them to occupy that ancient seaport under an arrangement beneficial to both parties. The Locrians may then have enlarged and improved the harbor, built new houses in the town, and plowed up and farmed a considerable portion of the surrounding plain. We hear of no more war between them and the Phocians after the peace made with Onomarchus; nor could he have taken a better way to disarm their hostility than by making to them such a concession. At the end of that war the Locrians must have felt that their title to this newly acquired district

Λοκροὶ οἱ Ἀμφισσεῖς, μᾶλλον δὲ οἱ προεστηκότες αὐτῶν ἄνδρες παρανομώτατοι, ἐπειργαζόντο τὸ πεδίον, καὶ τὸν λιμένα τὸν ἐξάγιστον καὶ ἐπάρατον πάλιν ἐτείχισαν καὶ συνῴχισαν, καὶ τέλη τοὺς καταπλέοντας ἐξέλεγον, καὶ τῶν ἀφικνουμένων εἰς Δελφοὺς πυλαγόρων ἐνίους χρήμασι διέφθειραν. The connection of the last clause with the preceding clauses proves that Æschines is speaking of recent acts.

[1] Æschines, Contr. Ctesiph. 72: *Καὶ τοὺς μὲν ἐναγεῖς καὶ τῶν πεπραγμένων αἰτίους μετεστήσαντο, τοὺς δὲ δί εὐσέβειαν φυγόντας κατήγαγον.*

was questionable and precarious. Although the Delphians in the first rejoicing after victory might not wish to disturb them in their possession, yet in the course of a short time they may have begun to think more seriously of it, especially if the improvements of the town and neighborhood of Cirrha were of such magnitude as to excite attention. As soon as the title of the Locrians became the subject of discussion, they would naturally be alarmed, and might endeavor by intrigue or otherwise to make interest for themselves with the Amphictyonic deputies. This may have afforded a color for the charge of Æschines against Demosthenes.

That there was any thing more however then a colorable pretense for such charge against Demosthenes, I altogether disbelieve. The only ground alleged by Æschines is, that he dissuaded his countrymen from taking any part in the hostile movement against the Locrians. But in this he only exhibited the zeal and foresight of a good statesman. His prediction was but too true, that Æschines was bringing an Amphictyonic war into Attica. The Athenians, though at first they disregarded the warning; considering it to have been dictated by private enmity, shortly afterwards came over to his views, and passed a resolution virtually condemning the acts of the Amphictyons. Æschines, to persuade his hearers that this resolution was not the genuine opinion of the Athenians, resorts to the stale device of asserting that it was irregularly and clandestinely obtained. But it is far more likely, that the people of Athens upon further inquiry and reflection became convinced, that the violent measures of the Amphictyons were uncalled for and unseasonable, that the affair of Cirrha did not concern them, and the most prudent plan was to keep themselves quiet, as Demosthenes advised.[1]

Of Æschines the least we can say is, that he acted with great indiscretion, and showed himself not a very fit person to manage any important business of state. Whether he was stimulated by the base motives which have been imputed to him, is a problem which no mortal can solve. Difficulties present themselves, whatever view we may be inclined to take. It can hardly be supposed that the course which things took was planned by Æschines; for no one could have foreseen that such results would flow from such causes, or that by the contingency which happened Philip would get the advantages which he did. Upon the Athenians declining to act against the Locrians, Philip had no *casus belli* against them as Amphictyonic leader, while he involved himself in a war with the Locrians, his former allies, at the risk also of displeasing the Thebans. The only compensation for this was, that he took the Athenians by surprise. It may however be thought, that the event which actually

[1] Mitford, who is always adverse to Demosthenes, thinks that his silence on the subject of this charge proves his guilt. (History of Greece, iv. chap. xli. s. 5.)

happened was not the most favorable one for Philip, who rather hoped that he should embroil the Athenians with the Locrians, and step in himself as the protector of the latter, drawing to his side the Thebans and other allies. Yet one would imagine it would better have suited Philip's purpose to get up a religious cry against the Athenians, so as to bring them into odium and disgrace with the Amphictyons, and excite perhaps a Sacred War against them, of which he might have the conduct. It is thus possible that the Locrian who declaimed so fiercely against Athens at Delphi was acting under his instigation, and that the reply of Æschines, made on the spur of the moment, accidentally turned the wrath of the assembly into another channel. It is by no means impossible, however, that the Locrian and Æschines were both Macedonian hirelings; yet that they had no definite object further than to create discord and confusion among the Amphictyons, which Philip might turn to his advantage according to circumstances. It is in this vague way that Demosthenes shapes his accusation.[1]

From a comparison of the two orators it appears, that the extraordinary meeting of Amphictyons was held at Thermopylæ at the time appointed, and attended by deputies from most of the states except Athens and Thebes. Cottyphus, being elected general, summoned the Amphictyonic tribes to take arms; their contingents however came in slowly, and not in sufficient numbers for the required purpose. Putting himself at the head of such force as he could muster, Cottyphus made a show of opening the campaign; but, not being strong enough to reduce the Locrians to submission, he contented himself with imposing terms upon them, in particular a pecuniary fine to be paid on an early day. These terms were not complied with; it was never desired by Philip's friends that they should be: accordingly at the ensuing autumnal[2] congress of Amphictyons it was proposed, as had been concerted by the Mace-

[1] Demosthenes does not pretend to say, that Philip marked out any particular course for Æschines or his other agents to pursue. Any war or confusion among the Amphictyons would be a gain to him; for he was sure then to be wanted: *'Επιχειρεῖ θεάσασθ' ὡς εὐ, πόλεμον ποιῆσαι τοῖς 'Αμφικτύοσι καὶ περὶ τὴν Πυλαίαν ταραχὴν· εἰς γὰρ ταῦτ' εὐθὺς αὐτοὺς ὑπελάμβανεν αὐτοῦ δεήσεσθαι.* De Coron. 276.

[2] Grote has taken the correct view of the chronology of these events. (See the learned notes to his History of Greece, xi. pp. 657, 664.) The extraordinary congress of Amphictyons was held at some time between the spring and autumn, but at what particular time does not appear. Philip was appointed general at the autumnal meeting, *εἰς τὴν ἐπιοῦσαν πυλαίαν*, (Demosth. De Coron. 277.) The *ἐαρινῆς πυλαίας* in the second Amphictyonic decree (ibid. 278) is clearly a mistake, except upon the improbable supposition that there were two decrees for the election of Philip, one in the spring of 339 B.C., and one in the autumn. The records cited in the oration of Demosthenes are certainly not to be relied

donian party, that Philip should be invited to subdue and punish the refractory people, who had dared to defy the general council of Greece. It does not appear by what deputies this motion was supported, or whether or by whom it was opposed: as however the tribes north of Thermopylæ formed a majority in the council, it was certain to be carried in the affirmative. Philip was invited; and eagerly embracing the opportunity, for which doubtless he was well prepared, he set out with his army for the south, proclaiming that he had taken arms in the cause of religion as the Greeks had requested him. He was speedily joined by the Thessalians and circumjacent tribes, and passing Thermopylæ with a force which neither the Locrians nor any single Grecian state could have resisted, he entered the north-eastern part of the Phocian territory. Had his sole purpose now been to prosecute the war which he had professedly come to conduct against the Amphissian Locrians, he would have pursued his march through Phocis towards their frontier. Instead of doing so, he halted suddenly at Elatea, and began to repair its ruined fortifications. By this step (as Elatea was on the confine of Bœotia, and commanded the entrance to that country) it became manifest, that his designs were against the Athenians, or the Thebans, or both.

How the Athenians viewed it, is plain enough from the celebrated description of Demosthenes. Whether Philip was openly at war with them or not, mattered but little. Had there been ten thousand treaties of peace between them registered on stone, the result would have been the same. Philip's approach was not the less dangerous, because he had made no proclamation of hostility. He had recent failures to avenge, losses at sea, and insults to his coast. Yet these were nothing compared with the intense desire which he felt to strike a mortal blow at the power of Athens. It was indeed a necessity, unless he meant to forego his ambitious schemes. The moment the Athenians received intelligence that he had occupied Elatea, the whole truth flashed upon them at once. Here at length was that terrible king of Macedon, whom Demosthenes had been so many years alarming them about. He was now ready to fall upon Attica, as he had fallen upon Olynthus; and where were they to look for defense? The whole city was paralyzed, until Demosthenes came forward to rouse the people from their stupor, and point out to them what means of defense and what hope remained. The Athenians were passive in his hands.

I shall not seek to describe in language of my own those scenes of excitement and terror, which are so vividly brought before our eyes by Demosthenes himself. The circumstances under which he rose to address his countrymen, his own counsel, and all the pro-

on for their dates, if they are for any thing else. I see no evidence for supposing that Æschines advocated the appointment of Philip.

ceedings of the popular assembly, are fully set forth in his most interesting narrative, to which I refer the reader.[1] Suffice it here to say, that under his advice, which was unanimously agreed to, a decree was drawn up,[2] offering alliance on the most honorable terms to the Thebans: an embassy was dispatched instantly to Thebes, with Demosthenes at its head; and the Athenians with a full muster of their military strength marched to Eleusis, in order to encourage their friends in Thebes, and to second the efforts of the embassadors.

The advance of Philip into their neighborhood was a thing by no means welcome to the Thebans. They had signified their disapproval of the late Amphictyonic movement by absenting themselves from the special congress. The appointment of Philip to conduct the war must have increased their uneasiness; and still more, his fortification of Elatea.[3] For some time past the Thebans had regarded Philip with no friendly eye. They were oppressed by the weight of their obligation to him, and felt a jealousy and a dread of his growing power, which they dared not exhibit or express. His garrison at Nicæa, which he had nominally given to the Thessalians, both gave them offense and kept them in awe.[4] He had taken possession of Echinus, a town on the Malian gulf, which formerly belonged to them.[5] He had transferred to himself the Peloponnesian confederacy, of which they had once been at the head.[6] The relation in which they stood to him was altogether painful and humiliating.[7] Yet whatever their grievances might be, there seemed no help for them: they were isolated from all alliances except those which were devoted to Philip. Athens was the only independent

[1] See ante, pp. 68—74. Orig. pp. 284—291. Diodorus, xvi. 84, has this description before his eyes.

[2] The decree cited in the oration (De Coron. 288—291) is clearly erroneous as to the archon and the month; perhaps also in the number of embassadors; for there are only five, and Demosthenes had proposed ten. See Grote, History of Greece, xi. 673, note 2. As to the merits of the decree itself there is a difference of opinion among critics. Schaefer and others think it verbose and inflated. (See ante, p. 72, note 3.) Lord Brougham and the Edinburgh Reviewer (cited by me, ante, p. 76, note 1,) think it a fine piece of composition. Grote considers it improbable that intermarriage should be offered by the Athenians to the Thebans in that state of the negotiation. But it was a great point with Demosthenes to make the most liberal and friendly proposals.

[3] How this would be regarded at Thebes, appears from Demosthenes, Philipp. ii. 69.

[4] Demosthenes, Orat. ad. Epist. 153. Æschines, Contr. Ctesiph. 73.

[5] Demosthenes, Philipp. iii. 120.

[6] See ante, p. 371, n. 2.

[7] See the remarks of Demosthenes upon their position after the peace, De Pace, 62.

power to which they could have recourse; but, though there gradually rose up at Thebes a party favorable to the Athenian connection, the prejudices against it were for a long time so strong as to render it almost hopeless. Ancient animosities had been increased by the events of the Sacred War, and especially by the course which things had taken at its close.[1] The Thebans had reason to complain of Athens for her intrigues with Philip, the violent language of her orators, and her endeavors to dismember Bœotia; while they were conscious that the retention of Oropus was an act of injustice on their own part.[2] Since the peace there had been little intercourse between the two cities. Border disputes had arisen, and troops were sent to guard the frontiers, though without leading to any actual conflict.[3] The inscription on the Athenian offerings at Delphi, whatever may have been the motive which prompted it, was an act hurtful to national feelings, and likely to aggravate Theban ill will to Athens.[4]

There had long been at Athens a party anxious for reconciliation with the Thebans; but it had not been popular. Æschines reproaches Demosthenes for belonging to it.[5] Since the spring meeting of the Amphictyons this party had been gaining strength, chiefly through the exertions of Demosthenes, who foresaw danger to Athens from the disturbances which had taken place at Delphi.[6] Divers embassies were about this time sent to Thebes, conducted by statesmen supposed to be most popular in that city. They were instructed (we may fairly presume) to offer an explanation of the affair of the shields—to sound the Thebans as to their views of the new religious question which had been agitated—to appease any hostile feeling which might have sprung up against themselves—and lastly, when the Amphictyons had passed the fatal decree which invited Philip into Greece, to bring about, if possible, a defensive alliance between Thebes and Athens. Meanwhile, however, all these attempts were counterworked by an opposite party. Philip kept his spies and agents in both cities, who informed him

[1] Demosthenes, De Coron. 237.

[2] See ante, pp. 260, 307, 308, 312.

[3] Demosthenes, De Fals. Leg. 446; c. Con. 1257.

[4] At the time when the Athenians presented these shields, they were flushed with their successes in Eubœa and the Propontis; and it is possible they may have given way to a foolish feeling of pride. Æschines, an anti-Theban, calls the inscription *τὸ προσῆκον ἐπίγραμμα*. (Contr. Ctesiph. 70.)

[5] Æschines, De Fals. Leg. 42: *Καὶ γὰρ πρὸς τοῖς ἄλλοις κακοῖς βοιωτιάζει.* Compare pp. 46, 47, and Contr. Ctesiph. 73, where he says of Aristophon, *πλεῖστον χρόνον τὴν τοῦ βοιωτιάζειν ὑπομείνας αἰτίαν.* See ante, p. 281.

[6] Demosthenes, De Coron. 275, 281.

of all that was going on.[1] Whilst he lay in apparent inaction at Pella, recovering from his wound, he was laboring by every engine of diplomacy to defeat the Athenian negotiations, and prevent a conjunction which might put a check upon all his ambitious schemes. And so well did he manage things, with the help of his ministers and partisans; so artfully did he work on the jealousies, the hopes, and the fears of the Theban people, that they were induced to pass decrees in his favor, rejecting the overtures of the Athenians: and when Philip set out on his march, it seemed impossible that any union could take place between Thebes and Athens.[2] In one thing, however, he failed. The Thebans refused to send any aid to the Amphictyonic expedition. They desired neutrality and peace.[3]

At length, Demosthenes and his colleagues arrived at Thebes. Philip's embassadors were already there, together with those of his allies, Thessalians, Ænianians, Ætolians, Dolopians, Phthiots. The Macedonian party were full of confidence, the friends of Athens in despondence and alarm. Demosthenes, at first, seeing how things stood, sent discouraging letters to Athens; but he quickly collected his energies to meet the exigency of the case. It was plain, the confidence of his adversaries was owing not merely to the assurances which the Thebans had lately given of their adhesion to the Macedonian alliance, but in a great measure, also, to the presence of Philip and his army. This, however, might operate in two ways. It intimidated the people; yet it also suggested thoughts favorable to a union with Athens. So long as Philip kept himself at a distance, the Thebans were content to be quiet, and not provoke his hostility by forming new connections. But if they were not to have the benefits of peace; if their territory was to be traversed by Philip's armies, or be made the theatre of war; and still more, if he designed to coerce them by keeping a strongly garrisoned fortress on their borders; his alliance was no longer the advantageous thing which it promised to be in the beginning. Such thoughts were sure to arise in the breasts of the Theban multitude, who had no corrupt interest

[1] Dinarchus (Contr. Demosth. 99) speaks of the traitors in Thebes. Compare Demosthenes, De Coron. 241, 286.

[2] Æschines, Contr. Ctesiph. 73. Demosthenes, De Coron. 281—284. Supposing the documents cited here to be partially genuine, it is certain that we have not all the documents referred to by Demosthenes in the oration. There must have been some decrees or answers of the Thebans, to which he refers by the words: *Τούτοις ἐπαρθεὶς τοῖς ψηφίσμας καὶ ταῖς ἀποκρίσεσιν.*

[3] Demosthenes, De Coron. 279: *'Ως οὐχ ὑπήκουον οἱ Θηβαῖοι.* I presume that Philip, soon after his nomination to be Amphictyonic general, solicited the Thebans to join him. They declined; and then he solicited the Peloponnesian states.

in Philip's friendship: and of these Demosthenes prepared to take advantage.[1]

A popular assembly was held, to consider whether the proposal of Philip or that of the Athenians should be accepted. The embassadors on both sides were introduced to the people. The Macedonians, holding already the character of allies, were allowed to have the first word.[2] They extolled the merits of the king of Macedon, enlarged upon the services which he had done the Thebans, enumerated the various causes of antipathy and jealousy which subsisted between Thebes and Athens, the many injuries which the Athenians had in a long series of years inflicted upon the Theban people. Now was the time, they said, for the Thebans to show their gratitude to Philip, and take vengeance upon long-standing enemies. But if they were unwilling to join in the invasion of Attica, Philip would be satisfied with their neutrality: let them only allow a passage to his army, and he would himself chastise the Athenians. If Philip had asked this of them before he lent them his aid in the Sacred War, they would have promised it easily: it would be unjust to refuse it because Philip had been generous and relied upon their honor.[3] By adhering to Philip's friendship they had every thing to gain; their own country would be secure, and they would share in the plunder of Attica; whereas, if they joined the Athenians, Bœotia would be exposed to warfare and pillage.[4]

Demosthenes rose to combat these arguments. Not a fragment of his speech is preserved. In the oration on the Crown he discreetly abstained from repeating any portion of it to the jury; as, however gratifying the recital might have been to his own feelings, it could at that time have answered no useful purpose. The position of affairs suggests to us the topics upon which he must have principally dwelt; and the substance of what he said may have been as follows:—

Men of Thebes, if this were a question only of punishing Athens, or even of destroying her, I might never have ventured to address this assembly. But it is a question which deeply concerns you and your own safety. Thebes is in no less danger than Athens; and as

[1] The seizure of Elatea turned the tide of Theban feeling in favor of Athens: *Μετέγνωσαν εὐθὺς, ὡς τοῦτ' εἶδον.* Demosthenes, De Coron. 278.

[2] Amyntas and Clearchus were the chief Macedonian envoys, according to Plutarch, in Vit. Demosth. 18. Python is mentioned by Diodorus, xvi. 85. But quære, whether he does not confound this with another occasion. See ante, p. 373.

[3] Aristotle, Rhetor. ii, 23. 6. Philochorus, apud Dionysium ad Amm. s. 11, pp. 739, 742: *Εἰ πρὶν βοηθῆσαι εἰς Φωκεῖς ἠξίουν, ὑπέσχοντο ἄν· ἄτοπον οὖν, εἰ, διότι προεῖτο καὶ ἐπίστευσε, μὴ διήσουσιν.* Aristotle cites this to illustrate a point of rhetoric—that a man should do out of gratitude for a past favor that which he would have promised to obtain it.

[4] Demosthenes, De Coron. 298, 299.

the Athenians would consider your subjection to Philip as one of the greatest calamities to themselves, such they conceive should be your feelings with regard to Athens. For if (which heaven forbid!) we should be disabled from lending assistance to you in the hour of need, what alliance, what protection will remain to you? All your Peloponnesian confederates have gone over to Philip. He commands the pass of Thermopylæ. He has surrounded you with his garrisons. The Thessalians, all the tribes of Pindus and Olympus, Oeta and Othrys, are devoted to him. Why do they come to invade Attica, and what mean they by this present embassy? We have no quarrel with the people of Thessaly, or with the Ætolians or Œtæans or any of them. They follow the king of Macedon against us, because they are his vassals; and they come here to dictate to you, what votes you shall give to-day. Dolopians and Perrhæbians would compel you, a free people, to render the same obedience to Philip which they are content to pay themselves. Their very presence here is an insult; and the whole conduct of Philip proves the light estimation in which he regards you. His envoys have reminded you of the obligations which you are under to him, and demand that they should be requited. The merit of an obligation depends on the motives of the party who confers it. Philip has shown, that the aid which he lent you was to further his own ambitious schemes and to make you subservient to them. There can be no gratitude, where there is no equality. He imagines that, having once assisted you, he is entitled to treat you as his inferiors. If he regarded you as allies on equal terms, he would have consulted you before his march; he would have asked leave for a passage through your territory before he approached the frontier. He has come without your permission, intending to make Bœotia the marching-road for his army; and he is now fortifying a post on your confines, in order to intimidate you. His conduct agrees with the language of his ministers. They threaten Bœotia with pillage, if you dare to refuse compliance with his will. The occupation of Elatea is the strongest proof, what Philip's opinion is both of himself and you. It proves that he distrusts you, that he regards you as doubtful friends; and for the best of all reasons, because he is conscious that he deserves not your friendship. It is but a short step from a suspicious ally to a declared enemy. At this very moment you are esteemed in no other light than as enemies, to be crushed on the first favorable opportunity. It is enough that you have deliberated about alliance with Athens; this alone he will never forgive: he expects from every people an unconditional and unhesitating obedience. Bethink you, how he treated the unhappy Olynthians. They assisted him against Athens; they helped him to deprive us of our Thracian dominions: yet, notwithstanding this, he attacked them without any provocation, and razed their city to the ground. Philip's enmity is the more to be dreaded, when it is not open and avowed. Every Grecian city is infested by his spies and agents. Among you, as among us, there are miscreants who would sell their country to Philip, that they may rule in it by his influence. These are the men who have hitherto contrived by their artifices to keep you and the Athenians asunder. They know that citizens of a free republic are the natural allies of the Theban people, whereas Philip will help his own hirelings to oppress their fellow-countrymen. Philip has the same motive for overthrowing your commonwealth that he has for destroying ours; for we both set an example of freedom to the other Greek states, which is an obstacle in his way to empire. But he declares no war against Thebes. He would be foolish to do so, if he can gain his objects without it. There will be no necessity for war, if, as he seems to expect, you submit to his commands without a murmur. If you are inclined, like us, to dispute Macedonian supremacy, then he considers it better to deal first with us, and with you on a more convenient occasion. It is thus that he proceeds step by step to reduce every Greek city to subjection. Can you be blind to his projects? Or are you afraid to resist them? I know not whether he calculates on your credulity or your fears. He came hither under a religious pretense, to chastise the Locrians for sacrilege: he never told the Amphictyons, whom he summoned to join his standard, that he was about to lead them against Attica: not till he is in within two days' march of our frontier, does he avow his real object. Who can safely trust a man, who thus ever dissembles his plans, till they are ripe for execution? Honor and good faith, which prevent other people from committing acts of wanton aggression, are no manner of restraint to Philip. He pays an ill compliment to your state, by supposing that you will aid and abet him in his treachery. It is plain, he imagines you are no longer the soldiers of Leuctra: he ranks you already among his dependents. Let him see that he is mistaken in his estimate. Prove to the Greeks, that you have the courage to stand up for their independence and your own. No middle course is open to you. These envoys indeed say, that Philip will be content with your giving him a passage through Bœotia. Mark the insidious nature of their argument, and the contempt which it shows of the Theban people. If the Thebans (they say) are unwilling to share with Philip the dangers of the field, he kindly permits them to stay at home. Why, if the war with Athens were just and beneficial to Thebes, and Philip had for the Theban people that respect which he ought to have, he would not be satisfied without their hearty co-operation. But he knows it is a war which by aggrandizing him must injure you; and therefore he tempts you to your ruin by offering you this base alternative. His orators are instructed to suggest this timorous counsel, in the hope that you will sacrifice your country to the desire of present ease. If Philip can succeed without your help, flatter not yourselves that you can be neutral with impunity. No! You must either be with us for Greece, or with Philip against her. If corrupt statesmen have already acquired such influence over your counsels, that they can persuade you to forget what is due to yourselves, and to disregard the dignity of the commonwealth, hearken to the call of Philip, obey his summons to arms, follow him to the walls of Athens, and be content, like Dolophians and Perrhæbians, to be the subjects of a prince whom Pelopidas brought as a hostage to Thebes. But if you would rather imitate those gallant men who raised your country to greatness and renown, then join with us in resisting an aggressor who comes to despoil us of all that is most dear and valuable. You have now the opportunity, which may never come again, of defending Hellenic liberty against barbarism, of blotting out other painful memories in the glory of one heroic struggle for your father-land. Arouse ye then, men of Thebes! Let the spirit of Epaminondas awaken in the bosom of every man sentiments worthy of his country. The Athenians will fight by your side. They that helped you when the Spartan had seized your acropolis, will not desert you now. Are there any in this assembly who look on Philip as invincible? Have we not driven him in confusion from the walls of Perinthus and Byzantium? Have we not expelled his tyrants from Eretria and Oreus? And shall we not now chase him from your frontiers, from the strongholds which he has chosen for his sallying-places against the Greeks? What need of many words? Our troops are already at Eleusis: at your call they will march to Thebes, and enable you to bid defiance to this man who now so insolently threatens you. Nor do we stand alone in the conflict. Achaia, Corinth, Megara, other states are our allies, who will not permit the sacred soil of Greece to be trampled on by a barbarian. But if you, men of Thebes, adopt that course which your true welfare requires, the war will speedily be brought to an issue. For when Philip sees that Athens and Thebes are firmly united, he will lower his arrogance, he will yield as he did at Byzantium, to a combination too powerful for him to conquer. His hopes are founded on our discord. Let that cease; and he will retire in haste to Macedonia. That you, men of Thebes, understand your duties, and that all which I have said is in accordance with your own honest judgment, I know full well. There is but one thing which gives me any anxiety: the remembrance of those jealousies which have divided us, and which have brought so many evils upon Athens and upon you and the rest of the Greeks. They indeed would have long since died away, but for the traitors in both cities, who, bribed by the gold of Macedonia, have made it their business to foment and keep them alive. It is these persons that you should view with jealousy and suspicion; aye, that you should execrate and abhor: and when they appear to support by their voice or their presence the foreigner who has hired their services, let them see by unmistakable signs, that you know them, and that you will not suffer yourselves to be deceived and betrayed. The people of Athens have by this resolution, which has been read to you, deliberately recorded the feelings with which they regard the people of Thebes. It is their sincerest wish, that all former animosities be buried in amnesty and oblivion. They will remember only the mutual kindnesses which have passed between you; and that the Thebans are Greeks of the same nation as themselves, for whose dignity and prosperity they will consult as they would for their own. They offer you alliance, friendship, brotherhood. I conjure and implore you, men of Thebes, to receive this solemn act of the Athenian people in the same spirit in which it was decreed. You have heard from my lips the sentiments of my countrymen; and with a few more words I shall have discharged my duty. Be assured, O ye Thebans, that union with Athens brings you security and honor; connection with Macedonia is but another name for servitude. You are about to give your votes on a question of the deepest moment to yourselves and your posterity. May the gods so direct your counsels that you may decide as becomes Greeks and freemen!

These and other arguments, expanded into the glowing language and delivered with the energy of Demosthenes, carried the day. The Thebans voted alliance with Athens, and invited her troops into the city. A large body of their own civic force was encamped without the walls, while the Athenians were quartered in their houses among their women and children, and received with the kindest hospitality, of which by their strict discipline and good behavior they proved themselves fully worthy. It is touching to see these two people, late such deadly foes, now in the expiring day of Grecian freedom united as friends and brothers, preparing to issue forth to their last common battle-field, and to shed their blood together in the same sacred cause.[1]

Æschines, in the impotence of his malice, will not allow to his adversary the least share of merit in the success of this negotiation; urging that it was the force of circumstances, and not the eloquence of Demosthenes, which prevailed upon the Thebans to take the side of Athens. This wretched piece of sophistry, which it is not worth while to refute, has not found much favor either at Athens or elsewhere. Modern readers of history lament only that a speech which achieved so signal a triumph should be lost.

[1] Demosthenes, De Coron. 299, 300.

[2] Æschines, Contr. Ctesiph. 73. He says also here, that the Thebans sent for the Athenians to join them, before Demosthenes proposed one word of a decree for an alliance. Of course the treaty was not finally decreed until the return of Demosthenes from Thebes. But Æschines insinuates something more. Demosthenes frequently boasted of his triumph at Thebes, and not without reason. See De Coron. 278, 288, 308. His remarks in p. 298 are most just and forcible—that Æschines, while he allowed him no credit as an orator or an adviser, attributed to him all the failures in the war. Compare Dinarchus, Contr. Demosth.

At the time when all the Athenians were rejoicing in the consummation of the Theban alliance, Æschines never muttered a word of complaint against it; but long afterwards he found cause of reproach against his rival in the terms of the treaty, which he contended were too favorable to Thebes. It was agreed, he says, that the Athenians should assist the Thebans in maintaining their sovereignty over Bœotia; that two thirds of the expenses of the war were to be defrayed by Athens; that the command at sea was to be shared between the two countries, though Athens was to pay the whole expense; and the supreme command by land was given virtually to Thebes: there could be no necessity for making such concessions, because the Thebans were in much greater peril than the Athenians, and were only too glad to obtain their succor. To all this, however, Demosthenes himself furnishes a complete answer; that it was neither prudent nor possible, to stand bargaining about conditions, when Philip was ready to outbid them, and when there was not a moment to be lost. We may add, that a liberal and generous policy was not only the best means for securing the immediate object, but the wisest thing also for the future, that there might be an end to the jealousies which had so long kept Thebes and Athens at variance.[1]

The Thebans having thus decided in favor of alliance with Athens, both sides prepared for war. Of the events of the war a very imperfect description is given us in the few ancient works that remain. Of English historians, Grote is the only one who has taken a correct view of the campaign. Others, misled by the brevity of Diodorus, and also by the records cited in the oration on the Crown, have conceived that the whole war occupied but two months, from Scirophorion to Metagitnion (June to August), 338 B.C It has been already noticed, how inaccurate Diodorus is in the connection and general outline of history. Not only does he omit many important events, but he observes no proportion of length and brevity in his narrative, sometimes wearying us with prolixity of description, at other times cutting short matters about which we are curious to obtain further information. And as to the records in the published

91. Plutarch, in Vit. Demosth. 18, cites the words of Theopompus: Τὸ *μὲν οὐν συμφέρον οὐ διέφυγε τοὺς τῶν Θηβαίων λογισμοὺς, ἀλλ' ἐν ὄμμασιν ἕκαστος εἶχε τὰ τοῦ πολέμου δεινὰ, ἔτι τῶν Φωκικῶν τραυμάτων νεαρῶν παραμενόντων· ἡ δὲ τοῦ ῥήτορος δύναμις, ὥς φησι Θεόπομπος, ἐκριπίζουσα τον θυμῶν αὐτῆν, καὶ διακαίουσα τὴν φιλοτιμίαν, ἐπεσκότησε τοῖς ἄλλοις ἅπασι· ὥστε φόβον καὶ λογισμὸν καὶ χάριν ἐκβαλεῖν αὐτοὺς, ἐνθουσιῶντας ὑπὸ τοῦ λόγου πρὸς τὸ καλόν.*

[1] Æschines, Contr. Ctesiph. 73, 74. Demosthenes, De Coron. 306, 307. A crown of gold was conferred by the people of Athens on Demosthenes: De Coron. 302.

[2] Mitford, in his History of Greece, vol. iv. ch. xlii. s. 4, says with justice:—"The narrative of Diodorus seems to imply that, before the

editions of the oration on the Crown, we have seen that the dates are incorrect; and if this be so, it is impossible to draw from them any conclusions which are opposed to other and better evidence. From the comparison of various passages in Demosthenes, Æschines, Dinarchus, Pausanias, Plutarch, and Polyænus, it appears beyond all question, that a protracted war was carried on in Phocis, Amphissian Locris, and Bœotia; during which there was much maneuvering on both sides, and three or four battles were fought before that of Chæronea with various success, one of them occurring in the winter season;[1] that Amphissa was taken by Philip; that embassies were sent to Peloponnesus and other parts of Greece both by Philip and his adversaries, and the latter succeeded in obtaining auxiliaries; that negotiations for peace were opened by Philip; and that the Athenians and their allies exerted themselves to reassemble the scattered population of Phocis, and to fortify some of their more important towns. All this argues not only extended military operations, but diplomatic proceedings, councils of war, plans, preparations, and arrangements, requiring a much longer period of time than what Clinton and those who follow him allow to the campaign of the Chæronea. That Philip began his march from Macedonia soon after the autumnal congress of B.C. 339, at which he was appointed to be Amphictyonic general, and that the war lasted for ten or eleven months from that time to the August of the following year is the opinion of Grote, formed upon a juster view of the historical data which are left us.[2]

Philip, disappointed of that success at Thebes which he had reason to expect, redoubled his efforts to procure assistance from the Peloponnesians. They had already been requested to send contingents in aid of the religious war against Amphissa; but none of them had complied with the summons. His letters were now more

competition of oratory between Python and Demosthenes at Thebes, the army of the Athenian confederacy had taken that station near Chæronea which it occupied to the time of the decisive. battle. But Diodorus, abridging greatly, and perhaps often writing from memory, not unfrequently manages narratives so that it is difficult to guess whether he intends that the reader should take what precedes or what follows as prior in time; and he still oftener omits, as here, to notice intervening transactions necessary to connect parts of his story." It is fair to state, that Mitford has not fallen into the error of omitting the winter and autumnal campaign: (ibid. ss. 4, 5.)

[1] Demosthenes, De Coron. 300: *Τὰς πρώτας μάχας, τήν τ' ἐπὶ τοῦ ποταμοῦ καὶ τὴν χειμερινήν.* Clinton (Fasti Hellenici, 271), in order to make this square with his chronology, says: "The word *χειμερινήν* is probably corrupt; perhaps capable of another interpretation." It has accordingly been interpreted to mean "the battle of the storm." Schaefer, in the Apparatus Criticus, remarks that this should be *χειμέριον*.

[2] Grote, History of Greece, xi. p. 683.

pressing, yet not more successful than before. None of the Peloponnesians could be deceived by the religious plea which Philip set up; for they speedily heard the truth from the envoys on the other side; and the members of the old Theban confederacy would naturally be reluctant to make war upon their former ally, with whom they had had no quarrel.[1] In the meantime Philip remained at Elatea, which he had chosen for the base of his operations; and we may presume that he employed himself in strengthening his position, while he awaited the arrival of reinforcements.

Nor was Demosthenes idle. After arranging the terms of alliance at Thebes, he returned to Athens, and immediately passed a decree to ratify the treaty. He dispatched embassies to the Peloponnesian and other cities, to solicit succor: he went in person to some of them, and obtained considerable success. Aid was promised by the Achæans, Corinthians, Megarians, Eubœans, Leucadians, and Corcyræans. Contributions in money were furnished by some states, and a large body of mercenaries was levied.[2] An unwonted vigor was infused into the Athenian administration. The spirit of the people rose to meet the peril which hung over them. Under the advice of Demosthenes, they suspended some works that were going on for the improvement of the docks and arsenal; and they gave a still stronger proof of their warlike zeal, by repealing the law of Eubulus, and allowing the theoric fund to be used for the purposes of war. Thus was accomplished, under the pressure of stern necessity, a measure which Demosthenes had long in vain recommended. He was now (in all but military talents) the Pericles of the day: an energetic and powerful war-minister, counseling, directing, animating all.[3]

Having completed all those measures of preparation which required his presence at Athens or elsewhere, Demosthenes hastened back to Thebes, to assist at the councils of war. Such was the zeal and ability which he had displayed, that even the Theban commanders paid the highest deference to his judgment. Doubtless he

[1] Demosthenes, De Coron. 279, 301, 302. The letters which Demosthenes refers to in the last passage would appear, from the context, to have been written after the first successes of the allies against Philip. But it is impossible to rely upon such an argument. Philip's letters would never have disclosed that he had been defeated. The date was sufficiently vague for Demosthenes to refer them to the period which suited his purpose. That none of the Peloponnesians joined Philip, appears from Pausanias. See ante, p. 374.

[2] Demosthenes, De Coron. 306. Æschines, Contr. Ctesiph. 74, allows that ten thousand mercenaries were raised. Compare Plutarch, Vit. Demosth. 17. Vit. Decem. Orat. p. 851. Justin, ix. 3. "Legationibus Græciam fatigant."

[3] Philochorus, apud Dionysium ad Amm. xi. p. 742. Demosthenes, De Coron. 301, 302.

was incompetent to give advice on the details of military tactics; yet in concerting the plan of a campaign, many questions might arise which required the help of a statesman and diplomatist. So entirely was Demosthenes identified with the cause, that he would spare himself no personal labor where he could be useful, and would leave nothing to be done by others which he thought he could do better himself. Æschines, who charges him with mischievous interference, admits that his influence was great both in the assembly and in the camp.[1]

One of the first measures determined on by the allies was, to re-establish the Phocian people, and to put their country in a state of security against Philip. It has been related how at the end of the Sacred War the Phocian cities were destroyed, their population dispersed into villages, and large numbers of men driven into exile. The country was at this time in a perfectly defenseless condition, having neither a force of its own to resist invasion, nor shelter for a protecting army. The Thebans, who had been so instrumental in the depression of their neighbors, now repented of the mischief which they had done, and exerted themselves to repair it. This (says Grote)[2] evinced on their part the adoption of an improved and generous policy, worthy of the Panhellenic cause in which they had embarked. They marched with the Athenians into Phocis, restored the ruined cities wherever it was practicable, and brought back the scattered inhabitants: in some cases uniting together several communities, which would have been too weak to defend themselves singly. The work of restoration was complete and permanent. Ambrysus, a city in the south-western part of Phocis, commanding one of the passes into Bœotia, was fortified with a double wall of extraordinary strength, the building of which must have cost much time and labor,[3] During all this time, it is clear, the Athenians and Thebans must have held the command of the Phocian territory. That Philip, however, did not leave them wholly undisturbed, we may infer from the mention of two engagements—one called the battle by the river, another the winter battle; in which, according

[1] Æschines, Contr. Ctesiph. 74, 75. Demosthenes justly says of himself (De Coron. 288), Ἔδωκ' ἐμαυτὸν ὑμῖν ἁπλῶς εἰς τοὺς περιεστηκότας τῇ πόλει κινδύνους. Plutarch, Vit. Demosth. 18, says: Ὑπηρετεῖν δὲ μὴ μόνον τοὺς στρατηγοὺς τῷ Δημοσθένει ποιοῦντας τὸ προσταττόμενον, ἀλλὰ καὶ τοὺς Βοιωτάρχας· διοικεῖσθαι τὰς ἐκκλησίας ἁπάσας οὐδὲν ἧττον ὑπ' ἐκείνου τότε τὰς Θηβαίων ἢ τὰς Ἀθηναίων, ἀγαπωμένου παρ' ἀμφοτέροις καὶ δυνατεύοντος, οὐκ ἀδίκως αὐδὲ παρ' ἀξίαν, ὥσπερ ἀποφαίνεται Θεόπομπος, ἀλλὰ καὶ πανὺ προσηκόντως.

[2] History of Greece, xi. 682. Notwithstanding this, the Phocian soldiers in Alexander's army exhibited a most revengeful spirit against the Thebans. See Arrian, Anab. i. 8. Plùtarch, Vit Alexand. 12.

[3] Pausanias, x. chaps. 3, 33, 36; iv. 31.

to Demosthenes, the allies had so much the advantage, as to afford occasion for public rejoicings and thanksgiving at Athens.[1]

It was, perhaps, in the spring of B.C. 338 that Philip, either having serious misgivings about the issue of the contest, or, which is more probable, with the intention of misleading his adversaries or distracting their counsels, sent proposals of peace to Thebes. The Bœotarchs were inclined to consider them favorably, but were opposed by Demosthenes, whose counsel prevailed with the Thebans, and caused them to reject Philip's overtures. So far we may safely credit the statement of Æschines, who, however, goes on to charge his rival with the most unseemly conduct; viz. that he jumped up in the Theban assembly before the question had even been introduced, and swore that, if any one advised the making of peace with Philip, he would seize him by the hair and carry him to prison: and that, when the Theban magistrates had ordered the return of some Athenian troops for the express purpose of deliberating on the question of peace, Demosthenes became quite out of his mind, denounced the Bœotarchs as traitors to the cause of Greece, and said he would advise his countrymen to send an embassy to Thebes and ask for a passage through Bœotia to attack Philip: and that, by such menace, he forced the Thebans to continue the war. All these additions we may set down to the malice of the accuser. Whether Demosthenes acted imprudently in dissuading all pacific negotiations, we are unable to judge, for want of knowing the circumstances. If there was a chance of obtaining a real peace, it might have been advisable to treat with Philip. But if he was trying to negotiate separately with Thebes, with a view to create disunion or dissension between the allies, or if he was maneuvering to gain time or any other advantage, and if there was any danger that the allies would fall into the snare, we can only say, that Demosthenes, by defeating Philip's crafty design, acquired an additional claim to the gratitude of his country.[2]

[1] Demosthenes, De Coron. 300. There is no occasion to suppose with Reiske, that the battle by the river has any reference to the district of Parapotamii. Yet it is likely enough, that it took place near the Cephisus.

[2] Æschines, Contr. Ctesiph. 74, 75. There is a difficulty about the words—*τοὺς στρατιώτας τοὺς ὑμετέρους πάλιν ἀνέστρεψαν ἐξεληλυθότας, ἵνα βουλεύσησθε περὶ τῆς εἰρήνης.* Thirlwall interprets them thus,—"A body of troops, which had been sent perhaps to counteract the effects of Philip's proposals, was turned back by the Theban magistrates." (History of Greece, vi. 67.) I think him right in supposing, that it was only a division of the Athenian troops that were sent back: as to the purpose for which they were sent from Athens, his suggestion is very doubtful. Grote explains the passage differently—"They proposed, even before the negotiations had begun, to send home the Athenian soldiers into Attica, in order that deliberations might be taken concerning

The first advantage obtained by Philip over the allies was in forcing his way to Amphissa. It was important for him to accomplish the general object for which the Amphictyons had invited him into Greece. It would have discredited him with many of his followers, if he made it appear that he had come on a false pretense, or if he allowed himself to be baffled in his original purpose; whereas, if he succeeded in it, they would be encouraged to assist him in his own private enterprises. The road from Delphi to Amphissa, probably that which Philip took, traversed the declivities of Parnassus. The defense of it was intrusted to Chares and the Theban Proxenus, who commanded a large body of mercenaries furnished by the Athenians. They occupied the entrance of a defile, which they could have defended against very superior numbers. Philip, in order to draw them from their strong position, forged a letter from himself to Antipater, stating that he had postponed his expedition to Amphissa, and was about to march instantly for Thrace, where he heard the people were rising. He contrived that this letter should fall into the hands of the enemy. Chares and Proxenus, deceived by its contents, neglected their guard of the pass: upon which Philip, marching through without opposition, surprised and routed their army, and afterwards made himself master of Amphissa.[1] Æschines bitterly reproaches Demosthenes for having lent the mercenaries to the Amphissians, and for having thus divided the forces of the allies, and enabled Philip to attach and defeat them separately. For this there may be better ground than for most of his charges. The defeat of the mercenaries was a severe loss and discouragement to the allies, and perhaps it might have been avoided by keeping the whole army together. While the generals are chargeable with the immediate miscarriage, it is very possible that the plan of operations was badly designed.[2]

Philip, having inflicted due punishment on the vanquished people

the peace." (History of Greece, xi. 689.) The word *ἀνέστρεψαν* however points to an act done rather than one proposed to be done: while the context indicates that the main body of the Athenian troops was not separated from the Bœotian. A reinforcement may have been on its way from Athens, which the Bœotarchs ordered to return, with a request that the Athenians would deliberate on the question of peace. That they did deliberate appears from Plutarch, (Vit. Phocion, 16,) which Grote with much probability refers to this period.

[1] Polyænus, Strateg. iv. c. 2, s. 8, confirmed by Dinarchus, Contr. Demosth. 99. *Ἐπὶ δὲ τοῖς ξένοις τοῖς εἰς Ἄμφισσαν συλλεγεῖσι πρόξενος ὁ προδοτὴς ἐγένετο*, and the passage of Æschines cited below.

[2] Æschines, Contr. Ctesiph. 74, He accuses Demosthenes of taking the public money to pay mercenary troops who did not exist; also, of making a profit of those who were lent to the Amphissians. He says that he himself protested against this last measure, but does not state upon what grounds.

of Amphissa,[1] and having thus performed his promise to the Amphictyons, and given them increased confidence in his fortune and ability, resolved vigorously to push the war against the Athenians and Thebans. The intermediate steps are unknown to us. It appears, however, that shortly after the midsummer of 338 B.C., by which time he had received strong reinforcements from Macedonia, he was in a condition to strike a decisive blow. The allies, after the loss which they had sustained, retreated from Phocis, and took up a defensive position in Bœotia; whither Philip speedily followed them, taking (as it seems) the easiest road which led by the vale of the Cephisus from Panopeus to Chæronea.[2] Finding that they were posted on a hill commanding one of the passes, he began to ravage and plunder the adjacent country; upon which the allies quitted their vantage-ground, and descended into the plain to offer him battle.[3] They met not far from Chæronea; Philip encamping on the banks of the Cephisus, the Greeks near the temple of Hercules, on a stream called Hæmon. Plutarch says, he remembered an oak near the Cephisus, which the people of the country called Alexander's oak, because his tent was pitched under it.[4] Philip's army numbered above thirty thousand foot, and two thousand horse, consisting of Macedonians and troops from Thessaly and the north. The allied army, composed of Athenians, Thebans, Achæans, Corinthians and Phocians, were, according to Diodorus, inferior in number; according to Justin, greatly superior. The chief difference lay in the quality of the troops and their commanders."[5]

[1] Grote thinks it may be gathered from Diodorus, xviii. 56, that the sacred domain was restored, and those Amphissians who had taken a leading part against Delphi were banished. (History of Greece, xi. 687.)

[2] Pausanias, x. 4; x. 35. Strabo, ix. 407.

[3] Polyænus, Strateg. iv. 2. 14.

[4] Plutarch, Vit. Alexand. 7. Vit. Demosth. 19. He cites an ancient oracle, which thus predicted of the battle:—

Τῆς ἐπὶ Θερμώδοντι μάχης ἀπάνευθε γενοίμην
Αἰετὸς ἐν νεφέεσσι καὶ ἠέρι θηήσασθαι.
Κλαίει ὁ νικηθεὶς, ὁ δὲ νικήσας ἀπόλωλε.

Of which one explanation was, that the river Hæmon, which flows into the Cephisus, was anciently called Thermodon, but after the battle got a new name from the carnage which polluted its waters. A different explanation however was given, as he tells us, by Duris.

[5] Diodorus, xvi. 85. Justin, ix. 3. Pausanias, vii. 6, 5; x. 3, 4. Strabo, ix, 414. The account of Diodorus, as to the number of the Greek army, seems nearer the truth than that of Justin. The Theban and Athenian civic force would hardly exceed 22,000 foot. The Achæans, (judging from the succor which they lent in the Sacred War,) we may set down at 2,000: the Corinthians and Phocians at about the same. The mercenaries who returned to their standards, and possibly some contingents

The Macedonians had never yet fairly tried their strength against the best troops of southern Greece. Philip had frequently encountered small bodies of the Athenians in Thrace and Macedonia, and had generally, but not always, overcome them. He had defeated the standing army of Onomarchus; superior on the whole to any which a single Greek state could have brought into the field, yet consisting chiefly of mercenaries, not animated (it might be thought) with the spirit of citizen-soldiers fighting for their country. He had never engaged in a fair pitched battle with the heavy-armed infantry of Athens, Thebes, or Sparta, the leading republics of Greece. The present confederacy was the most formidable which had yet been arrayed against him; nor could he have been entirely free from misgivings as to the result. We can not doubt, therefore, that, in order to decide so important a contest, Philip took every precaution which became a prudent commander; and that he had collected around him not only a force powerful in point of numbers, but the flower of the Macedonian army, and especially the celebrated phalanx, which he had brought to perfection by his own training and discipline.[1] Of this it may here be proper to give a brief description.

The Macedonian phalanx, as organized by Philip, was an improvement on the order of battle already in use among the Greeks.[2] The long line of heavy-armed infantry, standing with spear and shield in close array, was called a phalanx.[3] In this way most of the Greek republican armies were drawn up for battle, the depth of the line varying according to circumstances. At Mantinea, in the Peloponnesian war, the Lacedæmonians were drawn up in a line of four hundred and forty-eight men, eight deep.[4] At Leuctra the Lacedæmonians stood twelve deep, the Thebans fifty deep.[5] The soldiers held their spears couched in two hands, the left arm being passed through the ring of the shield, which was also suspended by a thong from the neck, and covered the whole body down to the

from other states, may be reckoned at 4,000 or 5,000. In number of cavalry Philip was most probably superior.

[1] Mitford in his History of Greece, vol. iv. c. 42, s. 4, contends that Philip's was a miscellaneous Amphictyonic army, with a small proportion of Macedonians, and probably without the phalanx. In support of his opinion he cites Demosthenes, Philipp. iii. 123. which however is not in point.

[2] Diodorus, xvi. 3. *'Επενόησε δὲ καὶ τὴν τῆς φάλαγγος πυκνότητα καὶ κατασκευὴν, μιμησάμενος τὸν ἐν Τροίᾳ τῶν ἡρώων συνασπισμόν, καὶ πρῶτος συνεστήσατο τὴν Μακεδονικὴν φάλαγγα.* He refers, as Polybius does, to the descriptions of the close ranks (*πυκιναὶ φάλαγγες*) in Homer. See Iliad. xiii. 131; xvi. 214.

[3] Hence *ἐπὶ φάλαγγος ἄγειν*, opposed to *κατὰ κέρας*. See Schneider ad Xenoph. Anab. vi. c. 5, s. 25. *Ζυγὸν* is *a file.*

[4] Thucydides, v. 63.

[5] Xenophon, Hellen. vi. c. 4, s. 12.

knee.[1] In this order they made their charge, generally at a running pace, endeavoring to bear down the enemy by the force and pressure of their spears. Troops unprovided with good defensive armor were unable to withstand the shock of the heavy-armed Greeks. Thus the Athenians at Marathon, and the Spartans at Platæa proved themselves superior to the numerous hosts of Darius and Xerxes: after which the Persian infantry never dared to face the Greek in a fair field of battle.

Philip, having in his younger days seen and admired the well-trained battalions of Thebes, determined to introduce a similar discipline into the Macedonian army. He formed his phalanx upon the general model of the Greek, making some alterations which he thought would increase its efficiency. He adopted the shield and other defensive armor of the Greek infantry, but lengthened the spear and the sword, as Iphicrates had done for his Peltastæ. The Macedonian spear, called sarissa, was at first sixteen cubits or twenty-four feet long, though afterwards reduced to twenty-one feet.[2] The tactical arrangements, which Arrian and other writers describe as in use under Alexander or his successors, were substantially the same as those adopted by Philip. The whole phalanx, containing from sixteen to eighteen thousand men, was divided into battalions, each of which was drawn up sixteen deep.[3] The file was halved or doubled, if occasion required; but sixteen was the ordinary depth. When the phalanx advanced to the attack, there was a distance of three feet between the soldiers both in rank and file; the first five ranks couched their sarissas,[4] so that those of the first rank projected fifteen feet in front, those of the second rank twelve feet, those of the third nine, those of the fourth six, and those of the fifth three. Thus the soldiers in the first rank were guarded by five spears projecting on each side. The sixth and hinder ranks held their spears uplifted, resting on the shoulders of those before, and protecting them in some measure from the arrows and missiles that flew over their heads. The pressure from behind added to the force

[1] The arms of the ὁπλίτης are comprehensively described by Æschylus in the Persæ, v. 243:—

> Ἔγχη σταδαῖα καὶ φεράσπιδες σαγαί.
> *The spear for standing fight, and covering shield.*

He carried also, but seldom used, a short sword; and wore a helmet, cuirass, and greaves.

[2] Polybius, xviii. 12. Κατὰ μὲν τὴν ἐξ ἀρχῆς ὑπόθεσιν ἑκκαίδεκα πηχῶν, κατὰ δὲ τὴν ἁρμογὴν τὴν πρὸς τὴν ἀλήθειαν δεκατεσσάρων.

[3] In later times it was divided into ten battalions, each containing sixteen hundred men, a hundred in rank, and sixteen in file. (Livy, xxxvii. 40.) If all the battalions were in line, the whole phalanx would occupy about three-fifths of a mile.

[4] Supposing the spear to be of twenty-one feet.

of the whole battalion, by rendering it impossible for the front ranks to retreat.[1]

Such was the phalanx, whose very aspect, two centuries after its first formation, struck Paulus Æmilius with dismay.[2] Encountered front to front, and upon ground favorable to its operations, it was, as Polybius affirms, irresistible.[3] Its defects were, that it was unwieldy and slow in its movements, and not adapted to varieties of place and occasion. The perfect order and regularity, which were required for its efficient action, could not well be maintained except upon level ground, free from impediments, such as trees, bushes, ditches, streams, and the like. A plain perfectly suitable for the movements of so large a body could not always be found. Again, it could not act with advantage, if vigorously assailed in the flank and rear. The wheeling round to meet a flank attack was a difficult and dangerous evolution in the presence of an active enemy:[4] and if the phalanx were threatened on both sides, and the rear had to face about, every step which it made in advance had a tendency to open the files and break the continuity of the mass. Once thrown into disorder, the complex machine became utterly useless, and the individual soldier with his long weapon was ill fitted for a hand-to-hand combat. All these defects fully appeared in the wars with the Romans: especially at Pydna, where the legionaries, attacking the Macedonians on all sides at once, disordered their ranks, and breaking in at the openings, slaughtered them almost without resistance.[5]

[1] Polybius, xviii. 12, 13.

[2] Polybius, Fragmentum, xxix. 6. Livy, xl. 40, suppl. 3. "Progrediebatur interim Æmilius: utque aspexit quum reliquos Macedonas, tum eos qui in phalangem contributi erant, partim clypeis, partim cetris ex humero detractis, inclinatisque uno signo sarissis, excipientes Romanorum impetum, admiratus et illam densatorum agminum firmitatem, et vallum protentis sarissis horrens, stupore simul et terrore perculsus est, tanquam non aliud unquam tam terribile spectaculum conspicatus: ac postea id sæpius commemorare et præ se ferre solitus est."

[3] Polybius, xviii. 13—15. The advantages and disadvantages of the phalanx, as compared with the Roman legion, are here fully set forth. A good description is given in Rollin's Ancient History, lib. xiv. s.1.

[4] Polybius, xviii. 9. *Τῆς δὲ τῶν φαλαγγιτῶν χρείας ἀδυνάτου καθεστώσης ἐκ μεταβολῆς καὶ κατ' ἄνδρα κινδυνεύειν.* These manœuvres were perhaps better executed in Philip's and Alexander's time than in the later periods to which Polybius has reference. See Arrian's description of Alexander's arrangements before the battle of Arbela: (Anab. iii. 12.) from which indeed it appears that the light troops were called in aid, to protect the phalanx from attacks on the flank and rear.

[5] When the Italians attempted to close with the front ranks, and break their pikes, they fared no better than the Persians did at Platæa. (Livy, xliv. 40, suppl. 3.) "Illi prælongas Macedonum hastas aut ferro incidere, aut umbone impellere, aut nudis etiam interdum manibus aver-

The Greeks however, who fought the Macedonians in their own way, ranks meeting and spears crossing in the accustomed fashion, allowed them the full advantage of their improved organization and discipline.

While the phalanx constituted the main strength of Philip's army, it was supported by other troops, which had often followed him to victory. There were the foot guards,[1] who had been long talked of in Greece; from whom afterwards were taken the Hypaspists of Alexander, a body of men who wore the long shield of the phalanx, but carried shorter spears and lighter armor. Of these there were about six thousand. A select body of them, distinguished for their superior bravery, were called Argyraspids, from the bright silver plates on their shields.[2] Light troops of various kinds, slingers, archers, and javelin-men, were furnished by the Thracians, Pæonians, Illyrians, Agrianians,[3] and other warlike tribes of the north, who

tere. Hi ambabus firmiter comprehensas tantâ vi adigere in temere ac furore cæco ruentes, ut transfossis scutis loricisque transfixos etiam homines super capita projicerent." Æmilius however soon discovered the true way of proceeding: (Ibid. suppl. 4.) "Animadvertit peritus dux non stare ubique confertam illam hostium velut compagem, eamque dehiscere identidem quibusdam intervallis, sive ob inæqualitatem soli, sive ob ipsam porrectæ in immensum frontis longitudinem, dum qui superiora occupare conantur ab inferiora tenentibus, vel tardiores à citatioribus, et progredientes à subsistentibus, instantes denique hosti ab impulsis, inviti licet, necessario divelluntur. Ergo ut omnino rumperet ordinem hostium, et inexpugnabilem illam universæ phalangis vim in multa minutatim prœlia carperet, imperat suis, ut intenti quacunque rimas agere hostilem aciem viderint, illuc quisque impetu inferantur, seque cuneatim in hiantia vel tantillum spatia insinuantes strenuè rem agant." The result is described with equal clearness: (Ibid. 41.) "Neque ulla evidentior causa victoriæ fuit, quam quod multa passim prœlia erant, quæ fluctuantem turbârunt primo, deinde disjecerunt phalangem; cujus confertæ et intentis horrentis hastis intolerabiles vires sunt; si carptim aggrediendo circumagere immobilem longitudine et gravitate hastam cogas, confusâ strue implicantur; si vero ab latere aut ab tergo aliquid tumultus increpuit, ruinæ modo turbantur. Sicut tum adversus catervatim incurrentes Romanos et interruptâ multifariam acie obviam ire cogebantur; et Romani, quacunque data intervalla essent, insinuabant ordines suos. Qui, si universâ acie in frontem adversus instructam phalangem concurrissent, quod Pelignis principio pugnæ incautè congressis adversus cetratos evenit, induissent se hastis, nec confertam aciem sustinuissent.

[1] *Πεζέταιροι.* Demosthenes, Olynth. ii. 23. *Οἱ ὑπασπισταὶ τῶν ἑταίρων.* Arrian, Anab. i. 14.

[2] Diodorus, xvii. 57. *Τὸ τῶν Ἀργυρασπίδων πεζῶν τάγμα, διαφέρον τῇ τε τῶν ὅπλων λαμπρότητι καὶ τῇ τῶν ἄνδρων ἀρετῇ.* Justin, xii. 7.

[3] These four people are described by Alexander as *Τούς εὐρωστοτάτους τε τῶν κατὰ τὴν Εὐρώπην καὶ μαχιμωτάτους.* Arrian, Anab. ii. 7.

were now annexed to the Macedonian empire. The Pæonians and Thracians supplied squadrons of light horse: the heavy cavalry came from Macedonia and Thessaly.[1] It is not unlikely that there were Ætolians in Philip's army; as that people, afterwards the deadly enemies of Macedonia, were now ranked among his allies.[2]

The choicest of the troops opposed to him were the heavy-armed of Thebes and Athens. Twenty years before, the Thebans were considered the best soldiers of Greece. The military exercises, to which they partly owed their pre-eminence, were probably not discontinued; yet, that their discipline and energy had greatly declined since the battle of Mantinea, is shown by the events of the Sacred War. Among the Athenian ranks there were plenty of brave men; the whole body of them were animated with a good spirit: but they were deficient in that training, which teaches soldiers to act in combination, and converts a multitude into an army. It had been the boast of Pericles, that his countrymen fought well enough by their native valor, and did not need to prepare themselves by laborious drilling.[3] But Delium and many other battles proved how unsafe it was to rely upon such a principle. In the time of Pericles, indeed, the constant service for which Athenian citizens were called out was of itself a species of training. At this time they were little used to serving in person; many of them had never seen the face of an enemy in the field, and knew little of the art and practice of war beyond the use of their arms, which they learned in early years. How could such men, a mere national militia, be a match for the veterans of Philip, who had not only been the victors in numerous battles, but even in time of peace were exercised in toilsome marches, to keep them in perpetual activity?[4]

But if the soldiers of the allied army were not equal to those of Philip, still less were their commanders to be compared with him. Well might they have exclaimed—"Oh for one hour of Epaminondas!" He would have contrived some means, by charging on the flanks of the phalanx or otherwise, to counteract the skillful tactics of his adversary and turn the fortune of the day. But there was no man at all equal to the emergency. Phocion had been absent in the Ægean when hostilities began: on his return to Athens he declared himself favorable to peace; perhaps he expressed himself too

[1] Alexander led from Europe an equal number of Macedonian and Thessalian horse, fifteen hundred of each. (Diodorus, xvii. 17.) Philip's army at Chæronea could not have differed much from that which followed his son into Asia a few years after. See the descriptions in Arrian, Anab. i. 14; ii. 9; iii. 11, 12. **Thirlwall, History of Greece, vi. 147—149.**

[2] See ante, pp. 373, 389.

[3] Thucydides, ii. 39.

[4] Polyænus, Strateg. iv. 2, s. 10.

strongly against the war, and this prevented his obtaining an appointment, for which, of all his countrymen, he was the best fitted.[1] The Athenians were now commanded by Lysicles, Chares, and Stratocles; the Thebans by Theagenes; none of them fit to be at the head of an army. Demosthenes was with them, sanguine himself as to the result, and advising them to seek the enemy in spite of discouraging omens and unpropitious sacrifices:[2] but he could render no service in the hour of battle.

For a description of the battle itself we have but scanty materials. The best history of it is to be found in the comparison of the two armies. A few special incidents only are recorded. Athenians and Thebans rushed upon the bristling forest of sarissas, and fought with a valor worthy of ancient times and of a better fate. It is said that Philip, knowing the Athenians to be impetuous in onset but incapable of endurance, ordered his soldiers to keep on the defensive till the strength of their adversaries was exhausted. At one point so furious an attack was made by Stratocles, that the Macedonian line gave way; Stratocles drove before him the retreating phalangites, crying—"Let us chase them to Macedon;" but pressing on too hastily, he threw his own troops into disorder; when Philip directed a timely charge which put them to the rout. On the other wing Alexander, supported by the ablest of his father's generals, was opposed to the Thebans, and was the first to charge the hitherto invincible Sacred band. The contest was bloody, and for a long time doubtful. Alexander made extraordinary efforts to prove himself worthy of the post assigned to him. The Thebans, after obstinately disputing every inch of ground, yielded at last to the superior strength of their opponents. As soon as they had given way, Philip, determined not to be outdone by his son, led his phalanx in person against the Athenian line, and decided the victory. A fearful slaughter was made of the allied army, now broken on all sides. Of the total loss of the Thebans we have no account. Their general Theagenes was slain,[3] and the three hundred of the Sacred Band fell

[1] Plutarch, Vit. Phocion, 16.

[2] Æschines reproaches him for this: and also for his sneering at the Delphian oracle, which they had proposed to consult, and saying that the priestess philippised. (Contr. Ctesiph. 72.) *Οὐ περὶ τούτων Ἀμεινιάδης μὲν προὔλεγεν εὐλαβεῖσθαι καὶ πέμπειν εἰς Δελφοὺς ἐπερησομένους τὸν θεὸν ὅτι χρὴ πράττειν, Δημοσθενὴς δὲ ἀντέλεγε φιλιππίζειν τὴν Πυθίαν φάσκων, ἀπαίδευτος ὢν καὶ ἀπολαύων καὶ ἐμπιπλάμενος τῆς διδομένης ὑφ' ὑμῶν αὐτῷ ἐξουσίας; οὐ τὸ τελευταῖον ἀθύτων καὶ ἀκαλλιερήτων ὄντων τῶν ἱερῶν ἐξέπεμψε τοὺς στρατιώτας ἐπὶ τὸν πρόδηλον κίνδυνον.* Conf. Cicero, De Divinat. ii. 57.

[3] Dinarchus, seemingly without cause, denounces him as a traitor: *Ἄνθρωπος ἀτυχὴς καὶ δωροδόκος.* (Contr. Demosth. 99.) Timoclea, who after the capture of Thebes pushed the Thracian soldier into the well, was his sister. (Plutarch, Vit. Alexand. 12. Polyænus, Strateg. viii. 40.)

side by side, perishing to a man. Of the Athenians there fell more than a thousand, and two thousand were taken prisoners. Demosthenes, who had fought in the ranks, escaped with the fugitives to Athens. In one short day all his lofty hopes had been overthrown: all his toils and labors for the safety of his country and the independence of Greece had been rendered fruitless.[1]—"Hic dies universæ Græciæ et gloriam dominationis et vetustissimam libertatem finivit."[2]

The news of this dreadful calamity was speedily brought to Athens. It is said to have killed Isocrates, who at the age of ninety-eight was in the full possession of his health and faculties, but now abstained from food, heart-broken at the sad tidings of his country's defeat.[3] The general grief and terror may well be imagined; but they are described to us by an eye-witness.[4] It was uncertain for the moment, how many of the citizens had been slain or captured. Almost all capable of bearing arms, between the ages of twenty and fifty, had been sent out: and the hopes of defending Athens seemed to rest upon those who were past the age of active service. Women were seen standing at their doors in an agony of distress, asking every one that passed if their husbands, fathers, sons, or brothers were alive. Old and infirm men were walking about the streets

[1] Diodorus, xvi. 86. Pausanias, ix. 40. Plutarch, Vit. Alexand. 7; Vit. Pelopid. 18. Demosthenes, De Coron. 314. Demades, Fragment. 179. Polyænus, Strateg. iv. 2, s. 2, and s. 7. What is told in this book of Stratocles, is attributed to Theagenes in viii. 40. That Demosthenes was accused of cowardice in the field, of having shamefully deserted his post and thrown away his shield, is well known. (See Dinarchus, Contr. Demosth. 91. Æschines, Contr. Ctesiph. 74, 76, 89.) But, as Grote observes, the continued confidence and respect shown to him by his countrymen prove that they did not credit these charges. It seems that he only shared in the general flight of the army. A story is told in the Lives of the Ten Orators, p. 845—that, as he was running away, his cloak was caught by a bramble, and he, thinking the pursuers were behind him, cried *Ζώγρει*, "Take me alive!" This looks very like an invention of his enemies.

[2] Justin, ix. 3. Compare Lycurgus, Contr. Leocrat. 154. *Ἅμα γὰρ οὗτοί τε τὸν βίον μετήλλαξαν καὶ τὰ τῆς Ἑλλάδος εἰς δουλείαν μετέπεσε· συνετάφη γὰρ τοῖς τούτων σώμασιν ἡ τῶν ἄλλων Ἑλλήνων ἐλευθερία.*

[3] Pausanias, i. 18. *Πρὸς τὴν ἀγγελίαν τῆς ἐν Χαιρωνείᾳ μάχης ἀλγήσας ἐτελεύτησεν ἐθελοντής.* Milton refers to it in one of his sonnets:—

As that dishonest victory
At Chæronea, fatal to liberty,
Killed with report that old man eloquent.

The fact however has been contested. See Mitford's disquisition at the end of section 6, chap. 42, vol. iv. of his History of Greece.

[4] Lycurgus, Contr. Leocrat. 149, 152, 153.

with their mantles doubled up, as if girding themselves to perform the duties of the young. As the fugitives successively flocked in, the real extent of the disaster was ascertained, and the people, rallying from their first dismay, hastened to meet as became them the distressing exigency of the hour. It was no longer possible to act in co-operation with the Thebans; each of the allied cities was thrown entirely upon its own resources: and it was uncertain against which of them the conqueror would first advance. It was necessary to put Athens in a condition to sustain a siege, and that without any delay. Resolutions for that purpose, framed chiefly by Hyperides and Demosthenes, were immediately passed in full assembly, ordering (among other things) that the women and children should be brought in from the country; that the generals should be empowered to require for garrison duty the services of all residents in Athens, whether citizens or foreigners; that the members of the council should go down in arms to the Piræus, and execute what measures they thought best for its security; that slaves bearing arms for the commonwealth should be emancipated, aliens be made citizens, and the disfranchised restored to their rights. Energetic measures were taken for the restoring and strengthening the fortifications. Men of every age lent a helping hand for the national defense. The country (says Lycurgus) contributed her trees, the dead their sepulchres, the temples their arms. Patriotic citizens came forward with large donations of money for the public service, Demosthenes himself contributed liberally towards the repair of the walls, which he had been appointed to superintend. It was further deemed expedient to solicit aid from some of the nearest friendly states. Embassies were sent to Trœzen and Epidaurus: and subsidies were collected from some of the nearest islands. Demosthenes, who was sent on one of these expeditions, is reproached for it by Æschines and Dinarchus, as if he had deserted his country for fear of the enemy. We learn from Dinarchus, however, that Demosthenes was by a decree of the people appointed envoy, and it appears that at this time, notwithstanding the unfortunate issue of his counsels, he continued to enjoy the confidence of the Athenians; for not only did they pass divers decrees which he had moved for the public safety, but they appointed him to hold the office of a commissioner of grain, and afterwards conferred upon him a still higher proof of their esteem, by selecting him to speak the funeral oration in honor of their fellow-citizens who had fallen in battle. Further, when his adversaries, thinking their position strengthened by the peace, assailed Demosthenes with indictments and other legal proceedings, he obtained a triumphant acquittal upon all.[1]

[1] Lycurgus, Cont. Leocrat. 149, 153. Dinarchus, Contr. Demosth. 100. Æschines, Contr. Ctesiph. 76. Demosthenes, De Coron. 267 285, 309, 310, 320, 321, 329. Plutarch, Vit. Dec. Orat. 846.

To the general zeal displayed by the citizens of Athens a few disgraceful exceptions are recorded. There were men who left or attempted to leave the city, in order to secure themselves and their families: and the example was considered so dangerous, that a special decree was passed, making it treasonable to desert the country in such a way. One man who had embarked for Samos was apprehended by the Council of Areopagus, and on the same day sentenced to death. Autolycus, an Areopagite, was condemned for having sent away his wife and children, though he himself remained in Athens. But the most remakable case is that of Leocrates; who, as soon as he had heard that the battle was lost, sailed away clandestinely with all his family and moveable effects to Rhodes, where he reported that Athens was taken, that Piræus was besieged, and he was the only person who had escaped. The Rhodians, believing his story, sent out cruisers to commit piracy in the Ægean; and the merchants in the harbor unshipped the corn and other goods which they were about to export to Athens. When the real truth became known, Leocrates quitted Rhodes, and came to live at Megara, contriving by means of his friends to sell what property he had left at Athens. After the lapse of seven years he returned to his country, and was impeached by Lycurgus in the manner already mentioned.[1]

While we admire the spirit with which the people of Athens bore up against their misfortunes, and the generous support which they gave to Demosthenes in the hour of his humiliation, one is sorry to find an act of the Athenian public recorded, which it is impossible to view with the same approving eye. Lysicles, who had commanded the army at Chæronea, was on the accusation of Lycurgus brought to trial, condemned, and executed, apparently for no other reason than because he had lost the battle. Mitford conceives it to have been a bold stroke of the war party, who, knowing that popular vengeance would demand a victim, resolved to sacrifice Lysicles to secure their own safety.[2] Thirlwall seems to think, that the character of Lycurgus the prosecutor affords some proof of the justness of the sentence.[3] The extract from his speech, preserved to us by Diodorus, exhibits the Spartan-like severity of the speaker's character, but indicates no special ground of cowardice or misconduct, distinguishing the case of Lysicles from that of his colleagues or any other unfortunate generals. His words are these:[4]—"You, Lysicles, were the commander: a thousand citizens have fallen; two thousand have been made captive; a trophy has been raised

[1] Lycurgus, Contr. Leocrat. 149, 150. Æschines, Contr. Ctesiph. 39. Ante, p. 330.

[2] Mitford, History of Greece, vol. iv. c. 42, s. 5.

[3] Thirlwall, History of Greece, vi. 72.

[4] Diodorus, xvi. 88.

against Athens; and the whole of Greece is in servitude. When all this has taken place under your conduct and command, dare you to live, and to behold the light of the sun, and to make your appearance in the market-place: you that are a monument of shame and disgrace to your country?"

Whether the Athenians with all their preparations could have successfully defended themselves against Philip's army, had he advanced to besiege Athens, was not put to the trial. Philip adopted such prudent and conciliatory measures, that they were tempted to abandon the high ground of resistance to Macedonian power, and to accept terms of peace which he prescribed. It is said that in the first moment of victory Philip gave way to feelings of indecent triumph, and insulted over his fallen enemies. Having drunk to excess at the banquet, he walked over the field of battle, and sang in iambic verse the prefatory words of Demosthenes' decree, stamping with his feet and dancing to the cadence.[1] Visiting the Athenian prisoners, he derided their misfortunes, and was rebuked by Demades in the manner already related.[2] These were but the intemperate sallies of the moment. It is said however, that he at first refused the Athenians the customary permission to bury their dead, which they had sent a herald to demand. His object in so doing perhaps was, to prevent their opening any communication with the Thebans: and he may for prudential reasons have assumed an appearance of rigor, which he never meant really to exercise. Certain it is, he very quickly decided upon adopting lenient measures

[1] Plutarch, Vit. Demosth. 20—

Δημοσθένες Δημοσθένους Παιανιεὺς ταδ' εἶπεν.

In the Life of Pelopidas (18) he is represented to have expressed his admiration of the Sacred Band, whose bodies he saw on the field.

[2] Ante, p. 327. It may be thought that Demades, who is said to have been long before this engaged in the cause of Philip, would not have ventured to use such freedom with him. Demades however was a strange compound. It is certain that he was a man of consummate assurance; and it is not at all unlikely that he may have taken this way of introducing himself to Philip. The positive testimony of Diodorus is not lightly to be rejected; for, with all his faults of omission and negligence, he is too honest to record any thing destitute of authority. The accounts of Philip's conduct given by Diodorus and Plutarch are seemingly indeed at variance with those of other writers. Justin says, (iv. 4) —"Hujus victoriæ callide dissimulata lætitia est. Denique non solita sacra Philippus illâ die fecit: non in convivio risit: non ludos inter epulas adhibuit; non coronas aut unguenta sumpsit; et, quantum in illo fuit, ita vicit ut victorem nemo sentiret." Compare Ælian. Var. Hist. viii. 15. The different statements are perhaps not irreconcilable. Philip assumed a grave and severe deportment; but it gave way on one or two occasions to a fit of intemperance. What is more likely?

towards the Athenians. He entered into confidential discourse with Demades, who must have been already known to him as an opponent of Demosthenes and the war party at Athens; and whom he found to be a man of agreeable manners, and likely to be a useful instrument to serve his present purposes. The orator doubtless exerted his powers of persuasion to recommend a mild and pacific policy: and a careful reflection upon his position and prospects convinced Philip, that it was wiser to conciliate the Athenians than to drive them to desperation.[1] He therefore intimated his willingness to restore the Athenian prisoners without ransom: he burned the bodies of the slain, and sent a deputation carrying their bones to Athens. It was headed by his son Alexander and Antipater, who communicated the terms upon which he was willing to treat for peace. These, though not honorable, were much better than the Athenians had expected, and they were favorably received by the people: the war party could not venture under existing circumstances to advise a prolonged resistance. Demades, who had been sent home for this very purpose, framed a treaty of peace, which he carried in the assembly without any opposition: by the terms of which the Athenians renounced all their pretensions to naval sovereignty, and all their dominions in the Ægæan sea, except Lemnos, Imbrus, and Samos. Virtually, though not in words, they acknowledged Philip as the head of the Hellenic community. In exchange for these concessions, they obtained peace and present security, and a return of their prisoners; likewise the city of Oropus, which was transferred to them from the Thebans, but to recover which in such a way was more of a disgrace than an advantage. Votes of honor to Philip were passed in the assembly on the motion of Demades; who now, together with the other members of his party, began to regain credit and influence in Athens. Æschines boasted that he was on terms of friendship with the king of Macedon, and went on an embassy to his camp. Submission and subserviency were the order of the day.[2]

[1] Philip's title to the praise, which Polybius bestows upon him for his lenity to Athens, is upon good grounds disputed by both Thirlwall and Grote. The former observes, that after his severity to Thebes he had the less reason to dread the hostility of Athens; that it was by no means certain that he could have made himself master of the city and Piræus; the danger of a failure, and even the inconvenience of delay, was greater than the advantage to be reaped from it; he had more brilliant objects in view: time was precious to him, and it would have been wantonly to tempt his fortune, if by too grasping a policy he had raised unnecessary hindrances to his designs. (History of Greece, vi. 74.)

[2] Diodorus, xvi, 87; xviii. 56. Demades, Fragment. 179. Demosthenes, De Coron. 319, 320, 321, 352. Plutarch, Vit. Decem. Orat. 349. Pausanias, i. 25.

While Philip was carrying on peaceful negotiation with Athens, he was taking measures of a very different character against the Thebans. Towards them his conduct was as harsh as it was lenient to their allies. He not only exacted ransom for their prisoners, but made them pay a price for the burial of their dead. Yet this was nothing in comparison with what followed. Very shortly after the battle, he contrived to make himself master of Thebes itself. Whether he took it by surprise, or whether it was surrendered to him by the philippising party or otherwise, we are not informed. There are no Theban writers to give us any historical particulars about their countrymen. It may be presumed that Philip lost no time in following up his victory; and the severe loss which the Thebans had sustained at Chæronea must have materially impaired both their courage and their means for defense. Philip, having got possession of the city, treated it as the Spartans had done forty-four years before, subjecting it to all the rigors of military occupation. A Macedonian garrison was placed in the Cadmea. As a further check upon insurrection, Orchomenus and Platæa were re-established, and filled with a population hostile to Thebes. All the Bœotian towns were declared independent. Some of the principal Theban statesmen were put to death by Philip's order; others were banished; their property was seized for his use. He recalled a large number of exiles, three hundred of whom he formed into a council, invested with summary powers, both executive and judicial. One of their first acts was, to bring their political enemies to trial for having sentenced them to exile. The accused gloried in their crime, and courted the vengeance that was prepared for them. This was but a foretaste of what the unhappy Thebans were to suffer under an oligarchy devoted to the conqueror and upheld by his troops. Three years of domestic and foreign oppression drove them into a new war, which ended in the extirpation of Thebes.[1]

[1] Diodorus, xvi. 37; xvii. 8, 9, &c. Justin, ix. 4. Dinarchus, Contr. Demosth. 92. Pausanias, iv. 27; ix. 1 and 6. Arrian, Anab. i. 7.

APPENDIX X.

WHETHER CTESIPHON BROKE THE LAW.

THE two special grounds upon which Æschines contended that Ctesiphon had violated the law, were,

First, because he had proposed to crown Demosthenes, before he had rendered an account of his official administration, Demosthenes having been a conservator of walls, and a treasurer of the Theoric fund:

Secondly, because he had proposed to publish the coronation in the theatre of the Dionysian festival, at the performance of the new tragedies.

In support of the first proposition, Æschines[1] cites a law which expressly forbade the bestowing of a crown upon any magistrate or official personage who had still his account to render. Anticipating an objection, that the offices held by Demosthenes were not magistracies, such as the law applied to, but rather inferior agencies or employments,[2] he shows that by the law of Athens all offices to which the people elected were to be deemed of a magisterial character, and that all superintendents of public works, and all persons who were intrusted with any of the public money for more than thirty days, or who held a legal jurisdiction, were to be considered as holding such offices, and were subject to the usual scrutiny[3] before they entered upon their duties. A conservator of walls was clearly a superintendent of public works; and he also presided in a court of judicature. Demosthenes had been appointed to that office by the Pandionian tribe in pursuance of a decree of the people, and had had the disbursement of ten talents of the public money. He had been elected treasurer of the Theoric fund by the people in general assembly. It made no difference, whether or not he had expended any of his own money gratuitously. He was liable to render an account in one or both of the aforesaid characters, even though none of the public moneys had passed through his hands. It was a principle of the democracy, that no magisterial functionary should be irresponsible.

He then proceeds to the second point,[4] and produces a law, en-

1 For this part of the argument, see Æschines, Contr. Ctesiph. pp. 55—58.

2 Ἐπιμέλειαι, διακονίαι, πραγματεῖαι, *commissions, agencies, employments*, are distinguished from ἀρχαί, *magisterial offices*. See Schömann, De Comitiis, 308, &c.

3 *Δοκιμασία.*

4 Æschines, Contr. Ctesiph. 58—60.

acting that, if the council bestowed a crown upon any citizen, it should be proclaimed in the council-chamber, if the people, in the assembly, but not in any other place; the object of which law he declares to have been, that honors of this kind, which concerned the commonwealth and its members only, should not be ostentatiously displayed before foreigners. Ctesiphon had infringed this statute, for the pnrpose of making an idle parade of his friend's honors at the Dionysian festival, when a large number of the Greeks were present.

Upon this part of the case he anticipates the answer which we find to have been actually made—viz. that there was a law which permitted crowns to be proclaimed in the theatre, if the people authorized it by their decree. That law, says Æschines, is not inconsistent with the one upon which I rely: nor indeed can there be two inconsistent laws: but it relates to an entirely different matter. A bad practice had sprung up; that men, who possessed influence in foreign states, got crowns presented to them by those states, and then had them proclaimed in the theatre at home. To put a stop to such an objectionable custom, a statute was passed, making it unlawful for crowns given by foreign states to be proclaimed in the theatre, except under a special resolution of the Athenian people. The law which Ctesiphon violated, which defined the places where crowns were to be proclaimed, applied to those which were given at home.

To these arguments Demosthenes makes but a short reply.[1] He does not at all dispute his general accountability in respect of the offices which he had held. He denies, however, that he was accountable to the state for what he had expended out of his private purse; and he contends that the crown was bestowed upon him, not for the acts of which he had an account to render, but for his gifts, which were not the subject of account. With respect to the place of proclamation, he adduces a law (as Æschines had expected) seemingly at variance with that on which the prosecution was founded, and not admitting the construction which Æschines had put upon it. He censures Æschines for misrepresenting the object of the lawgiver in fixing the place of proclamation, and not seeing that the proclamation was for the benefit of those who conferred, not those who received the honor. He refers also to a variety of cases, in which decrees similar to that of Ctesiphon, and under similar circumstances, had been passed in favor of other men.

With regard to the contradictory laws, we have not sufficient data to form an opinion. Each of the orators accuses the other of garbling the law which he cites: and we have not the whole of the statutes before us to enable us to see which is right. But the defense which Demosthenes sets up as to the time of crowning we have

[1] See ante, pp. 46—51.

little difficulty in pronouncing to be sophistical. The law which enacted, that no public functionary who had not passed his audit should be crowned, meant that the honor should not be conferred either for official services or on any other account. Besides, the crown given by Ctesiphon to Demosthenes actually purported to be a requital of his official services: for those donations to the public, which were specially commended, related to the business of his administration. In any point of view, therefore, Ctesiphon had by his decree violated the letter of the Athenian law: but it is clear also, that he violated the spirit of it. For a magistrate might be very liberal in donations to the public, and yet might in some way or other grossly abuse his trust: he might be generous with the one hand, and squander the public money with the other. At his official audit the whole of his administration would be inquired into: and he would be liable to punishment, if in any particular he had seriously neglected his duty. But by commending him for one part of his conduct, while the other was kept out of view, the merits of the case were unfairly prejudged before it came to the auditors. And this is the very abuse of which Æschines complains: crafty orators got premature votes of honors for their friends, to screen them from charges for official misconduct.[1]

The precedents cited by Demosthenes prove no more than what Æschines admitted; that the law had often been broken before; not that it ought to be broken, or was not still in force. If any weight were attached to them, it concerned the penalty rather than the verdict of guilty or not guilty.

Had Æschines confined himself to these two questions upon the laws, it appears undeniable, that the verdict ought to have been in his favor. But this did not satisfy him. He wished to cast reproach upon the character and politics of Demosthenes; and therefore he introduced the third charge, which raised the issue, whether Demosthenes had deserved well of his country. By mixing the three issues together, he thought to insure success in the cause; and he expected that a verdict against Ctesiphon, on whatever

[1] Æschines, Contr. Ctesiph. 55. 'Εν γὰρ τοῖς ἔμπροσθεν χρόνοις ἄρχοντές τινες τὰς μεγίστας ἀρχὰς καὶ τὰς προσόδους διοικοῦντες, καὶ δωροδοκοῦντες περὶ ἕκαστα τούτων, προσλαμβάνοντες τούς τε ἐκ τοῦ βουλευτηρίου ῥήτορας καὶ τοὺς ἐκ τοῦ δήμου πόῤῥωθεν προκατελάμβανον τὰς εὐθύνας ἐπαίνους καὶ κηρύγμασιν, ὥστ' ἐν ταῖς εὐθύναις τῶν ἀρχῶν εἰς τὴν μεγίστην μὲν ἀπορίαν ἀφικνεῖσθαι τοὺς κατηγόρους, πολὺ δὲ ἔτι μᾶλλον τοὺς δικαστάς—ᾐσχύνοντο γὰρ οἶμαι οἱ δικασταὶ, εἰ φανήσεται ὁ αὐτὸς ἀνὴρ ἐν τῇ αὐτῇ πόλει, τυχὸν δὲ καὶ ἐν τῷ αὐτῷ ἐνιαυτῷ, πρώην μὲν πότε ἀναγορευόμενος ἐν τοῖς ἀγῶσιν ὅτι στεφανοῦται ἀρετῆς ἕνεκα καὶ δικαιοσύνης ὑπὸ τοῦ δήμου χρυσῷ στεφάνῳ, ὁ δὲ αὐτὸς ἀνὴρ μικρὸν ἐπισχὼν ἔξεισιν ἐκ τοῦ δικαστηρίου κλοπῆς ἕνεκα τὰς εὐθύνας ὠφληκώς· ὥστε ἠναγκαζοντο τὴν ψῆφον φέρειν οἱ δικασταὶ οὐ περὶ τοῦ παρόντος ἀδικήματος ἀλλ' ὑπὲρ τῆς αἰσχύνης τοῦ δήμου.

ground obtained, would be a triumph over Demosthenes, and would have the effect of disgracing him and his party in the eyes of all the Greeks. Hereupon arises a question—whether Æschines should have been allowed to succeed in his manœuvre, and obtain such an indirect triumph over his rival. Not that Demosthenes ever raised such a point for the consideration of his judges—he was too old an orator to admit that any part of his case was weak. It is a point, however, which the Athenians who decided the cause ought to have considered, and perhaps did consider—a question of ethical jurisprudence, upon which the merits of their decision very much depend. The reader will be better able to form his opinion upon this and other parts of the subject, after seeing in what light they are presented by the always just and clear-sighted Thirlwall:[1]

"Æschines had indicted Ctesiphon as having broken the law in three points: first, because it was illegal to crown a magistrate before he rendered an account of his office: next, because it was forbidden to proclaim such an honor, when bestowed by the people, in any other place than the assembly-ground in the Pnyx, but particularly to proclaim it, as Ctesiphon had proposed: and lastly, because the reason assigned in the decree, so far as related to the public conduct of Demosthenes, was false, inasmuch as he had not deserved any reward. Among these points there was one, on which it seems clear that the charge of illegality was well grounded. Though the superintendence of the repairs was probably not a magistracy in the eye of the law, which indeed forbade any one to hold two at once, the treasurership of the Theoric fund certainly was one, and one to which the law, which forbade the crowning of a magistrate still accountable, applied with peculiar force. As to the mode of the proclamation, it seems doubtful, whether the law on which the prosecution rested had not been modified by another, which declared that proclamation might be made, as Ctesiphon proposed, if the people should so decree; though Æschines speciously contended, that this exception was only meant to relate to crowns bestowed on citizens, not by the people, but by foreign states. But the third point, the truth or falsehood of the reason alleged in the decree, was that on which, according to the manifest sense of both the parties, of the court, and of all present at the trial, the case really turned. The question at issue was in substance, whether Demosthenes had been a good or a bad citizen. It was on this account that the court was thronged by an extraordinary conflux of spectators, both citizens and strangers. Hence the prosecutor, after a short discussion of the dry legal arguments, enters, as on his main subject, into a full review of the public and private life of Demosthenes: and Demosthenes, whose interest it was to divert attention from the points of law, which were not his strong ground, can scarcely find room for them

[1] History of Greece, vol. vii. 135.

in his defense of his own policy and proceedings, which, with bitter attacks on his adversary, occupies almost the whole of his speech.

"The spirit displayed by the tribunal, which decided in favor of Demosthenes on such grounds as he alleged, is at least as noble as that of the Roman senate and people, when they went out to meet and thank the Consul on his return from Cannæ. But the case may seem to exhibit the Athenian administration of justice in a much less favorable light. On one point at least it is clear that Ctesiphon's decree was contrary to law. The attempt made by Demosthenes to prove that the law, which forbade an accountable magistrate to be crowned, did not apply to his case, only shows the extreme looseness of legal reasoning which was tolerated in Athenian courts. It seems indeed to have been admitted, that there had been numerous precedents for whatever was illegal in the decree as to the circumstances of time and place. But this only proves the laxity which prevailed in the observance of the laws. It appears that, according to that theory of the constitution, which had been universally approved and acted on in the purest times, immediately after the expulsion of the Thirty Tyrants, the court which tried the author of a decree denounced as illegal was bound to compare it with the letter of the law, and to give judgment on the simple question of their strict agreement. But it is evident that the courts had afterwards assumed greater freedom; and it is not at all certain that this was repugnant, either to the spirit of the constitution, or to the practice of preceding ages, with the single exception of the short period in which the restoration of the democracy awakened extraordinary jealousy for the maintenance of the laws. The will of the people, declared in a decree, had been subjected to the revision of a tribunal which might be expected to possess superior means of information, to secure the people itself against the pernicious consequences of temporary measures into which it might be surprised. This seems to have been the general object, to which all others were subordinate; and for this purpose it might be necessary that in such cases the courts should be invested with an ample discretion, and should not be required to adhere to the letter of the laws, so as themselves to commit wrong, or to injure the commonwealth. The form of the proceedings was such, that a verdict against Ctesiphon must have been interpreted as a condemnation of Demosthenes: and it was the deliberate will, and the highest interest of the people, to show that it still honored the man who had not despaired of the commonwealth. It would have been better that the prosecutor should not have been able so to embroil the question: but where he did so, it was desirable that the court should have the power to decide on what it deemed the most important point."

THE END.

Anthon's Classical Series.

Latin Lessons. Latin Grammar, Part I. Containing the most important Parts of the Grammar of the Latin Language, together with appropriate Exercises in the Translating and Writing of Latin. 12mo, Sheep extra, 75 cents.

Latin Prose Composition. Latin Grammar, Part II. An Introduction to Latin Prose Composition, with a complete Course of Exercises, illustrative of all the important Principles of Latin Syntax. 12mo, Sheep extra, 75 cents.

A KEY to the Above is published, which may be obtained by Teachers. 12mo, Half Sheep, 50 cents.

Zumpt's Latin Grammar. From the ninth Edition of the Original, adapted to the use of English Students. By LEONHARD SCHMITZ, Ph.D. Corrected and enlarged. 12mo, Sheep extra, 75 cents.

An ABRIDGMENT of the Above. 12mo, Sheep extra, 50 cents.

Latin Prosody and Metre. From the best Authorities, Ancient and Modern. 12mo, Sheep extra, 75 cents.

Latin Versification. In a Series of Progressive Exercises, including Specimens of Translation from English and German Poetry into Latin Verse. 12mo, Sheep extra, 75 cents.

A KEY to the Above is published, which may be obtained by Teachers. 12mo, Half Sheep, 50 cents.

Cæsar's Commentaries on the Gallic War, and the First Book of the Greek Paraphrase; with English Notes, Critical and Explanatory, Plans of Battles, Sieges, &c., and Historical, Geographical, and Archæological Indexes. Map, Portrait, &c. 12mo, Sheep extra, $1 00.

The Æneid of Virgil. With English Notes, Critical and Explanatory, a Metrical Clavis, and an Historical, Geographical, and Mythological Index. Portrait and many Illustrations. 12mo, Sheep extra, $1 25.

Eclogues and Georgics of Virgil. With English Notes, Critical and Explanatory. 12mo, Sheep extra, $1 25.

Sallust's Jugurthine War and Conspiracy of Catiline. With an English Commentary, and Geographical and Historical Indexes. New Edition, corrected and enlarged. Portrait. 12mo, Sheep extra, 75 cents.

The Works of Horace. With English Notes, Critical and Explanatory. A new Edition, corrected and enlarged, with Excursions relative to the Vines and Vineyards of the Ancients; a Life of Horace, &c. 12mo, Sheep extra, $1 25.

Cicero's Select Orations. With English Notes, Critical and Explanatory, and Historical, Geographical, and Legal Indexes. An improved Edition. Portrait. 12mo, Sheep extra, $1 00.

Anthon's Classical Series, continued.

Cicero de Senectute, De Amicitia, and Paradoxa, and the Life of Atticus by Nepos. With English Notes, Critical and Explanatory. 12mo, Sheep extra, 75 cents.

Cicero's Tusculan Disputations. With English Notes, Critical and Explanatory. 12mo, Sheep extra, $1 00.

The Germania and Agricola, and also Selections from the Annals, of Tacitus. With English Notes, Critical and Explanatory. 12mo, Sheep extra, $1 00.

Cornelius Nepos. Cornelii Nepotis Vitæ Imperatorum Excellentium. With English Notes, &c. 12mo, Sheep extra, $1 00.

Terence. Terentii Comœdiæ, with English Notes, Metrical Tables, and an Essay on the Scanning of Terence, &c. 12mo, Sheep extra. (*In press.*)

First Greek Lessons. Containing the most important Parts of the Grammar of the Greek Language, together with appropriate Exercises in the Translating and Writing of Greek; for the use of Beginners. 12mo, Sheep extra, 75 cents.

Greek Prose Composition. Greek Lessons, Part II. An Introduction to Greek Prose Composition, with a complete Course of Exercises illustrative of all the important Principles of Greek Syntax. 12mo, Sheep extra, 75 cents.

Grammar of the Greek Language. For the use of Schools and Colleges. 12mo, Sheep extra, 75 cents.

A New Greek Grammar. From the German of Kühner, Matthiæ, Buttmann, Rost, and Thiersch; to which are appended Remarks on the Prouunciation of the Greek Language, and Chronological Tables explanatory of the same. 12mo, Sheep extra, 75 cents.

Greek Prosody and Metre. For the use of Schools and Colleges; together with the Choral Scanning of the Prometheus Vinctus of Æschylus, and Œdipus Tyrannus of Sophocles, to which are appended Remarks on the Indo-Germanic Analogies. 12mo, Sheep extra, 75 cents.

A Greek Reader. Principally from the German of Jacobs. With English Notes, Critical and Explanatory, a Metrical Index to Homer and Anacreon, and a copious Lexicon. 12mo, Sheep extra, $1 00.

Homer. The First Six Books of Homer's Iliad, to which are appended English Notes, Critical and Explanatory, a Metrical Index, and Homeric Glossary. New and enlarged Edition. 12mo, Sheep extra, $1 25.

The Anabasis of Xenophon. With English Notes, Critical and Explanatory, a Map arranged according to the latest and best Authorities, and a Plan of the Battle of Cunaza. 12mo, Sheep extra, $1 25.

Anthon's Classical Series, continued.

Xenophon's Memorabilia of Socrates. From the Text of Kühner. With Explanatory Notes, &c., by D. B. HICKIE, LL.D. First American Edition, corrected and enlarged. 12mo, Sheep extra, $1 00.

Manual of Roman Antiquities. From the most recent German Works. With a Description of the City of Rome, &c. 12mo, Sheep extra, 87½ cents.

Manual of Greek Literature. With a Critical History of the Greek Language. 12mo, Sheep extra, $1 00.

Manual of Greek Antiquities. From the best and most recent Sources. 12mo, Sheep extra, 87½ cents.

Manual of Greek and Roman Mythology. 12mo, Sheep extra.

Latin Syntax. Latin Lessons, Part II. Containing Latin Syntax, with Reading Lessons, and Exercises in double translation, on the basis of Kühner's. 12mo, Sheep extra. (Uniform with Latin Lessons, Part I.)

Ovid. Selections from the Metamorphoses of Ovid. With English Notes, Critical and Explanatory. 12mo. (*In press.*)

Euripides. The Hecuba, Hippolytus, Medea, and Bacchæ of Euripides. With English Notes, Critical and Explanatory. 12mo. (*In press.*)

Juvenal. The Satires of Juvenal. With English Notes Critical and Explanatory. (*In press.*)

Bigelow on the Useful Arts,

considered in Connection with the Applications of Science. With numerous Engravings. 2 vols. 12mo, Muslin, $1 50.

Boucharlat's Mechanics.

An Elementary Treatise on Mechanics. Translated from the French, with Additions and Emendations, by Prof. EDWARD H. COURTENAY. Plates. 8vo, Sheep extra, $2 25.

Boyd's Eclectic Moral Philosophy;

prepared for Literary Institutions and general Use. 12mo, Muslin, 75 cents.

Boyd's Rhetoric and Criticism.

Elements of Rhetoric and Literary Criticism, with copious Practical Exercises and Examples. Including, also, a succinct History of the English Language, and of British and American Literature, from the earliest to the present Times. On the Basis of the recent Works of ALEXANDER REID and R. CONNELL; with large Additions from other Sources. 12mo, Half Bound, 0 cents.

Brande's Encyclopedia.

A Dictionary of Science, Literature, and Art; comprising the History, Description, and Scientific Principles of every Branch of Human Knowledge; with the Derivation and Definition of all the Terms in general use. Illustrated by numerous Engravings on Wood. 8vo, Sheep extra, $4 00.

Burke on the Sublime and Beautiful.

Essay on the Sublime and Beautiful. A Philosophical Inquiry into the Origin of our Ideas of the Sublime and the Beautiful. With an Introductory Discourse concerning Taste. Edited by ABRAHAM MILLS. 12mo, Muslin, 75 cents.

Buttmann's Greek Grammar.

A Greek Grammar, for the use of High Schools and Universities. Revised and enlarged by ALEXANDER BUTTMANN. Translated from the 18th German Edition, by EDWARD ROBINSON, D.D., LL.D. 8vo, Sheep extra, $2 00.

Campbell's Philosophy of Rhetoric.

Revised Edition. 12mo, Muslin, $1 25.

Cicero's Orator.

Cicero's Three Dialogues on the Orator. Translated into English, by W. GUTHRIE. Revised and Corrected, with Notes. 18mo, Muslin, 45 cents.

Clark's Elements of Algebra.

Embracing, also, the Theory and Application of Logarithms; together with an Appendix, containing Infinite Series, the General Theory of Equations, and the most approved Methods of resolving the higher Equations. 8vo, Sheep extra, $1 00.

Comte's Philosophy of Mathematics.

Translated from the Cours de Philosophie Positive, by W. M. GILLESPIE, A.M. 8vo, Muslin, $1 25.

Crabb's Synonyms.

English Synonyms explained. With copious Illustrations and Explanations, drawn from the best Writers. 8vo, Sheep extra, $2 00.

Dickens's Child's History of England.

2 vols. or 1, 16mo, Muslin, $1 00.

Docharty's Arithmetic.

12mo, Sheep extra. (*In press.*)

Docharty's Institutes of Algebra.

Being the First Part of a Course of Mathematics, designed for the use of Schools, Academies, and Colleges. 12mo, Sheep extra, 75 cents.

Draper's Text-book on Chemistry,

for the use of Schools and Colleges. Carefully revised, with Additions. With 300 Illustrations. 12mo, Sheep, 75 cents.

www.ingramcontent.com/pod-product-compliance
Lightning Source LLC
LaVergne TN
LVHW021149110826
845150LV00005B/1171

* 9 7 8 1 4 2 5 5 4 6 9 6 0 *